DRAMA
for Students

Advisors

Erik France: Adjunct Instructor of English, Macomb Community College, Warren, Michigan. B.A. and M.S.L.S. from University of North Carolina, Chapel Hill; Ph.D. from Temple University.

Kate Hamill: Grade 12 English Teacher, Catonsville High School, Catonsville, Maryland.

Joseph McGeary: English Teacher, Germantown Friends School, Philadelphia, Pennsylvania. Ph.D. in English from Duke University.

Timothy Showalter: English Department Chair, Franklin High School, Reisterstown, Maryland. Certified teacher by the Maryland State Department of Education. Member of the National Council of Teachers of English.

Amy Spade Silverman: English Department Chair, Kehillah Jewish High School, Palo Alto, California. Member of National Council of Teachers of English (NCTE), Teachers and Writers, and NCTE Opinion Panel. Exam Reader, Advanced Placement Literature and Composition. Poet, published in *North American Review, Nimrod,* and *Michigan Quarterly Review,* among other publications.

Jody Stefansson: Director of Boswell Library and Study Center and Upper School Learning Specialist, Polytechnic School, Pasadena, California. Board member, Children's Literature Council of Southern California. Member of American Library Association, Association of Independent School Librarians, and Association of Educational Therapists.

Laura Jean Waters: Certified School Library Media Specialist, Wilton High School, Wilton, Connecticut. B.A. from Fordham University; M.A. from Fairfield University.

DRAMA
for Students

Presenting Analysis, Context, and Criticism on
Commonly Studied Dramas

VOLUME 26

GALE
CENGAGE Learning

Detroit • New York • San Francisco • New Haven, Conn • Waterville, Maine • London

Drama for Students, Volume 26

Project Editor: Sara Constantakis

Rights Acquisition and Management: Margaret Chamberlain-Gaston, Aja Perales, Kelly Quin, Robyn Young

Composition: Evi Abou-El-Seoud

Manufacturing: Drew Kalasky

Imaging: John Watkins

Product Design: Pamela A. E. Galbreath, Jennifer Wahi

Content Conversion: Civie Green, Katrina Coach

Product Manager: Meggin Condino

For product information and technology assistance, contact us at **Gale Customer Support, 1-800-877-4253.**
For permission to use material from this text or product, submit all requests online at **www.cengage.com/permissions.**
Further permissions questions can be emailed to **permissionrequest@cengage.com**

While every effort has been made to ensure the reliability of the information presented in this publication, Gale, a part of Cengage Learning, does not guarantee the accuracy of the data contained herein. Gale accepts no payment for listing; and inclusion in the publication of any organization, agency, institution, publication, service, or individual does not imply endorsement of the editors or publisher. Errors brought to the attention of the publisher and verified to the satisfaction of the publisher will be corrected in future editions.

Gale
27500 Drake Rd.
Farmington Hills, MI, 48331-3535

ISBN-13: 978-0-7876-8122-7
ISBN-10: 0-7876-8122-9

ISSN 1094-9232

This title is also available as an e-book.
ISBN-13: 978-1-4144-4938-8
ISBN-10: 1-4144-4938-0
Contact your Gale, a part of Cengage Learning sales representative for ordering information.

Printed in the United States of America
1 2 3 4 5 6 7 13 12 11 10 09

Table of Contents

ADVISORS ii

THE STUDY OF DRAMA ix
 (by Carole L. Hamilton)

INTRODUCTION xi

LITERARY CHRONOLOGY xv

ACKNOWLEDGMENTS xvii

CONTRIBUTORS xix

AGAMEMNON *(by Aeschylus)* 1
  Author Biography 2
  Plot Summary 2
  Characters 4
  Themes 6
  Style 9
  Historical Context 9
  Critical Overview 11
  Criticism 12
  Sources 19
  Further Reading 19

THE BEAR *(by Anton Pavlovich Chekhov)* . . . 20
  Author Biography 21
  Plot Summary 22
  Characters 23
  Themes 25

Style 27
Historical Context 27
Critical Overview. 29
Criticism. 30
Sources 39
Further Reading 39

BYE-BYE, BREVOORT (*by Eudora Welty*). . . 41
Author Biography 42
Plot Summary. 43
Characters 44
Themes 45
Style 47
Historical Context 48
Critical Overview. 49
Criticism. 50
Sources 61
Further Reading 62

CROSSROADS (*by Carlos Solórzano*) 63
Author Biography 64
Plot Summary. 64
Characters 66
Themes 67
Style 69
Historical Context 70
Critical Overview. 72
Criticism. 73
Sources 82
Further Reading 83

THE FLIES (*by Jean-Paul Sartre*) 84
Author Biography 84
Plot Summary. 86
Characters 90
Themes 92
Style 93
Historical Context 94
Critical Overview. 96
Criticism. 97
Sources 109
Further Reading 109

FLORENCE (*by Alice Childress*) 110
Author Biography 111
Plot Summary. 112
Characters 113
Themes 114
Style 116
Historical Context 117
Critical Overview. 119
Criticism. 120
Sources 133
Further Reading 133

ILE (*by Eugene O'Neill*). 135
Author Biography 136
Plot Summary. 136
Characters 139
Themes 141
Style 143
Historical Context 143
Critical Overview. 145
Criticism. 146
Sources 156
Further Reading 157

IMPOSSIBLE MARRIAGE (*by Beth Henley*) . 158
Author Biography 159
Plot Summary. 160
Characters 162
Themes 165
Style 167
Historical Context 168
Critical Overview. 169
Criticism. 170
Sources 182
Further Reading 182

MARTY (*by Paddy Chayefsky*). 183
Author Biography 184
Plot Summary. 185
Characters 187
Themes 190
Style 192
Historical Context 192
Critical Overview. 194
Criticism. 194
Sources 206
Further Reading 206

NOVIO BOY (*by Gary Soto*) 207
Author Biography 207
Plot Summary. 208
Characters 211
Themes 212
Style 214
Historical Context 214
Critical Overview. 215
Criticism. 215
Sources 223
Further Reading 223

THE POST OFFICE (*by Rabindranath Tagore*) 224
Author Biography 224
Plot Summary. 226
Characters 228
Themes 230
Style 232

Historical Context 232
Critical Overview. 234
Criticism. 235
Sources 245
Further Reading 245

SORRY, WRONG NUMBER *(by Lucille Fletcher)* 246
Author Biography 247
Plot Summary 247
Characters 249
Themes 251
Style 254
Historical Context 254
Critical Overview. 256
Criticism. 257
Sources 259
Further Reading 259

THE TRIALS OF BROTHER JERO
(by Wole Soyinka) 261
Author Biography 261
Plot Summary 262
Characters 265
Themes 267
Style 268
Historical Context 269
Critical Overview. 271

Criticism. 271
Sources 281
Further Reading 282

A WALK IN THE WOODS
(by Lee Blessing) 283
Author Biography 284
Plot Summary 284
Characters 288
Themes 289
Style 291
Historical Context 292
Critical Overview. 294
Criticism. 294
Sources 300
Further Reading 301

GLOSSARY OF LITERARY TERMS. . . . 303

CUMULATIVE AUTHOR/TITLE INDEX . . 341

**CUMULATIVE NATIONALITY/
ETHNICITY INDEX** 349

SUBJECT/THEME INDEX 355

The Study of Drama

We study drama in order to learn what meaning others have made of life, to comprehend what it takes to produce a work of art, and to glean some understanding of ourselves. Drama produces in a separate, aesthetic world, a moment of being for the audience to experience, while maintaining the detachment of a reflective observer.

Drama is a representational art, a visible and audible narrative presenting virtual, fictional characters within a virtual, fictional universe. Dramatic realizations may pretend to approximate reality or else stubbornly defy, distort, and deform reality into an artistic statement. From this separate universe that is obviously not "real life" we expect a valid reflection upon reality, yet drama never is mistaken for reality—the methods of theater are integral to its form and meaning. Theater is art, and art's appeal lies in its ability both to approximate life and to depart from it. For in intruding its distorted version of life into our consciousness, art gives us a new perspective and appreciation of life and reality. Although all aesthetic experiences perform this service, theater does it most effectively by creating a separate, cohesive universe that freely acknowledges its status as an art form.

And what is the purpose of the aesthetic universe of drama? The potential answers to such a question are nearly as many and varied as there are plays written, performed, and enjoyed. Dramatic texts can be problems posed, answers asserted, or moments portrayed. Dramas (tragedies as well as comedies) may serve strictly "to ease the anguish of a torturing hour" (as stated in William Shakespeare's *A Midsummer Night's Dream*)—to divert and entertain–or aspire to move the viewer to action with social issues. Whether to entertain or to instruct, affirm or influence, pacify or shock, dramatic art wraps us in the spell of its imaginary world for the length of the work and then dispenses us back to the real world, entertained, purged, as Aristotle said, of pity and fear, and edified—or at least weary enough to sleep peacefully.

It is commonly thought that theater, being an art of performance, must be experienced—seen—in order to be appreciated fully. However, to view a production of a dramatic text is to be limited to a single interpretation of that text—all other interpretations are for the moment closed off, inaccessible. In the process of producing a play, the director, stage designer, and performers interpret and transform the script into a work of art that always departs in some measure from the author's original conception. Novelist and critic Umberto Eco, in his *The Role of the Reader: Explorations in the Semiotics of Texts* (Indiana University Press, 1979), explained, "In short, we can say that every performance offers us a complete and satisfying version of the work, but at the same time makes it incomplete for us, because it cannot simultaneously give all the other artistic solutions which the work may admit."

Thus Laurence Olivier's coldly formal and neurotic film presentation of Shakespeare's *Hamlet* (in which he played the title character as well as directed) shows marked differences from subsequent adaptations. While Olivier's Hamlet is clearly entangled in a Freudian relationship with his mother Gertrude, he would be incapable of shushing her with the impassioned kiss that Mel Gibson's mercurial Hamlet (in director Franco Zeffirelli's 1990 film) does. Although each of performances rings true to Shakespeare's text, each is also a mutually exclusive work of art. Also important to consider are the time periods in which each of these films was produced: Olivier made his film in 1948, a time in which overt references to sexuality (especially incest) were frowned upon. Gibson and Zeffirelli made their film in a culture more relaxed and comfortable with these issues. Just as actors and directors can influence the presentation of drama, so too can the time period of the production affect what the audience will see.

A play script is an open text from which an infinity of specific realizations may be derived. Dramatic scripts that are more open to interpretive creativity (such as those of Ntozake Shange and Tomson Highway) actually require the creative improvisation of the production troupe in order to complete the text. Even the most prescriptive scripts (those of Neil Simon, Lillian Hellman, and Robert Bolt, for example), can never fully control the actualization of live performance, and circumstantial events, including the attitude and receptivity of the audience, make every performance a unique event. Thus, while it is important to view a production of a dramatic piece, if one wants to understand a drama fully it is equally important to read the original dramatic text.

The reader of a dramatic text or script is not limited by either the specific interpretation of a given production or by the unstoppable action of a moving spectacle. The reader of a dramatic text may discover the nuances of the play's language, structure, and events at their own pace. Yet studied alone, the author's blueprint for artistic production does not tell the whole story of a play's life and significance. One also needs to assess the play's critical reviews to discover how it resonated to cultural themes at the time of its debut and how the shifting tides of cultural interest have revised its interpretation and impact on audiences. And to do this, one needs to know a little about the culture of the times which produced the play as well as the author who penned it.

Drama for Students supplies this material in a useful compendium for the student of dramatic theater. Covering a range of dramatic works that span from 442 BCE to the 1990s, this book focuses on significant theatrical works whose themes and form transcend the uncertainty of dramatic fads. These are plays that have proven to be both memorable and teachable. *Drama for Students* seeks to enhance appreciation of these dramatic texts by providing scholarly materials written with the secondary and college/university student in mind. It provides for each play a concise summary of the plot and characters as well as a detailed explanation of its themes. In addition, background material on the historical context of the play, its critical reception, and the author's life help the student to understand the work's position in the chronicle of dramatic history. For each play entry a new work of scholarly criticism is also included, as well as segments of other significant critical works for handy reference. A thorough bibliography provides a starting point for further research.

This series offers comprehensive educational resources for students of drama. *Drama for Students* is a vital book for dramatic interpretation and a valuable addition to any reference library.

Sources

Eco, Umberto, *The Role of the Reader: Explorations in the Semiotics of Texts*, Indiana University Press, 1979.

Carole L. Hamilton
Author and Instructor of English at Cary Academy, Cary, North Carolina

Introduction

Purpose of the Book

The purpose of *Drama for Students* (*DfS*) is to provide readers with a guide to understanding, enjoying, and studying dramas by giving them easy access to information about the work. Part of Gale's "For Students" literature line, *DfS* is specifically designed to meet the curricular needs of high school and undergraduate college students and their teachers, as well as the interests of general readers and researchers considering specific plays. While each volume contains entries on "classic" dramas frequently studied in classrooms, there are also entries containing hard-to-find information on contemporary plays, including works by multicultural, international, and women playwrights.

The information covered in each entry includes an introduction to the play and the work's author; a plot summary, to help readers unravel and understand the events in a drama; descriptions of important characters, including explanation of a given character's role in the drama as well as discussion about that character's relationship to other characters in the play; analysis of important themes in the drama; and an explanation of important literary techniques and movements as they are demonstrated in the play.

In addition to this material, which helps the readers analyze the play itself, students are also provided with important information on the literary and historical background informing each work. This includes a historical context essay, a box comparing the time or place the drama was written to modern Western culture, a critical essay, and excerpts from critical essays on the play. A unique feature of *DfS* is a specially commissioned critical essay on each drama, targeted toward the student reader.

To further aid the student in studying and enjoying each play, information on media adaptations is provided (if available), as well as reading suggestions for works of fiction and nonfiction on similar themes and topics. Classroom aids include ideas for research papers and lists of critical sources that provide additional material on each drama.

Selection Criteria

The titles for each volume of *DfS* are selected by surveying numerous sources on notable literary works and analyzing course curricula for various schools, school districts, and states. Some of the sources surveyed include: high school and undergraduate literature anthologies and textbooks; lists of award-winners, and recommended titles, including the Young Adult Library Services Association (YALSA) list of best books for young adults.

Input solicited from our expert advisory board—consisting of educators and librarians—guides us to maintain a mix of "classic" and contemporary literary works, a mix of challenging and engaging works (including genre titles that are commonly studied) appropriate for different age levels, and a mix of international, multicultural and women authors. These advisors also consult on each volume's entry list, advising on which titles are most studied, most appropriate, and meet the broadest interests across secondary (grades 7–12) curricula and undergraduate literature studies.

How Each Entry Is Organized

Each entry, or chapter, in *DfS* focuses on one play. Each entry heading lists the full name of the play, the author's name, and the date of the play's publication. The following elements are contained in each entry:

Introduction: a brief overview of the drama which provides information about its first appearance, its literary standing, any controversies surrounding the work, and major conflicts or themes within the work.

Author Biography: this section includes basic facts about the author's life, and focuses on events and times in the author's life that inspired the drama in question.

Plot Summary: a description of the major events in the play. Subheads demarcate the play's various acts or scenes.

Characters: an alphabetical listing of major characters in the play. Each character name is followed by a brief to an extensive description of the character's role in the play, as well as discussion of the character's actions, relationships, and possible motivation.

> Characters are listed alphabetically by last name. If a character is unnamed—for instance, the Stage Manager in *Our Town*—the character is listed as "The Stage Manager" and alphabetized as "Stage Manager." If a character's first name is the only one given, the name will appear alphabetically by the first name. Variant names are also included for each character. Thus, the nickname "Babe" would head the listing for a character in *Crimes of the Heart,* but below that listing would be her less-mentioned married name "Rebecca Botrelle."

Themes: a thorough overview of how the major topics, themes, and issues are addressed within the play. Each theme discussed appears in a separate subhead, and is easily accessed through the boldface entries in the Subject/Theme Index.

Style: this section addresses important style elements of the drama, such as setting, point of view, and narration; important literary devices used, such as imagery, foreshadowing, symbolism; and, if applicable, genres to which the work might have belonged, such as Gothicism or Romanticism. Literary terms are explained within the entry, but can also be found in the Glossary.

Historical Context: this section outlines the social, political, and cultural climate *in which the author lived and the play was created.* This section may include descriptions of related historical events, pertinent aspects of daily life in the culture, and the artistic and literary sensibilities of the time in which the work was written. If the play is a historical work, information regarding the time in which the play is set is also included. Each section is broken down with helpful subheads.

Critical Overview: this section provides background on the critical reputation of the play, including bannings or any other public controversies surrounding the work. For older plays, this section includes a history of how the drama was first received and how perceptions of it may have changed over the years; for more recent plays, direct quotes from early reviews may also be included.

Criticism: an essay commissioned by *DfS* which specifically deals with the play and is written specifically for the student audience, as well as excerpts from previously published criticism on the work (if available).

Sources: an alphabetical list of critical material used in compiling the entry, with full bibliographical information.

Further Reading: an alphabetical list of other critical sources which may prove useful for the student. It includes full bibliographical information and a brief annotation.

In addition, each entry contains the following highlighted sections, set apart from the main text as sidebars:

Media Adaptations: if available, a list of important film and television adaptations of the play, including source information. The list may also include such variations on the work as audio recordings, musical adaptations, and other stage interpretations.

Topics for Further Study: a list of potential study questions or research topics dealing with the play. This section includes questions related to other disciplines the student may be studying, such as American history, world history, science, math, government, business, geography, economics, psychology, etc.

Compare and Contrast: an "at-a-glance" comparison of the cultural and historical differences between the author's time and culture and late twentieth century or early twenty-first century Western culture. This box includes pertinent parallels between the major scientific, political, and cultural movements of the time or place the drama was written, the time or place the play was set (if a historical work), and modern Western culture. Works written after 1990 may not have this box.

What Do I Read Next?: a list of works that might complement the featured play or serve as a contrast to it. This includes works by the same author and others, works of fiction and nonfiction, and works from various genres, cultures, and eras.

Other Features

DfS includes "The Study of Drama," a foreword by Carole Hamilton, an educator and author who specializes in dramatic works. This essay examines the basis for drama in societies and what drives people to study such work. The essay also discusses how *Drama for Students* can help teachers show students how to enrich their own reading/viewing experiences.

A Cumulative Author/Title Index lists the authors and titles covered in each volume of the *DfS* series.

A Cumulative Nationality/Ethnicity Index breaks down the authors and titles covered in each volume of the *DfS* series by nationality and ethnicity.

A Subject/Theme Index, specific to each volume, provides easy reference for users who may be studying a particular subject or theme rather than a single work. Significant subjects from events to broad themes are included, and the entries pointing to the specific theme discussions in each entry are indicated in **boldface**.

Each entry may include illustrations, including photo of the author, stills from stage productions, and stills from film adaptations, if available.

Citing Drama for Students

When writing papers, students who quote directly from any volume of *Drama for Students* may use the following general forms. These exam-

ples are based on MLA style; teachers may request that students adhere to a different style, so the following examples may be adapted as needed.

When citing text from *DfS* that is not attributed to a particular author (i.e., the Themes, Style, Historical Context sections, etc.), the following format should be used in the bibliography section:

"*Our Town.*" *Drama for Students*. Vol. 1. Ed. David Galens and Lynn Spampinato. Detroit: Gale, 1998. 227–30.

When quoting the specially commissioned essay from *DfS* (usually the first piece under the "Criticism" subhead), the following format should be used:

Fiero, John. Critical Essay on *Twilight: Los Angeles, 1992. Drama for Students*. Vol. 2. Ed. David Galens and Lynn Spampinato. Detroit: Gale, 1998. 247–49.

When quoting a journal or newspaper essay that is reprinted in a volume of *DfS*, the following form may be used:

Rich, Frank. "Theatre: A Mamet Play, *Glengarry Glen Ross.*" *New York Theatre Critics' Review* 45.4 (March 5, 1984): 5–7. Excerpted and reprinted in *Drama for Students*. Vol. 2. Ed. David Galens and Lynn Spampinato. Detroit: Gale, 1998. 51–53.

When quoting material reprinted from a book that appears in a volume of *DfS*, the following form may be used:

Kerr, Walter. "*The Miracle Worker.*" *The Theatre in Spite of Itself*. Simon & Schuster, 1963. 255–57. Excerpted and reprinted in *Drama for Students*. Vol. 2. Ed. David Galens and Lynn Spampinato. Detroit: Gale, 1998. 123–24.

We Welcome Your Suggestions

The editorial staff of *Drama for Students* welcomes your comments and ideas. Readers who wish to suggest dramas to appear in future volumes, or who have other suggestions, are cordially invited to contact the editor. You may contact the editor via e-mail at: **ForStudentsEditors@cengage.com.** Or write to the editor at:

Editor, *Drama for Students*
Gale
27500 Drake Road
Farmington Hills, MI 48331-3535

Literary Chronology

525 BCE: Aeschylus is born in Eleusis, Greece.

458 BCE: Aeschylus's *Agamemnon* is first produced in Athens, Greece.

456 or **455 BCE:** Aeschylus dies in Gela, Sicily.

1860: Anton Chekhov is born Anton Pavlovich Chekhov on January 17, in Taganrog, Russia.

1861: Rabindranath Tagore is born on May 7, in Calcutta, India.

1888: Anton Chekhov's *The Bear* is first published in Russian and will be published in English in 1916.

1888: Eugene O'Neill is born Eugene Gladstone O'Neill on October 16, in New York, New York.

1904: Anton Chekhov dies of tuberculosis on July 2, in Badenweiler, Germany.

1905: Jean-Paul Sartre is born on June 21, in Paris, France.

1909: Eudora Welty is born on April 13, in Jackson, Mississippi.

1912: Lucille Fletcher is born in Brooklyn, New York, on March 28.

1912: Rabindranath Tagore's *The Post Office* is published in Bengali and will be performed in English in 1913 in Dublin, Ireland, and London, England.

1913: Rabindranath Tagore is awarded the Nobel Prize in Literature for *Gitanjali*.

1916 or **1920:** Alice Childress is born October 12, in Charleston, South Carolina.

1917: O'Neill's *Ile* is published.

1922: Carlos Solórzano is born on May 1, in San Marcos, Guatemala.

1922: O'Neill is awarded the Pulitzer Prize for Drama for *Anna Christie*.

1923: Paddy Chayefsky is born Sidney Chayefsky on January 29, in New York, New York.

1928: O'Neill is awarded the Pulitzer Prize for Drama for *Strange Interlude*.

1934: Wole Soyinka is born on July 13, in Isara, Nigeria.

1936: O'Neill is awarded the Nobel Prize for Literature.

1941: Rabindranath Tagore dies on August 7, in Calcutta, India.

1942: Jean-Paul Sartre's *The Flies* is first produced in French in Paris, France. It will be produced in English in 1947, in New York, New York.

1943: Lucille Fletcher's *Sorry, Wrong Number* is first produced as a radio play.

1949: Alice Childress's *Florence* is first produced in New York, New York.

1949: Eudora Welty' *Bye-Bye Brevoort* is first produced in Westboro, Massachusetts.

1949: Lee Blessing is born on October 4, in Minneapolis, Minnesota.

1952: Beth Henley is born on May 8, in Jackson, Mississippi.

1952: Gary Soto is born on April 12, in Fresno, California.

1953: O'Neill dies of a degenerative nervous condition related to alcoholism on November 27, in Boston, Massachusetts.

1953: Paddy Chayefsky's *Marty* is first produced on live television.

1957: O'Neill is awarded the Pulitzer Prize for Drama for his posthumously produced play *Long Day's Journey into Night*.

1959: Carlos Solórzano's *Crossroads* is first published in Spanish and will be published in English in 1993.

1960: Wole Soyinka's *The Trials of Brother Jero* is first produced in Ibadan, Nigeria.

1964: Jean-Paul Sartre is awarded the Nobel Prize for Literature, which he refuses.

1973: Eudora Welty is awarded the Pulitzer Prize for Fiction for *The Optimist's Daughter*.

1980: Jean-Paul Sartre dies of a lung ailment on April 15, in Paris, France.

1981: Paddy Chayefsky dies of cancer on August 1, in New York, New York.

1986: Wole Soyinka is awarded the Nobel Prize for Literature.

1987: Lee Blessing's *A Walk in the Woods* is first produced in New Haven, Connecticut.

1994: Alice Childress dies of cancer on August 14, in Queens, New York.

1997: Gary Soto's *Novio Boy* is published.

1998: Beth Henley's *Impossible Marriage* is published.

2000: Lucille Fletcher dies of a stroke on August 31, in Langhorne, Pennsylvania.

2001: Eudora Welty dies of complications from pneumonia on July 22, 2001, in Jackson, Mississippi.

Acknowledgments

The editors wish to thank the copyright holders of the excerpted criticism included in this volume and the permissions managers of many book and magazine publishing companies for assisting us in securing reproduction rights. We are also grateful to the staffs of the Detroit Public Library, the Library of Congress, the University of Detroit Mercy Library, Wayne State University Purdy/ Kresge Library Complex, and the University of Michigan Libraries for making their resources available to us. Following is a list of the copyright holders who have granted us permission to reproduce material in this volume of *DfS*. Every effort has been made to trace copyright, but if omissions have been made, please let us know.

COPYRIGHTED EXCERPTS IN *DfS*, VOLUME 26, WERE REPRODUCED FROM THE FOLLOWING PERIODICALS:

American Drama, v. 14, winter, 2005. Copyright © 2005 American Drama Institute. Reproduced by permission.—*American Theatre*, v. 14, January, 1997. Copyright © 1997 Theatre Communications Group. All rights reserved. Reproduced by permission.—*Belles Lettres: A Review of Books by Women*, v. 10, fall, 1994. Reproduced by permission.—*Book Report*, v. 14, January–February, 1996. Copyright © 1996 by Linworth Publishing, Inc., Worthington, Ohio. Reproduced by permission.—*Booklist*, v. 93, April 15, 1997. Copyright © 1997 by the American Library Association. Reproduced by permission.—*Books & Culture*, v. 7, November–December, 2001 for "Wole Soyinka's Outrage: The Divided Soul of Nigeria's Nobel Laureate," by Alan Jacobs. Reproduced by permission of the author.—*Drama Survey*, v. 4, summer, 1965 for "The 'Oresteia' of Aeschylus," by Harry L. Levy. Reproduced by permission of the author.—*Journal of Negro History*, v. 81, winter–autumn, 1996. Copyright © 1996 Association for the Study of Afro-American Life and History, Inc., www.asalh.org. Reproduced by permission.—*Latin American Theatre Review*, summer, 1980. Copyright © 1980 by the Center of Latin American Studies, The University of Kansas, Lawrence, KS 66045, U.S.A. Reproduced by permission.—*Law-Now*, v. 26, December–January, 2001. Copyright © 2001 University of Alberta, Legal Resource Centre. Reproduced by permission.—*Literature in Performance*, v. 1, April, 1981 for "A Conversation with Eudora Welty," by Joanna Maclay. Reproduced by permission of National Communications Association.—*Long Island Business News*, v. 45, November 6, 1998. Copyright 1998 Long Island Commerical Review Inc. Reproduced by permission.—*Midwest Quarterly*, v. 48, spring, 2007. Copyright © 2007 by *The Midwest Quarterly*, Pittsburgh State University. Reproduced by permission.—*The Nation*, April 9, 1988. Copyright © 1988 by *The Nation Magazine*/The Nation Company, Inc. Reproduced by permission.—*The New Leader*, v. 71, March 21, 1988. Copyright © 1988 by The American Labor Conference on International Affairs, Inc. All rights reserved. Reproduced by permission.—*The New*

Republic, v. 134, February 27, 1956. Copyright © 1956 by The New Republic, Inc. Reproduced by permission of *The New Republic.*—***PHYLON: The Atlanta University Review of Race and Culture***, v. 48, fall, 1987. Copyright © 1987 by Atlanta University. Reproduced by permission of *PHYLON.*—***Ploughshares***, v. 21, spring, 1995 for "About Gary Soto," by Don Lee. Reproduced by permission of the author.—***Positions: East Asia Cultures Critique***, v. 15, 2007. Copyright © 2007 Duke University Press. All rights reserved. Used by permission of the publisher.—***Scholastic Scope***, v. 53, October 4, 2004. Copyright © 2004 Scholastic Inc. Reproduced by permission of Scholastic Inc.—***The Southern Literary Journal***, v. 27, fall, 1994. Copyright © 1994 by the University of North Carolina Press. Used by permission.—***The Southern Quarterly***, v. 53, January, 1995. Copyright © 1995 by the University of Southern Mississippi. Reproduced by permission.—***SubStance***, Issue 102. v. 32 no. 3, 2003. Copyright © 2003 by the Board of Regents of the University of Wisconsin System. Reproduced by permission of the University of Wisconsin Press.—***UNESCO Courier***, May–June, 1986; v. 47, January, 1994. Copyright ©1986, 1994 by UNESCO-WWAP. All rights reserved. Republished with permission of UNESCO.—***Western Folklore***, v. 14, July, 1955. Copyright © renewed 1983 by California Folklore Society. Reproduced by permission.

COPYRIGHTED EXCERPTS IN *DfS*, VOLUME 26, WERE REPRODUCED FROM THE FOLLOWING BOOKS:

Colecchia, Francesca. From an introduction to ***Crossroads and Other Plays, by Carlos Solorzano***. Edited and translated by Francesca Colecchia. Farleigh Dickinson University Press, 1993. Copyright © 1993 by Associated University Presses, Inc. All rights reserved. Reproduced by permission.

Contributors

Bryan Aubrey: Aubrey holds a Ph.D. in English. Entry on *The Trials of Brother Jero*. Original essay on *The Trials of Brother Jero*.

Catherine Dominic: Dominic is a novelist and a freelance writer and editor. Entries on *The Bear* and *Crossroads*. Original essays on *The Bear* and *Crossroads*.

Joyce M. Hart: Hart is an author and freelance writer. Entry on *Sorry, Wrong Number*. Original essay on *Sorry, Wrong Number*.

Neil Heims: Heims is a freelance writer living in Paris and the author or editor of more than two dozen books on literary subjects. Entries on *Novio Boy* and *A Walk in the Woods*. Original essays on *Novio Boy* and *A Walk in the Woods*.

Diane Andrews Henningfeld: Henningfeld is a professor of English who writes widely on literary topics. Entry on *Bye-Bye, Brevoort*. Original essay on *Bye-Bye, Brevoort*.

Sheri Metzger Karmiol: Karmiol has a doctorate in English Renaissance literature. She teaches literature and drama at the University of New Mexico, and she is also a professional writer and the author of several reference texts on poetry and drama. Entry on *Florence*. Original essay on *Florence*.

David Kelly: Kelly is a writer and instructor of creative writing and literature. Entries on *Agamemnon* and *Marty*. Original essays on *Agamemnon* and *Marty*.

Claire Robinson: Robinson has a master's degree in English. She is a teacher of English literature and a freelance writer and editor. Entry on *Impossible Marriage*. Original essay on *Impossible Marriage*.

Bradley A. Skeen: Skeen is a classics professor. Entry on *Ile*. Original essay on *Ile*.

Leah Tieger: Tieger is a freelance writer and editor. Entries on *The Flies* and *The Post Office*. Original essays on *The Flies* and *The Post Office*.

Agamemnon

AESCHYLUS

458 BC

Agamemnon is one of the most famous plays by Greek dramatist Aeschylus. First performed at the influential dramatic festival in Athens in 458 BCE, it is the first play of the trilogy called *The Oresteia*, which concerns events surrounding the return of Agamemnon, king of Argos and leader of the Greek army that invaded Troy. According to legend, Agamemnon was forced to sacrifice his own daughter's life before the goddess Artemis would allow the Greek ships to sail from their shore. In Aeschylus's play, Agamemnon returns to a trap that his wife, Clytaemnestra, has been plotting for ten years to avenge her daughter's death.

The Oresteia won first place at the Athenian festival the year that it premiered. It is now the only surviving trilogy by Aeschylus, who is credited as the first to have written interwoven trilogies for the competition while other playwrights were submitting three unrelated pieces. Over the centuries, this story has been familiar in cultures throughout the world, and has been the basis for hundreds of similar stories. It deals with issues basic to humanity and civilization, such as honor, responsibility, revenge, deceit, kinship, and power. Readers of *Agamemnon* might feel a sense of outrage over power usurped; however, by the end of the trilogy, it is clear how such outrage can lead to one senseless act of revenge after another.

Dozens of reliable translations of *Agamemnon* are available today. One of the most recommended is by Robert Fagles, published in the 1979 Penguin Classic edition of *The Oresteia*.

Aeschylus (AP Images)

AUTHOR BIOGRAPHY

The facts about Aeschylus's life are not considered verifiable because he lived centuries ago, and they have been pieced together from existing information. He is believed to have been born in 525 BCE at Eleusis, near Athens, the capital of modern-day Greece. His father, Euphorion, was from a noble family. When Aeschylus was young, he worked in a vineyard, and it is said that it was his devotion to Dionysus, the god of wine, that led him to become a playwright. (The earliest Greek dramas were written and performed for feasts in celebration of Dionysus.) Aeschylus fought in the Persian War, in battles at Marathon, Artemisium, Salamis, and Plataea. He earned distinction as a soldier. In his epitaph, which Aeschylus wrote for himself, he talked about his accomplishments in battle but not the awards he won in playwriting competitions, indicating that he treasured his life as a soldier more than his life as a writer.

Aeschylus was writing dramas for competitions before he served in the army. His first competitive piece was produced in 499 BCE for the dramatic competition at the City Dionysian Festival in Athens, and his first victory in competition

came in 484. After that, he became a regular if not constant winner, receiving first place about twelve more times. In all, he is thought to have written between fifty and ninety plays, of which only seven remain. The earliest remaining play is *Persians*, from 472 BCE, when he was fifty-three years old.

Aeschylus is known to have spent two distinctive periods of his life on the island of Sicily, then a center of wealth and power among the Greece states and now an autonomous region of Italy. It was in Athens, however, that he produced *The Oresteia*, a trilogy that includes *Agamemnon*, *The Libation Bearers*, and *The Eumenides*.

Aeschylus died in the city of Gela in Sicily in 455 or 456 BCE, at the age of sixty-nine. Two of his sons became dramatists: Euphorion (who also restaged many of his father's plays) and Euaeon.

PLOT SUMMARY

Agamemnon begins with a lone Watchman, standing guard on the roof of the house of Atreus, the royal dwelling in Argos, as he has stood watch for hundreds of nights before. He struggles to stay awake, assuming that this night will be no different than any other. He is so bored with his task that he begs the gods to free him. In his musings, he thinks of how difficult life has been in Argos under Clytaemnestra, who is ruling the land in her husband's absence, and longs for the security of the old times before the king, Agamemnon, sailed off to war.

The Watchman sees a light on the horizon and thinks that he is seeing the sun rise. After a moment, though, he realizes what it really is: the signal that he has been watching for all these years. After a brief dance of joy, he climbs down from the roof through a side entrance into the palace.

A crowd of old men, the Chorus, enters, discussing the events that have led to the current situation. It was ten years ago to the day that Agamemnon and his brother, Menelaus, sailed off with the entire Greek army to attack Troy. Since they do not know of the signal the Watchman has seen, they do not know what to make of the cry of excitement that Clytaemnestra lets out within the palace. They continue their discussion, imagining the sight of battle on the Trojan fields, waged to retrieve Menelaus's wife, Helen, who was abducted by Paris, the prince of Troy.

MEDIA ADAPTATIONS

- A film of this drama, directed and produced by Sir Peter Hall for the National Theater of Great Britain, was released on videocassette by Films for the Humanities, of Princeton, New Jersey, in 1983.

- A two-tape audio cassette version of *Agamemnon* was released in 1977 by Jabberwocky Studio of San Francisco.

- A more recent version of *Agamemnon* is included in Blackstone Audiobooks's 2007 compact disc release of *The Oresteia*, from a translation by Ian Johnston, directed by Yuri Rasovsky and performed by Hollywood Theatre of the Ear.

- A 1992 translation of *Agamemnon: A Tragedy by Aeschylus* by Peter Meineck, Graham Mitchell, and Dirk Obbink, performed by Aquila Productions of London, is available on videotape from Film Counselors Associates.

The members of the Chorus express the wish that they could have taken part in the battle, but they were deemed too old to fight and were therefore forced to stay home, feeling dishonored and useless.

Noting that Clytaemnestra and her entourage have appeared and lit the altar fires, they ask her what news she has heard of the war, but she does not answer and goes away, which prompts the Chorus to dwell on more details of how the war began. They recall the call to arms, the gathering of a thousand ships to sail against Troy, and how the goddess Artemis halted the invasion by holding back the wind so that the ships could not sail. As the seer Calchas determined, Artemis would not let the invasion go forward until Agamemnon killed his daughter, Iphigenia, in sacrifice to her. He did, and the winds became favorable again. The Chorus knows, though, that during the ten years that Agamemnon has been gone, Clytaemnestra has sat in the palace, growing angrier and angrier over the loss of her daughter.

The Leader of the Chorus approaches Clytaemnestra and asks why the altar fires are being lit. She tells him that the war with Troy is over and that the Greeks have won. When the Leader asks if she might have dreamed this, Clytaemnestra is offended. She explains to him the system of signal fires that she has arranged, in which one outpost lights a fire upon seeing the fire from the previous outpost, so that the message of the Greek victory can travel across land and sea as quickly as the speed of light. She hopes that the soldiers who went off to battle will not take too much time to plunder the city but instead will come home quickly.

As they talk about the abduction of Helen and the course that the war has taken, the members of the Chorus begin to doubt that Clytaemnestra's system of signal fires could work as well as she says it has. She is just a woman, they say, and is likely to be gullible enough to get excited over something that could just be a coincidence, or a trick. But then a Herald arrives, announcing that Troy has indeed fallen to the Greek troops. The Chorus welcomes him and tells him that they have lived in fear of their lives for the past ten years. They have only been able to survive Clytaemnestra's reign by keeping silent.

Clytaemnestra enters with her servants and rebukes the Chorus for doubting her word that the war was indeed ended. She gives orders for Agamemnon to be sent to her when he returns, and then she leaves. The Chorus expresses distrust in her motives. Asked about the fate of Agamemnon's brother Menelaus, the Herald says that his ship was lost in a storm after leaving Troy; though the men are presumed dead, they might show up again, a reference to Greek poet Homer's epic poem *The Odyssey*. The Herald leaves, and the Chorus ruminates on the tragic fate that is destined to befall all of the house of Atreus.

Agamemnon enters in a chariot that is heavy with treasures, the goods that he has taken from Troy as his plunder. This includes Cassandra, who rides in the back of the carriage, away from the audience. He arrives thanking the gods, praising those who died in the war, and promising to look into rearranging the city's system of justice.

Clytaemnestra enters and explains how difficult life has been for her while Agamemnon was gone. She mentions their child, who is gone but should be there. When Agamemnon looks startled that she would bring up the sacrifice of Iphigenia, he explains that she is talking about their son, Orestes, who has gone into exile with Strophios the Phocian, to keep him safe during the war. In the name of doing honor to her husband, the conquering hero, Clytaemnestra has her servants lay out tapestries on the ground, saying that his feet should never again have to touch plain soil. Agamemnon objects, saying that such treatment is only fitting for gods, but she tells him that he should feel he deserves to be revered above all other men because he is a war hero. Agamemnon gives in at length. As he dismounts onto the tapestries, Cassandra can be seen in the back of his chariot. He tells the servants to escort her into the house and treat her well, and then he enters the palace. Clytaemnestra follows him in.

After the Chorus expresses their foreboding once more, Clytaemnestra emerges from the palace and approaches Cassandra, inviting her inside. When she does not move or talk, Clytaemnestra goes inside again, furious, telling the Chorus to make her understand her new position as a slave in this house. Eventually, Cassandra does speak, but she talks in cryptic half-sentences about destruction and death; the Chorus assumes that she is remembering the war zone from which she recently came. The more she talks, the more the old men assume that she has been driven insane by the war and by being enslaved. They are amazed by her ability to correctly speak about the events that have occurred in the house of Atreus in the past though she comes from a land overseas, and they listen to how she came to have her particular powers. The god Apollo fell in love with her and gave her the gift of being able to tell the future, but she ended up rejecting him, so he added a curse, that all of her prophesies, though correct, would not be believed. The Chorus listens carefully, and true to the curse, they still are unable to understand what Cassandra's predictions of death have to do with Agamemnon and herself. When she eventually, reluctantly, goes through the doors, they are curious about why she seems so sad.

Soon, a cry rings out from within the palace, then another. The doors open to reveal Agamemnon's body, wrapped in bloody robes, lying across a silver cauldron, with Cassandra's dead body beside him. Clytaemnestra, with a bloody sword in her hand, steps forward and explains how she enacted the plan that she has worked on for years while he was gone. She lured him into a bath, she says, then wrapped him up in robes so that he could not fight and stabbed him again and again

until, on the third thrust, he died. The Chorus is horrified that she has killed the king, but Clytaemnestra defends herself on the grounds that he killed Iphigenia, their daughter, in sacrifice to the goddess Artemis. Her defense includes a reference to Cassandra, the concubine that Agamemnon brought home as a war trophy.

The Chorus declares that Clytaemnestra is either insane or horrifyingly evil, telling her that she will be brought to justice for killing the king. Clytaemnestra announces that she is not without defenses. She brings out Aegisthus, Agamemnon's cousin, who she says is going to rule by her side. Aegisthus has lived his life waiting for revenge on Agamemnon. His father, Thyestes, was the brother of Agamemnon's father, Atreus. Atreus and Thyestes competed for control of Argos. Once, after having banned Thyestes from the city, Atreus invited him back in and served him a feast. When he was nearly finished eating, Thyestes discovered that he was eating the flesh of his recently murdered children. He fled into hiding with his one surviving infant son, Aegisthus, who waited in exile until a time when he could return and take control of Argos.

The Chorus refuses to accept Aegisthus as their ruler. He calls his soldiers to make the Chorus comply. The soldiers draw their swords, and the old men of the Chorus raise their canes. Clytaemnestra prevents the imminent battle. Aegisthus swears that he will make them pay for standing up to him, and the members of the Chorus say that Orestes, who is in exile at the time, will return to save the city from the tyrant's clutches.

CHARACTERS

Aegisthus

Aegisthus, Agamemnon's cousin, appears at the end of the play as a conspirator who is going to help Clytaemnestra rule Argos once Agamemnon is dead. In different versions of the story, Aegisthus has an active hand in the murder of Agamemnon, though in the story that Aeschylus tells in this play, the murder is committed solely by Clytaemnestra.

As Aegisthus explains it, he has been in exile for his entire life, waiting for his chance to take the throne of Argos, which he feels is rightfully his. His father, Thyestes, was the brother of Agamemnon's father, Atreus, and had equal claim to the throne. The two brothers fought back and forth until Atreus invited Thyestes to a feast and tricked him into eating the bodies of his own children. Aegisthus survived and was raised out in the countryside, educated in hatred for Atreus and his sons, Agamemnon and Menelaus.

Within moments of taking control of Argos, Aegisthus shows that he will be a king who rules by intimidation. The old men of the Chorus object to the fact that their king has been murdered and that his replacement is the man who is going to marry the murderess, so Aegisthus commands their silence. To back up his command, he calls in armed guards, and is prepared to have his guards kill the citizens before Clytaemnestra calls the attack off.

Agamemnon

Although he is the title character of the play, Agamemnon only appears in it briefly. His importance to the story rests more on who he is, and on what he has done before, than on what he does onstage.

Ten years before this story begins, Agamemnon led the Greek army in an attack on Troy. Paris, the prince of Troy, had come to Argos and abducted Helen, who was the wife of Agamemnon's brother Menelaus, and the Greeks were honor-bound to fight to retrieve her. The invasion itself created some resentment among those who were left behind, especially the women. At one point in the play Agamemnon's wife Clytaemnestra speaks scornfully about the fact that all of the Greek men abandoned their homes and wives to defend the honor of another woman.

When the Greek ships were prepared to attack Troy, they were halted at Aulis by winds that pushed them back toward shore and not out to sea. The goddess Artemis required the sacrifice of Agamemnon's daughter, Iphigenia. Different versions of this story give different reasons for Artemis's demand, but in this play it is to atone for the blood of Greek soldiers who are going to be killed in the coming war. Agamemnon killed his daughter on an altar, earning him the hatred of Clytaemnestra, his wife and the girl's mother.

When he does appear in the play, Agamemnon is a humble man. He gives thanks to the gods for his victory and to the people of Argos, who have waited patiently for the army's return, and he vows to start immediately to rebuild the government. When Clytaemnestra tells him to walk on tapestries instead of walking in the dirt, he modestly states that he is not worth

such exalted treatment. He goes inside, and Clytaemnestra is able to bind him up and stab him while she is bathing him because Agamemnon naïvely does not suspect her hatred for him.

Cassandra

In Troy, Cassandra was a princess, the daughter of King Prium and Queen Hecuba. She arrives at Argos as the slave and concubine of Agamemnon, one of the spoils of war that he has earned for himself in his part of defeating the Trojans.

Cassandra has the power of foreseeing what will happen in the future, given to her by the god Apollo, who was in love with her. According to the version of the story she tells in *Agamemnon*, she had a relationship with Apollo but managed to avoid becoming pregnant with his child. In his anger, he put a curse on Cassandra so that her prophesies would be accurate but they would never be believed by those who heard them.

Arriving at Argos, she refuses to speak to Clytaemnestra or to leave Agamemnon's carriage and enter his palace. Her hesitance is first read as confusion about being in a strange land with people using a different language, and then as a refusal to admit that she is now a slave, but she eventually tells the Chorus that she knows she will be killed alongside Agamemnon when she enters the house. The old men think that she is confused or insane as she walks to the doom that she knows is coming.

Chorus

The Chorus is a group of old men of Argos who, they explain bitterly, were considered too old to participate in the invasion of Troy. They feel that they have suffered under Clytaemnestra's rule for the past ten years. They do not trust her judgment, particularly because they do not think a woman is fit to rule a country like theirs. They eagerly look forward to the return of their king, Agamemnon.

After Clytaemnestra murders Agamemnon and announces that Aegisthus will be the new king, the members of the Chorus threaten to rise up in rebellion. They stand up to the armed guards who face them with spears and swords, and are ready to face death before Clytaemnestra calls the guards down.

Clytaemnestra

According to tradition, Clytaemnestra was the daughter of Leda, who was also the mother of

Helen, Menelaus's wife. In *Agamemnon* she is presented as a jealous, vindictive woman who has been planning to murder her husband after he returns from leading the army in war.

In Agamemnon's ten-year absence, Clytaemnestra has ruled Argos. She has been an unpopular ruler. The Watchman who begins the play and the Chorus of old men who have been living in the town while the army was away complain about living under her command. There is no question that they look forward to Agamemnon's return because they find him to be a more fair and compassionate ruler than his wife. She seems to be a capable ruler whom the citizens of Argos underestimate because of her gender. For instance, she implements a series of signal fires that can carry a message almost instantly across thousands of miles of sea and land, but the Chorus dismisses her idea as a woman's wishful thinking. Their low esteem only makes Clytaemnestra angrier and crueler.

Upon Agamemnon's return, Clytaemnestra pretends to be a doting wife. Still, her speech indicates the anger that she harbors. She mentions their absent child, raising the memory of Iphigenia, whom Agamemnon sacrificed on an altar at the beginning of the war. Agamemnon shows himself uncomfortable until she coyly states that she was talking about their son Orestes, who is off in exile. She tells Agamemnon that he should walk on tapestries, sarcastically suggesting that he is too good to touch the ground while at the same time getting him used to the kinds of fine cloths that she will eventually bind him up in to kill him.

Clytaemnestra knows that she will not be able to rule Argos once she has killed Agamemnon, but she also knows that a man who took power from the king could inspire the necessary fear to rule. Part of her plan for murder includes positioning Aegisthus, with whom she has a relationship, on the throne, which she can no longer hold herself.

Herald

The Herald is a soldier who has been off to war with the Greek army. He arrives soon after Clytaemnestra has seen the signal fires and confirms what the fires have told her: the war is over, and the army is on its way home. Though his appearance in the play is only minutes after the light of the signal fires reaches Argos, readers can assume that much more time has passed between the two.

The Herald also brings news of a number of Greek ships that were lost in a storm after the war was over, including the one bearing Menelaus. He says that there were bodies floating in the water, but that other soldiers who were not accounted for might show up at home someday. His words echo the events in Homer's epic poem *The Odyssey*, in which Menelaus and his wife, Helen, are found, having been shipwrecked in Egypt.

Iphigenia

Iphigenia is the daughter of Agamemnon and Clytaemnestra. She was killed ten years earlier, sacrificed on an altar to the goddess Artemis. Clytaemnestra murders Agamemnon in revenge for having killed Iphigenia.

Orestes

Orestes is the son of Agamemnon and Clytaemnestra. He does not appear in the play, as he has been sent to live with a family friend, Strophios the Phocian, while his father was away at war. In the last scene, the Chorus predicts that Orestes will return to Argos to avenge his father's death, as he in fact does in *The Libation Bearers*, the second part of Aeschylus's trilogy, *The Oresteia*.

Watchman

The Watchman is the first character to appear in the play. He stands guard on top of the palace, looking out into the night for a signal. He has been there night after night over the course of the ten-year war and complains about the cold and the boredom of his task until, within the context of *Agamemnon*, he actually does see the signal fire that was lit far off on the horizon; then he runs inside to spread the word.

THEMES

Justice

The action of *Agamemnon* is mostly driven by the question of how justice would best be served. Agamemnon is a conquering hero, the leader of an army that triumphed after a decade of fighting. Looking at that aspect alone, he deserves a hero's welcome upon his return home. Clytaemnestra, on the other hand, views him differently. To her, he is the man who murdered her child, Iphigenia, the product of Agamemnon's own blood. In Clytaemnestra's mind, the military victory in Troy does not justify the sacrifice that Agamemnon made to achieve it.

TOPICS FOR FURTHER STUDY

- The name Cassandra is often used to identify people who, like the character in *Agamemnon*, accurately foretell the future but are not believed. Make a list of five or more people from the news who you think qualify as Cassandras and explain in a class presentation how the public rationalized ignoring each one.

- At times, the Chorus dismisses Clytaemnestra's ideas because they think that as a woman, she is behaving emotionally instead of following reason. Have sexist attitudes changed within your lifetime? Using examples from personal experience or from the news, write an essay in which you argue that sexism is either becoming outdated or here to stay.

- In the play, Clytaemnestra devised a new method for bringing news of the war back from Troy before the official messenger arrived. Design a new method for sending communications from one room of your school to another, and create a poster explaining your idea.

- Comparisons have been made between the Chorus of ancient Greek plays and the newscasters of today. Choose one news story from television or radio that involves a complicated family like Agamemnon's. Record it and write a short drama based on the events of the story. Incorporate the newscaster into the events of your play as one of the characters.

The play, therefore, raises complex questions about the nature of justice. On one hand, it is true that Agamemnon has the responsibilities of a leader, which sometimes might necessitate committing acts for the greater good that would not, individually, be acceptable in peacetime. Military leaders are not considered to be murderers when their actions are taken in the course of fulfilling their duties. Furthermore, Iphigenia's death was ordained by the goddess Artemis, a higher moral power than Agamemnon himself. Clytaemnestra, on the other hand, feels that justice is on her side. As she has him walk the blood-red tapestry into

"the home he never hoped to see," leading Agamemnon to his death, she announces "Justice, / lead him in!" Aeschylus asks whether certain acts can ever be considered just, regardless of the surrounding circumstances, and whether acting for one's country is just if it does clear and direct harm to one's family. Aeschylus does not answer these questions, though the other plays in *The Oresteia* go on to explore them with increasing subtlety.

Revenge

Clytaemnestra nurses her anger for ten years, waiting to take her revenge against her husband. Aegisthus waits even longer—his entire life since infancy—to exact his revenge, as his cause is more complicated and the crime committed against Aegisthus's family was even more barbaric. The offense that Aegisthus wants revenge for is unimaginable in its cruelty, but it was perpetrated by Agamemnon's father, not by the man Aegisthus intends to punish. His is a more theoretical hatred.

One question raised constantly in *The Oresteia* is this: how personal does an offense have to be in order to warrant revenge? Aeschylus complicates this question in *Agamemnon* by making those who have suffered wrongs also stand to gain earthly rewards from their vengeful actions. Clytaemnestra and Aegisthus feel entitled to act against Agamemnon because offenses were done against them, but like any conspirators who have no more motive than personal gain, they stand to take control of the country in the course of taking their revenge. In *The Libation Bearers*, Orestes returns to Argos to take revenge against his mother for the revenge she took against his father on behalf of her daughter, and then Orestes must defend himself and explain why he deserves revenge and when the cycle of revenge might be considered complete.

Jealousy

Although it is not the major motivator in this play, jealousy is certainly a driving force that stimulates the bad feelings between Clytaemnestra and Agamemnon. Early in the play, Clytaemnestra notes that she has watched over Argos while all of the men of the country raced to Troy to fight for the honor of another man's woman, reputedly the most beautiful woman in the world. Unmentioned is the fact that Agamemnon was one of Helen's suitors before Helen married his brother Menelaus. Later, Clytaemnestra clearly expresses her jealousy about her husband's involvement

Sicily theater where Aeschylus first staged his plays (© Barry Mason | Alamy)

with other women—not just Cassandra, the Trojan princess Agamemnon has brought back from the war as his concubine, but all of the women he probably had relationships with during the decade-long siege. She refers to Agamemnon, whom she has recently murdered, as "the darling of all / the golden girls who spread the gates of Troy."

Agamemnon is not jealous because he does not know about his wife's involvement with his cousin, Aegisthus. Clytaemnestra keeps Aegisthus's involvement in the murder plot a secret until after she has killed her husband. In other versions of this story, Aegisthus is an active player in murdering Agamemnon and Cassandra, but Aeschylus makes it clear that, though Aegisthus believes himself to be a driving force, the killing is motivated by Clytaemnestra's anger at being wronged.

Sexism

The traditional roles of men and women were clearly defined in ancient Greek society and are reflected in *Agamemnon*. This play is able to draw particular attention to those roles because of the situation in which it takes place. It is wartime and the king has been called away from the country, creating the unusual circumstance of the queen being left in charge for an extended length of time.

Clytaemnestra's rule of Argos is not popular with the Watchman or the old men in the Chorus. It is likely, though, that their dislike of her is caused by their own sexism, and not by any particular act of her own. They never mention anything that she may have done as their ruler that would have harmed or offended them, but they do complain, frequently, about her being a woman. Her plan to carry news across thousands of miles with a series of signal lights is ingenious, but after a while the Chorus comes to mock it as unreliable: "Just like a woman / to fill with thanks before the truth is clear. / —So gullible.... // rumours voiced by women come to nothing." Clytaemnestra, who is well aware that they dismiss her ideas because she is a woman, is defensive and more inclined to be a harsh leader because of it, showing that she has the same toughness as a man.

Sexist attitudes may be seen at the very heart of the play's action. Agamemnon and Clytaemnestra view the sacrifice of their daughter, Iphigenia, from different perspectives, and their perspectives coincide with traditional gender roles. Agamemnon views Iphigenia's death as a necessary loss in order to attain a military victory that will hopefully prevent further attacks, while Clytaemnestra sees it through the lens of her own immediate family, as a mother who has lost a child.

STYLE

Dialogue

Aeschylus is credited with adding a second actor on stage in his dramas, a technique that allowed his dramas to present their situations through the characters' dialogue. Originally, staged dramas were presented as recitations by a chorus, or group of actors, which told the story but did not act it out. By Aeschylus's time, there was generally one actor. He might change masks throughout a performance, indicating that he was different characters, but still, the dramatic possibilities were limited.

With the addition of a second actor, the issues examined in a play could be dramatized through dialogue. Instead of telling audiences what each character felt, the character could either say what he or she felt or try to hide his or her feelings. The other character could then accept what he or she was told or challenge it. One example of this in *Agamemnon* occurs when Clytaemnestra, talking about how she "wavered between the living and the dead" while her husband was away, abruptly starts talking about their child who is "gone, not standing by our side," and only after a while reveals that she is talking about Orestes, the son in exile, and not the daughter that Agamemnon sacrificed on an altar. "You seem startled," she tells him, letting audiences know the emotions felt by the masked actor playing Agamemnon. Without dialogue, his suspicions of her would have to be voiced directly, which would undercut the nature of suspicion.

Greek Chorus

The use of dialogue diminished the part of the Chorus in Greek drama, though it was still many years before the Chorus fell away. In *Agamemnon* the Chorus is used, as choruses traditionally were, to convey background information. Many audience members would have been familiar with the tales that dramas were based on, but there were also many different versions of those tales. The recitation by the Chorus would serve to show which details were important to this playwright's telling. By the time that *Agamemnon* was written, the Chorus had ceased to function as an objective narrator and was identified as a character itself. Usually, as in this play, it represented a group of citizens who were familiar with the other characters and who had a vested interest in the events that were transpiring. The Chorus in *Agamemnon* is even more specific than a group of citizens because it represents the old men who have been excluded from the war and have a very particular view of the situation of the play. They are resentful about being told that they are not good enough to fight and resentful about being left to take orders from Clytaemnestra, a woman.

HISTORICAL CONTEXT

The Trojan War

The events depicted in *Agamemnon* take place in the aftermath of the Trojan War, which is considered one of the most significant sources for Greek mythology. Aside from Greek descriptions, there is no direct historical evidence of when the war took place or who was involved. Archaeologists have found that the ancient city of Troy, in modern Turkey, overlooking the straits of Hellespont, was destroyed sometime around 1250 BCE, presumably by violence, and many assume that the war that brought it down was the basis for the legends of the Trojan War. The Athenian scholar Erastosthenes calculated in the third century BCE that the fall of Troy occurred around 1184 BCE, which is so close that historians assume that each calculation is talking about the same event.

According to tradition, the Trojan War began as a direct result of a competition of the gods. Three goddesses—Hera, Athena, and Aphrodite—asked Zeus to choose which was fairest, and Zeus put the task off to Paris, the prince of Troy. Each goddess offered Paris a bribe for his vote, and he accepted the one offered by Aphrodite. As goddess of love, Aphrodite was not the most beautiful one, but she could offer Paris the love of Helen, the most beautiful woman in the world and the wife of King Menelaus of Sparta. Some sources say that Helen fell in love with Paris, and some say that he came to Sparta and took her forcibly, since Aphrodite had promised her to him. Menelaus called together all of the great men of Greece who had been Helen's suitors before she had married him, a list that included Odysseus, Ajax, Patroclus, and Menelaus's own brother, Agamemnon, who led the army that set out to invade Troy. The siege lasted ten years, ending when the Greeks snuck in to the city hidden inside of a hollow statue, the famed Trojan Horse, given as a false peace offering.

Many writers of the classic Greek period wrote tales about the Trojan War, and so there are many

COMPARE & CONTRAST

- **458 BCE:** Women are not considered fit for public office; only in the case of an extraordinary event like a war would a woman like Clytaemnestra hold political power.

  Today: Political offices across the globe are open to people of either gender. For example, in 2005 Angela Merkel becomes the first chancellor of Germany.

- **458 BCE:** Polytheism, or belief in many gods, is common in major civilizations. The gods of ancient Greece and Rome are thought to have been actively involved in human affairs, motivated by the same desires that compel human behavior.

  Today: Polytheism still exists, but the three most prevalent religions—Judaism, Christianity, and Islam—are monotheistic, meaning they hold that there is only one god.

- **458 BCE:** One generation of a family might fight to take revenge for a wrong done to them in the generation before.

  Today: In first-world nations where all citizens have access to the legal system, most wrongs are handled through the courts.

- **458 BCE:** The murder of a ruler might not be punished if the murderers have enough political power to take control of the country.

  Today: Political coups still displace established governments, but there are international tribunals to prosecute the worst violations.

- **458 BCE:** Dramas like *Agamemnon* are attended by those who have citizenship—males of the upper class.

  Today: Live theater is available to all, regardless of financial standing or interest; however, people most frequently watch drama in the form of movies or television.

variations to each story, as well as intricate details available about the histories of each character. The most authoritative sources are *The Iliad*, concerning events in the final year of the war, and *The Odyssey*, concerning the ten-year journey home of Greek hero Odysseus and his crewmates. These works are credited to the epic poet Homer, though historians believe that the two books might have been written by several different authors between 900 and 700 BCE. It is certain that Aeschylus, as well as many of the audience members who would have attended performances of his works, would have been familiar with Homer's accounts of the Trojan War and its aftermath.

Greek Dramatic Competitions

Of all of the examples of ancient Greek drama that exist today, all but one come from the springtime festivals of Dionysus Eleuthereus in Athens that began in the sixth century BCE. The festival was originally a celebration of the god Dionysus, the god of wine and creativity. By the sixth century, however, the drama, which had been staged as a minor part of the festival, had grown in prominence to become an important focus each year. Three playwrights were allowed to submit three dramas each year, as well as a short, rowdy comedy, called a satyr play. Each year, three wealthy citizens were also chosen and assigned to provide financing for the staging of the competition plays, and ten judges were chosen, one from each of the city's "tribes," or *phylai*. Winners of the dramatic competitions were recognized with a crown of ivy. Eventually, as dramas evolved from poetic speeches recited by choruses to dramatizations of scenes by distinct characters, a class of professional actors evolved out of the festivals of Dionysus Eleuthereus, also called the Dionysia.

As the competitions developed, the standards became more structured. Each poet's three competition works came to be linked by a

Staging of The Oresteia, *with Agamemnon on the right, at Olivier Theatre/National Theatre, London* (Photostage)

theme, and plays eventually constituted trilogies following the lives of the same characters. Aeschylus's trilogy *The Oresteia*, of which *Agamemnon* is the first play, is the one remaining intact trilogy to have survived to this day. It won first prize at the Athenian festival. Its corresponding satyr play, *Proteus*, concerns the travels of Menelaus as he returns from the Trojan War.

Aeschylus won the festival thirteen times over the course of his long lifetime. Sophocles, who competed against the much older Aeschylus, managed to beat him in competition and went on to win seventeen more times, including for his *Oedipus* trilogy, which exists today. The other major tragedian of the period was Euripides, who was born after Aeschylus's death. He won the Athenian dramatic festival only three times during his life (and once after his death), but he is considered one of the most important writers of the time, writing several works that survive today, including *The Bacchae*.

CRITICAL OVERVIEW

Aeschylus is considered the father of Greek tragedy, the first of the trio of writers, including Sophocles and Euripides, who have come to represent the golden age of Greek drama. Winning the Athens drama festival, his trilogy *The Oresteia* earned him recognition from the start and has been one of the most influential works of the Western canon ever since. He is credited with putting more than one character at a time on the stage and building his plays around complex moral dilemmas, setting standards for drama that remain in place today. Admiration for Aeschylus has been constant throughout the centuries, exemplified in the quote by Victorian poet Charles Algernon Swinburne, who Albin Lesky reports in *A History of Greek Literature* once referred to *The Oresteia* as "the greatest achievement of the human mind." Though not all critics praise the works with the exuberance that Swinburne lavished on it, there are none who would deny its importance to Western culture.

Some critics have identified *Agamemnon* as being the weakest of the three plays in the trilogy. It introduces themes that are not developed until the later plays and is uneven in its presentation of characters, as when the title character merely passes through for a few pages. Most critics, however, do not find this to be a problem of the play so much as a conceptual problem on the part of those who would try to stage it on its own, out of the context of *The Oresteia*. As John Herington notes in his essay "No-Man's-Land of Dark and Light" in *Aeschylus's* The Oresteia: *Modern Critical Interpretations*,

> To stage *Agamemnon* on its own makes rather less sense than to perform the first movement of a Beethoven symphony on its own. The leading themes of the *Oresteia* are, it is true, introduced in *Agamemnon*, but in a confused and confusing way, for this play depicts a world in moral chaos, a world in which there seem to be no fixed principles left to hold on to.

The few weaknesses of *Agamemnon* are therefore not considered the fault of the playwright; rather, they are integral to the themes of the complete work.

CRITICISM

David Kelly

Kelly is a writer and an instructor of creative writing and literature. In this essay, he looks at the ways in which Aeschylus builds believable characters in Agamemnon.

Agamemnon, the first play in Aeschylus's Oresteian trilogy, is a mature work, written in the final years of the life of one of the most skillful dramatists who ever lived. The trilogy examines critical issues of what it means to exist in society, pitting rules against emotions and individual rights against collective rights in ways that have had a broad impact on the development of legal theory throughout Western civilization. In *Agamemnon*, people do terrible things to other people, who then hold onto their grievances, nurturing them until almost everyone has forgotten the original offense. The offended then strike in retribution, and a new generation, knowing only the latest attack, starts planning a reciprocal retribution. This cycle twists its way through *The Libation Bearers* to *The Eumenides*, where the gods hold a trial to decide that the string of retribution, which could conceivably extend forever, must be cut short somewhere.

EVEN READERS WHO APPROACH *AGAMEMNON* AS AN EXAMPLE OF GREEK THEATER MUST ADMIT THAT CLYTAEMNESTRA MIGHT STAND FOR ONE THING OR ANOTHER, BUT SHE WOULD NOT BE A CREDIBLE REPRESENTATIVE OF THOSE TRAITS IF AESCHYLUS HAD NOT MADE A CREDIBLE HUMAN BEING OUT OF HER."

Agamemnon handles these social issues with a free-flowing grace that was not common at the time. For modern audiences, it might seem a little too verbal, with long speeches giving background that does not seem necessary. Parts that may bore modern audiences, though, become more interesting if readers and viewers remember that the play was written at a time when the custom was to direct *all* of the language and action to the audience, not to the other characters on the stage. *Showing* instead of *telling*, which is the standard for the modern era, was unheard of in Aeschylus's day. Making minor allowances for the different dramatic customs of the time, one can find much of interest in Aeschylus's characters. They are believable, rounded characters who exist beyond their symbolic functions.

The play opens with the Watchman standing atop the house of Atreus, the palace, looking down on the square below while lazily reminding himself that his attention should be on the horizon in case there are any developments in the ten-year-old Trojan War. The Watchman is poised to open up the new, post-war world to Greece, and he is...well, bored. Like any other low-paid functionary who has been at an unexciting, repetitious job for a year, he is not thinking of his place in history but instead is praying that the gods might relieve his cramps and keep him awake. Another playwright might have used this character just to shout out the news that the signal fires have announced the end of the war, but this Watchman does not even think that the grand scope of things can be more important than his own nagging complaints. Aeschylus has made him human.

His counterpart is, of course, the Herald who arrives later, bringing the actual, verifiable

WHAT DO I READ NEXT?

- Readers who have started the story of the house of Atreus in *Agamemnon* will want to read the rest of *The Oresteia* (458 BCE). In *The Libation Bearers*, Orestes, the son of Agamemnon and Clytaemnestra, returns to slay his mother and her new husband Aegisthus in retribution for his father's death. In *The Eumenides*, Orestes stands before a tribunal of the gods, who are charged with passing judgment on the whole concept of vengeance. All three books can be found in a new translation by poet Ted Hughes, commissioned by the Royal National Theater and published by Farrar, Straus and Giroux in 1999.

- Agamemnon and Cassandra are supporting characters in William Shakespeare's 1602 play *Troilus and Cressida*. Many editions are available, including the 2007 Folger Shakespeare Library version from Washington Square Press.

- *The Living Art of Greek Tragedy* (2003), by Marianne McDonald, examines three ancient Greek playwrights whose works are known and influential to this day: Aeschylus, Sophocles, and Euripides. Her discussion of these writers and their works shows the relevance of each in the modern world.

- Like *Agamemnon*, Shakespeare's *Hamlet* (written c. 1601) begins with a sentry keeping watch at night and follows a series of actions and counter-actions that are taken in the name of revenge. It too is available from the Folger Shakespeare Library from Washington Square Press, in an edition published in 2003.

- In his comedy *The Frogs*, first performed at the Festival of Dionysus in 405 BCE, Aristophanes dramatizes a scene with Euripides and Aeschylus competing in Hades for the title of "Best Tragic Poet" before the god Dionysus, who, despairing of the state of modern tragedy, can take one of the playwrights back to the surface to revive his festival. *The Frogs* is available in *Aristophanes: The Complete Plays*, published in 2005 by NAL Trade.

---

news that the war in Troy is indeed over. The Herald, more than the Watchman, is used to deliver background information to the audience, though Aeschylus does not sacrifice much in the way of character to achieve this. The Herald is a soldier, and as the old men of the Chorus make clear when they complain about being left behind during the invasion, this culture honors military involvement, and soldiers claim the right to walk with pride. He has also probably done this before—brought people news and seen their reactions to him, merging the messenger with the message. It would be natural that a person in his position would have an inflated sense of his own significance. And since his character would credibly be this way, Aeschylus only stretches the boundaries of credibility a little when he has the Herald talk at length about facts that are only slightly related to the plot of the drama, such as the storm that took the Greek

fleet and his own personal confidence that Menelaus, Agamemnon's brother, will show up again some day. Even for one who is used to holding his listeners' attention with the news he brings, the Herald comes off a little more like a source of background information than a person invested in the actions onstage. Aeschylus uses him primarily as a vehicle for delivering information to the audience, but that use is perfectly suited to who this character is.

Though the Herald is primarily important for delivering information, Cassandra is, oddly, the opposite. In theory, a character who can see the future would seem to be an ideal contrivance for a playwright to foreshadow what is coming up next to the audience, but in Aeschylus's situation, there was no need for that because he was dealing with old, familiar tales that most members of his audience would know. Instead of using Cassandra to tell the audience new information, then, he uses her in *Agamemnon* for emotional effect. She is barely coherent, raving, driven mad by her knowledge of the horrible death that awaits her. Since dramatic convention would not allow Aeschylus to put the actual massacre of Cassandra and Agamemnon on the stage, Cassandra experiences it moments before it happens, a powerful dramatic substitution. As fans of horror movies will attest, the anticipation of a gruesome deed is generally much more gripping than witnessing it would be because it forces the audience to participate with their imaginations. From the moment she steps out of the shadows to talk, Cassandra is a character in the process of dying. Aeschylus could hardly have conjured up a character more worthy of his audience's attention.

About Clytaemnestra as a character little needs to be said. She is one of the world's great protagonists, a woman whose complexity far exceeds her function in the story. The unwillingness to accept the sacrifice of her daughter Iphigenia has burned for a decade because it has been fueled by more than just her sense of justice, but by the obstinacy that is embedded deeply in her personality. In her idea of having signal fires transmit information across miles in a second, one can see her genius; in her anger at those who doubted it would work, one can see the pride that drives her. Clytaemnestra stands alone against the forces that disapprove of her, including the basic sexism of her society (which Aeschylus shows to be a useless, blinding affectation) and the populace's outrage at having their king murdered. She is only a credible character because Aeschylus has made her a person who might be able to stand up to such pressures and dismiss them. Even readers who approach *Agamemnon* as an example of Greek theater must admit that Clytaemnestra might stand for one thing or another, but she would not be a credible representative of those traits if Aeschylus had not made a credible human being out of her.

While Clytaemnestra is a thoroughly memorable, believable character, the same can hardly be said about her husband, Agamemnon, the king of Argos, the leader of the victorious army, who comes off as the vaguest, most ill-defined character onstage. Again, this is not really a sign that Aeschylus did not know what to do with this character, but is in fact a sign that he knew exactly what he was doing. Agamemnon only passes through onstage briefly, yet given the brief time he is in the drama that bears his name, he makes a distinct impression as a humble man, ready to settle down to the business of ruling just minutes after returning from a ten-year siege. Some critics have pointed out the fact that he does, at his wife's urging, consent to walk into his palace on a beautiful set of tapestries that would be more fitting for a god than a mortal, claiming that this is meant to be the evidence that Agamemnon has abandoned his humility to hubris, and therefore has earned the death brought down on him. But hubris, the inflated sense of self-importance, is a character trait, not a solitary act. Given the brevity of Agamemnon's appearance here, there is just no way of telling whether he is swept up by Clytaemnestra's persuasiveness or by the thrill of his triumphant return home, or if he really believes himself on level with the gods. Agamemnon appears, is flattered, resists flattery, and then gives in to it. For such a brief walk-through appearance, he establishes himself as a credible person.

The only character in *Agamemnon* to come off as hollow is Aegisthus. He is a cartoonish representative of evil who is not brave enough to kill his enemy himself but lets a woman do it instead; not honest enough to admit that the murder is Clytaemnestra's achievement, he takes credit for it; not sympathetic enough to make others see that the massacre of his brothers and sisters and the humiliation and befouling of his father gives him a right to strike against Agamemnon; and not regal enough to take control of Argos without brute power. He does not have the conflicting morals that fill out a well-drawn, human character—not even a minor character like the Watchman, torn between duty and boredom—but Aegisthus does provide the template for generations of villains to come. In putting Aegisthus in this play, Aeschylus has siphoned off much of the hatred that might otherwise be directed toward Clytaemnestra, allowing audiences to see her more clearly, in all of her human weakness.

Agamemnon is usually read in a school situation, as a text for learning about Greek morals and the development of the standards of Western civilization. Ancient texts probably need to be viewed that way, at least some of the time. But looking at the drama as a drama, appreciating Aeschylus as a playwright and not as a poet or philosopher, it turns out that his works stand up on their own. In particular, the characters that

> AESCHYLUS HAS BEEN CALLED THE FATHER OF TRAGEDY AND IS THE FIRST GREAT WRITER IN THIS GENRE. HE STAGED AND ACTED IN HIS PLAYS AND WAS RESPONSIBLE FOR GREAT INNOVATIONS SUCH AS THE INTRODUCTION OF TWO SPEAKING ACTORS PERFORMING ON STAGE TOGETHER."

he develops to populate this play, using traditional, familiar materials, are as fresh and real as any characters written in the twentieth or twenty-first century. They are not primitive at all. They are rounded and multifaceted. They are real.

Source: David Kelly, Critical Essay on *Agamemnon*, in *Drama for Students*, Gale, Cengage Learning, 2009.

Rob Normey

In the following essay, Normey provides biographical information on Aeschylus and discusses the modern relevance of The Oresteia.

The terrorist attacks on September 11 and its aftermath have astounded and altered all of us in ways impossible to measure. The enormity of the tragedy in New York and Washington may be beyond the ability of works of literature to encompass in any truly meaningful way. Nonetheless, I was most interested in a discussion the superb Eleanor Wachtel had with a panel on *Writers and Company* (CBC Radio for those of you out of the loop) after the attacks. Roger Shattuck, the distinguished academic critic (*Proust, Forbidden Knowledge*) offered the observation that we would do well to read Aeschylus' *Oresteia*.

I can report that I have taken him at his word and worked my way through the trilogy in Robert Fagles' translation. The *Oresteia* is made up of *Agamemnon,The Libation Bearers* and *The Euminides*. Aeschylus also wrote a satyr play with comic elements which was performed with the tragedies, but this has been lost. I won't try to draw links between the *Oresteia* and the recent acts of carnage but assure you that the trilogy has an abundance of political and moral meanings.

Aeschylus has been called the father of tragedy and is the first great writer in this genre. He

staged and acted in his plays and was responsible for great innovations such as the introduction of two speaking actors performing on stage together. Previously, the practice was to limit the interaction to one speaking actor and the chorus. Aeschylus was a formidable presence in Athenian society in the golden age of that remarkable city-state.

He valiantly fought at Marathon in the famous victory over the expansionist Persians in 490 BC. This soldier citizen also fought at Salamis. Indeed, despite his prowess as a playwright, it is his contributions as a warrior that are identified in his epitaph on a tombstone in Sicily:

> Aeschylus of Athens, Euphorion's son, this tomb covers,
> Who died at wheat-bearing Gela;
> His valour of high repute the grove of Marathon would attest
> And the long-haired Mede who came to know it well.

Aeschylus wrote over 90 plays, of which 7 have survived complete along with a number of fragments. His plays, including the *Oresteia,* were awarded a number of prizes in the fiercely competitive society of fifth century Athens. Nonetheless, in the years after his death his tragedies appear to have been far less popular with Greek audiences than the more accessible plays of his younger contemporaries, Sophocles and Euripides. Referring to Aeschylus' inspired interweaving of extended metaphors and his grand manner, Sophocles commented that the first tragedian must have composed while under some form of Dionysian intoxication.

Aeschylus wrote the *Oresteia* in 458 BC at the age of 67, two years before his death. It is believed that he was producing the work in Sicily at the time of his death. It was first performed at the famous Great Dionysia Festival, an annual festival of immense religious significance. The festival took place in the ninth month of the Greek calendar, roughly corresponding to our March. Tribute was offered to Dionysus, god of fertility and celebration.

The trilogy weaves myths concerning the cursed House of Atreus with incidents from the Trojan War into a gripping revenge saga. The House of Atreus is shot through with hubris and savagery. One of the ancient patriarchs, Pelops, won the hand of his bride through a ruse which killed her father—a reckless, deathly chariot ride which may have been the origin of the Olympic

Games. Pelops had two sons who feuded with one another. Atreus is reported to have lured his brother Thyestes to his banquet hall for a reconciliation. Atreus then proceeded to serve Thyestes his own children's flesh. Aghast at this barbaric act, Thyestes cursed Atreus and his descendants and fled into exile with his remaining son Aegisthus.

Atreus had two sons, Agamemnon and Menelaus, who jointly ruled the kingdom of Argos and married two sisters, Clytemnestra and Helen. Menelaus we will recall was dismayed to learn that his beautiful wife Helen had committed infidelity with the dashing Paris and fled with her lover to Troy. This was the famous event triggering the Trojan War. Agamemnon is established as commander-in-chief of the Greek forces. Before he can lead his troops across the sea, he is given an omen. He considers it necessary in light of the message he receives to sacrifice his own daughter, Iphigenia, to the goddess Artemis in order to set sail for Troy.

Agamemnon takes the story up as a watchman awaits the long-anticipated return of the king and his troops. Peering into the night, he makes out the light from torches which have been stationed along the route to the palace. The lighting of the torches signals that Agamemnon has returned after ten long years! This play of light and dark, together with a sequence of other key images and metaphors will be woven throughout the trilogy with powerful dramatic intensity.

This first play is at root a domestic tragedy. It asks its original audience in the severely patriarchal society of ancient Greece to contemplate the disruptive and frightening presence of a woman plotting to murder her husband, the leader of the entire community. Given Agamemnon's exalted status, the play is a political tragedy as well. Clytemnestra intends to punish her husband for the callous sacrifice of their daughter. We are made to experience the fear pervading the community, represented by the Chorus, as this formidable woman meticulously carries out her bloody deed, with the assistance of her lover, Aegisthus.

First she orchestrates a deeply ironic homecoming ceremony, convincing Agamemnon that he should overcome his scruples and accept the dangerous honour of treading on blood-red tapestries she has laid out for him. Her ability to play on his overweening pride tells us much about the flawed nature of the king.

Clytemnestra is less successful in manipulating the king's consort, Cassandra, a Trojan princess. Agamemnon has taken her as war booty. Cassandra is left on stage with the Chorus and gradually reveals to it her amazing powers of prophecy as an initiate of Apollo. She foretells in vivid and despairing detail the sorry end that awaits both herself and Agamemnon. She further foretells the appearance of a stranger who will avenge their deaths.

In *The Libation Bearers,* a similar pattern of extended preparation for the central confrontation of protagonists is developed in lines of sombre beauty and grandeur. Piercing oratory is exchanged between Orestes (son of Agamemnon) who returns to Argos in disguise, and his mother, from whom he has been separated for many years. The debate crashes to a close with the reminder that Orestes is under an injunction from Apollo to avenge his father's death. As the Chorus laments:

> It is the law, when the blood of slaughter
> wets the ground
> It wants more blood/
> Slaughter cries for the fury
> Of those long dead to bring destruction
> On destruction churning in its wake.

The cycle of bloody revenge thus appears to exemplify Nietzsche's aphorism: "All that exists is just and unjust and equally justified in both."

The Eumenides opens with Orestes being pursued by the Furies, primordial beings who rise up from the earth to demand his blood. They are hastened on by Clytemnestra's wandering spirit. Orestes has fled to the shrine of Apollo at Delphi in order to pray and seek purification. The young prince attempts to justify his deed, but the Furies adamantly refuse to exonerate him. They begin to sing a "binding song" which will cast a spell that will lead to a painful death. The goddess Athena arrives in time to protect him. She seeks to arbitrate the seemingly insoluble conflict.

The scene shifts to Athens. After praying at Athena's shrine on the Acropolis, Orestes makes his way to the Areopagus, the Athenian court. In a magnificent foundation myth, Aeschylus imagines a brilliant and auspicious beginning for the real court that played such a part in the polis of his time. Athena with her wisdom and reputation for fairness persuades both sides to agree on a trial in which "the first men of Athens" will sit as jurors and will cast their ballot stones after hearing all of the evidence. The trial scenes must be experienced directly. Modern readers will no doubt find it difficult to fathom Apollo's argument to the effect that Orestes should be acquitted because a woman is not really a parent of a child, just a "nurse to the seed." For good measure, he adds that it is man who is the source of life. At the very least, some may be mollified to note that it is not he, but Athena, displaying her wisdom as a goddess, who presides over the trial. By a close margin, Orestes is acquitted. Athena then respectfully persuades the Furies to forego their lust for vengeance and become respected guardians of Athens. She thus brings about a remarkable reconciliation. The Furies are transformed into the Euminides or kindly ones and will now channel their energies for good.

In dramatizing the transformation from a society governed by tribal laws of revenge to a society governed by the rule of law, fulfilled by independent judges and jurors, Aeschylus also entered the debate, which absorbed Athenians in 458, over the exact role of the Areopagus. Critics differ on where precisely Aeschylus stood on certain reforms proposed by the radical Pericles. It seems evident to me that he supported moderate democratic reforms to the degree that they would not seriously impair the basic functions of the court. In any event, on a deeper level, it is rare to experience a drama that so powerfully dramatizes the contribution that a fair and impartial court system makes to democratic civilization.

Source: Rob Normey, "*Oresteia*: A Bright New Day for Civilization," in *LawNow*, Vol. 26, No. 3, December–January 2001, pp. 44–45.

Harry L. Levy

In the following excerpt, Levy identifies the central theme in Agamemnon: *the problem of good and evil.*

The unending fascination of Greek drama, both in its original form and in modern adaptations, is constantly confirmed here in the United States and abroad by stage presentations. As countless lectures, symposia, and articles attest, the ancient Greek drama off-stage serves as a plentiful source of serious discourse for scholars and thinkers of our own time. The reason is obvious: the great Greek dramaturgists discerned and presented in striking form some of the most crucial problems with which thoughtful human beings of all ages and all cultures must perforce concern themselves. And so it is with the *Oresteia*, the great trilogy of Aeschylus: the *Agamemnon*, the *Libation-Bearers*, and the *Eumenides*.

> THE GREEK DRAMATISTS BOLDLY CONFRONT THE FACT THAT EVIL EXISTS: THEY HOLD THAT IT SPRINGS, SOMETIMES FROM THE MACHINATIONS OF THE GODS, SOMETIMES FROM THE FAULTS OF MEN."

The *Oresteia* commences with the return of Agamemnon from Troy and his slaughter by his queen and her paramour, tells us in the *Libation-Bearers* of the vengeance taken by Agamemnon's son Orestes, now grown to manhood, and ends with Orestes' persecution by the Furies of his mother, and his final release from the hounding of these monsters, who, changed to Eumenides, "The Kindly Ones," become a pillar of the Athenian polity. That, in brief, is the story: but what is the meaning of it as Aeschylus presents it? Richmond Lattimore, a superb translator and interpreter of Greek drama, thinks that he finds the answer, at least so far as the first two plays are concerned, in the dynamic contradiction between hate and love—he speaks of hate-in-love in the *Agamemnon*, and love-in-hate in the *Libation-Bearers*. For a full explication of his provocative theory, I refer you to his own writings.

But I should like to suggest to you that the problem which is central to the *Oresteia* is, if not altogether different from love and hate, at least more general: the problem of good and evil. The Greek dramatists boldly confront the fact that evil exists: they hold that it springs, sometimes from the machinations of the gods, sometimes from the faults of men. When evil comes into being, and harms or threatens to harm the lives of men, how are they to meet it? Shall they return evil for evil? This is the ancient law of the Near East, an eye for an eye and a tooth for a tooth, the *lex talionis,* the law of retaliation. Our trilogy is a study of the actual operation of this law in the first two plays, and of its partial setting-aside in the third.

The first play, the *Agamemnon,* centers upon a double retaliation: a single act of violence intended by each of its two perpetrators to avenge a different wrong. Clytemnestra, Queen of Argos, and her lover Aegisthus, as we have seen, murder

Agamemnon, returning victorious from the Trojan war. The murderer-in-chief is not the man Aegisthus, but the woman Clytemnestra. Aeschylus makes much of this point, and it bears upon the problem of the relative position of man and woman in the structure of the Greek family, a topic to which we shall return.

Let us dispose at once of the minor retaliator, Aegisthus. He was avenging the horrible murder of his own brothers by Agamemnon's father, Atreus: one explosion in what we may call in modern terms a chain-reaction of evil, into the details of which it would be beside our point to go.

But what of Clytemnestra? What does she avenge by the killing of Agamemnon? It is the ritual slaughter of her and Agamemnon's daughter Iphigenia, whom Agamemnon had killed at Aulis as a sacrifice to angered divinities. The sacrifice was performed in order that the Greek fleet might have safe passage to Troy. Now let us break into the chain at this point and consider this single link. Had Agamemnon not killed Iphigenia, he would not have been slain in turn by Clytemnestra. Then the specific chain-reaction of which we are speaking would not have occurred. Could Agamemnon have avoided the killing of his daughter, when the prophet had told him that this was the only way to secure the safe-conduct of the fleet to Troy? Yes, he could: but it would have meant renouncing the *lex talionis* at this point; he would have had to forego the revenge which he felt he and the other Greek princes were in duty bound to exact from Paris, the seducer of Helen.

Here, then, we have in this chain of events what seems to me the first clear instance of the decision of human will in the face of evil. That Paris' act had been evil, a breaking of the laws of gods and men, those primary laws governing the sanctity of the family and of the host-guest relationship, none could deny. That Paris' crime deserved punishment none could gainsay. But who was to punish him? The wronged one, says old Near-East tradition, the wronged one, if he is still alive; the wronged one, supported if he is alive, and replaced if he is not, by his kinsmen. Had it been simply a matter of exacting penalty for an abominable crime, who, according to the morality of that early time, would have raised an objection? But here the gods intervene: to accomplish his mission of retaliation, Agamemnon must sacrifice one of his own blood, his

beloved daughter, who had often joined with her clear maiden voice in his sacrifices to the gods. Agamemnon's anguish at the need for the choice is narrated by the Chorus. But anguished or not, he made his choice between his duty as a father and his duty as a ruler and warrior; he killed his daughter.

The girl is killed; the fleet sails; Agamemnon's host is victorious over the Trojans, and our heroic general returns in glory, to boast to the people of Mycenae that he has avenged the wrong done to Menelaus. In the vainglorious speech, there is no word of pity for the death of his innocent daughter; this is forgotten. So far is he from feeling any pity for one who must die so that his grand plans may advance, that he speaks with self-righteous assurance of using surgery to amputate any offending element in the state, all unconscious—a nice instance of dramatic irony—that the first victim of the knife is to be himself.

Well then, evil for evil: Paris has done wrong, Troy has been destroyed, Iphigenia has been cut down, to use Catullus' phrase, like a flower at the edge of the meadow, when it has been touched by the passing plowshare. Evil for evil, and there an end. But no: there is the seed of new evil here, for Clytemnestra, a woman with a man's will, does not accept Agamemnon's choice. He has killed her daughter; he must die in his turn. He dies, and Clytemnestra exults: "This is Agamemnon, my husband: he is dead; his death is the work of my own right hand, the work of a righteous craftsman. And that is that!" To the avenger, that is always that; the wrong is requited, the game is over. Nowhere does Clytemnestra show any wavering, any sense of a need for choice between slaying her king and husband, or leaving unavenged the evil of her daughter's death. Her womanliness comes out only in the fervor of her desire—vain hope—to have peace, now at last, to have an end of bloodshed. So ends the *Agamemnon*, the first great act of the trilogy: but just before the close, the Chorus foreshadow the next act. They speak of their longing for the return of Orestes, Agamemnon's young son, who has been sent away to stay with a prince in mainland Greece. Let him come back, they pray, to avenge his father's death. Upon whom? Upon the pair of murderers, they say. What of the fact that one of them is his mother? They take no note of that directly . . .

Source: Harry L. Levy, "The *Oresteia* of Aeschylus," in *Drama Survey*, Vol. 4, Summer 1965, pp. 149–58.

SOURCES

Aeschylus, *Agamemnon*, in *The Oresteia*, translated by Robert Fagles, Penguin Books, 1979, pp. 120, 135–37, 163.

"Aeschylus and His Tragedies," http://www.theatrehistory. com/ancient/aeschylus001.html (accessed July 22, 2008); originally published in *The Drama: Its History, Literature and Influence on Civilization*, Vol. 1, edited by Alfred Bates, Historical Publishing, 1906, pp. 53–9.

Herington, John, "No-Man's-Land of Dark and Light," in *Aeschylus's* The Oresteia: *Modern Critical Interpretations*, edited by Harold Bloom, Chelsea House Publishers, 1988, p. 121.

Lesky, Albin, *A History of Greek Literature*, Thomas Y. Crowell, 1966, p. 256.

Oxford Dictionary of the Classical World, s.v. "Tragedy, Greek."

Sommerstein, Alan Herbert, "Aeschylus," in *Who's Who in the Classical World*.

FURTHER READING

Euripides, *Iphigenia at Aulis*, translated by Don Taylor, BiblioBazaar, 2008.
> Originally published in 406 BCE, about a half century after Aeschylus's death, this play concerns the events surrounding the sacrifice of Iphigenia, which is the basis for Clytaemnestra's revenge in *Agamemnon*.

Fagles, Robert, and W. B. Stanford, "The Serpent and the Eagle," in *The Oresteia*, Penguin Press, 1979, pp. 13–97.
> This analysis of Aeschylus's trilogy, written by one of the most respected twentieth-century scholars of ancient Greek literature, gives readers an in-depth overview of the times, as well as of Aeschylus's innovative methods.

Gere, Cathy, *The Tomb of Agamemnon*, Profile Books, 2006.
> This book considers the archaeological discovery of the city of Mycenae, where the story takes place, and the burial vault believed to be that of the real, historical Agamemnon. It includes much information about burial rites and beliefs of King Agamemnon's lifetime, which would have been about seven centuries before Aeschylus's.

Herington, John, *Aeschylus*, Yale University Press, 1996.
> Herington is considered one of the great Greek scholars of the twentieth century. In this book, he offers a comprehensive examination of the playwright's life and career.

The Bear

ANTON PAVLOVICH CHEKHOV

1888

One of Anton Chekhov's minor dramatic works, *Medved* (*The Bear*, sometimes translated as (*The Boor*) was written in 1888 and apparently held in low esteem by Chekhov, who described it as "a silly little French vaudeville," as Vera Gottlieb notes in *The Cambridge Companion to Chekhov*. Yet much of Chekhov's literary income was earned through performances of *The Bear* and similar plays. Better known for his short stories and longer dramas than for such farces, Chekhov is considered a master of nineteenth-century, Russian realism. (Realism involves an attempt to depict people, environments, and objects as they exist in everyday life.) Even in comic, one-act plays such as *The Bear*, he vividly depicts details of the everyday lives of common people. The action of such works is driven by the characters and their interactions with one another. In *The Bear*, a widow, who mourns for her husband seven months after his death, is approached by one of his creditors, a man in dire financial circumstances who desperately requires the money that the widow's husband owed him. The exchange between the widow and the creditor quickly progresses from polite to explosive, and the creditor, who expresses his negative opinion of women in general, is transformed by the spirit with which the widow argues with him. Yet the two agree to duel, and the widow's willingness to meet this challenge compels the creditor to profess his love for her. The play ends with the pair embracing. Despite Chekhov's disparaging remarks about *The Bear*, it

Anton Chekhov (*Public Domain*)

is known from his letters that he took the composition of such plays as seriously as he viewed the writing of his fiction and lengthier dramas.

Medved was originally published in 1888, in Moscow, Russia, and was later translated as *The Bear* by Julius West in *The Plays by Anton Tchekoff*, published by Charles Scribner's Sons in 1916. The work is also available in *The Cherry Orchard & Other Plays*, published by Grosset and Dunlap in 1935 and in *Plays by Anton Chekhov, Second Series*, published by Hard Press in 2006.

AUTHOR BIOGRAPHY

The third son of Pavel Egorovich Chekhov and Evgeniia Iakovlevna Morozova, Anton Pavlovich Chekhov (sometimes spelled Tchekoff) was born on January 17, 1860, in the city of Taganrog, Russia. (Chekhov's birthday is sometimes alternately listed as January 29, 1860, and the day of his death as July 15, 1904, instead of July 2, 1904, because two calendars were in use in the

nineteenth century—the Julian calendar and the Gregorian calendar. The calendars differ in the way they calculate leap years.) Chekhov's father, an authoritarian man and a devout Orthodox Christian, owned a general store where Chekhov and his older brothers worked. The business ultimately failed, and in 1876, Pavel Chekhov fled from his debts and took his family to Moscow, where his two eldest sons lived. Anton Chekhov remained in Taganrog to finish secondary school. After finishing school in 1879, Chekhov received a local scholarship and enrolled in the medical school at Moscow University. In 1880, Chekhov published his first story in the journal *Strekoza* (Dragonfly). Thus began his prolific career as a short story writer, through which he supported his family. He continued to pursue his medical studies and graduated from Moscow University in 1884. The same year, using the pseudonym A. Chekhonte, he published his first collection of short stories, titled *Skazki Mel'pomeny* (Tales of Melpomene). Chekhov also opened a medical practice in 1884 and discovered, following his first pulmonary hemorrhage, that he suffered from tuberculosis. Over the next several years, Chekhov increasingly contributed to well-respected literary magazines and was praised as a talented newcomer in the world of literary fiction. Despite the critical praise Chekhov received during this time period, some reviewers felt that he shouldn't use his talent on trivial short stories.

Chekhov wrote the full-length play *Ivanov* in the fall of 1887, and it was produced in November of that year. It was published the next month and became a theatrical success. In 1888, Chekhov focused on his dramatic works, honing *Ivanov* and completing smaller works, including *The Bear*, which was published that year. In 1890, after months of planning the arduous and ambitious journey, Chekhov left for Sakhalin Island, a Russian prison colony (a community of prisoners and their families). He remained there for several months, gathering information for a census and material for a book. Following another year of various travels, Chekhov purchased a small estate south of Moscow, where he lived, wrote, and served the surrounding community as a physician. In the late 1890s, Chekhov's illness began to intensify, and he spent the winter of 1897 in Nice, France, with other tuberculosis sufferers. After returning to Moscow, Chekhov met an actress, Olga Knipper, who was to act in his play *Diadia Vania* (Uncle Vania), published in 1897 and produced in 1898. In addition to playwriting, he began to edit his earlier works of short fiction for another collection. He courted Olga, and the two traveled to Yalta, in what is now Ukraine, where Chekhov was having a new home built. In 1901, Chekhov and Olga married in Moscow. His last play, *Vishnevyi sad* (The Cherry Orchard), premiered in Moscow in 1904 and enjoyed the acclaim of theatergoers and critics. It was published the same year. In Badenweiler, Germany, a resort town where he and Olga had traveled to rest, Chekhov succumbed to tuberculosis; he died on July 2, 1904.

PLOT SUMMARY

A play in one act, *The Bear* takes place in a single setting, that of the widow Elena Ivanovna Popova's home. The scene opens with Popova staring at a photograph. Her elderly footman (servant), Luka, is arguing with her. Luka bemoans the fact that Popova never leaves the house, that she has grieved too long the death of her husband Nicolai Mihailovitch. Luka exclaims that it has been an entire year since she has left the house. Telling her about the regiment stationed nearby, Luka informs Popova that the soldiers are handsome and that each Friday there is a ball at their camp. Luka also states that Popova's beauty will fade and that when she finally seeks to be admired by the officers, they will not look at her, adding, "It will be too late." In reply, Popova professes that she will never stop mourning Nicolai. Admitting that Nicolai was cruel and unfaithful to her, Popova insists that she will "be true till death," thereby proving to her late husband her own constancy and goodness. Luka insists that she stop talking this way and encourages her to go out for a walk or have one of the horses, Toby or Giant, harnessed so that she may go for a drive and visit neighbors. At the mention of Toby, her husband's favorite horse, Popova begins to weep and orders Luka to feed the animal an extra ration of oats.

A bell rings, and Popova, wondering who could be visiting her, instructs Luka to turn the person away. In his absence, she returns her gaze to the photograph. Speaking to it, Popova affirms her faithfulness once more and chastises her husband for his adultery. Luka reappears and informs Popova that a gentleman has arrived who demands to be seen despite Luka's efforts to send him on his way. She agrees to see the man, and as Luka leaves, Popova comments on her annoyance with people.

MEDIA ADAPTATIONS

- In 1938, *The Bear* was adapted as a Russian film titled *Medved*, produced by Belgoskino and directed by Isidor Annensky. The cast included Olga Androvskaya, Mikhail Zharov, and Ivan Pelttser.

- In 1950, the Columbia Broadcasting System (CBS) television program *Nash Airflyte Theatre* produced an episode titled "The Boor," based on Chekhov's *The Bear*. The episode was directed by Marc Daniels and written by Ellis Marcus.

- In 1961, *The Bear* was adapted as a Czechoslovakian film titled *Medved*, written and directed by Martin Fric. The cast included Jan Werich and Stella Zázvorková.

- A remake of the 1961 Czechoslovakian film, *Medved*, *The Boor* is a 1996 Canadian-made, English-language film version of Chekhov's *The Bear*. The film was directed and written by Ian Thompson and distributed by Faust Films. The cast included Clyde Whitham and Colm Feore.

She suggests that perhaps entering a convent might be necessary. A man enters, yelling at Luka, and then politely introduces himself to Popova as "Grigory Stepanovitch Smirnov, landowner and retired lieutenant of artillery." Smirnov states that he has come regarding an urgent matter and further explains that Popova's husband died owing him over a thousand rubles. Additionally, Smirnov states, he must pay the interest on his own mortgage the next day, so he requires the money Nicolai owed him immediately. Popova informs Smirnov that while she currently does not have the money, her steward will arrive from town in two days, and upon his return, she will instruct him to settle the debt with Smirnov. Popova adds that it is "exactly seven months" since the death of her husband and that her current "state of mind" is such that she cannot attend to financial matters. An argument ensues between the two. Smirnov reiterates his dire need for the money, and Popova continues to insist that she does not have the cash to spare. Smirnov becomes more and more agitated, shouting and cursing at Popova. He tells her of the other people who owe him money, who also have an excuse as to why they cannot pay him. Popova chastises him for his language and tone of voice and exits the room. (Some editions of the text omit the stage direction indicating Popova's departure at this point, but it is clear that she leaves, as a stage direction for her reentrance appears shortly afterward.)

In Popova's absence, Smirnov continues to rant, stating that he has been "too gentle" with the people who owe him money, but that Popova might find out what he is really like. Concluding his tirade, he states that he will remain at Popova's house until she pays him. Complaining to Luka about what he believes is "silly feminine logic," Smirnov demands that Luka bring him some water. After bringing Smirnov the water he requested, Luka announces that Popova is ill and will not see him. Smirnov yells out the window to his driver, ordering him to unharness the horses, and then demands a glass of vodka from Luka. Shortly after Luka arrives with the drink, Popova reenters the room and asks that Smirnov stop shouting. However, both Popova and Smirnov resume yelling at one another about the debt, and Popova accuses Smirnov of being rude and not knowing how to properly behave around women. He begins to tease her, and attempts to shower her, sarcastically, with French pleasantries. Smirnov then launches into an extended speech about the lover he used to be, the women he used to woo, and how he believes all women are, in the end, unfaithful. This goads Popova into her own tirade about her cheating husband and her faithfulness. The argument returns to financial matters, and when Popova asks Luka to show Smirnov out, the creditor refuses to leave. Popova and Smirnov continue to shout at one another, while Luka wails in fear. Popova accuses Smirnov of being a boor, a bear, a monster, and a Bourbon (a derogatory reference to the French), and Smirnov is shocked that she would have the nerve to insult him. He suggests that she only feels free to do so because she is a woman and will not be subject to the same repercussions that a man would. Insisting that she pay for her insults and that if she wants "equality of rights" she will certainly get it, Smirnov challenges Popova to a duel. She accepts the challenge instantly and leaves to get her husband's pistols.

Smirnov ponders the spirit and nerve Popova possesses, marveling at her acceptance of the challenge. He admits to himself that he is no longer angry with her. Returning with the pistols, Popova asks Smirnov to show her how to use them. A fearful Luka departs, seeking the coachman and gardener to help prevent a catastrophe. Smirnov offers instructions to Popova, but informs her that he has no intention of shooting her. She asks him why he will not and accuses him of being afraid. Smirnov then confesses that he likes her. Popova responds with laughter. When Smirnov admits that he is nearly in love with her, Popova expresses her hatred of him. Threatening to shoot him, Popova remains adamant in the face of Smirnov's increasingly passionate proclamations of love. He even proposes to her but gets up to leave when it seems as if she will not have him. Popova stops him before he goes. Her brief speech that follows alternates between commands that he leave and insistence that he remain. When Smirnov moves toward the door, she asks where he is going but then yells at him to get out. As she continues to vacillate, Smirnov approaches her and embraces her. Despite Popova's protestations, Smirnov kisses her, just as Luka returns with the gardener, the coachman, and various workmen, all armed with tools. Popova turns to Luka and tells him not to give Toby any oats at all.

CHARACTERS

Luka

Luka is Popova's servant, an elderly footman. He speaks to his mistress in a familiar, fatherly way. Insisting that Popova has mourned her husband long enough, Luka describes his own brief mourning period following his wife's death. Luka advises Popova to visit the neighbors and to visit the soldiers' camp and attend their weekly balls. After Smirnov's arrival, Luka becomes increasingly fearful of the gentleman's shouting and insistence on remaining at Popova's house until he is paid. Luka is positively panic-stricken when Popova and Smirnov agree to a duel. Remaining politely deferential to Smirnov, Luka attempts on several occasions to ask Smirnov to leave, but when Smirnov responds with hostility and threats, Luka "clutches at his heart" and claims illness and shortness of breath. Weeping, he begs Smirnov to leave. Despite Luka's fear, he remains protective of Popova and departs to find reinforcements, leaving Smirnov and Popova alone together. Luka returns some time later with various workmen armed with an axe, a rake, a pitchfork, and poles. The men discover Smirnov and Popova kissing instead of arguing or dueling.

Elena Ivanovna Popova

Elena Ivanovna Popova is the widow of Nicolai Mihailovitch, who has been dead for seven months. She remains deep in mourning for her husband, and has vowed to mourn him for the rest of her life in order to prove her faithfulness to him. Despite Smirnov's initial show of respect for her, Popova is curt and abrupt. However, she does not attempt to shirk her husband's debt; rather, she offers to pay Smirnov within a few days, after her steward has returned from town. After she leaves and reenters, the stage direction indicates that her eyes are "downcast," perhaps suggesting that Popova is attempting to remain civil and respectful. When Smirnov refuses to leave, she quickly becomes fiery, insistent. When their ensuing argument turns to the topic of faithfulness, Popova's pain at having been betrayed by her husband reveals itself. Yet, as she affirms her intentions to remain faithful to him and mourn him until her death, her grief appears to transform into spitefulness and anger. Smirnov points out that even though she has chosen the life of a shut in, she still powders her face, hinting that she might in fact be interested in attracting a man. Indeed, though she is initially dismissive of Smirnov's compliments and insistence on his love for her, Popova hesitates when he attempts to leave. Confused, both with Smirnov's change of heart and by her own fluctuations in emotion, Popova cannot decide if she wants Smirnov to stay or depart. She continues to resist him until he embraces and kisses her. Following the kiss, though, Popova emphasizes the transference of her affections from her dead husband to Smirnov. She tells Luka not to reward the horse Toby with a ration of oats after all, demonstrating that she will no longer indulge her memories of her late husband. Significantly, it is Smirnov who sold the oats to Popova's husband, and it is this debt that he has come to collect; Popova is now aligning herself with her husband's creditor. By denying the horse the oats her husband purchased from Smirnov, and by transferring her affections to this man in particular, Popova not only rejects her husband's memory but snubs him as well. Her actions, while symbolic of the end of her mourning period, seem petty, as it is the innocent horse—whose only crime is having been the husband's favorite—who is punished.

While Popova's spirit impresses Smirnov, the fact that she is won over in such a short time by only his persistence and his kiss suggests that Popova may be as fickle as some of the other women whom Smirnov has already ridiculed. Additionally, Popova displays a capacity for deception. As Smirnov observes, she claims to want to shut herself off from society, yet she continues to be concerned about her appearance. Furthermore, she is clearly a strong-willed woman, unafraid of expressing her views, yet she attempts in various instances throughout the play to portray herself as more demure and reserved than she actually is. She apparently behaves this way for the sake of propriety, and yet she shows a blatant disregard for what her society deems proper by first verbally insulting Smirnov and then agreeing to the duel with him. Popova is a study in contradiction, and as such is the source of some of the play's humor. She is also a representation of both Chekhov's ability to create subtle, mutable characters with flaws and depth, and his willingness to do so even in a "simple" play.

Grigory Stepanovitch Smirnov

Grigory Stepanovitch Smirnov enters the play with a polite request of Popova, asking her to pay him the money Nicolai Mihailovitch, her husband, owed Smirnov for oats for horse feed. Popova's repeated response that she will be unable to pay him transforms Smirnov's demeanor from polite to hostile. He stubbornly intends to remain in her house until she pays him, and as their argument intensifies, he taunts and teases her. While Popova has reprimanded Smirnov for not knowing how to properly speak to a woman, he twists her desire to be treated respectfully into an opportunity to tease her about the way he believes women like to be wooed. He recounts stories about the women he has loved, who have been unfaithful to him. His challenge to a duel stems from Popova insulting him repeatedly, and Smirnov feels that if a man had carried on in such a manner, a duel would be the obvious way to address the situation. Yet his surprise at her response to the challenge triggers a transformation in his feelings for her. He feels that at last he has found a "real woman." He finds that not only is he not angry with her any longer but that he actually likes her. As he explains to her the proper way to hold and fire a pistol, he begins to notice her physical beauty.

By the time Popova is ready to go into the garden to have the duel, Smirnov has resolved to shoot his pistol into the air to spare Popova. The more she insists she hates him, the more Smirnov falls for Popova. On his knees, he confesses his love for her. Popova continues to resist his advances but in a manner that is hesitating enough to give Smirnov hope. Emboldened by her confusion, which suggests to Smirnov that Popova might be willing to consider him as a suitor, Smirnov kisses her.

THEMES

Death and Mourning

In Chekhov's *The Bear*, death, grief, and mourning are portrayed in a comic, lighthearted manner. Popova's husband has been dead only seven months, but her melodramatic comments, combined with Luka's exaggerations and comic reactions to Popova's grief, make the serious issue of death something to joke about. From the beginning of the play, Luka amplifies Popova's response to her husband's death, and through his exaggeration of the situation, he turns Nicolai's death and Popova's grief into something other than a serious event and an appropriate response. Furthermore, he attempts to legitimize the fact that he finds Popova's grief silly. Luka opens the play by chastising Popova for sitting in her house and not enjoying herself, adding that every other living creature is able to enjoy itself, even the cat outside. He claims Popova has not left the house in an entire year, even though we learn later that it has only been seven months since Popova has become a widow. In response, Popova defends herself, but her comments reflect an arguably exaggerated view of grief, in that she plans to grieve forever. She states that she will never go out again, as her life is over anyway; her husband is dead, and she has "buried" herself "between four walls." Luka, trying to be practical, replies that although Popova's husband *is* dead, it was God's will, and Popova has been right to mourn him. Yet she cannot mourn forever, he insists, explaining that when his own wife died,

he grieved for her as well. He cried for a month, and "that's enough for her." The "old woman," as he repeatedly calls her, was not worth him wasting any more of his life on grief. Luka continues to complain about Popova never leaving the house due to her grief. He jokes that they live like spiders, never seeing the light of day, and that the mice have devoured his livery (uniform). Popova will not be swayed, and she expresses her determination to prove how much more faithful to her husband she was and will be than he ever was to her. She even bursts into tears at the mention of her husband's favorite horse. While Luka chides Popova for her extended mourning, Smirnov scoffs, believing that her mourning is really all a show, so that others will find her "mysterious" and "poetic." Finally, after Smirnov's feelings for Popova transform from anger into love, her grief dissolves as Smirnov kisses her. Because Popova's grief has already been the object of jokes since the beginning of the play, it does not come as a shock by the play's end that she is willing to put her grief aside and embrace Smirnov.

Love and Faithfulness

For Popova, love was something she felt for her husband until his death, and faithfulness became a duty, a point to prove afterwards. Readers learn in her opening exchange with Luka that Popova loved her husband, Nicolai, even though he treated her cruelly at times; she also admits that he was unfaithful to her. But Popova vows to be faithful to Nicolai until her own death, to show him how *she* loves. Alone and speaking to Nicolai's photograph, Popova states that she will show him how loving and forgiving she can be and asks if he is ashamed. Promising to keep herself locked away and faithful until her death, she calls him a "bad child," and bitterly recalls how he deceived her and left her alone for weeks at a time. After Smirnov's appearance, when their discussion has shifted from financial matters to matters of the heart, Smirnov makes a speech about the women he used to love, and how passionately he loved them. Yet he has been deceived by them, he insists, and asks Popova if she has ever known a woman "who was sincere, faithful, and constant." Popova, whose own life has been scarred by an unfaithful husband, rails at Smirnov, stating that the best man she ever knew, her husband, could not manage to be faithful. She describes the depth of her love for Nicolai, how she worshipped him. Popova discovered, she tells

TOPICS FOR FURTHER STUDY

- *The Bear*, given its romantic themes and use of comic elements, was a precursor of the modern romantic comedy, a popular film genre. Rewrite *The Bear* as a modern romantic comedy short film screenplay or as a television situational comedy. Base your modern version of the play on a situation similar to Chekhov's, involving a mourning widow and an unlikely suitor. How will the setting differ from Chekhov's? What will the dialogue sound like? How will you develop your characters fully? Attempt to convey the sense that they are like everyone else, with common flaws and shared experiences, thereby helping to give your work the widespread appeal Chekhov's play enjoyed.

- Select one of Chekhov's full-length dramas, such as *The Cherry Orchard* or *The Seagull*. Compare it to *The Bear*. What elements do the plays share? What techniques does Chekhov employ in the longer drama that he does not use in the farce? Also, research the critical and popular reception of the longer drama. *The Bear* was criticized by some of the literary elite at the time for being too simplistic a format for Chekhov, yet the public flocked to see productions of *The Bear*. Was the longer drama you chose popular among audiences? Was it praised by the literary critics of the time? Write an essay in which you compare the two works and analyze their reception among critics and audiences.

- In *The Bear*, Popova and Smirnov are both land owners, and both have servants, facts which suggest a degree of wealth. At the same time, though, Smirnov is desperate for the money Popova's husband owed him. His need for the money, the fact that Popova's husband had not paid him, and Popova's inability to provide quick payment all suggest that even as landowners, Popova and Smirnov do not have access to much wealth. Research the state of the landowning class in Russia during the late nineteenth century. Were they a wealthy group? Did they farm their land and sell their goods for a profit, or were they only earning enough to provide for their families? Share your findings in an oral report.

- In *The Bear*, Chekhov does not reveal how Popova's husband, Nicolai, died. Write a short story that takes place just before his death, from his point of view. Describe his relationship with his wife and the circumstances surrounding his death. Consider including a discussion of an interaction between Nicolai and Smirnov, in which the latter sells Nicolai the oats for which Smirnov demands money in *The Bear*. Make sure that your story is consistent with Chekhov's characterizations in *The Bear*.

Smirnov, "a whole drawerful of love-letters," following Nicolai's death. She has since admitted to herself what she probably suspected when Nicolai was alive—his trips away from home were opportunities for him to be unfaithful. Yet, in spite of Nicolai's deception and adultery, Popova states, she continues to remain faithful and will do so "to the very end." Her faithfulness, as her comments indicate, seems to be generated by her need to spite Nicolai after his death, to prove to

him that she is stronger and better than him. As her whisperings to his picture suggest, she simply wants Nicolai to have the decency to feel ashamed of his actions. By the end of the play, as she begins to be swayed by the force of Smirnov's feelings, Popova shows a willingness to abandon her futile bitterness. In this sense, her embrace of Smirnov may be seen as an openness to a new relationship, despite the emotional risks involved.

Chekhov theater group *(© Mary Evans Picture Library | Alamy)*

STYLE

French Vaudeville

Chekhov described the style in which *The Bear* was written as French vaudeville, which in this context refers to a short, light, comic play. It has alternately been deemed a farce, or a comic play featuring verbal humor, parody, unlikely scenarios, and a fast-paced plot. The essential element in a vaudeville or farce is comedy. Comic situations allow for the revelation of comic characterizations. Often, comic characters become caricatures, that is, exaggerated versions of a personality type, but critics have often observed that Chekhov managed to endow such characters with three-dimensional personalities. For example, Popova may exhibit some stereotypical characteristics, such as the fickleness in affection demonstrated by how easily Smirnov wins her over. At the same time, she is bolder in her reactions and much sharper with her wit than a typical caricature in this genre. While some French farces were complex and well-crafted, notes Vera Gottlieb in *The Cambridge Companion to Chekhov*, Chekhov intended his farces to be light and entertaining, rather than suffused with deeper

meaning. However, critics have observed the parallels between farces such as *The Bear* and Chekhov's more serious plays and stories. A characteristically Chekhovian feature, for example, is that the *The Bear* lacks the finality of an uplifting ending. While Popova and Smirnov embrace and may marry, it is clear from their earlier actions that their relationship will remain a volatile one.

HISTORICAL CONTEXT

The Reign of Alexander III

Czar Alexander III, ruler of the Russian Empire, came into power following the assassination of his father, Czar Alexander II, in 1881; he ruled until his death in 1894. A more conservative ruler than his father, Alexander III reversed policies that limited the authoritarian power of the czardom. Alexander III also sought to preserve Russia's cultural identity and protect the empire from Western liberalism. Governmental policies organized under the autocratic administration—one in which political power is held by one

COMPARE
&
CONTRAST

- **1880s:** At the time Chekhov is writing *The Bear*, the Russian Empire is ruled by Czar Alexander III, who succeeded to this position following the death of his father, Czar Alexander II. The czar is the sole ruling authority, and Alexander is an extremely conservative ruler who is intolerant of political dissent.

  Today: Russia is ruled by both a prime minister and a president, who serves as the official head of state; executive power is shared by these two positions. Former President Vladimir Putin, who served in this position from 2000 to 2008, is appointed prime minister in 2008 by his hand-picked successor to the presidency, Dmitry Medvedev. Medvedev becomes president after winning the general election in 2008.

- **1880s:** Political dissidents (individuals who speak out against the government and Czar Alexander II) in Russia, as well as individuals convicted of a variety of crimes, are sent to prison colonies, such as Sakhalin Island, for extended periods of time. Prisoners are required to perform hard labor and often contract serious illnesses at the penal colonies. Often their families live with them in such communities, and the colonies grow when infants are born to the inmates. Chekhov later visits Sakhalin Island, where he assists the prison doctor and gathers census information.

  Today: The penitentiary system in Russia today is criticized for being severely underfunded, resulting in overcrowding and various other problems. Prison officials have difficulty providing enough food for prisoners and securing enough fuel to heat facilities. Obtaining sufficient medicine for the many inmates infected with HIV and tuberculosis is also a problem.

- **1880s:** Plays are a popular form of entertainment in Russia. These include serious dramatic works shown in fine theaters, as well as lighthearted farces shown in vaudeville houses. These theatrical forms of entertainment compete with nightclubs and restaurants for attendees. Despite the economic struggles of the lower, working classes, urbanization and industrialization provide an upper-middle-class population with the financial means and leisure time to enjoy such activities. Chekhov is able to support his literary efforts through the widespread production of plays like *The Bear*.

  Today: Russians enjoy an evening out as much as their nineteenth-century contemporaries did. Modern, middle-class Russians more often prefer film over live stage performances, and their choices include Hollywood (American) blockbusters, intellectual films by Russian directors such as Alexandr Sokurov, and Russian box office hits by directors such as Nikita Mikhalkov.

---

nonelected ruling figure—were designed to promote the supremacy of Russian nationalism, the Russian language, and a single religion, Eastern Orthodoxy. Alexander III enforced his harsh policies with the help of a secret police force. Political dissidents, including writers such as Chekhov's Russian contemporary Fyodor Dostoyevsky, were either executed or sent to forced labor camps, or penal colonies, in remote areas in Siberia.

While avoiding any direct confrontation with the authorities, Chekhov voluntarily visited Sakhalin Island, a Russian prison community, in order to document the living conditions and record statistics for a census. In addition to the political repressiveness of Alexander III's rule, there were great disparities among the social classes' basic living conditions. Chekhov lived in fear of poverty for much of his life. He was the grandson of a freed serf. (Serfdom was essentially a form of slavery in which agricultural laborers were legally bound to serve a landowner.) His father became somewhat wealthy as a merchant but was forced to flee with his family from the city of Taganrog, Russia, to Moscow, Russia, to escape the debts he had accrued when his business failed. Chekhov joined his family in their crowded basement apartment in Moscow after he completed his schooling. Although trained as a physician, Chekhov could not always depend on his medical practice for an income, and his income from writing was at times barely enough to provide a living for himself and his family. Still, Chekhov was better off than many Russians. Much of the country was gripped by a severe economic depression during the end of the nineteenth century. An increasingly industrialized nation, Russia was producing vast amounts of coal, iron, steel, and oil at the turn of the century. Such industries were powered by low-paid laborers, essentially the working poor, who endured deplorable living and working conditions. A small middle class consisting of professionals like doctors, lawyers, and entrepreneurs, such as merchants and industrialists, was slow to expand. Society was largely polarized between the poor working class and the aristocratic, wealthy upper class. The oppression inherent in the authoritarian czarist government fueled the growing discontent among the struggling agricultural classes and the emerging proletariat (working class). These factors ultimately contributed to a massive social revolution in post-World War I Russia.

Russian Literary Realism

At the time when Chekhov was honing his literary skills, Russian literature was characterized by the social realism that developed under novelist Leo Tolstoy (1828–1910), whom Chekhov admired, and Ivan Turgenev (1818–1883). Social realism developed as a reaction against the idealized view of the world explored by the romanticism of the earlier part of the nineteenth century. Social realists focused on the details of the daily lives of working-class people. They sought to depict the world as it existed. Chekhov adapted this type of realism, in his short stories and full-length dramas, to his own ends, portraying the ordinary occurrences in his characters' lives in a rich and honest way. He took pains to capture the colloquial (relating to the language of familiar conversation) tone of his subjects' speech, and he resisted the use of any forced

plot elements. Rather, he let the characters and their interactions pace his stories. His farcical works, however, given that they adhered to the standards of the vaudeville genre in their use of exaggerations, unlikely scenarios, satire, and parody, could not be described as wholly realistic, even though they were in some ways similar to Chekhov's realistic works. For example, Chekhov's short plays, like his other works, are largely character-driven rather than plot-driven. Unlike many of his predecessors, Chekhov avoided topics that strayed toward metaphysics (a branch of philosophy pertaining to the nature of reality) or religion. By the end of the nineteenth century, however, literature was moving more toward abstraction and symbolism and away from both realism and idealism. This new movement was referred to as the decadent movement and was disparaged by Chekhov.

CRITICAL OVERVIEW

When Chekhov wrote *The Bear*, he had already established an impressive literary reputation. Contemporary critics in the late 1880s and 1890s often viewed *The Bear* and Chekhov's other light-hearted farces as somewhat beneath him. Chekhov himself was known to speak dismissively of such dramatic efforts. However, in *The Cambridge Companion to Chekhov*, Vera Gottlieb points to letters in which Chekhov states that he took the writing of vaudevilles to be a serious literary endeavor. Modern critics like Gottlieb focus on the relationship of Chekhov's short farces to both his longer dramas and his exemplary short stories. Gottlieb argues that Chekhov's "short plays require redefinition within the context of the theatrical conventions of the time *and* as a major and serious part of Chekhov's achievement." Gottlieb also demonstrates how in Chekhov's short stories, full-length dramas, and short plays, including *The Bear*, Chekhov alternately addresses the serious and the trivial. Other critics focus on the reasons why his farces were so successful *as* farces.

Harvey Pitcher, in "Chekhov's Humour," an essay from *A Chekhov Companion* asserts that *The Bear* and another farce called *The Proposal* were Chekhov's best in this genre, particularly in the way they employed the "comedy of situation" as a means of exploring the "comedy of characterisation." Pitcher further emphasizes the "comic psychological inevitability" that is so effective in the *The Bear*. The transformations Popova and Smirnov undergo by the play's end are demonstrative of a complete psychological process, he maintains. Like Pitcher, biographer Philip Callow observes in *Chekhov: The Hidden Ground* that of all of Chekhov's vaudevilles, *The Bear* was the most successful. Callow also quotes Chekhov as saying that he lived "on the charity of my *Bear*." The popular little play helped to financially support the modest dramatist.

CRITICISM

Catherine Dominic

Dominic is a novelist and a freelance writer and editor. In this essay on The Bear, *she argues that Popova and Smirnov display sympathetic and realistic qualities that enable them to transcend their one-dimensional, farcical roots.*

In Chekhov's short stories, it is often noted that an absence of plot is compensated for by complex characterizations. The interaction between the characters creates the action in the story. The extent to which the characters in the farce *The Bear* may be viewed as psychologically complex is debatable; yet, just as in his short stories, it is the interaction between the characters, in this case the grief-stricken Popova and the volatile Smirnov, that generates the action in the play. Few outside forces are at work; rather, it is the powerful force of their two personalities that sparks the play's energy and compels Popova out of her state of grief. On the surface, both Popova and Smirnov appear to be characters typical of a farce, a lighthearted play in which the comedy arises from ironic situations, parody, wordplay, and other forms of verbal humor. Popova's grief is made to appear overblown and is therefore sarcastically mocked, while Smirnov's negative attitudes toward women are humorously challenged by an odd attraction to Popova, which arises out of her loathing of and desire to duel with him. Despite the inherent comedy in this unlikely scenario, Popova and Smirnov both possess a past that is marred by betrayal and loss. It is this solemnity in the characters that balances the play's intentional frivolity and distinguishes the characters as something more than stock farce stereotypes, even if they are not the deeply complex and fully developed characters of Chekhov's acclaimed longer plays or finest short stories.

WHAT DO I READ NEXT?

- *Anton Chekhov's Short Stories*, edited by Ralph E. Matlaw and published in 1979 by W. W. Norton, is a collection of some of Chekhov's finest short stories, culled from his numerous publications. Chekhov's literary reputation was built largely on the basis of his short stories.

- Leo Tolstoy, author of *War and Peace*, was highly regarded as a writer by Chekhov. *Great Short Works of Leo Tolstoy*, published in 2004 by Harper Perennial Modern Classics, is a collection of several of Tolstoy's shorter novels.

- Dmitry Vasilyevich Grigorovich was an esteemed writer and a highly regarded literary critic who advised Chekhov on his literary career. In *D. V. Grigorovich: The Man Who Discovered Chekhov*, published by Avebury in 1987, author Michael Pursglove discusses Grigorovich and his mentor relationship with Chekhov.

- *Daily Life in Imperial Russia*, published by Greenwood Press in 2008 and written by Greta Bucher, provides an examination of life in Chekhov's Russia. Bucher discusses such topics as industrialization, class conflict, work and labor issues, health, fashion, and traditions and rituals.

Popova is described in the *dramatis personae*, or character list, for *The Bear* as "a landowning little widow, with dimples on her cheeks," a description that gives the reader an overall impression of pleasantness. "Little" makes her seem vulnerable and nonthreatening, while "dimples" suggests a smiling face. Yet readers are introduced to her grief first through Luka's chastising and then through Popova's own words. Although Luka thinks there is something abnormal about the way Popova grieves—shutting herself away from the world and not leaving the house—and about the length of time she has been grieving (believing it has been "a whole year"), the fact remains that Popova

> IT IS THIS SOLEMNITY IN THE CHARACTERS
> THAT BALANCES THE PLAY'S INTENTIONAL
> FRIVOLITY AND DISTINGUISHES THE CHARACTERS AS
> SOMETHING MORE THAN STOCK FARCE
> STEREOTYPES, EVEN IF THEY ARE NOT THE DEEPLY
> COMPLEX AND FULLY DEVELOPED CHARACTERS OF
> CHEKHOV'S ACCLAIMED LONGER PLAYS OR FINEST
> SHORT STORIES."

has lost a husband whom she professes to have loved dearly. Furthermore, she is not an elderly woman whose husband died after many years of marriage. Luka describes Popova as "young and beautiful." Presumably she had been looking forward to a lifetime of loving Nicolai, and he was taken from her at a young age. We also learn, through Popova, that her husband Nicolai has actually been dead for only seven months, not the "whole year" Luka has indicated. While Luka exaggerates and trivializes Popova's grief, it is not unreasonable to assume that a young woman who loved her husband would grieve for him for seven months. Add to this grief the fact that he was unfaithful to Popova, and her pain becomes even deeper and more understandable. Her sorrow at losing her husband is compounded by her feelings of bitterness and betrayal. In terms of romantic comedy, the fact that Nicolai was a *cheating* husband will make many readers despise him. His adultery enables the reader to therefore root for Popova—with a clear conscience—to find a new love. From a human standpoint, however, the combination of the betrayal and the untimely death of a beloved spouse does not lend itself to rapid emotional or psychological healing. Rather, seven months, or even "a whole year," may not be enough time for a person to feel healed, whole, and ready for new relationships.

Popova's grief is colored with melodramatic comments for comic effect. She states her determination to bury herself within the four walls of her home and vows to wear widow's weeds (black clothes indicating she is in a state of mourning) until "the very end." Yet her speech to Smirnov about her love and grief for Nicolai is poetic,

heartfelt, and heartbreaking. She states that she loved her husband with all her being, "as only a young and imaginative woman can love," and that she gave him everything she had to give, that she "breathed in him." Her insistence on remaining faithful to him until her own death appears to be driven by her desire to prove to him how love and faithfulness should be, and by her desire to shame him. These intentions are mocked by Smirnov in a manner designed to heighten the comedy of the situation. He teases her, suggesting she is playing up her grief to attract attention, and adds that although she may appear to be sequestering herself, she nevertheless powders her face and takes the time to make herself attractive. Despite Smirnov's suspicions, Popova's intense need to prove that she is better than her dead husband is suggestive of the extent to which Nicolai's betrayal has wounded her. Smirnov may accuse Popova of manipulation, and she may at times behave in a melodramatic fashion, particularly at the play's end, when she vacillates so rapidly between wanting Smirnov to stay and wanting him to leave her home. But Popova cannot be viewed as a shallow stereotype, the pawn of farcical elements, or a caricature used simply for comic ends. Throughout the play, Popova remains a woman who has loved deeply and has suffered greatly. Her eagerness to argue and then to duel with Smirnov, as well as her reluctance in the last scene of the play to wholeheartedly accept his advances, suggest that while she may be taking the first tentative steps toward a new romance, her grief and bitterness remain just below the surface of her brave exterior.

Like Popova, Smirnov possesses a few characteristics of a typical farce character, but he also has a deeper, more serious nature that is revealed mainly through his long speech on the women he has loved. When Popova accuses Smirnov of not knowing how to act around women, he launches into a tirade in which he recounts the details of his past love life. One could easily dismiss Smirnov as a misogynist (a man who hates women), but a closer look at the insults he hurls at women as a group is suggestive of the fact that Smirnov, like Popova, has been wounded quite deeply by an unfaithful partner. His impertinent comments that mock Popova's grief and insult her personal integrity are delivered in a way that highlights Smirnov's own comic coarseness and emphasizes the characteristics in Popova that are meant to be viewed as amusingly frustrating. For example, he teases Popova in French, as a mock-suitor, when she claims he is speaking in an inappropriate way to her. He also laughs at her concern for her physical appearance. Smirnov continues, stating that he has "refused twelve women" but then admitting that nine women have refused his affections. He has made a fool of himself for love, he confesses, suffering intensely, sacrificing much, loving "passionately, madly, every blessed way." Now, however, he holds women in very low esteem. Although he insults the intelligence of women and finds them to be shallow, his greatest grievance is that he finds women to be deceitful by nature; he declares them incapable of loving deeply. While he has suffered for love, Smirnov claims that he has loved shallow and conniving women. He also believes that most women, with the exception perhaps of "freaks and old women," are unable to be faithful and true. Given the length, intensity, and focus of this passionate speech, it seems that Smirnov was once capable of love, but painful experiences with unfaithful women have changed him. In fact, when he begins to acknowledge the ways in which Popova differs from the women he has known, he becomes angry for allowing himself to feel emotions he attempts to reject. Popova is different from other women, not only because of her defiant spirit, which impresses Smirnov, but also because of her willingness to prove her faithfulness to her dead, cheating husband. The issue of fidelity seems to matter as much to Popova as it does to Smirnov.

Smirnov's situation is quite comic; he professes his love to Popova over pistols, which he has just shown her how to fire and with which she is eager to shoot him. The humor largely overshadows his own sense of loss and betrayal, as well it should, given that the play is intended to be a farce. Nevertheless, the reality of the pain and suffering of love, betrayal, and loss grounds both Smirnov and Popova. They remain appealingly real and human, rather than evaporating into the stereotypes of blustering misogynist and hysterically grieving widow.

Source: Catherine Dominic, Critical Essay on *The Bear*, in *Drama for Students*, Gale, Cengage Learning, 2009.

Anton Chekhov

In the following excerpt from one of Chekhov's letters, the author tells a friend about the cholera epidemic that occurred after the publication of his play The Bear.

> " I HAVE AN IMPATIENT DESIRE TO EAT, DRINK, AND SLEEP, AND TALK ABOUT LITERATURE—THAT IS, DO NOTHING, AND AT THE SAME TIME FEEL LIKE A DECENT PERSON."

To A. S. Suvorin....

Melihovo,

August 1.

My letters chase you, but do not catch you. I have written to you often, and among other places to St. Moritz. Judging from your letters you have had nothing from me. In the first place, there is cholera in Moscow and about Moscow, and it will be in our parts some day soon. In the second place, I have been appointed cholera doctor, and my section includes twenty-five villages, four factories, and one monastery. I am organizing the building of barracks, and so on, and I feel lonely, for all the cholera business is alien to my heart, and the work, which involves continual driving about, talking, and attention to petty details, is exhausting for me. I have no time to write. Literature has been thrown aside for a long time now, and I am poverty-stricken, as I thought it convenient for myself and my independence to refuse the remuneration received by the section doctors. I am bored, but there is a great deal that is interesting in cholera if you look at it from a detached point of view. I am sorry you are not in Russia. Material for short letters is being wasted. There is more good than bad, and in that cholera is a great contrast to the famine which we watched in the winter. Now all are working—they are working furiously. At the fair at Nizhni they are doing marvels which might force even Tolstoy to take a respectful attitude to medicine and the intervention of cultured people generally in life. It seems as though they had got a hold on the cholera. They have not only decreased the number of cases, but also the percentage of deaths. In immense Moscow the cholera does not exceed fifty cases a week, while on the Don it is a thousand a day—an impressive difference. We district doctors are getting ready; our plan of action is definite, and there are grounds for supposing that in our parts we too shall decrease the percentage of mortality from cholera. We have no assistants, one has to be doctor and sanitary attendant at one and the same time. The peasants are rude, dirty in their habits, and mistrustful; but the thought that our labours are not thrown away makes all that scarcely noticeable. Of all the Serpuhovo doctors I am the most pitiable; I have a scurvy carriage and horses, I don't know the roads, I see nothing by evening light, I have no money, I am very quickly exhausted, and worst of all, I can never forget that I ought to be writing, and I long to spit on the cholera and sit down and write to you, and I long to talk to you. I am in absolute loneliness.

Our farming labours have been crowned with complete success. The harvest is considerable, and when we sell the corn Melihovo will bring us more than a thousand roubles. The kitchen garden is magnificent. There are perfect mountains of cucumbers and the cabbage is wonderful. If it were not for the accursed cholera I might say that I have never spent a summer so happily as this one.

Nothing has been heard of cholera riots yet. There is talk of some arrests, some manifestoes, and so on. They say that A., the writer, has been condemned to fifteen years' penal servitude. If the socialists are really going to exploit the cholera for their own ends I shall despise them. Revolting means for good ends make the ends themselves revolting. Let them get a lift on the backs of the doctors and feldshers, but why lie to the peasants? Why persuade them that they are right in their ignorance and that their coarse prejudices are the holy truth? If I were a politician I could never bring myself to disgrace my present for the sake of the future, even though I were promised tons of felicity for an ounce of mean lying. Write to me as often as possible in consideration of my exceptional position. I cannot be in a good mood now, and your letters snatch me away from cholera concerns, and carry me for a brief space to another world. . . .

August 16.

I'll be damned if I write to you again. I have written to Abbazzio, to St. Moritz. I have written a dozen times at least, so far you have not sent me one correct address, and so not one of my letters has reached [you] and my long description and lectures about the cholera have been wasted. It's mortifying. But what is most mortifying is that after a whole series of letters from me about our exertions against the cholera,

you all at once write me from gay Biarritz that you envy my leisure! Well, Allah forgive you!

Well, I am alive and in good health. The summer was a splendid one, dry, warm, abounding in the fruits of the earth, but its whole charm was from July onwards, spoilt by news of the cholera. While you were inviting me in your letters first to Vienna, and then to Abbazzio I was already one of the doctors of the Serpuhovo Zemstvo, was trying to catch the cholera by its tail and organizing a new section full steam. In the morning I have to see patients, and in the afternoon drive about. I drive, I give lectures to the natives, treat them, get angry with them, and as the Zemstvo has not granted me a single kopeck for organizing the medical centres I cadge from the wealthy, first from one and then from another. I turn out to be an excellent beggar; thanks to my beggarly eloquence, my section has two excellent barracks with all the necessaries, and five barracks that are not excellent, but horrid. I have saved the Zemstvo from expenditure even on disinfectants. Lime, vitriol, and all sorts of stinking stuff I have begged from the manufacturers for all my twenty-five villages. In fact Kolomin ought to be proud of having been at the same high school with me. My soul is exhausted. I am bored. Not to belong to oneself, to think about nothing but diarrhœa, to start up in the night at a dog's barking and a knock at the gate ("Haven't they come for me?"), to drive with disgusting horses along unknown roads; to read about nothing but cholera, and to expect nothing but cholera, and at the same time to be utterly uninterested in that disease, and in the people whom one is serving—that, my good sir, is a hash which wouldn't agree with anyone. The cholera is already in Moscow and in the Moscow district. One must expect it from hour to hour. Judging from its course in Moscow one must suppose that it is already declining and that the bacillus is losing its strength. One is bound to think, too, that it is powerfully affected by the measures that have been taken in Moscow and among us. The educated classes are working vigorously, sparing neither themselves nor their purses; I see them every day, and am touched, and when I remember how Zhitel and Burenin used to vent their acrid spleen on these same educated people I feel almost suffocated. In Nizhni the doctors and the cultured people generally have done marvels. I was overwhelmed with enthusiasm when I read about the cholera. In the good old times, when people were infected and died by thousands, the amazing conquests that are being made before our eyes could not even be dreamed of. It's a pity you are not a doctor and cannot share my delight—that is, fully feel and recognize and appreciate all that is being done. But one cannot tell about it briefly.

The treatment of cholera requires of the doctor deliberation before all things—that is, one has to devote to each patient from five to ten hours or even longer. As I mean to employ Kantani's treatment—that is clysters of tannin and subcutaneous injection of a solution of common salt—my position will be worse than foolish; while I am busying myself over one patient, a dozen can fall ill and die. You see I am the only man for twenty-five villages, apart from a feldsher who calls me "your honour," does not venture to smoke in my presence, and cannot take a step without me. If there are isolated cases I shall be capital; but if there is an epidemic of only five cases a day, then I shall do nothing but be irritable and exhausted and feel myself guilty.

Of course there is no time even to think of literature. I am writing nothing. I refused remuneration so as to preserve some little freedom of action for myself, and so I have not a halfpenny. I am waiting till they have threshed and sold the rye. Until then I shall be living on *The Bear* and mushrooms, of which there are endless masses here. By the way, I have never lived so cheaply as now. We have everything of our own, even our own bread. I believe in a couple of years all my household expenses will not exceed a thousand roubles a year.

When you learn from the newspapers that the cholera is over, you will know that I have gone back to writing again. Don't think of me as a literary man while I am in the service of the Zemstvo. One can't do two things at once.

You write that I have given up Sahalin. I cannot abandon that child of mine. When I am oppressed by the boredom of belles-lettres I am glad to turn to something else. The question when I shall finish Sahalin and when I shall print does not strike me as being important. While Galkin-Vrasskoy reigns over the prison system I feel very much disinclined to bring out my book. Of course if I am driven to it by need, that is a different matter.

In all my letters I have pertinaciously asked you one question, which of course you are not obliged to answer: "Where are you going to be in the autumn, and wouldn't you like to spend part of September and October with me in Feodosia

or the Crimea?" I have an impatient desire to eat, drink, and sleep, and talk about literature—that is, do nothing, and at the same time feel like a decent person. However, if my idleness annoys you, I can promise to write with or beside you, a play or a story.... Eh? Won't you? Well, God be with you, then.

The astronomer has been here twice. I felt bored with her on both occasions. Svobodin has been here too. He grows better and better. His serious illness has made him pass through a spiritual metamorphosis.

See what a long letter I have written, even though I don't feel sure that the letter will reach you. Imagine my cholera-boredom, my cholera-loneliness, and compulsory literary inactivity, and write to me more, and oftener. Your contemptuous feeling for France I share. The Germans are far above them, though for some reason they are called stupid. And the Franco-Russian Entente Cordiale I am as fond of as Tolstoy is. There's something nastily suggestive about these cordialities. On the other hand I was awfully pleased at Virchow's visit to us.

We have raised a very nice potato and a divine cabbage. How do you manage to get on without cabbage-soup? I don't envy you your sea, nor your freedom, nor the happy frame of mind you are in abroad. The Russian summer is better than anything. And by the way, I don't feel any great longing to be abroad. After Singapore, Ceylon, and perhaps even our Amur, Italy and even the crater of Vesuvius do not seem fascinating. After being in India and China I did not see a great difference between other European countries and Russia.

A neighbour of ours, the owner of the renowned Otrad, Count X, is staying now at Biarritz, having run away from the cholera; he gave his doctor only five hundred roubles for the campaign against the cholera. His sister, the countess, who is living in my section, when I went to discuss the provision of barracks for her workmen, treated me as though I had come to apply for a situation. It mortified me, and I told her a lie, pretending to be a rich man. I told the same lie to the Archimandrite, who refuses to provide quarters for the cases which may occur in the monastery. To my question what would he do with the cases that might be taken ill in his hostel, he answered me: "They are persons of means and will pay you themselves...." Do you understand? And I flared up, and said I did not care about payment, as I was well off, and that all I wanted was the security of the monastery.... There are sometimes very stupid and humiliating positions.... Before the count went away I met his wife. Huge diamonds in her ears, wearing a bustle, and not knowing how to hold herself. A millionaire. In the company of such persons one has a stupid schoolboy feeling of wanting to be rude.

The village priest often comes and pays me long visits; he is a very good fellow, a widower, and has some illegitimate children.

Write or there will be trouble....

Source: Anton Chekhov, "To A. S. Suvorin," in *Letters of Anton Chekhov to His Family and Friends*, translated by Constance Garnett, Macmillan, 1920, pp. 306–15.

Julius West

In the following excerpt from an introduction to a collection of Chekhov's plays, West discusses Chekhov's comedies, including The Bear, *and the Russian sense of humor.*

The last few years have seen a large and generally unsystematic mass of translations from the Russian flung at the heads and hearts of English readers. The ready acceptance of Chekhov has been one of the few successful features of this irresponsible output. He has been welcomed by British critics with something like affection. Mr. Bernard Shaw has several times remarked: "Every time I see a play by Chekhov, I want to chuck all my own stuff into the fire." Others, having no such valuable property to sacrifice on the altar of Chekhov, have not hesitated to place him side by side with Ibsen, and the other established institutions of the new theatre. For these reasons it is pleasant to be able to chronicle the fact that, by way of contrast with the casual treatment normally handed out to Russian authors, the publishers are issuing the complete dramatic works of this author. In 1912 they brought out a volume containing four Chekhov plays, translated by Marian Fell. All the dramatic works not included in her volume are to be found in the present one. With the exception of Chekhov's masterpiece, *The Cherry Orchard* (translated by the late Mr. George Calderon in 1912), none of these plays have been previously published in book form in England or America.

It is not the business of a translator to attempt to outdo all others in singing the praises of his raw material. This is a dangerous process

and may well lead, as it led Mr. Calderon, to drawing the reader's attention to points of beauty not to be found in the original. A few bibliographical details are equally necessary and permissible, and the elementary principles of Chekhov criticism will also be found useful.

The very existence of *The High Road* (1884), probably the earliest of its author's plays, will be unsuspected by English readers. During Chekhov's lifetime it was a sort of family legend, after his death it became a family mystery. A copy was finally discovered only last year in the Censor's office, yielded up, and published. It had been sent in in 1885 under the *nom-de-plume* "A. Chekhonte," and it had failed to pass. The Censor of the time being had scrawled his opinion on the manuscript, "a depressing and dirty piece—cannot be licensed." The name of the gentleman who held this view—Kaiser von Kugelgen—gives another reason for the educated Russian's low opinion of German-sounding institutions. Baron von Tuzenbach, the satisfactory person in *The Three Sisters,* it will be noted, finds it as well, while he is trying to secure the favours of Irina, to declare that his German ancestry is fairly remote. This is by way of parenthesis. *The High Road,* found after thirty years, is a most interesting document to the lover of Chekhov. Every play he wrote in later years was either a one-act farce or a four-act drama.

In *The High Road* we see, in an embryonic form, the whole later method of the plays—the deliberate contrast between two strong characters (Bortsov and Merik in this case), the careful individualization of each person in a fairly large group by way of an introduction to the main theme, the concealment of the catastrophe, germ-wise, in the actual character of the characters, and the creation of a distinctive group-atmosphere. It need scarcely be stated that *The High Road* is not a "dirty" piece according to Russian or to German standards; Chekhov was incapable of writing a dirty play or story. For the rest, this piece differs from the others in its presentation, not of Chekhov's favourite middle-classes, but of the moujik, nourishing, in a particularly stuffy atmosphere, an intense mysticism and an equally intense thirst for vodka.

The Proposal (1889) and *The Bear* (1890) may be taken as good examples of the sort of humour admired by the average Russian. The latter play, in another translation, was put on as a curtain-raiser to a cinematograph entertainment at a London theatre in 1914, and had quite a pleasant reception from a thoroughly Philistine audience. The humour is very nearly of the variety most popular over here, the psychology is a shade subtler. The Russian novelist or dramatist takes to psychology as some of his fellow-countrymen take to drink; in doing this he achieves fame by showing us what we already know, and at the same time he kills his own creative power. Chekhov just escaped the tragedy of suicide by introspection, and was only enabled to do this by the possession of a sense of humour. That is why we should not regard *The Proposal, The Bear, The Wedding,* or *The Anniversary* as the work of a merely humorous young man, but as the saving graces which made perfect *The Cherry Orchard.*

The Three Sisters (1901) is said to act better than any other of Chekhov's plays, and should surprise an English audience exceedingly. It and *The Cherry Orchard* are the tragedies of doing nothing. The three sisters have only one desire in the world, to go to Moscow and live there. There is no reason on earth, economic, sentimental, or other, why they should not pack their bags and take the next train to Moscow. But they will not do it. They cannot do it. And we know perfectly well that if they were transplanted thither miraculously, they would be extremely unhappy as soon as ever the excitement of the miracle had worn off. In the other play Mme. Ranevsky can be saved from ruin if she will only consent to a perfectly simple step—the sale of an estate. She cannot do this, is ruined, and thrown out into the unsympathetic world. Chekhov is the dramatist, not of action, but of inaction. The tragedy of inaction is as overwhelming, when we understand it, as the tragedy of an Othello, or a Lear, crushed by the wickedness of others. The former is being enacted daily, but we do not stage it, we do not know how. But who shall deny that the base of almost all human unhappiness is just this inaction, manifesting itself in slovenliness of thought and execution, education, and ideal?

The Russian, painfully conscious of his own weaknesses, has accepted this point of view, and regards *The Cherry Orchard* as its master-study in dramatic form. They speak of the palpitating hush which fell upon the audience of the Moscow Art Theatre after the first fall of the curtain at the first performance—a hush so intense as to make Chekhov's friends undergo the initial emotions of assisting at a vast theatrical failure. But the silence was almost a sob, to be followed,

> HE WAS AN UNTIRING WORKER, AND BETWEEN HIS PATIENTS AND HIS DESK HE LED A LIFE OF CEASELESS ACTIVITY. HIS RESTLESS MIND WAS DOMINATED BY A PASSION OF ENERGY AND HE THOUGHT CONTINUALLY AND VIVIDLY."

when overcome, by an epic applause. And, a few months later, Chekhov died....

Source: Julius West, "Introduction," in *Plays: Second Series,* by Anton Tchekoff, translated by Julius West, Charles Scribner's Sons, 1916, pp. 3–6.

Marian Fell

In the following introduction to a collection of Chekhov's plays, Fell provides biographical information on Chekhov and discusses the commercial success of The Bear, *which Chekhov allegedly wrote overnight.*

The last years of the nineteenth century were for Russia tinged with doubt and gloom. The high-tide of vitality that had risen during the Turkish war ebbed in the early eighties, leaving behind it a dead level of apathy which lasted until life was again quickened by the high interests of the Revolution. During these grey years the lonely country and stagnant provincial towns of Russia buried a peasantry which was enslaved by want and toil, and an educated upper class which was enslaved by idleness and tedium. Most of the "Intellectuals," with no outlet for their energies, were content to forget their ennui in vodka and card-playing; only the more idealistic gasped for air in the stifling atmosphere, crying out in despair against life as they saw it, and looking forward with a pathetic hope to happiness for humanity in "two or three hundred years." It is the inevitable tragedy of their existence, and the pitiful humour of their surroundings, that are portrayed with such insight and sympathy by Anton Tchekoff who is, perhaps, of modern writers, the dearest to the Russian people.

Anton Tchekoff was born in the old Black Sea port of Taganrog on January 17, 1860. His grandfather had been a serf; his father married a merchant's daughter and settled in Taganrog, where, during Anton's boyhood, he carried on a small and unsuccessful trade in provisions. The young Tchekoff was soon impressed into the services of the large, poverty-stricken family, and he spoke regretfully in after years of his hard-worked childhood. But he was obedient and good-natured, and worked cheerfully in his father's shop, closely observing the idlers that assembled there, and gathering the drollest stories, which he would afterward whisper in class to his laughing schoolfellows. Many were the punishments which he incurred by this habit, which was incorrigible.

His grandfather had now become manager of an estate near Taganrog, in the wild steppe country of the Dun Cossacks, and here the boy spent his summers, fishing in the river, and roving about the countryside as brown as a gipsy, sowing the seeds of that love for nature which he retained all his life. His evenings he liked best to spend in the kitchen of the master's house among the work people and peasants who gathered there, taking part in their games, and setting them all laughing by his witty and telling observations.

When Tchekoff was about fourteen, his father moved the family to Moscow, leaving Anton in Taganrog, and now, relieved of work in the shop, his progress at school became remarkable. At seventeen he wrote a long tragedy, which was afterward destroyed, and he already showed flashes of the wit that was soon to blaze into genius.

He graduated from the high school at Taganrog with every honour, entered the University of Moscow as a student of medicine, and threw himself headlong into a double life of student and author, in the attempt to help his struggling family.

His first story appeared in a Moscow paper in 1880, and after some difficulty he secured a position connected with several of the smaller periodicals, for which, during his student years, he poured forth a succession of short stories and sketches of Russian life with incredible rapidity. He wrote, he tells us, during every spare minute, in crowded rooms where there was "no light and less air," and never spent more than a day on any one story. He also wrote at this time a very stirring blood-and-thunder play which was suppressed by the censor, and the fate of which is not known.

His audience demanded laughter above all things, and, with his deep sense of the ridiculous, Tchekoff asked nothing better. His stories, though often based on themes profoundly tragic, are penetrated by the light and subtle satire that has won him his reputation as a great humourist. But though there was always a smile on his lips, it was a tender one, and his sympathy with suffering often brought his laughter near to tears.

This delicate and original genius was at first subjected to harsh criticism, which Tchekoff felt keenly, and Trigorin's description in *The Sea-Gull* of the trials of a young author is a cry from Tchekoff's own soul. A passionate enemy of all lies and oppression, he already foreshadows in these early writings the protest against conventions and rules, which he afterward put into *Treplieff's* reply to *Sorin* in *The Sea-Gull*: "Let us have new forms, or else nothing at all."

In 1884 he took his degree as doctor of medicine, and decided to practise, although his writing had by now taken on a professional character. He always gave his calling a high place, and the doctors in his works are drawn with affection and understanding. If any one spoke slightingly of doctors in his presence, he would exclaim: "Stop! You don't know what country doctors do for the people!"

Tchekoff fully realised later the influence which his profession had exercised on his literary work, and sometimes regretted the too vivid insight it gave him, but, on the other hand, he was able to write: "Only a doctor can know what value my knowledge of science has been to me," and "It seems to me that as a doctor I have described the sicknesses of the soul correctly." For instance, Trigorin's analysis in *The Sea-Gull* of the state of mind of an author has well been called "artistic diagnosis."

The young doctor-writer is described at this time as modest and grave, with flashes of brilliant gaiety. A son of the people, there was in his face an expression that recalled the simple-hearted village lad; his eyes were blue, his glance full of intelligence and kindness, and his manners unaffected and simple. He was an untiring worker, and between his patients and his desk he led a life of ceaseless activity. His restless mind was dominated by a passion of energy and he thought continually and vividly. Often, while jesting and talking, he would seem suddenly to plunge into himself, and his look would grow fixed and deep, as if he were contemplating something important and strange. Then he would ask some unexpected question, which showed how far his mind had roamed.

Success was now rapidly overtaking the young author; his first collection of stories appeared in 1887, another one in the same year had immediate success, and both went through many editions; but, at the same time, the shadows that darkened his later works began to creep over his light-hearted humour.

His impressionable mind began to take on the grey tinge of his time, but much of his sadness may also be attributed to his ever-increasing ill health.

Weary and with an obstinate cough, he went south in 1888, took a little cottage on the banks of a little river "abounding in fish and crabs," and surrendered himself to his touching love for nature, happy in his passion for fishing, in the quiet of the country, and in the music and gaiety of the peasants. "One would gladly sell one's soul," he writes, "for the pleasure of seeing the warm evening sky, and the streams and pools reflecting the darkly mournful sunset." He described visits to his country neighbours and long drives in gay company, during which, he says, "we ate every half hour, and laughed to the verge of colic."

His health, however, did not improve. In 1889 he began to have attacks of heart trouble, and the sensitive artist's nature appears in a remark which he made after one of them. "I walked quickly across the terrace on which the guests were assembled," he said, "with one idea in my mind, how awkward it would be to fall down and die in the presence of strangers."

It was during this transition period of his life, when his youthful spirits were failing him, that the stage, for which he had always felt a fascination, tempted him to write *Ivanoff*, and also a dramatic sketch in one act entitled *The Swan Song*, though he often declared that he had no ambition to become a dramatist. "The Novel," he wrote, "is a lawful wife, but the Stage is a noisy, flashy, and insolent mistress." He has put his opinion of the stage of his day in the mouth of Treplieff, in *The Sea-Gull*, and he often refers to it in his letters as "an evil disease of the towns" and "the gallows on which dramatists are hanged."

He wrote *Ivanoff* at white-heat in two and a half weeks, as a protest against a play he had seen at one of the Moscow theatres. *Ivanoff* (from Ivan, the commonest of Russian names) was by no means meant to be a hero, but a most ordinary, weak man oppressed by the "immortal commonplaces of life," with his heart and soul aching in the grip of circumstance, one of the many "useless people" of Russia for whose sorrow Tchekoff felt such overwhelming pity. He saw nothing in their lives that could not be explained and pardoned, and he returns to his ill-fated, "useless people" again and again, not to preach any doctrine of pessimism, but simply because he thought that the world was the better for a certain fragile beauty of their natures and their touching faith in the ultimate salvation of humanity.

Both the writing and staging of *Ivanoff* gave Tchekoff great difficulty. The characters all being of almost equal importance, he found it hard to get enough good actors to take the parts, but it finally appeared in Moscow in 1889, a decided failure! The author had touched sharply several sensitive spots of Russian life—for instance, in his warning not to marry a Jewess or a blue-stocking—and the play was also marred by faults of inexperience, which, however, he later corrected. The critics were divided in condemning a certain novelty in it and in praising its freshness and originality. The character of Ivanoff was not understood, and the weakness of the man blinded many to the lifelike portrait. Tchekoff himself was far from pleased with what he called his "literary abortion," and rewrote it before it was produced again in St. Petersburg. Here it was received with the wildest applause, and the morning after its performance the papers burst into unanimous praise. The author was enthusiastically fêted, but the burden of his growing fame was beginning to be very irksome to him, and he wrote wearily at this time that he longed to be in the country, fishing in the lake, or lying in the hay.

His next play to appear was a farce entitled *The Boor*, which he wrote in a single evening and which had a great success. This was followed by *The Demon*, a failure, rewritten ten years later as *Uncle Vanya*.

All Russia now combined in urging Tchekoff to write some important work, and this, too, was the writer's dream; but his only long story is *The Steppe*, which is, after all, but a series of sketches, exquisitely drawn, and strung together on the slenderest connecting thread. Tchekoff's delicate and elusive descriptive power did not lend itself to painting on a large canvas, and his strange little tragi-comedies of Russian life, his "Tedious Tales," as he called them, were always to remain his masterpieces.

In 1890 Tchekoff made a journey to the Island of Saghalien, after which his health definitely failed, and the consumption, with which he had long been threatened, finally declared itself. His illness exiled him to the Crimea, and he spent his last ten years there, making frequent trips to Moscow to superintend the production of his four important plays, written during this period of his life.

The Sea-Gull appeared in 1896, and, after a failure in St. Petersburg, won instant success as soon as it was given on the stage of the Artists' Theatre in Moscow. Of all Tchekoff's plays, this one conforms most nearly to our Western conventions, and is therefore most easily appreciated here. In Trigorin the author gives us one of the rare glimpses of his own mind, for Tchekoff seldom put his own personality into the pictures of the life in which he took such immense interest.

In *The Sea-Gull* we see clearly the increase of Tchekoff's power of analysis, which is remarkable in his next play. *The Three Sisters,* gloomiest of all his dramas.

The Three Sisters, produced in 1901, depends, even more than most of Tchekoff's plays, on its interpretation, and it is almost essential to its appreciation that it should be seen rather than read. The atmosphere of gloom with which it is pervaded is a thousand times more intense when it comes to us across the foot-lights. In it Tchekoff probes the depths of human life with so sure a touch, and lights them with an insight so piercing, that the play made a deep impression when it appeared. This was also partly owing to the masterly way in which it was acted at the Artists' Theatre in Moscow. The theme is, as usual, the greyness of provincial life, and the night is lit for his little group of characters by a flash of passion so intense that the darkness which succeeds it seems wellnigh intolerable.

Uncle Vanya followed *The Three Sisters,* and the poignant truth of the picture, together with the tender beauty of the last scene, touched his audience profoundly, both on the stage and when the play was afterward published.

The Cherry Orchard appeared in 1904 and was Tchekoff's last play. At its production, just before his death, the author was fêted as one of Russia's greatest dramatists. Here it is not only country life that Tchekhoff shows us, but Russian life and character in general, in which the old order is giving place to the new, and we see the practical, modern spirit invading the vague, aimless existence so dear to the owners of the cherry orchard. A new epoch was beginning, and at its dawn the singer of old, dim Russia was silenced.

In the year that saw the production of *The Cherry Orchard,* Tchekoff, the favourite of the Russian people, whom Tolstoi declared to be comparable as a writer of stories only to Maupassant, died suddenly in a little village of the Black Forest, whither he had gone a few weeks before in the hope of recovering his lost health.

Tchekoff, with an art peculiar to himself, in scattered scenes, in haphazard glimpses into the lives of his characters, in seemingly trivial conversations, has succeeded in so concentrating the atmosphere of the Russia of his day that we feel it in every line we read, oppressive as the mists that hang over a lake at dawn, and, like those mists, made visible to us by the light of an approaching day.

Source: Marian Fell, "Introduction," in *Plays,* by Anton Tchekoff, translated by Marian Fell, Charles Scribner's Sons, 1915, pp. 3–10.

SOURCES

Callow, Philip, "Medicine and Humor," in *Chekhov: The Hidden Ground,* Constable, 1998, pp. 34–57.

Chekhov, Anton, "The Bear," in *The Cherry Orchard & Other Plays,* Grosset and Dunlap, 1936, pp. 138–55.

Finke, Michael, "Anton Chekhov," in *Dictionary of Literary Biography,* Volume 277, *Russian Literature in the Age of Realism,* edited by Alyssa Dinega Gillespie, Thomson Gale, 2003, pp. 54–79.

Gottlieb, Vera, "Chekhov's One-Act Plays and the Full-Length Plays," in *The Cambridge Companion to Chekhov,* edited by Vera Gottlieb and Paul Allain, Cambridge University Press, 2000, pp. 57–69.

Pitcher, Harvey, "Chekhov's Humour," in *A Chekhov Companion,* edited by Toby W. Clyman, Greenwood Press, 1985, pp. 87–106.

Turkov, Andrei, "Introduction," in *Anton Chekhov and His Times,* compiled by Andrei Turkov, University of Arkansas Press, 1995, pp. ix–xv.

FURTHER READING

Brooke, Caroline, *Moscow: A Cultural History,* Oxford University Press, 2006.

> Chekhov lived in Moscow for much of his life, and his greatest dramatic works premiered there. In this volume, Brooke explores the many cultural rebirths Moscow has experienced and studies its appeal to the writers, artists, and composers who, throughout history, made the city their home.

Frank, Stephen P., *Crime, Cultural Conflict, and Justice in Rural Russia, 1856–1914*, University of California Press, 1999.

> Frank examines the relationship between crime, punishment, and social order in rural Russia. The time frame the author focuses on encompasses Chekhov's life, and Frank's work illuminates the historical and social contexts of Chekhov's stories and plays.

Gottlieb, Vera, *Anton Chekhov at the Moscow Art Theatre: Archive Illustrations of the Original Productions*, Routledge, 2005.

> Gottlieb, a prominent theater historian, provides a collection of photographs from the original productions of Chekhov's plays at the Moscow Art Theatre (MAT) and also offers translations of the introductions to the productions by the theater director and the literary manager at the MAT.

Rayfield, Donald, *Anton Chekhov: A Life*, Northwestern University Press, 2000.

> Rayfield, a noted Chekhov scholar, offers a biography of Chekhov that is praised for its rich detail and comprehensive documentation.

Bye-Bye, Brevoort

EUDORA WELTY

1949

Although the Mississippi writer Eudora Welty is well known for her many short stories, novels, essays, and photographs, as well as for her fine ear for catching the speech patterns of the South, *Bye-Bye, Brevoort* is her only published play. A one-act farce, the play was first performed at a summer theater in Westboro, Massachusetts, in 1949. More notably, *Bye-Bye, Brevoort* was included in the 1956 off-Broadway production, *The Littlest Revue*. The play was published for the first time by Palaemon Press for the New Stage Theatre in Jackson, Mississippi. This edition is no longer in print and difficult to obtain; however, in 1991, editor Daniel Halpern included *Bye-Bye, Brevoort* in his book, *Plays in One Act*, a readily available source.

Bye-Bye, Brevoort is the story of three elderly ladies who live in the Hotel Brevoort, an actual building in New York City that was torn down shortly after Welty wrote her play. The three women entertain a gentleman caller for tea, while wrecking balls and workers destroy the hundred-year-old Brevoort. The humor derives from the women's refusal to notice that their home is falling apart as they continue their outdated rituals. While hilarious, the play also suggests a more serious theme, the destruction of the old to make way for the new.

Eudora Welty (Getty Images)

AUTHOR BIOGRAPHY

Eudora Alice Welty was born on April 13, 1909, in Jackson, Mississippi, to Chestina Andrews Welty and Christian Webb Welty. Her mother was a former schoolteacher and her father was an insurance executive. Welty's mother encouraged her daughter in all creative pursuits. Her father, an amateur photographer, also was very influential in his daughter's life. Welty was the eldest child in the family and the only daughter. The family members were great readers and placed a high value on learning. As a child, she visited the Andrew Carnegie Library daily and was allowed to take out two books per day.

Welty spent her entire childhood in Jackson. She began her college education at the Mississippi State College for Women, and completed studies for her bachelor's degree at the University of Wisconsin in 1929. From there she went to New York City, where she began studies in advertising at the Columbia University Graduate School of Business in 1930. Welty's father died of leukemia in 1931 and she returned to Jackson. Between 1931 and 1934, she edited copy for the local radio station and also wrote for the *Commercial Appeal*, a Memphis newspaper. During the Great Depression, she secured a job in the publicity department of the Works Progress Administration, where she wrote articles and advertising. The job also allowed her to travel throughout Mississippi, and she took a great many photographs during this time.

In 1936, after several years of submitting stories to magazines, Welty published her first short story, "Death of a Traveling Salesman," in the magazine *Manuscript*. In the same year, an exhibition of her Depression pictures was mounted in New York.

It took two more years for Welty to receive national attention. The publication of "Why I Live at the P.O." and "The Worn Path" in the *Atlantic Monthly* assured her of her place in twentieth-century American literature. In 1941, Welty's first collection of short stories, *A Curtain of Green and Other Stories*, was published to great critical success. In the same year, she also released the collection *The Wide Net and Other Stories*, following this book with the novella *The Robber Bridegroom* in 1942. Welty published her first full-length novel, *Delta Wedding*, in 1946. After this publication, she immediately began work on another project; however, she was unsure whether she was writing a series of connected short stories or a novel. In spite of urging from her agent, publisher, and friends to finish the project, she chose to put it aside when she went to New York City in 1948 to work with the writer Hildegarde Dolson on a musical revue. When she returned to Jackson in the summer of 1948, she completed both the material for the revue, including *Bye-Bye, Brevoort*, and the final two stories for her project. Published as *The Golden Apples*, the collection of connected short stories received critical acclaim and popular success. The stories are still considered to be some of Welty's finest fiction.

During the 1940s, Welty divided her time between Jackson and New York, finally returning to Jackson for good in the 1950s when her mother and her brothers became ill. For fifteen years, she cared for her mother and her brothers and consequently had little time for her literary endeavors.

After the deaths of her family members, she published two novels, including *Losing Battles* (1970) and *The Optimist's Daughter* (1972), a work that garnered the Pulitzer Prize for Welty in 1973. Welty also contributed to the field of writing with the 1978 book of essays *The Eye of the Story*, and her autobiographical *One Writer's Beginnings*. This book, published in 1984, is one of her most popular works, and is used in college classrooms across the United States and the United Kingdom.

Over her lifetime, Welty received many honors for her writing. In addition to her 1973 Pulitzer Prize, she also received the National Book Critics Circle Award, the American Book Award, numerous O. Henry awards, and the Gold Medal of the National Institute of Arts and Letters. In 1980, President Jimmy Carter awarded Welty a Presidential Medal of Freedom. This is the highest award that the President can bestow on a civilian. The French government inducted her into the French Legion of Honor the same year. In 2000, Welty was inducted into the National Women's Hall of Fame in Seneca Falls, New York.

Welty died at ninety-two from complications of pneumonia on July 22, 2001, in Jackson, Mississippi. Her work continues to be widely anthologized, and critical interest in her writing has increased since her death.

MEDIA ADAPTATIONS

- An original cast recording of *The Littlest Revue*, an off-Broadway musical with a score by Vernon Duke and Ogden Nash that included *Bye-Bye, Brevoort* as one of its sketches, was released on LP by Epic Records in 1956. The recording was rereleased on audio CD by Painted Smiles in 1995.

PLOT SUMMARY

Bye-Bye, Brevoort is a one-act farce, written as a sketch to be included in a longer musical revue. The setting of the play is the sitting room of Millicent Fortescue, an elderly resident of the Brevoort Hotel who does not seem to notice that the entire building is being demolished to make way for a new building. The time of the play is 1948, just a few years before the real Hotel Brevoort, a Manhattan landmark, was torn down.

As the play opens, Fortescue announces that it is time for four o'clock tea to her friends who live across the hall, Agatha Chrome and Violet Whichaway, both elderly women who, like Fortescue, wear hearing aids. All three women are dressed to the hilt: Fortescue is in lace, Chrome wears silk, and Whichaway is in tweeds. Fortescue calls for Evans, her maid, to set the tea table, then recalls that she has sent Evans out for petits fours, little frosted cakes suitable for high tea. Fortescue's oblivion to the world outside her door is made clear when she says she will have to send the Brevoort out to find Evans if she does not return soon. In truth, there is no one at the front desk, or anywhere else in the hotel, save for the wrecking crew making their way toward Fortescue's apartment.

At this moment, Evans arrives, riding a bike and dressed in an elaborate, old-fashioned maid's costume. She knows that the building is being torn down, but continues to humor the old women, although she makes wise cracks throughout the play. Fortescue is appalled that Evans has ridden her bicycle through the lobby and asks if anyone saw her. Evans replies that only men with dynamite and axes were there. Fortescue is relieved that no one with a lorgnette (a pair of handheld glasses favored by the upper class) has seen her maid. Evans begins setting the tea table, pulling out an elaborate tea service, china, glasses, vases, and a cake platter from behind a screen.

Fortescue announces that they will be joined for tea by Desmond Dupree, an elderly gentleman who regularly calls on the ladies. All three are in a flutter because he is coming. Dupree is clearly an aging ladies' man.

Dupree arrives. He says that he has had quite a bit of difficulty getting to the apartment due to low-class people in the hallways sawing on the walls. He does not seem to understand the significance of this, but rather deplores the caliber of people hanging about the corridors of the hotel.

Offstage, the sounds of the demolition are growing louder. Items in the apartment begin to vibrate and shake. The four elderly people complain about the traffic noise and their disgust with the numbers of lower-class people they are coming into contact with at the Brevoort.

Meanwhile, as Evans serves tea, she recites verses from Henry Wadsworth Longfellow's poem, "The Wreck of the Hesperus," the tale of a boat that meets its destruction. The building is shaking so much at this point that Dupree drops his teacup. Meanwhile, the voices of the wrecking crew can be heard just offstage as they draw closer to the apartment. Fortescue instructs Evans to telephone the Brevoort management, but of course, no one can get through.

At this moment, the wrecking crew breaks down the door. They enter, and try to persuade the group to leave the building. At this point, a carrier pigeon arrives with the message that the management is no longer at the Brevoort and advising the residents to do whatever the wrecking crew tells them to do. Fortescue attempts to resume the tea party while the Wreckers begin carrying furniture off the stage. Fortescue tells Evans to call for fresh tea to be sent up on the dumbwaiter, a device that carries items from floor to floor. When the dumbwaiter signals, Evans extracts a tea tray loaded with lighted dynamite sticks. Evans places the tray on the tea table, and the four residents place napkins in lap and prepare to eat. The Wreckers next begin carrying off the women in their chairs. Evans jumps on the back of one of the Wreckers and is carried off stage. Dupree is the final resident remaining on stage. The stage directions state that he "opens his collar and bares his throat, as one going to the guillotine." The Wreckers light his cigarette with a dynamite stick, and Dupree exits. Amidst the noise of the destruction, "The Marseillaise," the national song of France, associated with the French Revolution, begins to play. The last Wrecker leaves, carrying a portrait of the original inhabitant of the suite, Aunt Emmaline. Her fingers are in her ears. The walls collapse as the curtains close.

CHARACTERS

Agatha Chrome
Agatha Chrome is an upper-class, elderly resident of the Hotel Brevoort. She wears a floral silk dress and a hat. Her apartment is across the hall from Millicent Fortescue's. Like Fortescue, she seems oblivious to the destruction of the hotel and continues to partake in the high tea ritual. Like the other characters of *Bye-Bye, Brevoort*, Chrome is a caricature of a particular type of old woman. Her name suggests Agatha Christie, a famous English mystery writer. Christie's novels depicted English upper-middle-class society, complete with the disregard for upsetting events and the insistence on maintaining a "stiff upper lip" in all circumstances.

Desmond Dupree
Desmond Dupree is an upper-class, elderly gentleman who makes a point of joining the ladies for high tea on Thursdays. He wears a chesterfield jacket and yellow gloves, and carries a furled umbrella. He has a reputation as a ladies' man, and despite his age, continues to flirt with the women. He, along with the women, is aghast at the lower-class people milling about in the Brevoort. In actuality, these are the Wreckers. At the end of the play, he is the last of the elderly people to exit, as if he is going to his own execution. The Dupree character would be a recognizable stereotype for Welty's audience; like his female counterparts in the play, he represents a bygone era, one that Welty seems unsympathetic to. What was considered suave, charming, and dashing in the nineteenth century, for example, is portrayed by Welty as seedy and ridiculous at the time of the writing of the play. One might imagine an elderly Peter O'Toole playing this role with a great deal of irony.

Evans
Evans is Fortescue's maid. She wears a very elaborate maid's uniform, more suitable to the nineteenth century than to the twentieth. She is very active, riding into the apartment on her bicycle and roller skating places. She is not of the same class as the elderly women, as is evident from her language. While she is kind to the guests, and not disrespectful, she is a wisecracker and makes many funny remarks, often depending on puns for her humor. She is the comic element in the play. Nothing seems to faze Evans; although she knows that the Brevoort Hotel is being torn down, she continues to carry out her tasks as instructed. While the elderly women in the play are a parody of upper-class, clueless women, Evans is not a parody of a servant. To have made her so, Welty would have had to exaggerate her servitude. Rather, Evans is a representative of a whole new class of servers, people who are sure of themselves, cocky, and not at all daunted or intimidated by wealth. Although she is clothed in an outmoded uniform, she rides a bicycle and roller skates through the hotel. Such actions suggest that she has little respect for the past, as represented by the building. At the same time, she is neither cruel nor confrontational with the elderly people in the play. Rather, Welty uses Evans in this skit in the conventional role of the Fool, a theater tradition that extends back as far as Shakespeare. While the Fool can function as

comic relief in a play, the Fool is, at the same time, the wisest character in a play, as well as the most honest. The Fool character typically cloaks his or her wise and honest remarks with jokes, puns, and humor. In this way, the character to whom he or she is speaking can take the Fool at his or her word while the audience can read the truth beneath the surface. In *Bye-Bye, Brevoort*, Evans serves this function through her comic asides and her general demeanor. She clearly knows the score as far as the building is concerned, but she continues to humor the elderly women by serving their tea. She is by far the funniest character in the play and is absolutely essential for its success. One might imagine a young Carol Burnett playing this role; Evans is a larger-than-life character whose over-the-top antics provide the comic backdrop to the destruction of a way of life.

First Wrecker

The First Wrecker is the head of a three-man crew who are in the process of dismantling and demolishing the Brevoort. He is clearly lower-class, as is evident from his dialect. He is trying to get the elderly people to leave, and eventually he and his men carry the women offstage.

Millicent Fortescue

Millicent Fortescue is an upper-class, elderly resident of the Brevoort Hotel. She is dressed in lace, and also has a parasol with her. The action of the play takes place in the apartment she has lived in for many years after inheriting it from her Aunt Emmaline. The furnishings in Fortescue's apartment are heavy Victorian pieces and bric-a-brac. Her goal throughout the play is to continue to serve tea, a four o'clock ritual she has always upheld. She continues to behave throughout the play as if she is the one in charge of not only the tea party but the entire building. She appears oblivious to the wreckage around her and continues to order items such as hot water from the hotel when it is clear that the Brevoort is about to collapse. Like the other characters in the play, she is a caricature rather than a developed character. Because the action of the skit takes place in her dwelling, she can be considered the main character of the play, and the other characters take their lead from her. Welty has little sympathy for Fortescue; the character acts as if she is a member of the English peerage. In so creating Fortescue, Welty is satirizing Americans who emulate the English, as if it makes them more refined or of higher status.

Violet Whichaway

Violet Whichaway is the third upper-class, elderly resident of the Brevoort. She, too, lives across the hall from Millicent Fortescue. She is dressed in tweeds with white shoes and stockings and a hat. She favors an ear trumpet to cope with her deafness. She, too, seems unaware of the noise and destruction just outside her door. Welty, in this character, satirizes the English landed gentry, a class of people who live on large estates in England. Like the others, her deafness suggests that she is unable to hear the new age as it arrives at her door. Indeed, it is unlikely that she hears anything at all that she does not want to hear. In addition, her name suggests that she does not know "whichaway" she is going.

The Wreckers

The Wreckers have been tasked with tearing down the Hotel Brevoort. When the elderly people will not leave the premises at their request, they physically remove the women, carrying them offstage. The Wreckers are representative of a class of people the elderly characters regard as Philistines or barbarians. In the play, they represent the modern generation's complete disregard for the structures and traditions of the past. Their only concern is to tear down the building without any thought as to the lifestyles they are destroying. They work without sympathy and have disdain for the characters they are displacing. At the same time, because Welty's parody of the upper classes is so acute, her attitude toward the Wreckers is slightly ambiguous. On the one hand, she demonstrates that the values of the Victorian world are not appropriate for the time. On the other, The Wreckers, as symbols of the new age, seem to act without respect or regard for the past. They appear as ignorant as the elderly people. Welty seems to suggest that neither group is responding to changing times with either rationality or compassion.

THEMES

Change

Although *Bye-Bye, Brevoort* is a farce, meant to amuse the audience through its slapstick comedy and physical humor, the play nonetheless has several serious themes. One of these concerns the nature of change. At the time Welty was writing *Bye-Bye, Brevoort*, many nineteenth-century

TOPICS FOR FURTHER STUDY

- *Bye-Bye, Brevoort* is very brief; therefore, it could be easily staged during a class hour. Assemble a cast and crew from your classmates, and then prepare and present a staging of *Bye-Bye, Brevoort*. You will need to appoint a props person, stage manager, director, and actors.

- Research the history of the Brevoort Hotel, using both the library and the Internet. Find pictures of the hotel from its construction in 1854 to its destruction around 1950. What stands in its place today? Why was it torn down? Prepare a multimedia presentation for the class using the images and information you have uncovered.

- Many important twentieth-century writers have come from Mississippi, including Welty, Tennessee Williams, Richard Wright, and William Faulkner. Imagine that you and a group of your friends want to visit the locations where these writers lived, worked, and set their stories. Using the Internet and the library, research your trip and assemble maps, informational brochures, travel routes, photographs, and an itinerary. Prepare a multimedia presentation for your class including music, artifacts, food, images, and readings describing your trip.

- Read Welty's *The Golden Apples*, written in the same year as *Bye-Bye, Brevoort*. What similarities do you find in theme or style? Write a paper in which you compare and contrast the two pieces of work.

buildings in New York City, such as the Brevoort Hotel, were being slated for destruction in order to make room for new buildings. It was a time of rapid change, when not only old buildings, but also old traditions were being destroyed. In this sketch, Welty demonstrates ambivalence toward the changes. On the one hand, the elderly people living in the last remaining apartment of the Brevoort are silly in their attempts to maintain their traditions as the hotel crumbles around them.

Welty seems to be suggesting that the Brevoort and its residents are symbolic of the old order, crumbling away under the pressure from a new order brought about by modernism, World War II, and technology. However, she does not seem to wholeheartedly approve of destruction for destruction's sake. The members of the wrecking crew are not presented in a favorable fashion, either. They are crude, brutish men who exhibit no sympathy for or understanding of tradition. Evans, it seems, is the only character who appears to take in both worlds. The most interesting character in the play, and the funniest, she is perhaps a stand in for Welty herself, laughing at both the dinosaurs and the philistines.

Social Class

A second serious concern of *Bye-Bye, Brevoort* is that of social class. This is made apparent throughout the play as the elderly people are all depicted as upper-class, while the members of the wrecking crew and Evans, the maid, are depicted as lower-class. Welty accomplishes this through her descriptions of their costumes, their accents, their possessions, and their expectations.

One apparent attribute of the upper class in this play is their unwavering expectation that they deserve to be served by others. This is evident in the way that Fortescue orders Evans around. Moreover, they are completely oblivious to anything but their own needs. Thus, in spite of the noise in the corridor and ongoing explosions, the elderly people in the play believe that the Brevoort Hotel will continue to fulfill their every whim, including providing them with hot, fresh tea. A second attribute is their sense of superiority. The three women, as well as Dupree, complain that unsavory characters are in the hall. Indeed, all are scandalized when Dupree reports that some of the skaters in the park have beards. Fortescue immediately believes that this is something that the Brevoort should eliminate.

While Welty portrays the upper class as empty-headed and selfish, she does not render the wrecking crew in any better light. These men speak English with accents associated with the uneducated, they are rude to the inhabitants of the apartment, and they demonstrate no sympathy or understanding to the elderly people being forced out of their homes. In short, Welty portrays them as brutes. Of all the characters, the only one described sympathetically is Evans. She is lively, and although her English is not always proper, she demonstrates a quick wit and fine

Wrecking ball hitting wall *(© 2008 | Jupiterimages)*

intelligence. As such, she symbolizes, perhaps, a future in which class distinction is eliminated.

Aging

It would be easy to assume that Welty is simply satirizing the elderly in this play. She does not portray any of the elderly characters in a positive light. They are stereotypical of old people who do not understand their surroundings nor are considerate of those around them. However, it is also possible to consider aging in terms of the Hotel Brevoort. This building was an important landmark in the city of New York. Through its doors passed some of the most powerful people of the nineteenth century. At the same time, it stood for a class of people and an array of values rendered obsolete by World War II and technology. The essential thematic question concerning aging that Welty raises in this place is this: do aging buildings and aging people deserve to be destroyed? Or ought the modern age pay attention to their knowledge and historical significance? This is not to say that the old is inherently superior to the new, nor the elderly wiser than the young. It is to say, however, that the old might have something to offer the new, and that it is up to young people to distinguish what is valuable enough to be saved, and what must be discarded. This is a serious task. The fact that a building or a group of people are aging does not necessarily mean they must be discarded.

Farce

Most critics and biographers writing about Eudora Welty identify *Bye-Bye, Brevoort* as a farce. A farce is a short, funny play, often filled with slapstick and broad jokes, which finds its humor in the paradox of incongruous situations. That is, a farce will be funny to an audience because the situations it portrays do not fit together. For example, in *Bye-Bye, Brevoort*, Fortescue and her cronies insist on their afternoon tea ritual. This ritual is ridiculously pushed up against the demolition of the entire hotel. The humor is that the elderly people refuse to read the situation accurately, and their elaborate tea ritual is wildly out of place in a collapsing building.

In addition, *Bye-Bye, Brevoort* has its share of silly, broad jokes meant to elicit a laugh from the audience. For example, at the crucial moment in the tea ritual, Evans produces a tea tray loaded with lighted dynamite sticks. Thus, the one plot of the play, the destruction of the Brevoort, collides with the second, the afternoon tea at Fortescue's apartment. The scene is rendered even sillier with Evan's proclamation, "TNT is served, mum." Again, the juxtaposition of TNT and tea is both incongruous and funny.

Finally, farces often are highly satiric and parody, or imitate for the purpose of ridiculing, social institutions. In the case of *Bye-Bye, Brevoort*, Welty is poking fun at a whole class of people who do not see that the world they have grown up in is crumbling around them. Instead of seeing the world for what it is, this social class refuses to acknowledge change in the world. Likewise, she also parodies the brutish wrecking crew by painting them with a broad stroke as well. She suggests that those involved in wholesale destruction are just as culpable for the world's problems as are the self-delusional upper classes. Farce is the vehicle that allows Welty to compare these two very different worldviews in a funny and light-hearted manner.

Wordplay and Allusions

Throughout *Bye-Bye, Brevoort*, Welty relies on wordplay for much of the humor of the skit. Puns, considered by many to be the lowest form of humor, are important structural devices for the play, and demonstrate Welty's keen concern with the nuances of language. For example,

COMPARE
&
CONTRAST

- **1940s:** Victorian architecture and decorative arts, characterized by ornamentation and elaborate detail, are being replaced by modern architecture and design, with their emphasis on simplicity, sleekness, function, and rejection of elaboration.

  Today: Beginning in the last quarter of the twentieth century, postmodern architects react to the stark smoothness of modern architecture with a playful and ironic return to surface ornamentation and what is known as "neo-eclecticism." That is, architects and designers use diverse styles and decorations, often wittily juxtaposed.

- **1940s:** The Hotel Brevoort, one of the most famous Greenwich Village landmarks, noted for its connection to writers, artists, and the very wealthy, is slated for demolition at the end of the decade.

  Today: The large Brevoort Apartments complex stands in the location of the former

hotel and is a premier Fifth Avenue residence once again.

- **1940s:** Many famous old buildings, including the Mark Twain house, located close to the Hotel Brevoort, are torn down, regardless of their historical significance.

  Today: Significant New York City landmarks are protected by the Landmark Preservation Commission, begun in 1963, to prevent the wholesale destruction of important historical sites.

- **1940s:** Welty is beginning to publish the short stories, novels, and essays for which she will become famous. *Bye-Bye, Brevoort* is written, but not published, and is an obscure item in Welty's corpus of work.

  Today: Critics consider Welty to be one of the most important writers of the twentieth century. Although *Bye-Bye, Brevoort* is not often staged, the work is being published in literature anthologies designed for high school study.

---

she plays on the similarity of sound between "tea" and "TNT" to set up the biggest joke of the skit, the juxtaposition of a very proper high tea party with the explosions associated with the destruction of the Brevoort. In addition, Welty utilizes allusion, or references to other works of literature, to create comedy. Evans's reciting of Henry Wadsworth Longfellow's poem, "The Wreck of the Hesperus," for example, pokes fun at the nineteenth-century artistic sensibilities of the three elderly ladies while also connecting the wrecking of the famous ship with the wrecking of the Brevoort. In addition, Welty parodies the famous last scene from Charles Dickens's *A Tale of Two Cities*, when Sidney Carton must face the guillotine. Carton's fate is tragic in the novel; associating the has-been ladies' man, Desmond Dupree with Carton is a humorous incongruity. Carton, after all, is about to lose his life.

Dupree is just leaving a crumbling apartment. Welty's inclusion in the stage directions that the French national anthem, "The Marseillaise," should be playing amidst the noise of the destruction adds further irony to the scene.

HISTORICAL CONTEXT

The Hotel Brevoort

In order to understand much of the humor in *Bye-Bye, Brevoort*, it is important to understand something about the building Welty uses for her setting. The Brevoorts were a family of Dutch settlers who purchased farmland in 1714 in what is present day Greenwich Village in New York City. They held this farmland for many, many years, growing wealthier all the time. In

1824, Henry Brevoort built a large mansion on Fifth Avenue, and in 1854, the Brevoort family created a posh hotel out of three adjoining houses on Fifth Avenue. According to the Museum of the City of New York, the Brevoort Hotel was a favorite place for visiting European dignitaries to stay while in the United States during the 1860s. By all accounts, it was a luxurious and magnificent building.

In 1902, the Brevoort Hotel was purchased by a French restaurateur, Raymond Orteig. In his able hands, the Brevoort Café became one of the most sophisticated and popular eateries in New York. Many of the most important writers of the early twentieth century chose the Café as their favorite gathering place. In spite of this popularity, the milieu began to change shortly after World War I. Many of the old mansions in Greenwich Village were being replaced by high-rise buildings. In 1927, Orteig offered a $25,000 prize for the first person who would fly across the Atlantic Ocean non-stop. This feat was accomplished, of course, by Charles Lindbergh, who instantly became an international hero. When he returned to New York City, he was feted by a ticker tape parade, and received his prize money at a ceremony at the Brevoort Hotel.

Two important historical events impacted the future of the Brevoort Hotel: Prohibition and the Great Depression. In 1920, the United States passed a constitutional amendment that made it illegal to sell or purchase alcohol. Bars and restaurants across the nation went out of business as a result, particularly after the 1929 New York Stock Exchange crash, which resulted in the Great Depression. Orteig was forced to sell the Brevoort in 1932, although the hotel remained open, the home to an aging clientele who recalled the glory days of the great residence. After 1945, with economic recovery and the return of the veterans of World War II, change in Greenwich Village accelerated. The remaining old hotels, apartment buildings, and houses were demolished quickly and new, sleek high-rise apartments took their place. The Brevoort Hotel closed as a hotel in 1948, and ordered its permanent residents to vacate the premises at that time. The Museum of the City of New York states that the Hotel Brevoort and the other buildings on its block were all razed in 1954 to make way for the nineteen-story Brevoort

Three elderly ladies (© *Paul Doyle* | *Alamy*)

Apartments. Using the events of her own time, Welty satirized both the shabby elegance of the old hotel as well as the rush to destroy old buildings so prevalent in the post-war United States when she wrote *Bye-Bye, Brevoort*.

In 1981, the Brevoort Apartments were converted to cooperatives, flats that are owned outright rather than rented. The Brevoort Apartments continue to stand in the location of the old Hotel Brevoort, and the name is once again associated with very wealthy, upper-class residents.

CRITICAL OVERVIEW

Eudora Welty is one of the most highly regarded twentieth-century American writers. In an obituary appearing in the July 24, 2001, *Washington Post*, Bart Barnes links Welty with William Faulkner, Flannery O'Connor, Allen Tate, Tennessee Williams, and Robert Penn Warren as the "key figures in the movement that created a Southern literary renaissance during the 1930s, '40s and '50s and made Southern writing a major force in 20th century American literature." Likewise, Albin Krebs, writing in the July 24, 2001, edition of the *New York Times*, writes that Welty's work is "notable for [its] imagery, sharp dialogue and fierce wit."

Nonetheless, *Bye-Bye, Brevoort* is a much different kind of literature than that which Welty is generally noted for. John Burt, writing in *The Columbia Companion to the Twentieth-Century American Short Story*, writes that "Eudora Welty is a practitioner of the arts of subtlety and indirection, opening out the inner lives of her characters with perfect judiciousness and impartiality into radiance, but always by means of restraint." While such a comment holds true for Welty's short stories and novels, *Bye-Bye, Brevoort* is not in the least restrained nor subtle. A broad farce poking fun at outmoded traditionalists, heavy-handed modernists, and the class consciousness of both, *Bye-Bye, Brevoort* allows the reader to see another side of the talented Mississippi writer.

There are very few contemporary critical responses to the play. As Ann Waldron reports in her book *Eudora: A Writer's Life*, the play was first performed as part of the revue *Lo and Behold*, staged by a summer repertory company in 1949. Waldron writes,

> A review was damning: "Fair enough for a silo tryout, *Lo and Behold* doesn't have anywhere near the staying power to make a bid for the long stretch....[The skit] by Eudora Welty lacks sock....Furlow's songs are pleasant, but have no distinction."

A few years later, Brooks Atkinson wrote a short review for the *New York Times* of the 1956 off-Broadway production *The Littlest Revue*, which included *Bye-Bye, Brevoort* as one of its sketches. Atkinson described the show as a "bright, gay gambol," singling out *Bye-Bye, Brevoort* for special notice: "Eudora Welty's caricature of the old inhabitants of the old Brevoort is wry and enjoyable."

The most comprehensive critique of the play is by noted Welty scholar Peggy Whitman Prenshaw. Her article "Sex and Wreckage in the Parlor: Welty's *Bye-Bye, Brevoort*" appeared in the January 1995 issue of the *Southern Quarterly*. Prenshaw makes the case that although Welty never wrote "for the stage in any sustained way," she was, however, "deeply attracted to and

influenced by drama." Prenshaw details the circumstances surrounding the writing of *Bye-Bye, Brevoort* and traces both the performance and publication history of the play. She argues that the writing of *Bye-Bye, Brevoort* is closely connected to the writing of *The Golden Apples*, Welty's acclaimed collection of short stories, as Welty was working on both at the same time. Further, according to Prenshaw, "The farcical skit she wrote at the time she was conceptualizing the organizational whole of *The Golden Apples* helped her discover her main pattern."

While *Bye-Bye, Brevoort* has been largely overlooked critically and is not well-known among her readers, Welty's growing stature means that all of her work is undergoing increasing critical scrutiny. In this context, *Bye-Bye, Brevoort* may begin to receive more attention.

CRITICISM

Diane Andrews Henningfeld

Henningfeld is a professor of English who writes widely on literary topics. In the following essay, she examines the issues of social class, colonialism, and revolution that are satirized in the farce Bye-Bye, Brevoort.

Bye-Bye, Brevoort is a very short and very funny play. Using the devices of farce, the sketch mocks both the old and the new in its tale of the elderly residents of the Hotel Brevoort who insist on afternoon tea while the hotel is demolished around them. There is a darker side to the farce, however, one that Welty craftily hides within the broad slapstick comedy. Peggy Whitman Prenshaw, in a perceptive 1995 article from *The Southern Quarterly*, argues that the theme of *Bye-Bye, Brevoort* "is doubtless the most familiar and venerated one in dramatic and fictional literature—the mutability of human life, the inevitable, unavoidable passage of time and its consequence for human beings." She further notes, "The ladies' response—flat-out denial—might as easily have been rendered tragically or heroically, but in *Bye-Bye Brevoort*, Welty pulls them through comically by the skin of their teeth." While Prenshaw has tapped a central theme of the play, it is possible to generate yet another serious reading. *Bye-Bye, Brevoort* is not only about the passage of time in human life, it is also about the colonialism and class structures prevalent throughout the nineteenth

WHAT DO I READ NEXT?

- Welty wrote *The Golden Apples* (1949) at the same time she was writing *Bye-Bye, Brevoort*. This collection of connected short stories is considered by some critics to be Welty's best work.

- Students seeking additional information about Welty and her work should visit the University of Mississippi's Mississippi Writers page located at http://www.olemiss.edu/mwp, where they will find ample biographical and bibliographical help (first posted February 1998).

- Nathan Silver's expanded and updated book *Lost New York* (2000) offers photographs and essays about important sites since destroyed in New York City.

- In 1984, Peggy Whitman Prenshaw edited a large collection of interviews with Eudora Welty spanning forty years of conversations with various writers. *Conversations with Eudora Welty* is an important book for any student to peruse in order to understand Welty's career and writing.

- Welty's *One Writer's Beginning* (1984) remains the classic memoir for readers and writers alike.

- *Welty: A Life in Literature* (1987), edited by Albert J. Devlin, is a collection of critical essays by scholars from the publishers of *The Mississippi Quarterly*.

century, which were passing away in the twentieth. In this play, Welty provides a cautionary tale for the upper classes: failure to attend to the disparity between their lifestyles and those of the lower classes can lead to revolution and destruction.

During the eighteenth and nineteenth centuries, many European countries and, to a lesser degree, the United States, established colonies in various countries around the world, most notably in India and Africa. Under the guise of

> WHEN THE DISPARITY BETWEEN THE HAVES AND THE HAVE-NOTS GROWS SO EXTREME THAT THE COMMON PEOPLE HAVE ABSOLUTELY NOTHING LEFT TO LOSE, REVOLUTION BECOMES AN OPTION."

spreading Christianity to these places, Europeans exploited the natural and human resources of other continents. By the mid-twentieth century, many of the colonies had asserted themselves as independent nations, sometimes through violent revolution. India, for example, became a sovereign nation in 1947, after a number of years of turmoil. The loss of empire was difficult for the British and other Europeans, particularly for those upper-class people who had made their homes in places like India, Africa, and Southeast Asia. These people had enjoyed a very luxurious lifestyle at a very low cost, made possible by the work of the indigenous people of the colonies, who earned little money for their efforts. Indeed, the disparity in the lifestyles between the colonizers and the colonized led to discontent and, ultimately, uprisings.

While India, Africa, and Indo-China might seem far afield from the Brevoort Hotel in New York City, there are many clues scattered throughout *Bye-Bye, Brevoort* to suggest that Welty was considering the outcome of class disparity and colonial discontent. The fact that Welty wrote the play as a farce does not mean that she was unaware of some of the most important historical and political situations of her day. To begin with, the clothing that she assigns to the three elderly women in the Brevoort mimics British colonial clothing. Silks, tweeds, and lace were all common accoutrements of upper-crust British society. Fortescue's lace parasol is another clue: not only were parasols stylish during the nineteenth century, they were a necessity for colonial women who found themselves in much sunnier climes than England. In addition, Welty suggests that she is mocking not only the British but also Anglophile Americans who put on a show of being British by her use of dialect for the women and Dupree. For example, Welty's spelling of the word *can't* when it comes from Fortescue: "I cawn't think why they don't make vehicles go *around* the island!" Likewise, the word *terribly* becomes "teddibly" in Dupree's line: "Teddibly good of you."

In contrast to this parody of upper-class British accents, the wrecking crew demonstrates their own dialect. When the First Wrecker encounters the tea party in Fortescue's flat, he says, "Annuder nest of 'em. You can't smoke 'em out.... Foist we'll see if dey won't come out nice." Because language is one of the most common markers of social class, it is clear that Welty wants the audience to see these workers as from a very different socioeconomic and educational level than the tea party group. At the same time, however, she is parodying the differences in language use between the colonizers and the colonized, using the workmen as stand-ins for their African or Indian counterparts. It is as if the native New York working class is a completely different species, at least from the perspective of Fortescue and her crew.

There is another striking passage in the stage directions which suggests that Welty was considering colonial class structure when she wrote the play: the workers pick up the settee that Fortescue is sitting on and carry her offstage. Welty writes, "She takes up her lace parasol and opens it over her head. Rides out with it over her, as in a howdah." A howdah (also spelled houdah) is a fancy carriage affixed to the top of an elephant, used to carry very wealthy people, particularly in India. The visual image would be recognizable to any member of the original *Bye-Bye, Brevoort* audience as a reference to colonialism.

There is other less obvious and more symbolic evidence that the subject of *Bye-Bye, Brevoort* is class conflict, colonialism, and revolution. All three of the elderly women wear hearing aids, and apparently have difficulty hearing. They are not disturbed by the explosions and yelling coming from just outside their walls. Likewise, European colonials were "deaf" to the plight of the indigenous people of their colonies. They failed to hear the warnings that the discontent among these people was rising to a fever pitch. Chrome says at one point, "Riff-raff. Best *not* to notice them." Ultimately, it is the refusal of the upper-class colonizers (and for that matter, the upper classes in any number of twentieth-century countries, such as Russia and China) to hear the wails of the downtrodden masses that led to their overthrow. When Whichaway says broodingly, "There are moments when I seem to notice something over and beyond the noise of traffic and falling portraits," it is possible to read Welty's undercurrent. The "something" Whichaway hears is the crumbling of an entire way of life, soon to be taken away by the death and destruction of revolution.

That death is on her mind is only referred to obliquely. When Dupree enters the apartment, Fortescue tells him, "Dear Desmond. You're looking frightfully crepey." "Crepey" refers to facial and neck wrinkles and comes from the word *crepe*, meaning a piece of densely wrinkled fabric or paper. One of the most common uses of crepe is for denoting mourning. In the nineteenth and early twentieth centuries, people wore crepe bands around their arms at funerals and often homes where a death occurred were signified by crepe decorations. The members of the tea party at Fortescue's are nearing their own deaths due to age. In addition, whether they realize it or not, they will soon be mourning the complete passage of their way of life.

Finally, several important revolutionary images are embedded in *Bye-Bye, Brevoort*. One of the darkest is just after the group discovers that they cannot reach anyone by phone as the noise outside their door grows louder. Fortescue says, "Often I console myself by pretending the traffic noises are simply pistol shots—the riffraff *murdering* one another." While this comment is meant to be funny, it is impossible to hear it without considering the literal meaning. Fortescue, as a member of the upper class, is hopeful that the lower classes will kill themselves off with guns. This comment demonstrates a basic lack of human compassion and the complete disconnect between the upper class and the lower class. In addition, it also suggests that the violence Fortescue would like to see among the lower classes will soon be turned on her and members of her class. Her "pretending" is like that of the colonial master and the upper-class tyrant, and is reminiscent of the line famously (if erroneously) attributed to Marie Antoinette when she was told that the people of Paris could not buy bread: "let them eat cake."

While the funniest moment in the play may be as Dupree is led off the stage to the strains of "The Marseillaise," it is also a grim reminder of the death and destruction that France endured at the end of the eighteenth century. During the French Revolution, many aristocrats and upper-class people were led from their homes to the guillotine, where they literally lost their heads.

While this scene has been romanticized by writers such as Charles Dickens in *A Tale of Two Cities*, the truth is that the streets of Paris ran red with blood. When the disparity between the haves and the have-nots grows so extreme that the common people have absolutely nothing left to lose, revolution becomes an option.

In reading or watching *Bye-Bye, Brevoort*, one should not forget that the writer was also a photographer who traveled through rural Mississippi in the depths of the Great Depression, recording images of the poor. She knew first-hand the distance from glittery New York City restaurants and apartments to the destitute sharecropper's cottage, and she knew the history of the French and Russian revolutions, when the masses rose up against the rich. She also had the recent evidence of uprisings in India and Africa, when the colonized took back their countries. Welty's warning, therefore, to her audience is that they should pay attention, not be deaf, watch the culture carefully, and work for social justice, equality, and the dignity of all people.

Source: Diane Andrews Henningfeld, Critical Essay on *Bye-Bye, Brevoort*, in *Drama for Students*, Gale, Cengage Learning, 2009.

Peggy Whitman Prenshaw

In the following excerpt, Prenshaw traces the publication and production history of Bye-Bye, Brevoort.

Eudora Welty's place in twentieth-century American letters owes to her achievement in fiction and nonfiction prose. Since the publication of her first short story in 1936, "Death of a Traveling Salesman," her work has steadily drawn increasing readership and critical praise. Although her celebrated ear for the nuances of spoken language have won many admirers for the dialogue she creates in her fiction, she has never undertaken to write for the stage in any sustained way or to redirect her fictional career in the direction of the theater. She has nonetheless been deeply attracted to and influenced by drama, both American and European, the consequence of which one quickly discovers in reading her fictional, autobiographical and critical works.

In the opening section of *One Writer's Beginnings,* entitled "Listening," Welty locates in her childhood love of oral storytelling the dramatic impulse that she credits for shaping her career as a writer. "Long before I wrote stories," she notes, "I listened for stories." She depicts herself as an intense audience, willingly giving herself over to

> THE LADIES' RESPONSE—FLAT-OUT DENIAL—MIGHT AS EASILY HAVE BEEN RENDERED TRAGICALLY OR HEROICALLY, BUT IN *BYE-BYE BREVOORT*, WELTY PULLS THEM THROUGH COMICALLY BY THE SKIN OF THEIR TEETH."

suspenseful absorption in the dramatic conversation surrounding her. "Listening children know stories are *there*. When their elders sit and begin, children are just waiting and hoping for one to come out, like a mouse in a hole" (14). In this account of her early apprehension of stories and how they are made, she repeatedly invokes theatrical images and tropes: "It took me a long time to realize that these very same everyday lies, and the stratagems and jokes and tricks and dares that went with them, were in fact the basis of the *scenes* I so well loved to hear about and hoped for and treasured in the conversation of adults" (15).

Welty is an intensely "scenic" writer, one whose prose richly communicates visual and aural detail. Even in the stories that are most devoted to the interior life and rendered in a lyrical, poetic style, the action is grounded, realized, *staged* in a habitation that waits upon the reader to part the curtain and see the drama unfold. The "dramatic instinct" that she refers to in *One Writer's Beginnings* is even more apparent, however, in the fiction dominated by dialogue, in such works as "Petrified Man" or, most notably, in the novel, *Losing Battles*. There are also the special, one might even say radical, examples of dramaturgic technique employed in the service of fiction in the narrated monologues: "Why I Live at the P.O.,""Shower of Gold" and *The Ponder Heart,* brilliant transpositions of the spoken tale to the written story. Still, as Welty herself acknowledges on many occasions, writing dramatic fiction differs essentially from writing plays. In a 1980 interview, Joanna Maclay asked whether she had "ever thought of writing for the theatre." Welty responded: "It would be my dream. I realize now how much I would have to learn. In fact, I found out by trying it for myself. I thought, 'I love dialogue and I've worked hard on it in my stories, and I think I've gotten to a certain degree of competence in that.' But I found that that did not apply when it comes to writing for the theatre. Of course, any person who has ever performed knows how little that really applies" (Prenshaw 270).

Welty's dream of writing for the theater has to date been realized only once, in a one-act farce entitled "Bye-Bye, Brevoort." Although she has been an interested on-looker in the stage productions of *The Ponder Heart* (1956) and various stage and film adaptations of her fiction, she has not participated directly in the scripting or staging of these. In her description of the Welty collection at the Mississippi Department of Archives and History, Suzanne Marrs describes a small group of typescripts of unpublished, unproduced dramas by Welty, including "The Waiting Room," circa 1935, which Welty designated "a farce for a Little Theatre," seven other short sketches written, along with "Bye-Bye, Brevoort," for a revue entitled, *What Year Is This?* and a number of scenes from a screenplay adaptation of *The Robber Bridegroom,* written in collaboration with John Robinson (73f.). Of this group of manuscripts, the only one that has seen production or publication is "Bye-Bye, Brevoort," the "skit" or "sketch" that to date constitutes Welty's theatrical canon. This short play, published by Palaemon Press in 1980 for New Stage Theatre in Jackson, Mississippi, and limited to a run of 476 signed copies, has been reprinted in *Plays in One Act* (1991), edited by Daniel Halpern.

"Bye-Bye, Brevoort" was first staged in 1949 at a summer repertory theater, the Red Barn Theatre, in Westboro, Massachusetts, as part of the musical revue, *Lo and Behold.* The director was Paul Lammers, and music and lyrics were composed by Brown Furlow, a Mississippian with a degree in music from Louisiana State University who, according to the playbill for *Lo and Behold,* was also "working on the music for the Eudora Welty-Hildegarde Dolson revue, *What Year Is This?* from which the sketch 'Bye-Bye, Brevoort' was borrowed."

The sketch was most notably produced, however, as part of the Off-Broadway production, *The Littlest Revue,* which opened at the Phoenix Theatre in New York City, 22 May 1956. According to cast information carried in the *New York Times* on 23 May, Ben Bagley "conceived, cast and assembled" the revue, and Ogden Nash and Vernon Duke wrote most of the lyrics and music. Sketches were written by "Nat Hiken, Billy Friedberg, Eudora Welty,

Mike Stewart, George Baxt, Bud McCreery, Allan Manings and Bob Van Scoyk." Brooks Atkinson reviewed the production, noting that "time for the annual May dance having turned up, the Phoenix is celebrating with a bright gay gambol . . . for friends and subscribers," one that offers "a uniformly high standard of intelligence and humor." Among the cast principals were Charlotte Rae, Larry Storch, Tammy Grimes and Joel Grey, whom Atkinson described as "a versatile young man with a professional voice and manner . . . who can sing, dance and perform with the greatest of ease and affability." Of "Bye-Bye Brevoort," Atkinson writes that "Eudora Welty's caricature of the old inhabitants of the old Brevoort is wry and enjoyable." He goes on to praise Ben Bagley for holding "polite interludes of sentiment and romance" to a minimum, noting that Bagley "is more interested in topical humor." Atkinson concludes by declaring the revue "uniformly light, skillful and knowing." He applauds Paul Lammers, who "has attended to the staging with imagination and gusto," Laus Holm's settings, which are "both inventive and attractive," and Alvin Colt's "pleasant" costumes.

Welty wrote the sketch in 1948, collaborating with Hildegarde Dolson in a plan that called for the two of them each to write a variety of short pieces for the projected revue, *What Year Is This?* In 1977 Welty told her friend Jane Reid Petty, an actress and director in Jackson, Mississippi, that she had written "a lot of musical sketches that were done at the Phoenix Theatre in New York." She continues, "Then Hildegarde Dolson, a delicious writer, teamed with me to write a musical. We worked all one summer in New York but Lehman Engel, another Jacksonian, read it and said, 'You'll never get anywhere because there's not a blackout in it.' And you know, he was right. We never did get anywhere. But it was a wonderful excuse to see all the shows on Broadway that season" (Prenshaw 207).

According to correspondence quoted by Michael Kreyling in *Author and Agent,* Welty went to New York in the early summer of 1948 to work on the revue with Dolson, interrupting her progress on *The Golden Apples* collection. The timing was particularly significant in Welty's career. For the two years following the 1946 publication of her first full-length novel, *Delta Wedding,* she had been at work on the new collection— "a kind of a novel (or something)," she had said early in its composition (Kreyling 117).

In March 1948, however, she wrote her agent, Diarmuid Russell, that she was still undecided about the shape of the book, that, despite all the encouragement to produce another novel, there was nothing "novelish about the book." Further, in the face of mounting pressure to complete the collection that spring, she declared her intention to wait upon a shaping conception for the whole: "I intend to go on as fancy takes me and maybe the nucleus of the stories still to come…what I've done so far doesn't define it" (Kreyling 142). It was in the gestational interim that followed, an interim bounded by the writing of the two stories that would complete *The Golden Apples,* "Sir Rabbit" and "The Wanderers" (initially titled "The Hummingbirds"), that she composed "Bye-Bye, Brevoort." In fact, Kreyling reports that after Welty returned to Jackson in mid summer, "revue and stories alternately claimed the writer's time. The revue was allocated strictly limited blocks of time, '3 weeks only…and be done with it,' while the stories 'started coming in my head so fast' that they made a shambles of all agendas" (143). While the farcical sketch rightly warrants attention for its wit and spirited broad humor, its composition at a crucial moment in the writing of what many critics regard as Welty's richest and most complex literary achievement, *The Golden Apples,* perhaps even more compellingly claims notice for "Bye-Bye, Brevoort."

The play is set in contemporaneous New York City (circa 1948) in a residential hotel, the Brevoort, which during the course of the play's action is wholly demolished. The cast of characters includes three old ladies (Millicent Fortescue, Violet Whichaway and Agatha Chrome) who refuse to acknowledge the destruction of their home and way of life, blithely insisting upon their teatime ritual and the entertainment of a gentleman caller, Desmond Dupree, "an old sport in a chesterfield, with a furled umbrella…and yellow gloves" (483). The farce consists chiefly in the situational absurdity of their high Victorian manner in the face of mass wreckage and their rigid refusal to respond in any way to the mounting noise of the demolition crew. But Welty also develops comic humor through word play, prop gags, burlesque routines, incongruous literary allusions, costuming and a host of other familiar devices of stage farce.

Word play, for example, opens and closes the one-act. Miss Fortescue, in whose room the action takes place, speaks the first line, "Tea

time! Tea time!" and never wavers from her insistence that the tea service go forward. In the concluding moments, Evans, the maid and the interlocutor between the zany world of the ladies and the actual, if riffraff, world of the house wreckers, delivers a tray with lighted sticks of dynamite: "TNT is served, mum." Many other such jokes abound, including one particularly funny and revealing one that plays upon the word "slipping." The ladies quiz Evans about wearing bicycle clips through the hotel lobby, wondering aloud whether standards might be slipping. "Millicent—is Evans slipping—or the Brevoort?" Chrome asks, just as a loud crash issues from off stage, Evans's retort. "We'll go down together," is typical of her hard-edged, no nonsense manner, but it also catches the hint of pathos that underlies the farcical humor.

It is Evans who contributes the main action to the skit—she is in constant motion from beginning to end, fetching cheese straws and tea, entering the set "in cape, parcel in both hands and purse swinging from teeth…riding a bicycle." She distributes tea napkins to the ladies and to Dupree as in a game of "drop-the-handkerchief": in fact, she occupies the center of most of the farcical stage business. There is a "large dark oil painting of a lady ancestor in an ornate frame" that falls on cue, which is recovered, remarked upon and rehung by Evans. At the moment the wreckers break down the door and enter, it is Evans who "steps to the door as it falls." In the harum-scarum final action of the play, the wreckers remove the seated ladies, chairs, settee and all, and Evans, never one to stand by passively, leaps on the back of one of the crew, riding "piggyback, showing her bicycle clips attached to her long drawers."

Welty sustains a playful satire throughout the skit, exposing three old "relics" who are oblivious to a changing world outside their walls, relics who are worthy of being "museum pieces." In fact, they refer to a letter from the Metropolitan Museum that insists they take care of themselves! The theme of the farce is doubtless the most familiar and venerated one in dramatic and fictional literature—the mutability of human life, the inevitable, unavoidable passage of time and its consequence for human beings. The ladies' response—flat-out denial—might as easily have been rendered tragically or heroically, but in "Bye-Bye, Brevoort," Welty pulls them through comically by the skin of their teeth….

I HAD NEVER THOUGHT OF IT IN THAT WAY, BUT LAYING A PATTERN ALLOWS YOU TO EXPERIMENT. DOES IT WORK BETTER HERE, OR HERE? I PROBABLY DID GET THAT FROM SEWING. IT GIVES YOU MORE MANEUVERABILITY."

Source: Peggy Whitman Prenshaw, "Sex and Wreckage in the Parlor: Welty's *Bye-Bye Brevoort*," in *Southern Quarterly*, Vol. 53, No. 2, 3, January 1995, pp. 107–16.

Sally Wolff

In the following interview, Welty uses sewing as a metaphor for her writing process.

"Yes, I have heard that this happened,..." Eudora Welty replied, as we talked about events that took place in Mississippi during the Civil War. I was inquiring about an incident at the beginning of her story "The Burning" in which a mounted Union soldier rides his horse into the foyer of a plantation house. Her spoken response, similar to her literary one, draws on a deep sense of Southern heritage, folklore, and history. In her story, Welty initially focuses on hearth and furnishings, stressing thereby the intrusion, disruption, and calamity, as well as the lasting scars of soldierly conflict, on domestic order and setting.

Welty: ... In Natchez [Mississippi], in one of the old homes, they say you can see a long mark on the cabinet in the hall where the spurs from the soldier's boot scratched the wood as he rode into the house.

It was common for the soldiers to go through the house and take things, and burn down the houses, even the schoolhouse. Sherman put everything to the torch. I've seen photographs that were made of Jackson. It looked like Vietnam. Jackson was burned three times. We were on the way between east and west, and Sherman burned every time he came through. Jackson was called Chimneyville because all that was left standing were the chimneys. He was thorough.

Wolff: A good number of your characters drown, or you describe their deaths in drowning terms. Judge McKelva's face, for instance, in The

Optimist's Daughter, appears "quenched," as if "he had laid it under the surface of dark pouring water and held it there." Has anyone in your family drowned?

Welty: No, no one close to me has drowned. There's a lot of water in Mississippi, though. Mark Twain said, laughing at himself, that he didn't know how to dispose of characters, so he drowned all of them. They would go out in the yard to hang out the clothes and fall in a bucket of water or drown in the well.

Wolff: That is how Clytie drowns.

Welty: I hadn't realized the similarity; yes, she falls into the rain barrel. I didn't know what to do with her, either.

My mother was scared of drowning. Mother was terrified of drowning. She was afraid of her children drowning. She was scared for us to go swimming, and though she was a fearless woman in other circumstances, she didn't want me on a boat to go to Europe.

In West Virginia, people had no way to get anywhere except by water. The mountains went down to the rivers. Folks had to go by boat on water. My mother went that way when she took her father to Baltimore. She took him first on a raft, which was even scarier. She was pretty fearless.

People's lives did end in the water there. Those are treacherous rivers. They are icy and rapid, and if you tried to walk on stones, the water would just sweep you down. It had a power to it, but it was exciting. The roads were almost non-existent then. West Virginia was a pretty young state when she was there.

My father had us all have swimming lessons, and we swam here in Livingston Lake. It was just like warm milk.

Wolff: Where did your mother go to school?

Welty: My parents had to work hard to get the money for school. My mother taught school every year to get enough money to go to summer school. She eventually graduated from a teaching college in West Virginia down the river from Charleston [West Virginia]—one of the state colleges.

She showed me the careful notes she had taken in school. She showed me the maps she kept of Dante's *Inferno.* Her father had brought books back from Virginia in a barrel, "up river."

The course of the interview shifts. What is the significance, for her, of a rural setting in stories such as "A Piece of News,""The Wide Net," and

"Death of a Travelling Salesman," which are essentially about love?

Welty: I learned a great deal about Mississippi when I worked for the W.P.A. and traveled around the state. For the first time I saw that Mississippi was a rural world—I found it much easier to write about than a town. It's a simpler society to describe. It was a different world if you went outside the city. I got to know it pretty well with my journalistic jobs and the W.P.A.

Wolff: What did you see?

Welty: What I discovered was the people in the rural setting. Their lives didn't change with the times. They were poor. Their conditions didn't change and were really terrible. It was all so much worse than I could have imagined. They had no radios, no TV's. They were living in small shacks and cabins and were cut off from things.

These people were the opposite of what they easily might be—pinched and bitter. A friend of mine also had to go into rural areas to buy land for the roads, and, oh! the tales he told me of poverty he saw.

I discovered still more by visiting all the county seats. It was an education that I had again when I attended the M.S.C.W. It was the first state college for women in the country. At the time, everybody could go to school there, and it was cheap to go there. Some students were ill-educated. The teachers were the best educated people around. The school had a cross-section of girls from the rest of the state and many from poor homes. But their families were happy. Their mothers sent them baskets of fried chicken from home. They were good country people. It was a poor, poor time in history, when I look back.

Wolff: How did this understanding affect your writing?

Welty: These stories are all part of the same rural setting. You have to set the stage for a story. You have to have something to identify it. I used to take all the county newspapers and read them all. That's what got me interested in what went on in the State of Mississippi. Just the naked news.

The newspapers back then would have letters from little towns in the paper, by the family of the reporter or the correspondent. What Ruby Fisher reads in the newspaper was the kind of thing that would be in these newspapers: "So and So became shot," or "The Sunday visitors in

town were. . . ." That gave me a picture of what life was like, much as I think it did for Faulkner. I did know people like that. They are the material of Southern gothic. Jackson was not typical of Mississippi at the time because of its size. It's the only place of its size in Mississippi.

Wolff: You have written a great deal about love.

Welty: I suppose I have. What other kind of story is there? It's the basis for any kind of structure of the story—narrative and plot—the drive, the spirit, what makes the human. It's the center of all the stories. Human relationships are all that matter. What other human relationship would be as complex, as true, as dramatic an emotion?

Wolff: The marriage of Becky and the Judge seems to possess qualities which make it one of the best.

Welty: Well, it lasted the longest.

Wolff: In the earlier versions of your novel The Optimist's Daughter, *up through its publication in the* New Yorker, *Philip Hand, the husband of the protagonist, Laurel Hand, does not appear. Why did you decide to omit the scenes you had first written about their courtship?*

Welty: There wasn't time for any of it. I played Laurel down from the beginning—she's the eyes. But when I started developing the novel more, I decided to concentrate on Phil's death rather than on the earlier material. I wanted to imply more than I said about Phil.

It wasn't that more material didn't exist. World War II was still fresh in my mind. So many details come to mind that fit. My use of him changed. He remained the same. That was his function in the novel. I wanted to convey his reality. Everything had to be in its proportions, since he was in a short novel.

Writing makes its own contribution. I see things when I go back and re-read that I'd forgotten were in the novel. But they do exist in it.

Wolff: Is it correct that you decided to add Philip Hand during the year after the publication of the New Yorker *story, since the next set of revisions contain the first references to him?*

Welty: The reason I did not publish it in novel form for one year was to give it time. Lots of things came to me during that year. I was able to make right use of what I had. I didn't want anything to cloud over the last section. I really love that part when Laurel thinks of him going around the house. I just sat down at the typewriter—that's the way I revise—just sit down with the manuscripts.

Wolff: Did you base your characterization of Phil on your friend John Robinson?

Welty: Everybody is asking about John Robinson these days. No, I did not. He did not have Phil's character. My brother made a bread-board and had double-jointed thumbs and goes with the character. My brother saw action in the war. Walter went through the battle at Okinawa. But I felt I had too much about Chicago, so I kept things out that were not contributing to what I was trying to do. Also, I didn't know where a young married couple would live in Chicago. I knew a number of painters who went to the Art Institute and the first art gallery I went to, and that has meant the most to me.

Some of the language was Walter's as I think I've said. I use names, too. I keep a list of Mississippi towns. There was a Banner. I remember the exact ways things were said. Some of the remarks for *Losing Battles* came right out of the mouths of people helping me when my mother was ill.

Wolff: Phil was killed six weeks after Laurel married him, his body was never found, and he was eaten by birds he would have known and loved. What is the source in your imagination for the violence of this death?

Welty: I knew so much of that. My brother died of rheumatoid arthritis before he was forty. It was his life—he wanted it.

Wolff: When Phil cries for the life he wanted, isn't that also Laurel's wanting it, and yours?

Welty: It is a communication between them—that's what she felt, too. She's the one who could hear it. It was a reality to her. That was the meaning it had for her: she got the meaning. It was not lost on her.

Wolff: The image of Phil with his mouth open like a funnel is similar to a description you wrote of George Fairchild in an early version of Delta Wedding. You describe him as "a figure strangely dark, alone as the boogie man, back of them all, and seemed waiting with his mouth set open like a drunkard's or as if he were hungry."

Welty: It's almost like a trance or a dream. I've seen people like that before. Nothing physical can be invented. If you think about French and Italian art of the thirteenth-century period, it had people with grimaces like that.

Wolff: Is his open-mouthed image more suggestive of horror, fear, or longing?

Welty: Longing. That would be more like it, I think.

Wolff: Your other portrayals of marriage have happier endings.

Welty: Yes. I like Jack and Gloria. She has this idea that "We're gonna get off to ourselves." She thinks it'll work. She is naive in thinking she can do it—get away from the family.

Wolff: Your metaphorical writing often involves sewing, threading, or referring to cloth or parts of dresses: in The Optimist's Daughter, for example "It seems to Laurel that the voice could have torn cloth." Why do you often think in sewing terms?

Welty: People had to sew back in my mother's day. Babies had a regular trousseaux of hand-made and embroidered clothes, all done in the home. They sewed tea napkins—you know, small linen napkins with scalloped edges. People embroidered all day long—underclothes even. There was not much money to buy clothes, so people did sew a lot and provide for their own. We had a sewing woman who came and spent the day at our house. People knew sewing women.

Once my mother had just embroidered a beautiful dress for me, with pretty wreaths and hoops in the pattern. I was at a friend's house for a party. We were playing outside, and I was hiding near the woodpile. Another girl spotted me hiding and brought a whole pile of kindling down all over me. My dress was dirty and torn. When I got home, I saw Mother outside, and I prayed and prayed to Jesus to mend my dress before Mother came in from milking the cow. She had worked so hard on the dress.

Wolff: You have said that when you are revising your work, you cut pages apart and pin them together in some other configuration. Is revising a story or a novel like pinning a dress pattern?

Welty: Yes, in a sense. I had never thought of it in that way, but laying a pattern allows you to experiment. Does it work better here, or here? I probably did get that from sewing. It gives you more maneuverability. I did so much revision as it was.

I got some of that from working in newspapers, where you worked with long rolls of paper on your typewriter and where you were really able to patch something together.

Wolff: Do you plan stories by certain patterns? For instance, the weather often figures in your stories about love. In "A Piece of News" the storm accompanies the marital crisis, as it does in The Optimist's Daughter during Laurel's crisis.

Welty: I plan a story by its dramatic sense, not by a particular pattern. That's the dramatic end of writing. But the weather is an important part of a story. The weather depends on the crisis; the crisis is coming out of the weather. The crisis is the cause of the weather.

Wolff: Do you sew?

Welty: No. But my mother did. She tried to teach me to embroider. My mother had to leave the room when I threaded the needle—she couldn't stand to watch. I wasn't good at all.

Collecting stories, and stitching them, together with tradition and memory, into a whole cloth, is the essence of Eudora Welty's fiction. In her discussion of sewing, with implication for the literal and the figurative, Welty's memory reaches back to childhood and pins the floating images into patterns, establishing a chronology, as do her books of fiction and photographs. She says she was not "good" at sewing, although her mother tried to teach her. But perhaps without knowing, her mother bequeathed her the tools; her daughter would find her own art of embroidery.

Source: Sally Wolff, "The Domestic Thread of Revelation: An Interview with Eudora Welty," in *Southern Literary Journal*, Vol. 27, No. 1, Fall 1994, pp. 18–24.

Joanna Maclay

In the following interview with Maclay, Welty discusses the similarities between a short story writer and a dramatist.

...MACLAY: Throughout your career, you've entertained many audiences with readings from your own works. Do you have any favorite stories that you enjoy reading aloud publicly?

WELTY: Well, purely for reasons that help me, I want to read something with lots of conversation and plenty of action, which eliminates many of my stories to begin with. When I read for an audience, I wouldn't choose those very quiet stories that are interior or are more meditative, more contemplative. So I take stories that have something in them that I think would keep an audience interested.

JM: Do you find that you read stories that have more comedy in them, then?

> OF COURSE, IT'S TRUE THAT WE'RE ALL (NOVELISTS AND PLAYWRIGHTS) DEALING WITH HUMAN RELATIONSHIPS AND THE DRAMAS THAT ARISE FROM THAT; BUT I DON'T THINK YOU COULD WRITE THE FIRST LINE ALIKE IN A NOVEL AND IN A PLAY."

EW: Yes, and I think that's because I usually use the form of dialogue when I want to write a comic story. So it works out that way. Also, it's nice to hear the laughter of people. I must say, that goes to my head and makes me feel very fine. You feel that your audience is really listening to you. And that kind of experience encouraged me, because I hadn't ever thought of myself as a "reader" of my stories out loud, until I was just sort of talked into it once. Then I found I enjoyed it so much. I like the give and take of audiences. But I still don't think of my stories as being spoken when I'm writing them. I think of them as on the page, because as a reader I think in terms of the word and working with the word as I see it written. On the other hand, I never wrote a word that I didn't hear as I read.

JM: Do you mean you sound out a story when you write it?

EW: I just *hear* it when I'm writing it. It comes to me that way. In everything I read, I hear the voice of I know not who. Not my voice. I hear everything being read to me as I read it off the page. I used to think all people read that way; but I gather this is not so. But I have learned one important thing from reading aloud: it's a marvelous acid test for right or wrong. You hear every flaw come back to you. You learn things about where to cut, where you've said something more than once. Something may not look unnecessary or redundant on paper; but when you speak it, you know.

JM: Is it this kind of experience with reading out loud that leads you, for example, to cut out parts of "Petrified Man" when you read it aloud?

EW: Yes, I do cut out some of that story when I read it. That was a very early story and I didn't know then the benefits of close revision and cutting. I wasn't in the habit of going back and checking about things like repetitions. I hadn't learned then how really strict a form dialogue is. As you know, and as I am proving with every word I say, we don't make very strict sense in conversation, because so much is done with gesture and with mutual understanding between the two people talking. Put on a page, that's gone. And I hadn't learned that sort of thing.

JM: Have you ever had any occasion to encourage novice writers to read their stories aloud?

EW: Well once, after I had begun reading my own work aloud and had found what I had learned from that, I did a writing workshop here in Jackson at Millsaps College. That year was my first experience with such. I knew nothing about it and we had to make up our own rules. I said that I did not believe you could teach writing, but I thought that in the workshop we could find out things for ourselves by writing and bringing our stories to the class and reading them aloud. We would work with specific pieces, not with generalities about writing. So we did that, and I made each writer read his own work. They would say, "I wanted to let so-and-so read mine," or "You read it"; and I said, "No, part of the responsibility goes away if you don't read your own. You're the one who wrote this and you're answerable to yourself. You're the one who teaches yourself. When you hear your own voice saying it, you learn."

JM: Do you now ever read a story of yours aloud while you're in the process of writing it?

EW: I would be too self-conscious to do that, because while I'm writing a story it's all so interior to me, regardless of whether or not it's in conversation, that I'm still too deep in it. I think you would have to have finished writing it and have a complete story, and then you could try reading it out loud.

JM: I gather then that you never write a story with an eye to its being performed, as the playwright does?

EW: No, I don't. I have a completely different end in view.

JM: Well, have you ever thought of writing for the theatre?

EW: Oohh! It would be my dream. I realize now how much I would have to learn. In fact, I found out by trying it out for myself. I thought, "I love dialogue and I've worked hard on it in

stories, and I think I've gotten to a certain degree of competence in that." But I found that that did not apply when it comes to writing for the theatre. Of course, any person who has ever performed knows how little that really applies.

JM: I asked that question because many of your stories are, for lack of a better phrase, highly theatrical.

EW: Well you proved that in your own performance of "Why I Live at the P.O." and "Petrified Man." But then you had the talent of performing and your physical and personal presence to give it. You also had other people, all the theatrical elements. You concealed my weaknesses with that performance. And you also did it as a reading of that story. You weren't trying it out as something written as a play for a playgoing audience. And the difference between writing a story and writing a play would require a different procedure, a different end in view, different everything. But I love the challenge of writing drama, and I would adore to because I love the theatre.

JM: There are obviously certain similarities you as a narrative writer have to a playwright. For example, you both must be concerned vitally with dialogue.

EW: Certainly.

JM: Yet as a story writer, and particularly as a novelist, you don't have time constraints the playwright has.

EW: And also, things that a performance can give by acting have to be conveyed in a novel in many other ways. The short cut which a play can do and convey in silence or by an action still has to be conveyed in a novel. But the novel must use other means. Also, you don't employ the feeling of urgency in writing a scene in a novel that you would when writing a drama. The urgency should be there in a novel, but it is an urgency of its own kind, not something that should happen, be made overt, in a certain number of minutes. When the point has to be conveyed in a drama, not a word can be wasted, and I think it would be a marvelous discipline for a novelist. When I wrote *Losing Battles,* I was also trying to challenge myself to see if I could try to express everything in dialogue and action and not enter inside anybody's mind. And I never did go inside anybody's mind until the last chapter, when I went inside the little boy's mind—I couldn't resist that. I wanted everything to be brought to the outside and presented openly, in action. That impulse determined the setting, the kind of people who would be in the story, the sort of occasion it would be. I wanted to see if I could meet this sort of challenge, and it captivated me to try it. I think that's why I wrote so much that I never put in the finished novel, because I just couldn't stop. It just proliferated into scene after scene, in which I would try to do something five or six different ways and then pick the one I wanted. It was so much fun. But that didn't teach me to write a play. It just taught me to write a novel in dialogue. Of course, it's true that we're all (novelists and playwrights) dealing with human relationships and the dramas that arise from that; but I don't think you could write the first line alike in a novel and in a play. From the start, from the very beginning, they start out on two different roads. And that's something I had to learn.

JM: Would you ever consider rewriting any of your stories as plays?

EW: From the writing point of view, I wouldn't be interested in rewriting anything I've written as a story into a play. I'd want to start from scratch. I would have to. Once I've done something as a story, to me those people who make the story are enclosed in that world and you can't take them out.

JM: You've said that you believe that writing short stories comes out of a lyric impulse.

EW: I feel that, yes.

JM: Is this different in some way from the story-telling impulse?

EW: It may not be. I love the told story, and I can see how certain stories and novels are descended from it. But that is, in a way, lyrical. The tale certainly appeals to the emotions that everyone feels—a sort of community of emotions—through the senses, through the ears and the voice. And I think a short story does the same thing. Often, also, the old tales dealt with a single strand of experience, just as a short story does. In the same way as lyric poetry does, it follows its own path through a certain space and time, and is a whole in itself.

JM: Do you think that's somehow different from the dramatic impulse?

EW: I don't think so; I think it's connected up with it.

JM: Then do you think there is something within a particular artist that propels him or her to move in one direction primarily as his or her natural medium, for whom there is a natural impulse toward the lyric or the dramatic?

EW: I can only answer for myself. Of course we all know of people who can write in any medium. But I know my own limitations. I think I'm a short story writer naturally. I know I could never write a poem, and I never intended to write a novel. Every single one of my novels came about accidentally. That is, I thought I was writing a long story. When the scope was revealed to me and the story revealed itself as something that needed developing as I went along, then I had to discard that and go back and begin over with the long length and scope in my mind. Every time I wrote anything long, I never dreamed it was going to be a novel. That includes the longest one, *Losing Battles*. And most of my novels are pretty short, like *The Optimist's Daughter*. I consider those as long stories, because they almost never relax the tension I tried to start—which is the way a story goes. . . .

Source: Joanna Maclay, "A Conversation with Eudora Welty," in *Literature in Performance*, Vol. 1, No. 2, April 1981, pp. 68–82.

SOURCES

Atkinson, Brooks, Review of *The Littlest Revue*, in the *New York Times*, May 23, 1956, p. 37.

Barnes, Bart, "Writer Eudora Welty Dies; Voice of American South," in the *Washington Post*, July 24, 2001, p. B07.

"Brevoort Hotel with Mark Twain House," Web site of the Museum of the City of New York, http://www.mcny.org/collections/abbott/a029.htm (accessed July 15, 2008).

"Brevoort to Close as Hotel," in the *New York Times*, July 17, 1948, p. 17.

Burt, John, "Eudora Welty," in *The Columbia Companion to the Twentieth-Century American Short Story*, edited by Blanche H. Gelfant, Columbia University Press, 2000, p. 569.

"Farce," in *The Harper Handbook to Literature*, edited by Northrop Frye, et. al., Longman, 1997, p. 195.

Krebs, Albin, "Eudora Welty, A Lyrical Master of the Short Story, Is Dead at 92," in the *New York Times*, July 24, 2001, p. A1.

Kreyling, Michael, "Eudora Welty," in *Dictionary of Literary Biography*, Vol. 102, *American Short-Story Writers, 1910–1945, Second Series*, edited by Bobby Ellen Kimbel, Gale Research, 1991, pp. 335–50.

Prenshaw, Peggy Whitman, "Sex and Wreckage in the Parlor: Welty's *Bye-Bye Brevoort*," in the *Southern Quarterly*, Vol. 33, Nos. 2–3, January 1995, pp. 107–16.

Vande Kieft, Ruth, "Eudora Welty," in *Dictionary of Literary Biography*, Vol. 2, *American Novelists Since World War Two*, edited by Jeffrey Helterman, Gale Research, 1978, pp. 524–37.

Waldron, Ann, *Eudora: A Writer's Life*, Doubleday, 1998, p. 187.

Welty, Eudora, *Bye-Bye, Brevoort*, in *Plays in One Act*, edited by Daniel Halpern, Harper Perennial, 1991, pp. 459–66.

"Wreckers Attack the Old Brevort," in the *New York Times*, January 28, 1954, p. 29.

FURTHER READING

Folpe, Emily Kies, *It Happened on Washington Square*, JHU Press, 2002.

    This book offers a description and history of the area around Washington Square, the heart of Greenwich Village, and the location of the Hotel Brevoort, which is mentioned in the book. It also contains many historic images.

Kreyling, Michael, *Understanding Eudora Welty*, University of South Carolina Press, 1999.

    This book offers an overview of Welty's professional life and close readings of some of her fiction, as well as an analysis of *One Writer's Beginnings*.

Marrs, Suzanne, *Eudora Welty: A Biography*, Harcourt, 2005.

    An excellent recent biography of Eudora Welty, written shortly after the writer's death and containing a detailed account of the period surrounding the writing of *Bye-Bye, Brevoort*.

Welty, Eudora, *One Time, One Place: Mississippi in the Depression: A Snapshot Album*, University of Mississippi Press, 1996.

    This book is a remarkable collection of Welty's photographs taken during the years she worked for the Work Projects Administration. It offers readers the chance to see another side of Welty's artistic talents.

Crossroads

CARLOS SOLÓRZANO
1959

Carlos Solórzano's *Cruce de vías* (published in Spanish in 1959, translated and published in English as *Crossroads* in 1993) is one of the playwright's one-act dramas. The action of the play is abstract and symbolic; it concerns a character called the Man, who is waiting for a woman with whom he has engaged in a romantic correspondence. The two have never seen each other and have arranged to finally meet at a railroad crossing. The characters have no names. Their interaction fails to yield a deeper human connection, as the Woman, aging and fearing rejection, refuses to reveal herself to the Man. The Man believes he is waiting for someone much younger. The other characters in the play include the vague Flagman and several individuals dressed in gray who collectively form the Train. Through these characters, Solórzano explores the universal themes of longing, fear, and hopelessness. The stage directions describe the stage as sparsely decorated and darkened, and indicate that the characters are moving unnaturally, "mechanically." Such elements, combined with the symbolic nature of the characters, shroud *Crossroads* in an abstractionism (pertaining to ideas rather than realistic events) that marks the play as representative of the avant-garde (experimental) school of drama, with which Solórzano has identified himself.

Originally published in Spanish in 1959 by Mexican publisher El Unicórnio, *Cruce de vías* was translated into English by Francesca Colecchia

and published by Associated University Presses in *Crossroads and Other Plays by Carlos Solórzano* in 1993.

AUTHOR BIOGRAPHY

Born May 1, 1922, in San Marcos, Guatemala, Solórzano grew up in a wealthy, prestigious family. His father, José María Solórzano, was an engineer and a coffee farmer. His mother, Elisa Fernández Barrios, divorced José Solórzano but devoted herself to her six children, of which Carlos was the youngest. His great grandfather, Justo Rufino Barrios, was president of Guatemala from 1871–1888. As a young boy, Solórzano was educated at home by German tutors. He later attended a Marist school, where he received a traditional, strict, Catholic education. During this time, Guatemala was ruled by the dictator Jorge Ubico, and much of the country lived in fear of his tyranny. Solórzano and his family were shielded from much of what went on outside their home. He graduated from high school in 1939 and intended to travel to Europe to continue his studies in Germany, but the onset of World War II prevented him from traveling abroad. Instead, Solórzano attended Universidad Nacional Autonóma de Mexico (UNAM), where he studied architecture and literature and earned degrees in both subjects in 1946. Solórzano explored, in both his masters's thesis and doctoral dissertation, the complexities of the relationship between faith and reason found in the writings of Spanish philosopher Miguel de Unamuna. Solórzano's work reflects similar concerns. In 1946, Solórzano married Beatriz Caso, and three years later the couple traveled to Paris, France. Solórzano had received a 1949 Rockefeller Award for advanced studies at the world-renowned Sorbonne in Paris. Immersed in the culture and creative atmosphere of Paris, Solórzano pursued a literary career as a dramatist. Heavily influenced by avant-garde postwar French thinkers and writers, Solórzano developed his own experimental style. In 1952, he returned to Mexico with a completed script of the play *Doña Beatriz, la sin ventura* (*Doña Beatriz, the Luckless Woman*). He was appointed director of the new Teatro Universitario (University Theater) at UNAM, a position which he held for ten years. After *Doña Beatriz, the Luckless Woman*, Solórzano wrote several other full-length dramas, including *Las manos de Dios* (1956; translated as *The Hands of God*, 1968), which is his best-known and most highly acclaimed work. The controversial play treats religious themes through the use of prison imagery. In 1958, Solórzano presented a dramatic trilogy of one-act plays that he wrote at different times but that share similar religious themes. *Cruce de vías* was published in Spanish in 1959 (translated as *Crossroads* in 1993) and is subtitled "A Sad Vaudeville." Several years later, Solórzano turned from drama to fiction, publishing three novels including *Las celdas* (1971, title means "The Cells"). In 1974, his son, Diego, died in a hunting accident. After Diego's death, Solórzano refused a Fulbright Visiting Artist Award and only continued teaching. Later, Solórzano and his wife had two daughters. In addition to his position as director of the University Theater at UNAM, Solórzano also served as director of the Museo Nacional de Teatro, and as a career professor at UNAM. In 1985, he was named professor emeritus by the university. He has also received numerous awards and honorary degrees and served as the president of the Mexican Center of the International Theater Institute of the United Nations Educational, Scientific, and Cultural Organization (UNESCO) from 1999 to 2000. In 2001, he was recognized by the University of Buenos Aires in Argentina, receiving the Armando Piscépolo Award for his international prominence in theater.

PLOT SUMMARY

According to the stage directions, the one-act play *Crossroads* opens on an empty, dark stage. A clock hanging from the ceiling displays the time, five o'clock. The character of the Flagman stands at one end of the stage, repeating that the "trains from the North travel toward the South." Eventually the Train, which consists of three gray-clad actors moving uniformly with their arms pantomiming the motion of train wheels, moves across the stage. The last man moves free of the Train as if he were jumping from it, and the Train disappears offstage.

After comparing the time on his watch with the clock, a young, male character, known in the play as the Man, discusses with the Flagman whether or not the latter has seen a woman wearing a white flower. Wondering aloud if the woman he is supposed to meet will actually be wearing a yellow flower, the Man consults a letter, then confirms that the flower is indeed supposed to be white. Making vague comments that the Man indicates are unhelpful, the Flagman often shrugs and seems indifferent to the Man's plight. The Man goes on to explain how, through an advertisement in a magazine, he became acquainted with a woman with dark hair and blue eyes; she sent him a photograph. The Flagman's responses do not always seem to correspond with the Man's side of the conversation. The Man accuses the Flagman of speaking nonsense. A train whistle sounds, and the Flagman begins another repetitious chant, this time stating that trains from the South are traveling north. The Train crosses the stage once more.

The Man is disappointed, as he has not seen the woman he is waiting for exit the train as it passed by. Renewing his conversation with the Flagman, the Man contemplates the paradox the Flagman has presented him with—that the "impossible's always true." For a moment, the Man seems to agree with the Flagman, explaining that it seems impossible that he is supposed to be finally meeting this woman, and yet the anticipated meeting is the only event in his life of which he is actually certain. Toward the end of this discussion, the character of the Woman appears from behind the Man. She is tall and slim, her face is veiled, and she is wearing a white flower, which she tears from her dress when the Flagman raises his lantern to examine her. The Man has shielded his eyes from the sudden brightness of the light. The Man suspects the Woman is the one he has been waiting for, but she is coy and elusive and will not let him see her face, nor will she admit that she is in fact the woman who has been corresponding with him and has agreed to meet with him. However, she admits this to the Flagman and reveals her face to him. She is an elderly woman, and she tells the Flagman that she has sent the Man a younger photograph of herself.

The Woman tells the Man about a friend who is ugly but has sent retouched, older photos of herself to men, whom she agrees to meet. Yet when the men arrive at her door, she only watches them through the window and fantasizes about them, refusing to let them see her as she really is. The Man asks the Woman why she would tell him this, but she does not answer. Instead, she asks him about fear, and whether

he has felt afraid that the life he has been waiting for will never happen. Asking him to close his eyes, the Woman continues to press him about fears of solitude and aging, and above all else, loneliness. She urges the Man to not be overcome by time, to fight time, which is the enemy of the woman for whom he has been waiting. Having fallen under the spell of her voice and her words, the Man is confused when he opens his eyes and finds himself "held by the Woman's two hands." The Woman has lifted her veil, and he sees that she is old. He determines that she is not the woman for whom he was waiting.

When the Woman realizes the Man is unwilling to accept the possibility that she is *the* woman, she tells him that she does not believe the one he is waiting for is coming. She offers him the white flower she hid in her purse. The Man takes it from the Woman, excited by the knowledge that the woman he has corresponded with must have been there at some point. The Woman chastises him, telling him that she has already told him "that there's but a moment to recognize one's self, to close one's eyes." When the Man still seems eager to find whom he is looking for, the Woman says that all he can do now is wait, the same as everyone else does. She takes back the flower and walks away. The Man hesitates a moment, beginning to run after her but then stopping himself. The Flagman begins to repeat his refrain from the beginning of the play, stating that the trains from the North are traveling south.

The Train crosses the stage, and the Woman, waving the flower dejectedly, boards the Train, which leaves with the Woman pantomiming its movement with her arms, just as the other individuals who make up the Train do. The Woman, though, does so in a "writhing and anguished" manner. The Man speaks to the Flagman about the Woman, still believing that she was not *the* woman. The Flagman knows the truth—that the woman the Man sought was in fact the same woman who spoke to him—and also seems to be irritated that the Man has failed to ascertain this fact. While the Flagman's side of the conversation has been previously characterized by his indifference and vague attitude, the stage directions state that he now speaks to the Man in a harsh manner. The Man, though, remains confused and grows irritated with what he perceives to be the Flagman's obtuseness. Following another train whistle, the Train returns to the stage, and the Man hides his head in his hands in despair. The

Flagman calls out his now-familiar refrain regarding the direction the Train is moving, and the Train crosses the stage once more.

CHARACTERS

The Flagman

As the play opens, stage directions state that the Flagman stands at one end of the stage, opposite a semaphore (a signaling device that, in this case, alternates between the flashing of a green and a red light, which indicates the arrivals and departures of the Train). Holding a lantern, he is described as standing in a stiff way and possessing an indifferent demeanor. The Flagman speaks the first words of the play "in an impersonal voice," as he looks off into the distance. Intoning repeatedly the statement that the trains are traveling from the North to the South, the Flagman guides the movement of the Train with the rhythm of his words. His refrain, combined with the coordinated movement of the semaphore and the Train, provide the only structure of the play. Throughout the play, the Flagman is vague and often confusing in his interactions with the Man and the Woman. He does not even confirm his own identity when the Man asks if he is the Flagman. Emphasizing his mysterious nature, the Flagman's response to the Man is that he is called "by many names." In addition to refusing to acknowledge his identity, the Flagman insists that everyone looks the same to him. When the Man asks if he has seen the Woman for whom he is waiting, the Flagman replies that "they all look alike." Later, the Woman questions the Flagman, asking him why he did not tell the Man about her, and the Flagman appears not to know who the Man is. The Woman points out that there is only one man there. Despite his extensive conversation with the Man, the Flagman says he has forgotten about him. According to the Flagman, men and women appear to be interchangeable, the trains all go to the same place, and the impossible is "always true." He remains impassive and indifferent in all his interactions with the Man and the Woman, until the end of the play, when the Man has failed to recognize the Woman's true identity. At this point, the Flagman is finally roused out of his apathy when, according to the stage directions, he speaks "harshly" to the Man. The Flagman's response indicates his understanding of the Man's failure in comprehension, but he

does not explain the situation in a way the Man can grasp. The Man consequently accuses the Flagman of being useless. At the close of the play, the Flagman speaks the same, monotonous refrain as at the opening, "The trains from the North travel toward the South."

The Man

The Man enters the play as part of the Train. He disembarks the Train and approaches the Flagman. From his first interaction in the play to his last, the Man remains confused and frustrated. He attempts to communicate with the Flagman about a woman he is looking for, someone he says he has "been waiting for for many years." The Flagman's refusal to answer questions in a direct manner pushes the Man from his originally polite though confused demeanor to irritation, particularly when the Flagman informs the Man that it is not his job to answer questions. Yet the Man continues to talk to the Flagman despite his apparent disinterest. When the Woman arrives and will not show him her face or tell him who she is, the Man assumes she is not the one he is looking for and he continues to wait. However, he listens to her speak of the fear of waiting for "something that never happens." After finally confessing to her that he has been at times at least a little afraid, the Man closes his eyes and listens to her talk about waiting for the ideal person he has dreamed of. When he opens his eyes to finds that she is old and touching him, he once again becomes confused. "For a moment," he says to the Woman, "I thought you were her," but he dismisses this notion as a "wild dream." When she shows him the white flower, the Man becomes excited, certain that the woman he expects to meet must have been at the crossroads, but that he has missed her. After the Woman says she does not think that person is coming and boards the train, the Man, now dejected and sad, speaks to the Flagman again. The Flagman only perplexes the Man further, and he hides his head in his hand as the Train crosses the stage for the last time. The Man is the only character in *Crossroads* who does not comprehend the circumstances or the implications of his failure to recognize the Woman's true identity. His self-delusion appears almost willful, because, for a moment, he seems prepared to believe the Woman is the one with whom he has corresponded. He refuses to accept that the Woman is the same person with whom he has formed an emotional bond; the Man's sorrow, frustration, and confusion therefore seem to be the inevitable outcomes of his own decisions.

The Train

The Train is formed by three men, dressed in gray clothing, who mechanically pantomime the movement of a train's wheels with their arms. The Man is the last person forming the Train when it first appears on stage, and the Woman joins it at the play's end.

The Woman

The Woman does not arrive on the Train, but has been waiting for some time at the crossroads for a man she has corresponded with. She enters the scene from behind the Man, and she is described as tall, slender, and wearing a veil and a white flower. When the Flagman shines his lantern at her, she removes the flower from her dress, and turns her back on the Man. He is ready to dismiss her when she turns toward him, yet the Woman engages the Man in conversation. She does not admit that she is the woman for whom he has been waiting, nor does she reject the notion. Rather, through her ambiguous statements and stories about fear, loneliness, and aging, she attempts to open the Man's mind to the possibility of accepting her for who she truly is. Able to temporarily intrigue and mesmerize the Man, the Woman, who has asked him to close his eyes, removes her veil. His response when he opens his eyes and sees her clarifies for the Woman that it is impossible for the two to develop a relationship. She therefore covers her face again and tells him good-bye. Joining the Train, the Woman moves in an unnatural manner that emphasizes her pain and sorrow. Like the Man, the Woman practices her own self-delusions, assuming that no man would be interested in her if they knew her age or saw her face. She has lured men to her under the false pretenses represented by the retouched photograph, never giving any of them a chance to truly get to know her. While she does finally show her face to the Man, the Woman delays this revelation, attempting to forestall the moment when she might be rejected. Yet by postponing this moment and not announcing her true identity the instant she sees the Man, the Woman creates a situation in which the Man's confusion intensifies, making him wary and bewildered. Having sent him the

same retouched photograph, she has created a situation in which the Man can only feel confused at best and duped at worst. Before they even meet, she assumes the worst of him—that he would only judge her by her appearance. Her interaction with him, dishonest from the start, was unlikely to produce better results than her earlier attempts to connect with the men she attracted to her, who she watched, while she waited "behind the windows." The Woman, like the Man, ensures that the outcome of the attempted meeting will be negative. Through her fear of rejection, the Woman guarantees her continued loneliness.

THEMES

Longing, Loneliness, and Idealized Love

The Man and the Woman in *Crossroads* represent the idea of longing. Both seem to be yearning to satisfy a physical and emotional desire for connection, and both appear to crave a long-term, loving relationship. Their connection was forged through a correspondence they established before the onset of the play. The reader learns that the Woman placed an advertisement in a magazine stating that she was seeking a young man with whom to "establish relations" so that she would not have to live alone. The Man responded to this advertisement, she replied to his response, and they exchanged photographs of one another. Although the Flagman insists the Woman has something to sell, that everyone, in fact, "sells something," the Man defends her, saying that she is simply shy. He will not accept the idea that the Woman placed the advertisement in order to sell herself in any way; he longs for the idea of perfection and clings to the notion that a beautiful but shy woman was reaching out to him. The words the Man uses in relation to the Woman are always extreme: he tells the Flagman that his meeting her is "the only certain thing" in his "whole existence." Desperate to discover if the woman who has appeared is the one he has been seeking, he becomes upset and tells the Woman that it is "absolutely necessary" that he see her face. His emotional need for the idea of her, the idea of someone looking for him, is intense. For her part, the Woman is as much consumed by her

TOPICS FOR FURTHER STUDY

- *Crossroads* was written as an avant-garde or experimental drama. Study the differences between realism and avant-gardism in drama and rewrite the play as a realist drama, revising the dialogue and naming the characters as necessary. Consider the following questions as you revise the play: How will the Man and the Woman's interaction take place? Will the Man still be unable to discern the Woman's true identity? If not, how will his discovery alter the play? What will be the overall tone of the play?

- Although Solórzano avoids direct references to Mexican history, politics, or current events in his plays, he has stated that his work in general is influenced by Mexican culture. Research the cultural history of Mexico during the late 1950s, when *Crossroads* was written. How might the characters or setting in the play be reflective of Mexican culture at the time? How does the general mood of the play relate to the pervading cultural attitudes in postwar Mexico? Write a report on your findings.

- Compare Solórzano's *Crossroads*, a one-act play, with one of his full-length dramas, such as *Las manos de Dios* (title means "The Hands of God"). How do the plays differ in terms of Solórzano's dramatic technique, tone, and style? Is the longer play written in the realist genre or as an avant-garde drama? Write a critical essay presenting your analysis.

- Critics have observed how Solórzano was influenced by the work of artists, writers, and thinkers in post-World War II Paris. Research the philosophies and works of such figures, including the Algerian-born French author Albert Camus and French playwright Antonin Artaud. Do you see evidence of the existentialism of Camus in *Crossroads*? How did World War II contribute to Artaud's and, subsequently, Solórzano's employment of avant-gardism? Give a class presentation in which you explore the influence of such authors on Solórzano, citing examples from *Crossroads*.

---

fear of rejection as she is by her need for the Man. She wonders whether he will be able to understand that an "unsatisfied longing" remains strong within her, that she now needs him more than when she was younger. She speaks of the faces, of the strong bodies, which she watched from her window, although she tells the Man the observer was her friend. Her remarks point to her physical desire, but before long, she comments on her fear of being alone. She dreads the "solitude of the heart that tries hard every night to prolong its cry against the silence." She is looking for a partner. Yet both the Woman and the Man are deluded by the idea of romantic perfection. She asks him whether he too has waited for "someone invented by you, to your measure," and he answers that yes, he thinks this is what

he has been waiting for. This delusion intensifies their longing as well as their disappointment, for such an idealized mate exists for no man or woman. Soon, when the Man opens his eyes, his disappointment is made manifest, as is the Woman's, when she realizes the Man could never love someone who is older and less attractive than the woman in the photograph, and he sees that she is certainly not the dark-haired beauty he expected. Their mutual expectations—a longing for idealized love and the satisfaction of desire—yield disappointment, despair, and the realization of their shared fear of loneliness.

Time and Aging

The prospect of experiencing extreme solitude in old age intensifies the fear of loneliness explored

Hands touching *(© Franco Vogt | Corbis)*

in *Crossroads*. It is unclear whether the Woman is more afraid of aging or loneliness, for in her mind the two are linked. She fears the "solitude of . . . a body alone, that inevitably ages," as much as she fears the "solitude of the heart." The Woman implores the Man to fight this enemy, time. Yet when he sees her unveiled, he cannot accept time's effects on the Woman, whom he begins to believe is *the* woman. It is easier for the Man to believe that the Woman is not the one he has sought. For a moment, she cannot comprehend that he has given up on her so easily. She entreats him to recall what he has just said about being able to recognize, with his "eyes open," the voice of his ideal woman. The Man, though, claims to feel confused and stupid, stating that it was "ridiculous" of him to think that she was the Woman. Although the Man dismisses the possibility of her being *the* woman, the Woman makes a final effort to reveal her true identity to him by showing him the white flower, the one by which he was to recognize her. She lies, however, telling the Man that she has simply picked it up. She cannot do what she begged the Man to do, to fight time. By not revealing herself to the Man, the Woman lets time win; she agrees to let her aging appearance dictate the unfolding of events at the crossroads.

STYLE

Avant-Gardism

The style Solórzano employs in *Crossroads* has been described as avant-garde, experimental, and absurdist. Rather than depicting in a realistic manner characters who participate in a series of events, Solórzano's characters are unnamed and can be understood as representations of universal human responses to love, desire, and fear. Noting in the stage directions that the characters will move "mechanically, like characters in the silent movies," Solórzano emphasizes the disconnection between reality and his drama by forcing the actors to move about the stage in an unnatural manner. All elements of the play are representational rather than realistic; the train, for example, is depicted as the idea of a train, captured by three actors, dressed in gray, pantomiming the rhythmic motion of a train's wheels. In reality, a flagman typically serves at a railway crossing as a source of information, an indicator of the trains' direction and destination. Solórzano's Flagman appears to be useless as a source of information, a fact the Man points out on more than one occasion. The Flagman seems forgetful and makes statements that confuse the Man and the audience, as when he announces that the trains "come and go, but they end up meeting one another" and that the "impossible's always true." Despite the apparent disconnect between a symbol (the Flagman) and what this symbol *should* represent (information, knowledge), the Flagman in the end is aware of the reality of the relationship between the Man and the Woman. He understands that the Man has failed to recognize the Woman as the person he came to the crossroads to meet, and he scolds the Man for this failure to comprehend the situation. Through such experimental techniques, Solórzano urges his audience to look beyond the surface of the simple story of a thwarted romantic opportunity and see the way fear and delusion shape the lives of the characters and lead them to despair rather than love.

Vaudeville

Another example of the avant-garde nature of the play is Solórzano's experimentation with form. He subtitles the play "A Sad Vaudeville." Traditional vaudevilles are short and fast-paced plays featuring comic elements such as verbal and physical humor and parody, or imitation for the purpose of ridicule. Given that the essential element in a vaudeville is comedy, Solórzano's describing his work as a sad vaudeville indicates that the work contains some elements of inversion and irony. Characters in traditional vaudevilles, for example, are often caricatures, or stock figures who behave in predictably humorous ways. Solórzano's characters, however, rather than being comic caricatures, serve more as archetypes, or representative figures, for the lonely, desperate men and women seeking meaningful relationships. The incorporation of pantomime in the play is another example of Solórzano's inversion of vaudevillian elements. In *Crossroads*, characters pantomime the repetitive, mechanical movements of a train, whereas in a traditional vaudeville, pantomime is employed for comic effect.

HISTORICAL CONTEXT

Postwar Mexico

In the decades immediately following World War II (1939–1945), Mexico attempted to restabilize an economy damaged by poor resource management prior to and during the war. Mexico joined the United Nations in 1945, and the following year Miguel Alemán Valdés was elected president. Valdés promised to further industrialize Mexico, create more extensive irrigation systems to aid agricultural development, and address the problem of an inequitable distribution of wealth. With loans from the U.S. Department of Treasury and the International Monetary Fund, the Mexican government was able to restabilize the value of the peso, the basis of Mexico's currency. Governmental elections established the prominence of President Valdés's party, the Institutional Revolutionary Party (Partido Revolucionario Institucional, also known as PRI). In 1952, Adolfo Ruíz Cortines, also a member of PRI, was elected president of Mexico. An amendment passed by the legislature during Cortines's tenure gave Mexican women the right to vote. In 1958, the year before Solórzano's *Crossroads* was published, Adolfo López Mateos was elected president of Mexico. The women enfranchised under Cortines's presidency had voted in their first presidential election. Mateos, like his predecessor, was a member of PRI, but he differed from previous presidents in his insistence that the Roman Catholic Church should not interfere in Mexico's attainment of its political, revolutionary goals. During his later tenure, Mateos pursued measures designed to aid the working class, although many poorer workers and landless peasants grew increasingly discontent with their economic circumstances. Despite the often turbulent nature of Mexican society and politics during this time period, Solórzano, unlike some of his contemporaries, chose not to address specific political or social issues pertaining to Mexico in his work. Rather, his dramas employ a broader, more universal approach.

Theater of the Absurd

The horrors of World War II changed the world of theater, a transformation that began in Paris, France. In Paris, the playwright Antonin Artaud (1896–1948) sought to restructure traditional dramatic forms in order to reflect the collapse of values and sense that he perceived had occurred in the aftermath of the war. Realism was incapable of reflecting the new, postwar world accurately. In Francesca Colecchia's introduction to *Crossroads and Other Plays by*

COMPARE & CONTRAST

- **1950s:** In post-World War II Mexico, theater undergoes a transformation. The traditional realism of Mexican theater, exemplified by dramatists such as Luisa Josefina Hernández, remains strong, but a new, experimental, expressionist type of drama is being explored by playwrights such as Emilio Carballido and Carlos Solórzano.

  Today: A theatrical revival in the 1980s, in the form of a project organized by Carlos Solórzano called the Teatro de la Nación, or National Theater, has revitalized Mexican theater to the point that it still thrives today in many forms. Modern Mexican theater includes a number of genres, including experimental, lyrical, classical, and traditional Mexican drama.

- **1950s:** Most Mexican dramas are staged in the theaters of Mexico City, which is the heart of Mexico's artistic community.

  Today: Mexico City remains the center of Mexican theater production, although the provinces of Mexico are also beginning to generate their own strong dramatic programs.

- **1950s:** In Mexico, only one major political party can be identified as significant in terms of its control of the government (the presidency, the lower house of Congress, and the Chamber of Deputies). The Institutional Revolutionary Party (or Partido Revolucionario Institucional, also known as PRI) is comprised entirely of civilians and represents the peasantry, the working class, as well as professionals and businesspeople. The party retains control of the government from 1929 through 1997.

  Today: Several political parties hold power in the Mexican government, rather than one party in complete control. In addition to PRI, the parties include the Party of the Democratic Revolution, the National Action Party, and the Green Ecological Party.

- **1950s:** Passenger train travel between Mexican cities, such as the train travel that provides the backdrop to Solórzano's *Crossroads*, is made possible by Ferrocarriles Nacionales de México, the state-owned railroad company of Mexico, operational since 1938.

  Today: Extensive passenger train travel is no longer available in Mexico, since the Mexican government discontinued subsidies to intercity passenger trains in 2000.

Carlos Solórzano, she quotes an interview by Teresa Méndez-Faith with Solórzano in July 1982. In the interview, Solórzano states that Artaud shared with Latin Americans "a certain distrust in reality, a certain kind of anxiety in the presence of certain dark forces of nature." Artaud's vision of the transformation of theater manifested itself in the development by later dramatists of the "Theater of the Absurd." This type of drama was characterized by absence, most notably an absence of sense and logic, as well as an absence of a direct correlation between language and meaning. Absurdist theater was also described as avant-garde and experimental. Such developments in drama interested Solórzano when he studied in Paris in the early 1950s. The influence of Artaud's thinking on French philosophy, literature, and drama became apparent in Solórzano's writing following his return to Mexico in 1952. While some of his works employ a harsh realism, others are clearly experimental, exhibiting the disconnection between word and meaning and employing the use of symbols and allegory (the expression of generalizations or truths about human life through fictional characters). Critics such as Colecchia and Frank Dauster have characterized Solórzano's work as both avant-garde and absurdist in nature.

Commuter train *(© Sepp Spiegl / vario images GmbH & Co.KG / Alamy)*

CRITICAL OVERVIEW

The one-act play *Crossroads* is considered in some ways representative of Solórzano's body of work but by no means counted among his most notable dramatic efforts. The full-length play *Las manos de Dios* is generally regarded as the most powerful and well-crafted of Solórzano's literary works. Despite the praise *Las manos de Dios* has garnered, criticism of Solórzano's work is still not widely available in English; the majority of scholarly analyses of his plays and fiction is in Spanish. Many of Solórzano's writings were not even translated into English until the 1990s. Francesca Colecchia offered the first English translation of *Crossroads* in 1993, and her introduction to Solórzano's plays provides a comprehensive overview of the dramatist's themes and style. In this introduction to *Crossroads and Other Plays by Carlos Solórzano*, Colecchia observes that as a playwright, Solórzano creates "characters representative of concepts." Certainly this general statement applies to the characterization of the Man and the Woman in *Crossroads*. Colecchia also observes

that the primary conflict in *Crossroads* is "between reality and expectations." Whereas Colecchia describes the play as "bittersweet" in tone, critic Frank Dauster, in his 1964 essay "The Drama of Carlos Solórzano" (appearing in *Modern Drama*), finds that the play "takes on an atmosphere of sheer absurdity, of hopeless loss." Solórzano accomplishes this, Dauster maintains, through the mechanical, stylized movement of the characters, and through his "deliberate destruction of all illusion" in the play. Like Dauster, Wilma Feliciano, in a 2005 *Dictionary of Literary Biography* essay on Solórzano, studies the elements of the absurd in *Crossroads*, stating that there is a disruption between words and their meanings in the play. Feliciano further underscores that the creation of a gap between words and communicated information is a technique that is characteristic of absurdist drama. Through his usage of experimental methods, absurdist techniques, and symbolic characterization in *Crossroads*, Solórzano explores a dramaturgy absent of dramatic realism. Colecchia and Dauster agree that Solórzano rejects the conventionalism of Mexican theater that existed in the country in the aftermath of World War II, which focused on specific, regional political concerns. Rather, Solórzano is more interested in approaching broad, universal concepts; his writings, Dauster stresses, "are infused with a sense of humanity and human dignity."

CRITICISM

Catherine Dominic

Dominic is a novelist and a freelance writer and editor. In this essay, she examines the absurdist elements in Crossroads, *suggesting that such an approach to the play exposes Solórzano's nihilistic view of human relationships.*

Critics state that Solórzano's works tend to focus on universal themes like love, desire, loss, ritual, and death. In *Crossroads*, the playwright examines the concepts of loneliness, aging, disillusionment, and desire through the nameless characters of the Man and the Woman. Given the universal approach Solórzano employs, and the fact that the Man and the Woman are unnamed, the characters may be viewed as representations of humanity in general, of every man and every woman who yearns for another person both physically and emotionally. The characters seem to symbolize, or stand for, the idea that men and women need each other desperately but delude themselves in a way that ensures their separation. The play may be read as one about the failure of men and woman to communicate honestly and effectively and to create and sustain loving, satisfying relationships. Such a reading may be viewed as a cautionary tale through which the audience apprehends that fear, expectation, and deception lead to loneliness, despair, and grief.

Yet symbols in absurdist theater often do not correspond to the expected meaning. Words are a type of symbol, meant to convey a particular meaning, but as critics such as Frank Dauster and Wilma Feliciano point out, a gap between language and meaning exists in *Crossroads*. The Man gets the sense, for example, that he and the Flagman are not even "speaking the same language," for the communication seems garbled, confused. An alternate approach to the play explores the characters as absurdist symbols, that is, as inversions of their expected, universal representations. However bleak the first type of reading may be, the latter approach to

> IF THE MAN AND THE WOMAN REPRESENT EVERY MAN AND EVERY WOMAN, THEN IN THIS ABSURDIST, NIHILISTIC APPROACH TO THE PLAY, WE ARE ALL *NO ONE.*"

the play, one that fully explores the absurdist disassociation between symbols and meaning, yields a nihilist understanding of Solórzano's drama. (Nihilism is a philosophical system of thought that focuses on the possibility that nothing in the world truly exists or possesses meaning. This philosophy is generally regarded as a rejection of religious and moral principles.) The characters of the Man and the Woman, while typically interpreted as universal, allegorical representations of humanity, may alternately be viewed in terms of absence. Not only do they lack names, but they, along with the Flagman, are devoid of a sense of personal identity. They are unable to be perceived by the other characters for who they actually are, arguably failing to even accept their own selfhood. If the Man and the Woman represent every man and every woman, then in this absurdist, nihilistic approach to the play, we are all *no one*.

From the outset of the play, the Flagman's words emphasize the slippery notion of identity, the absence of correspondence between symbol and meaning. When the Man, interested in the train schedule, questions the Flagman, the Flagman responds that trains do not stop at this particular crossroads, ever. Clearly confused by the Flagman's words, the Man asks if he is indeed the flagman at this crossing. The Flagman states that he is called by a variety of names, and when the Man asks if he has seen a particular woman, he states that all the women look alike. Interestingly, the Flagman does not say that all the women look alike *to him*, only that they all look alike. He states his perception as fact, and through such habits creates a world in which the Man will question his own perceptions as well as the Flagman's. One's very ability to accurately perceive what appears to be the real world becomes destabilized at the crossroads.

WHAT DO I READ NEXT?

- *Las manos de Dios* (title means "The Hands of God") is Solórzano's most well-known and highly regarded play. A full-length drama, it was originally published in Spanish in 1956 and is available in translation in *Crossroads and Other Plays by Carlos Solórzano* (1993), translated and edited by Francesca Colecchia.

- The work of Antonin Artaud influenced the development of Solórzano's vision for his drama. *Antonin Artaud: Selected Writings* offers a selection of Artaud's writings. This collection was translated from French by Helen Weaver, includes an introduction by Susan Sontag, and was published in 1976 by Farrar, Straus and Giroux.

- *The Theatre of the Absurd*, by Martin Esslin, was originally published by Doubleday in 1961 and first employed the term "theater of the absurd" to describe this particular experimental genre of theater. Esslin's work was reissued in 2004 by Vintage Books.

- *Mexican Plays* (2008), edited by Elyse Dodgson, offers a collection of modern Mexican dramas. By comparing these modern plays with Solórzano's work, one can study the developments in Mexican theater.

Flustered, the Man insists that a flagman *ought* to be able to answer questions, even though the Flagman asserts that this is in fact not his job. The conversation between the Flagman and the Man continues to be filled with contradictions and paradoxes. When the next train arrives and he does not see the Woman disembark from it, the Man, who is described in the stage directions as "disillusioned," states that the woman was not on the train. The Flagman tells the Man, "He's never coming." When the Man asks him whom he is talking about, he says, "The man we're waiting for." Confused, the Man informs the Flagman that he is waiting for a woman, not a man, but the Flagman insists that "it's all the same." The idea of a woman, or a man, in the world of the play is "all the same." In this sense, the Man does not represent a man, and the Woman does not represent a woman. Their identities are reduced to nothingness.

Such disjunctions between symbols and meaning intensify when the Woman enters the play. Having already deceived the Man into meeting her by sending him a photo that no longer represents what she looks like, the Woman is determined to keep her identity a secret, at least until she can ascertain the Man's feelings. Although she has misrepresented herself, the Woman tells the Man, as he questions her about her identity, that she is now the woman she has "always wanted to be." Despite the Man's insistence, the Woman refuses to show her face. Feeling "tortured" by her refusal and his own confusion, the Man begins to bemoan the absurdity of the situation. If the Woman is the one he agreed to meet at the crossroads, she would come straight to him, he believes. Aware of the Flagman's suspicions regarding her identity, the Woman asks the Flagman why he did not tell the Man that she was at the crossroads all along, wearing the white flower. The Flagman, though, does not seem to know whom the Woman is talking about, saying he has forgotten the Man all together. All of these factors—the Flagman's inability or refusal to retain the knowledge of the Man's identity; the Man's acknowledgment of the absurdity of his circumstances, not knowing the Woman's true identity; and the Woman's claim that she is who she has always wanted to be, while still hiding herself—point to the elusiveness of identity in the world of *Crossroads*.

As the conversation between the Woman and the Man continues, they speak of their mutual desire to find an ideal person with whom they can share their lives. The Woman speaks of "waiting for that voice, the one of someone invented by you, to your measure," and the Man agrees. He too has been waiting for a person such as this. Yet both the Man and the Woman do not fulfill the requirements of what the other is looking for: neither can exist in the desired capacity for the other person. The Man fails the Woman in that he forms a judgment of her based on her appearance, even after he has the opportunity to converse with her and to realize that she is the woman with whom he has fallen in love through their previous correspondence. The Woman fails the

Man in her initial deception and in her refusal to be forthright with him after their meeting. Such shortcomings on the Woman's part suggest her inability to accept her own identity. In not realizing who he is to the Woman, the Man's self-knowledge is called into question. The Woman addresses their mutual lack of self-awareness when she tells the Man that "there's but a moment to recognize one's self."

After the Woman departs on the train, the Flagman reappears in the scene. As the Man questions him again about the woman wearing the white flower, the Flagman tells him he has seen "the one you aren't looking for, and the one you're looking for I didn't see." His convoluted response suggests that he has seen the Woman, but not the idealized woman the Man is seeking, because the latter does not exist. In the end, the Flagman's statement that "it's all the same" is accurate. The Man and the Woman both fail to be what the other expected. They have failed to exist for one another and for themselves as unique individuals. Both, presumably, as the Woman says, will keep waiting for ideas that cannot become reality, she behind her windows, he at the crossroads. In their waiting, their refusal to associate themselves with the progress of life, they cement their nonbeing and become symbols of nothingness. By depicting the Man and the Woman in such an absurdist manner, by divorcing them as symbols from their universal representations of men and women, Solórzano presents a desolate, nihilist view of human identity and relations.

Source: Catherine Dominic, Critical Essay on *Crossroads*, in *Drama for Students*, Gale, Cengage Learning, 2009.

Francesca Colecchia

In the following introduction to Crossroads and Other Plays, *Colecchia discusses Solórzano's existential influences and the conflict between expectation and reality in his play* Crossroads.

No history of the modern theater in Latin America, and more specifically Mexico, can be considered complete without the name of Carlos Solórzano. Born in 1922 in San Marcos, Guatemala, the son of a wealthy engineer and landowner and the great grandson of Justo Rufino Barrios—a former president of that Central American country, he enjoyed all the comforts and privileges such circumstances entail. He received his earliest education from German

> *CRUCE DE VÍAS* OFFERS A BITTERSWEET LOOK AT THE CONFLICT BETWEEN REALITY AND EXPECTATIONS AS THE MAN FAILS TO RECOGNIZE THE WOMAN AS THE PERSON WITH WHOM HE HAS FALLEN IN LOVE VIA THE MAIL. SHE, TOO TIMID AND TOO COWED BY PRIOR REJECTIONS, FAILS TO IDENTIFY HERSELF TO HIM."

tutors. At ten he was sent to a Marist school where the strict discipline and the insistence on a traditional religious formation contrasted with the more liberal attitude reflected at home by his father.

Born just after the dictatorship of Estrada Cabrera (1898–1920), Solórzano grew up during the first years of Jorge Ubico's (1931–44)—periods during which most Guatemalans knew only fear, uncertainty, and tyranny. Until he went to Europe at the age of sixteen, Solórzano knew almost exclusively the secure comfort of his home and the highly structured education offered by the Marists. The favored circumstances that characterized the first years of his life offered a marked contrast to the oppression experienced by his less fortunate compatriots.

In spite of his Gautemalan origin, Solórzano is most closely identified with Mexico and the theater of that country where he went to study and has lived since 1939. He holds a degree in architecture from the Universidad Nacional Autónoma from which he later obtained a master's as well as a doctorate in literature. In 1948 he went to Paris where he studied drama on a grant from the Rockefeller Foundation.

The years spent in France studying at the Sorbonne introduced Solórzano to the vital and innovative theater activity in Paris in those days. At the same time, it acquainted him with the major developments and themes in the history of theater, past as well as present. His sojourn in Europe brought him into contact with leading dramatists and men of letters, among them, Albert Camus, Emmanuel Roblés, and the Belgian playwright Michel de Ghelderode.

On his return from Paris, he was appointed director of the Teatro Universitario, a position that he held for ten years. He also served as director of the Museo Nacional de Teatro, a project that came to an end with the death of the Mexican dramaturg Celestino Gorostiza. At present he is "Professor de Carrera" at the Autónoma where he founded the program Carrera de Arte Dramático, and currently teaches two courses: Crítica Dramática and Teatro Ibero-americano. In 1985 he was named Professor Emeritus, and on 25 September 1989 he received the Premio Universidad in the area of "Aportación Artística y Difusión de la Cultura." Earlier the same year he received the Premio Nacional de Literatura "Miguel Angel Asturias" in Guatemala, an honor which, in his words, "...me llenó de satisfacción." Solórzano has traveled widely, representing Mexico at international theater festivals. He has also taught as a visiting professor in several American universities, among them Southern California, Kansas, and Columbia.

Solórzano has contributed to journals and newspapers in Latin America, Europe, Puerto Rico, and the United States. At different times he was correspondent for *Rendez-vous du Théâtre* as well as for *Primer Acto,* and drama critic for *Siempre.* At present he serves as editor for Latin America for an ambitious undertaking known as *Enciclopedia Mundial del Teatro Contemporáneo.* In addition to his dramas, his publications include two novels—*Los falsos demonios* (1966) and *Las celdas* (1971)—two works about Latin American theater—*Teatro latinoamericano del siglo XX* (1961) and *El teatro latinoamericano en el siglo XX* (1964), and three drama anthologies—*El Teatro hispanoamericano contemporáneo* (1964), *Teatro guatemalteco contemporáneo* (1964), and *Teatro breve hispanoamericano* (1971).

Despite his ventures into the novel and criticism, Solórzano's major contribution to Spanish-American letters lies in his drama. Though not as extensive as that of many of his contemporaries, his theater nonetheless offers the reader a provocative and imaginative presentation of those questions which most preoccupy modern man from a universal rather than national or regional focus. His theater comprises: *Doña Beatriz* (1952), *El hechicero* (*The Wizard,* 1954), and *Las manos de Dios* (*The Hands of God,* 1956)—all full-length plays, in addition to the following one-act pieces: *Los fantoches* (*The Puppets,* 1959), *Cruce de vias* (*Crossroads,* 1959), *El crucificado* (*The Crucified,* 1959), *La muerte hizo la luz* (*And Death Brought Forth the Light,* 1951), *El sueño del ángel* (*The Angel's Forty Winks,* 1960), *Mea culpa* (1967), and *El zapato* (*The Shoe,* 1966).

As a reading of critical studies of Carlos Solórzano's plays suggests, his dramas may be considered from different perspectives. In his *Carlos Solórzano y el teatro hispanoamericano* Esteban Rivas groups the Mexican author's plays on the basis of their thematic emphasis. For example, he places *Los fantoches* together with *El crucificado* because both have a common point of departure: the Mexican folk customs during Holy Week; while he pairs *Mea culpa* with *El sueño del ángel* because both deal with the concept of sin and the feeling of guilt that it engenders. A more recent study by Ostergaard utilizes a semiological approach to analyze *Las manos de Dios, El sueño del ángel,* and *El crucificado.* On the other hand Rosenberg sees ritual and the inversion of accepted values at the core of *Las manos de Dios* and to a lesser degree in the two one-act plays mentioned above.

If opinions about the Mexican playwright's theater vary, so also do the plots of the individual works. *Doña Beatriz,* his first play, narrates the tragic story of Beatriz de la Cueva who, upon the death of her sister, married Pedro de Alvarado, the brother-in-law she had coveted, and accompanied him to the New World. Unfortunately she did not share her husband's enthusiasm for the young continent or his insatiable desire to conquer new lands. The failed relationship with her husband, the marriage of her brother Rodrigo to Leonor, Pedro's mestizo daughter, her religious fanaticism, and her loathing of the natives drove her to refuse all offers of help, and she died in the flood that inundated the city.

El hechicero is a reworking of the legend of the philosopher's stone in which Merlin attempts to save his people from starvation by promising them the formula for the stone, a formula he has yet to perfect. However his estranged wife, Casilda, with the aid of Lisandro, her brother-in-law and lover, kills her husband only to discover that neither she nor Lisandro can decipher the formula. A series of ironic twists brings this play to a close. Merlin's ashes are scattered over the barren fields, fertilizing them so that they bring forth the crops needed to save the people, Beatriz, his daughter, convinces Casilda Lisandro has lied to her and really has the precious formula, leading Casilda to kill him.

The trend toward the abstract, toward characters representative of concepts, noted in the first full-length dramas by the Mexican dramatist, appears more strongly in the most powerful of his full-length plays, *Las manos de Dios,* a work in which the author tries to adapt the traditional auto sacramental to modern drama techniques. This play, set in an unidentified small town in Latin America dominated by the Amo and the Señor Cura, tells the story of Beatriz, a young woman who seeks the freedom of her younger brother who was imprisoned because he publicly demanded the return of his land unjustly seized by the Amo. No one in the town offers Beatriz a solution to her plight until the Forastero (Stranger), actually the Devil, convinces her to bribe the Carcelero (Jailer) to set her brother free by offering him jewels that she steals from the statue of the Eternal Father located in the church. The theft is discovered and Beatriz is bound to a tree, lashed by the townspeople, and left to die alone save for the Devil.

Solórzano's short plays challenge the public equally. Themes and concerns articulated in the longer works are reiterated in these pieces. As Frank Dauster has noted, all of them share the same rebellious spirit of *Las manos de Dios.* Through the use of puppets customarily burned by the Mexicans on Holy Saturday, *Los fantoches* explores the reason for man's existence and his relationship with his maker, while *El crucificado* examines the question of reality as the peasant Jesus, chosen to play the role of Christ in the Holy Week pageant, assumes the identity of Christ and is indeed crucified. Both *El sueño del ángel* and *Mea culpa* look at the issue of guilt and responsibility, but from different points of view. In the former, the problem is individual as the Woman struggles with her Guardian Angel, considered by some as the personification of her conscience, who forces from her the admission and expiation of her sin. In the latter, the issue, which initially seems an individual concern, takes on another dimension as the author accuses the institutional church, in the character of the old bishop. Utilizing the play-within-a-play technique in *La muerte hizo la luz,* the author looks at the amoral and self-centered manipulation so common to politics. *Cruce de vías* offers a bittersweet look at the conflict between reality and expectations as the Man fails to recognize the Woman as the person

with whom he has fallen in love via the mail. She, too timid and too cowed by prior rejections, fails to identify herself to him. *El zapato,* the only play by Solórzano that has an adolescent as its protagonist, deals with the difficult struggle of young people to realize their independence. As Rivas points out, the shoe, with which the youth debates, is "symbol of the father . . . and paradoxically, spokesman of the inner I of the youth."

All artists, irrespective of their genre, have been affected in greater or lesser degree by other artists. Solórzano is no exception to this rule. One cannot point out the specific influence of every single author, playwright or otherwise, to have ever come within his ken. Nonetheless, four seem to be especially reflected in Solórzano's work: Unamuno, Camus, Artaud, and Ghelderode.

The Mexican playwright's admiration of Unamuno found early expression in his master's thesis, *Del sentimiento de lo plástico en la obra de Unamuno* (1944) and his doctoral dissertation, *Espejo de novelas* (1945), both of which plumb the Basque philosopher's thought and personal motives. A careful reading of both treatises reveals Solórzano's total comprehension and assimilation of the Spanish philosopher's thinking. What he gives his public is genuinely original work imbued with the spirit of his intellectual mentor. Unamuno's influence upon Solórzano's work is neither momentary nor capricious, but pervasive and persistent. Perhaps the word *agitar,* to agitate,—a key word in the works of both men—best illustrates the intimacy of the philosophical and aesthetical bond between the two. In "Mi religión", an essay from his *Mi religión y otros ensayos breves,* Unamuno states, "I do not know whether anything of what I have done or what I may do in the future is to remain for years, for centuries after I die; but I do know that if one tosses a stone into a shoreless sea, the waves will form around it without ceasing, though becoming weaker. To agitate is something. If, thanks to that agitation, another comes after me who does something lasting, in it will endure my work." As Rivas has observed, "To agitate for Solórzano implies to move, to make the spectator think," thus underscoring the unwillingness of either Unamuno or Solórzano to accept anything without question simply because it exists.

Other echoes of Unamuno appear in Solórzano's theater. A preoccupation with death, its rationale, its apparent finality, and its absurdity is common to most of his dramas, while the notion of every man a Christ is most evident in *The Crucified.* His characters wrestle with the problem of existence and the issue of man's sense of inborn guilt concluding repeatedly as in *The Angel's Forty Winks,* "I'll pay for all my sins, expecially that of having been born." They cry out as Beatriz does in *The Hands of God,* "to understand, to know why we've been made this way . . . and why the only answer to our misfortune is death." Unamuno's concern with immortality, as well as his concept of life and death as a struggle and that struggle as man's tragedy also figure significantly in the Mexican playwright's theater.

If the influence of Unamuno that pervades Solórzano's theater is more philosophical and ideological, that of his fellow dramatists, Camus, Artaud, and Ghelderode, is more specific. The Mexican dramatist frankly acknowledges the impact of these writers on his work. In an interview with Teresa Méndez-Faith in July of 1982 he made the following observations.

Camus
While ascribing much of the philosophical concern and skepticism in his opus to Camus and the years spent in the post–World War II intellectual/artistic ferment of Paris, he attributed his first play, *Doña Beatriz,* directly to the influence of the French writer. "I was fascinated by an historical work by Camus, *Caligula,* taken from Suetonius, where to strict truth he [Camus] gave an existential content. Then I took an event from the history of Guatemala: the death of doña Beatriz de la Cueva."

Artaud
Of Artaud, whom he had never met personally, he said, "When I theoretically encountered Artaud . . . I found that he expressed a series of attitudes which we Latin Americans share, a series of appreciations as, for example, a certain distrust in reality, a certain kind of anxiety in the presence of certain dark forces of nature. That was something all of us Latin Americans have and that Artaud wanted to systematize in the theater." Rivas has suggested more specific evidence of Artaud in Solórzano's theater including the religious and ritualistic nature of the dramatic presentation and the poetic dimension of theater.

Ghelderode
Solórzano's observations about Ghelderode suggest a close affinity with the Belgian dramatist whom he knew personally. Of him he said,

"Camus as well as Ghelderode—above all the latter with his hallucinatory world, the use of popular motifs and at times even folkloric ones—leave a very strong impression on me." In an article about the Belgian dramatist that appeared in *Siempre* Solórzano wrote, "In his theater converge motifs from diverse sources: from vernacular fables and medieval farces to the lucid spirit of psychoanalytic introspection, which shows us, without extenuating circumstances, the contradictions of the human soul." Given the many similarities between the two, Solórzano might have been writing about his own theater. A strong anticlerical position characterizes the works of both men who see an almost exclusive concern for the material on the part of the clergy that obviates their responsibility to the faithful. Both share other themes in common, among them: an almost obsessive concern with death, an existential view of man, and a profound preoccupation with good and evil and the accompanying problem of guilt.

In more than half of Solórzano's plays the anticlerical motif appears as an essential consideration in the evolution of the plot as well as the theme. Its specific articulation varies in the individual works. It extends from the author's criticism of the intrusion of the Church in civic affairs and in the relations between husband and wife that we find in *Doña Beatriz* to the more wide-ranging charge of insensitivity to, and lack of concern for the fundamental needs of its communicants in *The Hands of God,* to the more radical suggestion in *Mea culpa* that the Church has sinned against man and should ask his forgiveness. This anticlerical bias is not directed against the essence of moral teaching. Rather it opposes the religious establishment and more specifically the selective interpretation of religious teaching that it has at times extended to its communicants. Born of close observation and considered reflection, the Mexican playwright's anticlericalism often appears hand in hand with his concern with man's freedom to exercise his own will.

During an interview with Esteban Rivas in 1966, he stated that, "to sin is to choose . . . and to be master of one's own conscience: choosing is man's greatest good." In his discussion of *The Hands of God,* Dauster noted that, "for Solórzano good and bad have very specific meanings: freedom and oppression." Considered together, these two statements synthesize Carlos Solórzano's firm belief, in a manner reminiscent of Camus, in the right and responsibility of every man to the determination of self. Whatever impedes or prohibits this is immoral.

The Mexican playwright brings a cosmopolitan perspective to his theater, reflecting the diverse influences in his own intellectual, spiritual, and aesthetic formation. The dramatist's intimate knowledge of both classical and modern theater not only as literature but as a performing art, and his experience as director of the Teatro Universitario increased his awareness of the technical and plastic aspects of mounting a play. This experience accounts for the singular and varied facets of his theater. These qualities, coupled with his perception of and preoccupation with those basic questions which trouble man in a society that often seems hostile and impersonal, explain the challenging uniqueness of his theater.

In Mexico, as in most Latin American countries, the post–World War II period saw a flurry of dramatic activity. Many of the new works that appeared were a reaction to the violence and horror of that conflagration. Parallel with the growth in theater is the emergence of an interested and dedicated audience that looked to the theater for a discussion of those problems which it shared in common with all men. The majority of new works dealt with some variation of what Solórzano calls, "a major concern: the incompatibility between original human nature and man's historical experience."

Two major trends emerge in postwar Mexican theater: one, a conventional nationally oriented drama often with a regional emphasis; and the other, an avant-garde drama with a more universal focus. It is to the latter that Solórzano belongs. Openly identifying himself with this movement in Mexican theater, he has said of it, "it aspired from the beginning to treat universal themes without losing touch with our motifs, our people, or our language." Thus, rather than ignore the specifically Mexican, Solórzano uses it as a point of departure in most of his plays. Finding his inspiration in Mexican customs, history, and problems, he looks beyond their ethnic circumstance, transforming them to the more basic questions confronting all.

Source: Francesca Colecchia, "Introduction," in *Crossroads and Other Plays*, edited by Francesca Colecchia, translated by Francesca Colecchia, Farleigh Dickinson University Press, 1993.

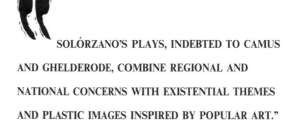

SOLÓRZANO'S PLAYS, INDEBTED TO CAMUS AND GHELDERODE, COMBINE REGIONAL AND NATIONAL CONCERNS WITH EXISTENTIAL THEMES AND PLASTIC IMAGES INSPIRED BY POPULAR ART."

Tamara Holzapfel

In the following essay, Holzapfel examines Solórzano's absurd plays, which "combine regional and national concerns with existential themes" and include Crossroads.

The complexity of contemporary theatre and the lack of a unified methodological approach to its study make it difficult to give a systematic account of any one trend in Spanish American theatre. Thus it is with the "absurd," a term that from the beginning was applied loosely and to a wide spectrum of plays. Now that it has long been assimilated into the general esthetic of the theatre and has been recognized as defining not a notion of "pure" absurdity, but simply a diverse and unprogrammatic movement, we can attempt to provide an overview of its manifestations in Spanish America, from an early stage in plays concerned with existential themes to the direction it is taking today. The absurd movement together with Brecht's theories of the theatre are perhaps the most salient innovative tendencies that have contributed to the revitalization of the stage and to the creation of a flourishing theatre throughout Spanish America.

There are many dramatic authors today in Spanish America, many of them quite famous, who have seen their works performed abroad in Spanish and in translation. It is true, however, that Spanish American drama has not yet achieved the degree of originality attained by the novel. But like the novel, the theatre has grown in professionalism and sophistication and many of the old problems of distinction are beginning to vanish. For instance, it is increasingly meaningless to distinguish between socially committed and avant-garde dramatists. Beforc, that is before 1950, the two groups denoted differences in mentality. But in the 1950's, the decade that witnessed the emergence of absurd drama and the rediscovery of Brecht's political theatre, a new dramaturgy came into being in Spanish America. Such important authors as René Marqués, Carlos Solórzano, Osvaldo Dragún, and Emilio Carballido were fusing sociopolitical concerns with universal themes and experimental forms. Marqués, using existentially anguished characters, deplores the colonial condition of Puerto Rico in poetic dramas that draw on a variety of formal techniques taken principally from North American Naturalism. Solórzano's plays, indebted to Camus and Ghelderode, combine regional and national concerns with existential themes and plastic images inspired by popular art. Distancing effects, the kind we associate with Brecht's theatre, and a clownesque style characterize Dragún's *Historias para ser contadas,* a series of one-acts that criticize the inhumanity of modern society in true stories from contemporary Buenos Aires. Contemporary Mexico is the scenario in the majority of Carballido's fantastic plays imbued with existential ideas and inspired by the theatre of Cocteau and Giraudoux or the medieval mortality play. The importance of existentialism in these authors cannot be underestimated. Existential ideas were fundamental in the creation of a theatre that could be called modern, contemporary and universal. Moreover, the sporadic instances of existential absurdity in these and other Spanish American dramatists helped to prepare the way for the acceptance of absurd theatre by Spanish American audiences.

Absurd theatre, as it is well known, adopted existential philosophy but developed a new expression of the theatre that became the dominant mode in Europe and the Americas in the sixties. The label "Theatre of the Absurd" came into universal usage upon the appearance, in 1961, of Martin Esslin's book with that title. Esslin, who borrowed the word "absurd" from Camus, who in turn had taken it from Kierkegaard, stripped it of its religious and metaphysical implications and used it to define the new dramaturgy. However, he applied the label rather broadly to a variety of avant-garde plays, thereby creating many misunderstandings about what the theatre of the absurd was all about. Today, "theatre of the absurd" has come to denote, in much the same way as the word "kafkaesque," segments of "real" life, disjointed or impenetrable experiences and, more specifically, plays that are self-contained, that do not comment on our experience or seek to heighten and rearrange it, but create rich new patterns of experience itself.

The absurdist revolution was initially, like all such movements of cultural change, a bewildering experience for many spectators. But as Beckett and Ionesco, along with other innovative French authors, began earning respect and admiration in scholarly and intellectual circles, audiences became more enthusiastic about the new theatrical mode, and in the 1960's the pull toward absurdity became widespread and all powerful.

In Spanish America the beginnings of absurd theatre can be traced back to as early as 1949, the publication date of Virgilio Piñera's *Falsa alarma.* But it is only in the decade of the sixties that a significant number of playwrights working in this vein emerges. George Woodyard, writing in 1969, identifies only five absurd dramatists: Elena Garro, Griselda Gambaro, Virgilio Piñera, Antón Arrufat and Jorge Díaz. This list can be easily augmented, however: Isaac Chocrón, Román Chalbaud, José Triana, Maruxa Vilalta, José de Jesús Martínez, Carlos Fuentes, Julio Ortega, and Eduardo Pavlovsky are among the better known authors who have written at least a couple of plays in the absurdist mode. Recent criticism and anthologies of Spanish American plays also attest to the preeminence of this genre.

Unfortunately, because of the initial misunderstanding created by Esslin himself about absurd theatre, many dramatists have denied their affiliation with the movement, and some critics have followed suit choosing vaguer labels, such as "nonrealistic" or "avant-garde," labels that could also be used to refer to the experimental theatre of protest or to plays that are fantastic, poetic, surrealistic, or what-have-you. "Absurd theatre" on the other hand, is a more precise descriptive phrase when it refers to plays lacking an obvious plot and story-telling, and which are characterized by a radical devaluation of language. Absurdist language tends to be banal and illogical. The poetry emerges instead from concrete and objectified images of the stage itself. In renouncing rational argument about the absurdity of the human condition—as existential playwrights had done—the theatre of the absurd presents it in terms of concrete stage images. These may be violent and grotesque, for the theoretical writings and staging experiments of Antonin Artaud, the exponent of the theatre of cruelty, prepared the way for the absurd theatre in France. This theatre does not have a message and is open to many levels of interpretation.

It is important then to keep in mind that when speaking of absurd theatre the reference is not to some notion of "pure" absurdity but to a movement in the theatre that definitely broke with the conventions of the past. Strindberg, Pirandello, Brecht, Ghelderode, the Surrealists, and Artaud had in their own way sought alternatives to a theatre that insisted on being "lifelike" and that tended to propose moral, psychological, or social solutions. Absurdist writers, generally as different from one another as Beckett and Ionesco, differed from their predecessors in that they were, in Richard Gilman's words, "structurally more extreme, they dispensed more completely with considerations of orderly plot, character development, progress toward a dramatic climax and so on. Beyond that they seemed to lack even minimal points of reference to the outside world."

Spanish American absurdist plays, like their European and North American counterparts, are a diverse lot and generally do not attempt to present pure absurdity. Sometimes this is especially obvious, as in René Marqués' *El apartamiento,* his only play cast in the absurd mode. In form the play is a Beckettian monodrama and communicates an almost overwhelming sense of anguish through isolation. But the presence of the Indian, representing the primitive man of Ibero-America with his original creative powers intact, symbolizes the ultimate possibility of liberation of Puerto Rico and Ibero-America. Other playwrights are more subtle in their allegorizing.... But I think that it is indisputable that in the plays Gambaro wrote during the 1960's, *Las paredes, El desatino, Viejo matrimonio, Los siameses,* and *El campo,* she developed a personal idiom within the convention of the theatre of the absurd. Characters lacking individuality, sparse action subordinated to the spirit of the play, a sense of metaphysical anguish at the absurdity of the human condition, the use of non-rhetorical language integrated with gestures, the importance of the *mise-en-scéne,* all these elements present in her plays are the properties of the theatre of the absurd.

In a recent study of the theatre of the absurd in Cuba, Terry L. Palls applies absurdity in the broader sense that I am using here. Her study defines the theatre of Piñera, Arrufat and Triana as revolutionary theatre concerned with the individual rather than the group.... The dramatic

action of Triana's complex play, *La noche de los asesinos,* for example, consists of a demonic game played by three children obsessed with the need to murder their parents. As is typical of absurd theatre, this play is presentational in nature and open to many interpretations. Montes Huidobro and Kirsten Nigro suggest that the forbidden games may have at least two different meanings. In one instance and on a more universal level they are the proem to a holy and necessary shedding of blood; in another, they imply a cyclical nature of history, particularly that of Cuba.

This tendency to allegorize national as well as universal reality seems to me to be the distinctive mark of absurd drama in Spanish America. A strong critical sense toward an unjust social order has traditionally permeated Spanish American literature, and given the present-day socio-economic situation and political conditions, it is not surprising to encounter the "denuncia en el aquí y el ahora" even in form-conscious literature such as the new novel and the theatre of the absurd.

Recent criticism has noted that a shifting away from the absurd mood in theatre is occurring in European and North American drama. In Spanish America the direct mode of absurdity also seems to have run its course. Modified forms of the absurd continue to appear. However, no major absurdist playwright has emerged in recent years, while some of the better known dramatists of the absurd are turning toward a more representational theatre. In Cuba the production of absurdist plays stopped altogether after 1969. Since what became known as the "first" Padilla affair (1968–69), new restrictions on the arts have been instituted that demand a more concrete reflection of the author's political commitment. In Chile, too, the political situation has had strong repercussions on the arts. The most significant plays produced since the coup combine an obvious historical and political commitment. Thus Jorge Díaz, whose previous work was characterized by an absurdist orientation, has written a documentary play, *Mear contra el viento.* Based on Jack Anderson's ITT memoranda, it is an intensely political indictment of foreign involvement in Chilean affairs.

But elsewhere in Spanish America manifestations of the absurd continue to appear. The Argentine Julio Ardiles Gray produced his first absurdist play, *Vecinos y parientes,* in 1973, and has continued writing in this vein. Another Argentine,

Eduardo Pavlovsky, has been active in the theatre since 1961 and, together with Griselda Gambaro, is an important contributor to a theatre that, as he puts it, "se expresa en un lenguaje distinto buscando la síntesis a través de la imagen y no de la palabra." A practicing psychoanalyst, this author employs abundant psychological material, especially the language of psychodrama. His plays are all conceived in the absurdist mode, although the analytic element, which of necessity is logical, tends to contradict the essentially illogical nature of absurdity. Also, his later plays may be more properly categorized in the subgenre of the theatre of cruelty.

On the whole, however, the trend seems to be away from the conventional standards of absurdity, away from strictly presentational form. Argentina's Griselda Gambaro has, in the present decade, branched out in other directions. Her initial departure from absurd theatre came with *Información para extranjeros,* a play that goes beyond absurdity to incorporate characteristics of Julian Beck's Living Theatre and Richard Schechner's Environmental Theatre. Her play of 1976, *Sucede lo que pasa,* structured along the lines of soap opera, is closer to representational theatre.... A similar case in point is the theatre of Mexico's Maruxa Vilalta. While in her previous work she relied entirely on the allegorical and expressionistic symbols characteristic of absurd theatre, her double-prize-winning play of 1975, *Nada como el piso 16,* is reminiscent of the kind of play developed by Harold Pinter. Pinter, who can hardly be labeled an absurdist, however, is not likely to have written as he has without the example set for him by a Beckett and an Ionesco. Similarly, Vilalta has benefited from her assimilation of absurdist techniques so brilliantly displayed in her previous work. In *Nada como el piso 16* she succeeds in developing the idea of game playing as an action metaphor. The situation is absurd but the form is representational since she uses individualized characters and emphasizes action. The play won two prizes that year because of the excellence of its overall quality and because it was perceived by Mexican critics as a play that brought something new and fresh to the theatre.

Finally, I want to mention the young Mexican writer José Agustín, who has never been directly affiliated with the theatre of the absurd but whose dramatic works *Abolición de la propiedad* and *Círculo vicioso* are perhaps symptomatic of how a younger generation of dramatists will benefit from the lessons of absurdity. These writers will no longer be called absurdists, but they are not likely to write as well without the example of those who were. On first impression, the two plays by Agustín seem to be very different from one another. They certainly are different in theme and stageability. The first is heavily encumbered with the gadgetry of the modern sight and sound industry but develops the conflict between only two characters. The second is more conventional in form but uses a larger number of characters and the conflicts are more complex. There are however some important elements that these plays have in common: the specialized idiom of "la onda" and an absurd situation that perpetuates itself in circularity. The language is especially noteworthy. The hip slang and a constantly flowing play on words serve as a kind of logic-destroying device. It is a truly "absurd" idiom since an uninitiated audience would find it partly incomprehensible and would have to rely to a greater extent on the stage events to clarify the situation. Still, both these plays are conceived as representational drama, and, as I have said before, they may simply be indicative of the eventual fate of absurdity in Spanish American theatre.

It may well be that absurdity is on its way out, to be replaced by a theatre that refuses to distort reality to the same extent. But, as Gilman has noted, "the kind of distortion that absurdity brought into being was necessary, healing in a profound way." Absurdity brought into sharper focus a world that had been obscured by our conventional way of looking at it. And whatever comes next will undoubtedly benefit from its having forced us to look at the known, unexamined world in a new way.

Source: Tamara Holzapfel, "Evolutionary Tendencies in Spanish American Absurd Theater," in *Latin American Theatre Review*, Summer 1980, pp. 37–42.

SOURCES

Banham, Martin, "Mexico: The 20th Century," in *The Cambridge Guide to Theatre*, Cambridge University Press, 1995, pp. 726–28.

Crabb, Jerome P., "Theatre of the Absurd," in Argosy University's Theatre Database, http://www.theatredatabase.

com/20th_century/theatre_of_the_absurd.html (accessed July 20, 2008).

Colecchia, Francesca, "Introduction," in *Crossroads and Other Plays by Carlos Solórzano*, translated and edited by Francesca Colecchia, Associated University Presses, 1993, pp. 7–16.

Dauster, Frank, "The Drama of Carlos Solórzano," in *Modern Drama*, Vol. 7, No. 1, May 1964, pp. 89–100.

Feliciano, Wilma, "Carlos Solórzano," in *Dictionary of Literary Biography*, Vol. 305, *Latin American Dramatists*, edited by Adam Versényi, Thomson Gale, 2005, pp. 316–29.

"The History of Mexico: Postwar Mexico," *History.com*, http://www.history.com (accessed July 20, 2008); originally published in *Funk & Wagnalls New Encyclopedia*, World Almanac Education Group, 2005.

"The History of Mexico since 1945," in *Encyclopedia Britannica Online* (accessed July 20, 2008).

"Mexican Political Parties," in *Encyclopedia of the Nations*, http://www.nationsencyclopedia.com/Americas/Mexico-POLITICAL-PARTIES.html (accessed July 21, 2008).

Mexlist Passenger Train Information, http://www.mexlist.com/pass.htm (accessed July 21, 2008).

Solórzano, Carlos, *Crossroads* in *Crossroads and Other Plays by Carlos Solórzano*, translated and edited by Francesca Colecchia, Associated University Presses, 1993, pp. 19–28.

FURTHER READING

Feliciano, Wilma, "Myth and Theatricality in Three Plays by Carlos Solórzano," in *Latin American Theatre Review*, Fall 1991, pp. 123–33.
Feliciano examines *Los fantoches, El crucificado*, and *Las manos de Dios*, arguing that in these plays Solórzano explores the obsession of Mexican religion with such conflicting notions as sacrifice and salvation.

Joseph, Gilbert M., and Timothy J. Henderson, eds., *The Mexico Reader: History, Culture, Politics*, Duke University Press, 2002.
This collection of essays and articles by various authors offers a comprehensive introduction to the history and culture of Mexico.

Larson, Catherine, and Margarita Vargas, eds., *Latin American Women Dramatists: Theater, Texts, and Theories*, Indiana University Press, 1999.
In this essay collection, trends and developments in Latin American theater in general, and in dramas by women in particular, are explored.

Rosenberg, John R., "The Ritual of Solórzano's *Las manos de Dios*," in *Latin American Theatre Review*, Spring 1984, pp. 39–48.
Rosenberg maintains that Solórzano, in *Las manos de Dios*, uses the drama as a means of breaking the pattern of Latin American Christian ritual and inspiring his audience with a desire for freedom.

The Flies

JEAN-PAUL SARTRE

1942

The Flies, by Jean-Paul Sartre, is one of the foremost examples of existentialist writing by one of the world's most prominent existentialist writers. Indeed, *The Flies* is one of Sartre's best-known works. Existentialism was an early twentieth-century intellectual movement that explored, outside of moral or scientific constraints, the existence and experience of the individual. The movement tended to espouse the idea that the individual has total free will and therefore the utmost responsibility for his or her actions. It also explores the repercussions of this freedom. *The Flies* demonstrates these principles through a retelling of the Greek myth of Electra and Orestes. The characters in the play learn that their gods are powerless and that, as human beings, they possess an innate freedom, which cannot be negated.

First produced in Paris at the Théâtre de la Cité in 1942 as *Les Mouches*, the play was published in French in 1943. It was translated and performed in New York City as *The Flies* in 1947. A separate English translation was published, along with Sartre's play *No Exit*, in 1947. Still studied and performed today, a more recent edition of *The Flies*, still in print, can be found in *No Exit and Three Other Plays*, 1989.

AUTHOR BIOGRAPHY

Jean-Paul Sartre was born June 21, 1905, in Paris, France, the only child of Jean-Baptiste

Jean Paul Sartre (AP Images)

and Anne-Marie Sartre. His father, a naval officer, died of a fever when Sartre was almost seventeen months old. Sartre subsequently spent his childhood with his mother and his maternal grandparents. Isolated without friends of his own age, Sartre entertained himself by reading. As a student, he began attending the École Normale Supérieure in 1924, earning a doctorate in philosophy in 1929. While there, he befriended fellow student Simone de Beauvoir, who became a noted intellectual and feminist. The two were sometimes romantically involved, had a lifelong friendship, and influenced each other's work throughout their respective careers.

Following his graduation, Sartre was drafted into the French Army, where he served uneventfully from 1929 to 1931. Afterwards, he began teaching at the Lycée le Havre. While there, he began writing his first novel, *La Nausée*, which was published in 1938. Translated into English and published as *Nausea* in 1949, the book was

and remains a critical success. Shortly after leaving his teaching post, Sartre studied at the Institut Français, from 1933 to 1935. There, he began reading the works of such philosophers as Martin Heidegger, whose writings heavily influenced Sartre's own philosophies. This influence, and the solidification of Sartre's emerging existential themes can be seen in his 1939 publication *Le Mur* (translated as *The Wall and Other Stories* in 1948). The collection, like his novel, was an immediate success.

Later that same year, however, Sartre was again drafted into the army, this time due to the outbreak of World War II. He had not served long before he was captured, and he spent nine months in Germany as a prisoner of war. Returning to Paris as a civilian in 1941, Sartre resumed his teaching and writing career, and he also participated (albeit minimally) in the Resistance (the movement against the German occupation of

France). Around this time he began writing his seminal existential work, setting forth the philosophies of existentialism in *L'Être et le néant: Essai d'ontologie phénoménologique*. The work was published in 1943 and translated into English as *Being and Nothingness: An Essay on Phenomenological Ontology* in 1956. Arguably at the peak of his writing career, Sartre also wrote his best-known plays during this period, *Les Mouches* (published in 1943, translated as *The Flies* in 1947) and *Huis clos* (published in 1945; translated as *No Exit* in 1947).

By the end of World War II, Sartre had established his writing career and was no longer teaching. He also founded the periodical *Les Temps Modernes*. His standout works from this period include the three-volume novel *Les Chemins de la liberté*, published from 1945 to 1949 (translated as *The Roads to Freedom*, 1947–1950). Sartre also wrote a great deal of literary criticism drawing on his existential ideals. In 1945, he was awarded the French Légion d'honneur for his work, which he refused based on the belief that to accept an organization's award was to make his work subject to that organization's powers.

By the 1960s, Sartre had once again turned to writing philosophy. As important as his first major philosophical work, albeit more optimistic, *Critique de la raison dialectique: Precede de Question de methode* (translated in 1976 as *Critique of Dialectical Reason: Theory of Practical Ensembles*) was published in 1960. Sartre's next significant publication was his 1964 autobiography *Les Mots* (translated as *The Words* in 1964). Also in 1964, Sartre was awarded the Nobel Prize for Literature, which he also refused, and was the first Nobel laureate to do so. In 1965, Sartre adopted his occasional mistress Arlette Elkaïm as his daughter, and she became the sole beneficiary of his estate after his death. By the 1970s, Sartre's health was failing, and he succumbed to a lung ailment on April 15, 1980, in Paris.

PLOT SUMMARY

Act 1

SCENE 1

The Flies is set in Argos, Greece. The opening scene depicts a statue of Zeus, "god of flies and death," in the town square. Elderly women dressed in black worship the statue. Orestes and the Tutor enter the square and ask the women

for directions, but they spit on the ground and run away. Orestes notes that though he was born here, he has been away so long that he does not know his way around. The Tutor makes fun of the town's backward and unfriendly customs. He then asks a boy for directions, but the boy babbles at him, speaking nonsense. A bearded man passes by, and the stage directions state that the man is Zeus in disguise. The Tutor says the bearded man has been following them for some time, but Orestes has not noticed.

The square is filled with flies, and the Tutor brushes them away from himself and from Orestes. Zeus approaches them and says that his name is Demetrios and that he is from Athens. They suddenly hear screams coming from the town's palace. Zeus tells them that the screams signal the beginning of a local festival, called Dead Men's Day, held in remembrance of the murder of Argos's former king, Agamemnon— killed fifteen years ago to the day. Zeus says he was in Argos when Queen Clytemnestra and her lover, Ægistheus, killed the king. Ægistheus then usurped the throne and has ruled Argos with Clytemnestra ever since. Orestes curses the gods for allowing such a thing to happen, and Zeus replies, "Don't blame the gods too hastily. Must they always punish? Wouldn't it be better to use such breaches of the law to point a moral?" Zeus adds that the flies swarming the town were sent by the gods "as a symbol."

Zeus asks a passerby, an old woman dressed in black, if she is in mourning. She replies that the whole town is in mourning. Zeus tells the woman that she was happy about Agamemnon's murder, which she denies. She says the town is remorseful for allowing the murder to occur by not warning the king of the plot, and that the townspeople do nothing but pray for forgiveness. Orestes grows suspicious of Zeus's identity since he knows so much about the town and its people. Zeus ignores Orestes' suspicions, but he says that the townspeople's repentance is dear to him. When Orestes questions him about this statement, Zeus corrects himself and says that he meant it is "dear to the gods." Orestes is shocked to hear that the gods would enjoy the people's fear and repentance.

Orestes learns from Zeus that Agamemnon and Clytemnestra had a daughter named Electra. She was too young to remember her father, and she still lives in the palace with her mother and her father's murderer. Zeus says that Agamemnon and Clytemnestra also had a son, named Orestes, but he was also murdered. At this remark, Orestes is about to reveal his identity, but the Tutor stops him. Zeus says that while some still believe that Orestes is alive, he would rather the boy were dead. Orestes then introduces himself as Philebus from Corinth and asks Zeus why he wishes Orestes were dead. Zeus answers that if Orestes claims his rightful place on the throne and brings his people joy, then the people will no longer be penitent, which will in turn anger the gods. He foretells that such a thing would "bring disaster . . . a disaster which will recoil" on Orestes. Zeus then shows them a magic trick to keep the flies from bothering them and goes on his way.

Orestes wonders if the strange man was a god, but the Tutor chastises him for believing in such nonsense. Orestes says he has no memories of Argos, that it would have been his home but is not now. He suggests that they leave, and the Tutor is relieved to hear that Orestes does not harbor any plans of revenge. Just as they are about to leave, Electra enters the square and approaches the statue of Zeus. She mocks the statue, calling it an empty idol. Electra notices Orestes, and he introduces himself, as he did with Zeus, as Philebus from Corinth. When Electra introduces herself and Orestes realizes that she is his sister, he asks the Tutor to leave, which he does. Electra tells Orestes that though her mother is the queen, she is treated as a servant in the palace. Orestes wonders why she does not run away, and Electra replies that she is "waiting for—for something." She hints that she is waiting for Orestes and wonders whether he will be brave and reclaim the throne or be cowardly and slink away from Argos.

Clytemnestra calls for Electra as she enters the square, and Orestes tries to hide his shock at seeing his mother for the first time. He describes her face as "drawn and haggard" and thinks she has "dead eyes." Clytemnestra and Electra squabble and then Clytemnestra introduces herself to Orestes. In turn, he introduces himself once again as Philebus from Corinth. Clytemnestra immediately tells him of her crimes and remorse, revealing that the only thing she truly regrets is allowing her son to be taken from her. Electra asks Orestes to attend the ceremony commemorating Agamemnon's death, and she leaves to get ready. When they are alone, Clytemnestra asks Orestes to leave, because she has a feeling that he will bring ruin on the town, and then she

also leaves the square to prepare for the ceremony. Shortly afterward, Zeus returns and states that he has been helping the Tutor find horses for their departure. Orestes says he has decided to stay. Zeus hides his disappointment and offers to be Orestes' guide.

Act 2

SCENE 1

The scene begins at a cavern in Argos; the entrance is blocked by a large boulder. It is believed that the cavern reaches into the underworld, and when the boulder is removed from the mouth of the cavern, the spirits of Argos's dead will enter the town and stay for twenty-four hours. During this time period, the dead pester all the people who transgressed against them during their lifetimes. On the day commemorating Agamemnon's death, the boulder is removed, and the townspeople wait in dread. A crowd has gathered for the ceremony, and Zeus enters with Orestes and the Tutor. The Tutor belittles the superstitious townspeople, but Zeus tells him that in the gods' eyes, the Tutor is no better than the people of Argos. Ægistheus and Clytemnestra enter, but when Ægistheus finds that Electra is not there, he sends his soldiers to retrieve her. They return empty handed, unable to find her. Ægistheus and Clytemnestra begin the ceremony without her, but not before Ægistheus promises to have Electra punished.

The High Priest of Argos comes forward and removes the boulder from the mouth of the cavern, calling forth the dead and instructing them to inflict their revenge on the living. Ægistheus goads the crowd, and they cry for mercy. The men repeatedly chant, "Forgive us for living while you are dead." When Ægistheus mentions Agamemnon, Orestes cries out, "I forbid you to drag my father's name into this mummery." Before Ægistheus fully registers what has been said, Electra appears wearing a white dress—everyone else is dressed in black. The crowd is shocked by her sacrilege, a violation of the traditional black garb worn during Dead Men's Day. Electra claims, though, that the ghost of her father is happy to see her in white. She dances with joy and says that the dead do nothing to stop her. As she dances, more and more people begin to question what they have been told about the dead and their vengeance. Some people in the crowd also begin to question Ægistheus. Zeus, aggravated by Electra's display, uses his powers to push the boulder over the mouth of the cavern. The townspeople interpret this occurrence as a bad omen and become fearful once more of the gods' powers.

Ægistheus says that he cannot kill Electra on the holiday, so he banishes her from the palace and orders that any man who sees her in the city tomorrow must kill her. The townspeople are pleased with this ruling, and they head back to their homes. Ægistheus and Clytemnestra return to the palace. Afterward, Orestes reveals his identity to Zeus (who overheard Orestes' earlier cries) and asks him to leave him alone with his sister. Zeus departs with the Tutor. Once they are alone, Orestes offers to help Electra to escape, but she refuses. She wants to stay in the city and find vengeance, and she plans to hide in the Temple of Apollo, where no one can harm her. She refuses to leave Argos until her brother arrives and they take their revenge on Ægistheus and Clytemnestra together.

Orestes reveals his identity to Electra, but he says that he does not want revenge, he only wants to rescue his sister. Though Electra believes Orestes, she prefers to think of him as Philebus, because he is not the Orestes of her dreams. Electra tells him to leave Argos, calling him her "noble-souled brother," and saying, "I have no use for noble souls; what I need is an accomplice." Orestes refuses to leave, but Electra feels he is innocent and will be corrupted if he stays in Argos. Orestes then says that he has no home to go to and that only Argos can be his home. Electra replies that the townspeople will never accept him and that nothing he can say or do will ever make Argos his home.

At an impasse, Orestes asks the gods for a sign as to whether he should stay or go. Unnoticed, Zeus has been eavesdropping on their conversation. At Orestes' request, Zeus causes a ring of light to appear around the boulder. Both Electra and Orestes take this as a sign that he should leave. Disheartened, Orestes appears to have an epiphany, and he chooses to renounce the gods and ignore their wishes. He announces that "something has just died" and declares, "There is another path—*my* path." He now plans to kill Ægistheus and Clytemnestra and to relieve the city of its suffering by making himself a vessel for its guilt. Electra says that Orestes is finally acting like the brother she has always imagined, and she accepts him and his plans.

SCENE 2

Electra and Orestes sneak through the palace, hiding when two soldiers appear. One soldier hears a noise and is suspicious, but the other soldier thinks it is only the spirits of the dead.

Clytemnestra and Ægistheus enter, and the soldiers leave. Believing that they are alone, Ægistheus tells Clytemnestra that he is tired of keeping the people of Argos fearful and repentant, and that he has never had remorse for his actions. Clytemnestra tries to comfort him, but Ægistheus is afraid it will displease Agamemnon's spirit. Clytemnestra reminds Ægistheus that she invented the myth of the spirits in the cavern, and he replies that he is so tired that he forgot. Clytemnestra leaves the room, and Ægistheus talks to himself, muttering that he is as empty as a "desert." He invokes Zeus and says, "I'd give my kingdom to be able to shed a tear." Zeus appears and warns Ægistheus of the plot to kill him. Ægistheus seems to welcome the thought of his death, but Zeus tells him that he must not allow himself to be murdered.

Ægistheus asks Zeus why he was allowed to kill Agamemnon while Orestes is not allowed to kill him. Zeus explains that he made a "profit" on Agamemnon's death: "For one dead man, twenty thousand living men [are] wallowing in" remorse. Ægistheus replies, "I see what lies behind your words. Orestes will have no remorse." Zeus admits this and talks about how he and Ægistheus are similar. They are both only able to rule by fooling men into believing they are not free. Zeus says that because "Orestes knows that he is free," the gods have no power over him. Ægistheus ultimately agrees to stop Orestes from killing him, and Zeus leaves. Immediately afterward, Orestes and Electra jump out from their hiding place. Ægistheus refuses to defend himself, and Orestes stabs him with a sword. He says he will feel no remorse because he is "only doing what is right."

Electra appears frightened by the sight of Ægistheus dying, and Orestes chastises her for it. Orestes goes to find Clytemnestra, but Electra changes her mind and does not want her killed. Despite this, Orestes goes to kill her alone, leaving Electra with Ægistheus's body. Electra is instantly filled with remorse for what she has done, although she pretends that she is happy. After all, her life's dream has finally come to pass. Clytemnestra's screams are heard in the background and then Orestes returns. He tells her that they are free, but Electra replies, "I don't feel free." She also states that they are murderers. Orestes tells her,

> I have done *my* deed, Electra, and that deed was good. I shall bear it on my shoulders.... The heavier it is to carry, the better pleased I shall be; for that burden is my freedom.

As they talk, it becomes harder for Electra to see Orestes through the swiftly thickening swarms of flies. Orestes does not care about the flies, but Electra thinks the flies are staring at them. Indeed, the flies have transformed into the Furies, "the goddesses of remorse." As they stand over Ægistheus's body, soldiers begin to pound on the palace door, and Electra and Orestes escape to the Temple of Apollo.

Act 3

SCENE 1

Electra and Orestes sleep in the temple beneath the statue of Apollo as the Furies wait nearby. They gloat over Electra and Orestes, planning to devour the sleeping pair with remorse. Orestes and Electra awake, and Electra is shocked by Orestes' peaceful, guilt-free face. Orestes is equally shocked by Electra's tormented, guilt-ridden appearance. Orestes observes that Electra now has the "dead eyes" that her mother had. "What use, then, was it killing her?" Orestes asks Electra, "when I see my crime in those eyes, it revolts me." The Furies begin speaking to Electra, pushing her further into despair as they describe her mother's death. Orestes tells Electra not to listen to them. He says they want to turn her against him and that "once you are alone . . . they will fling themselves upon you." Electra cries out as the Furies torture her, and Orestes says, "It's your weakness [that] gives them their strength."

Orestes points out that the Furies do not speak to him because they cannot hurt him. Although he feels anguish at the memory of Clytemnestra's death and Electra's subsequent pain, he asks, "But what matter? I am free. Beyond anguish, beyond remorse. Free. And at one with myself." Electra replies that though the Furies scare her, Orestes scares her more. The Furies tell Electra, "Only the suffering of your body can take your mind off your suffering soul." Convinced, Electra goes to them, and they attack her as she screams in pain. Zeus appears and tells the Furies to leave her alone. He chides Orestes and Electra for their crimes, but Orestes mocks him. Orestes admits that he does not regret the murders or the pain he has caused his sister. He tells Zeus, "[Electra] is dearer to me than life. But her suffering comes from within, and only she can rid herself of it. For she is free."

Zeus mocks and threatens Orestes, but when Orestes challenges him, Zeus backs down. Zeus turns to Electra and tells her that he will protect her from the Furies and absolve her as long as she repents her crimes. Electra says that she always wanted Ægistheus and Clytemnestra dead, and asks Zeus how she can regret her crime. Zeus tells Electra that she only thought she wanted them dead, but that she never truly wanted the murders to happen. As Electra begins to believe him, Orestes warns her that "it's *now* you are bringing guilt upon you. For who except yourself can know what you really wanted? Will you let another decide that for you?" Zeus tells Orestes and Electra that if they repent, he will make them rulers of Argos. Orestes mocks this offer as well. Zeus replies that Orestes will be cast out by his own people, but Orestes is not troubled by this threat. Zeus then goes into a tirade, stating that he created the universe and that everything in it is good. He says that Orestes is "like a splinter" in all that is good and that nature will "revile" him.

Orestes is not frightened by Zeus's rage. He states that while Zeus may be "king" of the universe, he is "not the king of man." Though Zeus made humans, he made them free. Zeus replies, "Let me tell you it sounds much like an excuse, this freedom whose slave you claim to be." Orestes responds, "Neither slave nor master. I *am* my freedom." Electra exclaims that Orestes is being blasphemous. Zeus adds that Orestes' freedom "means exile." Orestes agrees to this statement, but he says that nevertheless, he must show the people of Argos that they, too, are free. Zeus asks, "What will they make of it?" Orestes replies, "What they choose. They're free; and human life begins on the far side of despair."

Zeus indicates that he pities Orestes; yet Orestes states that he pities Zeus. As Zeus is about to leave, he tells Electra that she must choose sides between them. Electra begins to go with Zeus, telling Orestes, "Would to God that I had never known you!" Orestes tries to persuade her to stay, but she still follows Zeus. As soon as Electra exits the temple, the Furies begin to descend upon her. She calls out after Zeus, promising to do as he wishes. Orestes pities her fate, and soon afterward, the Tutor arrives with food. The Furies try to stop the Tutor, but he appeases them with the food that was meant for Orestes. He tells Orestes that the townspeople have gathered outside of the temple in an angry mob. Orestes commands the Tutor to open the doors to the temple, and he calls out to the crowd. He tells them that he is Agamemnon's son, and the crowd grows quiet. All of the flies of Argos have gone, gathered solely around Orestes in the form of the Furies. For the first time since Orestes' arrival in Argos, the sun is shining.

Orestes tells the mob that he does not want to be king. He declares, "As for your sins and your remorse...all are mine, I take them all upon me. Fear your dead no longer; they are *my* dead." The crowd parts for Orestes as he exits the temple and makes his way out into the world, the Furies following after him.

CHARACTERS

Ægistheus

Ægistheus is the king of Argos. Before he was king, Ægistheus was Clytemnestra's lover. He killed her husband, King Agamemnon, and usurped the throne. Ægistheus also had Agamemnon and Clytemnestra's young son, Orestes, taken to be killed, and made their daughter, Electra, a servant in her own palace. Ægistheus first appears in act 2 during the ceremony of the dead, which mourns Agamemnon's murder. He torments the crowd with their guilt to the point that they cry (unheeded) for mercy. Ægistheus pretends to tremble at the thought of Agamemnon's spirit, and he makes a great show of repenting his crime. Indeed, in private, he admits that he regrets nothing; he concocted the ceremony of the dead as a means to control the people of Argos, and he is fully aware that he, like Zeus, is only able to rule by fooling the townspeople into believing they are not free.

Since his power depends on this belief, Ægistheus is extremely agitated when Electra almost succeeds in proving that the ceremony is a farce. He tells her, "I suffered your presence in the palace out of pity, but now I know I erred." Though Ægistheus says that he cannot kill Electra on the holiday, he banishes her from the palace and orders that any man who sees her in the city the next day must kill her. Later, alone in the palace, Ægistheus admits that he is weary of his charade of power and the fear that he must maintain. He is so weary that when he learns of Orestes' plan to kill him, Ægistheus practically welcomes his own end. Ægistheus has also come to believe his own lies, as when Clytemnestra tries to comfort him, and he is afraid it will displease Agamemnon's spirit. Ægistheus has no remorse but makes it seem like he does (and instills it in his people). In awe of Orestes' proud defense of his actions and lack of regret, Ægistheus acknowledges his confusion in his last remarks before dying.

Agamemnon

Exactly fifteen years before the setting of the play, Agamemnon, king of Argos, was murdered by his wife's lover, Ægistheus. Though Agamemnon is dead before the play begins, his spirit is imagined to hover over Argos on the anniversary of his death. Agamemnon's death is also essential to all of the events that ensue throughout the play, and for this reason he is an important character.

Clytemnestra

Clytemnestra, queen of Argos, plotted with her lover, Ægistheus, to kill her husband, Agamemnon, allowing Ægistheus to usurp the throne. She also allowed her lover to take her son, Orestes, and have him killed, the only act she truly regrets. Clytemnestra forces her daughter, Electra, to work as a servant in the palace. She also does not take responsibility for making Electra a servant, claiming that it was ordered by Ægistheus. At one point, Clytemnestra warns Electra that they are alike, that she was once like her daughter and that "nothing good" came of it. In another perceptive moment, she asks Orestes (whom she only knows as Philebus) to leave, because she fears he will ruin them. Described as having "dead eyes," Clytemnestra is consumed with remorse at allowing her son to be taken from her. It is likely that, for this reason, she renounces her own will, becoming little more than a figurehead who does Ægistheus's bidding. Throughout the play, she is not shown to take any actions or make any decisions. Perhaps this is why her dying moments are not portrayed; her screams are merely overheard.

Demetrios

See Zeus

Electra

Orestes' sister and a servant in the palace, Electra is the only person of Argos who refuses to feel remorse for something that she did not do. She longs for her brother to arrive, imagining that he will kill Ægistheus and Clytemnestra in revenge for Agamemnon's murder. Perhaps Electra also imagines that she and Orestes will rule together joyfully in their place. Ultimately, however, Electra comes to regret the killings, and she wishes that she had never met Orestes. In this way, Electra becomes a foil (contrast) to Orestes. Where he is brave, she is fearful. Where he feels no remorse, she feels repentance. Where he challenges the gods and mocks them, she sees blasphemy. By the play's end, Electra agrees to repent in exchange for Zeus's protection from the Furies, "the goddesses of remorse," who hound her penitent soul. Initially a joyous, rebellious, and beautiful young woman, Electra possesses her mother's "dead eyes" after the murders, perpetuating the cycle of violence and remorse into which she was born. Electra is unable, or unwilling, to recognize her freedom, and her end underscores Orestes' own triumph.

Furies

In the beginning of the play, Zeus comments that the flies plaguing Argos are "a symbol." Later in the play, it becomes clear that they symbolize the Furies, "the goddesses of remorse." Furthermore, the flies feed on rotting meat, while the Furies feed on rotting souls. This is why they are so successful in their attacks on Electra, whose soul is quickly devoured by guilt. Orestes tries to warn Electra, saying, "It's your weakness [that] gives them their strength." Despite this, the pain the Furies cause Electra is less frightening to her than Orestes' lack of remorse. The Furies tell Electra that "only the suffering of your body can take your mind off your suffering soul," and Electra believes them. In the end, however, the Furies choose to let Electra escape and pursue Orestes instead. This is partly because Electra gains Zeus's protection in exchange for her repentance. The Furies also believe they can wear Orestes down, and that though "his little soul is stubborn," "he will suffer for two [himself and Electra]." In fact, as Orestes soon takes the remorse of all of the people of Argos upon him, he suffers for far more than two.

High Priest

The High Priest of Argos officiates over the ceremony of the dead, removing the boulder from the cavern and calling forth the spirits of Argos's dead. He calls Electra a "profaner" for daring to wear white and dance with joy during the ceremony, and he chastises the crowd for listening to her. He perpetuates the townspeople's fear and prevents them from understanding that they are free, though it is likely he is also unaware of this fact.

Orestes

Orestes is the protagonist of *The Flies*. He is often referred to by critics as an existential hero, because he embodies all of the values and principles inherent in existential belief. At the beginning of the play, Orestes does not wish for revenge; he only mourns the childhood that he never had. Upon meeting his sister, Electra, he calls himself Philebus from Corinth. Witnessing her circumstances and that of the town, Orestes begins to reconsider his decision. His mind is forever changed, however, when Zeus sends him a sign in an effort to make him leave Argos. At this very moment, Orestes has an epiphany. He announces that "something has just died" and then declares, "There is another path—*my* path." Orestes then plans to kill Ægistheus and Clytemnestra and to relieve the city of its suffering by making himself a vessel for its guilt.

Because, during his epiphany, Orestes realizes that he is free, Zeus admits that he no longer has any power over Orestes. Nevertheless, Zeus makes Ægistheus promise to stop Orestes from committing murder, because he fears that if the people of Argos realize they are free, then he will lose control over them as well. Orestes, however, succeeds, and though the murders and his sister's remorse pain him, he remains steadfast in his knowledge that he is free. Despite his sister's appeals, Zeus's arguments, and the Furies' presence, Orestes will not surrender his will—and to renounce his actions (the murders) is to renounce his will. He acknowledges that he will be in "exile," but he still wishes to tell the people of Argos that they too are free, even if it leads to their own exile. Orestes states that "human life begins on the far side of despair." For this reason, it seems essential that Orestes does not take the throne, not only because Zeus wishes him to rule in the same manner as Ægistheus but also to prove to the people of Argos that he has committed a righteous act (not motivated by a desire for power, a power that Orestes knows to be an illusion). This action, or lack thereof, paves the way for Orestes to take on the sins and remorse of the townspeople.

Philebus

See Orestes

Townsfolk of Argos

The townsfolk of Argos are not aware that they are free, and they are subjugated by remorse and fear. Therefore, both Ægistheus and Zeus are able to rule over them. The townspeople take on a single character, that of the mob, both during the ceremony and in the play's final scene. During the ritual, Electra easily leads them to question their beliefs, and the falling boulder quickly convinces them that Electra is a blasphemer who should be punished. At the end of the play, the townspeople are more clearly a mob in their cries for Orestes' blood. However, they grow quiet when he reveals his true identity, and they part for him as he makes their sins his own.

Tutor

The Tutor is Orestes' servant and traveling companion. He is also the man who has educated Orestes. The Tutor's defining characteristic is that he sees religion as a superstitious and backward tradition for small-minded people. It is likely that this belief has influenced Orestes to some extent. Though the Tutor does not wish for Orestes to exact revenge on his father's murderers, he supports Orestes regardless, as is seen when he brings food to Orestes in the Temple of Apollo and placates the Furies with it.

Zeus

Though Zeus is acknowledged in the play to be the creator of the universe, he is described as the "god of flies and death." Like Electra, he acts as a foil to Orestes, albeit in a less direct manner. At their first meeting, Zeus hides his true identity from Orestes and the Tutor, calling himself Demetrios. Zeus's main function as a foil is performed in his debates with Orestes in act 3. This is especially true when Zeus explains the consequences of freedom to Orestes, who embraces freedom nonetheless. Zeus tells Orestes that he will be cast out by his own people, that he will be "like a splinter" in all that is good and that nature will "revile" him. Orestes does not care, observing that while Zeus may be king of the universe, he is "not the king of man." Zeus adds that Orestes' freedom means exile. Orestes agrees that it does. By the end of their debate, it appears that they have arrived at a semblance of mutual respect through mutual pity. Zeus pities Orestes for his exile, while Orestes pities Zeus for his attempt to convince men that they are indebted to their creator. Though Zeus does his best throughout the play to undermine Orestes, he is ultimately rendered powerless by Orestes' knowledge that he is free, subject to no man and no god.

THEMES

Freedom

Existential philosophy focuses on the ultimate freedom of the individual. All constraints (social, cultural, moral, or otherwise) are an illusion.

TOPICS FOR FURTHER STUDY

- Sartre's relationship with Simone de Beauvoir has long been of interest to literary historians. Study their relationship and give a class presentation based on your research. Based on your research, do you believe Beauvoir influenced Sartre's writing in any way? Discuss your findings in your presentation.

- Research the existentialist movement and write a paper that summarizes your findings. Based on what you have learned, why do you think Sartre is considered one of the foremost existential philosophers? How did he develop his version of existentialist philosophy? How was it unique?

- Study the German occupation of France during World War II, paying particular attention to the influence of the occupation on French literature and culture. Pretend that you are a writer in France during that time. Write a week's worth of diary entries describing the daily impact of the war, your fears and concerns, and your imagined participation in the Resistance Movement or an underground writers' community.

- With several of your classmates, perform a scene from *The Flies*. After the performance, in a short presentation to your class, discuss your interpretation of the scene and how your performance influenced your understanding of the play.

According to existential thought, humankind is largely unable to process absolute freedom, which is why humans thrive under constraint. Constraint offers a sense of security by placing manageable boundaries on freedom. This central theme regarding freedom, and man's experience of it, is illustrated in *The Flies* in several ways. Though the Tutor has taught Orestes that religion is nothing but superstition, Orestes is religious in some ways. He wonders if Demetrios (Zeus in disguise) is a god, and he prays to the gods for guidance. However, when the sign that he asks for comes, Orestes realizes that whether he listens or not is immaterial. The gods have no power over him, because he is free.

Following this realization, Orestes demonstrates his freedom, accepting both the good (the ability to act without remorse) and the bad (being cast out from society) consequences of his actions. Given that existentialism is founded on the idea of absolute freedom, Orestes embodies the figure of the existential hero. Unfortunately Electra, who once believed in her freedom, ceases to do so after the shock of Ægistheus's death. When Orestes tells Electra that they are free, Electra replies, "I don't feel free." Although Orestes feels anguish at the memory of Clytemnestra's death and Electra's subsequent pain, he says, "But what matter? I am free. Beyond anguish, beyond remorse. Free. And at one with myself." Nothing that Zeus can say or do convinces Orestes that he is not free. Even Zeus admits that he made man free, though he did it so that they "might serve" him. Earlier in the play, however, it is acknowledged that both Ægistheus and Zeus are only able to rule because they convince their subjects that they are not free. Electra, in contrast to Orestes, initially believes that she is free but renounces her freedom as soon as its consequences ensue.

Remorse

The constraints of guilt, remorse, sorrow, and repentance are all imposed upon the people of Argos and relished by Zeus, who is empowered by them. These constraints not only deny freedom, they also obscure it. By refusing to own their actions through repentance, the characters deny their freedom; they are not even aware that they have autonomy. This can be seen in Clytemnestra's "dead eyes" and her refusal to take responsibility, instead ascribing her actions to Ægistheus's rulings; the townspeople's fear of the spirits who are said to come and inflict revenge on those who harmed them during their lives; and, most prominently, in Electra's change of heart after the murders of Ægistheus and Clytemnestra. Orestes comments astutely when he says that "the most cowardly of murderers is he who feels remorse." In this statement, Orestes indicates that it is cowardly to reject one's own actions; to reject one's actions is to deny one's freedom to act. In this regard, to feel remorse is not only to reject one's freedom but also to disown it.

Orestes and his sister, Electra (© Bettmann / Corbis)

The flies that Zeus initially calls "a symbol" later transform into the Furies, who in turn represent remorse. The Furies tell Electra, "Only the suffering of your body can take your mind off your suffering soul," meaning that the pain of freedom can be alleviated by the shackles of remorse. Indeed, remorse is attractive to both the people of Argos and to Electra, because it allows them to retroactively avoid responsibility for their actions. For instance, when Zeus tells Electra that she only thought she wanted Clytemnestra and Ægistheus dead, but that she never truly desired the murders to happen, Electra begins to believe him. Yet Orestes tells Electra that to "let another decide...for you" in an attempt to evade responsibility is the very act that will heap "guilt upon you."

STYLE

Rhetoric

Simply put, rhetoric is the art of communicating effectively. On a more practical level, it is the art of communicating ideas. In this manner, *The Flies* is a play meant to promote existential rhetoric. The third act, in which Orestes argues that he is free, is a prime example of rhetoric. Orestes not only communicates that he is free but also identifies the repercussions of freedom. While promoting these ideas, Orestes argues that the consequences of freedom are preferable to those of slavery, both blind and willing. This latter example of rhetoric is predominantly included in his arguments with Electra, while the former are included in his arguments with Zeus. Other examples of existential rhetoric in the play include the Tutor's ridicule of religion, and Zeus's discussion with Ægistheus, in which both admit that they are only able to rule by tricking their subjects into believing that they are not free.

Greek Tragedy

The Greek myth of Electra exists in many guises and variations. It appeared in dramatic form throughout Greek history, in Aeschylus's *Oresteia* trilogy, which was first performed in 458 BCE; in Euripides' tragic play *Electra*, written around 410 BCE; and in Sophocles' tragic play *Electra*, which was likely written between 409 and 410 BCE. Sartre's *The Flies* is based on the Electra myth, though it is revised to suit an existential agenda. Indeed, the play both contains and flouts (contradicts or challenges) the style and characteristics of a Greek tragedy. On a general level, tragedies often include death and are either sad or serious in tone. In this manner, *The Flies* can easily be classified as a tragedy. Central to Greek tragedy, however, is the hero's reversal of fortune (usually from good to bad, rather than vice versa), which is brought on by the hero's moral or character flaws. While Orestes is inarguably the hero and he does see a reversal of fortune, it is not entirely clear whether that reversal is good or bad. It is also unclear whether that reversal is derived from a flaw or a strength.

HISTORICAL CONTEXT

Existentialism

Existentialism, an early twentieth-century philosophy that focused on exploring the existence and experience of the individual outside of moral or scientific constraints, tended to support the idea that the individual has total free will and therefore the utmost responsibility for their actions. Existentialists recognized that the knowledge of total freedom often gives rise to despair. Nevertheless, they believed that right and wrong are uncertain or arbitrary, and that morality is predominantly a tool for denying oneself of freedom and responsibility. Indeed, existential belief posits that the ultimate sin is to deny the true nature of one's freedom by abdicating it and therefore denying one's responsibility. The reverse of this, imposing one's will on another individual, was also considered a sin. Both, according to existentialists, are called "bad faith."

Founded in part by nineteenth-century philosophers Friedrich Nietzsche and Søren Kierkegaard, the existentialist movement was at its strongest from the 1930s to the 1950s. Beginning with 1930s works by German philosophers Karl Jaspers and Martin Heidegger, the movement peaked in the 1940s in France, led by Sartre, Albert Camus, Beauvoir, and Gabriel Marcel. The movement is perhaps most notable for the wealth of literature it produced. Canonical works by Sartre and Camus all reflect existential beliefs. Writers whose works predated the peak of existentialism, such as Franz Kafka and Fyodor Dostoevsky, were nonetheless claimed by the movement as well. Furthermore, the popularity of existentialism is largely derived from its historical context. In the face of the atrocities of World War II and the Holocaust, Europe struggled to redefine what it meant to be human in a world that permitted genocide. Thus, earlier modes of thought and expression were no longer sufficient. In this manner, the philosophy merges well with absurdism, an artistic movement that took place in conjunction with existentialism. Existentialism also gave rise to the philosophical movement of phenomenology, which predominantly explored the nature of firsthand experience, namely how a person experiences the "other," or that which is outside of oneself.

Occupied France

Following the defeat of the Allied Forces in the Battle of France during World War II, the French signed an armistice on June 22, 1940, ceding the western coast of France and northern France to the Germans. France was believed to have had a superior military, and its surrender came as a blow to the French people. The remaining southeastern portion of the country was governed by Marshal Philippe Pétain from the temporary capital of Vichy. Thus, the unoccupied area was known as Vichy France. However, in 1942, when Allied Forces invaded North

COMPARE & CONTRAST

- **1940s:** The prevailing philosophy of the day is existentialism, which explores the existence and experience of the individual outside of moral or scientific constraints, with the idea that the individual has total free will and thus absolute responsibility for his or her actions. Leading existentialist thinkers include Sartre, Martin Heidegger, and Karl Jaspers.

  Today: There is no dominant philosophy; rather, there are several loose offshoots derived from post-postmodernism, which reacts to and opposes postmodern irony. Post-structuralism, however, which prevailed in the 1970s, is perhaps the most recent movement with a definitive philosophy. Post-structuralism questions and challenges the structures in language and systems of thought. Leading post-structuralist thinkers include Jacques Derrida and Michel Foucault.

- **1940s:** The German occupation of France ends in December 1944, following the Invasion of Normandy (D-Day) on June 6, 1944,

  by the Allied Forces (mainly British, American, and French troops). World War II ends in 1945.

  Today: There has not been a third world war; however, war across continents, involving alliances, still occurs. On March 19, 2003, the United States invades Iraq with British, Polish, and Australian military support. The invasion is declared a success on May 1, 2003, but as of 2008, troops are still engaged in the conflict.

- **1940s:** Anti-Semitism is central to Nazi policies, and Jews in occupied France are forced to wear a yellow star on their clothing. Many Jews are deported and sent to concentration camps.

  Today: Anti-Semitism in Europe has been in decline since World War II. However, a slight reversal of this trend begins in 2000 with a statistically significant rise in hate crimes, such as beatings and vandalism.

Africa (just south of Vichy France), the Germans occupied all of France. From 1940 to 1944, while under German occupation, France suffered food shortages, curfews, and forced deportation of Jews and laborers. Even Vichy France, while unoccupied, was not much better off. The French democracy was revoked and Pétain ruled with dictatorial powers.

Thus, some French citizens were opposed not only to the occupation but also to the government in the unoccupied zone. French General Charles de Gaulle escaped to London, England, and arranged for French troops that were not captured by the Germans to join with British forces; this group became known as the Free French. In France, the Resistance was stimulated in small pockets through illegal publications and underground political organizations. Sartre cofounded one such group,

Socialisme et Liberté, in 1941. However, the organization was not successful, and Sartre mainly focused on his writing from then on. Members of the Resistance also hid Jews and Allied soldiers, and they destroyed the railroad lines used by supply trains to German troops. The German occupation of France finally came to an end in December 1944, following the Invasion of Normandy on June 6, 1944, by the Allied Forces.

Sartre was writing at the peak of his career in this war-torn environment. Certainly, it is difficult to ignore the remarkably bleak tone of French intellectuals and artists at the time, and Sartre was no exception. *The Flies* was written halfway through the French occupation and, aside from its existential leanings, the play's presentation of characters who mistakenly think they are subject to gods with powers beyond human

Olga Dominique in a 1951 production of Les Mouches *(The Flies) at the theatre of Vieux-Colombier in Paris (Lipnitzki / Roger Viollet / Getty Images)*

control has been frequently interpreted as a metaphor for French citizens living under the German occupation. The play, in a sense, is a call to arms and a condemnation of complacency.

CRITICAL OVERVIEW

Though the initial reception of *The Flies* was somewhat ambivalent, the play has withstood the test of time and is now acknowledged as a significant contribution to twentieth-century literature. Though second in popularity to Sartre's play *No Exit*, *The Flies* is still considered to be one of Sartre's best dramas. Both plays, written within a few years of one another, are predominantly valued for the insight they shed on existential thought. Timothy J. Williams, writing in the *Midwest Quarterly*, comments that *The Flies* is "possibly the best introduction to the philosophy of Sartre." Williams adds that it "contains all the essential elements of his existentialist thought" and notes that it is "one of Sartre's least ambiguous works." Commenting on the political undertones in the play, Williams observes that "many post-war critics find an anti-Vichy message in the play, or view it even as a clarion call to resistance." Seconding these opinions in *Sartre Studies International*, Sam Coombes writes that "the implications of the portrayal of Orestes as an allegorical representation of resistance to the German occupation and to the Vichy regime are readily apparent." Coombes, like Williams, believes that *The Flies* "stages an opposition between the inalienably free subject defined in that work and the influence of an oppressive ideology perhaps more clearly than anywhere else in Sartre's fiction."

Commenting on the play and on Sartre's initial reception in the United States, *Hudson Review* critic Gerald Weales states that Sartre's "work was the first European work to come to us after the end of World War II." Thus, Weales finds that "Sartre brought a supposedly new philosophy, one which could be used as [an] excuse or banner." Weales adds that "the freedom of the existential hero became, for some people...a kind of license, a lifting of moral restraint." He further observes, "On the other hand, the freedom of the existential hero... could be seen and was seen as a positive philosophy, a road by which a man might make his tough way through a world" that, following World War II, was felt to have been one "which God had deserted and in which the [old] economic and psychological determinisms could no longer be used as excuses."

WHAT DO I READ NEXT?

- Sartre's 1964 autobiography, *Les Mots*, was translated as *The Words* in 1964. The volume focuses on Sartre's childhood and early years, providing insight into some of the events that shaped his emerging philosophies.

- Like *The Flies*, the play *Huis clos* (published in 1945, translated as *No Exit* in 1947) demonstrates Sartre's existential beliefs in dramatic form. It is perhaps his best-known play.

- In hindsight, Franz Kafka is often classified as an existential writer. His most famous story, *Die Verwandlung* (1915), was translated as *The Metamorphosis* in 1937. It features a man who awakes one morning to find that he has been transformed into a giant insect.

- Albert Camus was a leading French existentialist writer and one of Sartre's contemporaries. His best-known work is *L'Étranger* (1942), published in English as *The Stranger* in 1946. The story portrays a young man who is to be executed for a murder that was supposedly cold-blooded, when in fact the protagonist was acting in self-defense.

CRITICISM

Leah Tieger

Tieger is a freelance writer and editor. In the following essay, she explores the aspects of Greek tragedy in The Flies.

Traditionally, the Greek myth of Electra in its many variations is defined as a tragedy. Yet, while Sartre's *The Flies* is indeed based on the Electra myth, the play's status as a tragedy is questionable. In order to ascertain whether or not *The Flies* can be called a tragedy, one must consider the classic characteristics of Greek tragedy and subsequently apply them to Sartre's play. Greek philosopher Aristotle (384-322 BCE) asserted in his *Poetics* that the defining feature of a tragedy is the hero's reversal of fortune (usually from good to bad), which is known in

Greek as *peripeteia*. This reversal is brought on by the hero's hubris (pride) or moral or character flaws (often called the tragic flaw or *hamartia*). Related to this reversal of fortune, the hero often comes to an epiphany (sudden realization), or *anagnorisis*. As an added dimension, the audience undergoes a *catharsis* (purifying emotional experience) upon experiencing a well-made tragedy. The phenomenon of catharsis, according to Aristotle, is derived from the fear or pity that the audience feels during the course of the tragedy.

Inarguably, peripeteia occurs in *The Flies*, but whether that reversal is for good or for ill is not entirely certain. Orestes begins the play as an innocent person; he does not plan to avenge his father's death and instead wishes to pursue the peaceful life he has enjoyed as a child raised by strangers. Yet Orestes mourns the rightful

> **ON A SURFACE LEVEL, ELECTRA'S FORTUNE MOVES FROM BAD TO GOOD. ON A DEEPER LEVEL, THOUGH, HER FORTUNE PROGRESSES FROM GOOD TO BAD. NOTABLY, THE REVERSE IS TRUE OF ORESTES."**

childhood that he was robbed of and says that he does not have a home or a people to call his own. No matter how peacefully he may choose to live his life, Orestes will always be a man whose inheritance was taken from him. When Orestes realizes that he is free, though, he feels empowered to take his revenge. Orestes murders Ægistheus, his father's murderer, and commits matricide, killing his mother, Clytemnestra. Though he feels anguish at the thought of these murders, and also at his sister's subsequent horror, Orestes acknowledges that his distress does not matter, because he is free and therefore "beyond anguish... beyond remorse... and at one" with himself. Orestes has become an exile who embraces his banishment. He wants to bring his fellow people to their own exile (what he believes is freedom), because, as Orestes states, "human life begins on the far side of despair."

In one sense, Orestes experiences a reversal of fortune from good to bad. He was once innocent, but he loses this purity and becomes an outcast, abhorred by nature and man alike. In an existential interpretation, however, Orestes' reversal is one that goes from bad to good. Where he was once ignorant of his very nature, Orestes has come to understand that he is free, able to act without remorse, and no longer subject to the gods or man. He crosses "the far side of despair" and claims his "human life." However, when one considers that Orestes takes the sins of Argos's people upon him, it becomes more difficult to define the reversal of fortune as either good or bad. Certainly, Orestes appears to be a tragic and heroic figure as the crowd parts for him and the Furies follow, but is this a good or bad fate? To most, Orestes' fate appears to be bad, though an existentialist may perceive it as good. Given that existentialism is founded on the idea of absolute freedom, Orestes embodies

the figure of the existential hero. Yet when he takes on the sins of his townspeople, he becomes an unequivocal hero.

Considering hamartia, Orestes does not appear to have a tragic flaw. This is especially true when he is viewed as an existential hero. According to existential thought, the tragic flaw of human existence is the denial of freedom. Thus, Orestes is the only character in *The Flies* who distinctly lacks hamartia. However, if one views Orestes' reversal of fortune as progressing from good to bad, then Orestes' tragic flaw is his lack of remorse, which is seated in the knowledge that he is free. It is this flaw that makes him a murderer; causes him to be forever hounded by the Furies; and separates him from the gods, mankind, and his own sister. Since existential values subvert the play's classification as a tragedy, though, it is Electra—not Orestes—who is a more tragic (and flawed) character.

It seems far more clear, with or without an existential viewpoint, that Electra experiences a reversal of fortune from good to bad as brought about by a tragic flaw. Electra begins the play as a joyful, rebellious, and beautiful young woman who is full of life. When Electra faces her remorse (her tragic flaw) at the murders of her mother and Ægistheus, she is hounded by the Furies. Also, her beauty is replaced by the "dead eyes" that were once her mother's, and she agrees to rule Argos as a repentant subject of Zeus. Even so, Electra's lot has improved on a material level. She is no longer a lowly maid and is on the cusp of becoming the queen of Argos. On a surface level, Electra's fortune moves from bad to good. On a deeper level, though, her fortune progresses from good to bad. Notably, the reverse is true of Orestes. If we are to judge the play's outcome by the characters' inner lives, rather than by outward circumstances, Electra is certainly a more tragic, flawed character than Orestes.

The trait of anagnorisis as it appears in *The Flies* is perhaps easiest to quantify in a straightforward manner. Certainly, Orestes experiences an epiphany. After asking the gods for a sign, which he receives in the form of a ring of light surrounding the boulder, Orestes realizes that "a change has come on everything." He announces that "something has just died," and declares, "There is another path—*my* path." This sudden realization precedes and, in fact, causes his reversal of fortune, rather than being derived from it.

Regardless of cause and effect, this epiphany still meets the criteria of anagnorisis. Electra, however, does not appear to experience an epiphany of any sort. Certainly, she experiences a change of heart through her remorse for the murders, but this can hardly be labeled an epiphany. Indeed, Electra's remorse is mere reaction, little more than squeamishness at the sight of Ægistheus's blood. The best she can offer while standing beside Ægistheus's body is that she "didn't realize how it would be." Considering this aspect of Greek tragedy, it is Orestes, and not Electra, who is assigned the role of tragic hero—existential or otherwise.

Addressing the catharsis that the audience is intended to feel in reaction to *The Flies* is a difficult proposition, especially when one considers that an emotional experience is subjective and is unique to each audience member. However, given that Aristotle proposes that catharsis is brought about via the experience of fear and pity, one can assess whether or not the text of the play is likely to evoke these emotions. It seems fair to argue that the play evokes pity, if not for the murder victims and the perpetually mourning villagers, then certainly for Electra and Orestes. Regardless of the divergent paths that the brother and sister choose, both ends are unenviable and positively pitiable. Electra becomes a slave to her repentance and to Zeus, and Orestes is cast out of society, doomed to be hounded by the Furies. Yet the only possible fear that can be felt in the play is derived from Electra's fear of freedom and of the Furies, or, perhaps, her fear of what her long-nursed desire for murder has wrought. Admittedly, this theory is something of a stretch, making it hard to define the play as cathartic based on Aristotle's two-pronged criteria (pity and fear). Furthermore, Sartre's intention in writing *The Flies* appears to be to demonstrate existential principles. Thus, the play's end achieves less of a catharsis and more of an edification (an educational or enlightening experience).

While the play does meet Aristotle's qualifications, especially peripeteia, hamartia, and anagnorisis, it does so predominantly on a surface level that does not consider the values of existentialism. *The Flies* also meets these criteria when both Electra and Orestes are considered alternately as the tragic hero. Still, the cathartic nature of the play in either reading is somewhat questionable. In general, when *The Flies* is read

> INDEED, IT WOULD SEEM THAT THE MOST IMPORTANT FACTOR IN DETERMINING THE 'RIGHTNESS' OF A COURSE OF ACTION IS THE ATTITUDE EXHIBITED TOWARD THE ACTION BY THE AGENT. THEREFORE, ONE POSSIBLE MESSAGE OF *THE FLIES* IS THAT WHILE REMORSE INVALIDATES AN ACTION, SHAMELESSNESS IS A KIND OF VINDICATION."

exclusively as an existential play, it largely fails to meet the definition of a Greek tragedy.

Source: Leah Tieger, Critical Essay on *The Flies*, in *Drama for Students*, Gale, Cengage Learning, 2009.

Timothy J. Williams

In the following excerpt, Williams discusses Sartre's The Flies *and his view of individual freedom and human existence.*

Jean-Paul Sartre summarized his philosophy in three words: existence precedes essence, thereby abandonning all *a priori* definitions of a human being. According to Sartrean existentialism, before a person can complete the statement "I am . . . *something,*" he or she must acknowledge the primary reality of human existence: "I am." Whatever follows this realization of the mere fact of existence can only result from action. Every individual is absolutely free— Sartre says that people are *condemned* to be free—and we totally define ourselves by our actions, we create ourselves through our choices. The "authentic" individual must confront this existential reality by accepting responsibility for actions and refusing to invoke any external standards, religious or philosophical, to justify personal choices. Such an individual is overwhelmed by the full implications of this radical freedom and experiences moral anguish and a sense of absurdity in recognizing that everything is ultimately arbitrary. The result is alienation from the great majority of people, who will not appreciate this freedom, and the free individual must endure a profound despair born of absolute moral solitude and from the certainty that there is no metaphysical hope.

Reading *The Flies* (*Les mouches*) is possibly the best introduction to the philosophy of Sartre. His first dramatic work, it is comparatively brief, yet contains all the essential elements of his existentialist thought. It is also one of Sartre's least ambiguous works, certainly much clearer than the 1938 novel, *Nausea* (*La nauseé*). Gabriel Marcel, the Christian existentialist and Sartre's contemporary, considers *The Flies* a "manifesto" of existentialism (*L'heure théâtrale,* 189). Despite this relative clarity, opinions about the fundamental meaning of this play are varied, just as are assessments of Sartre's ultimate achievement in philosophy. One particularly interesting detail about *The Flies* is that it was first staged during the Nazis' occupation of France. Since many post-war critics find an anti-Vichy message in the play, or view it even as a clarion call to resistance, the fact that *The Flies* was allowed on a Parisian stage in 1943 has had to be explained. Typically, Sartre's freedom to produce his play has been attributed either to the "stupidity" of the German censors, or to their "artistic liberalism" (Brosman, 73). However, critics do not seem to have considered an equally obvious possibility, and one that has profound implications for the interpretation of the play and the overall assessment of Sartre's philosophy. It is possible that the German censors were correct, ultimately, in detecting nothing dangerous in the message of *The Flies,* at least nothing that would challenge their totalitarian program for a subjugated Europe.

Like other French writers of the twentieth century (Anouilh, Camus, Giraudoux), Sartre expounded his ideas by reviving ancient Greek themes and characters, in this case by reworking the myth of Orestes and Electra. The thoughts and deeds of this brother and sister illustrate opposing reactions to the propositions of Sartrean existentialism as they confront the moral dilemma of vengeance against the murderers of their father, King Agamemnon of Argos. But the spectator (or the reader) of Sartre's dramatic recreation must keep in mind that all is not as it appears. Though Sartre has exploited many aspects of the Greek myth, he most decidedly does not wish to recreate classically-inspired tragedy. Whereas in Greek theater tragedy often seems to arise from the distance separating people from the divine, atheistic existentialism admits to no possibility of a chasm to be bridged, for nothing lies beyond mankind, nothing but the void.

In the opening scene of *The Flies,* Orestes has returned to Argos with his tutor, but, significantly, under the assumed name of Philebus of Corinth. Though he knows his true family history, Sartre's Orestes has yet to really discover himself. Far from being driven by the gods to avenge the death of his father, he seems merely curious to see the city and palace that might have been his to rule. Otherwise, he appears to have no concrete plan of action. His ill-defined character at this point in the play can be taken as a literal illustration of the Sartrean notion that "existence precedes essence" (Marcel, *L'heure théâtrale,* 187). Zeus, disguised as a citizen of Athens, has been anxiously following the travelers for some time. It becomes clear that he would like Orestes to depart from Argos, fearing that the stranger will profoundly disturb the piety of its faithful citizens. But from the outset, Zeus shows himself to be utterly powerless to obtain his ends, and this is the key to understanding his role. He appears to be very active in the play, but in fact accomplishes nothing. Long before he himself acknowledges his impotence, we understand him to be a mere figurehead, the shadow of a belief system that is entirely illusory.

The unfriendly inhabitants of Argos are immersed in their annual period of repentance for the crime of having allowed their king to be slaughtered. Orestes reacts with a mixture of curiosity and aversion toward the Argives' frantic cult of contrition. This commemoration of "Dead Men's Day" has been interpreted as Sartre's mockery of the theme of national guilt that was promoted by the Vichy government during the Nazi occupation (Brosman, 74). It is also possible—unavoidable, really—to interpret the Argives' unceasing cries of "*Ayez pitié de nous*" ("Have mercy on us") as an attack on the Christian idea of sin and redemption (Marcel, *L'heure théâtrale,* 183) and more specifically, the Catholic Church and its penitential liturgy (Cawdrey, 51). In any case, Zeus, the figure of the gods and upholder of religious belief, delights in the expressions of remorse and acts of mortification, whereas the skeptical Orestes is clearly irritated by the entire proceeding. When Aegistheus invokes the name of the dead King Agamemnon while presiding over the religious ceremonies, Orestes erupts with his first flash of anger: "I forbid you to drag my father's name into this mummery."

It is Electra, however, who first speaks of action, of retribution, a vengeance of which she has long dreamt. But she seems unable to act alone. After lamenting her deplorable treatment at the hands of her murderous mother and stepfather, Electra tells Philebus (Orestes in disguise) that she has never had the courage to flee, but believes that she will not have to endure her situation forever. For the present, she is merely "waiting for something" or someone to put all aright. Thus, Electra is presented as violent in speech, but passive and timorous in behavior, which explains why she ultimately recoils in horror when Orestes finally executes his murderous plan.

And whence comes the plan of action? This is probably one of the most difficult and weakest moments in the play. The decision to act against Aegistheus and Clytemnestra has followed Orestes's prayer to the gods to show him the way: "I am weary" he says, "and my mind is dark; I can no longer distinguish right from wrong. I need a guide to point my way....O Zeus,...make plain your will by some sign; for no longer can I see my path." There is then an inexplicable flash of light around the stone that seals the tomb of Agamemnon, a phenomenon which, of course, offers no real help. Is it a natural event or does it signal some epiphany? If the latter, the divine will would still have to be interpreted. But quite suddenly, following the taunts of Electra, Orestes experiences an enlightenment, a sudden awareness that he is totally alone in an indifferent universe: "Until now," he proclaims, "I felt something warm and living around me, like a friendly presence. That something has just died. What emptiness! What endless emptiness, as far as the eye can reach!"

Though overwhelmed by this feeling of absolute solitude, Orestes is emboldened by his new-found freedom, and declares that he will no longer take orders, neither from men nor gods. He asks Electra to guide him to the royal chambers so that he might strike without delay. Now, we have already been told that Orestes has been raised free from prejudice and superstition and that he is "free to try his hand at anything," but he has also been tutored in the importance of not committing himself. Why should he now be determined to avenge a crime in which he has no crucial stake? As we learn later in the play, Orestes has no interest in assuming the throne, and in fact leaves Argos at the first opportunity. How does an awareness of the fact of human freedom suddenly create the desire to avenge a wrongful murder? For that matter, what is a

wrongful murder? Sartre might reply that existentialism does not answer the question of what one ought to do, but merely that once having decided on a course of action, there are no grounds for remorse or repentance. Indeed, it would seem that the most important factor in determining the "rightness" of a course of action is the attitude exhibited toward the action by the agent. Therefore, one possible message of *The Flies* is that while remorse invalidates an action, shamelessness is a kind of vindication.

When Orestes makes clear what he intends to do, Zeus attempts to intervene by warning Aegistheus of the danger. His will is that the king should strike first against this impious son of Agamemnon. Aegistheus, weary after fifteen years of upholding the guilt of his remorseful subjects, shows little interest in saving himself. He is merely curious about two things. First, why does Zeus, who permitted the murder of Agamemnon, now wish to prevent the crime of Orestes? The answer is that the crime of Aegistheus was "clumsy and boorish," a crime of passion, a crime that did not "know itself," and that was soon regretted. As such, it was a useful crime for the gods, keeping the whole city of Argos in fear and trembling, a fear of which the gods have need for their very existence. Orestes, on the other hand, will commit his deed in cold blood, and will not have a trace of remorse. Why, then, does Zeus himself not destroy Orestes? The god explains: "Once freedom lights its beacon in a man's heart, the gods are powerless against him. It's a matter between man and man, and it is for other men, and for them only, to let him go his gait or to throttle him." The reader is to understand, of course, that the gods are not real, that they are mere projections of human fear, ceasing to exist for one who no longer fears the burden of absolute freedom.

The brief encounter between Orestes and Aegistheus reveals the thoughts of the young man just as he strikes down his enemy: "Justice is a matter between men, and I need no god to teach me it. It's right to stamp you out, like the foul brute you are, and to free the people of Argos from your evil influence. It is right to restore to them their sense of human dignity." Although the course of action is expressed in noble terms—the suppression of evil, the restoration of human dignity—there is nothing in the play to justify the use of such terms. What is justice and how is it to be dispensed if each individual is radically free to choose and to validate any course of action? Why exactly is the crime of the tyrant Aegistheus more evil than the impending crime of Orestes? Indeed, what is a crime, and what is a tyrant? If such stinging questions occur to readers of *The Flies,* their effect is likely to be deadened by the relentless stream of Sartre's anesthetizing prose. It is at this point that the incoherencies of the play begin to accumulate. As Marcel observes, one cannot entertain the idea of justice "without reestablishing a certain order, a genuine order—that of unwritten laws—in opposition to the exterior and corrupt order established by the tyrant" (*L'heure théâtrale,* 188, my translation). Of course, the very idea of inferred, *essential* laws is impossible according to Sartrean existentialism.

Zeus makes a final effort to turn Orestes back into the fold, to rejoin the faithful in their religion of remorse and repentance. Orestes will have none of it. He tells Zeus, the god of lightning, that freedom came crashing down on him like a thunderbolt: "I knew myself alone," he explains, "utterly alone in the midst of this well-meaning universe of yours. I was like a man who's lost his shadow. And there was nothing left in heaven, no right or wrong, nor anyone to give me orders." Thus, the radical, personal freedom of Orestes is accompanied by darkness, for the light has simply gone out of his universe. In perhaps the most famous line that Sartre ever penned, Orestes reveals what existentialist man must confront in order to live authentically: "Human life begins on the far side of despair." Neither God, nor the universe, nor history, nor culture, nor family can provide a ground for existence. All is ultimately arbitrary and meaningless. Unlike the common person, Orestes must find his own *raison d'être* every day of his life: "Foreign to myself—I know it. Outside nature, against nature, without excuse, beyond remedy, except what remedy I can find within myself." Zeus warns that this attitude will mean exile, and asks Orestes what he intends to do with his new-found freedom. "The folk of Argos are my folk," Orestes declares, "I must open their eyes." In one of several passages that echo Nietzsche's Zarathustra and that mock the Gospels, Zeus replies: "Well, Orestes, all this was foreknown. In the fullness of time a man was to come to announce my decline. And you are that man it seems."

The flies are the furies, the goddesses of remorse. They set upon Electra, who has quickly repented of the vengeance she long desired, accepting the falsely exculpatory version of the crime offered by Zeus. Orestes angrily rejects the casuistry of Zeus. In vain, he pleads with his sister: "Electra! It's now that you are bringing guilt upon you. For who but yourself can know what you really wanted? Will you let another decide that for you? Why distort a past that can no longer stand up for itself?" Because Orestes refuses to doubt himself, the flies can do him no harm. They must disperse to let him pass as he bids farewell to the Argives and marches bravely toward a new day.

Whatever Orestes does with himself, armed with his new freedom, his destiny will have nothing to do with Zeus, with the citizens of Argos, with his sister, Electra, or even with the Orestes who has just killed Aegistheus. For existentialist man, all manifestations of the past—one's own *vita,* one's culture, human history, even the past of the universe, Creation itself—all these are meaningless. Only action in the present moment has significance. But wouldn't the prospect of absolute moral relativity weighing upon a given act have a rather paralyzing effect on any plan of concrete action? Just as it would be impossible to imagine any prolongation of *The Flies,* any sequel recounting further purposeful adventures in the life of Orestes, it is difficult to conceive of an existentialist program of coherent social activism of any sort, and this reality has certain parallels with the life of Orestes's creator....

Source: Timothy J. Williams, "Sartre, Marcel, and *The Flies:* Restless Orestes in Search of a Café," in *Midwest Quarterly*, Vol. 48, No. 3, Spring 2007, pp. 376–89.

Allan Stoekl

In the following excerpt, Stoekl examines the possibility that Sartre knowingly and willingly took the place of an unfortunate Jewish professor in 1941, using Les Mouches *(The Flies) as the basis for his argument.*

Recently much debate has turned around Jean-Paul Sartre's alleged duplicity during the Occupation: did he or did he not knowingly replace, in 1941 at the Lycée Condorcet, a Jewish professor who had been deprived of his post simply because he was Jewish? Did this make Sartre a knowing, albeit passive, accomplice to Vichy racial policy—an accomplice, like millions of others in wartime France, in that he was, with

> AM I SAYING THAT SARTRE WAS A FASCIST, EVEN A NAZI? NOT AT ALL. PERHAPS WE DO SEE HERE THE OUTLINES OF SARTREAN EXISTENTIALISM AS IT WOULD HAVE DEVELOPED IF THE GERMANS HAD WON THE WAR, IF THE OCCUPATION HAD CONTINUED INDEFINITELY. WE CANNOT KNOW."

an apparently clean conscience, willing to take advantage of another's—a Jew's—misfortune?

At this late date, it seems difficult to adjudicate this issue and proclaim Sartre's bad faith. We can never know for certain what he knew, and when he knew it. To try to understand Sartre's problematic position under the Occupation, I think one must go to the actual writings we have at our disposal: his essays, plays, and interviews. Failing this, we will always be constrained to judge him based on innuendo, negatively: what he wasn't doing, but should have done; what he may have known, and yet did not act upon. I think if we turn to his writings, or at least one of them, we will be confronted with a different problem. The question of Sartre's shadow-collaboration turns not around what he knew, or what we can know about his knowledge, but around what we can and cannot know about what wartime audiences knew and did not (could not) know of the supposed message of Sartre's wartime drama.

Was Jean-Paul Sartre's play *Les Mouches,* published in April 1943 and first performed that June in Occupied Paris with the approval of the German censor, a Resistance play? Was it meant to convey a pro-Resistance message? The debate has swirled for a number of years, giving rise to accusatory books, such as Gilbert Joseph's *Une si douce occupation,* arguing that Sartre never was a Resistance figure, and that the works he published under the Occupation were harmless, and hardly noted for their insurrectional fervor. On the other hand, defenders—starting with Sartre himself after the war—have argued that key wartime works such as *Les Mouches* were really calls to resistance, given censorship, however, it was necessary to mask the message with,

for example, the setting of ancient Greece. Sartre even argued that the drubbing administered by collaborationist critics was proof that they understood the play's true intent: an argument for human freedom, in opposition to the Vichy doctrine of remorse and eternal penitence for the sins of the Third Republic. Sartre's foes, on the other hand, are quick to respond by recalling that *Les Mouches* was produced in a theatre whose name had been changed (from Le Théâtre Sarah-Bernhardt to Le Théâtre de la Cité) to please the anti-Semitic occupier, that the director (Charles Dullin) dabbled in collaboration, that Sartre himself gave interviews to a (fairly mild) collaborationist paper (*Comœdia*), and so on. Finally, the seeming trump card: if the Resistance emphasis of the play was so clear, why did the censors pass it in the first place?

Ingrid Galster, in her book *Sartre, Vichy et les intellectuels,* has done a lot to set the record straight. After carrying out exhaustive research, which involved reading virtually every review of the play printed in Occupation-era papers—even the ones in German, published both in Paris and Berlin—she concludes that, in effect, neither side is right. On the one hand, clearly there were audience members "in the know," able to perceive the message of freedom and place it in the context of the Resistance. On the other hand, she argues, the collaborationist critics who roasted the play perceived absolutely no Resistance message: what they saw was a long, talky play that offended them mainly because it recalled Sartre's earlier works, such as *La Nausée,* perceived as a celebration of nausea—a disgusting book by a disgusting author, hardly the uplifting reading that the new era demanded. In addition, rightwing critics objected to the whiff of the avantgarde they perceived in the play's sets and costumes, which evoked for them the heyday of left-leaning aesthetic scandals of the prewar years—the bad old days. Moreover, one German critic, writing for the Paris German-language newspaper distributed to the occupying soldiers, actually saw in *Les Mouches* a celebration of a Nietzschean-Nazi superman.

Despite the thorough and excellent research it displays, Galster's book still leaves us with an unanswered question: how is it possible for a work to be read, or seen, by two communities, and found to have different "messages"? We need more than just the observation that both critics and supporters of Sartre were (and are) misguided. Were the collaborationist critics and the censors simply obtuse? Did Sartre really put one over on them? If so, why did even Michel Leiris—certainly an ally of Sartre and a man with impeccable credentials on the left—not stress the importance of the Resistance message in his review of the play, in a Resistance paper? One can go on: if Resistance message there was, it was so subtle that no one appears to have been moved by it to resist: in today's jargon, the play at the time of its first production got no "traction" as a call to Resistance. On the contrary: one German critic actually implied that it was a (rather mystifying) call to collaboration.

What's needed, I think, is a model of writing and reading that will allow us to see the larger social and political ramifications of a work based on specific communities of interpretation. It may be that Sartre was writing neither for the Resistance community of readers—real or potential—nor for the collaborationist one; rather, he was writing a polyvalent work that could be read in different ways by different groups: what would be manifest for one group would be a thematic black hole for the other, impossible to recognize or comprehend. This is not to say that the play is simultaneously a perfect work of collaborationist ideology and a call to heroic Resistance; instead, I would argue that the play puts forward certain *idéologèmes,* hardly a complete collection of them on either side, that allow it to pass muster among at least certain members of two, ferociously opposed, communities of readers. I am not saying that Sartre was consciously double-dealing; all we can know about what he was doing was what he himself wrote, in the play and in contemporary interviews; his later, post-Liberation comments are obviously tendentious, self-serving, and partisan (though not necessarily wrong). They do not and cannot take into account what Sartre would have said about the play if the Germans had won the war....

First, as Orestes tells us in Act II, Scene VIII, to be free is to suffer: it is the pain of one who literally bears the consequences of his free act.

> I have done my deed, Electra, and that deed was good. I shall bear it on my shoulders as a carrier at a ferry carries the traveler to the farther bank. And when I have brought it to the farther bank I shall take stock of it. The heavier it is to carry, the better pleased I shall be; for that burden is my freedom.

Beyond this quiet and self-effacing—but joyful—suffering, there is the affirmation of liberty as strength and self-affirmation in the present. Orestes proclaims in Act III, Scene I:

> It's your [Electra's] weakness that gives them their [the Furies'] strength. Mark how they dare not speak to me. [...] And the anguish that consumes you—do you think it will ever cease ravaging my heart? But what matter: I am free. Beyond anguish and memory. Free. And in agreement with myself. You mustn't hate yourself, Electra. Give me your hand; I won't abandon you. (translation modified)

Electra's remorse—her memory—is her weakness; conversely, the affirmation of the crime, in dread, is purely in the present, without memory. This is strength, nobility, but also, of course, toughness. Orestes is no sob sister: he commits his crime, the most horrible, the unthinkable—matricide—and affirms it, forgets its monstrosity, carries it, ultimately, secretly (for who else could understand? How could he communicate it?), and joyfully.

We know the conventional reading: remorse is Pétain's message, to resist it is to opt for freedom, and by extension, for the Resistance. (The critique of remorse is a major theme of the play, of course; but how great, really, was the cult of remorse in Pétainiste France? Was it as overwhelmingly important as it is in Jupiter's Argos?) But remorse in the play is presented not so much as the product of a government—that of Aegistheus—as it is a kind of "natural" fatality, the product of Jupiter's will. What Orestes fights against is less the remorse-doctrine of a single, oppressive government as it is the "natural" tendency to accept remorse by refusing to step up and commit brutal, horrifying crimes. Such is the case with Electra, who has longed for Aegistheus's death, but who refuses to take responsibility for it—who, in other words, caves in to the will of Jupiter.

Sartre's Orestes is an example of what I've called "existentialist fascism." That term might seem overly provocative, but consider: a lonely, elite hero, breaking brutally with the past, showing nothing but contempt for accepted morality, willingly commits a crime universally judged indecent, monstrous. Freedom is a heavy burden to carry, but its very heaviness, its antisocial and cruel (even masochistic) aspect, is what gives it significance. Freedom is the refusal to compromise, to back down, to remember, because all these are functions of remorse, of weakness. Freedom is monstrously violent, and its repetition in society—if there is to be repitition—is set off only by the lone, violent actor: Orestes himself, who, one assumes, will be such a figure of revulsion that no one can or will be able to remember him. That is the paradox of freedom: it is propagated through a public act, but one that renounces memory and that will itself be forgotten or hidden from memory.

This . . . can be read as a pseudo-Nietzschean freedom, but also that of the SS man, carrying out his duties, affirming his own personal freedom by carrying out a monstrous, but "necessary," crime. An SS man who (we might remind Dr. Buesche) expects no glory, no reward, no recognition, and whose glorious acts are a heavy burden that will of necessity always remain hidden, will never be celebrated or remembered, by himself or by others (and might very well be condemned). In 1943 Himmler proclaimed: "To have endured this [the sight of hundreds of corpses] and at the same time to remain a decent person [. . .] this has made us tough, and is a page of glory never mentioned and never to be mentioned [. . .]". In other words the burden, and paradoxically also the glory, will be outside memory.

Was the critique of remorse in *Les Mouches* an oblique critique of Pétain? Recall that Vichy was criticized not only by the left and the Resistance, but also by the right: French fascists who admired the Nazi cult of strength and violence (one thinks of *Je Suis partout,* Brasillach, Drieu la Rochelle) had little use for the endless lecturing coming from senile and impotent killjoys like the Maréchal . . . "Français, vous avez la mémoire courte" indeed.

Am I saying that Sartre was a fascist, even a Nazi? Not at all. Perhaps we do see here the outlines of Sartrean existentialism as it would have developed if the Germans had won the war, if the Occupation had continued indefinitely. We cannot know. What we do see is a handful of *idéologèmes* that make possible the reading of the play—no matter how cursory a reading—as a pro-fascist statement. Again, my point is not that Sartre was a fascist, but only that there are enough bits and pieces of ideology in the play to allow a hasty reading of the play as pro-fascist.

The significance of this is that people reading inattentively—the censors, easily bored collaborationist critics, puzzled Nazis—could have read or seen the play and not even noticed its putative message, because for them it would blend effortlessly into the collaborationist propaganda they produced and consumed every day.

But the postwar Sartre and his apologists were probably correct as well: the play *was* a call to Resistance; the young people who saw it at the Théâtre de la Cité and applauded its encomiums to freedom really *were* thinking ahead to the Liberation. Just as a quick reading could allow fascists to find nothing objectionable in Sartre's statements or in the larger themes of the play, so, too, young Resistance sympathizers could jump to the conclusion that the play was a celebration of the Resistance and an attack on Vichy.

My point is that both sides were "right," and neither was. Sartre wrote a protean work whose very strength was that it could be read from either side. To say this is to say more than what Sartre himself said—that he had to conceal a critique of Vichy and a celebration of the Resistance in a play set in ancient Greece, in order to get his "message" across. There is no question of concealment—unless it is a concealment of the sort carried out in Poe's "Purloined Letter," where the "hidden" letter was always there, visible, available if it only could be recognized. The strength of the play is that it presents two sets of complementary blind spots for two different audiences: fascists could see the play, ignore a vaguely provocative reference to "dignity" (the dignity of being a magnificent criminal) and see, no matter how lackadaisically, an affirmation of individual violence that transcends common, bourgeois morality. Resistance partisans, on the other hand, could (and did) ignore those elements, and fasten on the few hints within the play—again "dignity," the killing of Aegistheus as a house-cleaning by which the fascists are (apparently) eliminated, "freedom" as a personal benefit to be derived through democracy—that would lead them to perceive a celebration of the Resistance. For fascists, the play's flies would recall the filth that Occupation propaganda associated with Jews and misfits; for fans of the Resistance, the flies are symbols of the parasitical, petty remorse that characterizes the mindset of the loyal Pétainist citizen. Each community of readers has its blind spots, and these blind spots are symmetrically opposed; what I see, no matter how haphazardly, is precisely what is invisible to the other person—and vice versa. . . .

Source: Allan Stoekl, "What the Nazis Saw: *Les Mouches* in Occupied Paris," in *SubStance*, Vol. 32, No. 3, 2003, pp. 78–91.

Oreste F. Pucciani

In the following interview, Pucciani presents Sartre with questions about his writing style, topics, and love for literature.

[The highlight of last year's theatre season in Paris was the opening of Jean-Paul Sartre's newest play, *Les Séquestrés d'Altona*. Oreste Pucciani, in France last spring, interviewed M. Sartre for *TDR* concerning his new play.]

PUCCIANI: From remarks of yours which I have read here and there, I gather that your ideas of engaged literature have changed since you published Qu'est-ce que la litterature? in 1948. Simone de Beauvoir has told me that you no longer feel that people can be changed by literature; that one of your greatest impressions of Cuba was that the Cuban people have been changed.

SARTRE: Yes. To an extent that is true. I remain convinced, however, that if literature isn't everything, it is nothing.

PUCCIANI: What precisely do you mean by that statement?

SARTRE: I mean that a writer, a novelist cannot deal with the slightest concrete detail of life without becoming involved in everything. If I want to describe a scene—Saint-Germain-des-Prés, for example—I am immediately caught up in all the problems of my time. I may try to avoid these problems, limit my world and deal only with a small fragment of reality. But actually I cannot. Look at Jouhandeau. I like Jouhandeau very much, but Jouhandeau has limited himself to the world of a couple: Lise and Jouhandeau. This sort of writing, however interesting, is bound to produce monsters. The writer cannot *not* be engaged. In one way or another all writers

know this. Yet they don't accept it. Consequently, when they do try to deal with their own times, they end up by writing detective stories. Look at the last volume of Durrell.

PUCCIANI: Isn't this a different sort of engagement from engagement as you saw it in 1948? The engagement of 1948, as I understand it, was essentially an engagement of content over form.

SARTRE: Yes. Content over form, if you will. But I have certainly evolved since 1948. In 1948 I was still naïve—the way we are all naïve. I still believed in Santa Claus. Up to the age of forty! I believed, as you say, that people could be changed through literature. I no longer believe that. People can certainly be changed, but not through literature, it would seem. I don't know just why. People read and they seem to change. But the effect is not lasting. Literature does not really seem to incite people to action.

PUCCIANI: Is it perhaps because literature reaches people within their essential solitude?

SARTRE: Yes. There is certainly that. But there is something, for example, in a political meeting—and I do not mean that political meetings are in any way superior to literature!—which has a more lasting effect. Direct political action seems to be more *effective* than literature. I think it perhaps comes from the fact that we writers don't know too well what we are doing. The situation of the writer today is very strange. Today the writer has more means at his disposal than ever before and yet he seems to count for so little. It's incredible. Today everyone is known; everyone knows each other. A writer of relatively little importance can easily be as famous or more famous than Baudelaire or Flaubert in their time. Look at my own career. I started around 1938 with *La Nausée*. There had been a few things before; nothing much. Then with *La Nausée* I had a nice *succès d'estime*. Now look at what has happened. In a way I should actually have fewer means at my disposal than I do. And yet what does it all amount to? There is a kind of impotence about being a writer today. I think the realization of that is the difference between my position today and my position in 1948.

PUCCIANI: You have mentioned impotence and that brings me to the Séquestrés d'Altona. *As I see it, the great theme of the play is "sequestration." But the corollaries of "sequestration" are impotence and power. Do you agree?*

SARTRE: Yes, Certainly that is so. But the play is really about torture.

PUCCIANI: It is an engaged play?

SARTRE: Yes. But it is not the play that I really wanted to write. I wanted to write a play about French torture in Algeria. I especially wanted to write about the sort of chap who tortures and who is none the worse for it. He lives perfectly well with what he has done. It never comes out unless he starts boasting some night in a café when he's had a little too much to drink.

PUCCIANI: Why didn't you write that play?

SARTRE: For the simple reason that there isn't a theater in Paris that would have produced it!

PUCCIANI: So you chose to set it in Germany?

SARTRE: Yes. After all, no one is going to contradict me if I say the Nazis committed torture.

PUCCIANI: Would you explain the title of the play to me?

SARTRE: Well, I used to be very fascinated by the "sequestered life." You know the sort of thing I mean. There is a common myth—it was very common in my youth—about the writer or the poet who locks himself up and just writes and writes because he can't help himself. It's his nature to be a writer and that's all there is to it. Of course, I no longer subscribe to that sort of nonsense, but I used to be very fascinated by it. Now I subscribe to the point of view that a writer writes because he has something to say. Anyway...I wanted to show this sort of sequestration in terms of liberation. As you say, the whole theme of the play is sequestration from the beginning. Léni is a *séquestrée* because she is incestuous. Old Gerlach is the powerful industrialist—*un grand bourgeois*—who is a *séquestré* because of his class. Frantz is also a *séquestré* from the beginning. The first sign that Frantz was really guilty of torture, that he was actually the first to torture, is his reaction to the Jewish prisoners. He was disgusted by their dirt and their degradation rather than revolted by their plight. This is not the sort of reaction to have. You can see from that that he was going in for such abstractions as "human dignity" and that sort of thing.

PUCCIANI: It seems to me that one might say in the final analysis that Frantz was a good man because he committed suicide.

SARTRE: Yes. Provided you say *because* he committed suicide. Actually, the terms "good" and "bad" have no meaning in history. The more one goes along, the more one realizes that the "good" were "bad" and that the "bad" were "good." It is a sort of mystification. The terms really mean nothing. There is no justice in history. Frantz comes to face what he has done; so does his father. They have to commit suicide. But the production of the play didn't really put the meaning across. Ledoux as old Gerlach wasn't what I intended.

PUCCIANI: With reservations Reggiani was very good.

SARTRE: Yes. With reservations.

PUCCIANI: The recent German production in Essen was apparently quite different. Gerlach was, I gather, much more what you intended. The powerful over-bearing industrialist.

SARTRE: Yes. But that was odd too. The Germans apparently cut out the scene where Frantz eats his medals. You remember, they are made of chocolate. At one point he and Johanna eat them. Very strange. Frantz should—he must—*eat* his medals.

PUCCIANI: I noticed that. But I thought the German version was an improvement. I didn't at all like that particular scene.

SARTRE: Really? Why?

PUCCIANI: I thought it out of keeping. It was a trick.

SARTRE: How strange. No one has criticized that. It was very successful on the stage.

PUCCIANI: I know. The audience laughed. But I didn't feel they should have.

SARTRE: Oh, but the audience must laugh! I have learned that if you don't give audiences a chance to laugh when you want them to, they will laugh when you don't. Besides, there is no point in some empty gesture like tearing off the medals or that sort of thing. There is no meaning in that. After all, the medals would remain intact. But if Frantz eats them, that means he eats them every day. The medals disappear. They are digested.

PUCCIANI: But what is the point of that?

SARTRE: You forget that we have heroes in France. They must be made to feel the insult that is intended. They must suffer a little for what they represent.

PUCCIANI: I have frequently heard your play criticized as being a drame bourgeois. *This strikes me as unfair. I see the first, third and fifth acts as deliberately* bourgeois; *the "downstairs" reality. But the "upstairs" reality is quite different. That is* avant-garde. *There are two levels: physical and metaphysical.*

SARTRE: Yes. Exactly. That's exactly it. Perhaps not "metaphysical," but still that's it. We must start with the *bourgeois* world. There is no other starting point. In this sense Existentialism is a *bourgeois* ideology, certainly. But this is only the starting point. In a different sort of world, theatre itself would be different. So would philosophy. But we have not reached that point. In a society of permanent revolution, theatre, literature would be permanent criticism, permanent contestation. That is a long way off. But it is entirely wrong to call my play a *drame bourgeois*. *Bourgeois* drama exists only for the purpose of eliminating the problem it deals with. This is not the case in the *Séquestrés*. There is an actual liberation in the two suicides. There is no secret mystery that is revealed. There is a dialectic.

PUCCIANI: To come back to the title of the play again, would you tell me just why you chose that title? I mean almost etymologically.

SARTRE: Well, you know what it means. In French a person who shuts himself up or who is shut up is called a *séquestré*. I don't know if you are familiar with Gide's *Souvenirs de la Cour d'assises*. Perhaps you recall the *Séquestrée de Poitiers?*

PUCCIANI: Yes. I wondered if there were an echo of that.

SARTRE: Definitely.

PUCCIANI: Your play is then actually an act of personal engagement?

SARTRE: Yes. Quite. I still believe in engaged literature.

PUCCIANI: Mauriac has said that you are the real séquestré. *I wonder what you think about that? Your play reflects your concern for the writer's impotence; his frustration in power.*

SARTRE: Well, no. I'm not a *séquestré*. No one has locked me up and I haven't locked myself up.

PUCCIANI: I once said in an article about you that engaged literature means la litterature au pouvoir. *I wonder what you think about that.*

SARTRE: Yes. That's correct. As a kind of ideal statement. But one should add immediately that it must be understood that literature will never be given this power. If it were, it would no longer exist. Look at Malraux. This is a great danger for literature. As a matter of fact, one of the reasons for my own evolution in this regard is that I became aware, after 1948, that I was in the process of constructing an ethic for the writer alone. *Une morale de l'écrivain.* I wanted to get away from that. I wanted to deal with all problems. Not just with the world of the writer.

PUCCIANI: I would like to ask you something about Existential psychoanalysis. I am reminded of this because of Frantz's "madness." Could one not say that Existential psychoanalysis is psychoanalysis for normal people whereas Freud requires a category of the "pathological"?

SARTRE: Certainly Existential psychoanalysis is concerned with normal people. Conventional psychoanalysis as it is practiced today in America and France is a plague. It encloses the individual in his malady. There is no way out.

PUCCIANI: This is somewhat erratic now, but I would like to raise another question of engagement. I have often heard Existential engagement criticized—by my students, for example—on the grounds that it is a doctrine for heroes. I remember one student's asking me: "How can the little people be engaged?"

SARTRE: That is very interesting. Yes. That may be a problem. But I wonder if there is not a difference there between France and the United States. I should imagine that in California, for example, where everything more or less works well . . .

PUCCIANI: Hm!

SARTRE: . . . yes, badly, well, but it more or less works . . . I should imagine there would be a lack of *cadres* for engagement. But this is not true of France. There are many *cadres* here where a student like the one you mention could find a place for individual action. And I mean both on the Right and on the Left.

PUCCIANI: This brings me to a last question about engagement and the effectiveness of the writer. There is great interest in Existentialism. In California, for example, which is very remote from your world. I wonder if that interest could exist if you had not given literary form to your work?

SARTRE: Literature is certainly very important. Yes, I know what you mean. And I do believe that we must continue to give literary form to our work. It is the writer's only chance, as I have said everywhere. At the same time, literature is not the only way. This should not be taken to mean, however, that literature should not be engaged. I am not offering any alibis. I am less sanguine than I used to be, but I still believe the writer can help—if it is only to prevent the worst from taking place.

Source: Oreste F. Pucciani, "An Interview with Jean-Paul Sarte," in *Tulane Drama Review*, Vol. 5, No. 3, March 1961, p. 12–18.

SOURCES

Cohen-Solal, Annie, *Jean-Paul Sartre: A Life*, edited by Cornel West, translated by Anna Cancogni, New Press, 2005.

Coombes, Sam, "The Early Sartre and Ideology," in *Sartre Studies International*, Vol. 9, No. 1, June 2003, p. 54.

Flynn, Thomas, *Existentialism: A Very Short Introduction*, Oxford University Press, 2006.

"Jean-Paul Sartre," in *Nobel Prize in Literature 1964*, http://nobelprize.org/nobel_prizes/literature/laureates/1964/sartre-bio.html (accessed July 23, 2008).

Kedward, Roderick, *Occupied France: Collaboration and Resistance, 1940-1944*, Wiley-Blackwell, 1991.

McManus, Barbara F., "Outline of Aristotle's Theory of Tragedy in the *Poetics*," in *College of New Rochelle CLS 267 Topics Web page*, http://www.cnr.edu/home/bmcmanus/poetics.html (accessed July 30, 2008).

Oesterle, J. A., "*Poetics* (Aristotelian)," in *New Catholic Encyclopedia*, 2nd ed., Vol. 11, Thomson Gale, 2003, pp. 433–35.

Sartre, Jean-Paul, *The Flies*, in *No Exit and Three Other Plays*, Vintage Books, 1955, pp. 49–127.

Weales, Gerald, "Whatever Happened to Jean-Paul Sartre," in the *Hudson Review*, Vol. 13, No. 3, Autumn 1960, pp. 465–69.

Williams, Timothy J., "Sartre, Marcel, and *The Flies*: Restless Orestes in Search of a Cafe," in the *Midwest Quarterly*, Vol. 48, No. 3, Spring 2007, p. 376.

FURTHER READING

Beauvoir, Simone de, *Adieux: A Farewell to Sartre*, translated by Patrick O'Brian, Pantheon, 1984.
> Beauvoir's intimate memoir traces her tumultuous relationship with Sartre and tells of Sartre in his final days. She also shows how they shaped one another's ideas and writings over time.

Boyd, Douglas, *Voices from the Dark Years: The Truth about Occupied France 1940-1945*, History Press, 2007.
> This study contains first-person testimonials from French citizens who lived under the German occupation, providing a day-to-day look at life in France from 1940 to 1945.

Heidegger, Martin, *Being and Time*, translated by John Macquarrie and Edward Robinson, Harper Perennial Modern Classics, 2008.
> Heidegger's work was extremely influential on Sartre's philosophies. It is likely that Sartre was familiar with *Being and Time*, first published in French in 1927. Indeed, the main title of his first major philosophical work *Being and Nothingness* is too similar to *Being and Time* to be coincidental.

Sartre, Jean-Paul, *Being and Nothingness: An Essay on Phenomenological Ontology*, translated by Hazel E. Barnes, Washington Square Press, 1993.
> First published in French in 1943, this book sets forth the foundation of Sartre's existential philosophies and of existentialism as a movement. It informs readings of Sartre's fiction and provides insight into the history of twentieth-century thought.

Florence

ALICE CHILDRESS
1949

Childress's first play, *Florence*, a one-act play given her mother's name, was written in 1949 but not published until the following year in *Masses & Mainstream* (October 1950), a predominately communist magazine that published African American literature. Childress produced the first performance of *Florence* at the American Negro Theatre in New York City in 1949. The setting for the play is a segregated railroad station in which a black woman and a white woman wait for a train to take them to New York City. The play focuses on the corrosive effects of racism and stereotyping and how prevalent they were during this period. Childress uses realism to depict the prejudices that many white people had about African Americans. She also challenges ideas about what should constitute a suitable career for African American women. Florence's mother, who initially does not support her daughter's dream of becoming an actress in New York, changes her mind about her daughter's career when she is faced with the racial stereotypes put forth by a white woman. The white woman, Mrs. Carter, is so firmly entrenched in her own vision of the truth that she has no interest in learning that she is wrong. Childress's first play also reveals the difficulties that black actors face when trying to find work in the white-dominated theatrical world. *Florence* was first presented off Broadway by the American Negro Theatre. Childress directed and starred in this first production of the play. *Florence* is available in *Wines in the Wilderness:*

Alice Childress (*G. Marshall Wilson | Ebony Collection | AP Images*)

Plays by African American Women from the Harlem Renaissance to the Present (1990), edited by Elizabeth Brown-Guillory.

AUTHOR BIOGRAPHY

Alice Childress was born either October 12, 1916, or October 12, 1920, in Charleston, South Carolina. Her birth name might have been either Herndon or Henderson, and it is thought that her mother's name was Florence. While the facts surrounding her birth and parentage are in doubt, what is known is that as a small child she was taken to New York to be raised by her grandmother. Childress, who dropped out of high school after two years, was raised in Harlem in New York City by her grandmother, Eliza Campbell. Campbell had only an elementary school education, but she was an accomplished storyteller whose talent sparked in Childress an early

interest in telling stories. Although her formal education ended early, after her grandmother's death in the early 1930s, Childress continued to educate herself during hours spent reading at the public library. She was married to Alvin Childress during the 1930s, with whom she had a daughter, Jean. Childress was very private about her personal life, so little is known about her relationships or her daughter, but it is known that the couple divorced after Alvin took an acting job on television and moved to Hollywood. Childress would later marry Nathan Woodard in 1957.

Childress had joined the American Negro Theatre (ANT) in Harlem when she was twenty, with an appearance in *On Strivers's Row*. Childress was an actress and director with ANT for ten years and appeared in some of their biggest hits, including *A Midsummer Night's Dream*, *Natural Man*, and *Anna Lucasta*. She wrote her first play, *Florence*, in 1949. This one-act play examines the prejudice of both white and black people and establishes the direction many of Childress's subsequent plays would take. She followed this early success with another play, *Just A Little Simple* (1950), an adaptation of the Langston Hughes novel, *Simple Speaks His Mind*. Childress's third play, written in 1952, *Gold Through the Trees*, became the first play by a black woman to be professionally produced on the American stage. Childress's next play, *Trouble in Mind* (1955), focused on a topic she knew well—the difficulties black women face as actresses. This play was very successful, and Childress became the first woman to win the Village Voice Obie Award, for the best original off-Broadway play of the 1955–1956 season. A revised edition of this play was published in *Black Theatre: A Twentieth-Century Collection of the Work of Its Best Playwrights*.

Childress next composed *Wedding Band* (1966) and *Wine in the Wilderness*. The latter was written for public television in 1969 and was the first play broadcast by WGBS Boston as part of the series "On Being Black." This was followed by another one-act play, *String* (1969), which was an adaptation of a Guy de Maupassant short story, "A Piece of String." Another one-act play, *Mojo: A Black Love Story*, followed in 1970.

Childress continued to write plays, including two for children—*When the Rattlesnake Sounds* (1975) and *Let's Hear It for the Queen* (1976). Childress also wrote several novels. The first, *Like One of the Family: Conversations from a Domestic's Life* (1956), was based on conversations with black domestic workers. She also wrote several novels for young adults, *A Hero Ain't Nothin' but a Sandwich* (1973), *A Short Walk* (1979), *Rainbow Jordan* (1981), and *Those Other People* (1989). Childress received several awards, including the first Paul Robeson Award for Outstanding Contributions to the Performing Arts from the Black Filmmakers Hall of Fame in 1977. In 1993, Childress received the Lifetime Career Achievement Award from the Association for Theatre in Higher Education. Childress was working on a memoir about her great-grandmother, who was born a slave, when she died of cancer on August 14, 1994, at Astoria General Hospital in Queens, New York.

PLOT SUMMARY

Florence opens as a middle-aged black woman walks on stage and sits down on a bench on the "Colored" side of the railway station waiting room. A low railing separates the setting into a "White" waiting room and a "Colored" waiting room. A young black woman follows behind the older woman and immediately begins to chide the older woman about their early arrival. The younger woman is Marge, who tells her mother that she must force Florence, Marge's sister, to come back home because her son needs her. Mama and Marge also exchange some words about the rent, which is going to be late because the money is being used to try and bring Florence home. Marge reminds Mama to eat the lunch that was packed for her and buy coffee for her lunch before she boards the train, since black passengers are not permitted to enter the dining car. Before she leaves the station, Marge tells Mama that Florence must be forced to return home. Mama reminds Marge that Florence was in a play for two weeks, but Marge replies that her sister's role was as a maid, which only reinforces Marge's argument that there is no future for a black woman as an actress. After Marge leaves, the porter walks in and begins to mop the floor on the white side of the waiting room. He asks Mama if she is going on a trip. When Mama replies that she is going to New York to see Florence, the porter responds that his son in Atlanta saw Florence in a colored film. This is further evidence that Florence has had some success as an actress. The porter next warns Mama that if she needs to go the bathroom, she must use

the colored men's bathroom, since the bathroom for colored women is out of order.

At that moment a well-dressed white woman, Mrs. Carter, comes rushing in and immediately begins to give the porter orders, addressing him as "Boy!" After being reassured that the porter will watch her bags, Mrs. Carter sits down on the white side of the waiting room. Mrs. Carter begins to speak to Mama and explains that after only two days in this small town, she is bored and eager to return home. She insults Mama by asking if she lives in the small town that has her "bored to tears." Mrs. Carter explains that she has only come south to cheer up her brother, whose most recent novel has earned such poor reviews that he has given up writing. When Mama explains that she has never heard of this novel, Mrs. Carter begins to explain the plot, which involves a light-skinned Negro woman who is smart and ambitious but who commits suicide because she is not white. Mrs. Carter explains that all blacks are filled with self-hate because they are not white. When Mama challenges this view of blacks, providing examples of light-skinned blacks who are quite happy and successful, Mrs. Carter abruptly stops the conversation and insists that the subject is too controversial to discuss with a black woman. Mrs. Carter seems genuinely distressed to have upset Mama and tries to reassure her that she is not a racist. She even claims to have "eaten with Negroes." When Mama begins to ignore Mrs. Carter, the white woman sits for a few minutes pretending to read a book, but soon enough she tries again to engage Mama in conversation. In response to Mama's explanation that she is going to New York City to see her daughter, Florence, who is performing on the stage, Mrs. Carter assumes that Florence is a singer, saying, "You people have such a gift" for spirituals. When Mrs. Carter learns that Florence is a dramatic actress, she begins to express pity for Florence, whom she thinks must be pathetically depressed over having chosen a career at which she cannot possibly succeed. Mrs. Carter is also an actress, and she has not had much success. She cannot conceive of the possibility that a black woman could have either talent or success.

When Mrs. Carter brags about all her contacts on the stage, Mama asks if there is any way that the woman can help Florence. Mrs. Carter is quick to say yes and explains that she can get Florence work with a woman who is a writer and director. Mama is excited until she learns that the work Mrs. Carter is proposing for Florence is as a domestic servant, cleaning house. At this point, Mama becomes so upset that she grasps Mrs. Carter by the arm, alarming the white woman, who suddenly understands that she has upset Mama but does not know how. Mama tells Mrs. Carter that she should go back over to the white side of the waiting room, and Mrs. Carter quickly retreats into the "White ladies" bathroom. Just then the porter enters to tell Mama that the train is almost at the station. Mama writes something on a piece of paper and puts the note and the check that she was carrying to pay for Florence's return ticket home from New York into an envelope. She asks the porter to mail the envelope for her and tells him that the note to Florence tells her to "keep trying." The play ends as Mama leaves the stage.

CHARACTERS

Porter Brown

The porter has one foot in the white world and one foot in the black world. By virtue of his job, he moves across the color barrier and the Jim Crow laws that separate white from black. He tells Mama that the bathroom for black women is out of order and that she must use the bathroom for black men, since the law forbids her to use the bathroom for white women. His role is to maintain order, as defined by law, but there is never any doubt that he belongs on the black side of the line. While he is permitted to walk on the white side of the waiting room, he only does so to mop the floors, and when Mrs. Carter enters, she addresses him imperiously as "Boy!" This is clearly a derogatory address for a man who is described as being about fifty years old.

Mrs. Carter

Mrs. Carter is a white woman. She sees herself as tolerant and liberal in her thinking, but her words define her as a racist. She refers to the porter, a man many years her senior, as "boy." Her examples of tolerance include having "eaten with Negros." Mrs. Carter worries about her brother, who is an unsuccessful novelist. He writes about a culture that he neither understands nor is capable of experiencing, which may be why his books do not sell. Mrs. Carter fails to understand that merely observing a different world does not

make the observer an authority. Mama tries to explain that the story Mrs. Carter's brother is telling is not true, but Mrs. Carter rejects this explanation. Mrs. Carter cannot accept that a black woman could know more than her white brother. Mrs. Carter's offer to find Florence a position as a domestic reflects her conviction that if a white woman cannot succeed as an actress, a black woman certainly cannot succeed. Mrs. Carter has no interest in hearing the truth and is blind to her own racism. The depth of her racist ideology is further seen in that the job she presumes is most appropriate for a young black woman is that of a domestic servant. Mrs. Carter genuinely believes that she is doing a good deed in arranging for a black woman to work as a servant. She understands the laws that separate black and white people and is unwilling to challenge those laws.

Florence Whitney

Although Florence never appears in the play, she is the focus of Mama's journey and the reason Mama is sitting in the train station. Florence is a young widow who moved to New York to try and find success as an actress. Although she has not yet achieved stardom, Florence has achieved some small successes on the stage, a fact that encourages her to remain in New York, but she continues to need her mother's financial assistance to survive. Mama explains to the audience that Florence has not felt right about living in the South since her husband was murdered when he tried to vote. Because her husband died while trying to fight injustice, Florence feels she cannot accept the discrimination that black people have been forced to endure for so long. Florence knows that it is only by challenging oppression that black Americans will be able to have the same opportunities as white Americans. Florence is more courageous than her sister Marge and is willing to take risks that her sister will not take.

Mama Whitney

Mama is on her way to New York City to bring her daughter Florence home. She is a strong black woman who is not intimidated either by her daughter Marge or by the white woman, Mrs. Carter. When they first arrive at the railway station, Marge speaks to her mother as if she is so naïve and inexperienced that she cannot be trusted to travel by herself to New York. Ironically, Mama tolerates all this mothering from Marge because

Marge is her daughter, but Mama grows less patient with every new warning and bit of advice. She finally complains that Marge is treating her like she is "a northern greenhorn." Mama remains polite, but her responses to Marge suggest that she is ready for her daughter to return home, which is exactly what Mama encourages Marge to do. Mama is also polite to Mrs. Carter, even though the woman is insulting and racially insensitive. Only in her conversation with the porter does Mama appear to relax. Their conversation is natural and easy. If Mama seems only slightly impatient with Marge, she is less reticent when confronted with Mrs. Carter's racism. Mama is brave enough to contradict the stereotypes that Mrs. Carter offers about black women. Mama is not at all intimidated by the white woman, who breezes into the station wearing furs and jewelry, which she dumps casually on the bench. Mama remains polite and in control until Mrs. Carter insults Florence by offering to find her a job as a domestic servant, as if that is the only job for which a young black woman is qualified. Mama then grabs Mrs. Carter by the arm and tells her to return to her side of the waiting room. Such an action takes courage and strength.

Marge Whitney

Marge is Florence's sister. Although the audience never meets Florence, she is clearly a contrast to her sister, Marge. Marge thinks she must accept her place as a black woman living in a segregated world, while Florence challenges the notion that she cannot succeed in the career she has chosen. Marge wants Florence to return to the South and give up her dream of succeeding in a career dominated by white people. Marge has been helping her mother raise Florence's child, since the young widow moved to New York, but now Marge argues that the child needs his mother. She rejects the idea that Florence might be happier or more successful away from home. When Mama reminds Marge that Florence has not felt right about living in the South since her husband was murdered when he tried to vote, Marge responds that other people do not feel right about living in the South and that Florence would not feel right no matter where she lived because "she must think she's white!" These words reveal that Marge does not understand her sister's need to fight against a system of oppression. Marge has no desire to challenge her role in the world. She does not understand why

Florence would apply for a job at a department store that does not hire black people for positions that deal with the public; she does not understand that it is only by challenging oppression that circumstances will change. Marge is not as brave as Florence. Marge lacks her sister's courage and instead focuses on forcing Florence to accept the rules that define black people as lesser human beings.

THEMES

Limitations and Opportunities

The characters in *Florence* are constrained by racist laws that limit their opportunities for change. Marge sees herself as unable to change either herself or the world in which she lives. Racism has created emotional and mental limitations that have convinced Marge that she must continue to know her place and not try to resist or challenge the status quo. In a real sense, Mrs. Carter is also the victim of an oppressive society that makes her incapable of recognizing that her brother's failure to be a successful writer is also a result of laws and customs that oppress black people, while creating an artificial view of a world that is not real. Mrs. Carter's brother romanticizes racist images to such a degree that he limits his own success as a novelist. While Mama initially seems to accept the limitations placed on black people, by the end of the play she is in agreement with Florence. She understands that the only way to change a racist world is to challenge racism and thus force white people to acknowledge the rights of black people to have the same opportunities as those provided to white people.

Racism

The title of Childress's play is named after one of Mama's daughters, Florence, but the character for whom the play is titled never appears. The play is only peripherally about Florence Whitney. The play is about racism. Racism lies at the center of a law that prevents blacks and whites from crossing the artificially constructed line that keeps these two groups separate in the American South. Childress uses her play as a way to examine how legal authority and social custom serve as forces to maintain racism within society. The actions and words of the characters

TOPICS FOR FURTHER STUDY

- Drama is meant to be seen and heard and not simply read. With one other student from your class, choose a section of dialogue from *Florence* to memorize and then present to your classmates. After you have completed your mini-performance, ask each of your classmates to write down at least one thing that they learned from hearing and seeing your performance of the play that they did not know just from reading it.

- Beah Richards, Aishah Rahman, and Lorraine Hansberry are three black female playwrights who were contemporaries of Childress. Choose one of these writers to research in some depth, and then write a report in which you outline the kinds of plays this playwright composed, the themes she addressed and characters she created, and why she chose to write.

- Near the end of the play, the audience learns that Florence's husband was murdered when he tried to vote. Research voting laws and restrictions that were used to keep black men and women from voting in the United States. Prepare a poster presentation in which you use photos and diagrams to illustrate the history of minority disenfranchisement in the United States, the enactment of

the National Voting Rights Act of 1965, the voter registration movement, and current concerns regarding minority voting rights.

- Staging is important in bringing the images of a written play to life for a theatrical audience. Draw or illustrate in some way one of the images that Childress's play created in your mind as you were reading. You may also use photography. Then write an essay that explains how you chose the image and what you think the image adds to your understanding of this drama.

- Imagine for a moment that you are a producer and you plan to stage this play on Broadway. Prepare an oral report in which you explain which contemporary actors you would choose to play the four roles and why you would select them. Pay special attention to the characterizations that you will be creating and how these actors would portray these four characters. Give examples of other characters played by the chosen actors and describe how your expectations for the roles would demand similar or different performances from the actors. Your analysis of the characters and actors should include enough information to support your choices.

---

reveal that racism is more than white oppression of black people. When Marge expresses her belief that black people need to know their own place, she is helping to maintain the racism that oppresses her. Racism is also denoted by the separate but unequal bathroom signs designated for white and black use. The bathroom for black women is labeled "Colored women," while the bathroom for white women is labeled "White ladies." The implication is clear—black women are not ladies. Because the bathroom for black women is out of order, Mama is told she must use the bathroom for black men, even though doing so is humiliating. She may also lose the

sense of personal space and privacy that women expect in using a public restroom.

Stereotypes

Mrs. Carter tells Mama that her brother has written a novel, which has not been reviewed favorably by the critics. Her brother is so discouraged that he is no longer able to write. Mrs. Carter's brother has written a book based on stereotypes. She explains that her brother has written about Negroes, but upon hearing the description of the plot, Mama says that his work is not true. Mrs. Carter's brother cannot

"Colored Waiting Room" sign (© Corbis)

know or understand the black experience because he cannot comprehend or identify with a world he has not experienced. The laws that separate blacks and whites also keep each group from each other's world. Because Mrs. Carter's brother cannot know what it means to be a black person, he is forced to rely upon stereotypes to construct his characters. As a result, his characters, for whom his sister claims her brother "suffers so," are not real enough to capture a reading audience. This would-be novelist creates a young black woman who is described as lovely, intelligent, and ambitious, but because she is not white, she kills herself. Readers are supposed to believe that this young woman, who wants to be a lawyer, is so ashamed of being black that she does not want to live. The novel is a failure because the stereotypical characters are so unreal. When Mama offers examples to support her argument that this fictional character is not based on reality, Mrs. Carter rejects the idea. All that she knows about black life is what she has learned from cultural stereotyping. She thinks that black women are satisfied to work as domestics, housekeepers, and servants, because that is how she and her friends employ them. Mrs. Carter cannot imagine that a young black woman can be a successful actress because it is so hard for a white woman to succeed on the stage. Mrs. Carter accepts the stereotypes that define black women

as less talented and thus less successful than white women. Because legal traditions and social customs keep whites and blacks from intermingling, all that they can know about one another are the stereotypes of the past.

STYLE

Realism

Realism is a literary movement that began in the nineteenth century and continued to influence literature in the twentieth century. In general, realism is an effort by a writer to depict a world honestly and truthfully. Realist writers usually depict the lives of ordinary people who struggle to survive in the lower or middle class. Such writers often espouse a democratic ideal, using realism as a way to argue for equality. Realists are concerned with ethical issues and with ordinary events. They often reject the traditional forms of a genre. For example, Childress rejects the traditional five-act play in favor of a one-act play that depicts the struggles this family faces against oppression and racism. There is no heroic sacrifice, just ordinary people doing what they must do to survive. Mama is not a dramatic hero. She is an ordinary mother who is willing to sacrifice to help her daughter. She does not have much money, and she will be late paying the rent because she is using the money to take the train to New York. Childress's point is that Mama is just like any other mother who sacrifices for her children. She suffers because her daughter lacks the opportunities that white daughters receive. She is a recognizable human being, the type of person that realism seeks to illuminate.

One-Act Dramatic Structure

Florence is a one-act play with prose dialogue, stage directions, and no interior dialogue. There are no soliloquies, and thus, the thoughts of the characters are reflected in their speeches, and all action must occur on stage. The actors address one another and not the audience. In ancient Greek plays the sections of the drama were signified by the appearance of the chorus and were usually divided into five acts. This is the formula for most serious drama from the Greeks to the Romans and through the Renaissance, including Elizabethan playwrights such as William Shakespeare. The five acts denote the structure of dramatic action: exposition, complication or rising action, climax, falling action, and catastrophe or resolution. The five-act structure was followed until the nineteenth century when playwright Henrik Ibsen combined the last two acts into one act. During the twentieth century, audiences became more accustomed to three-act plays. One-act plays have been performed since the Greek period, but they were much less common then. Since the end of the nineteenth century, however, one-act plays have been more widespread. Early in the twentieth century they were associated with vaudeville and comedy, but more recently one-act plays have featured serious themes and are often presented with other one-act plays at a single performance.

Childress's one-act play mostly follows the traditional structure of dramatic action. The exposition is at the beginning of the play when the audience learns that Florence has left the South to escape memories of the death of her husband. She has had some success but is now in need of money to help her survive while she looks for more work. The complication or rising action occurs when Mrs. Carter and Mama clash over the notion that a black woman would kill herself because she is not white. The climax is the point of a drama when the action takes a dramatic turn. In this case, it occurs when Mama realizes that Mrs. Carter is offering a domestic job to Florence because she assumes that is the most suitable work for a black woman. The falling action signals the resolution of the plot. This occurs when Mama decides to send money to Florence and continue to support her efforts to escape the South. The catastrophe is usually the death of the hero, but there is no catastrophe in this play.

HISTORICAL CONTEXT

Jim Crow Laws

When Mama and Mrs. Carter are forced to sit in areas designated for "Colored" and for "Whites" and required to use bathrooms labeled for "White ladies" and "Colored women," they are experiencing laws and customs put in place through Jim Crow laws. The term *Jim Crow* is thought to have originated in a song by that name sung by black-face minstrels performing early in the nineteenth century. The term eventually became identified with state and local laws that mandated segregation in public facilities. These laws were first enacted after Civil War Reconstruction ended in 1876, at which point many southern states began to create laws that segregated black people. Some laws were designed to separate blacks from whites on public transportation, such as on trains, as Marge notes when she warns Mama that she will be unable to eat in the dining car on the train. In some states, miscegenation laws made it illegal for a black person to marry a white person. Poll taxes and literacy tests prevented many black citizens from voting. Sharecropping practices prevented black farmers from owning their own land, while separate school systems kept black children from receiving an education equal to that received by white children. Eventually, nearly all public facilities were segregated to keep black and white people apart. Public restaurants, theaters, drinking fountains, and bathrooms all contained restrictions against white and black people mingling together. Violence, most commonly lynching, prevented many black people from taking action against Jim Crow laws. A major step toward change came in 1954, when the Supreme Court ruled in *Brown v. Board of Education* that segregated public schools were unconstitutional. However, schools would remain segregated for many more years. The passage of the Civil Rights Act of 1965 and the Voting Rights Act of 1965 brought an end to legalized segregation.

Segregation in the New York Theater

Mama's daughter Florence is a struggling actress in New York. Her efforts mirror those of Childress, who was herself a struggling black actress. The primary venue for black actors at the time was the American Negro Theatre (ANT), which was a part of the Federal Theatre Project, a product of the Great Depression that was designed to create jobs. The depression of the 1930s created unemployment for white actors and stage workers, but the effect on black actors was more significant, simply because there were already far fewer opportunities for black actors and stage crew. In white productions, black actors were cast as domestic help or as slaves who loved their masters and thus were content with their lives. Most often, though, black people were depicted as comic figures, such as in minstrel shows. Dramas were written by white playwrights whose views of black life were skewed by their

COMPARE
&
CONTRAST

- **1940s:** *Negro Digest* begins publication in 1942 and proves that there is an audience for magazines that focus on the black experience. In 1945, *Ebony* magazine begins publishing the first U.S. picture magazine directed at a black readership. The magazine sells out its initial press run. Another magazine directed to a black audience, *Masses & Mainstream*, in which Childress would publish *Florence*, is introduced in 1948.

  Today: There are more than twenty U.S. magazines directed toward a black audience, including *African American Golf Digest*, *Black Enterprise*, and *Black Issues in Higher Education*. *Ebony* is still being published.

- **1940s:** In 1947, Jackie Robinson becomes the first African American baseball player allowed to play major league baseball. Although he is a member of the Brooklyn Dodgers team, Robinson is still subject to segregation under the Jim Crow laws and cannot stay at the same hotel as the white players when the team plays in the American South.

  Today: Major league sports teams are fully integrated, and African American players are common in baseball, football, and basketball. On many teams, African American players dominate team rosters.

- **1940s:** In 1948, President Harry S. Truman signs an executive order that requires the U.S. military to desegregate all armed forces. Prior to this time, black soldiers fought in both World War I and World War II, but the armed forces were segregated and black servicemen were placed in separate units.

  Today: A Pentagon study reveals that 75 percent of African American military personnel have experienced racially offensive behavior, according to a November 1999 article in the *Washington Post*.

- **1940s:** The first African American to win an Academy Award (Oscar) is Hattie McDaniel, for her supporting performance as "Mammy" in the 1939 film *Gone With the Wind*. It would be twenty-four years before another African American actor, Sidney Poitier, would win an Oscar as an actor in a lead role, for his performance in *Lilies of the Field*.

  Today: In 2002, Denzel Washington and Halle Berry receive Oscars for their respective leading roles in *Training Day* and *Monster's Ball*. This marks the first time an African American performing in a leading role has won an Oscar since Sidney Poitier in 1964, although a number of African Americans have won Oscars for supporting roles or for composing music for films in the intervening years.

---

ignorance of the real world. ANT was established in Harlem, New York, in 1940 as a way to train black actors and to provide them the opportunity to appear on stage in productions that would depict black life in the United States more accurately. ANT staged eighteen plays, including *Anna Lucasta*, which starred Childress. This play was so successful that it eventually was produced on Broadway, where it ran for more than 950 performances. ANT helped to launch the careers of Sidney Poitier, Ozzie Davis, Ruby Dee, and Harry Belafonte, as well as many others. ANT also provided a forum for black playwrights, whose work was intended to depict the reality of black life. By the end of the 1940s, ANT was disbanded, and while there were more roles for black actors on the New York stage, the roles had not improved beyond the stereotypes of the past, which is why Childress began writing plays, including her first drama, *Florence*.

Jazz singer *(Bruce Ayres / Stone / Getty Images)*

CRITICAL OVERVIEW

The New York theater world, and especially plays presented on Broadway or even Off Broadway, have always been eagerly watched and reviewed. Even during the 1940s, including the World War II years, New York theater productions were generally well reviewed—unless, of course, the play was presented at the American Negro Theatre. Plays written by black playwrights and starring black actors did not receive the kind of press coverage that greeted most other New York theater productions. Accordingly, there is little evidence of how *Florence* was greeted by the public. Moreover, little was written about Childress at her death in 1994. In a very brief obituary printed by the *New York Times*, Sheila Rule notes the controversies that surrounded some of Childress's work and that her children's book *A Hero Ain't Nothin' but a Sandwich* has been the object of censorship by school districts. Childress's most famous play, *Wedding Band*, an interracial love story, was not produced in New York until several years after it was written in the early 1960s, due to the controversial nature of the subject. Rule, who lists Childress first as a novelist and actress and last as a playwright, provides little critical discussion of Childress's accomplishments or her contributions as an author.

It has been the province of literary critics, rather than theater critics, to assess Childress's legacy as a playwright and author. In an essay in *Black Women Writers (1950–1980): A Critical Evaluation*, Samuel A. Hay writes that *Florence* is typical of Childress's plays in that the author is "interested in a well-crafted situation" and that she is capable of changing "her dramatic structure" to fit the requirements of plot. Both these comments suggest a playwright of considerable talent who possesses the knowledge to make the dramatic genre fulfill her needs. This ability, according to Hay, "sets Childress apart" from other playwrights. She is capable of switching the "protagonist-antagonist functions" and of creating "several other revolutionary changes in order to support her political and ethical concerns." Childress, then, fits a tradition of playwrights who are capable of crafting "well-structured plays which aim to show how things ought to be, or where they have gone wrong."

This is, of course, what Childress does in *Florence* when she shows that racism cannot be defeated until people are able to recognize their own deeply buried prejudices.

In an essay in *African American Review*, Will Harris provides another critical evaluation of Childress's importance as a playwright. Harris refers to *Florence* as "revolutionary" in "its staging of a black feminist ideology." Childress, according to Harris, is one of the early black women playwrights who was capable of taking the prevailing image of black women as servants and transforming it "into a potent symbol" of strength. Childress's ability to transform negative images of black women into strong positive images of strength and resilience is an important legacy that Childress leaves for her readers and for those who are privileged to see her plays performed. Although it is rare to see a performance of *Florence*, both Hay and Harris make clear that Childress's contributions to theater and her images of strong black women should be remembered.

CRITICISM

Sheri Metzger Karmiol

Karmiol has a doctorate in English Renaissance literature. She teaches literature and drama at the University of New Mexico, and she is also a professional writer and the author of several reference texts on poetry and drama. In this essay on Florence, *Karmiol discusses Childress's message about racism and the oppression that black women face.*

Alice Childress noted in her essay "A Woman Playwright Speaks Her Mind," published in *Freedomways* in 1966, that the United States extended basic rights and opportunities to foreign visitors and to immigrants that it did not offer to black Americans. International travelers who visited the United States were free to travel, seek shelter in hotels, and eat at restaurants that black Americans were barred from entering. Visitors could ride public transportation and were not forced to sit in the back of a bus or to surrender their seats for the comfort of white passengers. Segregation denied these freedoms to black citizens. This injustice is manifest in Childress's play *Florence* when Mama Whitney and Mrs. Carter are seated on opposite sides of the divided railway station, when Mama must use the men's bathroom because she is not permitted to use the bathroom

WHAT DO I READ NEXT?

- Childress's play *Wine in the Wilderness* (1969) examines what it means to be a black American in a segregated and racist society. The play examines several of the issues touched upon in *Florence*, including the lack of opportunities provided to African Americans.

- *The Wedding Band*, another play by Childress, examines racism and intolerance through the eyes of a couple trying to find acceptance for their interracial love affair. Because the play's subject was so controversial in its time, *The Wedding Band* was not produced until 1966, several years after it was written.

- *A Raisin in the Sun* (1959), by Lorraine Hansberry, explores segregation, racism, and the lack of economic opportunities that beset African Americans.

- Maya Angelou's autobiography, *I Know Why the Caged Bird Sings* (1970), details her childhood in rural Arkansas. Readers are introduced to racism and segregation as the author confronts these realities, and they are also exposed to the importance of family in shaping the African American experience.

- *In Search of Our Mothers' Gardens* (1974), by Alice Walker, is an autobiographical essay that argues for the importance of matrilineage, or descent as traced through the maternal line, in the growth of a young black girl.

- The collection *Black Theatre, USA: Plays by African Americans: The Recent Period, 1935–Today* (1996), by Ted Shine and edited by James V. Hatch, includes plays by Childress, Langston Hughes, Lorraine Hansberry, Abram Hill, and James Baldwin, as well as many plays by less well-known playwrights.

labeled "White Ladies," and when Mama must bring a sack lunch on the train because she is not allowed to enter the dining car. Childress thought that writing was an important way to tell the truth

CHILDRESS USES HER SHORT PLAY
FLORENCE TO EXPLORE BOTH THE OBSERVABLE AND
THE UNSEEN SYMBOLS OF RACISM THAT OPPRESSED
WOMEN IN 1940S AMERICAN LIFE."

about racism and that a black woman writing about black women's lives was an essential step in exposing the destructiveness of racism. Childress uses her short play *Florence* to explore both the observable and the unseen symbols of racism that oppressed women in 1940s American life.

In *Florence*, two women sit on opposite sides of the color line in a segregated railway station. The conversation between them gives voice to Childress's concerns about the insidiousness of racism and the extent to which it permeates American society. The railway waiting room is divided by a low railing that creates two separate areas within the room, one for "White" passengers and another for "Colored" passengers. The railing can be easily crossed, as both Mama and Mrs. Carter do at separate times in the play, so the audience understands that the railing is a symbol of division and not simply a barrier designed to keep white and black passengers on different sides of the room. As Elizabeth Brown-Guillory notes in her book *Their Place on the Stage*, the railing is "a physical and emotional barrier between whites and blacks." It is one of the symbols that Childress uses to remind her audience that black and white people have been kept apart by artificial barriers. That the barrier fails actually to separate the two women illustrates that their basic humanity is the same. When each woman is impelled by emotion to confront the other, she easily crosses to the other side. When Mama challenges Mrs. Carter's defense of her brother's notion that a black woman would commit suicide because she is not white, she crosses the railing and moves one foot into the white side of the room. Similarly, when Mrs. Carter offers to find employment for Florence as a domestic, her excitement at being able to help Mama moves her to the colored side of the room. Brown-Guillory explains that the railing serves a purpose, even though it does not

effectively separate white and black. According to Brown-Guillory, "Conversations and actions are structured around this dividing line that reminds the audience that there are special limitations placed on blacks and whites." When Mama has had enough of Mrs. Carter's conversation, she reminds her that "it's against the law" for Mrs. Carter to cross over to the colored side of the room. With those few words, Childress reminds the audience that while laws may separate black and white, ignorance and bias present barriers that are much harder to overcome.

The special limitations placed on black and white that Brown-Guillory observes also remind the audience that black and white passengers are not only separate but they are treated as unequal as well. The separate bathrooms are a reminder that even in matters of physical need, black passengers must be kept separate from white passengers. It is not enough, though, that the bathrooms are labeled White and Colored. They are also labeled "White ladies" and "Colored women." The immediate implication is that "Colored" women are not ladies. The word "ladies" suggests a social status that is missing from the word "women." Ladies have a higher social position than other women. In the aristocracy, the wife of an aristocrat is simply titled "Lady." Even in the United States, where supposedly equality eliminates social class, the term "lady" denotes a woman of refinement, of social position, and of manners. The use of the word, woman simply designates a person of the female gender, a human being who possesses certain feminine, and largely biological, characteristics. This common term suggests nothing extraordinary beyond a woman's humanness. The division of these two groups of female into "ladies" and "women" in *Florence* is taken one step further when the porter tells Mama that "if you go to the restroom, use the Colored men's." According to the porter, the bathroom for "Colored" women is out of order, and so Mama must use the men's bathroom. This middle-aged woman must debase herself in order to use the bathroom. As if the humiliation of separate seating in the waiting room and separate bathrooms for white and black people is not sufficient, Mama must also use the "Colored" men's bathroom and, as Brown-Guillory reminds readers, "risk having her privacy invaded," should a man walk in on her. In this way, Childress reminds her audience that separate is also unequal. White women, who are defined by the signage as superior to black women, are not forced to submit themselves to a degrading experience to meet their physical needs. Racism has implications beyond the obvious separate bathrooms; it also strikes deeply into the very definition of what it means to be a human being.

Mrs. Carter is Childress's reminder that even those who think themselves open-minded, generous, and tolerant can themselves be guilty of racism. Childress maintains in a 1993 interview with Shirley Jordan, published in *Broken Silences: Interviews with Black and White Women Writers*, that people, including black people, who say they know nothing about racism are failing to look beyond the obvious. Childress claims that everyone has "heard, felt, and seen racism, but many do not wish to see it." It is "comforting," according to Childress, to deny racism and painful to admit it exists. For example, Mrs. Carter defends herself to Mama as someone who is not a racist. She has given money "to a Negro college for scholarships," and she has "eaten with Negroes." These are surface expressions of tolerance. Racism is much deeper and more carefully hidden. For instance, when Mama explains that her daughter is trying to make a living on stage, Mrs. Carter automatically assumes that Florence is a singer, telling Mama, "You people have such a gift" for music, especially spirituals. Mrs. Carter sees nothing wrong with referring to Florence as one of "you people," as if she is not an individual with talents that extend beyond the stereotypes that Mrs. Carter uses to define black people. Mrs. Carter's complete unawareness that she is racist suggests that racism is deeply ingrained into American life. A woman who thinks of herself as liberal and tolerant of differences can with a few words reveal how deeply racism permeates her thinking.

In her interview with Jordan, Childress expresses concern that white women who work hard for equal rights do not understand that the struggle for equality is more complex and more difficult for black women. It is not sufficient to have the same opportunities as black men; black women want to have the same opportunities as white women. Childress explains that "the greatest barrier between white and black women is racial." White women cannot understand the struggle of black women because they have not experienced racism. Mrs. Carter's remarks illustrate Childress's point. When told that Florence wants to be a dramatic actress, Mrs. Carter

responds that Florence's attempt is "pathetic." Mrs. Carter reveals that she is an actress who has not worked in six months. She claims to be well known, and if she, a white woman with so many contacts in the business, cannot succeed, the implication is that Florence will never be a success. To Mama's argument that Florence was encouraged to be an actress because she has talent, Mrs. Carter states that "there are loads of unscrupulous whites up there" who cannot be trusted to be honest in assessing Florence's talent. Since it is obvious that a black woman cannot have the talent to succeed as an actress, Mrs. Carter is willing to help Florence find a position as a domestic. It never occurs to Mrs. Carter that she is being condescending or insulting or racist. She does not understand Mama's anger and quickly retreats to the "White ladies" bathroom to hide until it is time to board the train. Mama's response to Mrs. Carter's racism, her cowardice, and her condescension is to send money to help Florence. Rather than force Florence to return home to the hatred, racism, and restrictive blindness of the South, Mama uses Mrs. Carter's racism as the impetus to help her daughter succeed. It is clear that Mama does not have much money; in fact, the trip to New York to bring Florence home creates a significant financial hardship. More important than money, though, is the need to help one black woman survive in a world that devalues her.

Florence reveals how black women face oppression on two fronts: they are discriminated against both as women and as African Americans. It is this illumination of racism and its insidious pervasiveness that makes *Florence* a drama worth studying. In her 1966 essay, "A Woman Playwright Speaks Her Mind," Childress contends that black women writers need to tell the story of black women who have struggled to survive. In *Florence*, Childress does just that.

Source: Sheri Metzger Karmiol, Critical Essay on *Florence*, in *Drama for Students*, Gale, Cengage Learning, 2009.

Olga Dugan

In the following excerpt, Dugan discusses Childress's works, including Florence, *and identifies their importance in the history of dramatic literature in the United States.*

In *Their Place on the Stage: Black Women Playwrights in America* (1988), Elizabeth Brown-Guillory declared that "Alice Childress is the only black woman in America whose plays have been

"CHILDRESS WROTE *FLORENCE* IN KEEPING
WITH PRINCIPLES OF CONTENT, FORM, AND
COMMITMENT TO WHICH SHE REMAINED TRUE
THROUGHOUT THE YEARS SHE FOCUSED ON
PLAYWRITING."

written, produced, and published over a period of four decades." Childress wrote seventeen plays. Six have a history of both production and publication. Four of these plays, appearing on stage between 1949 and 1969 when she was writing and working exclusively in and for the American theatre, have procured for her many coveted awards, and great visibility. But it is still the norm to walk into popular bookstores and not see any plays by Alice Childress on the shelves. And it is possible to finger through publishers' catalogues under author, title, or subject and not find a listing for Childress, or discover that the few single editions of her plays have long been and remain out of print. This should not be since over the last twenty years, Childress's plays have been important subject matter for critical evaluation of the history of dramatic literature in the United States.

Through historical-critical analysis of modern American drama in general and of black drama in particular, as well as black feminist criticism, feminist theories of dramatic criticism, and a resurgent wave of curricular inclusion of "drama as literature," critics have analyzed Childress's plays ultimately as "literature to be performed." But they also maintain in their analyses the fabulist view of the playwright as a storyteller, as an interpreter of reality. In their works, Samuel Hay, C. W. E. Bigsby, Carlton and Barbara Molette, Mance Williams, Genevieve Fabre, Emory Lewis, and Loften Mitchell reevaluate the themes of racial injustice and the struggle for human rights at the center of the stories Childress's plays tell. They all conclude that critics need to reconsider her plays as serious contributions to the literary and theatrical histories of how drama functions in American culture and society.

Elizabeth Brown-Guillory, Margaret B. Wilkerson, John O. Killens, Trudier Harris, Rosemary

Curb, and Jeanne-Marie A. Miller have written books and articles examining the generation of Childress's strong black female protagonists, and her subjectivity of black women's issues concerning legal, educational, social, political, and economic struggle in this country. These scholars link Childress's plays to a literary tradition of black women writers from the New Negro Renaissance to modern and contemporary movements.

In the same vein, Gayle Austin, Helene Keyssar, and Janet Brown explore plot and theme as ideological structures of a feminist premise and method of presentation in drama. They include Childress's plays among those of women dramatists from the United States and Europe in studies that reveal a dialogue on the "political poetics" of women's drama.

Finally, anthologists Elizabeth Brown-Guillory, Margaret B. Wilkerson, Mari Evans, James V. Hatch and Ted Shine, and Lindsay Patterson reveal Childress's significance as a dramatic theorist and consummate craftsperson. Moreover, these anthologists have made the plays, at least those already previously published and produced, available for study that has led to a number of academic essays and doctoral theses.

This writer aligns herself with the scholars, teachers, and playwrights who have given voice to the demand for a critical hearing, long overdue for African-American theorist and playwright Alice Childress, and her contributions to American drama. In 1993, just a year before her death, when I told Ms. Childress personally about my own literary-historical studies of the plays, she only smiled at me and replied firmly, "tell the truth." I have taken up the challenge to do so. In this article I discuss a theory of black self-determinist theatre that emerges from the essays Childress wrote over two decades. This theory establishes the central theme of black self-determination in *Wine in the Wilderness,* representative of the three other plays, *Florence,Trouble in Mind,* and *Wedding Band,* that account for the greater portion of Childress's significant contributions to the history of American drama and to the African-American intellectual tradition.

Meeting Alice Childress
Alice Childress was born in Charleston, South Carolina on October 20, 1920. When her parents separated, the five-year old went to live with her maternal grandmother in Harlem. Eliza Campbell raised and befriended her granddaughter, and she

also helped to educate the mind and spirit of the young writer who had yet to discover her potential. At Public School 81, Julia Ward Howe Junior High School, and Wadleigh High School, Childress received a typical public education, but she was no typical student. Even then she was developing her convictions about writing. Childress left high school after only three years of study. The deaths of her grandmother and mother forced her to continue her education at the public library and work to make ends meet. She also began the struggle to become an actress. Her training was not formal, but on-the-job.

Childress began acting when she joined such future theatrical legends as Ruby Dee and Ossie Davis in helping Abram Hill and Frederick O'Neal establish the American Negro Theatre (ANT) in the 1940s. Her experience with ANT laid the foundation for the twenty years in which she was most active as a playwright in the legitimate theatre. She underwent a "conversion experience" largely due to the racism that crippled the company. In "A Candle in a Gale Wind," Childress presented a brief account of the ordeal that made her a writer with a vision: "I had started a 'career' as an actress with the American Negro Theatre, went to Broadway with *Anna Lucasta,* was nominated for a Tony Award. Radio and television work followed, but racism, a double black-listing system, and a feeling of being somewhat alone in my ideas caused me to know I could more freely express myself as a writer" (115). Childress recognized a calling in her talent as a writer, and she determined to write plays that vindicate black people.

With ANT's production of *Florence* in Harlem in 1949, and its publication in 1950, Childress began her professional career as a playwright. As Samuel Hay writes in *African-American Theatre, Florence* "radically altered the African-American 'Mama' stereotype" (26). Mrs. Whitney, "Mama" in the play, became a prototype for the black heroines Childress created over the next two decades. The playwright's primary goal was to redress the black image, especially of women, on and off national and international stages. Childress wrote *Florence* in keeping with principles of content, form, and commitment to which she remained true throughout the years she focused on playwriting.

Childress's grandmother, and the years she spent at the library trying to read at least two books a day, provided her with a material and spiritual education that influenced her principles of writing. Eliza Campbell taught Childress that observing was not enough, that she should write down the "thoughts" she found "worthy" of "keeping" ("Candle": 114). She did so and eventually found writing to be a way of putting her world into perspective, of taking control of how she expressed herself in it.

At the public library, Childress read and evaluated form ("Candle": 115). Knowing the "difference of structure in plays, books, short stories," and so on taught her how to use conventional elements and themes to accommodate her "own thought and structure patterns." She also became acquainted with works that would profoundly influence her understanding of literature, especially drama, as a vital tool for social change. Alongside the Bible, books on African-American history, and Shakespeare, she read and studied the drama, novels, and poetry of others who had long committed themselves and their art to telling the truth. She aligned herself with Walt Whitman and Paul Laurence Dunbar, who "approached ordinary people with admiration and respect because these poets realized that every human being has endless possibilities." She also admired Sean O'Casey and Sholem Aleichem, who "celebrated the poor Irish and the poor Jews, as Paul Laurence Dunbar honored the poor Black slave through love, understanding and truth" ("Human Condition": 10). Each of these writers had what Childress called "an urge to mold clay" or a sense of drama that made them dramatists, which they put to use in creating art dedicated to the common desire for all oppressed peoples—liberation.

Childress's on-the-job training was rounded off by her experiences in other branches of the theatre. She excelled in administrative positions. As co-founder of ANT, she served as a theatre consultant. As a co-founder of The Harlem Theatre Movement, she sat on its board of directors. Furthermore, she was a key member of the Author's League of the Dramatist Guild, acting in negotiations to establish equity standards for actor's salaries in off-Broadway productions. Childress affiliated herself with the Harlem Writer's Guild and the New Dramatists in the 1950s and 1960s. Finally as a scholar and historian of dramatic literature, she wrote proposals and received grants from the John Golden Fund for playwrights in 1957 and the Rockefeller

Foundation. And in 1968, she held an appointment at the Harvard-Radcliffe Institute for Independent Study. Much of the time Childress might have called "spare," she spent lecturing and attending conferences as a keynote speaker on drama. But for all of her accomplishments, it was as a drama theorist and playwright that she came nearest her goal to help provide useful theatre by, for, and about black people.

A Theory of Black Self-Determinist Theatre

Childress's theory of black self-determinist theatre begins and ends with her views on the meaning and function of theatre for African-Americans. Written between 1951 and 1969, her seminal essays constitute a theory of black self-determinist theatre, which she worked hard to bring into reality through her own work during the peak of her career as a playwright. Childress linked the meaning of black theatre with the great need to represent African-Americans on the stage in images and through stories that vindicate their collective and individual identity. "I have learned that I must watch my people in railroad stations, in restaurants, in the fields and tenements, at the factory wheels, in the stores, on the subway. I have watched and found that there is none so blind as he who will not see" ("Negro Theatre": 62). She defined the word "theatre" as being "derived from the Greek meaning to see or view" (61), and deduced that "a Negro people's theatre" is all about "the opportunity of seeing and viewing the Negro people" in an effort "to inspire, lift, and eventually create a complete desire for the liberation of all oppressed peoples" (63). Childress held fast to this same definition or rather description of what theatre means to the African peoples in America. She wrote that "black communities have always had black theaters," and declared that "we will continue to need them, even when, if ever, this land is free of racism. Theater serves as the mirror of life experience and reflects only what looks into it; everyone yearns to see his own image once in a while" ("My Thing": 9).

Childress envisioned the function of black theatre as twofold. Given the humanist nature of all art, Childress maintained that the usefulness of theatre as well as any art form was synonymous with its concern primarily for human beings and their values, capacities, and achievements. "There will be no progress in art without peace," she warned, "a lasting peace throughout the world" ("Negro Theatre": 63). She extended this insight to her view of a humanistic function of "Negro people's theatre" as "a guide," lighting "the way to all that we may glean the precious stuff from that which is useless." The "precious stuff" is what would make black theatre *useful* in enhancing black people's understanding not only of themselves, but of themselves among others who have also known oppression. Experiences of collective struggles and individual triumphs would "be heard around the world" through a black theatre that systematically seeks "out every artistic expression...to study and teach not only what has been taught before[,] but [also to] found and establish a new approach to the study of the Negro in the theatre, dance and arts" (63). "We shall take advantage of the rich culture of the Chinese, Japanese, Russian, and all theatres," Childress contended. The advantage here has to do with African-Americans expanding their knowledge of themselves and of their own theatre by discovering theatres that represent the lives of people(s) who experience this world differently. The other part of the advantage is what the black theatre could give back to the world. "Last but not least," the educational duty of the powerful movement she envisioned would be to offer "courses in the cultural background of the minority groups in this country" (63).

Childress's view of the theatre's humanistic function is balanced by her view of its political function in the history of the American theatre. She insisted that the workings of black theatre are inextricably connected to the self-determination of the African-American people: a "black theater here and there does not signify 'turning away' from commercial television, motion pictures and theater. It is one reaction to being turned away" ("My Thing": 9). At the same time, Childress claimed *white theater* does exist despite people's not saying so bluntly, and that it "is separatism." She charged that this "theater functions even though the greater part of what it turns out fails," while only a few *"plays by black writers"* get *"presented on Broadway"* (9). Her use of italics betrays the voice of resistance that heretofore did not deny that black theatre, as with all American theatre, was financially dependent on the "so-called mainstream." She also made clear that black theatre relied heavily on its own manpower, its conviction to advance subjects that promote truth about the people(s) it represented, and its ability to cope, however many plays by black writers Broadway ignored. "The time is over for asking or even demanding human rights, in and out of the theater. We no longer *ask* for manhood or womanhood or dignity; all we can do is express what we have to the degree that we have it," Childress protested. In the words of a warrior still fighting the good fight, she added that "[s]oon we may have to read our works on the sidewalks of inner-city and 'mainstream' Broadway. Time is up. I've a play to write that may never be seen by any audience anywhere, but I do my thing. Who has ears to hear, hear...all others, later." In 1969, National Educational Television (NET) broadcasted its production of the most political and yet humanistic play in the personal repertoire Childress had been carefully building since 1949. And three years later, Samuel French published *Wine in the Wilderness* for what has become an international audience.

At the core of Childress's theory of black self-determinist theatre are her views on the relationship between the individual black playwright and a collective black theatre. Perhaps the most complicated of Childress's arguments, they delineate the writer's role as the central source and resource of a powerful movement. In the black writer was the soul of the black theatre. For Childress, the development and growth of black playwrights and actors "into real people's artists," represents the congruity between the humanistic function as an end, and the political as a means to that end ("Negro Theater": 63). She included herself as a playwright when she explained that real people's artists "must be sure that through our interpretation the world and our next door neighbor may see and view the Negro people." As with the black theatre, the function of a real people's artist—or in Childress's case the black playwright—is humanistic within the context of long-term goals. "Where is truth? Where are the schools that will teach us Negro art forms?" Both will be needed if the writer is to project black people in their own terms, and is to view them as one of many participants in a world community where equality of all begins with the knowledge and respect of one another's differences.

With regard to the method used to reach this goal, the function of the black playwright according to Childress is decidedly political. Childress urged writers to take a self-determinist route towards gaining the "time, study and research" needed to cultivate an "understanding and projection of Negro culture" ("Negro Theatre": 62).

The greater part of her theory delineates a method for self-expression by which black playwrights can make the African-American people [the] subject of plays for a theatre that she believed would be dedicated to "telling the truth" about their many experiences, and to promoting their well-being.

Childress's method of self-expression demands that the writer make a personal investment in the subject. She pointed out the deliberate lack of "interest" that modern American educational and theatrical institutions were taking "in the cultural or historical background of the Negro people" ("Negro Theatre": 61). As a result most artists "can only 'suggest' an African," she argued, "because we have been divorced through education from much of our cultural heritage." Therefore, the first step of her method is to attain self-knowledge. The black writer must "turn within" him or her*self* "for guidance" to portray black people.

Since the ultimate goal is to educate others, the black writer is to go on to the second step of defining the black self on a collective level, first by examining African art forms that already exist, and then by turning searching eyes toward the people themselves. Finally, in a third step of the method, the writer's self-knowledge and self-definition incur with the act of literary mimesis. The real people's artist has the responsibility of giving aesthetic expression to observations of "neighbors, the community, the domestic workers, laborers, white-collar workers, churches, lodges, and institutions" ("Negro Theatre": 62). "These things," Childress was convinced, "we must learn to duplicate."

Childress insisted upon this third step. She believed that emphasis on the real-life situations, conditions, and circumstances of black people formed the core value for black theatre. She saw these as sources to which black writers must turn in order to project black culture. She also valued the past and cautioned writers never to overlook it: "be wary of those who tell you to leave the past alone and confine yourselves to the present moment. Our story has not been told in any moment,...and our history is not gone with the wind, it is still with us" ("Negro Woman": 16). Her point is that the independence and self-government of the black-theatre relies on black writers turning out "plays...about these things" (17).

"These things" were not on view elsewhere in the 1940s and 1950s. Stories of African-American men and women either misrepresented them or simply did not take them seriously as proper subject matter for literature. Depicting black self-determination would redress the false images of blacks so commonly presented on the stage and in film, and it would provide images where there were none. In an instance concerning the black woman in American literature, Childress argued that "the general popular American drama, television, motion pictures and radio" nearly omitted the Negro woman as important subject matter ("Negro Woman": 14). Furthermore, they misconceived her strengths "as faults" and freely produced grossly distorted images because of prejudice and ignorance among average American citizens. If the black woman was not the "empty and decharacterized faithful servant," she was the demoralized hussy or at best an overtly religious, ball-busting matriarch. It was up to writers committed to truth to "tell her story, with the full knowledge and appreciation of her constant, unrelenting struggle against racism and for human rights" (19). In this way, she would attain "her rightful place in American literature" as significant to the history of this country she helped to build with "soap suds and muscle."

Childress understood that if "plays ... about these things" were not produced and published, the creation of such plays would not receive financial support. She saw little hope of "escape" from this reality: "any attempt to 'buy our own' puts us in the position where they ["white power"] can cut off our supply lines, via unions and real estate holdings, at a moment's notice" ("Literary Lions": 86). Bleak though this may sound, however, Childress was not a fatalist. She believed in "black writers establishing a 'black aesthetic,'" despite her reservations about their finding "a way to earn some minimum living within the white economy" (36). That black theatre was economically in a "subservient position" was a *fact* to her, and that was all it was, a fact (86). *"Soon we may have to read our works on the sidewalks of inner-city and 'mainstream' Broadway"* ("My Thing": 9). For Childless, the soul of black theatre was not in where it would or could be housed; it was in the politics of its relationship to black people. The control of black theatre Childress placed in the hands of black playwrights.

To turn out plays depicting black self-determination was fundamentally the heart beat of black theatre as Childress viewed it. Its future depended on the "pouring out [of] what is still largely unusual" ("Literary Lions": 36). On the one hand, the *unusual* was a determination against racist determinism. "I have ever been in the position of having to study and understand the 'greatness' or meanness of others and of making whatever adjustment to exist in their world," Childress lamented, recounting an experience with which black people are still all too familiar (86). The *usual* was "the oppressed forever studying the oppressor, deferring self-expression to self-censorship" in an appeal to the "goodwill" of those who afflict pain, and being left "bitter" or at best "numb." A *bitter* Childress exclaimed that "we have cajoled, pleaded, tommed, protested, achieved, rioted, defied, unified ... you name it! But white supremacists have dug their heels into the ground and will settle for nothing less than out-right confrontation in the streets of America" (87).

On the other hand, the *unusual* was not merely a reaction to white supremacy. The black theatre she envisioned was a form of self-expression, and in this Childress located its greatest significance. It was a theatre that would express her feelings without censure; that favored truth over the good will of those who oppressed her. Whether of bitterness or of happiness, self-expression was the evidence and means of creating an independent and self-governed black theatre. ...

Source: Olga Dugan, "Telling the Truth: Alice Childress as Theorist and Playwright," in *Journal of Negro History*, Vol. 81, No. 1/4, Winter–Autumn 1996, pp. 123–36.

Susan Koppelman

In the following essay, Koppelman gives a brief overview of Childress's life, accomplishments, and works, including Florence.

Alice Childress, award-winning playwright, novelist, actress, director, and lecturer, died in New York on Sunday, August 14, 1994. Many considered her the greatest African American woman playwright in the history of this country. Her work has been praised for its powerful and frank treatment of racial issues, the compassionate but unflinching characterizations she created, and the broad appeal of her work. Her ability to personalize social issues such as poverty, racism, addiction, and child abuse mobilized those who saw her plays and read her novels to take action on behalf of social justice.

She was born in Charleston, South Carolina, on October 12, 1920, was educated at public schools in Harlem, and, as a midlife adult, was a scholar at the Radcliffe Institute for Independent Study. She studied acting with Venzella Jones and Nadja Romanov.

Among her many honors was the coveted Obie Award for the best original Off-Broadway play for *Trouble in Mind* in 1956, which she also directed. For her famous 1973 novel, *A Hero Ain't Nothin' but a Sandwich* (which revolutionized writing for young adults by introducing the nitty-gritty realities of urban life in following a young boy's struggle with drug addiction), she received awards from the Jane Addams Peace Association, a National Book Award Nomination, the Lewis Carrol Shelf Award, an Outstanding Book of the Year Citation from the *New York Times*, and the Best Young Adult Book citation from the American Library Association. In 1975 she received the Sojourner Truth Award from the National Association of Negro Business and Professional Women's Clubs.

She wrote the screenplay for the film of *A Hero*, starring Paul Winfield and Cicely Tyson and was honored for this work with the first Paul Robeson Award for Outstanding Contributions to the Performing Arts and election to the Black Filmmakers Hall of Fame in 1977. Another young adult novel, *Rainbow Jordan*, was named an outstanding book of the year by the *New York Times* in 1982, a School Library Journal best book of 1981, and an honorable mention for a Coretta Scott King Award.

Miss Childress spent 11 years with the American Negro Theater in New York City as an actress and director, belonged to the Harlem Writers Guild, and acted in such plays as *Anna Lucasta, The World of Sholom Aleichem, The Cool World,* and in the title role of her own play, *Florence,* on and off the Broadway stage and on television. She can be seen in the 1968 Paramount film *Uptight.*

With her husband of 37 years, musician and composer Nathan Woodard, Alice Childress wrote the musical plays *Young Martin Luther King* (originally titled *The Freedom Drum*), *Martin Luther King at Montgomery, Alabama,The African Garden, Gullah,* and *Moms: A Praise Play for a Black Comedienne* (based on the life of Jackie "Moms" Mabley). Their long and happy marriage provided a model of mutual respect and collegiality to many young artists

they mentored, helping the artists learn mutually to accommodate and support the creative careers of those they love. They travelled widely, visiting and performing in many countries on three continents.

Her play *Wedding Band: A Love/Hate Story in Black and White,* a story of interracial love (first produced at the University of Michigan in 1966), was co-directed by Childress with Joseph Papp as part of the New York City Public Theater's Shakespeare Festival in 1972 and adapted for television and broadcast by ABC in 1973. Producer-director Debbie Allen plans a production of this play.

Childress's book of dramatic monologues, *Like One of the Family: Conversations from a Domestic's Life,* first published in 1956, was reprinted with an introduction by Trudier Harris in 1986 by Beacon Press. The monologues were published first as a column in *Freedom*, a newspaper edited by Paul Robeson, and continued in the *Baltimore Afro-American.* These short, provocative, and inspiring pieces are often read aloud today from pulpits and in classrooms. Her adult novel, *A Short Walk,* first published in 1979, traces African American history from the turn of the century to the mid-century civil rights movement by following the life of Cora James, born in Charleston, through her struggle to survive in Harlem in the 1940s. The novel's depiction of African American experience ranges from the Marcus Garvey movement to the vaudeville circuit.

Childress received the Radcliffe Graduate Society Medal in 1984, the African Poets Theatre Award in 1985, and the Harlem School of the Arts Humanitarian Award in 1987. She is survived by her husband and one granddaughter; her daughter, Jean Lee, predeceased her. Mr. Woodard remarked that Alice Childress's final message to us was "God Bless Us All."

Source: Susan Koppelman, "Alice Childress: An Appreciation," in *Belles Lettres: A Review of Books by Women,* Vol. 10, No. 1, Fall 1994, p. 6.

Elizabeth Brown-Guillory

In the following essay, Brown-Guillory discusses the roles of black characters in the plays of Lorraine Hansberry, Ntozake Shange, and Childress, including the play Florence.

Alice Childress, Lorraine Hansberry, and Ntozake Shange, three outstanding contemporary black women playwrights, are crucial links

> FLORENCE IS A POSITIVE IMAGE OF BLACK WOMANHOOD; SHE REFUSES TO USE RACISM AS AN EXCUSE FOR NOT TRYING TO IMPROVE HER LIFESTYLE. SHE REPRESENTS THOSE BLACK WOMEN WHO REFUSE TO DESPAIR IN THE SIGHT OF SEEMINGLY INSURMOUNTABLE OBSTACLES."

in the development of black women playwriting in America. These three playwrights, whose perspectives and portraits are decidedly different from those of black males and white playwrights, have created images of blacks which dispel the myths of "the contented slave," "the tragic mulatto," "the comic Negro," "the exotic primitive," and "the spiritual-singing, toe-tapping, faithful servant."

Childress, Hansberry, and Shange have created credible images of blacks, such as "the black militant," "the black peacemaker," "the black assimilationist," "the optimistic black capitalist," "the struggling black artist," and "the contemporary black matriarch." However, three images which appear most frequently in the plays of these black women are "the black male in search of his manhood," "the black male as a walking wounded" and "the evolving black woman."

The black male in search of his manhood, a product of the ambivalence fostered mainly by the continued disinheritance of blacks after World War II and the Korean War, is a major new image in contemporary literature. Functioning in this role, the black male struggles to realize who he is and what his function in life is to be. In his essay, "Visions of Love and Manliness in a Blackening World: Dramas of Black Life from 1953–1970," Darwin T. Turner states:

> Ironically, as black dramatists examine their characters more critically, often they seem less polemical and more compassionate because, in the black world, they perceive not only individuals searching for manhood and love but even more pathetic figures too impotent to search for manhood or to achieve a relationship of love....

Plays by Childress substantiate Turner's claim because the image of the black male in

search of his manhood is shown either as a creature who is in the process of becoming a mature human being or one who is too incapacitated to search for manhood. His insecurity of his own identity and values renders him generally passive. He vacillates between integration and separatism. He has yet to establish a philosophy about how to succeed or cope in American society.

As he strives to overcome personal problems and to achieve responsible maturity, the confused black male may castigate blacks and opt to align himself with whites who he feels will validate his manhood. Though he may reject his ethnicity during the search, he reaches maturity when he realizes that his manhood does not hinge upon his acceptance by anyone but himself.

John Nevins, a black male in search of his manhood, appears in Childress' 1955 Obie award-winning drama, *Trouble in Mind,* a play which centers around the frustration blacks feel because of the limited and demeaning roles available to them on the American stage. John, in his early twenties, hopes to prove his manhood by becoming a successful actor. A novice among his veteran-actor co-workers, John dreams of making money regardless of what must be sacrificed. When the white director, Al Manners, appears, John immediately becomes a "yes-man," indicating that he is neither assertive nor self-respecting.

Nevins's self-effacement is apparent during the rehearsal of *Chaos in Belleville,* Childress' play within a play, a device which she learned from Shakespeare, one of her principal influences. When Al Manners asks John if he can object in an artistic sense to the word *darkies,* John placatingly replies:

> No I don't object. I don't like the word but it is used, it's a slice of life. Let's face it, Judy wouldn't use it, Mr. Manners wouldn't...

John eagerly compromises his opinions to keep his role in *Chaos in Belleville* in order to "make it" in the theatre and, thus, define his manhood.

When his black co-workers display anger at his "Tomish" remarks, John aligns himself with one of the white actresses, Judy, hoping that she will validate that he is a man. Not only does he seek approval or direction from Judy, but he also turns to Al Manners. However, Manners, during an argument over interpretation, unthinkingly makes the mistake of implying that John could not be compared to his son because John is black and his son is white. Angered by this remark and encouraged by his black co-workers to assert himself, John examines his values and decides that racial pride means more to him than success in a play that degrades blacks. Boldly he declares, "They can write what they want but we don't have to do it." John moves in the direction of maturity as his black peers help him to become whole.

Whereas John Nevins eventually asserts himself, Sheldon Forrester, one of John's co-workers, typifies the image of the black who is too impotent to search for manhood. Sheldon chooses to sacrifice dignity for minor roles on the American stage. He has no self-respect, and he chastises those blacks who affirm themselves. Sheldon has been worn down and perceives that it is futile for a black male to try to function as a man in American society. Ironically, Sheldon defines his manhood in terms of success at projecting that he is not a man among white men. He brags that his denial of self has helped him to survive in the world and says that blacks ought to "take low" in order to keep whatever jobs are issued out to them. The audience sees Sheldon's spinelessness when he aims his remarks at his co-worker, Millie:

> I hope the wind blows her away. They gonna kick us until we all out in the street . . . unemployed . . . get all the air you want then. Sometimes I take low, yes, gotta take low. Man say somethin' to me, I say . . . "yes, sure, certainly." That ain't tommin', that's common sense. You and me . . . we don't mind takin' low because we tryin' to accomplish somethin' . . . Well, yeah, we all mind . . . but you got to swaller. . . .

Sheldon has neither the courage nor the determination to become a whole person.

Like Sheldon, Teddy is a black male in search of his manhood in Alice Childress' *Mojo: A Black Love Story*, a play which deals with the need for black men and women to be supportive of each other both in and out of love relationships. At the beginning of the play, Teddy is searching for his manhood in his relationship with his white girlfriend, Berniece. He wants very much to please her so that she, as he says, will make him feel like a man. Teddy's devotion to his status symbol is apparent when he makes the following comments: "Aw, baby, I aint callin you white folks, you wild, yallerheaded, fine thing, you! They all white folks but you . . . you somethin else. I'll be there . . ."

Later when Teddy argues with his black ex-wife, Irene, he displays insecurity and his need for affirmation from a white woman:

TEDDY. Git offa my back, Reeny . . . that's one thing bout that simple Berniece . . . she make me feel like a man. She's white but she make you feel like. . . .

IRENE. Feel like . . . feel like . . . I been hearing that all my days . . . sound like my poppa . . . "I wanta feel like a man." You wanta be a man . . . forget that feel like . . . feel like. . . .

TEDDY. If you wasn't on your way to the hospital I'd knock the hell out of you, for underminin me. Berniece knows how to make you feel pleasant.

Towards the end of the play Teddy, with the help of Irene, does begin to insist that he is a man, not a child needing approval. His growing confidence in himself is demonstrated when he lovingly reaches out to comfort Irene who is soon to be hospitalized.

Childress' sensitive treatment of the black male in search of his manhood reflects her vision that black men and women can become whole only when they not only join forces but resources as well. Childress' Teddy represents those black males who refuse to let poverty and bad luck keep them from growing into fine black men who accept responsibility for their families.

Unlike the black male in search of his manhood is the black male as a walking wounded. Whereas the former struggles for direction and identity, the latter knows exactly who he is and is painfully aware of the fact that he is oppressed in American society. He not only survives but survives whole. Though physical and/or emotional blows are heaped upon him, he is neither fragmented nor abusive to his women. He is fully aware of his roots and is proud of his heritage.

The black male as a walking wounded insists that he be treated like a human being. A contented slave he is not; instead, he struggles to free himself and others from oppressive forces. Because of a positive sense of self, he can and does reach out to others. He especially has a strong sense of family togetherness, a trait which his African fathers brought with them to America. In short, this character, which is diametrically opposite to the image of the incorrigible black beast that dominated the American stage for so many decades, refuses to be anybody's sacrificial lamb and boldly keeps going in spite of his wounds.

Though Childress, Hansberry, and Shange have created credible images of black men, the females in plays by black women have much more dimension and are more finely tuned than the males, These black women characters are not...like Karintha and Carma in Jean Toomer's *Cane* or Bessie Mears in Richard Wright's *Native Son*. Nor do they resemble the countless "black mammies" who were created to represent black womanhood, such as Dilsey in Faulkner's *The Sound and the Fury,* Berniece in Carson McCullers' *The Member of the Wedding,* Addie in Lillian Hellman's *The Little Foxes,* or Ella Swan in William Styron's *Lie Down in Darkness.* Doris Abramson in *Negro Playwrights in the American Theatre 1925–1959* includes the following Hansberry quote which demonstrates her rejection of the then popular images of blacks:

> One night, after seeing a play I won't mention, I suddenly became disgusted with the whole body of material about Negroes. Cardboard characters. Cute dialect bits. Or swinging musicals from exotic sources.

Additionally, Cynthia Belgrave in "Readers' Forum: Black Women in Film Symposium," comments on the inaccurate and narrow images of black women on the American stage:

> If you're strong and stoical you're a matriarch, and if you're weak and sensual, you're a whore. Of course there are no equitable gradations in between.... The Black woman is at the mercy of everybody. When we finish kicking people, let us kick the Black woman again.

...In her essay, "Images of Black Women in Plays by Black Playwrights," Jeanne-Marie A. Miller contends that the images of black women are not only peripheral in plays by whites, but the portraits of black women in plays written by black men are, generally, radically different from the images of black women in plays by black women:

> In the plays written by Black males, Black women's happiness or "completeness" depends upon strong Black men. Thus, Black women playwrights bring to their works their vision, however different, of what Black women are or what they should be.

In short, Miller calls for an inclusion of the caricatures of black women playwrights when the images of black writers are the subject of discussion.

Mary Helen Washington in *Black Eyed-Susans: Classic Stories By and about Black Women* makes a strong case in the following lines for studying black women writers:

> What is most important about the black woman writer is her special and unique vision of the black woman.... One of the main preoccupations of the black woman writer has been the black woman herself—her aspirations, her conflicts, her relationships to her men and her children, her creativity.... That these writers have firsthand knowledge of their subject ought to be enough to command attention.

Childress, Hansberry, and Shange view black women from a special angle. One image which dominates their plays is "the evolving black woman," a phrase which embodies the multiplicity of emotions of ordinary black women for whom the act of living is sheer heroism. This creature emphasizes understanding and taking care of herself. Not always a powerhouse of strength, the evolving black woman is quite fragile. Her resiliency, though, makes her a positive image of black womanhood. Self respecting, self-sufficient, assertive, these women force others around them to recognize their adulthood....

Florence in Alice Childress' *Florence,* may be classified as an evolving black woman. As the play opens, Florence's mother, Mrs. Whitney, and her sister, Marge, discuss Florence, who has moved to New York because she views the South as too confining for a black woman desirous of improving her lifestyle. Characteristically, Florence strives to survive in a hostile world. Placed in the position of supporting herself and her son because her husband was killed by whites in the South, Florence dreams of becoming an accomplished actress. She chooses to relocate in order to fulfill those dreams.

Though Florence has not met with much success, except for the several times that she has played the part of a maid in plays, she is determined to find a way to make a name for herself in the theater. Florence is a positive image of black womanhood; she refuses to use racism as an excuse for not trying to improve her lifestyle. She represents those black women who refuse to despair in the sight of seemingly insurmountable obstacles. Instead of applying for public assistance, she sets out to become self-sufficient in a profession that she considers dignified. It is her determination to succeed after her husband's death which makes her a character truly to be admired.

The evolving black women in Childress' *Wine in the Wilderness* and Ntozake Shange's *For Colored Girls Who Have Considered Suicide/When the Rainbow is Enuf* are preoccupied with themselves because they have been disappointed by the men who have come into their lives. These are women who have had their share of "deferred dreams" and are no longer willing to play the role of "woman-behind-her-man" to men who appreciate neither their submissiveness nor their docility. These women rebel and claim that no man is ever going to oppress them again. They are not women who give up on men or feel that all men are insensitive beasts; instead, they are women who have become independent because of their fear of being abused physically and/or emotionally in subsequent relationships.

The image of the black woman in these two plays is that of a woman who has to "sing the blues" before she is able to make some sense out of the chaos in her life. Though black women who are abandoned in Childress' and Shange's plays bewail their losses, emphasis is placed on their ability to survive in a world where they are forced to care for themselves. The evolving black women in these plays fight back after they have been bruised, and they work toward improving their lifestyles.

Tommy Marie in Alice Childress' *Wine in the Wilderness* is an evolving black woman. When a young, black, middle-class artist, Bill Jameson, chooses to include Tommy in his triptych, she gets the impression that he is interested in starting a relationship with her. However, though Bill seduces her, he merely intends to use her to capture the image of, as he describes it, "the dumb chick whose had her behind kicked until it's numb."

When Cynthia, a bourgeois friend of Bill, tries to tell Tommy that she is not good enough for Bill and that she must not look upon him as a possible provider, Tommy Marie flaunts her independence:

> Tommy's not lookin' for a meal ticket. I been doin' for myself all my life. It takes two to make it in this high priced world.... I have a dream too. Mine is to find a man who'll treat me just half-way decent...just to meet me half way is all I ask, to smile, to be kind to me. Somebody in my corner. Not to wake up by myself in the mornin' and face this world alone...I'm so lonesome...I want somebody to love. Somebody to say... "That's alright," when the world treats me mean.

Tommy typifies the evolving black woman in that she dreams of finding a man who will love and share with her, but it is apparent in her comments that she has equipped herself to survive alone if she must....

> I don't have to wait for anybody's by-your-leave to be a "Wine in the Wilderness woman." I can be it if I wanta,...and I am. I am. I am. I'm not the one you made up and painted, the very pretty lady who can't talk back,...but I'm "Wine in the Wilderness"...alive and kickin' me...Tomorrow-Marie, cussin' and fightin' and lookin' out for my damn self 'cause ain' nobody else around to do it, dontcha know.... That's "Wine in the Wilderness,"...a woman that's a real one and good one. And yall just better believe I'm it.

...James V. Hatch contends that Tommy Marie is a positive image of black womanhood because she is honest, and she is not living under the illusion of false reality. Hatch suggests that she is a survivor who refuses to despair:

> True, Tommy "hopes" that Bill will seriously fall for her, but if he doesn't, she is prepared to move on. She is a sensible woman without pretense. The beauty of *Wine in the Wilderness* is in part due to the author's sensitive treatment of Tommy whose warmth, compassion, inner dignity, and pride make her more of a woman than Cynthia will ever be. Alice Childress has created a powerful, new black heroine who emerges from the depths of the black community.

At the end of the play, Tommy is confident that if Bill Jameson does not see her worth and beauty, another male will. What is important to note is that Alice Childress has created an image of a woman whose inner strength will protect her as she searches for a stable relationship in which there is reciprocity....

Alice Childress, Lorraine Hansberry, and Ntozake Shange are contemporary black women playwrights whose visions or perspective[s] are different from black males or white writers. To exclude black women playwrights as a source for examining black life is to omit a large piece of the human puzzle. These three major women writers are important because they, too, like black women writers in other genres, supply America with plausible, and in some cases unique, images of black men and women.

Some have dared to ask, "Do black women playwrights really depict black life?" Unequivocally, they do, but these images must be viewed in conjunction with the images created by black males in order to create an accurate picture of black life. Others have asked, "Do black women playwrights represent the majority of blacks?" These selected playwrights do not create images which represent the majority of blacks; no two or three writers can, or should have to try. However, these three women playwrights present a vital slice of life, and it is up to many more black writers to capture the multitude of images of blacks.

Perhaps, the most important question to be asked is "Will society be different after meeting the characters in the plays of black women?" The answer is yes, significantly so. When blacks turn to theater for better ways to live, Childress, Hansberry, and Shange offer them a multiplicity of options via black characters who come from the heart of the black community. Contemporary black women playwrights uniquely give to the American stage a view from the other half.

Source: Elizabeth Brown-Guillory, "Black Women Playwrights: Exorcising Myths," in *Phylon*, Vol. 48, No. 3, Fall 1987, pp. 229–39.

SOURCES

"African American World: Timeline," http://www.pbs.org/wnet/aaworld/timeline.html (accessed June 27, 2008).

"American Negro Theatre," *BlackPast.org: Remembered & Reclaimed,* http://www.blackpast.org/?q = aah/american-negro-theatre (accessed June 27, 2008).

Brown-Guillory, Elizabeth, *Their Place on the Stage*, Greenwood Press, 1988, pp. 54–55.

Childress, Alice, "A Woman Playwright Speaks Her Mind, " in *Freedomways*, Vol. 6, Winter 1966, pp. 14–15.

———, *Florence*, in *Wines in the Wilderness*, edited by Elizabeth Brown-Guillory, Praeger, 1990, pp.110–21.

Davis, Ronald L. F., "From Terror to Triumph: Historical Overview," in *History of Jim Crow*, http://www.jimcrowhistory.org/history/overview.htm (accessed June 27, 2008).

"Feature Presentation: African American Oscar Winners," in *Black Film Center/Archive*, http://www.indiana.edu/~bfca/features/oscars.html (accessed August 27, 2008).

Harmon, William, and Hugh Holman, *A Handbook to Literature*, 11th ed., Prentice Hall, 2008, pp. 178–79, 456.

Harris, Will, "Early Black Women Playwrights and the Dual Liberation Motif," in *African American Review*, Vol. 28, No. 2, Summer 1994, pp. 205–21.

Hay, Samuel A., "Alice Childress's Dramatic Structure," in *Modern Black American Poets and Dramatists*, edited by Harold Bloom, Chelsea House, 1995, pp. 57–58; originally published in *Black Women Writers (1950–1980): A Critical Evaluation*, edited by Mari Evans, Anchor Press, 1984, pp. 118–19.

Jordan, Shirley M., "Alice Childress," in *Broken Silences: Interviews with Black and White Women Writers*, edited by Shirley M. Jordan, Rutgers University Press, 1993, pp. 28–37.

"Magazines About African Americans," http://www.ncbuy.com/shopping/magazines/search.html?action = intoff&intid = 2000 (accessed June 27, 2008).

Maguire, Roberta S., "Alice Childress," in *Dictionary of Literary Biography*, Vol. 249, *Twentieth-Century American Dramatists, Third Series*, edited by Christopher Wheatley, The Gale Group, 2001, pp. 30–39.

Rule, Sheila, "Alice Childress, 77, a Novelist, Drew Themes from Black Life," *New York Times*, August 19, 1994, p. A24.

Rusie, Robert, "Broadway 101: The History of the Great White Way, Part IV, A Bright Golden Haze 1940–1950," http://www.talkinbroadway.com/bway101/6d.html (accessed June 27, 2008).

"Survey on Race Pits Facts vs. Attitudes," in the *Washington Post*, November 26, 1999, http://findarticles.com/p/articles/mi_qn4179/is_19991126/ai_n11734836 (accessed June 27, 2008).

Trager, James, *The People's Chronology*, Henry Holt, 1992, p. 895.

FURTHER READING

Austin, Gayle, "Black Woman Playwright as Feminist Critic," in *Southern Quarterly*, Vol. 25, No. 3, Spring 1987, pp. 53–62.

Austin argues for the importance of reading Childress's plays as strong pro-feminist works. Although this essay provides some general observations about Childress, Austin's primary focus is on two of Childress's texts, *Wine in the Wilderness* and *Trouble in Mind*.

Hill, Errol G., and James V. Hatch, *A History of African American Theatre*, Cambridge University Press, 2006.

This book presents a thorough history of African American theater and its traditions. This text discusses several different formats, including vaudeville and minstrel shows, as well as dramatic theater.

Packard, Jerrold M., *American Nightmare: The History of Jim Crow*, St. Martin's, 2003.

Packard traces the origination of slavery as a legal institution and of Jim Crow laws, which were common throughout the United States. He also provides a detailed look at segregation and the court cases that brought an end to Jim Crow.

Ritterhouse, Jennifer, *Growing Up Jim Crow: The Racial Socialization of Black and White Southern Children, 1890–1940*, University of North Carolina Press, 2006.

The author explores how children learned the unwritten and carefully socialized rules of segregation. This book investigates how parents taught their children about segregation and how the differences between public and private behaviors were defined during this period of American history.

Watson, Steven, *The Harlem Renaissance: Hub of African-American Culture, 1920–1930*, Pantheon, 1996.

This book covers the literature and art of the Harlem Renaissance, which took place when Childress was a child growing up in New York City. The book includes art, photographs, and poetry, as well as information about important literary and artistic figures of this time.

Ile

EUGENE O'NEILL
1917

Ile, first performed in 1917 and published in 1919, is among the earliest dramatic works of Eugene Gladstone O'Neill, who went on to become the leading American playwright of his generation. Its title represents pronunciation of the word *oil*, referring to whale oil, in the dialect, or specialized language, of New England whale fishermen. O'Neill came from a family of actors, so he naturally turned to the stage as a profession after his health failed, ending his first chosen career as a merchant sailor. Most of O'Neill's early plays reflect, as does *Ile*, his experiences at sea. Like all of O'Neill's earliest work, the play consists of only one act and runs little more than twenty minutes in performance. For this reason, it is still among the more commonly performed of O'Neill's works, especially by amateur and student groups. It is also frequently anthologized and is included in O'Neill's 2007 collection from Yale University Press, *Collected Shorter Plays*. *Ile* explores what O'Neill considered to be fundamental incompatibilities between the temperaments of men and women, and, brief as it is, touches upon autobiographical themes that would be prominent in his mature work, especially in his posthumously premiered masterpiece, *Long Day's Journey into Night*. The setting of *Ile* aboard a whaling ship trapped in the ice for a year, under the command of a ruthless and fanatical captain, inevitably recalls themes found in Herman Melville's novel *Moby Dick*, particularly humans' alienation from nature and each other.

Eugene O'Neill (AP Images)

AUTHOR BIOGRAPHY

Eugene Gladstone O'Neill was born in New York City on October 16, 1888, in the bedroom of a hotel suite on Times Square where his parents were living while his father James played on Broadway. James O'Neill was a successful actor who eventually gained great economic, if not artistic, success, in the then-popular genre of melodrama, in particular playing the title role in *The Count of Monte Cristo* more than four thousand times. As he grew older, the younger O'Neill spent much of his time at the family home in New London, Connecticut, and, growing fascinated with the romantic image of life at sea, became a sailor after being suspended from Princeton University. When sailing was denied him due to ill health, he turned to professional writing, first as a reporter and poet, but, by 1916, as a professional playwright, becoming intimately involved with the avant garde Provincetown Players. This group first performed all of his early plays.

Ile was first performed in November and December of 1917 in Greenwich Village in New York City by the Provincetown Players. This group originally came together in Provincetown, Maine, during the summer of 1915. The group's founding members met while vacationing and soon invited other like-minded writers, actors, and directors, including O'Neill. After an essentially amateur season in Maine, they relocated to Greenwich Village in New York and continued to work toward artistic rather than financial success. They premiered all of O'Neill's early plays between 1916 and 1918. Like *Ile*, these were all one-act dramas on nautical themes. *Ile* was first published in 1919 in *The Moon of the Caribbees, and Six other Plays of the Sea*, an anthology of O'Neill's early one-act dramas.

O'Neill soon moved beyond the purposefully small and unprofessional productions of the Provincetown Players and became one of the leading playwrights produced on Broadway. He won the Pulitzer Prize for Drama in 1922 for *Anna Christie* and again in 1928 for *Strange Interlude*. He won it a third time posthumously in 1957 for *Long Day's Journey into Night*, which he wrote in 1942 but held back from performance during his lifetime. This play, like *Ile*, was intensely autobiographical, and so the two works share many themes despite their separation in time and the consequent difference in O'Neill's artistic maturity. After a series of failed marriages, in 1929 O'Neill married Carlotta Monterey and lived in Europe until returning to the United States in 1937. In 1936, O'Neill was awarded the Nobel Prize for Literature. He died on November 27, 1953, in Boston, Massachusetts, of a degenerative nerve disease probably related to his life-long alcoholism (a condition he shared with his older brother Jamie and his sons, Eugene Jr. and Shane). Many consider O'Neill the greatest of all American playwrights.

PLOT SUMMARY

Ile is set aboard the whaling ship *Atlantic Queen* just before 1:00 p.m. one day in late June of 1895. The ship is frozen in the ice of the Bering Sea. The entire action takes place inside the captain's cabin. The printed text of the play begins with a detailed description of the cabin. There is nothing exceptional about the cabin per se, but O'Neill draws the reader's attention to certain facts. The first of these is that there is an organ in the cabin and also a feminine sewing basket. This second item suggests a woman is aboard ship, an unusual circumstance on a whaling voyage in 1895. Also, there is no rolling or pitching, motions felt almost universally while at sea. In fact, there would be nothing unusual in a stage production not showing such motions (which would be technically quite demanding), but O'Neill makes a point of mentioning and explaining their absence. The lighting in the cabin is meant to suggest that it is "one of those gray days of calm when ocean and sky are alike dead."

The steward enters the cabin and begins to clear away lunch dishes left on a table in the middle of the room. But he is soon distracted from this task by a desire to spy on the person behind the door in the rear of the cabin. He makes sure he is unobserved and goes over to the door and presses his ear against it to listen, cursing at what he hears. He hastens back to his work when Ben, a young cabin boy, enters. The conversation between the two establishes the dramatic conditions of the play. The Atlantic Queen has been frozen in an ice field in Arctic waters for nearly a year and has harvested only a miniscule amount of whale oil. The two-year contracts of the crew are up on the day of the play, making the captain's continued authority over the men ambiguous. The ice has been breaking up and it would be possible to sail to the south, though the north, with its whaling, remains ice-bound. The ship's supply of food is running low and they would be lucky to make it to a port before running out if they headed south immediately. Ben has heard a rumor that the crew intends to mutiny if the Captain does not immediately head south and the steward agrees that the situation warrants such drastic action.

The two crewmen conclude that Captain Keeney is crazy, and further, appealing to traditional ideas about insanity, that he is being punished by God. The sin being punished is also the first act that the men judge to have been mentally unsound: Keeney bringing his wife on board for the duration of the voyage. She is the one the steward was surreptitiously checking out through the door at the rear of the stage. Her reaction to the intolerable isolation of the last year locked in the ice has been to retreat further and further away from reality. She has gone from being a friend to the entire crew, mitigating the captain's harshness, to a withdrawn figure never seen by the crew who speaks only to her husband. All she is capable of doing to distract herself is sewing, and she spends most of her waking hours weeping, as the steward heard her doing through the door.

When Ben and the steward hear the captain coming down the companionway steps to his cabin, they immediately cease their conversation. The steward goes back to his job of clearing the lunch dishes while Ben furiously pretends to be cleaning the organ in the cabin. Keeney soon enters with the second mate Slocum. Keeney clears the two men out of the cabin with threats of violence, but not before noting that he is fully aware that they were "gossipin'," that is, talking about subjects subversive of Keeney's command of the ship, as they indeed were.

Once they are alone, Slocum explains what he called Keeney down into the privacy of the captain's cabin to say. With the contractual obligation of the crew expiring today, he fears the crew will cause trouble if Keeney does not order a southward course back to port. Keeney responds that he is well aware of the situation. This conference is interrupted when Mrs. Keeney comes out of her room. She announces that she wants to go up on deck, but her husband tries to dissuade her, making excuses about the weather being unsuitable. He tries to interest her in her organ as a distraction, but she replies, "I hate the organ. It puts me in mind of home." She notices that the ice has broken up to the south and renews her impulse to go up on deck to see it better, but Keeney convinces her not to and sends her back to her cabin on the excuse that he has to discuss the ship's business with Slocum.

Once Mrs. Keeney is gone the captain admits to Slocum that he didn't allow her on deck because he expects trouble from the crew. He inspects his own revolver and makes sure Slocum has his. He does not expect to have to do more than brandish them to quell any rebellious impulse in the crew, but is fully prepared to shoot if necessary. He likens the crewmen to dogs too submissive to rebel against their master. Slocum correctly infers from this that Keeney does not intend to return to port, citing the rational reasons why he might choose to do so, namely that the ship's store of food is running low and that Keeney might be subject to legal action for damages if he keeps the ship out past the crew's contractual obligation. Keeney responds by taunting him, suggesting that he might join in a mutiny, a charge that Slocum absolutely denies. Keeney agrees it is unlikely because Slocum has been his protégé for ten years and Keeney himself trained him in the whaling business. He adds, "No man kin say I ain't a good master, if I be a hard one," as though he merely considers Slocum a better breed of dog than the rest of the crew. Slocum suggests another reason for heading home, that it would be better for Mrs. Keeney, who is "ailin' like." Keeney bristles at this, and tells his subordinate to mind his own business. However, he reveals to Slocum why he will not turn back, and the admission brings forth an excessive outpouring of primitive emotions. He would feel humiliated before rival captains to return to port without a full consignment of oil. He also suggests that he has seen evidence that the ice northward of the ship is breaking up.

Keeney's tirade is interrupted by a renewed bout of weeping heard from Mrs. Keeney through the closed door. In this interval, Joe the harpooner intrudes uninvited into the captain's cabin. As a harpooner, Joe would have been a natural leader among the crew, and in fact he has come here to make the crew's demands to the captain; even so he cannot bring himself to do more than sheepishly wait to be noticed by the captain, which he soon is. Joe announces that the men wish to send a deputation to the captain. At first Keeney wants to respond by cursing them, but then agrees to see them as he inevitably must. In the interval before the deputation's arrival, Slocum suggests summoning the other officers, but Keeney insist he can take care of the matter alone.

Joe and five crewmen soon return. Acting as their leader, Joe points out that the men's contracts are finished and the food is running low. He demands on behalf of the crew to return to port. Keeney refuses, citing the imminent breakup of the northern ice floe and the chance to fill the ship's hold with oil. Joe then expresses the crew's decision to cease to work the ship except as necessary to return home, arguing that any possible legal action in the future would support this decision. Keeney reminds them that he is the legal authority while they are at sea and threatens to imprison anyone who does not obey his orders. Joe then declares that the men have no choice except to mutiny and take the ship home themselves. It is at this moment that Mrs. Keeney reemerges from her room, although none of the other characters notice in the excitement of their heated argument. She sees her husband hit Joe in the face, knocking him unconscious. The other crewmen seem likely to attack and overpower the captain, but they are cowed before Keeney and Slocum's pistols. They meekly withdraw,

dragging Joe's unconscious body with them. Keeney believes he has triumphed over them and sends Slocum up on deck to keep order. Only once the crisis is past does Keeney hear his wife's hysterical sobs and turn to attend her.

When Keeney calms his wife down to the point where she can talk, she simply says, "Oh, I can't bear it! I can't bear it any longer!" What she cannot bear is the brutality on the part of the crew and especially on the part of her husband, but most of all, a refrain of intolerable conditions that she repeats throughout the play: "the ice all around, and the silence." In a brief monologue, she admits that she demanded to come on this voyage over her husband's objections. Her whole identity was attached to Keeney's heroic reputation in the whaling community (she could not even continue as a schoolteacher lest the fact of his wife working should become a reproach); therefore she felt she needed to witness him in his own element, in command of a whaling expedition. "I guess I was dreaming about the old Vikings in the storybooks and I thought you were one of them," she tells him. However, she realizes how mistaken she was: "And instead.... All I find is ice and cold—and brutality!" She pointedly refers to the violence she witnessed him use to quell the mutiny, but also, no doubt, implicitly includes his whole demeanor as a ship's captain. She begs him to return home at once with increasing hysteria, which Keeney wishes to attribute to some physical disease such as a fever, rather than to her deteriorating mental condition or, even more accurately, to her discovery of the disjunction between his appearance and reality. He refuses to go home, insisting that the two months back to port must be extended by another two or three months to fill the ship with oil, and she demands to know why. "A woman couldn't rightly understand my reason," he tells her. She overheard his explanation to the mate of his fears of being humiliated by other captains, which she dismisses as "a stupid, stubborn reason." He retreats from that position, and also disclaims that he has any interest in the monetary profit or loss of the voyage since they are so well off from his lifelong success. But he cannot say precisely why he feels he must get his quota of oil, except that nothing but success would be right for him. Finally she reflects that if they turned back now they would reach their home port on or about their wedding anniversary. She makes a final appeal to the effect that if they do not return at once, she feels as though she will die. She demands that, if he loves her as he confesses he does, he must take her home.

Keeney finally agrees to take the ship back to its home port and so bring his wife home. She thanks him, but at that very moment Slocum comes into the cabin and announces that the ice to the north is breaking up. Casting aside all other thoughts, he receives the estimate from Slocum that the men will obey orders, and commands that the ship immediately head north in search of whales. He gleefully calls out, "And I was agoin' home like a yaller dog!" Mrs. Keeneny implores the captain to keep his promise—made but a moment ago—to head home, but he reverts to his monomania to get the whale oil at all costs, returning to his insistence that she is merely ill. He goes further, saying, "I got to prove a man to be a good husband for ye to take pride in. I got to git the ile, I tell ye." He rushes to go up on deck and personally supervise the operation of the ship, but hesitates when she starts to laugh hysterically and play the organ in a wild, chaotic way. He instead goes over and tries to get her attention, but she ignores him, even when he jostles her roughly by the shoulder. Keeney wants to convince himself that her unresponsiveness is some kind of mockery of him, but he finally comes to a different conclusion: "You said—you was a-goin' mad—God!" At that moment Slocum returns and reports that a large pod of whales has been sighted near the ship. Keeney determines he must go at once to personally lead the pursuit of the whales. He announces this to her, that they will go home just as soon as the ship is filled with oil and begs her not to go mad. He leaves, his wife taking no notice. As the curtain falls on the play, she continues to dissonantly play an unnamed hymn on her organ.

CHARACTERS

Ben, the Cabin Boy
Ben is a teenaged boy given to tricks such as making handstands on deck for his own amusement. Being so young, he was at one time Mrs. Keeney's special pet. He is keen to show his importance by repeating to the steward what he has overheard from other crewmen who are suggesting the possibility of mutiny, and also to join in by supporting the opinion that such a step might be necessary.

Joe, a Harpooner
Joe is "an enormous six-footer with a battered, ugly face." As a harpooner, he is the leader of one of the ship's boats actually involved in chasing whales. He was chosen by the crew to deliver their ultimatum to return home or face mutiny to Captain Keeney. At first he treats Keeney with the deference he is accustomed to, but when he lays out the demands of the crew, he summons up the courage to act with bravado, only to be knocked unconscious by Keeney.

Mrs. Annie Keeney
Annie Keeney, the wife of Captain Keeney, came along on the voyage—over Keeney's objections—out of admiration for her husband. "I used to dream of sailing on the great, wide, glorious ocean. I wanted to be by your side in the danger and vigorous life of it all. I wanted to see you the hero they make you out to be in Homeport." But it turned out nothing like she had hoped. "And instead.... All I find is ice and cold—and brutality!" The disparity between expectation and reality has had a profound effect on her. When she first came on board she acted as a ministering angel to the crew. At the beginning of the play, Ben the cabin boy and the steward praise her former character, but cannot do so without noting the drastic change in her, as the former says, "She useter be awful nice to me before—she got—like she is." To remove any doubt, the steward spells out how she now is: "she's near lost her mind." By the time the audience sees her emerge from her cabin, she is frightened and filled with dread, her eyes permanently red from weeping. She has lost weight from her depression.

When Mrs. Keeney finally confronts her husband in the climax of the play, she reveals that she has sacrificed everything for what she believed was his heroism. She gave up her career as a schoolteacher, which would have kept her occupied during his long voyages, because a hero could not have a wife who was independent of him. She finally gave up her home in order to come and see his heroism in action on the present voyage, but she realizes that it is nothing except brutality. After subsuming herself to him she is nothing but an empty shell, entirely dependent on him. When she sees that she too is to be subordinated to his pride, her individual identity is completely destroyed, the condition O'Neill describes as going mad.

Captain David Keeney
David Keeney, the captain of the *Atlantic Queen*, is about forty years old. He is just above average in height but possesses a massive barrel chest. His hair has gone gray and he wears it long in the nautical

fashion of the day. "His face is massive and deeply lined, with gray-blue eyes of a bleak hardness."

Before he is seen, the steward describes Keeney as "a hard man—as hard a man as ever sailed the seas." He emphasizes this by reminding Ben that Keeney would beat him simply for fooling around (making handstands on deck). At one point Keeney's temper and disrespect are demonstrated when he nearly strikes the steward for breaking a dish and being dilatory in his duties. He thinks better of it and tells the steward, "'Twould be like hitting a worm." These early threats of violence prefigure his suppression of the mutiny through fisticuffs and threats of gun play. It becomes clear that despite his dissatisfaction with the conditions and success of the voyage, the steward is personally in fear and awe of Keeney and the very sight of Keeney fills the steward with fear. The parallelism in phrases like the steward's "Damn him and damn the ice!" suggest that there is something greater than human about Keeney, that the steward is disposed to see him as a force of nature on equal terms with the elements of the sea and the weather. At the same time, he believes the captain's mental condition has become unstable. Keeney spends all of his time on deck staring at the pack ice to the north that separates them from the whaling grounds, and which blocks the fulfillment of the ship's mission when reason might suggest that the sensible course would be to look to the south and a return to port, admitting that the expedition has failed. In particular, he is treating those around him with increasing disregard. He treats the ship's crew like dogs and although he not overtly cruel to his wife, the mere continuation of their hopeless position at sea is oppressive to her. Finally the steward judges that Keeney is being driven mad by his obsession: "All he thinks on is gittin' the ile—'s if it was our fault he ain't had good luck with the whales. I think the man's mighty nigh losin' his senses." The captain's actions have driven the steward from an attitude of awed loyalty to one of bitter hatred and rejection, summed up in the curse that ends the initial conversation of the play: "God send his soul to hell for the devil he is!"

When his second mate Slocum all but demands that Keeney return to port, he admits to his subordinate why he will not consider the idea. He has no interest in the profit to be made from a full cargo of oil. Instead his motivation is pride. He cannot stand the thought of being humiliated before rival whaling captains by returning with a small consignment of oil. The

very thought of it sends him into a frenzy that causes him to strike the table top in wrath in lieu of any other target. Moreover, the idea of avoiding the mockery of his peers has assumed grandiose, almost theological overtones: "I got to git the ile! I got to git it in spite of all hell, and by God, I ain't agoin' home till I do git it!"

Keeney is briefly able to have his heart moved and relents in his quest, agreeing to go back to port when his wife begs him to do so. To her, Keeney can offer very little explanation of why the oil is so important to him (though he does consciously disavow the idea that it is pride), save that it is an essential part of his nature. In the end, he disavows everything else, even the love and sanity of his wife, to "git the ile."

Mate
See Slocum

Members of the Crew
The members of the crew have supernumerary roles (meaning that they appear on stage but have no spoken lines). They are not functionally different from Joe the harpooner who speaks for them. O'Neill may have had in mind the chorus of a Greek drama, who either all speak the same lines together or else allow a single member to speak for them. In this case it is significant that they never speak either to express their own opinions or to support what Joe tells the captain. From another viewpoint, the multiplication of crew members beyond Joe in the confrontation with the captain is necessary for the sake of realism.

Slocum
The ship's second mate is named Slocum. He is a tall, lean man who is about thirty years old. O'Neill describes his face as weather-beaten, which would probably today be termed "suntanned." He has been trained by Keeney over the course of the last ten years and is unwavering in his loyalty, despite his personal desire to end the voyage and return to port.

The Steward
The steward is an old man filled with anger and cursing; perhaps he feels slighted over not being advanced as rapidly as younger crewmen like Slocum. In any case, he holds Captain Keeney in a sort of superstitious dread and keeps to himself a terrible wrath against his injustice. This slips out only in occasional discourses and curses against his captain, spoken only when their object cannot possibly hear.

TOPICS FOR FURTHER STUDY

- What is the status of whaling in the modern world? Research how whaling functions in various nations, including among traditional peoples living around the Arctic Ocean, as well as in Norway and Japan. Write a paper comparing and contrasting the practice of whaling in the twenty-first century and in 1895.

- How have society's ideas of masculinity and femininity changed since O'Neill's day? How might a modern woman have reacted in Mrs. Keeney's place? Explore a modern female character's response to crisis in a short story.

- O'Neill was fascinated with ancient Greek drama. Even in *Ile*, the crew has some characteristics of a Greek chorus, and the action of the play follows many conventions of Greek drama, including the unity of time and space and the convention of not allowing more than three speaking characters on stage at one time. Later in life, O'Neill toyed with the idea of reviving the Greek practice of having actors wear masks with their dramatic emotions clearly displayed in a some-

what cartoonish form, to better show the audience members the feelings of the characters, which might not be easily discernable over the distance between the seats and the stage in a large theater. Design masks to represent the major characters of *Ile*. Bear in mind that dramatic changes in a character's feelings would have been shown by changing masks while offstage. For example, Mrs. Keeney might have one mask showing depression and another showing insanity.

- Read O'Neill's play *A Long Day's Journey into Night*. That play and *Ile* are generally considered to be among O'Neill's most autobiographical. Compare them to a biography of O'Neill. What facts or events of his life appear to influence both plays? How do the plays differ in their representations of the author's life? Write a critical essay comparing and contrasting the autobiographical elements of the two works and exploring what these different representations might reveal about the author.

THEMES

Humans versus Nature

Humans' relationship to nature is a common literary theme in American literature, especially in relation to man's journey to the limits, whether on the frontier or, as in O'Neill's play, on a whaling voyage. Nineteenth-century writers like Herman Melville and Jack London rejected earlier, Romantic ideas of nature in the work of Emerson and Thoreau—that man and nature were harmonious and that man could see the best part of his existence reflected in the natural world. Nature, therefore, becomes a powerful yet indifferent force that will dispense with man and man's ego-driven pursuits; nature can never truly be conquered. In *Ile*, Captain Keeney

succeeds in overcoming nature to the extent that by the end of the play he will "git the ile," but at a terrible cost.

Captain Keeney's profession as a whaling captain puts him in direct conflict with nature insofar as he must hunt down whales and venture through the most remote areas of the earth in the most extreme weather conditions. Yet O'Neill establishes a deeper conflict between Keeney and the natural world. Keeney is detached from the human world around him and focused on the weather and the ocean as if they might be his opponent in a chess match: "... He don't see nothin'. He just walks up and down like he didn't notice nobody—and stares at the ice to the no'the'ard." He seems to have a monomania for getting his quota of whale oil: "He won't look

Ship trapped in ice (© Corbis)

nowheres but no'the'ard where they's only the ice to see. He don't want to see no clear water. All he thinks on is gittin' the ile." To Keeney this represents victory over the elements. Keeney finally triumphs over nature with the breakup of the northern icepack and the resumption of a rich whale hunt:

> Hell! I got to git the ile, I tell you. How could I figger on this ice? It's never been so bad before in the thirty year I been a-comin' here. And now it's breakin'up. In a couple o'days it'll be all gone. And they's whale here, plenty of 'em. I know they is and I ain't never gone wrong yit.

His triumph comes at the expense of his wife's sanity. She, on the other hand, is ultimately defeated by nature. Whatever forces drive her mad, they are symbolized by ice. The ice is always mentioned in connection with her growing distance from reality, sometimes simply, "ice, ice, ice!"

Traditional Gender Roles

In *Ile*, O'Neill is remarkably concerned with issues of traditional gender roles. The play dramatizes the crossing of conventional gender boundaries, an act that drives the tension in *Ile*. The central conflict of the play comes about from Mrs. Keeney wanting to leave the home, a realm traditionally considered feminine, and join the whaling voyage, a realm traditionally considered masculine. Keeney tells his wife as much, saying, "I warned you what it'd be, Annie. 'Whalin' ain't no ladies' tea party,' I says to you, and 'you better stay to home where you've got all your woman's comforts.'" Keeney eventually conceives of his wife's presence on board as an attack on his masculine identity. He tells her, "Woman, you ain't adoin' right when you meddle in men's business and weaken 'em."

In the fictive world O'Neill creates, crossing traditional gender boundaries results in disaster. Ultimately, Mrs. Keeney's entrance into the male world of the ship brings about her ruin; her "madness" suggests that she has lost her ability to comprehend herself and the world. Interestingly, the steward suggests that Captain Keeney's decision to bring her in the first place was a sign of his madness. "Who but a man that's mad would take his woman . . . on a stinkin' whalin' ship to the Arctic seas," he remarks to Ben.

STYLE

Dramatic Unities

The ancient Greek philosopher Aristotle, writing a generation after the golden age of Greek Drama, set out in the first book of his *Poetics* to analyze what made the plays of Aeschylus, Sophocles, and Euripides so exceptional. One element that he identified is known as dramatic unity. This means that the performance represents real actions that could and do all take place in a single physical space convincingly represented by the stage set and in a time no greater than that occupied by the performance of the play. To put this in modern terms, a play with dramatic unity ought not to represent actions that take place over many different areas of the world or over years all compressed down into the time and space of the stage performance, but should be something like a real-time surveillance video of the action at a single point. Many playwrights, notably Shakespeare, have completely ignored this "rule," but O'Neill followed the dramatic unities insofar as possible, and in no play as strictly as in *Ile*, which takes place in a single small room (able to be shown convincingly in the tiny Provincetown Players' stage where it premiered) and in the space of only a few minutes time. In addition, in this play O'Neill follows the Greek practice of having no more than three speaking characters on stage at any one time.

Realism

Realism developed as a style in reaction to the emotional and dramatic excesses of the melodramas popular at the end of the nineteenth century, which relied on an unrealistic and artificial manipulation of the audience's emotions. European playwrights like Anton Chekov, Henrik Ibsen, and August Strindberg produced a new type of play that depended upon the development of realistic characters. Realist drama had a profound impact on O'Neill. In an early play like *Ile*, O'Neill used natural rather than exaggerated speech, actions, and plot devices to engage the audience's emotions directly, as if they were participating in events in the real world. He draws upon his own memories and feelings to create a fictional experience for the audience based on his real life.

One element of the realism in the play is the language used by its characters. The speech of the sailors, who comprise all but one of the characters, is markedly dialectical, not least in the use of "ile" for "oil" in the title of the piece.

The language is no doubt molded on that of the men O'Neill himself sailed with in his youth and on retired sailors that O'Neill knew in his New England boyhood who were of the generation of the play set in 1895. One purpose of the use of dialect was to make a sharp distinction from the stereotyped language of melodrama, of which O'Neill disapproved. Yet lines like the steward's description of Captain Keeeny, "He's a hard man—as hard a man as ever sailed the seas," today seem cliché and even melodramatic in their familiarity. Time and fame have not served O'Neill well in this respect. Much of the language of the play seems to verge on parody precisely because lesser writers have so frequently turned to the language here and in his other nautical-themed plays and thereby reduced it by overuse and transference to lower genres. Thus, to a modern audience, the language hardly seems to counter stereotypes.

HISTORICAL CONTEXT

The Provincetown Players

In the summer of 1915, a group of intellectuals vacationing in Provincetown, Maine, decided to form their own theater company, which became known as the Provincetown Players. They were dissatisfied with the theater being produced on Broadway, which often strove for popular appeal at the expense of artistic integrity and generally consisted of melodramas (a drama that focused on artificially heightened emotions at the expense of realism) and romantic comedies. They soon sent for O'Neill, whom the journalist Jack Reed knew to be writing plays in the new realist style popular in Europe. O'Neill was only too happy with this development because he saw it as a way of breaking with his father, who had, in O'Neill's view, thrown away an artistically promising career in favor of playing a single popular and profitable but artistically uninteresting role on Broadway, performing the lead role in a melodrama based on Alexander Dumas's novel *The Count of Monte Cristo* more than four thousand times. While some members of the Provincetown Players were professional writers, none had experience in the theater as directors, actors, or stage designers. However, they felt that their lack of experience would give their productions a direct simplicity that was preferable to the exaggerated

COMPARE
&
CONTRAST

- **1895:** Society views women as dependent upon men, for the most part in line with existing legal realities.

  1917: Women's social roles are rapidly changing, as evidenced by the fast-growing movement for women's suffrage, or the right to vote, which would become law in 1920.

  Today: Women have identical legal and political standing with men and generally have a similar range of social opportunities and roles.

- **1895:** The treatment and social recognition of mental illness is still largely based on pseudoscience and folk tradition.

1917: The treatment of mental illness is becoming more scientific because of the work of pioneering psychologists like William James and Sigmund Freud.

Today: The treatment of mental illness is a fully integrated part of scientific medicine.

- **1895:** Whaling is a major American industry; in particular, whale oil is used in lamps, the main source of indoor lighting.

  1917: Whaling has largely vanished from the American economy.

  Today: Whaling is illegal throughout the world (excluding Norway), except to satisfy the traditional rights of peoples indigenous to the Arctic and for scientific purposes.

---

and overwrought professional productions on Broadway. They immediately started to produce short plays by O'Neill and other writers in private houses in Provincetown and other unlikely venues, to considerable critical and even commercial success.

In 1916, they bought a brownstone in Greenwich Village, New York, and converted the living room into a tiny theater with a stage only ten feet wide, before which only 140 viewers could be crammed in, and over three years produced full seasons of new works, including O'Neill's *Ile* in 1917. This play was especially written for the Provincetown Players and tailored to the strengths and weaknesses of the amateur ethos of their productions. The Provincetown Players originally took pride in "mistakes" that replicated real life, such as lines misspoken and errors in blocking. The authors acted as unofficial directors of their own works, but really no one was in charge, leading to endless arguments on matters ranging from details of production to whether or not critics ought to be allowed in the audience. By late 1917, however, they were joined by Nina Moise, a recent graduate from Stanford University with a degree

in theater. She became the group's director, including directing *Ile*. She introduced some needed correctives to the group's excessive amateurism, but as a result most of the original members soon drifted away. Nevertheless the Players still remained a small independent theater that could afford to produce risky but important plays that Broadway would not touch, premiering many Pulitzer Prize-winning works besides O'Neill's. The company remained the premier avant garde theater in New York until 1929 when the economic disaster of the Depression caused it to close.

Herman Melville's Moby Dick

O'Neill's *Ile* has many commonalities with Herman Melville's 1851 novel *Moby Dick*, a similarity noted by critic Travis Bogard in his book *Contour in Time: The Plays of Eugene O'Neill*. Both works concern the captain of a whaling ship (Captain Ahab and Captain Keeney) who has transformed his commercial enterprise into an obsessive personal quest that is becoming increasingly irrational and destructive of everyone around him. Moreover, both seem to be carrying on some sort of personal struggle against nature and the world itself. Although we have no direct knowledge of the genesis of *Ile* (O'Neill kept a Work Diary in which he meticulously detailed his ideas, methods, and sources, but this does not begin until 1924), there can be little doubt that it was directly inspired by Melville's novel. *Moby Dick* originally received mixed reviews and failed to become an established classic, lapsing into obscurity shortly after it was published. The novel's moral ambiguity and metaphysical complexity did not find favor with contemporary audiences. However, in the wake of widespread intellectual and spiritual alienation felt during and after World War I, *Moby Dick* found a new appeal and quickly became recognized as an important work, if not the greatest American novel. The renaissance of Melville's novel swept through the New York intellectual community early in 1917, by word of mouth more than published criticism. *Ile* premiered on November 30, 1917, and was written over the preceding weeks or months, so O'Neill would certainly have been aware of the newly popular novel as he worked on his play. While O'Neill's reference to the symbolic structure of *Moby Dick* is superficial, that is to be explained by his relative inexperience as a playwright and the novelty of Melville's work, which could hardly have been well examined so quickly.

Ernest Shackleton's Expedition to Antarctica

At the beginning of *Ile*, Keeney's ship has spent the last year frozen in the pack ice of the Bering Sea (between Alaska and Russia). Contemporary audiences must have been reminded of the harrowing, real-life adventure of the expedition of Sir Ernest Shackleton (1914–17), which set out to cross the Antarctic continent but met disaster after being frozen in the ice for several months and eventually having their ship destroyed by the pressure of the ice on its hull. They sailed from Antarctica to Elephant Island and then to South Georgia in one of the ship's boats, during which time Shackleton had to face down a possible mutiny at pistol point. Shackleton himself reached the Falklands in June 1916 to organize the rescue of his men from Elephant Island (making worldwide headlines) and the entire crew returned safely to England on May 29, 1917, six months before the premiere of *Ile*.

The Whale Fishery

In the nineteenth century, whale fishing was a major American industry. It was centered in the port towns of New England such as Nantucket and New Bedford. Throughout most of the nineteenth century, whale oil-burning lamps were the primary source of illumination in American homes; however, by 1895, the use of whale oil was waning and, by 1917, the date at which *Ile* was written, it was completely replaced by a whole series of new technologies, including kerosene fuel for lamps (the first use that petroleum was put to), and the introduction of natural gas-burning jets, and finally by lightbulbs, as gas lines and electrifications spread to more and more American homes. For O'Neill, old stories of the whale fishery heard from retired sailors in his boyhood home of New London, Connecticut, especially his neighbor Captain Nat Keeney, were probably a source of deep nostalgia, contributing to his romantic desire to go to sea, and the later focus of his early plays on nautical themes. Ecological ideas related to modern concerns about whaling, although sometimes referenced in playbills of recent productions of *Ile*, could hardly have played any part in O'Neill's original inspiration, since ideas of that kind did not enter popular consciousness until the 1950s and 1960s.

CRITICAL OVERVIEW

Since *Ile* was an early and relatively minor work of O'Neill's, it has not received the same degree of critical attention as some of his more mature plays. An anonymous review of *Ile* in the *Dramatist* in July 1919, occasioned by the play's publication in *The Moon of the Caribbees*, is not terribly enthusiastic. The reviewer considers it inferior to the other plays in the volume because it is under-dramatized. While he seems to support the overall realistic tone of the play, he considers that the wife's descent into madness is arbitrary, and that the viewer, not having been shown why it is so, neither feels it nor understands it. Instead, he would prefer the viewer be made to experience the wife's change in mental condition for himself.

The biographers Arthur and Barbara Gelb, in *O'Neill: Life with Monte Cristo*, find sources for *Ile* in its author's New England background. According to the Gelbs, an old friend of the

O'Neill family, the retired whaling captain Nathanial Keeney, and O'Neill's friend novelist Mary Vorse passed on to him the Provincetown story of the whaling captain John Cook, which in its general content was nearly identical to the plot of *Ile*. Travis Bogard, in his book *Contour in Time: The Plays of Eugene O'Neill*, remarks on the similarity of Captain Keeney to Melville's Captain Ahab in *Moby Dick* and observes, "In Keeney, for the first time, O'Neill draws the character of a man who commits a decisive act of will." His earlier characters were generally tragic prisoners of fate. Margaret Loftus Ranald and Judith E. Barlow, each writing in *The Cambridge Companion to Eugene O'Neill*, note the criticism of both genders—each from the viewpoint of the other—that is a major theme of the play. Barlow also sees Mrs. Keeney as an early treatment of O'Neill's own mother, a point expanded upon by Jean Chothia in the same volume and by the Gelbs. Generally, *Ile* is viewed as representing an important stage of growth in O'Neill's work rather than being a masterpiece in and of itself.

CRITICISM

Bradley A. Skeen

Skeen is a classics professor. In this essay, he considers Ile *as a representation of basic human psychological drives.*

Ile is certainly not comparable to the great plays of O'Neill's mature period in the 1930s and 1940s, such as *Mourning Becomes Electra* or *Long Day's Journey into Night*. It is nevertheless of considerable importance in the development of O'Neill as a playwright. It is the first of his plays written after he became established as a playwright, at least in intellectual if not yet popular circles. It has a curious origin. The depictions of Mrs. Keeney's descent into madness and Captain Keeney's overbearing character are commonly taken to be reflections of O'Neill's own mother's drug addiction and his father's personality, types that he would return to over and over throughout his career. The play is also based on the stories of the sea he heard as a boy in the port of New London, particularly from his neighbor the retired seaman Captain Nat Keeney, who was also the basis for Captain Turner in *Long Day's Journey into Night*. Then, O'Neill's own years at sea in the merchant

WHAT DO I READ NEXT?

- Herman Melville's *Moby Dick* was published in 1851 and enjoyed a new vogue in 1917. It was likely an inspiration for O'Neill's *Ile*.

- O'Neill's play *Long Day's Journey into Night* was written in 1942 but not performed until 1956, after O'Neill's death. It explores some of the autobiographical elements also present in *Ile*, but in a more extensive and sophisticated fashion.

- Marc L. Songigni's *The Lost Fleet: A Yankee Whaler's Struggle against the Confederate Navy and Arctic Disaster*, published in 2007, is a general account of the New England whaling industry in the difficult era of the Civil War, but it also focuses on a single voyage to the Bering Sea by whaling captain Thomas William Williams, accompanied by his wife Eliza.

- In *The Anatomy of Madness*, published in 1985, medical historian Roy Porter gives an introductory account of the changing perception of mental illness through history.

marine contributed considerably to the realism of the depiction of ship life. But there were two more recent points of departure that must have impelled O'Neill to write in the direction he took. One was the new fashion for *Moby Dick*, which swept the New York intellectual community in 1917. Another was a story of local lore in Provincetown, Maine, told to O'Neill when he first joined with the Provincetown Players by the suffragette and novelist Mary Vorse, who acted as the group's patron. According to the story, as told in Arthur and Barbara Gelb's second biography of O'Neill, *O'Neill: Life with Monte Cristo*, Vorse knew a Captain John Cook who retired to Provincetown and who had quelled a mutiny on one voyage after staying at sea for over two years. On another voyage, Cook had taken his wife (not as rare an event as *Ile* suggests), who went mad—that is, when she returned home, she ceased to speak to anyone

> WHAT O'NEILL IS CONCERNED WITH IS THE CONFLICT BETWEEN TWO BASIC HUMAN DRIVES— THE WILL TO CONTROL AND THE DESIRE TO CREATE—THAT OPERATE AT ODDS WITH EACH OTHER YET MUST STRIKE SOME KIND OF BALANCE IN EVERY PERSON."

else and visibly spent the day talking to herself while going about her household chores. Supposedly this madness was the result of the monotony of the voyage and her witnessing the brutality necessary for her husband to control the crew. In any case, these events formed the backdrop of O'Neill's drama.

Ile is about the collision of two worlds that may, for the purpose of convenience, be called the masculine and the feminine, although those terms have here a symbolic rather than a literal sense. Any attempt to read the play in feminist terms, as the patriarchal oppression of an individual woman, would prevent the reader from coming to grips with the actual meaning of the drama. In *Ile*, the masculine principle, represented by Captain Keeney, is a drive for achievement and mastery. Keeney does not pursue the "ile," or oil, for profit, glory, or any other tangible, external reason. "Gittin' the ile" is what he must do to become a fully actualized human being. It represents the abstract qualities of discipline and success. Keeney's compulsion for the "ile" is his impulse toward justice and virtue and against compromise. Keeney cannot say precisely why he must "git the ile," but he knows if he fails it will destroy his identity as a man; it will reduce him to the position of a child taunted by his schoolmates:

> [D]'you s'pose any of 'em would believe that— any o' them skippers I've beaten voyage after voyage? Can't you hear 'em laughin' and sneerin'—Tibbots 'n' Harris 'n' Simms and the rest—and all o' Homeport makin' fun o' me? "Dave Keeney what boasts he's the best whalin' skipper out o' Homeport comin' back with a measly four hundred barrel of ile?"

The masculine principle has qualities which, viewed from outside, can be seen as deficiencies.

This principle is hard and brutal because it is only concerned with achieving its goal. Keeney, however, takes pride in the mixture of these qualities and does not see them as defects. "No man kin say I ain't a good master, if I be a hard one." Also, "I'm the law on this ship." That is how Keeney wishes to be perceived. Merely male beings, such as the crewmen, who do not fully possess this actualized masculinity are not men but animals, "dogs" in the sense that they must be controlled by those who *are* men. Keeney is momentarily driven by kindness to agree to give up the "ile" for the sake of his wife, and once he recovers he curses himself, "And I was agoin' home like a yaller dog!" Once the men are brought under control, "They're meek as lambs." Keeney's masculine identity is ultimately fulfilled, though held in check for a year by the ice, and it is clear that he will succeed in "gittin' the ile."

The feminine principle in *Ile* is represented by Mrs. Keeney. This idea is not as well developed in the play as is the masculine principle, but its character is clear enough. It is peace and repose instead of action; it is waiting instead of demanding. It delights in building up the self, not through mastery and dominance but through cultivation with creative pastimes such as art, music, and learning. (Ann Keeney has been a schoolteacher.) Religion, represented by the hymn she plays, is clearly feminine in this sense, but notably both of the Keeneys bear Biblical names. David was the king of Israel who wrested control of the kingdom through violence and conquest, bringing order to Israelite tribes who were little more than bands of brigands without his leadership. Ann, from the Hebrew *hannah*, means "grace." Defects associated with the feminine principle in *Ile* include weakness and passivity.

These masculine and feminine worlds or elements, O'Neill suggests, cannot be mixed. If they are, whoever mixes them must immediately fall into a despicable hermaphroditic state that truly represents neither principle. This is Keeney's judgment on the steward. "Instead of doin' your rightful work ye've been below here gossipin' old woman's talk with that boy." The two worlds can interact in only one way, through love, and this is the principle that built the Keeneys' once successful marriage. The blending of the masculine and feminine principles in love is necessary because it allows each principle to experience the virtues of the other. Keeney is kind to his wife because he loves her, and kindness is the opposite of his quality of brutality, which he finds necessary in the masculine sphere. They have a point of contact through the masculine's entry into the feminine sphere of the home; however, there seems to be some fault or flaw marring the marriage that O'Neill does not fully articulate. He indicates it by stating that the marriage does not have the usual result of offspring, but is sterile. Mrs. Keeney expresses the incomplete thought, "I sometimes think if we could only have had a child." What she means, no doubt, is that she would never, in that case, have asked to intrude into the masculine world of the whaling ship. So it was the incompletion of her feminine identity that led her to invade the masculine. Her ideas of what the masculine life of the ship would be like were a fantasy; she imagined that she would see her husband as a sort of Viking hero (in other words, a figure of melodrama, which was hateful to O'Neill). It is this mixing of the two spheres, for which Captain Keeney, in giving his consent, is as much to blame as his wife, that leads to disaster.

Once aboard the whaling ship, the feminine principle represented by Mrs. Keeney is stifled, as she is unable to connect with anyone. At first she is kind to the crew, especially the young cabin boy, Ben, who might in some sense be a surrogate son, but she grows increasingly distant and withdrawn over the course of the voyage. Throughout the play, she consistently blames this on the factors of silence and the ice that surrounds the ship. "All this horrible brutality, and these brutes of men, and this terrible ship, and this prison cell of a room, and the ice all around, and the silence." She feels that her mind is being distorted by these same factors. "I feel as if the cold and the silence were crushing down on my brain." When her husband notices a mad look in her eye, she explains, "It's the ice and the cold and the silence—they'd make anyone look strange." "The silence" represents her inability to connect with those around her, the profound alienation in the impossibility of bridging the gap between the feminine and the masculine. It is symbolized by the ice, a cold, numbing element, the opposite of the love that would more properly exist between the two gender types and the factor that cuts the ship itself off from the whole world. It is the brutality of the masculine, unalloyed with the kindness of the feminine, that prevents her connection.

Most of all, Captain Keeney fails to explain the whole meaning and character of his own existence to her, because the masculine is as unable to communicate with the feminine as the feminine is with the masculine. "You don't see my meanin'. I got to git the ile," he tells her. Thus Keeney's entire purpose in existence in unintelligible to her. It is no wonder that this alienation results in a breakdown in communication that is described as madness, the utter inability to convey meaning across the gap. Though the reader might at first think this madness affects only Mrs. Keeney, this is not the case. Captain Keeney is rendered equally unable to communicate with her. He refuses to accept her communication; he thinks it is a form of mockery or pretense, anything other than the direct communication it is. Having failed to understand her, he imagines that fulfilling his own masculine identity will somehow restore her. "I know you're foolin' me, Annie. You ain't out of your mind—be you? I'll git the ile now right enough." Keeney asserts, "I got to prove a man to be a good husband for ye to take pride in. I got to git the ile, I tell ye," believing in contradiction of any realistic assessment of the situation, and that his triumph will heal her suffering. Both are imprisoned in worlds that are each unable to communicate any longer with the other.

One should not attach the masculine and feminine symbols of O'Neill's play to the biological genders. The mere lack of communication between the sexes is not what he is discussing, though a lack of communication in his parents' marriage may inform his play on some level. What O'Neill is concerned with is the conflict between two basic human drives— the will to control and the desire to create—that operate at odds with each other yet must strike some kind of balance in every person. If the balance is struck poorly, the result is not madness in a clinical sense (and, indeed, one would be hard-pressed to diagnose or describe Mrs. Keeney's "madness" in psychiatric terms), but one fails to become a human being living up to his potential, a failure O'Neill characterizes as madness.

Source: Bradley Skeen, Critical Essay on *Ile*, in *Drama for Students*, Gale, Cengage Learning, 2009.

Edd Winfield Parks

In the following excerpt, Parks traces the development of O'Neill's philosophy in his dramas, including Ile.

> AS IN ALL GREAT PLAYS THERE ARE TWO CONFLICTS: THE INTERNAL STRUGGLE IN CAPTAIN KEENEY BETWEEN PRIDE AND COMPASSION; THE EXTERNAL STRUGGLE BETWEEN A CAPTAIN AND HIS CREW, A HUSBAND AND HIS WIFE, A MAN AND THE UNIVERSE."

For some twenty years (1936–1956), Eugene O'Neill's expressionistic dramas with their symbolic distortion of objective facts to reveal inner experiences were more popular in South America and especially in the Scandinavian countries than they were at home. The dramatist who in the 1920s had been awarded three Pulitzer Prizes was regarded mainly as of historical importance when in 1936 he was the recipient of the Nobel Prize. To many critics, it seemed a recognition (belated or, perhaps, undeserved) of work that might once have been exciting but that no longer seemed vital or particularly relevant. In the main, we failed to see in his work what the Scandinavians found in it.

Since 1956, there has been a tremendous upsurge of interest in O'Neill's plays. When *The Iceman Cometh* was produced in New York in 1946, it met with an exceedingly cool reception; ten years later, it was a brilliant success. So, at least as far as surface recognition was concerned, were the autobiographical plays, *A Moon for the Misbegotten* and *Long Day's Journey into Night*, as well as the historical play, *A Touch of the Poet*. The rather grim story of a tubercular prostitute, *Anna Christie*, has been turned into a musical comedy; the tragic *Desire Under the Elms* has been turned into a movie that follows with reasonable faithfulness the play itself and the movie script that O'Neill once prepared from it (the substitution of a foreign for a New England girl was made by O'Neill in the script).

This may be no more than jumping on the bandwagon, although only the musical comedy really seems a misguided and hardboiled attempt to gain financial advantage from a newly-found popularity. Yet there is little to indicate that we have yet recognized the ideas behind O'Neill's

plays—the ideas that today make him a living force in Sweden, Denmark, and Brazil. We have concentrated too much on the sense of doom and futility that pervades O'Neill's work. Undeniably this negative aspect is there. The man who was always "a little in love with death" was assuredly not an optimist when he dealt with life. Yet a reading of O'Neill plays indicates that he is not basically a deterministic writer, but rather that he has been attempting to find a philosophy that would reconcile a rationalistic view of the universe with man's need for something beyond rationalism—for a sense of the infinite beyond the finite.

Early in his career, O'Neill recognized this basic necessity, when he wrote in an essay that "the playwright today must dig at the roots of the sickness of today as he feels it—the death of the old God and the failure of science and materialism to give any satisfying new one for the surviving primitive religious instinct to find a meaning for life in." In the attempt to find that meaning and to state it in dramatic terms, O'Neill has temporarily embraced and then discarded many modern substitutes for religion, and has even attempted to re-state the Catholic concept of religion in the terms of modern psychology. Essentially he has been a mystic who used the trappings of realism, but a mystic uneasily aware that with the advent of scientific determinism came the need for a new symbolism.

For a new day in man's thought, a new and fresh power was needed. An instinctive, convinced belief in mythological gods and heroes (Hebraic as well as Scandinavian or Greek) was past; even the moral order no longer carried a vital power. Instead, that power was to be found in the scientific laws which were the true if inanimate rulers of the universe. Writers could no longer accept the myths of yesterday, as Herman Melville earlier had recognized when he wrote that "great geniuses are a part of their times; they themselves are the times, and possess a corresponding coloring." So for *Moby Dick* Melville used a scientific and natural symbolism: he took for a springboard into his exploration of the unknowable soul not an outworn mythology but the sea and a man's search for an actual and a symbolic white whale. Nature became the tragic force, and Moby Dick the *deus ex machina*. O'Neill's great master, Henrik Ibsen, made heredity a tragic force in *Ghosts;* however unjust it might be, it led as surely to irrevocable doom as ever the moral order had. These and many other writers created powerful literary conventions out of the scientific thought of the time.

O'Neill also has followed these modern conventions. In his first important play, *The Moon of the Caribbees,* he set man against nature, with the spirit of the sea intended to be the hero, and the man Smitty reduced to silhouetted gestures of self-pity. Smitty's sentimental posings, set against the revealing moods of the sea's eternal truth, reveal that he is out of harmony with nature and therefore no longer attuned to beauty. Only the noble savage, or in our time the natural man, can attain this harmony. O'Neill stated this theme explicitly when he tried to explain the meaning of a difficult and to many people a confusing play: the protagonist of *The Hairy Ape* is "a symbol of man, who has lost his old harmony with nature the harmony which he used to have as an animal and has not acquired in a spiritual way...The public saw just the stoker, not the symbol, and the symbol makes the play either important or just another play...The subject here is the same ancient one that always was and always will be the one subject for drama, and that is man and his struggle with his own fate. The struggle used to be with the gods, but is now with himself, his own past, his attempt 'to belong'."

O'Neill temporarily abandoned this immediate symbol, but throughout the plays the ultimate longing and the ultimate symbol remain the same: man's desire to find a satisfactory spiritual peace, a place "to belong" not only in this world but in relation to the universe. The quest was in part at least a personal one. Much later he was to write of himself that "I will always be a stranger who never feels at home...who can never belong."

For dramatic purposes, however, he turned back to the theme of man's struggle against nature; out of it, in fact, he wrote one of his greatest plays, *Ile*. Here a tight, just, hard-fisted New England sea captain who has failed for the first time to secure his quota of whale oil is faced with mutiny, and with the prospect of a wife slowly going insane from loneliness and fear; but when the ice breaks and the whales spout, the captain turns inevitably to the chase. The background is deliberately meager. All the overtones, the true background, are in the struggle shadowed forth rather than expressed between man and his ancient enemy, nature. As in all great plays there are two conflicts: the internal struggle in Captain Keeney between pride and compassion; the external struggle between a captain and his crew, a husband and his wife, a man and the universe. Because he is above all else the primitive man, the proud hunter, Captain Keeney makes his decision; and relentlessly, with nature as inexorable as ever were the Greek gods, tragedy results.

The play was satisfying, but to O'Neill the philosophy behind it was not. Man's spirit had to be reckoned with, as well as man's mind. Always the spirit seeks an assurance of immortality. If a rationalistic and mechanistic philosophy denies and to the rational mind proves that it cannot be found through religion, that the assurance can no longer be achieved through faith, then it must be sought elsewhere. In his own search, O'Neill fell temporarily under the sway of the idea that a man attains immortality through his descendants. This is the underlying motif of *The Fountain*. In a program note, O'Neill told the audience that "The idea of writing a 'Fountain' came on finally from my interest in the recurrence in folklore of the beautiful legend of a healing spring of eternal youth." So Ponce de Leon searches fruitlessly for this spring which will wash away the years and give him an earthly immortality; at last, when he has given up hope, he finds a vicarious immortality in the youth of his nephew: "One must accept, absorb, give back, become oneself a symbol."

This is the clearest affirmation that O'Neill's philosophy at that time could admit. The fountain was a symbol of life, tossing its little drops, its human beings, high in the air. They had myriad shapes and colors: some were caught in the light, others dropped dully back, and a few burst into an incandescent miniature rainbow. It did not greatly matter: more drops must be propagated that more drops may be tossed into the air, and absorbed back again into the whole.

Yet there is something more. According to this belief, the creative power, the strongest power in nature, would perform the age-long functions of mythic religion. For the man this concept was not finally satisfying; for the dramatist it proved exceedingly fruitful. It is out of this theme of creation and continuance that he wrote two of his finest plays, *The Great God Brown* and *Mourning Becomes Electra*. Even when he parallels, and deliberately suggests cross-comparison with, the ancient Greek legend of Electra, O'Neill endows his characters with psychological complications that we recognize (and he intends us to recognize) by such modern terms as repressions, frustrations, and fixations. But men and women today, like those in ancient Greece, can not resist forces stronger than themselves: the terms have changed, but the tragedy remains the same. In this play with its American setting and modern time of action, O'Neill is attempting to rephrase the motivations of classical tragedy so as to relate them to our own doubts, fears, and desires, but in the process to give us, also, faith in the creative life force.

In *The Great God Brown,* this is combined with the more dominant motif of the religion of art. O'Neill defines his purpose in this play as showing "the mystery any one man or woman can feel but not understand as the meaning of any event—or accident—in any life on earth." To give added depth, richness, and suggestiveness, he deliberately mixed what we think of as folklore and as revealed religion: Dion Anthony is in part Dionysius, and in part St. Anthony, and he returns for strength to Cybele, the pagan earth mother. But this mystical element serves to accentuate the importance of the individual, even as the use of masks to indicate an actor's public or private character emphasizes an individual's complexity. But one person is influenced and changed by others even as he acts upon them, as we grope in the world's half-light for a fuller illumination. Here the reader can identify himself with the characters, can fully comprehend the nature and intensity of their desires, whether or not he accepts the underlying philosophy.

That is not possible with all his plays, at least for most of us. O'Neill has embraced even more dubious philosophies. In *Dynamo* he envisioned a man who saw a new god in the whirling wheels of machinery and the weird power of electricity, but this study of a fantastic modernly-grounded religious mania was neither dramatically nor philosophically convincing. O'Neill also flirted briefly and tentatively with Marxianism in *Marco Millions,* but it was at best a half-hearted flirtation since he was, soon afterward, describing Communism as "the most grotesque god that ever came out of Asia." Sociological nostrums, especially the theory that man will quickly improve if only his environment be changed for the better, won his half-hearted allegiance in such plays as *All God's Chillun Got Wings* and *Desire Under the Elms.*

Whether his philosophical ideas had proved satisfying or not, he had consistently attempted to get beyond the literal and factual reality. Both the man and the dramatist seem ever in quest of a valid, tenable explanation of the meaning of life. In that quest he came to Christian Catholicism, and out of it he wrote the moving but only partially successful *Days Without End.* In this play meaning inheres not in the fountain or the dynamo or the sexual delta, but in the crucifix. He has not abandoned modern terms or modern psychology, and he continues to be concerned with man's essential dualism to such an extent that the two parts of the main character are played by two different actors. Somehow, too, there is little difference in the terms of his Christian characters and those of his earlier non-Christian ones: John Loving believes with the rationalistic part of his mind that "we are all the slaves of meaningless chance," but with the idealistic part that "a new Savior must be born who will reveal to us how we can be saved from ourselves."

If the play has too much of dramatic and philosophical debate in it to be quite successful as drama, it is the clearest statement we have of O'Neill's constant striving to find a satisfactory philosophy of life. It gives in epitome his own spiritual evolution: he is seeking the infinite behind the finite, searching for something that will add to the dignity of man. Whatever the terms employed, however unsatisfactory the explanations, O'Neill holds in this play that man's spirit is greater and ultimately more important than man's body. If at times he seems only to have a faith that man must have a faith, he has made an honest and unrelenting search for valid and tenable bases for a faith that will not deny scientific truths but will affirm a deeper, more positive spiritual truth.

"Man is involved in a web of circumstance, a web that is not of his own weaving." O'Neill had begun as a playwright with this deterministic philosophy of life and the universe; rather disconcertingly, he has partially reverted to it in his later plays. The disturbed and disturbing state of the world shook his lightly-rooted faith; even more directly, a serious personal illness in 1934 temporarily ended his dramatic activity; it developed into, or was later diagnosed as, the incurable, slowly ravaging Parkinson's Disease.

It may be too early to evaluate the work of O'Neill's darker years, but certain unmistakable trends seem dominant. He had turned back into his own past for dramatic material; increasingly he pinned his faith on human love and warmth to give a meaning to life; and he presented man lacking the will to act as being spiritually dead, however alive physically he might be. There is a cathartic quality in these plays, but the purging clearly was intended more for the author than for the audience: O'Neill was attempting to objectify by writing out of himself certain obsessive memories that long had haunted him. . . .

Source: Edd Winfield Parks, "Eugene O'Neill's Quest," in *Tulane Drama Review*, Vol. 4, No. 3, March 1960, pp. 99–107.

Ivan H. Walton

In the following excerpt, Walton explores O'Neill's portrayal of sailors and sailing in his plays, including Ile.

Students of folklore have long been aware of the extensive use literary artists have made of the folk materials current among the peoples whose lives they have delineated. It will come as no surprise to them to note the widespread and effective use America's outstanding dramatist, Eugene O'Neill, made in his plays of the folklore and what may be called the folkways of the sea—traditional sailor concepts and patterns of conduct he had learned from two years of firsthand experience aboard ocean-going ships and in waterfront areas before beginning his career as a dramatist.

His dominant and continuing interest in sailor ways is shown by the fact that fifteen of his first twenty-five plays produced on the stage following his first association with the Provincetown Players, that is, from 1914 to 1924, were concerned either directly or indirectly with this material. These plays include, in the order of their production, *Bound East for Cardiff, Thirst, Fog, In the Zone, The Long Voyage Home, Ile, The Rope, Where the Cross Is Made,* and *The Moon of the Caribbees*—all one-act plays; and *Beyond the Horizon, Chris Christopherson* (a year later made over into *Anna Christie*), *Diff'rent, Gold* (a four-act drama which includes the action in *Where the Cross Is Made*), *The Hairy Ape,* and *The Ancient Mariner* (a dramatic version of Coleridge's poem). To these should be added *Warnings,* a one-act play produced in 1914, and *The Second Engineer* (also called *The Personal Equation*), written during his year at Harvard (1914–1915), but apparently neither appeared on the professional stage. In 1925 *The Fountain* was produced, and three years later, *Marco Millions,* each with scenes

> SAILORS LONG, PERHAPS ALWAYS, HAVE HAD A SPECIAL LANGUAGE, A TRADITION OR FOLKWAY OF COMMUNICATING WITH EACH OTHER THAT TO A LANDSMAN MIGHT BE NEARLY UNINTELLIGIBLE, AND O'NEILL MADE USE OF IT IN DEVELOPING CREDENCE IN HIS CHARACTERS AND SITUATIONS."

on shipboard, but with no real sailors in either cast. However, in the trilogy *Mourning Becomes Electra,* first produced in 1931, O'Neill again made good use of his knowledge of the sea and the ways of sailors.

There seems to be no information available at this time as to whether or not any of the plays projected, sketched, or completed after the author's "temporary retirement" in 1934 were concerned with the sea. Of the two which he allowed to be published—*The Iceman Cometh* (1946) and *A Moon for the Misbegotten* (1952)—the first has its setting in a waterfront dive which is remarkably similar to those utilized in at least two of his first plays. A third full-length play of this period, *The Long Day's Voyage into Night,* whose title may possibly imply a connection with the sea, may not, according to the author's direction, be made public for a quarter century. O'Neill has withdrawn from production or publication *Thirst, Fog, The Ancient Mariner, Warnings,* and *The Second Engineer;* so they will not be considered here.

As the above list of plays well demonstrates, O'Neill has been equalled by few if any other dramatists and surely by none in his own country in his use of sailor life and the sea. And his delineations have the ring of authenticity, a result no doubt of his using folk materials derived from his own days as a sailor on and about the Atlantic.

According to one of O'Neill's letters, he made his first sea venture in 1910 after a few months of touring the American East and Middle West as assistant manager of his father's theatrical company. He was twenty-two years of age at the time he shipped on a Norwegian barque-rigged vessel from Boston to Buenos Aires. The trip lasted sixty-five days. While in the Argentine he had a series of shore jobs with branches of American firms in Buenos Aires and La Plata, and then became a "bum on the docks" and made friends with sailors, stevedores, and the down-and-outs. He worked only when he had to for money to purchase necessities, liquor, and waterfront entertainment at the "Sailor's Opera," which was evidently akin to the traditional American "free and easy shows" that catered to sailors in the larger ports of both oceans as well as in those of the Great Lakes. The ground floor provided a combination bar and vaudeville where professional entertainment was liberally supplemented by singing, dancing, yarning, and by the fighting of customers. The upper floors provided cheap lodgings as well as quarters for the ladies of the streets. In O'Neill's own words, the Sailor's Opera where he and his friends went for entertainment was "a large cafe to which all seamen automatically went. There the seamen yarned of adventures, drank, played cards, fought, and wallowed."

After some weeks or months of shore life, he shipped as mule tender on a cattle boat bound from Buenos Aires to Durban, South Africa, and return. Then followed a second prolonged period "on the beach" before he signed on a British tramp steamer as an ordinary seaman for New York. Back in his home city he obtained lodgings at three dollars a month at "Jimmy-the-Priest's," a waterfront vermin-infested dive which he described as "a hell-hole." He again "hung around the waterfront" as at Buenos Aires for some time and picked up an occasional job on a mail boat, and finally shipped as an able seaman on an American liner, the *New York,* to Southampton, England. He returned on the *Philadelphia,* and this trip ended his seafaring as a sailor. He still continued, however, to live among sailors at their customary places.

This two-year interval of sailoring came to an abrupt end when, after celebrating a winning streak at cards, he found himself on a railroad train well on his way to New Orleans. On arriving in that city he found his father's troupe there playing the perennial *Monte Cristo.* He was given a minor part and traveled the western Orpheum circuit before returning east to the family home at New London. Here, after a few months of working as a newspaper reporter, he developed a light case of tuberculosis of the lungs and spent the first half of the year 1913 in a sanitarium at Wallingford, Connecticut. Here,

where he had plenty of spare time on his hands, the urge to write came upon him, and he quite naturally turned to his own experiences in the theatre for form and to the sea for content.

His experiences as a sailor had a deep influence upon him, and in the following decade his unromanticized, unsentimentalized, and almost naturalistic re-creations of the violent lives of seamen and their waterfront associates, all untroubled by drawing-room standards, appeared on the Provincetown and New York stages with startling results....

The folkways of seafaring used by O'Neill can, for convenience, be divided into two groups—those concerned with sailor life aboard ship and those with the waterfront. And one of the first of the established patterns of sailor life aboard ship to be noticed by a reader is the persistently grim attitude of his sailors toward the sea itself. Shore poets sing of the freedom, inspiration, and beauty of the sea as they do of the "big open spaces" of the American West, but those who make their living in these places find life a pretty grim business. O'Neill's point of view is prevailingly that of the common sailor in the forecastle. The omnipotence and omnipresence of the sea dwarfs the sailor's puny powers. The crew of the whaler *Atlantic Queen,* stuck in the frozen ice floes of the Arctic, are driven to mutiny and Captain Keeney's wife to insanity by the overpowering sea and the attendant monotony and brutality....

Another folkway prominent in the plays of the sea is the sailor's glorification and exercise of brute strength. C. Jones writing of O'Neill against the background of his own sailor experience states that at sea, "a man with exceptional strength is usually the leader; each man wins or loses the admiration of his fellows in proportion to his ability to 'hold his own end up!'" The ample descriptive literature of life at sea and my own experience in listening to the talk of scores of ex-sailors in Great Lakes ports, many formerly from salt water, support this statement.

One will recall at once the admiration of the men in the stokehole for Yank in the opening scene of *The Hairy Ape.* The author writes of him that, "He seems broader, fiercer, more truculent, more powerful, and more sure of himself than the rest. They respect his superior strength—the grudging respect of fear." Yank rules the group by threatening physical violence. When Long has delivered himself of a tirade against "the damned capitalist class," Yank closes him up with, "Sit down before I knock you down!" and then asserts the superiority of all members of the stokehole crew over the passengers by saying, "We're better than they are, ain't we? Sure! One of us guys could clean up the whole mob wit one mit. Put one of 'em down here for one watch in de stokehole, what'd happen? Dey'd carry him off on a stretcher. Dem boids don't amount to nothin'."

Mat Burke in *Anna Christie* comes aboard the barge after five days in an open boat with three others, and he is the only one able to walk. Anna suggests that he go into the cabin and lie down, but Mat interrupts indignantly by boasting of his physical strength, and, when Anna is not impressed, he adds, "An' I can lick all the hands on this tub wan by wan, tired as I am!" Driscoll, Mat's counterpart in the *Glencairn* plays, also asserts his leadership over his shipmates by virtue of his superior strength.

Captain Keeney in *Ile* has shoulders and chest "of enormous proportions," and before he comes on the stage, the steward describes him as "a hard man—as hard a man as ever sailed the seas." His iron determination withstands his wife's pleading to turn homeward after two years in the frozen North to the point of her going insane, and when the crew threaten mutiny he knocks their leader to the deck with one blow of his fist, and when the ice floes open he orders his vessel on northward. Captain Bartlett in the opening scene of *Gold* is described as, "a tall, huge framed figure of a man. . . . There is a suggestion of immense strength in his heavy-muscled body. . . . His broad jaw sticks out at an angle of implacable stubbornness." And it will be recalled that he knocks Butler down with his fist when the latter refuses to acknowledge that the discovered chest of native trinkets contains gold and precious gems.

O'Neill's sailors are also all homeless world-wanderers—another widely accepted folk pattern of the sea. In the *Glencairn* plays Yank, Driscoll, Olson, Davis, Cocky, Smitty, Paul, Paddy, Ivan, and Swanson are all aimless wanderers over the face of the earth, as are Mat Burke and old Chris in *Anna Christie* and the stokehole crew in *The Hairy Ape*. Yank in the last-mentioned play states that he ran away from his home in Ireland when he "was a kid," and has not been back in fifteen years. Olson in *The Long Voyage Home* tells the harlot Freda in the

London waterfront dive that he has been planning to go to his home in Sweden for ten years: "But I come ashore, I take one drink, I take many drinks, I get drunk, I spend all money, I have to ship away for other voyage. So dis time I say to myself: Don't drink one drink, Ollie, or, sure you don't get home." But that night he is drugged and robbed and carried aboard the notorious *Amindra* bound on a two-year voyage "around the Horn."

Old Chris probably speaks for all of them when he confesses to his daughter:

> Ay don't know, Anna, why ay never come home Sveden in ole year. Ay vant come home end of every voyage. Ay vant see your mo'der, your two bro'der before dey was drowned, you ven you was born—ay—don't go. Ay sign on oder ships—go South America, go Australia, go China, go every port all over vorld many times—but ay never go aboard ship sail for Sveden. Ven ay got money for pay passage home as passenger den—ay forgat and ay spend all money. Ven ay tank again, it's too late. Ay don't know why, but dat's vay wit most sailor faller, Anna.

Even though Mat Burke expresses contempt for landsmen, he, like others of O'Neill's sailors, yearns for a fixed home and a family ashore. The dream, however, never materializes. Olson in *The Long Voyage Home* wants to go back to Sweden to his family farm, but as has already been mentioned, the omnipotent sea has its way. Captain Bartlett in *Gold* is obsessed with the idea of acquiring riches so that he can retire with his family in the country, but he is to be overtaken by madness. The dying Yank in the forecastle of the *Glencairn* as it moves slowly through a fog in the mid-Atlantic muses between spasms of pain to his friend Driscoll: "It must be great to stay on dry land all your life and have a farm with a house of your own—" But he is not to survive the trip. It is worth noting that the United States government during the nineteenth century established marine hospitals in all the larger American ports to care for the homeless and generally moneyless men of the American merchant marine who arrived in port ill or injured and with no claim on the community.

O'Neill's sailors, true to the folkways of the sea, are also inveterate grumblers. They grumble about their vessel and its owners, their officers, their food, their work, their pay, the weather; and by doing so, no doubt, they gain a temporary elevation of soul that comes from the fleeting superiority they thus gain over their straitened, monotonous lives. A good example is the opening scene in *Bound East for Cardiff* in which the sailors, off watch on the fog-bound steamer, are gathered in the dingy forecastle near the bunk of the mortally injured Yank. They complain at length of the incompetence of the captain and mate, and Olson suggests that Yank be given some food:

> Driscoll—Wud ye have him be eatin' in his condishun? Sure it's hard enough on the rest av us wid nothin' the matther wid our insides to be stomachin' the skoff on this rusty lime-jucer.
> Scotty—(*indignantly*) It's a starvation ship.
> Davis—Plenty o' work and no food—and the owners ridin' around in carriages!
> Olson—Hash, hash! Stew, stew! Marmalade, by damn! (*He spits disgustedly*.)
> Cocky—Bloody swill! Fit only for swine is wot I say.
> Driscoll—And the dishwather they disguise wid the name av tea! And the putty they call bread! My belly feels loike I'd swalleted a dozen rivits at the thought av ut! And sea-biscuit thet'd break the teeth av a lion if he had the misfortune to take a bite at one! (*Unconsciously they have all raised their voices forgetting the sick man in their sailor's delight at finding something to grumble about*.)

A groan from Yank brings them back to earth, but as the men put on their oilskins to go up on deck to relieve the old watch, they vent themselves freely on the weather.

O'Neill's sailors invariably indulge in this luxury at every opportunity: Olson in *The Long Voyage Home* when he explains why he is quitting the sea; Cocky in *The Hairy Ape* when he lets go on the life of the stokehole crew; Butler in *Gold* when he complains about being "forced to cook the swill on a rotten whaler!" and even Andrew in *Beyond the Horizon* when he describes sailor life to his brother Robert.

O'Neill's sailors grumble continually about their present lives, and the older ones whose experience goes back to the days of the wind-driven ships loudly assert, in true sailor folkway fashion, the superiority of sailing vessels over steamships. It will be recalled that the first sailor labor unions would not recognize steamboatmen as sailors or permit them to join the organizations.

Large numbers of sailors left the Atlantic for the Great Lakes when commercial sailing vessels became scarce on the oceans, and, finally at the turn of the century, left off sailing altogether when steamer competition on the Lakes drove the slower sailing vessels into retirement. Working on a steamship to them was not really sailing....

Sailors long, perhaps always, have had a special language, a tradition or folkway of communicating with each other that to a landsman might be nearly unintelligible, and O'Neill made use of it in developing credence in his characters and situations. His sailors are "shipmates" instead of friends, they "go below" instead of downstairs, and they use a "companionway" instead of a stairway. They go "aft" or "forward" instead of to the stern or front part of the vessel, they turn "to port" or "starboard" instead of to left or right, and they answer "aye" instead of yes. The ship's master when not present is always "the Old Man." Mat Burke's vessel went to "Davy Jones" instead of to the bottom of the sea. Smitty in *In the Zone* is no sailor because he cannot "box the compass," that is, name the thirty-two points clockwise around the compass card. Captain Brandt orders Lavinia to "belay" instead of stop when she slanders his mother. In *Diff'rent* Captain Caleb Williams tells Emma that her no-good parasitic nephew is a mean skunk from "truck to keelson" instead of from top to toe. When Captain Bartlett in *Gold* sees his schooner secretly leaving the harbor without him, he turns bewildered to his son Nat and asks, "Ain't that my schooner, boy—the *Sarah Allen* reachin' toward the p'int?" And a few minutes later he adds, "He's passed the p'int—and now headin' her out to sea—so'east by east. By God, that's the course I charted for her!"

Captain Dick Scott in *Beyond the Horizon* "goes aloft" to turn in, that is, upstairs to bed, and he reminds Andrew to pack his "dummage," his clothing and effects. His ship is to depart at "six bells," that is, at seven o'clock in the morning, to take advantage of the high tide. On a later occasion when he has climbed a hill on the Mayo farm to tell Andrew of a berth as second mate that is available on a steamer bound for Buenos Aires, he says, "God A'mighty, mountin' this dammed hill is worsern going aloft to the skys'l yard in a blow," and adds that as soon as he heard of the job he "'bout ship and set all sail" back to the farm to tell Andrew.

One familiar with the uninhibited nature of sailor speech will be a bit surprised at the watered-down nature of O'Neill's sailors' profanity.... We must remember, however, that O'Neill's *Glencairn* series antedated such plays as Anderson and Stalling's *What Price Glory,* Sherriff's *Journey's End,* and Kirkland's *Tobacco Road* by ten, fifteen, and twenty years, respectively....

Source: Ivan H. Walton, "Eugene O'Neill and the Folklore and Folkways of the Sea," in *Western Folklore,* Vol. 14, No. 3, July 1955, pp. 153–69.

Horst Frenz

In the following essay, Frenz comments on O'Neill's reputation abroad, pointing out the numerous translations and foreign editions of the author's works, including Ile.

In the history of the American drama there has been no writer who has established a wider foreign reputation than Eugene O'Neill. His plays have been produced in almost every important city of the world and have made a deep impression upon theater audiences, critics, and even publishers. In England, Germany, and Sweden, editions and translations appeared in print only a short while after the plays had reached the stage. The first British edition of a series of three of O'Neill's plays (*Plays: First Series: The Straw, Emperor Jones,* and *Diff'rent*) was issued in May, 1922, to be followed, during the next year, by three volumes containing thirteen plays. One of these volumes—*The Hairy Ape and Other Plays*—has been reprinted six times since. The Germans published a translation of *The Emperor Jones* (*Kaiser Jones*) as early as 1923, almost coincident with the first production of the same play in Berlin, and would have printed *Anna Christie* even earlier if its translator, the Hungarian Melchior Lengyel, had received the author's permission. There is no record of a German edition of this play. The first Swedish attempt to publish the American's works was made in 1924, when a collection under the title of *Tre Dramer: Emperor Jones—Ludna gorillan—Tran* was published by Albert Bonnier in Stockholm. In all these cases, the response of the reading public must have been satisfactory, for this publishing house, as well as Jonathan Cape in London and S. Fischer in Berlin, has continued to print other dramas by O'Neill.

In France, O'Neill is better known as a literary figure than as a playwright. This is reflected in the fact that the first three translations of his plays *Ile, The Moon of the Caribbees,* and *The Hairy Ape* appeared in French literary magazines (between 1928 and 1930). So far I have found only one Italian edition—*Anna Christie* translated by Luigi Berti and printed in 1938. Spanish editions have been sold not only in Spain but also in South American countries, for the publishers held the rights for both markets.

The play that has been printed most frequently—to judge from the foreign editions I have been able to locate—is *Strange Interlude.* The first British edition appeared in 1928, and there were four reprints between 1929 and 1936. In 1933, the German "Albatross Modern Continental Library" brought out an English edition, and *Excelsior,* a Chilean literary magazine, published "Extraño Interludio" in a 1937 issue. The play has also been translated into French and Rumanian. Perhaps in the opinion of one of the French critics, who said that *Strange Interlude* is more like a novel than a play, we have the explanation of why publishers in various parts of the world have felt that this play would appeal to the reading public.

The list of foreign editions of O'Neill's plays extends over seventeen years, from 1922 to 1939—an impressive record when we consider that the American playwright wrote most of his plays in the twenties.

Source: Horst Frenz, "Eugene O'Neill's Plays Printed Abroad," in *College English,* Vol. 5, No. 6, March 1944, pp. 340–41.

SOURCES

Barlow, Judith E., "O'Neill's Female Characters," in *The Cambridge Companion to Eugene O'Neill,* edited by Michael Manheim, Oxford University Press, 1998, pp. 164–77.

Bogard, Travis, *Contour in Time: The Plays of Eugene O'Neill,* Oxford University Press, 1972, p. 91.

Chothia, Jean, "Trying to Write the Family Play: Autobiography and the Dramatic Imagination," in *The Cambridge Companion to Eugene O'Neill,* edited by Michael Manheim, Oxford University Press, 1998, pp. 192–205.

Gelb, Arthur, and Barbara Gelb, *O'Neill: Life with Monte Cristo,* Applause, 2000, pp. 211, 612–14.

O'Neill, Eugene, *Ile,* in *Collected Shorter Plays,* Yale University Press, 2007, pp. 113–41.

———, *The Moon of the Caribees, and Six Other Plays of the Sea,* Boni and Liveright, 1919.

Ranald, Margaret Loftus, "From Trial to Triumph (1913–1924): The Early Plays," in the *The Cambridge Companion to Eugene O'Neill*, edited by Michael Manheim, Oxford University Press, 1998, pp. 51–68.

Review of *Ile*, in the *Dramatist*, July 1919, pp. 960–61.

FURTHER READING

Gelb, Arthur and Barbara, *O'Neill*, Harper, 1962.
    The Gelbs are journalists and historians of the Broadway Theater tradition. This is their first biography of O'Neill. This volume was not superseded by the later one, *O'Neill: Life with Monte Cristo* (2000). Rather, the two volumes reflect two different perspectives on O'Neill at an interval of forty years.

O'Neill, Eugene, *The Plays of Eugene O'Neill*, 3 vols., Modern Library, 1982.

This is a standard collection of O'Neill's complete dramatic works.

Tornqvist, Egil, *Eugene O'Neill: A Playwright's Theatre*, McFarland, 2004.
    Tornqvist, a leading drama historian in Sweden, deals with the major themes of O'Neill's works and gives individual treatment to the most important plays. O'Neill is viewed in Sweden as the successor to the Swedish playwright Strindberg as a realist and so has always been immensely popular in that country. This appreciation was a major factor in his winning the Nobel Prize, which was then selected by Swedish academics.

Verrill, A. Hyatt, *The Real Story of the Whaler: Whaling, Past and Present*, Appleton, 1916.
    This popular history of whaling was published just before O'Neill began to write *Ile*. It illuminates commonplace attitudes toward the whale fishery at the time of the play's composition, which form the background of *Ile*.

Impossible Marriage

BETH HENLEY

1998

American playwright Beth Henley's play *Impossible Marriage* was first produced on stage by the Roundabout Theater Company in New York City in October 1998. It was published in the same year in a hardcover edition by Stage & Screen, and appeared the following year in a paperback edition from Dramatists Play Service. *Impossible Marriage* was also included in the collection *Beth Henley: Collected Plays Volume II: 1990–1999*, published by Smith & Kraus in 2000.

Impossible Marriage is one of many Southern-flavored plays by Henley that reflect her Mississippi upbringing. The play deals with an impending, ill-fated wedding set at a country estate in Savannah, Georgia. It is a melodramatic black comedy of manners, full of overblown gestures and witty observations, and is reminiscent of the plays of the nineteenth-century Irish author Oscar Wilde. In its simultaneous comedy and seriousness, *Impossible Marriage* also has a flavor of Russian playwright Anton Chekhov, whom Henley has cited as an influence on her work. The main theme of the play is the conflict between civilization and passion. While critics consider it to be of secondary importance to Henley's best-known play, *Crimes of the Heart* (first produced in 1979), *Impossible Marriage* has proved a popular success.

Beth Henley *(Robert Pitts / Landov)*

AUTHOR BIOGRAPHY

Beth Henley was born Elizabeth Becker Henley on May 8, 1952, in Jackson, Mississippi, the second of four daughters of Charles Boyce, an attorney and Mississippi state senator, and Elizabeth Josephine Henley, an actress. Inspired by watching her mother rehearse for plays, the young Henley intended to become an actress. With this goal in mind, she earned a Bachelor of Fine Arts degree at Southern Methodist University in Dallas, Texas, in 1974.

While at college, Henley joined an acting group and wrote her first play, *Am I Blue*, which was produced at the university's Margo Jones Theatre in 1973 and published by Dramatists Play Service in 1982. From 1974 to 1975 Henley taught drama at the Dallas Minority Repertory Theatre. In 1975, she began graduate study in the Master of Fine Arts program at the University of Illinois, Urbana. However, she never completed the program. Instead, in 1976, she moved to Los Angeles to live with actor and

director Stephen Tobolowsky, with whom she would later collaborate on the screenplay for *True Stories* (released by Warner Bros. in 1986). Unsuccessful in finding acting roles, she threw herself into playwriting.

In 1978, Henley submitted a three-act play, *Crimes of the Heart*, to the Great American Play Contest sponsored by the Actors Theatre of Louisville, Kentucky. Based on Chekhov's play *The Three Sisters, Crimes of the Heart* is a black comedy about three sisters living in a small Southern town. It won the contest and was staged at the theater to considerable critical and popular acclaim. Nominated for the Susan Smith Blackburn Award in 1979, the play was produced on Broadway at the John Golden Theatre and published by Dramatists Play Service in 1981. It won the New York Drama Critics Circle Award for the best new American play, the Pulitzer Prize for drama, and a Tony nomination for best play, all in 1981. Many consider it to be her masterpiece.

Henley later adapted the play for a film version, also called *Crimes of the Heart* (released in 1986 by De Laurentiis Entertainment). The film received an Academy Award nomination for best adapted screenplay (1986).

Henley's next play was *The Miss Firecracker Contest*. The play was first produced in Los Angeles in 1980 and was published by Dramatists Play Service in 1985. Henley later adapted the play into a screenplay for a film, released as *Miss Firecracker* by Corsair Pictures in 1988.

Other plays by Henley include *The Lucky Spot*, produced in Williamstown, Massachusetts, in 1986 and on Broadway in 1987, and published by the Dramatists Play Service in 1987; and *Abundance*, produced in Los Angeles in 1989 and published by the Dramatists Play Service in 1990.

Henley wrote *Impossible Marriage* while she was pregnant. The play was first produced on stage by Roundabout Theater Company in New York City in October 1998 and was published by Stage & Screen in the same year. In the original production, the part of Floral was played by Holly Hunter, who has appeared in several of Henley's stage plays and in the film *Miss Firecracker*.

Henley's later plays include *Sisters of the Winter Madrigal*, published by Dramatists Play Service in 2001, and *Signature*, published by Dramatists Play Service in 2003.

As of July 2008, Henley lives in Los Angeles, California. She has one son, Patrick.

PLOT SUMMARY

Part One

Impossible Marriage opens in the garden of Kandall Kingsley. Sidney Lunt, son of the groom, enters and swipes at a row of flowers with his cane. Floral appears, heavily pregnant and upset. Kandall follows and Floral complains that she swept up the leaves but no one noticed. Floral's husband Jonsey enters. He has brought Floral chocolates to satisfy her pregnancy cravings. They wonder why they have not heard from the groom when the wedding is tomorrow. Floral and Kandall agree that the match between Pandora and Edvard is a bad one.

Pandora, in an exuberant mood, enters with the Reverend Jonathan Larence, who is to perform the ceremony. She is pleased that Edvard's son Sidney has arrived, as none of Edvard's children has spoken to him since his divorce. The Reverend congratulates Floral and Jonsey on Floral's pregnancy. Floral seems embarrassed.

Pandora announces that she will wear a pair of blue wings at her wedding. Changing the subject, Kandall asks the Reverend about his recent stay in Nigeria. Pandora says he is a good man, which he strenuously denies.

The company goes off for refreshments at the manor, leaving Floral and Pandora alone. Floral asks Pandora why she is marrying Edvard, who is over twice her age, short-sighted, a womanizer, and probably a drunk. Pandora insists that he is all she desires, but admits to doubts over his age. Floral predicts that she will end up being his nursemaid. Pandora, alarmed, asks Floral to break off her engagement. Floral tells Pandora she must make the decision. Pandora tries to settle the question by playing the traditional game of pulling the petals off a flower one by one. The verdict is that she will not marry Edvard.

Kandall returns and Floral tells her that the wedding is off. Kandall's first concern is to pick up the wedding cake to remove it from the sight of the townspeople, who would view it as a symbol of her family's impetuousness. Kandall and Pandora leave to collect the cake.

Jonsey enters and Floral tells him that Pandora is breaking off the engagement. Jonsey is shocked. Jonsey lovingly addresses Floral as his dear wife and the mother-to-be of his child. Floral is more interested in summoning Edvard so that she can break the bad news to him. Edvard arrives and apologizes for being late, explaining

that he was in a hotel fire. Floral tells him that Pandora wants to call off the wedding. Edvard is distraught. Pandora rushes in and greets him adoringly. Unable to bear Edvard's crying, she dismisses her doubts as natural pre-wedding jitters and accuses Floral of acting out of jealousy. Pandora and Edvard go off to the woods.

Kandall returns and reports that Pandora threw herself out of the moving car on their way to pick up the cake when she heard Edvard call her name. Floral comforts herself with the thought that Pandora can get a divorce, but Kandall replies that there is no precedent in the family. Kandall wishes that Edvard would conveniently die.

Sidney enters and Kandall claims the family is thrilled about the wedding. Sidney says that marriage is an outdated institution. He admits that he has never been in love. He has only come to deliver a private message to his father. Kandall takes him to find Edvard.

The Reverend enters. He and Floral discuss sincerity, which they agree is difficult to discern. Floral leaves. Pandora and Edvard enter from the woods. Kandall, Sidney, and Jonsey enter from the manor. Kandall greets Edvard effusively as a man of "global renown." Edvard does not recognize Sidney, saying that he is too old to be his son. Sidney gives Edvard a note from Margaret in which she threatens to kill herself if he marries Pandora. Edvard is tormented by his dilemma: if he marries Pandora, Margaret will kill herself, but if he calls off the wedding, he will be scorned by Pandora for capitulating to blackmail. Edvard leaves.

Jonsey enters from the woods and says that he has seen three red cardinals in the grove. Jonsey tells Sidney that when he was young he witnessed his father drowning in a boating accident.

Part Two

It is night. Pandora enters, dancing ecstatically. She calls to Edvard offstage to join her, but being short-sighted, he cannot see in the dark. Kandall asks the Reverend to bring candelabras. Jonsey, Kandall, Floral, and Edvard enter. Pandora again asks Edvard to dance with her, but he declines as he has eaten too much. Jonsey dances with her, and everyone praises his dancing and handsome looks. Pandora twirls herself into Edvard's arms and says that her love for him will last forever. Edvard points out that this is not necessarily so: his first marriage did not last forever. Pandora says that was because it was not a good marriage, but Edvard says it was good, until he met Pandora.

Floral reminisces about a bowl of goldfish that Pandora kept as a child. One of the fish died because she never fed them, but she refused to throw it away and the stench of rotting fish filled the house. Pandora could not understand why she had to throw out a fish just because it was dead, as she still loved it. Edvard says he felt his life was over until he met Pandora. He is determined to marry her and will not be held responsible if his ex-wife kills herself. Sidney says that if Edvard goes through with the marriage, he will kill himself too, and his brothers and sisters will do the same. Kandall, worried about scandal, says that the wedding is off, and asks the Reverend for advice. He says that people should be with those they love. Floral faints.

Pandora threatens to elope with Edvard if Kandall forbids the marriage. Kandall allows the marriage to go ahead. Sidney announces, "All must die," and goes off to the woods.

Floral talks deprecatingly about her appearance in her pregnancy. The Reverend abruptly goes off to the manor to pray. Pandora again calls him a good man, but Floral cautions, "Everyone isn't always what they seem." Floral goes off to the woods. Kandall goes with Pandora to the manor to fetch a dessert of cherries jubilee.

Jonsey asks Edvard if he (Edvard) is the father of Floral's child. Jonsey explains that he flirts with women to spread the myth that he is a womanizer, but it is all illusion. He and Floral pretend that the child is his. Jonsey leaves.

Kandall and Pandora enter with the dessert. Kandall apologizes to Edvard for Floral, who has carved into his wedding cake and eaten a large piece. Kandall is shocked that Floral ate the cake with her fingers. Kandall blames Floral's permanent anger on Jonsey's supposed infidelities. Floral had counseling from the Reverend, but he went to Nigeria about the time that she became pregnant.

Kandall reflects alone on the "impossible" wedding. Sidney enters and Kandall invites him to eat cherries jubilee with her. He cannot bear her kindness, as he has not come "as a friend of these proceedings" but "only to disrupt and annihilate." Kandall explains that they are on the same side, as neither wants to see the wedding take place. They drink champagne and gaze at the night sky. Sidney is haunted by the thought of his

mother committing suicide, but Kandall says his life would go on even if she did. Kandall reveals that she is terminally ill but has told no one. Sidney kisses her passionately and tells her he loves her, but he then berates himself and kicks down a row of toadstools. Kandall rebukes him for destroying the "fairies' houses." As Kandall goes off, Sidney tries to repair the toadstools.

Floral enters, covered in dirt and foliage, her hair tousled. She tells Sidney that she has been rolling down hills. Sidney leaves as the Reverend enters. The Reverend tells Floral that he has decided to leave the church. She says that he must not leave the church, just as she must not leave her marriage. He agrees, but only "because it is the right thing to say." Overcome with passion, he kisses her, but then draws back, feeling that their relationship is "impossible." Floral angrily rejoices that her child will come from a good home, "without any hint of scandal." Jonsey enters from the woods, and Floral kisses him. The Reverend leaves, unseen by Jonsey, for the woods. Floral and Jonsey pull apart and look sadly at each other.

Part Three

The following morning, all is in place for the wedding. Floral enters and apologizes to Kandall for eating the wedding cake, explaining that her hunger got the better of her. Kandall replies that they are supposed to be civilized human beings, not animals. Sidney enters and asks Kandall to forgive him, referring to his romantic overtures. Kandall exits to the manor. Floral suggests that Sidney prevent the marriage going ahead by shooting the groom. She tells him where in the house he can find a pistol. Sidney goes off to fetch it.

Floral warns Edvard that his life is in danger and advises him to leave before the wedding. Edvard admits to having doubts. Floral and Edvard discuss civilized behavior. Edvard is torn between his desire to escape all marriages and his love for Pandora.

Jonsey arrives and reports that the Reverend went missing that morning and has since been found weeping in a muddy ditch. Kandall enters and announces that the wedding will begin. Pandora enters in her bridal gear and wings. Sidney enters with a pistol and points it at Edvard. He threatens to shoot his father unless the wedding is called off. Pandora runs to Edvard, vowing never to leave him. The Reverend intervenes. Kandall tells Sidney that if he shoots the Reverend, she will never speak to him again. Distracted, Sidney accidentally shoots himself in the foot. Pandora again tells the Reverend that he is a good man. A bleeding Sidney begs the Reverend to help him, but the Reverend tears off his preacher's collar and announces that his life as a minister is over, as it has led only to "desperate, unquenchable desires." He storms off in the direction of the woods. Edvard calms Sidney by reciting a poem (Dylan Thomas's "The Lament") that he used to read to him when he was a child.

Sidney is carried into the house, and everyone except Kandall and Floral goes off. Floral confesses to Kandall that she guided Sidney to the pistol. She says that one day, Pandora will be grateful, as "once you are married you're stuck." Kandall disagrees, insisting that tradition keeps people sane. Floral says that the child she is carrying is not Jonsey's. Kandall advises her not to tell Jonsey. Floral says he probably knows, as they never consummated their marriage. She adds that she does not love him. Floral weeps and says that all along, she only wanted to emulate her parents, who loved each other. Kandall corrects her: she and her husband pretended to love one another so that the children would not get "the wrong idea about marriage." Kandall's advice is that eventually, they will all die and their troubles will be over. In the meantime, there will be a scandal, but she no longer cares. Kandall and Floral embrace.

Pandora enters, wearing her wings over her honeymoon suit. She and Edvard have decided to drive to a neighboring county, where a judge will marry them in a civil ceremony. She adds that Sidney's wound is not serious. Floral confesses to Pandora that she is jealous of her and has plotted against her wedding because her own marriage is miserable. Pandora, however, admits that she fears for the future: her charms are dependent on youth and will fade. She must seize her chance when she can.

Edvard and Jonsey enter, and Edvard admits to Floral that he has doubts about his marriage. He reflects on the symbolism (in Greek mythology) of Pandora's box, which contained both pestilence and hope.

Pandora and Edvard leave. Jonsey explains to Floral that he is impotent and only gives attention to other women to appear normal. Floral tells Jonsey that she must leave him. He objects, saying he will love her child as his own, but Floral wants reality, not pretence.

Sidney comes into the scene, and Jonsey tells him that he is so disturbed by Floral's snoring that he is going to divorce her. Floral agrees, and Jonsey leaves. Floral admits to Sidney that the gun suggestion was a mistake, but Sidney is pleased that he was able to tell his mother that the marriage did not take place and prevent her suicide, for the moment.

The Reverend enters. He says that while being with Floral would be "tricky," it would not be impossible. Floral says she wants to be with him forever. He replies that that is impossible, but in the meantime, "many things" can happen to them in their life together. He leads her out of the garden and into the woods.

Kandall enters, eating raspberries with her fingers. Sidney tells her that Floral has left with the Reverend, who is the father of her child. Kandall wonders if it is too late to change her life. She asks Sidney to kiss her. He declines and says he must go, but first asks for a raspberry. As the scene fades to black, he remains, eating berries with Kandall.

CHARACTERS

Kandall Kingsley

Kandall is the wealthy matriarch of the Southern country estate on which the action of the play takes place. She is a beautiful and elegant widow in her fifties, and the mother of Floral and Pandora. Throughout most of the play, her main concern is to preserve an appearance of civilized behavior, respectability, and decorum for her family. For example, in part one, when Floral temporarily persuades Pandora to cancel her wedding, Kandall's priority is to pick up the wedding cake so that there is no danger that it could be seen by the townspeople and become "an emblem of our impetuous hearts." She can be relied upon to change the subject or create a pleasant distraction whenever events begin to turn ugly or embarrassing.

As the chaotic events of the play unfold, Kandall's attempts to maintain a veneer of perfection begin to unravel. This change is also partly prompted from within herself, as she knows that she is terminally ill and is finally (in part three) able to admit that the image of the happy marriage that she projected within her family was a lie. Her inner development is symbolized by her willingness at the play's end to eat berries with her fingers, a behavior that previously appalled her, and is characterized by her readiness to enter a romantic relationship with the much younger Sidney. Finally, it seems that Kandall is on the brink of a new and more spontaneous phase of life.

Pandora Kingsley

Pandora is the twenty-year-old daughter of Kandall Kingsley and the younger sister of Floral Whitman. She is the bride-to-be whose forthcoming wedding to Edvard Lunt sparks the events of the play. Described as "the image of youthful exuberance," Pandora embodies the romantic hopes of youth, pushing aside the objections of other characters to her unsuitable marriage because of her love for Edvard. The wings that she dons for her wedding symbolize her whimsical and unworldly viewpoint. She has doubts about her marriage to Edvard and allows herself to be persuaded against it by Floral, but changes her mind as soon as she sees him. Her lone dance, in which Edvard does not join her, emphasizes her isolation in her idealized world. She is surrounded by more experienced and cynical characters who act as foils (contrasting or opposite characters) to her own nature.

Pandora justifies going ahead with her marriage on the basis that she knows that her charms will not age well, and that therefore she must seize her moment. This is probably a delusion, as the older Floral and the much older Kandall find that such moments of opportunity can occur at any age.

Reverend Jonathan Larence

The Reverend, as he is called in the play, is the minister who is engaged to perform the marriage ceremony. He is described as having "an innocent aura that can be alternately interpreted as idiotic and wise." He has recently returned from Nigeria, where he has been doing missionary or charity work. This prompts Pandora repeatedly to praise him as a good man, a charge that he strenuously denies—as it transpires, with reason. In part two it is revealed that Floral had marriage guidance counseling from him and became pregnant at around the time he left for Nigeria. His being discovered weeping in a ditch on the morning of the wedding suggests that there are hidden conflicts in his life, which finally come to the surface during the marriage ceremony. The Reverend

tears off his collar, renounces his ministerial vocation and runs off into the woods. The reason for his behavior soon becomes clear: he and Floral are in love and she is expecting his child. After Floral announces that she is divorcing her husband, the Reverend decides that his own relationship with her, though "tricky," is not impossible. He rises above the pretenses of his life in the church and embraces his own redemption in the form of a new life of passion with Floral.

Edvard Lunt

Edvard Lunt, Pandora's fiancé, is a worldly, decadent-looking, but attractive man in his fifties who has achieved global fame in some unnamed field. According to Floral, he has the reputation of being a philanderer and a drunk. He has divorced his wife of twenty-three years and left his seven children in order to marry Pandora, even though he is more than twice her age. The gap separating him from Pandora is obvious to everyone but her: he is too shortsighted to see her dancing in the dark, too staid and prone to indigestion to join her in the dance, and too experienced in relationships to harbor any illusions that their love will last forever. He veers between enchantment with Pandora's youthful charm and doubts about the wisdom of their union. His excuse for being late for the wedding—that he was in a hotel fire in which his documents were destroyed—does not inspire confidence. It adds to the existing impression of a murky and unaccountable past.

Edvard has a distant relationship with his family. He does not recognize his own son, Sidney, when he turns up for the wedding. In part one, Sidney describes him as a good man, but one who "doesn't know what to say to children" (the irony of which lies in the fact that Edvard is marrying a woman young enough to be his daughter). Edvard's notion of bonding with his children seems to have been reading poetry to them. He read Dylan Thomas's poem "The Lament" to the young Sidney, and recites it to him again to comfort him after Sidney shoots himself in the foot. This poem, significantly, is a lament for lost youth by the ageing poet. While an odd choice to entertain a young child, it could be viewed as an apt commentary on the ageing Edvard's relationship with the much younger Pandora, as well as veiled advice to the repressed Sidney to live his life with passion while he still can. Edvard tells Floral in part one, "I believe we are defined by the things we can no longer feel, dream, or accomplish." It becomes clear in the rest of the play that there are many things that Edvard can no longer feel, dream, or accomplish. He cannot feel the urge to dance in the night with Pandora, he cannot share her dream of love without end because he has seen love end, and he cannot marry without being haunted by the thought that his ex-wife may carry out her threat to kill herself. Nevertheless, his final decision to marry Pandora, whatever the risks, shows courage.

Sidney Lunt

Sidney Lunt is the son of Edvard Lunt and Margaret, Edvard's former wife whom Edvard divorced when he met Pandora. Although he is a young man in his twenties, Sidney seems old before his time, with his beard and wire glasses. Indeed, the reason his father gives for not recognizing him is that he looks too old to be his son, although this also shows Edvard's self-delusion in pursuing an ill-starred marriage with a woman young enough to be his daughter. Edvard acts younger than his age, whereas Sidney acts older than his. Unlike his father, Sidney takes a timid and cynical approach to life. He has never known love and the closest he has come to a relationship with a woman is a commercial relationship with a female ice-cream seller, whom he rejected when she gave him a type of ice-cream he did not like.

Sidney occupies the comedic role of antagonist. Traditional comedy often centers on the desire of a young couple to marry. This couple may or may not be the protagonists (main characters who drive the action forward). Their union is opposed and frustrated by the antagonist (from the Greek meaning *opposing actor*), often taking the form of an older parent or other relative who discounts love in favor of money or status. The broader conflict is thus between youth and age, love and material concerns, passion and cynicism, and life-affirming fertility and death-dealing decline.

Henley both establishes and subverts the role of antagonist in the character of Sidney. First, he is an atypical antagonist because, as Edvard's son, he is younger than the man who wishes to marry. Thus, in an ironic reversal, passion is embodied in the ageing Edvard, while cynicism is embodied in the young Sidney. Typical of the antagonist, however, is Sidney's entrance on the stage. It is marked by the anti-romantic act of striking a row of flowers with his cane and laughing in the manner of a cliché stage villain. His antagonist role is further cemented by his attempt to abort the wedding by aiming a pistol at his father.

But Sidney is not a very effective or committed antagonist. He has to be guided by Floral into borrowing a family pistol, and then he is distracted from shooting the Reverend, who intervenes to save Edvard and his bride, by Kandall's threat never to speak to him again. Sidney only succeeds in shooting himself in the foot. This action could stand as a metaphor for the way in which his growing capacity for love repeatedly undermines his half-hearted commitment to villainy.

This process of emotional development becomes more visible in part two. In an ironically detached reference to his role as antagonist, Sidney rejects Kandall's offer of cherries jubilee, as he has not come "as a friend of these proceedings" but "only to disrupt and annihilate." But later in the scene, his passion momentarily breaks through his desiccated personality enough for him to kiss Kandall passionately. Fighting his own nature, he immediately launches into a fit of self-hatred and, in an echo of his initial action in swiping at the flowers, kicks down a row of toadstools. It is clear that his action symbolizes his desire to destroy romantic ideals. But again, he is distracted from this attempt at villainy by his desire to please Kandall, who is upset for the fairies whose homes, she fancies, are the toadstools. Pulled back from his angry urge to kick out at love and beauty by his own growing love for Kandall, he desperately tries to repair the toadstools.

In the final scene, he verbally rejects Kandall's request that he kiss her and says he must leave, but his body tells a different truth. Kandall, having announced that she means to change her life, is eating the berries with her fingers, a practice she previously viewed as uncivilized. Sidney does not leave, but takes a berry from her, relishes it, and stays.

Floral Whitman

Floral is Kandall's eldest daughter and the elder sister of Pandora. She is married to Jonsey. Floral is arguably the most complex and interesting character in the play. She is the closest character to an authorial voice. This interpretation may be justified by the fact that Henley wrote the play when pregnant, as Floral is. Floral brings a degree of realism to the whimsical lives of the other women, trying to burst the romantic bubble of Pandora and indulging in spontaneous but uncivilized behavior that offends Kandall. Her cynical and embittered attitude to life may stem from her sterile marriage to Jonsey, whom she believes to be unfaithful.

In her own way, Floral is as subject to self-delusion as the whimsical Pandora and Kandall, as she and Jonsey keep up a pretence of a happy and loving marriage. They even pretend that the baby Floral is carrying is Jonsey's. When Pandora suggests that Floral despises Jonsey, Floral claims that her angry rejection of his offered gift of a drink was nothing but the cravings of pregnancy. Floral also fails to see that Jonsey's flirtations are simply an act to make him appear more normal. Once he reveals this to her, she realizes that her marriage is empty and that she is free to be with the man she truly loves and the real father of her child, the Reverend Jonathan Larence. When she allows him to lead her out of the garden at the end of the play, this is symbolic of her embracing a more passionate, risky, and meaningful life.

Jonsey Whitman

Jonsey is Floral's husband. He is a wealthy and pleasant but vacuous man who states in part two, "I never wanted an interesting life. I prefer a few familiar things: my estate; my yachts; my trusted staff and crew." He is charming, attentive, and considerate, ready to dance with Pandora when Edvard will not, and offering to massage his wife's feet with oils when they are swollen. He is happy to keep up the pretence that he and Floral have a loving and happy marriage and that the baby she is expecting is his. He is convinced of his own handsomeness, which he repeatedly mentions, and he flirts with other women to make himself appear normal. He has gained the reputation of being a womanizer, but as he says to Edvard, he has never had an affair.

Jonsey stages a conversation for Sidney's benefit in which he mentions Floral's supposed snoring as a reason why they must divorce. It is possible that Jonsey is motivated by a desire to shield Floral from more scandal rather than by a desire to preserve his own reputation. Such good manners would be typical of him. Jonsey's exit leaves the way clear for Floral to pursue her relationship with the Reverend openly.

THEMES

Civilization versus Passion

The main theme of *Impossible Marriage* is the conflict between civilization and passion. At the beginning of the play, the characters are victims of their own over-civilized behavior, which leads them to pretend to be something they are not. Floral and Jonsey tolerate their disastrous marriage and even pretend that Floral's baby is Jonsey's when both know better. They act the part of a loving couple, seemingly so that they can avoid unpleasantness. Jonsey pretends to be a womanizer, even though it leads Floral to become so angry that she has to enter counseling with the Reverend, with whom she falls in love. The Reverend carries out his ministerial duties and must listen to people praising him as a virtuous paragon, even though he is involved with Floral and is the father of her child. Kandall keeps up the image of the gracious hostess, presiding over the wedding and welcoming the guests, even though she is so against the match that she wishes Edvard would die. She allows her family to believe that she and her husband were in love and had a good marriage. More seriously, she is terminally ill but keeps it a secret so as not to "cast a shadow."

The impending wedding acts as a catalyst to bring everyone's secrets into the open. This has the effect of allowing the characters to let go of their pretences of civilized behavior and to live with greater spontaneity and passion.

The Repression and Liberation of Women

In choosing the tradition-bound society of the Deep South as the setting for the play, Henley has fenced in her female characters with a set of social conventions and expectations that are arguably more restrictive than those encountered elsewhere. Floral rebels against the expectations placed upon women in this highly artificial society. She embodies a state of barely contained rage. She is impatient with Jonsey's gallantries, such as fetching her drinks and giving foot massages. She counters Pandora's dance—an image of beautiful femininity—in part two by commenting vulgarly, "I wonder if I got these warts out here touching frogs." This remark, the second in which Floral refers to her warts, refers to the old folkloric belief that warts are contracted by touching frogs or toads. It also has many anti-romantic connotations. It subverts the fairy-tale tradition of kissing a frog

TOPICS FOR FURTHER STUDY

In Jackson R. Bryer's "Expressing 'The Misery and Confusion Truthfully': An Interview with Beth Henley," published in *American Drama*, Henley recalls writing *Impossible Marriage*: "I remember deliberately wanting to steal from Oscar Wilde. I went and read everything he wrote and I said, 'Give me some of that and some of that. Sprinkle it on me.'" Read any one of Oscar Wilde's comic plays. Write an essay in which you compare and contrast Henley's use of language in *Impossible Marriage* with Wilde's. Include in your essay an analysis of the dramatic strengths and weaknesses of Henley and Wilde's respective styles of language.

Henley is often praised as a playwright who is keeping alive an American regional voice on the stage. Research any aspect of the history and culture of the American South that you believe informs Henley's *Impossible Marriage*. Another way of looking at this question is to ask yourself what makes the play distinctively a work of the American South. Give a class presentation on your findings.

Henley has cited the nineteenth-century Russian playwright Anton Chekhov as an important influence on her work. In his interview with Henley, Bryer identifies "simultaneous comedy and seriousness" as an important quality of the work of both playwrights. Write an essay in which you consider how Henley's *Impossible Marriage* embodies this quality. You may, if you wish, refer to the work of Chekhov in your answer.

Henley's *Impossible Marriage* focuses on the pretences maintained by people who are determined, in varying degrees, to appear more respectable or civilized than they really are. Identify (without naming names or revealing personal information) some of the pretences maintained by people that you know or have met. You may, if you wish, include yourself. Analyze the reasons (for example, cultural, ethnic, gender-based, religious, or personal) why people maintain these pretences: what do they stand to gain and lose through maintaining or abandoning them? You may find the psychological concepts of compensation (covering up qualities or behaviors that the individual deems socially or personally unacceptable) and persona (the mask that people present to the outside world, as opposed to their real self) useful in pursuing your analysis. Lead a class discussion or write a report on your findings.

---

that turns into a prince, as here, the frogs only produce warts, and it carries a folkloric association with witches and old crones who lived outside respectable society, but were perhaps privy to unusual or forbidden wisdom.

"Warts and all" could be Floral's personal motto in *Impossible Marriage*. She is determined to puncture Pandora's romantic ideals, partly, as she admits later, out of jealousy, but also because she has an overwhelming drive to voice the unpleasant truth in a world of pleasant untruths. For example, she volunteers to break Pandora's engagement to Edvard when Pandora admits to doubts. She throws out the Southern belle ideals of hospitality and politeness to guests when, after Sidney tells of his strange relationship with the ice-cream seller, she announces bluntly, "This is a silly person." Breaking the rules of feminine decorum, she calls her pregnant body "gigantic" and "elephantine" and says she is able to "accommodate a circus under this tent" of a maternity dress. Floral says things that others dare not, in the process giving voice to the audience's feelings. Her outspokenness makes her the most likeable character in the play as well as the most rebellious.

Flower bouquet *(Kevin Walker | Taxi Japan | Getty Images)*

It is a frequent criticism of Henley's work, and of *Impossible Marriage* in particular, that the male characters are two-dimensional and unconvincing. In this play, however, that weakness could be seen as a strength to the play overall. The female characters are memorable, and the audience is impatient for these strong women to cease defining themselves in their relationship to the patriarchal Southern society and to their individual men, who seem oddly bloodless. While Floral and Kandall do enter new relationships with men of their choice by the end of the play, this time, the women are in control.

STYLE

Symbolic Setting

The setting of *Impossible Marriage* is an artificial and constricted one that reflects the theme of civilization versus passion. The general location of the play, the Deep South, evokes images of a

society deeply concerned with correct appearances. Intensifying these factors is the immediate setting of Kandall's garden, an artifice that is as carefully managed as the public image of her family.

The garden has exits in the direction of both the manor and the woods. The woods symbolize wildness and passion, and the manor symbolizes civilization. Characters exit to, and enter from, one or the other, depending on which principle is dominant in their psyche at that moment.

Melodrama

Impossible Marriage is often called a melodrama. The word *melodrama* derives from the Greek words for song and drama, and was originally used to refer to drama in which music was used to intensify the emotional effect. The term has come to mean drama in which extreme emotion is emphasized, and plot and action take precedence over character development.

Impossible Marriage is full of melodramatic incidents, such as when Sidney turns up at the wedding ceremony with a pistol and threatens to shoot his father, and when Floral runs off with the Reverend and he is revealed to be the father of her child. However, Henley undermines the melodrama with the absurd and the human. For example, Sidney fails to shoot his father and ends up shooting himself in the foot.

Comedy of Manners

Impossible Marriage is often described as a comedy of manners. Comedy of manners is a literary genre that satirizes the customs of a social group or class. The genre flourished in the Restoration period from 1660 to 1710 in England, in what has become known as Restoration comedy. Restoration comedy featured artificial plots involving sexual liaisons, stock characters, and witty, epigrammatic dialogue. The tradition of artificial plots and epigrammatic speech was taken up by the Irish playwright Oscar Wilde in plays such as *The Importance of Being Earnest* (1895).

In the case of *Impossible Marriage*, the class that is satirized is the upper-class society of the Deep South, with its preoccupation with decorum and propriety. The play also features stock characters and epigrammatic dialogue.

Epigrammatic Dialogue

Critics have commented on the epigrammatic, mannered, and unrealistic dialogue of *Impossible*

Marriage. An epigram is a witty, ingenious, or pointed saying tersely expressed, so epigrammatic dialogue is speech that embodies these qualities. An example is Sidney's remark, "Love has yet to avail itself to my scrutiny." One effect of such dialogue is to rob it of emotional power. Also, epigrammatic dialogue often results in the characters addressing the audience rather than each other. This reinforces the emotional distance between the characters.

Occasionally, Henley achieves a wit comparable to that of Oscar Wilde, as when Kandall comments acerbically on the disastrous marriage ceremony. Using the Wildean subverted cliché, she says, "Amazing. It has all gone off so much worse than expected." With the substitution of the word *worse* for the expected word *better*, Kandall sums up the series of uncomfortable revelations prompted by the marriage.

Southern Belle Archetype

Although slavery has ended and the South of the twenty-first century has a diverse economy, certain features of the antebellum (pre-Civil War) culture persist in the region. One cultural reference point implicit in *Impossible Marriage* and other literary works based in the South is the archetype (idealized model) of the Southern belle. This is a woman of the wealthy upper class whose family typically owns a country estate. She would be more likely to be a homemaker than to have a career outside the home, and would aim to be a good wife and mother, a gracious hostess, and an accomplished cook. She would cultivate traditional feminine and wifely virtues such as hospitality, charm, and beauty. Flirting would be part of her feminine appeal, but she must at the same time be chaste and above moral reproach. Critics of the Southern belle archetype point out its repressive influence on women, in that it tries to make them conform to a restrictive external set of criteria.

In *Impossible Marriage*, Kandall embodies many Southern belle virtues. A charming and elegant hostess, she tries to smooth over any embarrassing or uncomfortable episode with polite small talk and gestures of hospitality, as when she announces in part two that the wedding will go ahead:

> SIDNEY. Then all must die. (Sidney exits to the woods.)
> KANDALL. More champagne, please.

Pandora, with her whimsical femininity and willingness to subjugate her doubts about Edvard to her love for him, qualifies as a Southern belle. Floral, in contrast, is by nature antagonistic to this ideal and is increasingly honest about her attitude as the play progresses. With her talk of accommodating circuses under her maternity dress, her musings about warts, her blunt advice to Pandora about Edvard's unsuitability as a husband, and her barbaric behavior in carving into the wedding cake and eating it with her hands, she might be called an anti-Southern belle. Kandall's final desertion of the Southern belle ideal of chaste widowhood in pursuit of the much younger Sidney means that only Pandora remains in the Southern belle camp—and she, as Henley portrays her, is too young and inexperienced to know any better.

It is worth noting the symbolism of names in the play in relation to the Southern belle archetype. The name Kandall suggests the cliché expression, "to keep the candle burning," which means to keep alive a memory or tradition, in this case for the ways of the Old South. The symbolism is reinforced by Kandall's ordering the candelabra to be brought when the short-sighted Edvard cannot see in the dark. Delighted with the romantic light cast by the candelabra, Kandall says, with satisfaction, "The mood created."

Floral's name, suggesting Kandall's beautiful garden as well as the feminine dresses worn by Southern belles, was undoubtedly bestowed by Kandall in an exercise in wishful thinking. Floral does not live up to the Southern belle ideal of decorative decorum, but she does embody a different feminine archetype. Like her near-namesake Flora, the Roman goddess of flowers and spring, Floral is fertile and creative (significantly, the play is set in a garden in mid-May, when Flora's powers were at their height). Floral is pregnant with a baby and with new possibilities for the future. She finally rejects Kandall's tamed garden and allies herself with a wilder aspect of nature, the woods and hills that lie beyond.

HISTORICAL CONTEXT

The American South

The American Civil War (1861–65) cemented a division between Northern and Southern states of the United States. In 1861, thirteen Southern states seceded (disjoined) from the United States, or Union. Eleven of those states, including Georgia, where the play *Impossible Marriage* is set, joined together to form the Confederate States of America, or the Confederacy. The secession brought about the American Civil War. The war was primarily about different economic systems. The Southern states were heavily dependent on slave labor, which underpinned their plantation-based, agricultural economy. The Northern states were increasingly rejecting slavery and had a fast-expanding industrial economy. With the victory of the Union forces in 1865, all slaves were freed.

The states in the Deep South, a subregion that includes Georgia, were the most dependent on the plantation economy, the main crop being cotton. Savannah, where Kandall's country estate is situated, was one of the main centers for cotton, and it is likely that the estate was once a cotton plantation.

Many authors who have written about the South (notably William Faulkner in such novels as *The Sound and the Fury* [1929], and *Absalom, Absalom!* [1936]; Margaret Mitchell in her novel *Gone With the Wind* [1936]; and Tennessee Williams in plays such as *A Streetcar Named Desire* [1947]) emphasize in their work that while some aspects of the region changed as a result of the Civil War, others did not. The political and economic systems were transformed and the institution of slavery vanished, but many cultural mores, attitudes, and practices persisted. The latter half of the twentieth century saw the rise of a new generation of authors who, conscious of the South's history of slavery, identified racism as a prominent Southern trait and confronted its effects in their work. One of the best known of this group of authors is Alice Walker, whose novel *The Color Purple* (1982) explores the racism encountered by a young black woman in a predominantly white Southern culture.

Though the character of the American South has evolved over time, the South maintains a distinctive culture, and this is especially so in the Deep South. The Deep South is widely viewed as conservative and as embodying traditional values, such as an emphasis on the importance of family, strong religious convictions, propriety, and patriotism. As of 2008, there is no sign that Southern values are in decline. On the contrary, their perceived power and resilience gave rise in the early 2000s to a new term, *southernization*, which refers to the idea that Southern values and beliefs are being adopted throughout the United States.

In *Impossible Marriage*, the chief conflict is between the conservative Southern values embodied in Kandall and the more progressive and modern spirit embodied in Floral. Floral's behavior constantly shocks Kandall, who tries for much of the play to maintain the appearance of decorum that she has so carefully cultivated. In the end, this is a losing battle. Just as the old South had to change its economic and social structures after the Civil War, so Kandall gives up trying to hold on to the old ways. Ultimately, she enthusiastically embraces the new life of spontaneity and passion. It is significant, however, that Kandall's transformation occurs within her typically Southern garden surrounding her manor house. Kandall's partner in passion, Sidney, is invited to stay with her in the garden, tasting its delicious fruits. Henley, like Margaret Mitchell before her, seems to suggest that Southern life can adapt to changing times and values and that its beauty and charm will survive.

CRITICAL OVERVIEW

Henley's plays have often met with a mixed critical response, and *Impossible Marriage* is no exception. Ben Brantley, in his 1998 review of the play for the *New York Times*, compares the play unfavorably to *Crimes of the Heart*, remarking that "this comedy never breaks through its exterior to reveal a fractured human heart." Charles Isherwood, writing in *Variety*, calls the play "sometimes insufferably precious and sometimes disarmingly charming—and often both simultaneously." Isherwood is one of several critics who find themselves alienated by the "fanciful dialogue," which "keeps reminding us that these Southern madcaps aren't particularly convincing as flesh-and-blood human beings." Ishwerwood concludes, "The artificial grandiloquence of the talk and the plot's self-consciously addled air" make it hard to take seriously the characters' thoughts on "the need for both civilization and erotic abandon." In a similar vein, Mark Harris, in his review for *Entertainment Weekly* (1998), calls the play "mossy, overdrawn Southern-gothic whimsy."

Reviewing the play for the *Hollywood Reporter*, Frank Scheck judges it "a distressing step down" for the author of *Crimes of the Heart* and *The Miss Firecracker Contest*. In Scheck's view, the comic style "leans much too far toward the baroque and silly," the dialogue is "far more arch than it is enlightening," and the characters are "more irritating than endearing." The actors in this New York production, he notes, "struggle with the artificiality of what they are given to play."

Richard Scholem, in his review for the *Long Island Business News*, praises those aspects of the play that other critics condemn. Scholem calls it the "funniest, frothiest, finest comedy," with "bigger-than-life" characters who are "deliciously overwrought, over dramatic, over magnified and over the edge." He adds that they delight because although they are tragic, "we need not take any of them seriously."

Pamela Renner, reviewing the play for *American Theatre*, believes that its characters show a maturation from the "youthful infatuation and emotional disarray evident in [Henley's] 1980s works" on the grounds that they are more ready to accept the passage of time. Renner also notes that the "sense of delight" of Henley's earlier works is also to be found in *Impossible Marriage*, but the tone is softer and more mellow.

CRITICISM

Claire Robinson

Robinson has a master's degree in English. She is a teacher of English literature and a freelance writer and editor. In this essay, Robinson examines the nature of the redemption achieved by the characters of Beth Henley's Impossible Marriage *in light of the Greek myth of Pandora.*

In *Impossible Marriage*, Pandora's forthcoming wedding propels many of the characters out of their old lives of pretence and conformity. Change is long overdue, as is clear from the gap between the civilized pretence of their lives and the reality. In this gap arises tension, which demands resolution. They escape the old confines of civilized behavior and embrace lives of greater spontaneity, reality, and passion. But any notion that they are leaving their problems behind and heading for a paradisical new existence would be simplistic in the extreme. The nature of the journey they make, and the redemption they achieve, is central to an understanding of the play.

WHAT DO I READ NEXT?

Henley cites Chekhov as a major influence. In her interview with Jackson R. Bryer for *American Drama*, Henley points to Chekhov's play *The Cherry Orchard* (first published under its Russian name, *Vishnevyi sad*, in 1904) as a particular inspiration for her work.

Margaret Mitchell's novel *Gone With the Wind* (1936) is an illuminating study of the customs and mores of the Deep South before, during, and after the Civil War, particularly as they applied to women. The book is written from the point of view of the upper-class slave-owning society and is sympathetic to slavery.

Sarah Morgan: The Civil War Diary Of A Southern Woman, edited by Charles East and published in 1992, is a compilation of entries from the diary of the wife of a Confederate soldier during the American Civil War. Written between 1862 and 1866, the diaries were first published in 1913. Readers of *Impossible Marriage* may recognize in the self-absorbed Morgan a prototype of the more whimsical aspects of Henley's characters.

Mary Chesnut's Civil War, edited by C. Vann Woodward and published in 1981, is a classic diary account of the Civil War written between 1861 and 1865 by the wife of a prominent politician of the time. Chesnut's observant and well-informed account makes an interesting contrast to that of fellow diarist Sarah Morgan. Woodward's annotated edition won the Pulitzer Prize in History in 1982.

The journey that is explored in most detail is that of Floral. She appears to have remained in her sterile marriage to Jonsey so as not to upset him and her family. At the beginning of the play, their play-acting is committed, though largely unconvincing. This is shown graphically by Floral's attitude to her pregnancy. Though she is so heavily pregnant that the fact is obvious to all, she tries to play it down, saying, "Is it really that apparent? I'm carrying extremely small for my size." She wishes to minimize the pregnancy because Jonsey is not the father of her baby.

While Floral's mind leads her into lies, her body forces her to tell the truth. By part two, only hours have passed since she described her bump as "small," but she now talks of it as "gigantic" and "elephantine." Her shape has not changed, but her attitude toward life has. She is less able, and less willing, to pretend or to cultivate the appearance of propriety. While she may fool herself and others that she has a happy marriage, nature has its own language, and it cannot be denied a voice forever. It speaks through her growing pregnancy—with another man's child. This fact forces itself into everyone's awareness, most of all Floral's. She is losing control of her pretences, a process that is shown symbolically by her animalistic behavior in carving into the cake and eating it with her fingers. She blames pregnancy cravings, but her cravings for cake symbolize her desire for the Reverend, whose child she is carrying. Floral alerts the audience to this symbolic undertone when she tries to explain to Pandora her rejection of the drink Jonsey brought her only minutes after asking for it: "These cravings are very deep and reason does not speak to them." Her true feelings are breaking through her veneer of civilized pretence.

The job of maintaining civilized appearances is left largely to Kandall, who is appalled at Floral's treatment of the cake: "If this continues, we'll soon be searching for distant places in which she can be put out of our sight for long periods of time along with other criminals, lunatics and barbarians." Pandora backs up Kandall's attitude by pointing out another of Floral's sins against feminine propriety: "And she has warts, Mother. She has warts on her fingers."

Significantly, a wart, like a pregnancy, is a natural growth that is not under the control of the forces of civilization. There is much irony in the juxtaposition of Kandall's increasingly doomed attempts at keeping up appearances with the less photogenic reality. When Floral walks off barefoot "to go roll down a hill," an uncontrolled and uncivilized act which is especially dangerous during pregnancy, Kandall tries to distract everyone by changing the subject to the dessert of cherries jubilee. Significantly, while she goes off to fetch the dessert, Jonsey confides to Edvard that Floral's child cannot be his because he and his wife have never consummated their marriage. The effect is of tragedy covered with a fragile veneer of social niceties.

Kandall's carefully constructed world finally cracks when Floral tells her why she stayed with Jonsey: she wanted to emulate Kandall's happy marriage. Kandall admits that in reality, she did not love her husband. She hid the fact because, as she says to Floral, "You might have gotten the wrong idea about marriage." The irony lies in the fact that "the wrong idea" is, in this case, the truth. Kandall and Floral have been caged in falsehoods of their own making, condemning themselves to passionless lives for the sake of maintaining an image of respectability. Once Kandall has admitted this secret, she is able to rise above her previous obsession with avoiding scandal.

It is probable that Kandall's knowledge that she is terminally ill also enables her to gain a new perspective on life and see what is truly important. Significantly, she reveals this secret first to Sidney. Her gesture of trust and truth-telling emboldens him, prompting him to kiss her passionately. The two subsequently begin a romantic relationship. This relationship promises to rejuvenate the young man, who is old before his time, and to allow Kandall to move beyond the Southern belle virtues she previously cultivated.

However, the passionate life is not held up as a panacea, or cure-all. The most committed passionate relationship in the play is that between Edvard and Pandora, yet it carries undertones of impending disaster, mostly because of the mismatch in age, life experience, and energy between the two. Pandora is "the image of youthful exuberance." Edvard, in contrast, is over twice her age, ominously believes that "we are defined by the things we can no longer feel, dream, or accomplish," and is unable to join her in her night-time dance because he has eaten too much and does not feel the urge. Both parties have doubts about the match, and Edvard's final determination to go through with the wedding is, as the eighteenth-century English essayist and critic Samuel Johnson said (as quoted in *The Oxford Dictionary of Quotations*) about a second marriage, "the triumph of hope over experience."

Hope is the chief factor that propels all the characters into their new lives. The most hopeful character in *Impossible Marriage* is Pandora. In order to understand the undertones of the concept of hope as Henley uses it, it is important to consider the origin of the name Pandora. In Greek myth, Pandora was the first woman. She was created by the gods on the orders of Zeus, the king of the gods, in revenge against Prometheus, the first man, because he stole fire from heaven. She was modeled in the image of Aphrodite, the goddess of love, and so was extremely beautiful.

Pandora's name derives from the Greek for "all-gifted" or "the gift of all" because each of the gods gave her a power designed to bring about the ruin of man. She was also given a box to contain all these gifts, but was told never to open the box. Then she was sent to earth. Prometheus did not trust Zeus and stayed away from Pandora, but his brother, Epimetheus, was overwhelmed by her beauty and married her. It is noteworthy that Prometheus's name means "forethought," and Epimetheus's name means "afterthought." One of the gifts that Pandora had been given was curiosity. She was eager to find out what was in the box and, despite Prometheus's warnings, Epimetheus allowed her to open it. All the evils in the box flew out, and ever since, they have afflicted the world. Thus the term *Pandora's box* is used to mean a gift that is actually a curse.

Some accounts of the myth say that the last gift to fly out was hope, but other accounts say that hope alone remained in the box. Interpretation of this last element of the myth is debated. It could mean that hope is a blessing that remains accessible to man to enable him to bear all the other afflictions, or it could mean that hope is a blessing that is denied him because it is locked in the box.

A third possibility, and the one that is suggested in *Impossible Marriage*, is that hope is itself an evil. This is because it encourages people to be discontent with their present lot and to

desire something more, or something other, just as Edvard and Floral become discontented with their marriages. As Francesco Aristide Ancona writes in his psychological explication of the Pandora myth for the *Journal of Evolutionary Psychology*, "Hope Sinks: Pandora, Eve and the Obsession of Ahab," "Hope is what keeps us from ever being happy because it fuels the black hole in us, creating a constant expectation and desire for more." The message of the myth, Ancona concludes, is that "hope is evil."

Henley is not so categorical in her modern reworking of the Pandora myth. Rather, *Impossible Marriage* emphasizes the tantalizing ambiguity of the myth, as highlighted by Edvard. As Edvard and Pandora are about to leave Kandall's house to be married, Edvard says, "Pestilence and hope were in Pandora's box. Hope was the salvation. Or was it the final pestilence?"

Perhaps hope, embodied by the youthful and vivacious Pandora, is indeed a salvation, capable of rejuvenating the aging Edvard. As Edvard says on hearing how Pandora refused to throw out her dead fish, "I thought my life was over, then I met you." Hope enables Edvard to marry Pandora, for all their evident incompatibilities. Hope also drives a transformation in the lives of the other characters. It inspires Floral and the Reverend, and Kandall and Sidney, to embrace passion after a lifetime of self-denial and pretence. They hope they are taking the first step toward a better life. Beyond the world of good manners and propriety lies the promise of woods to be explored, berries to be eaten with the fingers, and hills to be rolled down. Perhaps the characters will find fulfillment. Pandora's impending marriage has acted as a catalyst to release this boxful of new possibilities for the characters.

On the other hand, hope may turn out to be a pestilence. The characters could end up recreating with their new partners the disappointment and pretence that dominated their old lives. Relationships that at present seem full of promise may fall apart, just as Edvard's first marriage did. In this case, disenchantment will breed further hope, for yet another and different life. It is ominous that one quality of Edvard's that is heavily emphasized is his shortsightedness, suggesting that in marrying Pandora, he has more in common with the gullible Epimetheus (afterthought) than the cautious Prometheus (forethought). This is also true of the other characters in the play. Only time will tell whether

> ALTHOUGH I MUST ADMIT THAT MORE RECENTLY IN THE PLAY *IMPOSSIBLE MARRIAGE*, I REMEMBER DELIBERATELY WANTING TO STEAL FROM OSCAR WILDE. I WENT AND READ EVERYTHING HE WROTE AND I SAID, 'GIVE ME SOME OF THAT AND SOME OF THAT. SPRINKLE IT ON ME.'"

the tempting gifts that lure the characters into the world beyond the garden will turn out to be blessings or curses.

Source: Claire Robinson, Critical Essay on *Impossible Marriage*, in *Drama for Students*, Gale, Cengage Learning, 2009.

Jackson R. Bryer

In the following interview, Henley offers insight into her career in theater, including her first productions, and her writing process.

Beth Henley's first professionally produced play, *Crimes of the Heart,* won the Pulitzer Prize and the New York Drama Critics' Circle Award in 1981 after a successful New York production (prior to New York, it had been done in Louisville, Baltimore, and St. Louis in 1979 and 1980). Her first produced play, *Am I Blue* (1974), was written while she was an undergraduate student at Southern Methodist University. Her works for the stage since *Crimes of the Heart* include *The Miss Firecracker Contest* (1980), *The Wake of Jamey Foster* (1981), *The Debutante Ball* (1985), *The Lucky Spot* (1987), *Abundance* (1989), *Signature* (1990), *Control Freaks* (1992), *Revelers* (1994), *L-Play* (1995), *Impossible Marriage* (1998), *Sisters of the Winter Madrigal* (2001), and *Exposed* (2002). This interview was conducted on September 30, 2002, in the Ina & Jack Kay Theatre of the Clarice Smith Performing Arts Center at the University of Maryland; the audience was composed of undergraduate and graduate students and faculty members. For significant assistance in preparing the transcription of the interview, I wish to thank Carolyn Bain.

JACKSON BRYER: Can you start by telling us about your first exposure to the theatre? As I recall, you became interested in theatre through your mother, who was an actress. Talk a little bit about your early interest in theatre and also about your time as a student of theatre.

BETH HENLEY: I grew up in Jackson, Mississippi, really in suburbia, so my mother was in community theatre plays. They were so magical for me, and one of the most exciting experiences was to go in and see little houses that were built for people to act in and then were torn down. I would also help her with her lines. I remember when she got to play Blanche DuBois and I got to hear those words over and over again when she was trying to learn her lines. Also, I liked to help her edit things. If she was doing a reading for a club or something, we'd have to make Blanche's speeches longer and cut out Stanley's—so I got into editing. Then, when I was a senior in high school, I was kind of bereft and she put me in an acting class. What I loved about the acting class was that you got to think all day long about a person that wasn't you, and figure out why they were sad and what they wanted, what they dreamed. I just loved being divorced from my own wretchedness. Then I went off to Southern Methodist University in Dallas. They had a really wonderful theatre department. I regret that I was so not grateful at the time to my professors. We're sort of innocently arrogant about just being young. The class I liked the best, that I think helped me the most, was my movement class because when I got out of high school, I was very hunched over. In movement class, you had to lie on the floor and get your alignment in to pass the class. You had to stand on your head for, I think, three minutes. That transformed me in a way that's hard to speak about. I also took Stage Combat, and I took a wonderful class in Theatre Styles where you'd do the Greeks and make your own mask. I remember sitting there with a death mask over me with straws coming out of my nose. I had a really good Theatre History class that, at the time, was excruciating. It was at nine in the morning, and I would sometimes go in jeans and my bedroom slippers. But actually that's kind of the way I learned about history. The only foothold I have in world history is through theatre history.

JB: All this time, you were doing this in order to become an actress?

HENLEY: Yes. I was sort of in the acting program. How I got in the acting program is a miracle. Oh, I know how I got in. Anyone could get in! You had to do a general audition for the school when you got in, and I chose to do, brilliantly I think, Willie from *This Property is Condemned*. And then I did Macbeth in *Macbeth*, which was the only Shakespeare I knew. Somehow, I was in the acting department.

JB: But it sounds like when you talk about your experience with your mother that, even if you weren't conscious of it, you were paying pretty close attention to the words.

HENLEY: Yes.

JB: Had you been interested in writing at all or were you always interested initially in being a performer—probably because your mother was a performer? Were you conscious of any interest in writing?

HENLEY: I wrote a play in sixth grade called *Swing High, Swing Low*. It was about Dolly, a girl who lives in the suburbs and goes to New York to be an artist. Actually, the character was named Dolly because when she came to New York, they said, "Hello, Dolly, hello!" And the parents back in the suburb were, "Kids. What's the matter with kids today?" I tried to direct as well as write this. I wasn't performing, and we got boys involved. It ended in a debacle. It never ever got on anywhere. It was a summer project. The next thing I wrote was in a writing class at night school. It was about a poor woman who worked at a dime store and who was all alone for Christmas in Laurel, Mississippi. I hadn't finished it and the teacher said, "Just read it anyway." I got up to read it, and I was so pained by its inadequacies that I crumpled up the paper and threw it on the floor and ran down the hallway and hid in the restroom for the rest of the afternoon. It's really interesting that whenever you do something that is so out of character, like having an emotional outburst, that you don't get in trouble. I guess they were horrified by the hysterics of a junior high schooler. After that I thought, "You know what? You're not smart enough to write." But when I got to SMU and decided to take a playwriting class, I said this isn't a bad idea. If I write characters, they could be as dumb as me, and I don't have to be very smart. It was kind of enlightening to become a playwright. I wrote a play called *Am I Blue,* which is about a young guy who's very straight and his fraternity's sending him to a whorehouse on his eighteenth birthday and he's a virgin. He meets this young sixteen-year-old girl who's all alone on the night of her prom and lives a very chaotic life. That was my first play that was actually done.

JB: After SMU you went to graduate school at the University of Illinois. What was the impetus behind that?

HENLEY: The impetus behind going to graduate school was a year after graduating from college spent in Dallas working at the dog food factory and Bank America and not having met success in my chosen field, which at that point was being an actress. I think I had a job in a children's theatre. I taught badly because I was into nihilism at the time and that's just not where you go with teaching. Then an old professor of mine went to run the art school at the University of Illinois in Champaign. He said he would give me a scholarship to go there if I would teach. I got there and somehow miraculously lived on two hundred dollars a month, which was what I got—and I was happy to have it. I did realize after being there for a year—I didn't complete my MFA—that if they had teachers as bad as me it wasn't a good sign. So I had to move on. I was just restless with being in school; so I went out to Los Angeles.

JB: You've spoken in other interviews about a time when several successful directors came to SMU. Can you speak a little bit about what it means to a person who is an undergraduate in theatre to have an actual, successful theatre professional present? What kind of impression did it make on you?

HENLEY: A searing impression. Somehow I got to be one of five of six actors that the directors would use as guinea pigs at this directing colloquium, where people pay to listen to and watch the directors direct. It was painful because I was a really bad actress. I remember I had just done an awful rendition of Juliet, and William Gaskill, this British director; said, "Now won't you just sit on that box and don't move!" Joseph Chaikin came and he read some stuff and he was so brilliant; that was glorious! I've never ever seen anything like that in my life. The spirit, the sort of human, animal, god energy of that guy was just unforgettable. Joseph Anthony came and we saw his film *Tomorrow,* which Horton Foote wrote. They were so artistic.

JB: Another story that you've told—and I don't know when this happened chronologically—is when you went to New York to see a production of The Cherry Orchard. *When was that?*

HENLEY: I was in college. We were having auditions the following year, so this was after my sophomore year. In the fall, I was going to have to audition for Chekhov's *Three Sisters*. I was reading it and it made no sense. I didn't get it. I probably had a bad translation anyway. I was like "How can I get into this character? Who are these people? They're stiff; they're not people you can really like." Then I went to see an all African-American production of *The Cherry Orchard* with Gloria Foster and James Earl Jones as Lopahin. I finally got it when he says, "They used to tell me I wrote like a pig." When he buys the cherry orchard, it's the happiest and most devastating moment of his life. It's so big how he did it, and I started having this sort of epileptic fit in the audience. I was crying and screaming; I was really euphoric because I understood how things could be simultaneously tragic and comic and so alive and so real. After that I understood Chekhov, but didn't get cast in *Three Sisters*. I did go on to write *Crimes of the Heart,* which is loosely based on *Three Sisters*.

JB: Don't you think also that the quality in Chekhov of simultaneous comedy and seriousness is something that characterizes many of your plays?

HENLEY: I like that edge. I like when I see it in writing if it's over the edge. Even something like the Marx Brothers is sort of brutal in how funny it is. Some really good things kind of swing both ways and I like to see people that can swing really, really, really sad and horrible and terrible and really, really, really beautiful and funny. I think Chekhov does that like nobody else. Shakespeare's up there, but . . .

JB: Isn't there something inherently Southern about that too, about combining the most grotesque and serious kinds of things with the funny, about being able to see the humor in the grotesque? Why is that? What is there about the South that makes that particularly true?

HENLEY: That's a good question. I think that people have to be able to see two sides of the coin to survive because it is a racist society and yet you're being raised by racists. So what are you going to do? There are these people who are feeding you, but they're chauvinist and racist. You kind of have to get a little perspective. You can't go with "They're just evil," and you can't go "Oh, I believe them, I love them." You kind of have to go "This is a little more complicated."

JB: You have to see them with two different sets of eyes.

HENLEY: At least two!

JB: Was Crimes of the Heart *the second play you wrote after* Am I Blue? *Were there other plays in between?*

HENLEY: I wrote one play that was only recently done. It was buried in a trunk. It's called *Sisters of the Winter Madrigal*. It was interesting for me to see it done after so many years; because I wrote it and I didn't realize what a rage I was in. I always think, "Oh, I'm not a feminist. I like men." But in this play there are these two sisters: one's a whore and one's a cow herder. One wants to marry the shoemaker's son, but the king wants her because of her hair and she ends up with her ear bit off; and the other one ends up with her arm chopped off. It's very Bergmanesque; there are all kind of pieces of them in the end.

JB: Who did it?

HENLEY: A friend of mine did it, Frederick Bailey. He and I had had a double bill back when my play was at SMU. We did his Vietnam play *The Bridgehead* and my blue play about two virgins. His play was first and ended with somebody getting shot in the head. Then they had to clean up the blood for my play. It wasn't a perfect double bill! But he is one of my favorite writers, and he's written a play and he wanted to do these two plays on the same bill; his new play is called *Dirty, Ugly People and Their Stupid Meaningless Lives*. I said sign me up! So he directed both of these pieces and so that's how it got done.

JB: What was is like seeing an early play like that? Do you say to yourself, "How could I have done that?"—or were you rather pleased with it?

HENLEY: I was touched that I was that enraged. I was happy to know I had that rage and happy that I'd written it then. That's what I was saying earlier. I'm always happy to have written anything because it's kind of a mark of who you were at the time if it's even vaguely honest—though you could never redo it. I couldn't recapture that sort of frivolous rage. It had its moments, so I was really pleased.

JB: Talk a little bit about how you came to write Crimes of the Heart.

HENLEY: My friend Frederick Bailey was doing *Gringo Planet,* a play of his, at the La MaMa Hollywood and he produced the whole thing for $500. I thought, "Maybe I could do that." I'd written the screenplay while I was out there and I said, "This would be perfect for Sissy Spacek. I love her! I'll call up her agent and see about her reading it." So the agent says, "We don't take unsolicited material. When you get a producer to produce it, we'll be happy to look at it." Then I called up producers and they said they didn't take unsolicited material. It was a catch-22 thing. I didn't really know how to get it to a producer or how to get it to an agent. Nobody's going to look at it unless it's a success. I wrote *Crimes of the Heart* kind of because I thought, "At least I can do this with my friends for my friends for $500 at the La MaMa." That's why in the very first draft I don't have them cut into the cake because I'm thinking of the budget! We can't have a different cake every night, so the lights go down as they cut it. That's also why it was one set, a kitchen, and modern clothes. I was really thinking practically when I wrote that play; I was thinking about producing it on my own.

JB: Was it done at La MaMa in Los Angeles?

HENLEY: No, it wasn't done at La MaMa. I didn't have $500! Actually, Bailey, who is so instrumental in my life, had won the Actors Theatre of Louisville playwriting contest with his play *The Bridgehead* the year before, and he sent my play in and it won the Actors Theatre of Louisville contest.

JB: And that was the first production?

HENLEY: That was the first production, and they were very adamant about it not having been produced anywhere. That's one sort of annoying thing to me about this. Plays are so much more special if they've never ever had a production, but I think you can really work on a play and make it better with each production. Anyway, that was the first place it was done.

JB: What was that like?

HENLEY: It was terrifying, number one. I remember not knowing what a cue light was because I'd never worked in a production that was high class enough to have a cue light. They kept saying, "Yeah, we'll do it with a cue light." And I was like, "Yeah, yeah, the cue light. What's the cue light?" But I had two glorious actresses in the parts of Lenny and Meg. Kathy Bates played the original Lenny and this wonderful actress, Susan Kingsley, played Meg and she was a genius at it. I don't know if I want to get into the ugliness of this, but the director's wife played Babe, and she wasn't as good as the others.

JB: What is it like when you go and you're involved in a production about which you have very definite ideas, and it isn't going entirely the way you want it to go?

HENLEY: It so depends on the production. The most glorious thing about working in the collaborative art is when you have somebody like Susan Kingsley or Kathy Bates who are better than your play. And you're just "Ahh." That is just extraordinary. You have a director that sees things in the play that you didn't envision and knows how to heighten them and move the rhythm of it and to cover up any faults and make all of the assets really glimmer. I'm very into the first production of the show. I love to see the rehearsals, to sit there throughout the entire rehearsal and hear it over and over because with repetition you can get a sense of what the rhythm of the lines is. When I first started, it was much harder because in the very first production of the play, I'm thinking, "I really don't know what is the director's fault, what's my fault, what's the actor's fault." It was very hard; they'd say, "Cut this" and I would say, "But I'm not certain that needs to be cut." Now I've gotten a lot clearer on how to sort that out, I think.

JB: And how do you sort all that out?

HENLEY: I have a lot of meetings in my living room and hear it again.

JB: In other words, today you'll go to rehearsal having a lot more ideas of how things should be, and how they should sound? With Crimes of the Heart, *when you got to Louisville was that really the first time you had heard the play read?*

HENLEY: I think I did have a reading at my house.

JB: But you hadn't worked on it?

HENLEY: I hadn't thought of the process, of somebody telling me to cut a line. I love to cut. My fault now is making my plays too short.

JB: Has that been a result of writing a lot of plays?

HENLEY: It's the result of writing plays and feeling the audience get restless. That to me is like "I want it to move. I want it to move!" Pace, you know. I don't want you looking restless. Because it's so excruciating when you're in the theatre and you can feel that "Why isn't this over?"

JB: Crimes of the Heart *was such a success. It must have been difficult to write the next play. You had a lot to live up to at that point, didn't you?*

HENLEY: When I went to Louisville, I had started on a new play, *The Miss Firecracker Contest.* That was always my inclination, to start on a new play before the other one gets done, because at least you'll have something to go back to if that play gets trashed. It took a long time for *Crimes of the Heart* to get on. It was done in Louisville and in Baltimore, and then in St. Louis. It was round and about before it was actually a big success, so I had time to work on other plays.

JB: Is Crimes of the Heart *the play through which you got involved with Holly Hunter?*

HENLEY: No. Holly auditioned for *The Wake of Jamey Foster.* There was a part of a seventeen-year-old orphan who's a burn victim, who's a romantic interest of one of the boys. It was so bizarre because Holly and I got stuck in an elevator; we were trapped in this elevator together at this very first meeting. So I thought, "Hmmm." I knew who she was because someone had said that this wonderful, wonderful actress was coming in, but I was too shy to talk very much. We got free. I loved her audition so much for *The Wake* that when we were replacing Mary Beth Hurt in the part of Meg on Broadway in *Crimes of the Heart,* I got her to do that, to be that replacement, but with the stipulation that when *The Wake* started she'd get out of *Crimes of the Heart.* So *Crimes* was the first play of mine she was in; then she was in *The Wake.*

JB: Some actors and actresses have a particular affinity to certain playwrights, and it seems to me that there's something about the way Holly Hunter presents herself on stage that makes her particularly good at the roles you write.

HENLEY: Absolutely. I'm really blessed.

JB: Have you ever written anything with her in mind?

HENLEY: Yes, I have. A play called *Control Freaks.* We were working at a theatre in Los Angeles together, the Met Theatre, and I wrote a play for her and three other actors and she ended up doing it in LA. She was wonderful. So that play I specifically wrote for her.

JB: Do you tend to do that often—write for specific actors or actresses?

HENLEY: Not really, no. Not generally.

JB: How would you describe your relationship with Holly Hunter? When she comes to the play, does she discuss the character with you a lot? Of is it more a matter of watching her and saying things to her through the director?

HENLEY: It kind of varies because we've worked together over so many years. She particularly likes to explore while she's working and not get a lot of feedback until she's reached the limits of her exploration. It's very fearless and sometimes very bad. That's another point about running a play with actors.

They'll risk being just terrible. Holly will come in with ideas that are just brilliant and she'll come in with this idea that makes no sense; she likes to really go with her instincts. Once she has those instincts in play, then you can shape more.

JB: Along with Holly Hunter, you've worked with some other tremendous actors over the course of your career, and you write so richly for actors. What do these great actors have in common in terms of making strong choices for your work?

HENLEY: That's a good question. I don't know. It's a deep, deep commitment and passion for investigating every facet of every moment. With Holly, it's the things that she'll do for the play, like learn to play the harp, learn to tap dance, learn to twirl a gun around, learn to play the piano.

JB: Have you ever dealt with actors, where in the end you know they're going to come up with something really, really good, but to get there you're going to have to let them do that kind of fearless exploration?

HENLEY: When we were doing *Control Freaks,* it was all about being out of control in rehearsals and then doing a play that is so utterly controlled. Every moment is basically choreographed, and then it explodes into this big mess—but it's a very thoughtful mess.

JB: I've heard playwrights and directors say that one of the talents of being a director and not simply a playwright at rehearsals is knowing that different actors work in different ways.

HENLEY: Yes, you have actors that are all over the board in how they've been trained and what they like and what they are used to or how they perform best.

JB: Do you speak to actors directly, or go through the director most of the time?

HENLEY: I'll speak to them directly if the director trusts me or if the director says, "What do you think of that?" Sometimes the director is so burned out talking to the actors, they'll say, "Now, Beth, what did you tell me?"

JB: Would you know in that situation if you had been given permission to talk to the actors or not?

HENLEY: Yes. I feel very much it's all sort of diplomatic and a sense of trust and deep respect. You can't just go in there and open your mouth until the cast and director feel comfortable with you.

JB: It took you a while to get away from the South, dramatically. But you have with the most recent plays not written as much about the South. What was the source of that change?

HENLEY: I guess, not living in the South. My first few plays took place in the South and even *The Lucky Spot* was in the thirties but in Louisiana. Then I moved further into the past into the Wyoming Territory for *Abundance* and then I just decided to thrust myself into the future and wrote *Signature,* which takes place in Los Angeles in 2052. Then I wrote *Control Freaks,* which is very much a Los Angeles play.

JB: You have said that one of the reasons you live in Los Angeles is because no one will bother you; everybody there is involved in film and so you can do your own thing and not feel you're competing with all the people in New York, where there are playwrights on every street corner.

HENLEY: Part of that is that New York has proved to be too much...for me to live and work [in]; I love New York so much. It's my favorite city but it's kind of nice to go back to Los Angeles and just not be inundated with what is the scene and what is hot or what is not. You're just left on your own in Los Angeles, and you can have a nicer place with a yard there

JB: You have also said that it's a little frustrating in LA because everything is film.

HENLEY: It's not a theatre town. It's film and television and that's—entertainment-wise—the heart of the city. Often people will be in plays to get into film and television; whereas, in Chicago or Seattle or New York, they're just in the plays because that's what their passion is.

JB: Do you feel that the people in LA support theatre? Are there audiences or do you find them so involved with film that theatre is a kind of secondary medium to them?

HENLEY: I tried to start a theatre in LA and failed miserably, but I was probably not meant to raise money.

JB: Are the theatres in LA supported pretty well? Do they get audiences?

HENLEY: The big places like the Taper do, but some of the smaller theatres, no.

JB: Is it frustrating? When you get your plays done, you don't usually get them done in LA, do you?

HENLEY: Not usually, although occasionally.

JB: Isn't it more likely to have a reading of a new play of yours in Washington or New York than in LA?

HENLEY: Absolutely.

JB: Are playwrights treated badly in Hollywood when they write for films or are they being treated with more respect by producers and directors than they have been in the past?

HENLEY: Here's the thing you have to know about being a screenwriter. I love writing for the screen. I love that they pay you a lot of money. You get to meet fancy people and eat really good food. But here's the thing: what you do as a screenwriter is you sell your copyright. As a novelist, as a poet, as a playwright, you maintain your copyright. If you write a fabulous screenplay, they pay you this chunk of money; it's theirs, they own it. I've always emotionally tried to detach myself from my screenwriting and just love doing it, enjoy doing it, and I try to do adaptations. I did write a couple of original screenplays, but I'd rather write plays. If you are a screenwriter, they can fire you at any moment, and the actors can change your dialogue. It's really a director's medium, where theatre is much more a writer's medium; in theatre, you have actor approval, you have director approval, you have not necessarily design approval, but at a point you do. They can't change anything, even stage directions, without your approval. Of course they have, I suspect; but at least not when you're on the premises!

JB: What was it like adapting Crimes of the Heart *as a screenplay? Didn't you have to detach yourself a little from that, almost have to not be the playwright who wrote the original play?*

HENLEY: That's a long story. I was working on *Crimes of the Heart* with Jonathan Demme, and they made us fly in from New York, to have a meeting where the producer told me I was the worst person to write this because I had written the play. So I tried to open it up, and I wrote a version of it and they said it was too much like the play. Jonathan Demme quit on principle because he didn't want to be the person to ruin this beautiful play. Then a couple of years later, I was in London and Bruce Beresford was hired to do *Crimes of the Heart* and I said, "They don't want me." He said, "Well, I want you and I told them I wanted you." And I read Demme's script and it veered too far from the play. I said, "Bruce, I got fired from it!" He said, "Oh, they don't know what they want." So I got rehired with Bruce Beresford who has brought a lot of plays to film. And he was lovely to work with and it was great; but it was on the verge of being catastrophic.

JB: It sounds like he had great respect for you as the writer of the play?

HENLEY: He's just a fun, smart guy who respects people; he wasn't afraid of any idea you had because he knows he's really smart. He's really experienced in what he's doing and he knows what he wants.

JB: And how much of that screenplay actually survived to be the screenplay of Crimes? *Was the screenplay that survived pretty much the screenplay you wrote?*

HENLEY: Very much, because he was very good as well. He wanted it short. He said, "Let's keep it short."

JB: But that's not always the case, is it?

HENLEY: No.

JB: Don't you have the kind of horror stories about Hollywood that other playwrights tell?

HENLEY: My horror stories are the screenplays that didn't get made; you get frustrated with that, but you still get paid this enormous amount for them. I figure that helps me with my theatre work.

JB: Talk a little bit about your play, L-Play.

HENLEY: I couldn't think what to write for a play. I was really fragmented in my life and so I kept scribbling. It's really painful when you're trying to come up with an idea for a play. I decided I would write a play called *L-Play,* which would have twelve different scenes, twelve totally different characters, and twelve different theatrical styles because I was into exploring different styles. The only unifying factor is that the names of the scenes start with an "L." This was completely stupid! But I proceeded in the face of this stupidness and it was really fun because it was a bit like an exercise for me. It was struggling with the fragmented nature of reality, like who is real, Donald Duck or Bergman, of just the different realities that come together in the fragmented world. The Learner and the Lunatic are the only reoccurring characters.

JB: You have said that frequently you write plays about characters who express some part of yourself you wouldn't express any other way. Often, it's part of yourself you're afraid of or that you wouldn't go out out in public with on your own.

HENLEY: The girl, Ashby, in *Am I Blue* didn't get invited to the prom and she is all alone and feels isolated. I did have friends at that age, but what you fear is not having friends. You fear that part of you is not acceptable to be exposed and I think that's a lot of what I look for in my characters. I wonder what their greatest fear is and what their greatest dream is and what the teaching is between the two. Usually their fear is holding them back from their dream, and their dream is giving them hope to fight against their fear. A lot of what I like to write about are things I'm confused about. When I was younger I kept thinking that I needed to write an important play, that I needed to help people understand something and improve the world and enlighten people—except I didn't know anything. This was the big problem. And then I read where Ionesco said: "Oh, I just like to write about my own confusion." I said, "Well, I can do that; I'm certainly confused." It was like this weight was lifted. I don't have to solve anything because there is nothing to solve. It's all a big mystery and if you can express the misery and the confusion truthfully, that might be something worth looking at.

JB: Too often we're looking for answers in plays when plays are really asking you to think. They're not actually looking to solve problems for you.

HENLEY: People say, "How do you want the audience to respond to your play." And I say, "As individuals!" I would feel horrible if everyone felt the same thing by the end of the day, and didn't have particular thoughts, particular notions, if some people weren't upset about something and some people enthralled by something.

JB: How do you start a play?

HENLEY: I think if you're any good you're aware of the notion that you can't start where you want to. I use a ton of notebooks. I write what is the theme and then I write all sorts of different themes; some of them never end up being the theme at all, and then I have images that I see.

I see some stage images; like for *Crimes of the Heart*, I see a knife cutting into a lemon. I see there is a birthday cake. I'm not sure whose birthday it is.

Or I see somebody roped; somebody's going to hang themselves, but I don't know if they're going to live or not. Images. I do images. I do theme. I do the style, and I've really gotten to be much more cognizant about the style. I have a section in my notebook just called dialogue, things I've heard that are intriguing to me, or read, that might go in this play. And then, there's dialogue for this particular character—what do they do, what is their dream, and what are their feelings? There's preparation before you do it; getting to page one is quite a mess and takes, for me, the most time and is the hardest because they're not talking to you yet. You're kind of planting the seeds so they will talk. When they start talking, don't edit them for a while; let them talk.

JB: Do you know where a play is going when you start?

HENLEY: No. That's the scariest thing and the most thrilling.

JB: In other words, when you saw that birthday cake, you had no idea that was the end of the play?

HENLEY: No, I didn't know that was the end of the play. I did know by the time I got to the third act that Babe was going to try and kill herself, but I didn't know that she wasn't going to kill herself up until the moment she didn't. I thought, "No, it's going to be a tragedy. I thought it was a comedy, but I guess it's going to be a tragedy because it's a tragedy when a character kills himself." And then it turned. I always think that although this is very frustrating for the writer, it's really key to writing something good because if you don't know where it's going, that means the audience doesn't know where it's going either. You have to be clever enough to take it to a wonderful authentic place by just letting the characters tell you where they need to go.

JB: When you start, do you know the general subject matter?

HENLEY: Usually, but in the play I'm writing now, as well as in *Exposed*, it wasn't that clear. It became clear in *Exposed* that this is all taking place in a winter solstice, the darkest night of the year. The play I'm working on now I call *The Men's Play* because all I knew was I wanted to write a play about men because I don't understand men anyhow.

JB: When you write a play, do you have a specific message you want your reader to get from it? What do you want people to get from Crimes of the Heart?

HENLEY: When I write a play, I don't—since I have no idea what the play's going to be—have a message in mind. But in looking at *Crimes of the Heart*, I can say that my impression as a theatregoer would be that it is a play about these three sisters coming to grips with a lot that happened in their past that left them stunted in different ways and going on from there in the final moment of the play. That's pretty bad, but that's why I'm not a theatre critic!

JB: Talk a little bit about the role of Barnette in that play. If you were there while an actor was doing the part, what would you say to him?

HENLEY: I would say, "Don't err on going too sweet." He's very, very committed to winning this case. He's very fiery and there's also a rage in him. Barnette's often wrongly done as a sweet old Southern boy, and it's kind of icky.

JB: How much do you feel like you consciously engage with work from prior literary traditions? You mentioned that Crimes of the Heart *is based on* Three Sisters, *and I was wondering if you intentionally wrote it that way or not.*

HENLEY: I think I probably did it subliminally with *Crimes of the Heart*. In fact, I know I did since I love *Three Sisters* so much and I'd rehearsed it over and over again, seeking the part of Irina. It was in my subconscious. Although I must admit that more recently in the play *Impossible Marriage*, I remember deliberately wanting to steal from Oscar Wilde. I went and read everything he wrote and I said, "Give me some of that and some of that. Sprinkle it on me." So I don't know. It's not usually very conscious, but it can be.

JB: What other kinds of dramatic literature influence you?

HENLEY: This is going to sound so boring, but Shakespeare. I've taken five years of Shakespeare class and . . . the more I just want to know him.

JB: What have you, as a playwright, learned from Shakespeare?

HENLEY: Shakespeare is one of those people, like Magic Johnson in basketball. You can't learn really because what they do is too superior to what humans can do. You just sit back in awe. Some playwrights you can read and kind of go, "Oh, here's how they do that." But Shakespeare... how'd he write that? Oh, it's so humbling.

JB: Are any of your characters based on people you know—or knew?

HENLEY: Sometimes they evolved from a couple of people I know. A couple of times I've said that person is so appealing to me I'm going to write a character just like them. That's only happened a couple of times. But by the time the character comes out in the play, it's no longer the person at all. People say, "I'm Babe aren't I?" And I say, "We just met!"

Source: Jackson R. Bryer, "Expressing 'the Misery and Confusion Truthfully': An Interview with Beth Henley," in *American Drama*, Vol. 14, No. 1, Winter 2005, p. 87.

Richard Scholem

In the following essay, Scholem presents a positive review of Henley's Impossible Marriage, *calling it "the funniest, frothiest, finest comedy to open in these parts for some time."*

It's impossible to keep a straight face watching Beth Henley's *Impossible Marriage* at Broadway's Roundabout Theatre.

That's because it is the funniest, frothiest, finest comedy to open in these parts for some time. Its characters are deliciously overwrought, over dramatic, over magnified and over the edge.

Set on a country estate outside of Savannah, Henley's *Impossible Marriage* hones in on the impending wedding of Pandora Kingsley (Gretchen Cleevely) and Edvard Lunt (Christopher McCann). Pandora's sister, Floral (Holly Hunter), her mother Kandall Kingsley (Lois Smith) and everybody in the audience agree that this marriage will be the mismatch of the ages.

It seems Pandora, a silly, childish screwball, who wants to be married in a fairy gown with big blue wings, is attracted to Edvard, an author, because he wrote her into one of his books, making her somewhat of a legend. Floral, her older sister, the very pregnant and very funny Holly Hunter, feels he is "repulsive" and "a hairy old goat" to boot.

While Lois Smith's mother Kandall, who can convulse an audience with a single word, pleads with Pandora not to marry a man who is "twice her age" and a myopic philanderer who divorced his wife of 23 years, leaving her and his children.

Finally, she points out, he has a ponytail and lacks character. Pandora's rejoinder is, "His character's not important; he's an artist." After all, this is a girl who refused to flush away her dead rotting pet fish because it "hadn't done anything wrong."

If this goofy, bigger-than-life Southern family is a looney tunes version of Tennessee Williams or a thoroughly fouled-up Faulkner, some of the people orbiting around them are downright Chekovian.

Take Sidney Lunt, Edvard's son, whom he does not recognize. Or Daniel London, who plays the role with just enough neurosis to be believable as a withdrawn worry wart, who looks as though he just wandered in from *The Cherry Orchard*. He announces upon entering that his mother plans to kill herself by jumping from the attic if her father marries Pandora.

Henley's bigger-than-life characters delight us because, though they are tragic, unpredictable and out of sinc, we need not take any of them seriously. Even if we wanted to it would be impossible. After all, here we have Floral telling Sidney to go "get a pistol to kill your father with and bring me more muffins." Floral's very proper, half crazy mother is much more upset about her eating wedding cake with her hands than the fact that her about-to-give-birth-daughter chooses to roll down muddy hills in her weakened condition.

But then the quirky Floral, beautifully played as a purposely exaggerated eccentric by Holly Hunter, has troubles of her own. Although she is so pregnant she "could accommodate a circus under this tent" (of a dress), she has never had sex with her handsome, but sappy, syrupy, adoring husband Jonsey (the preening Jon Tenney).

Keep your eye on the seemingly straight laced Rev. Jonathan Larence whom Hunter insists "is quite incapable of seducing a harlot in Dante's *Inferno*."

Christopher McCann does a marvelous, high camp rendition of the improbable, inappropriate, over aged groom, Edvard Lunt, and yet much like the other six gifted actors in Ms. Henley's comedic romp, manages to apply a residue of poignancy to the play's merriment. Just enough for us to care about these people, even as we laugh at them.

Source: Richard Scholem, "Henley's *Impossible Marriage* Impossibly Delightful," in *Long Island Business News,* Vol. 45, No. 45, November 6, 1998, p. 38.

SOURCES

Ancona, Francesco Aristide, "Hope Sinks: Pandora, Eve and the Obsession of Ahab," in the *Journal of Evolutionary Psychology*, March 2003, pp. 15–22.

"Beth Henley," in *Contemporary Dramatists*, 6th ed., St. James Press, 1999.

Brantley, Ben, Review of *Impossible Marriage*, in the *New York Times*, October 23, 1998.

Bryer, Jackson R., "Expressing 'The Misery and Confusion Truthfully': An Interview with Beth Henley," in *American Drama*, Winter 2005.

Cumberlege, Geoffrey, ed., *The Oxford Dictionary of Quotations*, 2nd ed., Oxford University Press, 1941, rev. ed., 1954, p. 272.

Harris, Mark, Review of *Impossible Marriage*, in *Entertainment Weekly*, October 23, 1998, p. 68.

Henley, Beth, *Impossible Marriage*, Dramatists Play Service, 1999.

Isherwood, Charles, Review of *Impossible Marriage*, in *Variety*, Vol. 372, No. 10, October 19, 1998, p. 84.

Renner, Pamela, "The Mellowing of 'Miss Firecracker': Beth Henley—and Her Impetuous Characters—Are Undergoing Transformations," in *American Theatre*, Vol. 15, No. 9, November 1998, p. 18.

Scheck, Frank, Review of *Impossible Marriage*, in the *Hollywood Reporter*, October 19, 1998, p. 7.

Scholem, Richard, "Henley's *Impossible Marriage* Impossibly Delightful," in the *Long Island Business News*, Vol. 45, No. 45, November 6, 1998, p. 38A.

FURTHER READING

Andreach, Robert J., *Understanding Beth Henley*, University of South Carolina Press, 2006.
> This book is an invaluable critical overview of Henley's plays, taken as a unified whole. Andreach discusses *Impossible Marriage* in considerable detail, linking it thematically and imagistically with Henley's other work.

Ayers, Edward L., and Bradley C. Mittendorf, eds., *The Oxford Book of the American South: Testimony, Memory, and Fiction*, Oxford University Press, 1998.
> This is an ambitious compilation of fiction and nonfiction writings about the American South. Selections include diaries, memoirs, letters, and essays from over fifty writers from the colonial period to the present. Featured authors include Olaudah Equiano, Charles W. Chesnutt, Thomas Jefferson, Mark Twain, Martin Luther King Jr., Alice Walker, and Maya Angelou.

Fesmire, Julia, ed., *Beth Henley: A Casebook*, Routledge, 2002.
> This compilation of critical essays on Henley's plays is a useful introduction to Henley's work. It includes discussions of *Impossible Marriage*, of the major literary and cultural influences on Henley, and of film adaptations of her plays.

Ruppersburg, Hugh, ed., *Georgia Voices: Nonfiction*, University of Georgia Press, 1994.
> This book is the second volume of a three-volume anthology of Georgia's literary heritage. It features nonfiction writings by native Georgians or long-term Georgia residents about key features of Southern life. Among the writers featured are James Oglethorpe, Henry Grady, Erskine Caldwell, Martin Luther King Jr., Alice Walker, Jimmy Carter, and Cherokee and Creek Native Americans.

Marty

PADDY CHAYEFSKY
1953

Marty, a teleplay by Paddy Chayefsky, was broadcast on live television in 1953, a time when such teleplays were common. It was such a tremendous hit that it was immediately optioned for film. The film version, only slightly different than the television version, was released in 1955 by Hill-Hecht-Lancaster Productions and is considered a classic of American cinema. It was nominated for eight Academy Awards, winning for Best Director, Best Picture, and Best Actor, as well as one for Chayefsky for Best Adapted Screenplay. It is one of only two films to win both the Best Picture Oscar and the Golden Palm at the Cannes Film Festival. Chayefsky is considered one of the greatest television and movie writers of all time.

Marty tells the story of Marty Pilletti, a mild-mannered, middle-aged butcher who lives with his mother. All around him, people tell him that he should find a girl, marry, and settle down, but every girl whom Marty talks to rejects him. He is convinced that he is a fat, ugly, little man who is destined to spend his days alone. When Marty finally does meet, at a dance, a girl who understands him, who has felt the rejection he has felt, Marty sees his family and friends suddenly change their attitude. Instead of telling him that he should be ashamed of himself for being single, they convince him that she is not good enough for him.

The teleplay script of *Marty* is available in *The Collected Works of Paddy Chayefsky: The Television Plays*, published by Applause Books in 1995.

Paddy Chayefsky (*Walter Daran | Hulton Archive | Getty Images*)

AUTHOR BIOGRAPHY

Sidney "Paddy" Chayefsky was born in New York City on January 29, 1923, to immigrant Ukrainian Jewish parents. He attended Dewitt Clinton High School in the city, and then went to City College, where he earned a bachelor's degree in accounting in 1943. He briefly attended Fordham University before going into the U.S. Army to fight in World War II. While in the army, he earned the nickname "Paddy," a traditionally Irish name, because he wanted to attend service at the Catholic church, even though he was Jewish. He was a private in the army until the end of the war in 1945, earning a Purple Heart when he was injured near Aachen, Germany. It was while he was recovering at a hospital near Cirencester, England, that he wrote his first hit, the musical play *No T.O. for Love*, which was produced by the army's Special Services and ran for two years at army bases throughout Europe before starting a commercial run in London's West End.

After the war, Chayefsky returned to New York and worked briefly in his uncle's printing shop. He became a gag writer for radio personality Robert Q. Lewis and wrote plays for radio and television, including a 1949 adaptation of Bud Selig's novel *What Makes Sammy Run?* for television. When his teleplay *Marty* was broadcast on May 24, 1953, as part of the National Broadcasting Company (NBC) live series *Philco Television Playhouse*, it was such a critical and popular success that a film version was immediately approved. Chayefsky's contract stipulated that the film, which was released two years later, could be written by no one but him. The film earned him an Oscar for Best Screenplay. It also won the Academy Award for best picture in 1955, the Golden Palm at the Cannes Film Festival, the Catholic Award, and the New York Film Critics Award.

After the success of *Marty*, Chayefsky shifted his focus from television to film, where he was to earn as much critical praise as he did for his television work. His work for Hollywood ranged from the screen adaptation of the Western musical *Paint Your Wagon* in 1969, to his Oscar-winning script for *The Hospital* in 1971, to the scathing satire of television news in *Network*, which earned him his third Academy Award in 1976. Throughout the 1960s, he also wrote several plays for the Broadway stage, and in 1978 he released his first novel, *Altered States*. His screenplay of the book was made into a film in 1980, but Chayefsky did not like the director's vision and so had himself credited as "Sidney Aaron."

Paddy Chayefsky died of cancer in New York City on August 1, 1981, at the age of fifty-eight.

PLOT SUMMARY

Act 1

Marty begins on a Saturday afternoon in a butcher shop in the Italian area of New York. Marty Pilletti, a butcher, is a thirty-six-year-old man who generally maintains a cheerful disposition, even when he is feeling pressure. In this opening scene, Marty is talking with Mrs. Fusari, who the script identifies as the Italian Woman. She is interested in hearing about the marriage of Marty's younger brother Nickie over the past weekend. She asks about other members of the family while Marty works, and he describes them to her: his brother Freddie was married four years ago; his sister Margaret is married to an insurance salesman; his sister Rose is married to a contractor and lives in Detroit; his sister Frances married two and a half years earlier. As the character identified as the Young Mother tries to hurry Marty, the Italian Woman takes the time to chastise the butcher for not being married yet. He tells her that he needs to move her along because the Young Mother is impatient. When he does send the Italian Woman away, though, the Young Mother steps forward and takes her turn hectoring him about still being single.

Later that day, Marty joins his friend Angie in a booth at a local bar. This is where they often end up on Saturday nights, talking about girls whom they have met. Angie, not content to spend yet another Saturday night out with his friend, suggests that they phone the girls whom they had escorted home from the movie theater about a month earlier. Marty is not interested in calling them, and would be fine with just going

MEDIA ADAPTATIONS

- *Marty* premiered on May 24, 1953, during the fifth season of the National Broadcasting Company (NBC) live series *Philco Television Playhouse*. This production starred Rod Steiger as Marty, Esther Minciotti as his mother, and Nancy Marchand as Clara ("The Girl") and was directed by Delbert Mann. It was briefly available in videocassette, and it is sometimes rebroadcast on television.

- The 1955 film version of *Marty*, starring Ernest Borgnine and Betsy Blair, is considered a film classic, being one of only two movies to have won both the Academy Award for Best Picture and the Golden Palm at the Cannes Film Festival. It also won Academy Awards for Best Actor (Borgnine), best director (Delbert Mann), and Best Screenplay (Chayefsky). Originally produced by Hill-Hecht-Lancaster Productions, it is available in DVD from MGM's Vintage Classics series.

- A musical stage adaptation of the film had a brief run beginning in 2002, directed by Mark Brokaw with a book by Rupert Holmes, music by Charles Strouse, and lyrics by Lee Adams. It premiered at the Huntington Theatre Company in Boston, and John C. Reilly starred as Marty.

bowling with Angie. "I'm a little, short, fat fellow," he explains, "and girls don't go for me, that's all." He tells Angie to feel free to call a girl for himself, but he does not want to go to the bother. Angie is displeased, but he sits back down and stays with Marty.

Time passes. The audience sees the clock changing from 4:50 p.m. to 5:45 p.m. and then sees Marty alone at the table, with three empty beer bottles in front of him. He finally gets up off of his seat and goes to the phone booth. He phones Mary Feeney, one of the girls whom he and Angie met at the movie theater. She does not remember him even as he reminds her of the theater, the fact that he is a butcher, or the fact that they took them out after the show. Finally, when she does remember him, Marty asks if she would like to go out, but she says that it is late to be calling her for a date that same night. She is busy the following week, and the next Saturday, and the Saturday after that, and Marty hangs up, depressed. As he leaves the bar, the Bartender asks about his younger brother's wedding, and Marty, almost reflexively, responds just as politely as he did for the ladies in his butcher shop that it was a nice wedding. The Bartender tells Marty that he should get married too.

The next scene takes place at Marty's house, where his mother is talking to his cousin Thomas and Thomas's wife, Virginia. They live with Thomas's mother Catherine in a small apartment with their new baby, and they are finding it difficult to get along. The most recent problem occurred three days earlier. Virginia was preparing milk for the baby's bottle and found herself so distracted by Catherine that she spilled some of the milk on the table; when Catherine complained that she was wasting expensive milk, Virginia's temper flared, and she threw the entire bottle of milk against the wall. Virginia apologized, but by then Catherine had already run out of the house. Marty's mother has already heard this story about Virginia's temper from Catherine, her sister. Virginia and Thomas suggest that it would make sense for the aunt to move in with Marty and his mother. Most of the people who live in that house have married and moved on, while the apartment that Virginia and Thomas share is so small that his mother does not even have her own bedroom. Marty's mother agrees, but says that they have to ask Marty.

Before Thomas and Virginia leave, Marty's mother asks if they know of any girls he can marry. Thomas suggests that he can find eligible girls at the Waverly Ballroom, where he used to meet girls when he was single.

Marty comes home, and Virginia and Thomas explain their situation to him while his mother goes off to prepare his dinner. He agrees that his aunt Catherine should move into the house. His mother comes back into the room just after they have left and suggests that Marty could meet girls at the Waverly Ballroom, using the same slang expression that Thomas used to describe the place, "It's loaded with tomatoes." Marty laughs, but when his mother presses him

to find a girl to marry, he becomes defensive. He describes the phone call to Mary Feeney, and her rejection of him. He is ugly, he tells her, and girls do not want to date him.

Act 2

When the second act opens, Marty and his friend Angie are at the Waverly Ballroom, standing off to the side with the other men who do not have dates, assessing the single women. Angie suggests that Marty should go and talk to a Short Girl, about twenty years old. Angie asks one of the girl's companions to dance, and she wearily agrees without a word, but the Short Girl tells Marty that she does not want to dance.

Returning to his place among the single men, Marty is approached by a Young Man with a proposition. The Young Man came to the ballroom with a blind date, but he has found another girl he likes better, so he offers Marty five dollars to pretend to be an old friend and escort his date home. Marty is aghast. He watches the Young Man walk off and find another man who is "stag," or unattached, and make the same offer. As Marty watches, they approach the Young Man's date, but she understands what is happening and sends them away. Passing by Marty, the Stag still insists that the Young Man owes him the five dollars that was offered.

Marty follows the dejected girl out to the fire escape and asks her if she would like to dance. She turns and falls into his arms, crying. Marty reaches back to close the door to the ballroom, then lets her continue crying.

Elsewhere, Marty's mother arrives at Thomas and Virginia's apartment to talk to her sister. She asks Catherine to come to live at her house, explaining that Thomas and Virginia and her baby need their privacy. Catherine responds by talking about feeling rejected and unwanted, and warns Theresa that she, too, will be left without a home to live in if Marty finds a girl to marry. In the end, though, Catherine agrees to come to her sister's house to live.

Meanwhile, Marty is dancing with Clara, the girl from the fire escape. She talks about the rejection she felt the last time she was at the Waverly Ballroom, when a young man called her ugly and said she would have no chance of getting someone to dance with her. Marty sympathizes with her. He is lonely too, he says. He recalls the kind of relationship that his father and mother had, noting that his father was an ugly man. From that, he has always drawn hope that there would be someone out there for an ugly man like himself. They dance together, contented in each other's arms.

Marty and Clara stop in at his house. He offers her some leftover chicken. Before leaving to take her home, Marty tries to kiss her, but she backs away. Marty feels rejected, but she says that she would still like to go out with him again. She accepts his offer to go out together the next night and says that it might be possible that they will be together to go out on New Year's Eve together; Marty, overcome with emotion, leans against her shoulder, crying.

They separate when Marty's mother comes in with the news that Catherine is going to move in. The mother explains Catherine's loneliness, and Clara offers the opinion that a mother should have a life of her own. Marty's mother, remembering what her sister told her about how lonely she will be of Marty marries, becomes defensive, and Clara backs down on her assertions. They say good night politely.

Act 3

It is Sunday, the morning after the previous two acts. Marty's mother and his aunt talk about the girl who was at the house with Marty when his mother came home the night before. His aunt warns her sister that he will marry her and then sell the house, as her own children did, leaving his mother no place to live. His mother does not take her seriously until Marty comes in and, noticing that some plaster has fallen from the ceiling, suggests that they should sell the house and look for an apartment. After that, she does what she can to sabotage Marty's relationship with Clara. She points out that Clara is not a very good-looking woman and refuses to believe that she is twenty-nine years old, as she claimed. She suggests that women with college educations have low moral standards. She tells Marty outright that she does not like Clara. When he leaves, she tells herself that she is no better than her sister Catherine.

Marty goes back to the bar. In the same booth he was at in Act 1 are Angie and other unattached men. One is telling the others about a book he read, featuring a tough detective who handles women roughly and is showered with their love in return. The others—a forty-year-old and a twenty-year-old—listen with rapt attention.

The men have heard that Marty was dancing with a homely girl at the ballroom the night before. Marty says that he enjoyed his time with Clara and wants to ask her out to a movie that night. Angie talks him out of calling her. When the conversation turns to the regular discussion of what movie or burlesque show the men can all go to that night, though, Marty suddenly realizes that he would be a fool to give up a chance for a relationship with a nice girl like Clara. He goes to the phone booth, but before dialing Clara's number he asks Angie when he is going to get married, taking satisfaction in the chance to use the very same line that everyone has been using on him throughout the teleplay.

CHARACTERS

Angie

Angie is Marty's friend. He is thirty-four years old and slight in build. He and Marty are so familiar with each other that when Marty sits down across from him at the table in the bar, Marty simply takes a section of the newspaper Angie is reading, without saying a word.

In the first act, Marty is content to just spend the evening with Angie, but Angie feels that, since it is Saturday night, they should try to get dates. When Marty backs away from calling girls, Angie leaves without him. Marty later catches up with Angie at the Waverly Ballroom, which is where unattached men go to find girls.

Although he has trouble getting women interested in him, Angie has high standards about women. When he talks about them with Marty, he always has judgments about their looks. This reaches a high point at the end of the teleplay, when Angie nearly convinces Marty that Clara is too homely for him. Marty realizes that Angie is too discriminating and he turns on his friend with the same line that people have been taunting him with, telling Angie that he ought to be ashamed of himself for not being married yet.

The Aunt

Marty's Aunt Catherine is a bitter woman. She has been living in a one-bedroom apartment with her son Thomas, his wife Virginia, and their infant baby when the teleplay begins. The young couple feels that Catherine is difficult to live with because she makes Virginia nervous and angry. When Virginia throws a bottle of milk against the wall, Catherine goes to her sister, Marty's mother, and says that bottle was thrown at her. Theresa asks Catherine if she would like to move into the house where she and Marty live, and Catherine points out that people have been conspiring against her, but still, she agrees to move. She nearly poisons Theresa's relationship with Marty by insisting that Marty will abandon her if he marries, just as she was abandoned by her son Thomas.

The Bartender

Soon after Marty has been rejected by Mary Feeney, whom he calls for a date, the Bartender, Lou, asks about his brother Nickie's wedding. Instead of being bitter, Marty answers politely that it was a very nice wedding. Without meaning to, the Bartender compounds the pain of Marty's rejection by telling him he should be married too, not realizing how aware Marty is that women do not find him attractive.

Mrs. Canduso

See The Young Mother

Catherine

See The Aunt

The Critic

In the last scene, on Sunday night, several single, dateless men are assembled at a table at the bar. The Critic is the man who has just finished reading a detective novel and is telling the others about it. He admires the way that the hardboiled detective in the book was cruel toward women, and how they loved him even more for it. It is clear that the Critic's knowledge about human relationships comes from books, not actual experience.

Clara Davis

See The Girl

Mary Feeney

Mary Feeney's name first comes up early in the first act, when Marty and Angie are sitting at the bar, trying to decide what to do that night. Angie reminds Marty that they met Mary and her friend at the movie theater a few weeks earlier and accompanied them home, and he suggests that they might call them again for dates. Later, after he has been left alone, Marty does call Mary Feeney. She is slow in remembering him and, when she does, she rejects one offer for a

date after another, leaving Marty to conclude that she is not interested in him.

Mrs. Fusari

See The Italian Woman

The Girl

Clara Davis is a twenty-nine-year-old history teacher at Benjamin Franklin High School, and a graduate of New York University. In the script, she is identified as "The Girl." She is not very good looking, having her looks criticized by Marty's friend Angie and by a young man who, in a story she tells, once walked past her at the Waverly Ballroom and went out of his way to insult her. When Marty first meets her, she has just been abandoned by her date, and she turns to him, a stranger, and cries on his shoulder. She and Marty have a long discussion on the night that they meet, showing great empathy for one another. When Marty tries to kiss her, she backs away, but makes it clear that her timidity does not mean that she does not like him. She goes on to kiss him again and lets him escort her home.

The Italian Woman

In the first scene, the Italian Woman, Mrs. Fusari, talks to Marty about his family while he cuts her order. When she hears that all of his brothers and sisters, including those younger than him, are married, she tells Marty that he should be ashamed that he is not married yet.

The Mother

Marty lives with his mother, Theresa Pilletti. In general, she is as shy and courteous as he is. When her nephew Thomas asks if her sister can move into the house, Theresa is willing to accommodate him, but she also says that she must ask Marty first. She starts the teleplay concerned about Marty, the only one of her six children who has not married. After talking with her sister Catherine, however, she becomes concerned that if Marty marries she will be abandoned, as Catherine was. She finds fault with the one girl who likes Marty, Clara, saying that Clara is lying about her age and that she is probably snobbish or morally corrupt because of her college education.

Marty Pilletti

Marty is a thirty-six-year-old butcher in New York. He is a quiet, courteous man who speaks with respect to his customers, to his relatives, and to the few women who will talk to him. He does not think that he has any chance with women because, as he states several times throughout the teleplay, he is "a fat, ugly little man."

Generally, Marty's problem with women is a minor part of his life because he associates with a group of men at the bar—most notably, his best friend, Angie—who are just as bad at dating. At the start of this teleplay, however, the situation has changed. The recent wedding of his brother brings attention to the fact that Marty is unmarried, and the fact that it was his younger brother makes people mindful of Marty's age. Older women are not shy about telling him that he should be married because they do not see him as fat or short or ugly, they just see him as a kind man who would be a good provider.

Marty is protective of Clara after watching her date abandon her, amazed that a man would treat a woman cruelly. When she shows her vulnerability, he is able to show his own vulnerability to her, telling her that he cries often. Thinking that it is what is expected of him, he does try to force her to kiss him when they are alone in his house, but when she rejects him he backs off, afraid that he has ruined their blossoming relationship. He is grateful that she is still willing to date him.

After being pushed to find a girl and marry her throughout the teleplay, Marty suddenly finds that no one wants him to date Clara. His mother, having seen how her sister feels abandoned by her own son, is afraid that Marty will marry and want his own life, leaving her alone. His friend Angie, who cannot find dates for himself, declares that Clara is not good looking enough to date. Marty almost gives in to peer pressure, only changing his mind at the last minute when he realizes that the men at the bar are going through the same tired process of deciding what to do for entertainment that they go through every night. He recognizes that he has almost let his one chance to date a kind woman go by. He decides that he is going to go out with Clara, and if things go well enough, some day he might marry her.

Theresa Pilletti
See The Mother

The Short Girl
Having been encouraged to go to the Waverly Ballroom to meet girls, Marty approaches the Short Girl to ask her to dance. She rejects him, leaving him feeling rejected, despondent, and angry when the Young Man asks Marty to help abandon his blind date.

The Stag
After Marty refuses to help him by taking his date home, the Young Man approaches another man, the Stag, and offers him the same deal that he offered Marty. They talk to Clara, but she can tell that these two men are not old friends at all, as they pretend to be, and she sends them away. The Young Man wants his five dollars back because the plan failed, but the Stag feels that he deserves the money for trying. "Stag" is slang for a man who goes to a social event without a date.

Thomas
Marty's cousin Thomas has the same gentle disposition that Marty has. Thomas is in an uncomfortable position, stuck between a wife and a mother who cannot get along with each other and feeling loyalty for each. He is apologetic about asking Marty to take his mother in, but he knows that she incites Virginia's temper, which is not good for their child.

The Twenty-Year-Old
The Twenty-Year-Old is one of the men who gather at the bar on Sunday night. He is impressionable, listening raptly to the ideas the older men have about women.

Virginia
Virginia is a young wife and mother, married to Marty's cousin Thomas. They live in a cramped little apartment with Thomas's mother, but Virginia and her mother-in-law, Catherine, do not get along. Catherine, she says, makes her nervous. Virginia's relationship with her mother-in-law is made even worse by Virginia's violent temper, as exhibited by the fact that, criticized for spilling a little milk and being wasteful, she reacts by smashing an entire quart of milk against the wall. Virginia is polite with the other characters in the teleplay, and seems to only have problems getting along with Catherine.

The Young Man
At the Waverly Ballroom, Marty is approached by a Young Man who thinks he has a problem. He came with a blind date and he found a girl

that he likes better. He offers Marty five dollars to pretend to be an old friend from the army and offer to take the blind date home. Marty is insulted by the idea and refuses. The Young Man finds another man willing to go along with it, but the girl, Clara, sees through their pretense and sends them both away.

The Young Mother

In the first scene of the teleplay, the Young Mother, whom Marty addresses as Mrs. Canduso, is shopping in Marty's butcher shop. She is in a hurry and is impatient while the Italian Woman being served ahead of her talks to Marty about his brother's wedding and tells him that he should be ashamed for not being married himself. When her turn comes, however, the Young Mother takes the time to chastise him as well.

THEMES

Marriage and Courtship

Marty begins the weekend after the marriage of Marty's younger brother, Nickie. Though Nickie does not appear in the teleplay, his marriage has a significant impact on Marty's life. Not only is Marty the only one of the six Pillettis still unmarried but he has also been overtaken by a sibling younger than himself, upsetting what people take to be the natural order. People in his neighborhood feel free to tell him that he ought to be married, and that he should be ashamed of himself because he is not. They treat Marty as if he is committing a crime against society by remaining single.

With all of the social pressure on Marty to find a girl and marry her, he holds firmly to his ideals. He does not want to go out with girls just because it is what is expected of him. When he sees how the Young Man, who is on a blind date with Clara, treats her, offering strangers a bribe to take her home, Marty's sense of decency is outraged. Though he has not had much experience with women, he knows better. His decency is rewarded when Clara becomes interested in him. When she envisions their relationship going on for months, all the way to New Year's Eve, Marty is moved to tears.

In the end, Marty's approach to marriage is level-headed and sensible. Having been pressured to find a wife when no suitable candidates

TOPICS FOR FURTHER STUDY

- In the years between the end of World War II in 1945 and the advent of television in the 1950s, many Americans socialized by going to dance halls like the Waverly Ballroom mentioned in the script. Select a partner from your class, research the music and the dances of that time period, and prepare a demonstration for your class of some of the dances that might have been done by couples who met at the Waverly.

- Paddy Chayefsky has been called the greatest writer of television's Golden Age. Obtain a script from a more recent television program that you think is well written, and prepare a chart that shows the similarities and differences between the script you selected and *Marty*.

- Marty nearly misses the chance to go out with Clara after his friends talk badly about her. Think about a time in your life when you decided against doing something because you did not think other people would approve. Write a work of fiction showing how things might have gone differently if you had followed your own impulses.

- In the final scene of the teleplay, the Critic tells his friends about the way Mike Hammer, a character in detective fiction of the time, wins the affection of women by treating them cruelly. Find a character in literature who you think exemplifies the ideal approach to relationships and a character who you think presents an unfavorable approach. Write an essay outlining "dating dos and don'ts," using excerpts and examples from your selected works and characters.

were around and then pressured to quit thinking of Clara as a suitable candidate, he decides that he will prostrate himself before her and "beg that girl" to marry him. He will not do this out of desperation, though, but only if the two "have enough good times together," which shows that he is approaching this relationship with hopes that are not unrealistic.

Family

One of the defining characteristics of Marty Pilletti is his devotion to his relatives, who play a significant role in his life. His strong connection to his family can be seen most clearly in the way that, in the very first scene, he rattles off the names and whereabouts of each of his siblings for the Italian Woman, showing that they are constantly on Marty's mind. It is also obvious in the fact that, at thirty-six, he still lives with his mother and takes care of her.

The other members of his family are just as devoted to their relatives. His cousin Thomas has been trying to watch over his mother, just like Marty has. Their circumstances are different, however—Thomas is married, has a child, and lives in a one-bedroom apartment, and his wife and mother do not get along. When they accept the fact that they cannot have Catherine living with them, Thomas's wife Virginia calls Thomas's brother Joe to talk to him about the problem before they come to Marty and his mother for help. When asked if he would mind if his Aunt Catherine moved into his house, Marty agrees immediately, without even listening to the circumstances of her leaving her son's apartment. Marty must know that his aunt is a difficult woman, but in his worldview there is simply no way to refuse a favor to a family member. This is why audiences can tell that, even though his Aunt Catherine has put worrisome thoughts into his mother's head, Marty will never abandon his mother if and when he marries.

Community

Marty's dedication to his family is mirrored in his steadfast commitment to the people around him who form his community. To the customers at his butcher shop, he is almost like a surrogate son. They can talk to him freely, ask personal questions, and give their opinions about how he is living his life. He is calm and patient with them, allowing them to state their opinions, which may be one reason why customers come to Marty's shop and talk.

Marty's easygoing manner does not ingratiate him to any of the women that he meets, but it does help him fit in with a circle of friends at the

School teacher *(Archive Holdings Inc. | Stone | Getty Images)*

bar. This community of single men might help him avoid loneliness, but they also nearly cost him the one chance that he has for a romantic relationship when his friends disapprove of Clara. Briefly, he is willing to accept their opinion that a woman like Clara is not good enough for him, even when there are those among them who have never met or seen her. Marty is devoted to his community of friends, but he stops himself just before allowing his devotion to sabotage the happy future that he knows is possible.

Beauty and Ugliness

Several times in this teleplay, Marty points out that he is not an attractive man. The people whom he feels he has to tell this to do not seem to recognize his physical shortcomings, though; they, including his mother and his friend Angie, are not looking at him as a prospective romantic partner, and so his looks mean little to them. Several times in the teleplay, however, he approaches women for a date and finds them completely uninterested, as happens with Mary Feeney, who does not remember him a few weeks after he escorted her home, and with the

Short Girl at the Waverly Ballroom. Though they avoid him, Chayefsky's script purposely does not make clear whether they really find him physically objectionable, or just uninteresting. The point is that romantic interest is just a matter of mindset and not of external beauty.

Marty makes this point when he tells Clara about his parents' marriage. His father, he says, was an ugly man, and yet Marty admired the depth of his devotion to Marty's mother, and her devotion to him. From observing them, he learned that good looks do not have to teleplay an important role in having a healthy relationship.

It is ironic, therefore, that Marty nearly gives up on his relationship with Clara because his friend Angie has seen her from afar and judged her a "dog." There is nothing in the script to indicate that Marty is repelled by her looks himself. When he speaks frankly about her homely looks, he does so in a completely objective way. Like most of the people he associates with, Marty does not put much importance on Clara's looks, which may be why he is unsure of how to act when his friends at the bar tell him to stay away from her because she is ugly.

STYLE

Slang Diction

Chayefsky wrote *Marty* using the sort of informal, colloquial style that would be common in the working class section of New York in the post-war years. This includes contractions that are specific to the Italian immigrant families whom these characters represent, as when the script contains the line "Watsa matter" for "what's the matter," or "lemme" for "let me," or "she spills a couple-a drops" for "a couple of drops." Chayefsky also includes particular phrases that would have been common in the community, such as when Marty tells his customer the price of the meat he has been cutting and asks, "How's that with you?" The characters' use of language frequently shows their lack of education. Marty's mother often uses incorrect grammar, as when she repeats herself and uses a contraction and an improper negative in saying, "My sister Catherine, she don't get along with her daughter-in-law, so she's gonna come live with us." The use of slang diction is very important in this teleplay for establishing who these characters are and why they see the world

the way that they do. Chayefsky has been frequently praised for his ability to hear how people from this particular neighborhood would speak and for being able to put the sound of their voices down on paper.

HISTORICAL CONTEXT

The Emergence of Television

Marty was written as a teleplay for television, broadcast on the *Philco Television Playhouse* on Sunday, May 23, 1953.

Though television became commercially available in the United States in 1940, the country did not really embrace it while World War II was going on. Resources were being drawn on by the war effort, and most households could not afford the costly television sets. When the war ended in 1945, however, the country found itself flush with a new prosperity that it had not known since before the stock market crash of 1929. Economic prosperity brought the means to expand television's range and also the leisure time that allowed people to sit back and watch the programs. The first television network, DuMont, began in 1946, connecting New York and Washington; NBC began regular broadcasts in 1947; CBS and ABC began in 1948.

When television was in its infancy, broadcast networks were hard pressed to find enough material to put on the air. Motion pictures with sound had only been around for about twenty years, limiting the existing catalogs. Sporting events were always popular, but events were not always being staged. There began a struggle to produce original programming for broadcast as the networks' range extended westward across the continent.

The model that was often followed for show content was that of the Broadway stage. Most of the networks grew out of the radio networks established in the previous decades and their executives were not used to thinking visually. Also, cameras were large, cumbersome, and difficult to move, so they were best suited for capturing shows from one stationary perspective, the way an audience member would watch a stage play. Most significantly, all four television networks were based in New York City, which was and still is the country's home for live theater. Television producers went to Broadway to recruit writers, directors, and actors, and the

COMPARE
&
CONTRAST

- **1950s:** Most Americans get their meat from a butcher shop like the one Marty runs.

  Today: In many cases, the function of the independent butcher shop has been incorporated into local supermarkets.

- **1950s:** A man who is in his mid-thirties and unmarried is unusual in the prevailing social structure. According to the U.S. Census Bureau, the average age at which most men in the United States marry is twenty-three.

  Today: People tend to marry later in life, if they marry at all. According to the U.S. Census Bureau, the average age at which men in the United States marry is around twenty-eight.

- **1950s:** Calling a woman to formally ask her for a date later the same day is considered an insulting breach of etiquette in the United States.

  Today: Social conventions are more relaxed. A man like Marty might call a woman on her cell phone, or send her an e-mail or text message, to see where she is going that evening and arrange to meet up with her and her friends.

- **1950s:** A teleplay like *Marty* is broadcast live, once. If it is a success, it might be adapted to a full-length movie for release in theaters.

  Today: Films that are made for television broadcast are often rerun on television; such films are seldom released in theaters but are usually made available on DVD soon after their release.

---

production values that they brought with them are evident in the shows they developed. For many, putting quality programming on the air was viewed as an important civic responsibility, a duty to use their new tool to bring culture to the nation.

Philco Television Playhouse was typical of the shows that ran on television at the time, part of a genre that included such classic series as *Kraft Television Theater*, *Actors Studio*, and *Studio One*. It premiered on October 3, 1948, and ran for seven years. Like many other series of the time, *Philco* was an anthology series, with different actors and writers for each episode. Also typical of the time was that it was broadcast live, and shows were only taped for broadcast in later time zones, not for permanent record. A recording of the original broadcast of *Marty* does exist, but the quality is not good enough to make it commercially available. Many shows from this period, which is commonly referred to as "The Golden Age of Television," have been talked about and written about, but are not available to be seen.

The writers who provided material for the teledramas of the 1940s and early 1950s often used television as a launching pad for great careers. In addition to Chayefsky, other writers who wrote for *Philco* include Horton Foote, Arnold Schulman, and Gore Vidal. Dozens of the actors who would become movie stars in the 1960s and 70s learned their trade acting in live television dramas. Directors who worked in teledramas and went on to influence Hollywood include Robert Altman, John Frankenheimer, Sidney Lumet, and Sidney Pollack.

As the 1950s wore on and television matured, live teledramas fell out of favor. Shows began relying on the multiple-camera structure, which situated several cameras around the studio to capture actions from different angles, giving television shows a look that was distinct from movies. Producers realized the benefits of filming shows. Not only could mistakes be edited out but reruns of shows proved to be a valuable part of television's financial structure. Audiences began to form emotional bonds to characters in continuing series and lost interest

Ernest Borgnine in the 1954 film adaptation of Marty *(United Artists / The Kobal Collection)*

in one-time teleplays. Television programming became more focused on how to create a product that was best suited for its medium, instead of copying the aesthetic principles used by radio, movies, or the stage.

CRITICAL OVERVIEW

Critics had little to say about *Marty* when it appeared on live television in 1953 because there was no way to preview it before the broadcast, and as soon as it was shown the networks and viewers had moved on to other things. But the fact that it was quickly adapted to film with a script also written by Paddy Chayefsky allowed many reviewers to go back and refer to Chayefsky's work on the teleplay in their nearly universal praise of the movie. For instance, Ronald Holloway, writing in *Variety*, suggests that, based on the evidence of *Marty*, more films should be made from television sources. Calling it a "sock picture" (show business slang for "socko," or powerfully successful), Holloway writes, "It's a warm, human, sometimes sentimental and an enjoyable experience." In the *Saturday Review*, Arthur

Knight expresses his hope that this adaptation will lead to more movies from television scripts. "For what this lovely, touching, wonderfully human picture reveals is that a fine TV script provides a better basis for a film than possibly any other source of movie material outside of the *bona fide* original," he writes. Like many reviewers, he particularly notes Chayefsky's ability to make his characters come alive:

> There must be millions of Martys. What makes this Marty exceptional is the fact that Chayefsky has created him so fully, with such warmth and humor and affection, that inevitably all the other lonely Martys who wonder how to spend their Saturday nights are reflected in his image.

The novelty of moving a television show onto the big screen was also noted in John McCarten's review of the film for the *New Yorker*. "A gentleman with the improbable name of Paddy Chayefsky has adapted a television script of his own devising into a movie called *Marty*," he writes, "and the end product is a remarkable tour de force." *Time* magazine's unnamed reviewer felt reservations about Chayefsky's "almost too clever script," but notes that

> at his best this writer, who was born and raised in a Jewish-Italian part of The Bronx, can find the vernacular truth and beauty in ordinary lives and feelings. And he can say things about his people that he could never get away with if he were not a member of the family.

Over the course of the next decade, Chayefsky came to be as well known for his work in movies as he was in live television, but even in reviewing some of the most influential films of their day (such as *The Hospital* and *Network*), critics usually identified Chayefsky as the man who wrote *Marty*.

CRITICISM

David Kelly

Kelly is a writer and an instructor of creative writing and literature. In this essay, he examines the understated elements of dramatic tension in Marty.

The nicest thing about Paddy Chayefsky's teleplay *Marty*, written for live television in the 1950s, is that it manages to introduce so many issues that are part of common life without dwelling on them. Life is presented in the teleplay, not explained; to use the old writers' adage,

WHAT DO I READ NEXT?

- The year after *Marty* was first produced, Paddy Chayefsky was back on the *Philco Television Playhouse* with another teleplay with a similar theme, *The Mother* (1954). It takes place in the same milieu and examines similar characters and themes. It is included in *The Collected Works of Paddy Chayefsky: The Television Plays*, published by Applause Books in 1995.

- Readers who are interested in film might want to compare Chayefsky's teleplay for *Marty* with the script for the film version, which won him an Academy Award in 1955. The film script is included in *The Collected Works of Paddy Chayefsky: The Screenplays, Volume I*, published by Applause Books in 1995.

- Shaun Considine's biography of Chayefsky, *Mad as Hell: The Life and Work of Paddy Chayefsky*, takes its title from one of Chayefsky's most famous screenplays, *Network*. In it, he compares Chayefky's personality to

Marty's. The book was published in 2000 by AuthorHouse.

- British comic writer P. G. Wodehouse took a lighthearted look at a situation not much different than Marty's in his 1927 novel *The Small Bachelor*. Although Wodehouse's George Finch lives in an upper-class world of servants and manor houses, readers can see that he and Marty suffer a similar fate. This book is available in a 2001 reissue from Penguin.

- Laura, one of the main characters in Tennessee Williams's classic American play *The Glass Menagerie*, is so socially isolated and awkward that she looks out across the alley from her apartment at a ballroom like the one Marty goes to, thinking that it is a place where great romance takes place. Williams's play, in contrast to Chayefsky's, is presented as an unrealistic memory play. First performed in 1944 and staged continuously since then, it is available in a 1999 edition from New Directions.

---

it is shown, not told. Like any good drama, *Marty* is driven by dramatic tension. The sources of tension are accepted as part of the characters' lives. This is what makes *Marty* seem so much like real life, where issues are dealt with but situations stay the same, the accepted background of everyday life.

In an essay called "Marty: Two Choices of Material," written to accompany the printed edition of the teleplay, Chayefsky wrote about working with common events and characterizations instead of showing people of grand appetites and emotions leading lives composed of highly significant moments. He attributed his ability to be subtle to the fact that he was using television as his canvas. Plays for the stage, Chayefsky wrote, require large, dramatic moments, the kind of telling incidents that will communicate to audiences the characters' inner

turmoil. Movies, too, rely on grand gestures, and are populated with characters who are more exotic and conspicuous than ordinary people. Both tell their stories in big, open places, to hundreds of people at a time, and have to communicate the emotions driving the story to the people at the back of the furthest balcony. Television, on the other hand, is better suited for interpreting ordinary life because it is such an intimate medium, bringing the story into people's homes on a box so small, for most of its history, that the most common camera technique in the 1950s was the close-up, which draws attention to every nuance of the actors' faces. This was the situation at the time when *Marty* was written, although things have changed since then. Wireless microphones let actors speak in the largest auditoriums without raising their voices above a whisper, for instance, and the

> EVEN THOUGH TIMES HAVE CHANGED, MARTY'S SITUATION IS STILL CONSPICUOUS—NOT ENOUGH TO QUALIFY HIM AS ONE OF THOSE LARGER-THAN-LIFE CHARACTERS WHO POPULATE THEATRICAL PRODUCTIONS BUT ENOUGH THAT AUDIENCES WILL ALWAYS WONDER WHAT MAKES A MAN LIKE MARTY TICK. THAT IS THE ESSENCE OF POWERFUL DRAMA."

distribution pipeline that brings movies to television within a few months of theatrical release has made the techniques for each mostly indistinguishable.

In his essay, Chayefsky refers to a few of the tensions that he feels are unstated in *Marty*, even though he refuses to analyze them for his readers. "I do not like to theorize about drama," he writes. "I suspect the academic writer, the fellow who can precisely articulate his theater." He mentions that the teleplay has overtones of homosexuality and the Oedipal complex, two popular issues in the 1950s, when Freudian psychoanalysis was at its prime, but he steers clear of explaining how each functions in his teleplay. He refuses particular interpretations of his work, though Chayefsky does not want to leave the impression that a work can be vaguely about unrelated events. There is enough drama in real life to feed any number of teleplays, he feels, without resorting to either the big significant moments that movies and stage plays require or the kinds of larger-than-life characters that are needed to hold audiences' attention in both of those outsized media.

While Chayefsky decided that it is not the author's place to explore the unresolved dramatic tensions that drive his work, there is nothing to say that readers should take the same hands-off approach. *Marty* might seem to be a plain, unaltered slice of life, but it only really seems that way to readers who are able to slip right past some very prominent issues. No teleplay would be as compelling to generation after generation as *Marty* is if it were not held together with the very basic tensions of life. The teleplay does not flaunt these tensions as openly as many artistic works, but they are there.

For instance, Chayefsky's work raises the eternal question of how one generation should behave toward the generation that came before it. Marty's mother, Theresa Pilletti, has the kind of divided emotions that make a character dramatic in traditional theater. She wants her son to evolve, to take a wife and start a family, but she has also seen, from the firsthand experience of her own sister, that, following marriage, a son might abandon his mother. Audiences, of course, do not consider Theresa to be in any real danger of finding herself shut out of Marty's life. He is such a thoroughly decent guy that there is little reason to believe he would not find some way to include his mother in his new life, if he were to marry, as it seems he probably will when the story ends. Still, the issue of one generation moving away from the past is brought up in *Marty*, and it is undeniably one of the teleplay's driving forces. Chayefsky does not examine what would happen if Marty and Clara start a life free of his mother, but within the world of the teleplay, such a thing could easily happen. After all, there is every reason to believe that Marty's cousin Thomas is just as nice a fellow as Marty is, but circumstances do lead Thomas to choose his wife and child over his mother. Furthermore, the teleplay clearly demonstrates that Marty's best intentions can be overridden when he is trying to please two opposing factions at once, so that he actually comes near letting the first girl he possibly could date slip away. In the teleplay, the issue of abandonment of the elderly is brought up by Marty's Aunt Catherine. She is presented as the sort of person who would be angry and paranoid no matter what life handed her, but her personality does not make the issue any less real.

A related issue driving the teleplay is the natural tension between mothers and their daughters-in-law. Chayefsky keeps this issue out of the center of the teleplay, but the volatile relationship between Catherine and Virginia is more than just a coincidence of two strong-willed women whose lives came into contact with each other. Though these two people happen to both be headstrong, there is also a sense that conflict would occur even between two mild-mannered people. There is a natural wariness between mothers who dominate their sons' lives and the women who take those sons away.

Marty's suspicions of Clara, who is educated and has the self-assurance to disagree with his mother when they first meet, is stoked by Aunt Catherine. Though Theresa exaggerates, his mother is correct to assume that Marty's relationship with Clara will alter, and most certainly diminish, his relationship with her. This is another existing issue that Chayefsky chose to not resolve, or even explore in depth, but is undeniably present in the teleplay, and audiences who see or read *Marty* cannot help but be aware of it on some level.

While these issues are pushed to the periphery, there is one that is central, as one of the teleplay's driving forces: society's perception of the unmarried man. This teleplay is, at its core, a love story, and the major obstacle to Marty and Clara's love is not his looks or her looks but Marty's uncertainty about how to handle his social position. When he was younger, being unmarried was not such a significant issue as it is at this point in Marty's life—customers and family members did not tell him he should be ashamed of who he is. In the teleplay, however, after a tender, honest start on the fire escape, social pressures make Marty approach Clara with a range of insincere and self-defeating gestures. He does not know how to behave because he is ashamed.

To the audience of 1953, an unattached thirty-six-year-old man may have seemed freakishly out of place in society, as so many characters in the teleplay are quick to point out. In the twenty-first century, however, audience members are not as quick to judge because divorce rates have risen, homosexuality is commonly accepted, and people are less assertive about when a person should be married. Along with relaxed social standards comes increased vigilance. Fewer people might find Marty odd, but those who do would be more likely to check his name on the local police department's list of sex offenders. Even though times have changed, Marty's situation is still conspicuous—not enough to qualify him as one of those larger-than-life characters who populate theatrical productions but enough that audiences will always wonder what makes a man like Marty tick. That is the essence of powerful drama.

The one other unexamined source of dramatic tension driving *Marty* is the mystery that men are to women and women are to men. This is, of course, an important part of Marty's

trouble in the teleplay, but Chayefsky only touches on one aspect of it—the consternation of the single man—without bringing the whole issue into focus. He shows how some single men are more than just insensitive, they are downright cruel. The Young Man at the Waverly Ballroom offers other men money to take his blind date off of his hands; Angie spreads the word through the bar that Clara is a "dog"; a youth insults Clara without provocation, merely because she looked at him expectantly. Chayefsky does not just show that single men are cruel, he also shows *why* they are that way, with the crowd of Marty's friends at the bar discussing the tough-guy antics of Mickey Spillane's character Mike Hammer as if this detective novel had any bearing on reality. These men are clueless, grasping at straws. Chayefsky does not explain why women keep rejecting Marty. As Marty explains in his moving speech about his parents' marriage, it is quite possible for people who are "ugly" to have fulfilling relationships. Either the women whom Marty approaches do not understand this, which could well be given the circumstances under which he meets them, or there is something about him—his awkwardness, his timidity—that makes them reject him. Chayefsky does not say.

Much is unsaid in *Marty*. Situations are presented with implied meanings lurking beneath their surfaces. Chayefsky purposely wrote this teleplay for broadcast on television, knowing that matters of ordinary life can resonate with television audiences in ways that do not require an author's explanation. This teleplay is meant to reflect life as it is, and that means that the dramatic tensions that other playwrights draw attention to are left for audiences to understand on their own.

Source: David Kelly, Critical Essay on *Marty*, in *Drama for Students*, Gale, Cengage Learning, 2009.

Éric Dentley

In the following essay, Dentley compares the film adaptation of Marty *to the play* Middle of the Night, *both by Chayefsky.*

One of the current topics of conversation in New York is Paddy Chayefsky, the first writer, I imagine, whose works have been adapted, not *to,* but *from,* TV. Nor is this fact all that is remarkable about the film *Marty* and the play *Middle of the Night*. Mr. Chayefsky draws on the everyday life of New York with so much ease and eager interest, you could believe for a moment that no one had ever been familiar with New York before. He has his eyes and ears open, he enjoys a lot of what he sees, hears, and he has the talent to communicate some of the enjoyment and many of the facts. Some of his humorous sallies—such as when the young husband in *Marty* bawls out his wife for her lunches out of cans and cellophane—are worthy of Odets. Nor, any more than Odets, are they merely literal transcripts of life. They are often closer to the comic strip. If a man says once: "That Mickey Spillane, boy, he sure can write," you can rest assured he'll say it three times. And, at his worst, Mr. Chayefsky will just give a character a tagline like: "what the hell?"

It is perhaps in the nature of the case that the film would be far superior to the play, for the talent of Mr. Chayefsky is wholly journalistic, and the camera is a better reporter of external facts than the stage will ever be. If Mr. Chayefsky's mentality is not to bother you, you need the constantly busy camera to keep your attention fixed on the streets, bars, kitchens, and bedrooms of Manhattan. In the role of a John Gunther "inside New York," Mr. Chayefsky is charmingly successful. Another valid comparison would be with De Sica, for *Marty* conveys a similar sense of relaxed identification with lower-class metropolitan life, not without a similar romanticism about it. Enjoining these things, you are prepared not to probe beneath the surface—until you see *Middle of the Night,* Mr. Chayefsky's play about a middle-aged widower (Edward G. Robinson) who woos and wins a married woman of 24.

Even then you may like what you find, provided only that your demands on the theatre are quite different from mine. What do you go to the theatre for? To recognize things out of the life you left behind you? To say of this actor; "He's just like Mr. Jones across the way," and of that: "Just like my husband!" and of this speech or the other one: "Just what mother always says!"? It is true that our theatre expends a lot of energy engineering such recognitions; and perhaps one day—1984?—drama will consist of absolutely nothing else. If so, Mr. Chayefsky is riding the wave of the future.

That he is certainly riding the wave of the present is best proved from the thematic substance of his works. Are you lonely? Plain? A little old, now, for marriage? Have you fallen in love

with a man old enough to to be your father? Or can't you manage to fall in love at all? Is your potency on the wane now you're past 50? Do you find call-girls sordid yet fail to find a satisfying alternative? As I think back to *Middle of the Night,* I have it all mixed up, somehow, with memories of "Mr. Anthony" on the radio years ago or Norman Vincent Peale in a magazine the other day. "Now tell me: do you think it'd be right for me to break with my husband?" "My dear, that is a question only you can answer." But I think this Shakespearean retort was uttered by Edward G. Robinson in reply to the leading lady. The whole play is like that except that, later on, Mr. Robinson stops being cagey and answers all questions, including the question: what is love? I am not going to reveal what his answers are. You can guess: for this author can be relied upon to tell you what you want to hear. *What you want to hear, not what a given character would say:* that is the formula. Or, one might express it, he doesn't write characters, he writes audiences.

When an author writes with his audience, not his characters, in mind, his writing is necessarily all calculation and contrivance. Which is why Mr. Chayefsky's intended eulogy to average humanity doesn't work out—or, rather, why the averageness works out, and not the humanity. Perhaps this is as it should be for the playwright of the age—this age of salesmanship, of what Riesman calls "outer direction," of conformity and uniformity. The idea of an "average man" is valid enough in certain fields—"the average man fills so many cans of garbage a day," etc. But much as we all love our average man, none of us will confess to *being* him: whatever our weakness, we feel too full of freedom and possibility to accept the title; and the artist, pre-occupied with such feelings, is interested precisely in the non-averageness even of the person stigmatized as average. Perhaps, outside his plays, Mr. Chayefsky would be unmodern enough to support the artist in this (for one deplores in him the abuse, not the absence, of intelligence); but, inside the plays, we truly get the average and not the unique, the preachment and not the truth, the facts and not the life of the facts.

The relation of such a play to performance is an annoying one. It is true that fine actors have always appeared in false and rubbishy plays. But the falsehood of, say, Sarah Bernhardt's vehicles by Sardou and the rest was overt and involved no deception: the falsehood of melodrama is even enjoyed as such. Since the rise of realism, human falsity can be wrapped up in facts and offered as genuine, realism being the vehicle of unreality. So here with Edward G. Robinson in *Middle of the Night*. Delmore Schwartz was saying recently that the acted emotions of Julie Harris went far beyond the written emotions of John Steinbeck; and Paddy Chayefsky owes it to Mr. Robinson, whose acting is wonderfully weighty as well as full of apt detail, that people will think there is a *man* in his play. There is a more cheerful way of looking at it: the stage is a form in which some of an author's deficiencies may be made good by actors. Out of a few rather empty lines Anne Jackson and Martin Balsam build handsome histrionic creations. Miss Jackson is one of the most skillful actresses we have.

Joshua Logan directed the actors well, though he had a heroine with whom no directing could do very much, and this author brings out Logan's weaknesses as much as his strength; for Logan too tends to make a fetish of the audience, and consequently to insult it with unworthy devices—such as, in this case, imitation-TV captions and imitation-TV background music.

Source: Éric Dentley, Review of *Marty* and *Middle of the Night*, in *New Republic*, Vol. 134, No. 9, February 27, 1956, p. 21.

Frank W. Wadsworth

In the following essay, Wadsworth critiques the works published in the collection Television Plays of Paddy Chayefsky, Marty *among them, concluding that while the works are insightful, they possess a "saccharine quality that does not reflect Chayefsky's own outlook on life."*

The appearance of *Television Plays of Chayefsky* is more than a passing moment in publishing history, marking the first time that the plays of a single television dramatist have been gathered together into one volume. Three hundred and forty years of wonderful theater have come and gone since a similar event—the first collected edition of plays by an English dramatist—occurred; yet, there is an interesting parallel to be observed between the arrival of Ben Jonson's *Works* in 1616 and Mr. Chayefsky's six plays in 1955. Jonson's dramas were the product of a highly commercial theater, and the literati who graced court affairs (the literary teas of the day) elevated their elegant noses at the thought that the author of writings designed to make money

> IN SPITE OF THE INTIMATE VIEW GIVEN US OF MARTY, WE KNOW HIM INCOMPLETELY, SUPERFICIALLY, NEVER BEING FAVORED WITH ANY FLASHES OF TRULY PROFOUND INSIGHT."

should have the temerity to consider his plays literature. Similarly, Mr. Chayefsky's plays are the product of a medium that few will deny exists mainly for the purpose of making money and that, according to the judgment of the purer literary circles, is therefore incapable of giving birth to anything of real value.

But Jonson's plays confounded the critics and, in spite of the commercial nature of the theater which begot them, turned out to be among the brightest achievements of English drama. As a result, it seems not unreasonable to ask, without implying in any way that the author is another Jonson, whether the six plays of Paddy Chayefsky do not also have intrinsic value as drama.

Messrs. Simon and Schuster, the publishers, seem to have some doubts, one notices, for their advertising of the volume has stressed Chayefsky's own analyses of his craft, which accompany the plays, rather than the plays themselves. As Franklin Fearing pointed out in the Fall, 1955, issue of the *Quarterly*, these analyses are of great interest and value to the would-be playwright. But for the student of the drama, at least, the main significance of *Television Plays of Paddy Chayefsky* is the appearance in print of six plays by a gifted young writer who is widely acclaimed as television's foremost dramatist. Here, at last, is a chance to form a literary judgment not only of one of the finest serious writers in this newest of entertainment media but through him, perhaps, of the literary potential of the medium itself.

This essay, therefore, will attempt to answer two questions on the basis of the evidence afforded by Chayefsky's six plays. First, can television drama validly be classed as literature? Second, if it can be so classed, to what extent is its value as literature affected by the peculiar demands of the television medium? Before turning to the answers, however, it will be helpful to summarize the major characteristics of the plays.

With the exception of *Holiday Song,* a realistic fantasy in the O'Neill tradition, the plays are brief, intimate dramas of lower- and middle-class life, designed to be played in fifty-odd minutes of viewing time. In keeping with their author's conviction that the television screen cannot effectively handle more than four people at any one moment, they seldom bring in view more than this number at once. Yet, there is no feeling of thinness, or of over concentration; for Chayefsky, aided by the spatial fluidity of his medium, makes constant use of the subplot, thereby filling his plays with a goodly number of people.

Since Chayefsky feels that the seemingly undramatic events of ordinary existence are far more significant to a modern audience than the great tensions of the traditional drama, his plays all look searchingly at the run-of-the-mill problems of run-of-the-mill people.

Marty, for example, details the coming of love to a squat, unattractive butcher of an Italian district in New York City and a thin, plain schoolteacher who at twenty-nine seems destined to be an old maid. It is a tender, moving story, revealing sympathetically the drabness with which love enters the life of the lonely and unbeautiful, and honest to the point of showing its hero's momentary wavering when he is reminded of the girl's homeliness.

Marty, The Bachelor Party, too, is a story of loneliness and love, this time of the loneliness of marriage and of the attempt to find that romantic-sexual excitement which the routine of lower middle-class existence can so easily destroy in the marriage itself. Chayefsky shows a young accountant's quest for excitement, setting it against a background of empty frustration personified by the other members of the bachelor party. Frightened by the thought of bringing up his unborn child on his small salary, troubled by a persistent but dimly understood longing for the body of some woman other than his wife, Charlie takes part in the bachelor party with sullen aggressiveness at first. Soon, inflamed by drink and the seeming erotic freedom of the Bachelor's unfettered life, he is loudly shouting that he wants to "find some women!" But a sodden tour of the city is unsuccessful ending in a bar graced only by one battered veteran of the city's streets. In his own frustration and in the loneliness of the Bachelor, Charlie recognizes the quiet virtues of his own marriage; and he returns to his wife with a new love and understanding.

One other play, *The Mother,* has this quality of hyperordinariness. *The Mother* is the story of a recently widowed woman of sixty-six who is determined to return to her old job as a seamstress in the garment industry in order to combat the loneliness of her new life. She is handicapped, however, by her aged ineptitude—it has been forty years since her last employment—and by the opposition of her daughter, a determined martyr out to protect her mother from the world even though her protection increases the misery of the old lady's remaining years. When, having been given a chance to show her skill, she mistakenly sews only left-hand sleeves, and is fired, the Mother is ready to concede defeat and to move in with her overly possessive daughter. But a single night reaffirms her determination to work, the only kind of life she has ever known, and to live out her last years in her own home, surrounded by her own possessions. The daughter, finally understanding her mother's determination, accepts it and, for the first time, directs her solicitude toward her own family.

Marty, The Bachelor Party, and *The Mother* are marked by a subdued realism of character and event that gives them the immediacy of ordinary, day-to-day existence. The problems that the characters face are the problems most of us face, cannot escape facing, and Chayefsky's characters come to them no better or worse equipped for a solution than do we. Compared with these three plays, *Printer's Measure* and *The Big Deal* suffer from an excess of theatricalism and contrived action—but only in terms of Chayefsky's own work, let me emphasize. Beside such landmarks of the realistic drama as *Street Scene* or *The Silver Cord, Printer's Measure* and *The Big Deal* are quiet indeed. Nevertheless, both plays smack of the unusual, not in relation to the events of literature, perhaps, but in relation to the ordinary events of life.

The Big Deal tells the story of Joe Manx, once a successful builder of houses, who for fifteen years as a bankrupt has been existing on big dreams and big talk. Joe is a theatrically effective figure as, scorning a humble, low-paying job, he goes from place to place trying to wangle the four thousand dollars that will enable him to get started on the unsound project that is his big deal. He is, in fact, a bit too theatrically effective, a bit too much the distillation of all such useless dreamers, so that when he finally goes to the daughter who has been supporting him and attempts to borrow her carefully saved five thousand dollars, we feel that the action is unfolding rather too patly. This is true also when she offers him the money without a moment's hesitation, and when he refuses it and decides then and there to take the humble job. The play is highly effective as theater, and it is quite possible that intelligent directing and acting could lessen the contrived effect; but *The Big Deal* does not have the simple, basic life rhythm that marks the action of *Marty* and the other two plays.

To a lesser extent, this is also true of *Printer's Measure,* the story of a proud old compositor faced by the challenge of a Linotype machine. In his picture of the old-fashioned craftsman with his fierce artistic integrity, Chayefsky has again come up with a type character, with the result that the action unfolds almost too logically to the moment when the compositor takes a sledge hammer and gives vent to his pent-up resentment by smashing the Linotype machine to bits. Dramatic, exciting—but shallow stuff compared to the deep, slow-moving emotions of *Marty,The Bachelor Party,* and *The Mother*.

The sixth play in the volume, *Holiday Song,* is written in a somewhat different vein. The story of an elderly Jewish cantor who temporarily loses his faith in God, it depends upon extraordinary coincidence (albeit based on a true occurrence) and a mysterious, angelic figure to return its central figure to belief. The play, as Chayefsky himself points out, is essentially a comedy—gentle, wistful comedy—probing Jewish traditions and temperament with kindly irony and revealing that the author's talents are not limited to a single approach to drama.

All six plays were highly successful on the television screen. *Marty,* of course, was made into a motion picture, one of the year's most distinguished. *The Mother* has, I believe, been sold to Hollywood. But a motion-picture version of a television play, no matter how faithfully it may attempt to follow the original, is bound to be a different work of art. Unless these plays also exist as literature, apart and distinct from the unique screening that gave them life, their artistic existence has been disappointingly ephemeral. I think that it can be demonstrated that they do exist as literature—and this in spite of the fact that the author himself is on record as stating "I do not write literature; I write drama, and drama depends entirely on how it is played." It is to this demonstration that I now turn.

In a thoughtful and provocative essay published some years ago, Professor Erwin Panofsky argued that the motion-picture script is subject to what he called the principle of coexpressibility; that is, unlike theater drama, which can express itself by words ("speech") "free and independent of anything that may happen in visible space," the motion-picture script exists only as an incomplete part of the visual movement, which is the heart of the finished production, the words alone leaving us either bored or embarrassed. Thus, he claims, good movie scripts seldom make good reading and usually go unpublished.

This does not necessarily hold true for good television scripts. The very limitations of live television force the playwright to pay more than lip service to the spoken word; at the same time, these limitations result in a kind of compressed visual action that can be effectively recreated in the playwright's expository inserts between the stretches of dialogue. Although the directions in the actual shooting script of a television play may, because of their strange format, offer a block to the imagination of the average reader, the more literary passages found in the final published version do not. These passages plus the dialogue result in a dramatic form that has not only a verbal magic rarely found in the motion-picture script but also a coexpressiveness unusual in the published drama. Thus, like the plays of J. M. Barrie, those of Paddy Chayefsky make extremely happy reading. For, whether he is fully aware of it or not, Chayefsky has clearly prepared his texts with the reader in mind, not only the would-be television playwright, but the average lover of published drama. If by literature one means a significant form of writing capable of existing in time independent of any ephemeral, nonliterary phenomena that might originally have accompanied it; then, Chayefsky has, in fact, been writing literature at the same time that he has been writing what he describes as drama.

Chayefsky's descriptive passages go beyond the exigencies of mere production. In *Holiday Song,* Sternberger, the elderly cantor who has lost his faith in God, is pictured as "a gentle little man in his fifties—a scholar, generally confused by the outside world. His lean, sensitive face is gaunt with inner pain." We are told that his eyes are "deep" and "pained" and "wide with some unknown fear." Here is visibility, clear and revealing, yet not so detailed as to destroy the necessity of the reader's own imaginative creation, that positive act which is one of the chief rewards of reading a play. This same quality characterizes Chayefsky's description of physical action which, by relying upon selected rather than exhaustive detail, encourages the reader to complete the picture. *Holiday Song* opens on Naomi, the cantor's niece, ironing, "nearsighted and intense." When she receives a visitor, she sits down "and straightens her skirt"; when she tries excitedly to tidy herself up for the appearance of a prospective husband, we are told

> She notices the kitchen towel lying on the table, picks it up, stuffs it into her apron. Then she realizes the apron is no costume in which to greet Brother George from Cleveland, hurriedly takes it off, looks nervously around for some place to put it, finally throws it into the grandfather's clock.

With such descriptive passages, Chayefsky makes us visualize the action of his drama. With such unobjective comments as the faintly ironic "Brother George," he sustains and clarifies the tone of the dialogue, thus giving the reading text the tonal direction that would come in production from the attitudes of the actors. When it appears that Naomi has found herself a husband, she reveals her excitement by starting to hum a Jewish wedding tune. Then, writes Chayefsky, "Slowly the wedding dance swells within her" and she begins to dance. The metaphorical "swells" is surely as revealing of Naomi's emotion and of Chayefsky's attitude toward it as any visual indication could be, and the whole paragraph of description becomes not simply a stage direction, a substitute for action, and therefore essentially an unorganic part of the play, but rather an integral part of the unity of the drama as literature.

Chayefsky's full stage directions, in other words, are essentially literary, conceived as organic parts of the experience of reading the play and written in a style harmonizing with the effect of the dialogue, simple, direct, and usually very effective. Occasionally, they become obtrusive, as when he tells us parenthetically that Cantor Sternberger's living room is plain because "(Cantors don't make very much money.)" Or when, after the old aunt in *Marty* has described for the Mother the loneliness of finding one's children all married, he writes "The aunt has hit home." But, in general the passages, simply and pungently written in the idiom of the play itself, and seldom technical in nature, give the reader a sense of words and movement that

only the most experienced, imaginative reader can get from the conventional dramatic text.

Even without this extra dimension, Chayefsky's plays could stand independent of the picture on the television screen. Unlike the motion picture with its vast, almost endless visual scope, the television drama is limited by the physical restrictions of current studios, by relatively small budgets, by, as the talented TV writer is well aware, the literal smallness of the televised image. As a result, the television play must perforce have something of the verbal distinction of the legitimate drama, its dialogue the central element, dominating the action rather than being dominated by it. And the real strength of Chayefsky's plays lies in words. I cannot think of any modern writer, whatever his medium, who better captures the essence of ordinary speech. By ordinary, I mean the everyday conversation of lower middle- or upper lower-class people, or whatever one wishes to call the vast army of little men and women who are America. Chayefsky's verbal stronghold, of course, is New York City and its environs (except in *The Big Deal*), and his dialogue normally reflects the idiosyncracies of this area. But his dialogue is so natural, so unforced and lacking in artificiality that it transcends its peculiarities and speaks to every one willing to listen.

Two qualities seem to me to characterize his handling of dialogue. First, he writes speech, not dialect. There is none of the heightening, none of the exaggeration and wrenching of words for special effect which mark so many efforts to capture the flavor of ordinary talk. This is not to say that Chayefsky's language is a literal reproduction, something taken from a tape. Chayefsky is too much the artist to fall into that old naturalistic trap. His language *sounds* like ordinary speech; it does not reproduce it. And his characters only *seem* to have the inarticulateness of ordinary men, actually speaking with the tongues of poets. His dialogue, in other words, is truly a work of art, superior, from the point of view of readability, even to such a master of realistic speech as James Farrell.

The other quality is harder to define, being in part the result of Chayefsky's firm grasp of characterization. It is a poetic quality, one revealing rich strata of subsurface meaning in lines of seemingly simple dialogue. It recalls the buried tensions of Hemingway, though here the vibrations are quieter, less disturbing. Take, for example, the revelation of loneliness in *Marty*. The play abounds in passages of quiet anguish, in which banal conversation is made vivid by the emptiness it seeks to cover. In the following bit of dialogue, two desperate men, each in his thirties and each monumentally unpopular with the girls, face the prospect of another lonely Saturday night:

Angie: Well, what do you feel like doing tonight?

Marty: I don't know, Angie. What do you feel like doing?

Angie: Well, we oughtta do something. It's Saturday night. I don't wanna go bowling like last Saturday. How about calling up that big girl we picked up inna movies about a month ago in the RKO Chester?

Marty: (Not very interested) Which one was that?

Angie: That big girl that was sitting in front of us with the skinny friend.

Marty: Oh, yeah.

Angie: We took them home alla way out in Brooklyn. Her name was Mary Feeney. What do you say? You think I oughtta give her a ring? I'll take the skinny one.

Marty: It's five o'clock already, Angie. She's probably got a date by now.

Angie: Well, let's call her up. What can we lose?

Marty: I didn't like her, Angie. I don't feel like calling her up.

Angie: Well, what do you feel like doing tonight?

Marty: I don't know. What do you feel like doing?

And the painful comedy continues, as it has night after night, the ineffable loneliness of the two young men crying out from under the seeming inanity of their talk.

The answer to the first of the two questions asked earlier—can television drama validly be classed as literature?—would seem, then, to be yes, it can. Chayefsky's plays in their published form not only retain something of the visual dimension of dramatic production but have, as well, the verbal richness of the legitimate drama. Let us turn now to the second question posed, and seek to determine the extent to which the demands of the TV medium affect literary excellence of these plays.

Perhaps most interesting from a technical point of view are the structural problems that

television production presents to an author. He is asked to do in less than sixty minutes a dramatic job comparable in many respects to that done by the legitimate dramatist in double the time. Chayefsky has been only partially successful in this difficult task of dramatic compression. In many ways, his plays are unusual in the skill with which the story has been fitted to the truncated hour normally devoted to full-length television drama. Shocking in the half-hour playlet, and still noticeable in the longer play, has been the television playwright's failure to proportion his drama successfully within the time limits of his medium. The result of this failure has been a rash of plays which are all exposition, plays in which the resolution, if it occurs at all, is hasty and startling in its inappropriateness. Chayefsky's dramas, on the other hand, indicate an awareness of the problems posed by the brevity of even the hour show; and they have a welcome architechtonic, getting under way easily and without dragging, developing their conflicts at some length, and resolving these conflicts with a certain care and thoroughness.

To perform this miracle, however, Chayefsky generally relies upon a second plot to act as a catalyst, using this subplot to bring the main conflict to a head. At least once, in *Printer's Measure*, this subplot is handled both awkwardly and obviously, for the introduction of the death of the narrator's father as a means of having the narrator desert old Mr. Healy, the compositor, is unconvincing. The shift in emphasis, at least temporarily, from Mr. Healy to the boy is unfortunate, since the author does not have time to develop the boy's story to the point where it becomes an organic part of the whole. This lack of unity is felt again, if to a lesser extent, in *Marty*, where the story of Marty's embittered old aunt seems proportionately long for its function of turning Marty's mother against the girl. To create this hurdle for Marty's love to overcome, Chayefsky is forced to introduce the distinct and rather unrelated troubles of the aunt and of her daughter and son-in-law.

Chayefsky handles the subplot much more effectively in the other plays, especially in *The Big Deal* and *The Mother*. He introduces it early and, particularly in *The Mother*, integrates it with the main action. His handling of the subplot is aided (as, to some extent in all the plays) by the fluidity of his medium, the photographic technique of fading from one scene to the next enabling the author to make the effortless transitions characteristic of Elizabethan drama.

One important result of this fluidity is the television playwright's freedom to go to his characters instead of being forced to assemble them on some few, static sets. Television does not, at present at least, offer the possibilities of the motion picture. But, by comparison with the limitations of the modern stage, the TV dramatist is in a position to poke his nose hither and yon with relative freedom. Because of this freedom, Chayefsky's plays have an intimate quality seldom if ever found in the legitimate drama. They reveal the ordinary with a loving attention to the little things of life. The mobile camera with its fondness for close-up scrutiny, emphasizes the familiar dialogue accompanying the ordinary actions of life. In this way, we get a kind of verbal close-up together with a visual one.

But Chayefsky's attention to the patterns of everyday existence does not result in quite so deep a probing of the human consciousness as he seems to think. He claims, in his analysis of *Marty,* to have "ventured lightly" into such things as the Oedipal relationship, reversion to adolescence, latent homosexuality. However much these themes may have been present in his mind when he was writing *Marty,* they do not seem to me to be embodied in the text of the play (as distinct from the motion picture); that is to say, they are not there in any recognizable form, for they cannot be proved by the play, any more than Hamlet's so-called Oedipus complex can be proved by the text of Shakespeare's tragedy. *Marty* concerns an outcast whose particular form of ostracism is adequately explained by his appearance and by the defensive mechanism he has created for it. The play examines the plight of this outcast tenderly and thoughtfully, showing his painful enfetterment in the chains of social custom and his eventual but somewhat reluctant escape. It does not go much deeper. In spite of the intimate view given us of Marty, we know him incompletely, superficially, never being favored with any flashes of truly profound insight.

This failure may come in part from the temporal limitations of television, since probing is a delicate, time-consuming task. It also stems from Chayefsky's avowed belief that television should avoid the greater tensions of traditional drama, for "there is more exciting drama in the reasons why a man gets married than in why he murders

someone." I suspect that this is not necessarily true. It is certainly doubtful, dramatically speaking, that all the minor crises in a man's life will reveal his inner self with the clarity that a single, unusual, soul-shattering event is capable of doing. Chayefsky, who is neither accurate nor wise in his criticism of the legitimate stage, draws a misleading comparison between the subdued realism of his own plays and the more flamboyant realism of the theater. If it is true that the theater cannot capture the intimate, ordinary quality of Chayefsky's plays, it is also true that he has not, at this writing, captured the penetrating quality of the best legitimate drama.

But what Chayefsky does he does well, revealing the patterns of everyday life not only with technical skill but with true understanding of their significance. For his attention to routine detail is no mere naturalistic decoration; it is the result of his awareness that such seemingly little things are the essence of ordinary existence. Whether it is the frustrating experience of being interrupted at a moment of petty triumph, as in *The Big Deal* when the wife tries to tell her husband of their daughter's engagement, or the failure to pick up a girl in a cheap dance hall, as in *Marty,* Chayefsky paints his everyday crises with loving care, understanding and making us understand that they are ordinary only in the sense that they occur as part of the normal pattern of life.

And Chayefsky sketches these crises not without humor, a humor ranging from the obvious, visual comedy of *The Bachelor Party* to the tear-provoking smiles of *The Mother.* Both *The Bachelor Party* and *Holiday Song* are funny, the former with its scenes of drunken revelry, the latter with its old-world Jewish flavor and its rather typed characters. Through all the plays, there runs a strain of kindly irony, seen in such episodes as Naomi's request that her uncle put off losing his faith for two weeks so that the loss won't inconvenience her search for a husband; the hilarious confession of the proud possessor of a hundred and eighty-nine dollar suit of imported Egyptian fabric that the suit is unbearably hot ("I'll be honest with you. I don't know how they manage in Egypt with it"); or the reply of one old lady to another who has accused her own son of wishing to "cast his mother from his house" . . . "Catherine, don't make an opera outta this." Finally, there is the admixture of tragedy and comedy with its gentle Chaplinesque appeal, which characterizes *Marty* and *The Mother* especially: Marty in the phone booth attempting to play the gallant; Marty trying with clumsy desperation to kiss the first girl who has ever liked him; and, perhaps the most poignant touch of all, but one still essentially comic rather than tragic, the bundle of sleeves, all for the left arm, that the Mother has sewn in her desperate attempt to hold her new job.

It would seem from what has been said that the medium of television offers mixed blessings to the serious writer. If the brevity of the performance creates structural problems sometimes difficult of solution, and limits the kind of psychological analysis feasible, the fluidity of the camera makes possible a unique intimacy which can be exploited with sympathetic understanding and quiet humor. But television exerts another form of control over the dramatist, this one thematic rather than technical, which would seem to place almost insuperable obstacles on the road to literary excellence. For television, as Paddy Chayefsky is painfully aware, is at present an advertising rather than an entertainment medium, with the result that the dramatist is prevented from writing about "almost anything that relates to adult reality." Such subjects as adultery, abortion, and the social values of our times are out, protests Chayefsky; and so the serious television writer, prevented from expanding "in breadth," must turn to "minutely detailed studies of small moments of life." Unfortunately, even these suffer from advertising necessity, as Chayefsky's own plays reveal.

For all their wonderful insight, Chayefsky's dramas do not ring completely true. Seemingly frankly realistic, they actually leave one too much aware of the pathos of life, too little aware of the tragedy. This impression is partly the result of the plays' having happy endings, at least in the sense that the people involved come to accept, more or less gracefully, the conditions in their lives against which they have been rebelling. Cantor Sternberger finds his faith; Mr. Healy, the compositor, accepts his lot, whatever particular interpretation one may attach to the ending of the play; Joe Manx takes the job as building inspector; Marty decides in favor of his homely girl; the Mother continues the good fight, as her daughter accepts the inevitable; Charlie returns to his wife unsullied and content—saved, as someone has remarked of Scott Fitzgerald's heroines, after hanging over the cliff.

Adding still more sugar-coating to the bitter pill of existence is the essential goodness of Chayefsky's characters. The people of his drama are fundamentally decent and, once we get to know them, likable in spite of some annoying surface traits. Thus, when the chips are down, Joe Manx in *The Big Deal* is capable of self-sacrifice; he cannot bring himself to take his daughter's savings. And the meddling aunt in *Marty* is a long way from being vicious; she is simply a lonely, deserted old woman with a crusty disposition. Similarly, the Bachelor in *The Bachelor Party* turns out to be a tired young man trying to fill up the corners of his loneliness with desperate revelry, not a smalltime Iago attempting to lead his married friends astray. In the same way, the selfish daughter in *The Mother* is finally capable of real affection.

Chayefsky's people are convincing enough as individuals. No one character is too good to be true, nor is the revelation of goodness under a harsh exterior unbelievable in any single instance. It is simply that it happens too often. Older ideas concerning original sin are not fashionable today, and we are lectured by those who should know to the effect that man is never bad, merely maladjusted. Nevertheless, individual experience teaches us that the world contains a fair share of people who are mean and vicious, wherever these traits may come from. And a world in which such people never appear, no matter how faithfully it presents appearances or examines the people who do inhabit it, is not a wholly true one.

That this saccharine quality does not reflect Chayefsky's own outlook on life, but comes from the necessities of his medium we may be sure. Indeed, his essays make it clear that he is uncomfortable in his bed, Procrustean rather than of his own making. But perhaps it is not altogether accurate to blame television alone for this sweetness; a wiser judgment might be inclined to view the fault as one rising out of the not infrequent inability of American culture to accept reality. Certainly American realistic literature, notably the drama, has seldom shown the honesty of the best European writing. In the field of the motion picture, this contrast is even more obvious. Thus, it would seem to be faintly un-American to fail to cater to the romantic immaturity that is the mark of a home-grown audience. And it would seem also to be rather unfair to blame the least pretentious of our artistic media for attitudes that, if it still panders to them, it at least did nothing to create.

Nevertheless, if television is to fulfill the great promise Paddy Chayefsky sees in store for it; if it is indeed to become the basic theater of our century, it will do well to face up to the harsh truth of life. To recognize that man can be mean and vicious and to honor him in spite of this requires infinite compassion and comprehension. Paddy Chayefsky appears to be a young man who has these attributes and, in addition, the literary skills to go with them. Perhaps this talented writer will one day be able to force television to discard the pathetic for the strange mixture of ugliness and beauty, evil and good, that is human existence. If he does, it will not be long before television will be producing a truly vital, powerful literature of its own.

Source: Frank W. Wadsworth, "The TV Plays of Paddy Chayefsky," in *Quarterly of Film Radio and Television*, Vol. 10, No. 2, Winter 1955, pp. 109–24.

SOURCES

Bird, J. B., "Paddy Chayefsky," in *Museum of Broadcast Communications*, http://www.museum.tv/archives/etv/C/htmlC/chayefskypa/chayefskypa.htm (accessed on August 1, 2008).

Chayefsky, Paddy, *Marty*, in *The Collected Works of Paddy Chayefsky: The Television Plays*, Applause Books, 1995, pp. 137–82.

———, "*Marty*: Two Choices of Material," in *The Collected Works of Paddy Chayefsky: The Television Plays*, Applause Books, 1995, p. 187.

Clum, John M., *Paddy Chayefsky*, Twayne Publishers, 1976.

"'Golden Age' of Television Drama," in *Museum of Broadcast Communications*, http://www.museum.tv/archives/etv/G/htmlG/goldenage/goldenage.htm (accessed August 1, 2008).

Holloway, Ronald, Review of *Marty*, in *Variety*, March 23, 1955.

Knight, Arthur, "If You Can't Lick 'Em, Join 'Em," in *Saturday Review*, March 26, 1955, p. 25.

McCarten, John, "Up From TV," in the *New Yorker*, April 23, 1955, p. 133.

"The New Pictures," in *Time*, April 18, 1955, http://www.time.com/time/magazine/article/0,9171,866248-1,00.html (accessed August 1, 2008).

U.S. Census Bureau, "Table MS-2: Estimated Median Age at First Marriage, by Sex: 1890 to Present," September 15, 2004, http://www.census.gov/population/socdemo/hh-fam/tabMS-2.pdf (accessed August 12, 2008).

FURTHER READING

Eco, Umberto, *On Ugliness*, translated by Alastair McEwen, Rizzoli Press, 2007.
Eco is one of the most distinguished fiction writers and critics of the late twentieth century. His book-length study of the history of ugliness points out just how intangible society's likes and dislikes are.

Freeman, Joshua, *Working-Class New York: Life and Labor Since World War II*, New Press, 2001.
Freeman's look at the people who populate Chayefsky's teleplay starts around the same time as *Marty* and extends to the current day.

Odets, Clifford, *Waiting for Lefty and Other Plays*, Grove Press, 1994.
Though playwright Clifford Odets's characters were more concerned with politics than romance, his plays took place in the same social setting as *Marty*, and his style has been compared to Chayefsky's. The title play in this collection, Odets's 1935 drama *Waiting For Lefty*, taps into the same bittersweet hopefulness that attracted audiences to Marty.

Wilk, Max, *The Golden Age of Television: Notes from the Survivors*, Truck Press, 1999.
Wilk is able to recreate the environment in which *Marty* came into being, giving readers a sense of the freedom and creativity that flowed in television's early days.

Novio Boy

GARY SOTO
1997

A one-act play in seven scenes, Gary Soto's *Novio Boy* is intended for junior high school and high school readers, performers, and audiences. Published by Harcourt in 1997, the play is set in a Mexican American neighborhood in Fresno, California, about two hundred miles north of Los Angeles. Soto suggests that this setting is adaptable to any region, as it is written in somewhat simple and colloquial English mixed with some Spanish. The *novio* of the work's title means "boyfriend" or "sweetheart" in Spanish. *Novio Boy* tells the story of ninth grader Rudy's first date with eleventh grader Patricia. The play focuses on his concern about what to say and how to behave during the date, obtaining the money to pay for the date, her anticipation, and his family's responses to this milestone in his social maturation. Mixed in with its treatment of typical teenage concerns are allusions to Chicano culture, referencing food, music, and radio programs.

Soto has also used the term *Novio Boy* for the name of a cat in his children's story, *Chato and the Party Animals*.

AUTHOR BIOGRAPHY

Gary Soto was born to working-class Chicano parents, or Americans of Mexican descent, Manuel and Angie Soto, in Fresno, California, on

Gary Soto (AP Images)

April 12, 1952. Manuel, like his Mexican-born parents, was a field and factory worker. He was killed, at the age of twenty-seven, in a work-related accident when Soto was only five years old. Soto, too, labored in the California fields as a grape and orange picker. After he graduated from high school in 1970, Soto was convinced he would not be admitted to California State University, Fresno, so he enrolled at Fresno City College, where he studied geography. Soto encountered the poetry of the American poet Edward Field in his college library. Identifying with Field's work, especially with his descriptions of alienation, Soto found power in words to express feelings that seemed inexpressible. After this event, Soto decided to become a writer rather than a geographer. He then applied to and was accepted at California State University, Fresno. There, from 1972 to 1973, he studied creative writing under the American poet Philip Levine. In 1974 he graduated magna cum laude, and in 1975, he married Carolyn Oda, the daughter of Japanese American farmers, although his mother would have preferred that he marry a Mexican American. In 1976 he received an M.F.A. in creative writing from the University of California at Irvine. During the same year,

Soto was a visiting writer at San Diego State University. In 1977 he began teaching as an associate professor in both English and Chicano Studies at the University of California, Berkeley.

In 1975 Soto won the Academy of American Poets Prize and the Discovery/*Nation* Prize. In 1976 he won both the United States Award of the International Poetry Forum and the University of California, Irvine's Chicano Contest Literary Prize. In 1978 Soto was awarded the Bess Hokin Prize by *Poetry* magazine. In the same year, Soto's *The Tale of Sunlight* was a finalist for the Lenore Marshall Poetry Award. In 1979 he was awarded a Guggenheim Fellowship and spent a year writing in Mexico City, Mexico. Soto also received a National Education Association fellowship in 1981. In 1984 he received the Levinson Award from *Poetry* magazine. *Living Up the Street: Narrative Recollections* won the American Book Award in 1985. Soto's one-act play, *Novio Boy*, was published in 1997. In the spring of 1988, Soto was the Elliston Poet at the University of Cincinnati, Cincinnati, Ohio. Since his book of poetry, *The Elements of San Joaquin*, was published in 1977, Soto's poetry has been widely published in numerous journals, including *Antaeus, Partisan Review, Paris Review, Poetry, Nation, American Poetry Review, North American Review*, and the *New Yorker*. He has also published *Baseball in April* and numerous other stories for young readers.

PLOT SUMMARY

Scene 1

The first scene of *Novio Boy* begins with the stage divided in half. Stage left, two boys, Rudy and Alex are hanging around in a backyard talking about girls. Stage right, two girls, Patricia Gomez and Alicia are sitting on a couch in a living room. Only the boys' section of the stage is lighted. Rudy begins talking about his upcoming date with Patricia, worrying that he will fail to impress her, because she is older than he. His friend Alex teases him, advising him to be honest and apologize to her for his physical appearance. Rudy retaliates, saying he is good-looking, that he looks like the actor Tom Cruise. Alex, more seriously, advises Rudy to make simple conversation with Patricia, asking her what her favorite color is. Most important, Alex has heard on a radio show, is to just keep talking. As the boys continue to talk, Rudy expresses his own disbelief that he is growing up and going on a date, when just a few days before, he and his cousin were playing with G.I. Joe action figures and Barbie dolls.

In addition to worrying about the impression he will make, Rudy is concerned about obtaining the money to pay for his date at a pricey steak house. Alex offers him a quarter and then shows him a love letter he recently received. He recounts his first date when he was nine years old and went to the playground with a girl, dressed up. Alex speaks of how another boy teased him when he saw him holding the girl's purse for her as she was drinking from a water fountain.

Scene 2

As the lights go down on Rudy and Alex, they come up on stage right, revealing Patricia, the girl with whom Rudy has a date, and her friend Alicia. The girls admire magazine pictures of handsome boys and gossip about Patricia's date with Rudy. Patricia tells Alicia how nice she thinks Rudy is, and the girls, like the boys, begin to contemplate how they are growing up, remembering how they played with Barbie dolls and G.I. Joe action figures. Alicia recalls how she got back at her brother after he used the head of her Barbie doll as a baseball by locking him out on the porch wearing just a pair of dirty underwear. The girls laugh, continue to look at the magazine, and talk about boys, tricks they play on their parents, and clothing. El Gato appears on the opposite side of the stage where Rudy and Alex sat before. El Gato is playing music, pattering, and announcing dedications. After a few minutes, the focus shifts back to the girls, who have been listening to the show. They think of calling in to his program but are too shy to do so. They ask each other to name the most important person they have ever talked to. They can only come up with advertising figures like the McDonald's clown and the San Diego Padres mascot, a man in a chicken suit. Then they reiterate their wish to call El Gato and ask him to play "Ninety-Six Tears," both girls' favorite song. Patricia says she cried exactly ninety tears once when a boy broke up with her, and the scene ends with both girls pretending to cry.

Scene 3

Rudy's mother is lifting weights to keep in shape. Rudy stands behind her, good-naturedly imitating her. He asks her about her first boyfriend, and she reminisces a bit. Rudy tells her he has a date and asks to borrow fifteen dollars from her. She balks at the amount and wonders if he is too young to go on a date. When he tells her the girl is older than he is, she is also taken aback. However, Rudy reminds his mother that his father is younger than her. She counters Rudy's argument by stating that she looks young. She challenges him to find wrinkles on her face and shows off her dark hair, admitting, though, that she colors it. Rudy's mother contemplates the idea of Rudy having a girlfriend and worries that soon he will leave her. She asks if the girl is nice. He says he thinks she is. His mother warns him to be "nice," like his father, whose virtues and business success she praises. Rudy's father now owns his own cement truck and is head of a crew of workers. She notes her job as a beautician and says that Rudy will be able to go to college.

When his mother leaves the room, Rudy does a few repetitions with her weights but quickly tires. His Uncle Juan enters with his guitar and, noticing that Rudy looks downcast, asks him why. Rudy denies he is troubled. Juan begins to play and sing a song but stops soon to ask him again what is wrong. Rudy explains he has a date but does not have the money to pay for it. Juan, an unemployed, aging hippie who plays his guitar on the street, tells Rudy not to worry about money. Rather, he emphasizes that it is important to make conversation on a date.

When Rudy's mother returns, Juan joins forces with Rudy to borrow some money from her. They flatter her, but she resists their blandishments and tells Juan he should find a real job. Juan surprises her by stating that he has a part-time job playing guitar and singing in a steak house. Rudy's mother softens and gives Rudy his birthday money a month early. As the scene ends, they smell something burning. It is the beans Rudy's mother is cooking, and she dashes into the kitchen.

Scene 4

The setting is the radio studio from which El Gato is broadcasting live. After dedicating a few songs to listeners, he introduces Mama Rosa, who gives advice about love, where to meet people, and how to concoct a love potion.

Juan is the next guest on the program. He publicizes his appearance at Steaks, Steaks, y Más Steaks, the same steak house that Rudy is planning to take Patricia to on their date. After some banter, Juan sings a song about a fight between tortillas and frijoles (beans) and their reconciliation. El Gato gives Juan coupons for a meal at a Cuban restaurant as payment for his appearance on the radio show and repeats the announcement of Juan's upcoming performance.

Scene 5

In the beauty parlor, Rudy's mother is doing Estela's hair. Estela gossips about a man she was interested in who turned out to be married. She says she wants her hair dyed red, laments the way she looks, and asks if Rudy's mother thinks "redheads have more fun." When Rudy's mother answers that one's attitude is more important than one's appearance, Estela misunderstands the word attitude and protests that she does not have an attitude, a joke that will continue throughout the play. When Rudy's mother states that her husband is a good man, Estela complains about her "three...no, four" husbands. She concludes that she might flirt with Juan if he were not so lazy. The women hear El Gato speaking on the radio and turn the volume up.

On his radio program, El Gato talks about love and takes questions from callers. Estela calls in and asks him the same question she asked Rudy's mother—if being a redhead increases attractiveness. El Gato answers as Rudy's mother did, saying attitude trumps appearance. Again Estela balks, saying she has no attitude. El Gato explains that he means personality when he says attitude and suggests the "inner self" is more important than the outer appearance, but Estela dismisses his comments as "nonsense" and hangs up on him. Rudy's mother puts Estela under a hair dryer and takes the next customer, who happens to be Rudy's date, Patricia. This is Patricia's first visit to the salon. As they talk about what Patricia wants done with her hair, Patricia mentions her upcoming date with a nice boy. Rudy's mother realizes Patricia is speaking of Rudy; however, Patricia remains unaware that the beautician is Rudy's mother. When Patricia says that Rudy hardly ever speaks of his mother except to say she is strict, Rudy's mother becomes comically upset and a little jealous. The scene ends as Estela comes out from under the hair dryer as a redhead and shimmies excitedly upon seeing her new look.

Scene 6

In an attempt to make money for his date, Rudy sets up a stand with Alex and hopes to sell apples. They speak of finding money and how Alex once burned his baby brother. Alex plays with a G.I. Joe action figure, and Rudy comments that he would not go into the army because he does not like uniforms. Alex talks about his intention to play football. They realize that they have not sold any apples. An old man enters the scene, and the boys successfully sell him some apples. In the course of the transaction, they learn that the man is a widower. They talk about dating, and when the old man complains that his life is boring and that he never goes out on dates, they encourage him to go out to a restaurant. The idea seems to spark his interest. The scene ends with Rudy and Alex reflecting comically on the fragility of relationships with girls.

Scene 7

The climactic scene of the play, Rudy's date with Patricia in the steak house, brings nearly the whole cast together on stage. The scene begins with Juan playing his guitar and telling the waiter that he will "wow the crowd." The waiter remarks that the boss expects Juan to draw a crowd. Rudy and Patricia enter, and Rudy checks his wallet, observing the restaurant's elegant atmosphere. The waiter seats them. Patricia says that it is a "discriminating restaurant," and Rudy takes the word *discriminating* in its negative sense. Patricia, though, promises him that she does not mean that the restaurant discriminates against Latinos. She affectionately calls him silly when he says the cloth napkin looks like a diaper. Juan sings a song, and Patricia says she thinks he is very talented. Rudy, embarrassed that his uncle is there, says he is just ok. The waiter brings them menus. A "moo" sound comes from the kitchen, and Patricia notes that "the food's really fresh." Rudy compliments a cat pin Patricia is wearing, which leads to a conversation about her cat, called Novio Boy, meaning "sweetheart boy." She shows him a picture of the cat, whose ear was ripped off in a fight. Patricia compares the cat to Rudy; she says that "he's small but he's valiant." Rudy, however, states that he is "against fighting," because when he fights, he gets beaten up.

The waiter returns, and Patricia places a large order. To avoid spending too much money, Rudy orders only crackers and a diet soda, saying that he has to watch his weight, because he is wrestling. They continue to talk; he compliments her, and she tells him she is learning to drive a car. She also mentions that her mother is "overprotective"; does not like her dating boys; and thinks that she is at the library, not on a date. However, Patricia reassures Rudy that he will not get into trouble and how highly she (Patricia) thinks of him. As they are talking, the old man to whom Rudy and Alex sold apples enters the restaurant and stops when he sees Rudy. They shake hands, and the old man tells him he is taking Rudy and Alex's advice and is doing something. He compliments Patricia and asks if Rudy can fix him up with her mother, but Patricia tells him her mother is already married. The old man then asks Juan if he knows a certain song and takes a seat. Rudy tells Patricia how he knows him and at the same time her beeper goes off. (The play was written just a few years before cell phones became ubiquitous.) Patricia tells Rudy that Alicia is paging her, and she goes outside for a moment to call her.

While Patricia is on the phone, Rudy asks Juan why he is there. Juan tells him he has a job playing guitar and singing at the restaurant and then gives Rudy some money to pay for his meal. Juan then addresses the audience, talking about his various girlfriends. When Patricia returns, Juan plays a romantic song. The waiter brings their orders, Patricia's hamburger and fries and Rudy's crackers and diet soda. Patricia offers to share her food, and together they discover they both like their fries with mustard. Rudy compliments Patricia's hair, noting that his mother is a hair dresser. As Rudy reads prepared compliments from a hidden sheet of paper, Alex enters the restaurant. Slipping the waiter a dollar, he gets a table near Patricia and Rudy. The old man recognizes Alex as the boy who sold him apples along with Rudy and notes how nice Patricia is but that her mother is married. Patricia stands near Juan as he plays, and Rudy and Alex talk about how Rudy's date is going. Patricia returns, and Alex goes back to his table. As Rudy and Patricia continue to talk, Rudy notices that the restaurant is full of familiar people. At that moment, his mother and Estela enter the restaurant. Slowly, Rudy realizes that he is surrounded by people he knows, and they are watching him. Nevertheless, he dances with Patricia. She offers to teach him to drive and offers to split the bill. He declines her offer to help pay for the meal. She says that she will pay next time, indicating that they will have another date. When Patricia must go home, she kisses Rudy on the cheek.

After Patricia leaves the restaurant, Rudy confronts his mother, asking her why she is spying on him. She denies knowing that he was taking his date to the steak house, but Estela points out that Rudy's mother styled Patricia's hair. Juan says their presence at the restaurant shows they are all "watching out for" Rudy, but they should have given him more space. The old man strikes up a conversation with Estela, and they go for a walk with Juan. Left alone with Alex, Rudy decides that he will gather up all his toys and other signs of his childhood and sell them at a yard sale in order to pay back everyone who lent him money for the date, indicating his passage into adolescence and his developing sense of responsibility.

CHARACTERS

Alex

Alex is Rudy's good friend. He is described as "big" and "awkward." On his first date, when he was nine years old, Alex took a girl to the playground and was embarrassed when another boy saw him holding the girl's purse as she drank from a water fountain. He advises Rudy as to how to act on his date, even during the date, when he comes to the steak house where Rudy has taken Patricia and helps Rudy by giving him money to pay for the meal.

Alicia

Alicia is Patricia's friend and confidant. Looking at a magazine, she giggles about the pictures of attractive boys and discusses Rudy with Patricia. She recalls the tricks she played on her parents when she was a kid and the fights she had with her brother. She is "scared" to call in to the celebrity radio disc jockey, El Gato.

El Gato

El Gato is a radio disc jockey. His broadcast style is lively but not combative. He plays records, interviews guests, takes on-air phone calls, and engages in discussions about love and money. Many of the characters in the play listen to his show. His show is one of the focal points of the community in the play.

Estela

Estela is a customer in Rudy's mother's beauty shop. She is beginning to age and is distressed by it. She has her hair dyed red in the hope that she will feel more youthful and have more fun with red hair. She has been married three or four times and admits she is unclear about the number. There is a recurring joke based on her repeated misunderstanding of the word *attitude*. She is rough in her manner and a little slow in her understanding, but she is a warm person, nevertheless.

Juan

Juan is Rudy's uncle, an aging hippie and street musician who has finally obtained a part-time job singing and playing guitar at a steak house. He is a guest on El Gato's radio show, where he sings a song and advertises his performance at the restaurant. He acts more like a brother to Rudy than an uncle. Although he talks as though he is a man of experience, Juan is nearly as financially dependent on his sister (Rudy's mother) as Rudy is.

Mama Rosa

Mama Rosa gives advice about love, discusses astrology, and offers recipes for love potions. She appears on El Gato's radio show, which many of the characters in the play listen to for advice.

Old Man

The old man is a widower who buys apples from Rudy and Alex. His life has been dull since his wife died. At Rudy and Alex's suggestion, the old man goes out to a restaurant, the same steak house where Rudy takes Patricia for their date. He meets Estela there and, along with Rudy's mother, goes on a walk.

Patricia Gomez

Patricia is an eleventh-grade girl whom Rudy asks out on a date. Older and taller than Rudy, she is attractive and knows how to drive a car. Although she lies to her overprotective mother by saying she is going to the library rather than on a date with a boy, she is a good-natured, responsible girl. Patricia likes Rudy; she tells him she thinks he is brave and sensible and even imagines marrying him when she is an adult.

Rudy

Rudy is a ninth-grader moving from childhood to adolescence. He works in the school cafeteria serving food and is nervous about his first date with Patricia, who finds him attractive. Rudy

teases his mother when she becomes vain, but he is amiable and responsible. He is not a tough kid and states that he does not like to fight because he gets beaten up. At an age when he has both childhood and adolescent interests, Rudy decides at the end of the play to get rid of his childish toys.

Rudy's Mother

Rudy's mother is a beautician. She keeps in shape by doing aerobic exercises with weights and dyes her hair to retain a youthful appearance. She tries to be stern when Rudy asks to borrow money from her but quickly softens. She is a responsible person who works hard, looks to rise socially and economically, and respects her husband, who is successful in business through hard work.

THEMES

Age versus Maturity

Novio Boy is a coming-of-age story about the anxieties and ambitions that Rudy faces growing up, especially as he makes the effort to transition from childhood to adolescence. He asks Patricia out on a date, gathers the money to pay for the date by selling apples, faces his past by talking about the toys he has enjoyed playing with, and attempts to enter his future by divesting himself of them. His date with Patricia becomes a rite of passage not just because it is his first date but also because so many characters from his past participate in it by watching the date happen at the restaurant.

The difference between age and maturity is an implicit theme in *Novio Boy*. Initially, in the play, a younger boy asks an older girl out on a date, and then he worries about appearing immature. The older girl is also aware that she is going out with a younger boy, but she is not disturbed by this fact at all. Her affection for him is, nevertheless, tinged with that of a mature person for a naïve person. In contrasting scenes, Rudy and his friend Alex and Patricia and her friend Alicia recall their childhoods and remark on how immature or naïve they used to be. When the scene shifts to the adults in the play, concern for age is still at the forefront of conversation. Rudy's mother worries that she has wrinkles, and she dyes her gray hair. Both Estela and Juan are examples of adults who have not

TOPICS FOR FURTHER STUDY

- *Novio Boy* concerns a boy's first date. Write a short story narrating your first date, including the circumstances, anxiety, and excitement involved. How do you go about making the date and preparing for it? What expectations do you have? How does the date compare with your expectations?

- Rudy's mother is a beautician, and she is concerned about losing her youthful looks. She exercises and dyes her hair. Her friend, Estela, has similar concerns. Rudy, too, is aware of his age, since Patricia is two grades ahead of him in school. Prepare a questionnaire that asks respondents about their attitudes toward aging, whether they cosmetically alter or enhance their looks, what they look for in a partner physically, and the relative importance of attitude and looks and whether or not the two subjects are related. Present the survey to an equal number of males and females. Compile your data in a report, analyzing how males and females differ, if at all, in their responses.

- Nearly everyone listens to the radio in *Novio Boy*. In an essay of at least five hundred words, discuss the importance of radio in, and its effects on, American culture. You may extend the scope of your essay to other media as well.

- *Novio Boy* presents a rather comfortable picture of life for Mexican Americans in California. There have been, however, serious labor and economic struggles waged in California over the last fifty years by the United Farm Workers (UFW) Union, founded by Cesar Chavez (1927–1993) for the rights of farm and field workers. Research the UFW and Chavez and present an oral report on the issues the union confronted, the methods it employed in the fight for workers' rights in California, and its significance for the rest of the country. Conclude your report by outlining the challenges Mexican Americans face in the workforce today.

---

attained maturity; Estela does not have a mature understanding of relationships, and Juan cannot support himself financially. The old man listens to Rudy and Alex's advice and attempts to recover his youth by going out to a restaurant and socializing with women. The resolution of the play comes with Rudy's decision to get rid of his childhood toys after realizing that he is maturing and wants to grow up.

Community

The importance of a community bound together by a common culture pervades *Novio Boy*. In the play, this entails a mixture of Mexican and American cultures. Therefore, the characters relate stories of experiences that seem typically American, like playing with action figures and dolls and listening to American music. They also share

experiences that involve Chicano food and music. Perhaps the play's strongest social link is El Gato's radio program, as it facilitates community-wide conversation. Relationships between individuals, however, contribute most to the sense of a community and a common culture, as the friendships of Alex and Rudy or Patricia and Alicia show. The final convergence of most of the characters in the steak house, as Juan remarks, shows a common concern for Rudy's well-being.

Gender Roles

Soto challenges traditional gender stereotypes in *Novio Boy*. Throughout the play, women are shown in positions of authority and strength, and men are portrayed as dependent on and subordinate to women. Patricia, for example, thinks that she might become a soldier after graduation.

Rudy, conversely, tells Alex he does not want to be a soldier, as he dislikes the uniforms. In addition, he does not like to fight, since he usually loses. When Rudy attempts to use his mother's weights, he quickly becomes winded. Alex recalls being teased when he was seen carrying a girl's purse for her as she drank from a water fountain in the park. Rudy's mother works out and shows off her muscles. His uncle, Juan, a usually unemployed street musician, is dependent upon Rudy's mother for his income. Estela is presented as being promiscuous in a way often attributed to males. Soto makes a point of having the waiter refer to the owner of the steak house as a female, reinforcing the role of women in authoritative positions in the play.

STYLE

Chicano Dialect

A dialect is a common speech shared by members of any particular social or cultural group. It includes slang and popular expressions and utilizes the straightforward sentence structure of everyday speech. The characters in *Novio Boy* use a dialect that blends English, Spanish, and slang. For example, the boys call each other "man," "bro," and "homes," and use expressions like "cool." The girls refer to each other as "girl" and use expressions like "cross my heart." Rudy's mother calls Rudy *m'ijo*, a term of endearment that comes from the Spanish *mi hijo*, meaning "my son;" and Estela *mujer*, meaning "woman" or "lady."

Throughout the play, Spanish words, phrases, and expressions are used alongside English ones. For example, when El Gato jokes about the best time to fall in love, he says, "*Pues* [well], I think it's the first of the month, when the *cheque* [check] comes in." Spanish figures so prominently in the dialect that there is a six-page glossary of Spanish words and expressions appended to the text to aid readers who are unfamiliar with the Spanish language. Through the mix of Spanish, English, and slang, Soto portrays Chicano culture linguistically.

Stychomathia

Originating in Greek drama, *stychomathia* is a dialogue in short, alternating lines, like a game of catch between the actors. In *Novio Boy*, Soto renews the classical form when he uses it to present the quick and abbreviated back-and-forth that characterizes a great deal of colloquial conversation in the play. This stylistic device reinforces the playful tone of the work.

HISTORICAL CONTEXT

Chicano Literature in the Twentieth Century

Chicano literature is an English-language literature of a people whose heritage is a literature composed in Spanish. It is a literature written by Mexican Americans, native to the United States, whose cultural identity is often more fundamentally American than Mexican and who are dedicated to integrating their experience of the two cultures in literature. Chicano literature is rooted in the sense of a Mexican past and partly in the popular nineteenth-century Mexican ballads celebrating heroic deeds, called *corridos*. However, the literary genre often focuses on Mexican American life experiences in the United States.

Chicano literature experienced an upsurge and renewed popularity in the late 1960s and the 1970s when Chicano poets, such as Rodolfo Gonzales; Luis Alberto Urista, writing under the pen name of "Alurista"; Jimmy Santiago Baca; Lorna Dee Cervantes; and Leroy V. Quintana began to write consciously and proudly about their culture and their roles as artists in the culture. Such writing brought a sense of Mexican American culture and history to a people who found themselves, largely in the American Southwest, relegated to a socially inferior status. The social condition, a prominent subject of Chicano literature, is featured in José Antonio Villareal's novel *Pocho*, which analyzes the experiences of Mexican immigrants living in the United States during the Depression in the 1930s. Social issues were also the subject of the poetry and fiction of this generation of Chicano writers. Luis Valdez formed El Teatro Campesino and presented plays like *Zoot Suit*, performed by and for striking migrant workers during the labor struggles of the 1960s and 1970s led by Cesar Chavez and Dolores Huerta. Chicano authors also wrote about crises of faith, relationships with the land, and experiences of urban life.

During the late twentieth century, Chicano novelists produced a rich body of work, including Rudolfo Anaya's *Bless Me, Ultima* (1972), which won the Premio Quinto Sol National literary award; Sandra Cisneros's *The House on Mango Street* (1984), which won the American Book Award; Denise Chávez's *The Last of the Menu Girls* (1986); and Tomás Rivera's *And the Earth Did Not Devour Him* (1987).

1960s Advocacy for Mexican American Labor Rights

Novio Boy does not necessarily address social or economic issues critically, except as they appear in Juan's comic persona or Rudy's adolescent problem of earning money for his date. However, Soto emphasizes these subjects in several of his other works, especially relating to Mexican Americans' experiences in his home state of California, where *Novio Boy* is set. The history of many Mexican Americans, especially in California, is linked to agricultural work, exploitation by growers, and the labor struggle of Mexican American farm workers. In 1966 several farm worker unions joined together to conduct a series of strikes and formed the United Farm Workers of America (UFW) union. In an effort to educate the next generation of Americans about these struggles, Soto wrote a biography of Cesar Chavez, one of the leaders of UFW reform, for children. Titled *Cesar Chavez: A Hero for Everyone* and illustrated by Lori Lohstoeter (2003), the book reflects Soto's esteem for Chavez and analyzes his role as an advocate for Mexican American rights. Chavez, Dolores Huerta, and other UFW leaders based their effort on the principles and practices of nonviolent philosophies as defined and deployed by Mohandas Gandhi during the Indian movement for independence from England. They also incorporated the nonviolent philosophies of Bayard Rustin and Martin Luther King, Jr., used during the U.S. civil rights struggle for racial equality in the 1950s and early 1960s. In *Cesar Chavez: A Hero for Everyone*, Soto examines Chavez's modest background during the Depression and his important role as a farm worker, labor organizer, civil rights activist in obtaining Mexican American labor rights.

CRITICAL OVERVIEW

Gary Soto is most noted for his poetry, which takes a hard and unaffected look at the oppressive conditions under which many Mexican

Americans live and labor. Julian Olivares, in a review for the *Latin American Literary Review*, states that Soto is "the most recognized Chicano poet in the American literary mainstream." *Revista Chicano-Riqueña* contributor Patricia de la Fuentes finds a kind of linguistic ambiguity that creates complexity and depth in Soto's poetry. La Fuentes identifies, for example, how Soto's use of the word *strokes* to describe the movement of the air in his poem "Wind," not only "accentuates the terror and aggression implicit in the action of the wind because it denotes hitting or striking a blow that wounds or destroys, an attack," but "also carries a denotation which is at odds with the implacable violence of the wind since it represents the diametrically opposite action of caressing, flattering, soothing."

Soto has also established himself as an author of books for children and adolescents. In these works—the greater part are short stories— and also in plays, such as *Novio Boy*, Soto portrays worlds free from the grim realities he describes in his poetry. Denise E. Agosto, a contributor to *School Library Journal*, calls *Novio Boy* "a hip, funny play" that "young actors should be able to perform ... with or without adult assistance."

CRITICISM

Neil Heims

Heims is a freelance writer living in Paris and the author or editor of more than two dozen books on literary subjects. In the following essay, he examines how Soto's background and audience influence Novio Boy.

Whether knowledge of an author's life is relevant or useful in interpreting or understanding his or her work is a matter of considerable debate. During much of the twentieth century, a school of literary thought called New Criticism asserted that biography is extraneous to an interpretation of literature, that a reader need consider nothing but the text in front of her or him. It suggested that literature presents a paradox that must be identified; works should be approached as if they contain a puzzle or a code to be broken. A work like Gary Soto's *Novio Boy*, regarded as a piece of dramatic literature, poses a problem for such critics. *Novio Boy* is a straightforward story of a Chicano

WHAT DO I READ NEXT?

- *A Memory of Two Mondays*, first published in 1956, is a one-act play by Arthur Miller. The play traces the maturing of a young man as he works in a warehouse in 1933 during the Great Depression, longing for a college education in a seemingly hopeless time.
- *The Catcher in the Rye* (1951), J. D. Salinger's only novel, traces the journey of Holden Caufield, a rebellious and angst-ridden teenager recently expelled from a college preparatory school. Holden explores an underground lifestyle in New York City and has a nervous breakdown, beginning a melancholy maturity.
- *Giant* (1952), by Edna Ferber, is an epic novel of family, culture, and class in Texas that focuses in part on the social status and challenges of Mexican American oil-field and farm laborers.
- *Soon to Be a Major Motion Picture*, published in 1979, is a cultural memoir by Abbie Hoffman, a leading social and political activist during the civil rights movement of the 1960s.
- *Cesar Chavez: A Hero for Everyone*, published in 2003 by Aladdin Books, is Soto's biography of the great Chicano labor organizer who, along with Dolores Huerta, led Mexican American workers through a successful strike against California grape and lettuce growers. Written for children, it sheds light on the values and Mexican American history that Soto wishes to impart to the next generation.

boy's first date. There are no weighty problems or tensions, no deep encounters with the self, others, morality, or society. At the end of the play, Rudy does decide to separate himself from his childhood by selling his old toys at a yard sale, but his approach to manhood still has a good deal of boyishness to it. Why not? He is

> THE RESONANCE IN *NOVIO BOY* COMES NOT FROM WITHIN THE PLAY ITSELF BUT PRECISELY FROM EXTERNAL FORCES, BROUGHT FROM EITHER THE EXPERIENCE OF ITS READERS OR THE CIRCUMSTANCES OF ITS PRESENTATION."

still a boy. The play is a good-natured, gentle comedy, more like a situation comedy made for television than a drama for the theater. The challenges he faces are conventional, and the outcome is what is typically called "heartwarming." There is little to explain, no buried meaning to excavate.

Eventually, the rigors of New Criticism gave way to critical methods that do take into account biography, historical period, culture, and other elements New Critics might consider extraneous. They suggest that knowledge of the events of an author's life and culture do inform a reading of an author's work. Some also place emphasis on how readers bring meaning to a work. These more holistic approaches help further illuminate a seemingly uncomplicated work like *Novio Boy*.

Novio Boy is an introductory play to be performed by and for young audiences. It is intended for performance; it comes to life on the stage, not on the page. *Novio Boy* is more a community event—a school production, for example—than a literary event. It is the type of play that thrives when the audience knows the actors in everyday life and the actors are aware that they are performing for an audience that knows them outside their roles, recognizes them inside their roles, and is rooting for them. *Novio Boy* involves familiarity, good will, and a communal and educative purpose that can be found more in the performance than in the text of the play. It demands of its performers not necessarily that they show great skill as actors but simply that they endeavor to perform.

The resonance in *Novio Boy* comes not from within the play itself but precisely from external forces, brought from either the experience of its readers or the circumstances of its presentation. Rudy is a sympathetic character who is concerned about obtaining the money to pay for his first date. He is also worried how his date, Patricia, will perceive him, especially since she is two years older than he, a significant difference in adolescence. Young audience members can identify with Rudy as he goes on his first date, is self-conscious about his physical appearance, and struggles to assert independence from his mother. *Novio Boy* also addresses Rudy's relationship with his mother. She recognizes that she and her son are growing older and that her son is becoming less dependent on her.

Here is where knowledge of Soto's life becomes illuminating. Soto's father was killed in a work-related accident when Gary was only five years old, leaving him and his siblings to be raised in near poverty by their mother. Absent from *Novio Boy* are strong male figures, as they were from Soto's own childhood. In the play, though, the sting is removed and absence does not signify loss and deprivation, but a congenial exercise in refocusing. Although the cast of *Novio Boy* is balanced in terms of male and female characters—six males and five females, excluding the callers on El Gato's radio program, influential male figures seem to be missing from the play.

However, their absence is not presented as problematic. Rudy's father is absent from the action of the play, but he is not absent from Rudy's life. Rudy's mother mentions him as a model for Rudy. His father has succeeded in getting "his own cement truck" and becoming the boss "of his own crew." Rudy's mother, however, is presented not only as a strong character because of her presence in the action of the play but as a provider for her family. She works as a beautician and supports her brother, Juan. Rudy's mother's customer, Estela, adds a comic dimension to the absence of men in the play as she speaks of her "first three husbands." When asked by the old man if she is married, Estela answers "sometimes." The presence of three such transitory men, as Estela presents them, actually indicates the absence of a man of significance in her life. Juan, intended as a comedic figure is nevertheless a weak male figure, unable to provide for himself or hold a steady job. He is not a model for Rudy in this sense, although this issue is hardly emphasized. Rather, he is characterized as a source of affection and camaraderie for Rudy. Rudy himself is far from macho—he is winded by exercise, reluctant to fight, and disinterested in the military. Patricia, on the other

hand, imagines the possibility of becoming a soldier. Nevertheless, she admires Rudy's dislike of fighting and is charmed by his romantic words. The absence of strong males in the community of the play is transformed into an absence not of men but of machismo (an exaggerated sense of masculinity).

Another important biographical fact about Soto is that he is an American of Mexican descent. He grew up as social, political, and economic issues in Mexican American communities took on national prominence. During this time, Dolores Huerta, Cesar Chavez, and other labor activists of the United Farm Workers of America (UFW) union were striving to end discrimination against and exploitation of Mexican American workers in the fields and factories of agricultural enterprises, particularly in California, where Soto was born and raised. Racial drama is not represented in this play about members of a Chicano community. Yet many Mexican Americans, including Soto, have experienced social struggles like exploitation, poverty, and discrimination. These issues formed the context of Soto's childhood and remain contemporary problems for numerous Mexican Americans. Significant themes of social adversity are evident in Soto's poetry and adult fiction. Rather than writing about social issues and confronting them dramatically and thematically in *Novio Boy*, however, Soto has made the work itself tacitly confront those issues by presenting an alternative reality, a reality as familiar and as tame as that depicted in a generic situation comedy for television. In the play, Soto dramatizes cultural assimilation. He does not depict experiences of oppression and exploitation. Instead, he celebrates the comfortable sense of being an included and accepted member of mainstream American culture.

Issues, thus, that might have defining importance for a Chicano audience, such as economic exploitation and social oppression, are not addressed in *Novio Boy*. Rather than analyzing the difficulties that beset many Mexican American communities, Soto presents in *Novio Boy* a young Mexican American dealing with adolescence as any other boy his age does. The Chicano reality that Soto depicts is as American as an after-school television special, and its language and setting are straightforward and familiar to young Mexican American students. Soto thereby enables students who read and perform *Novio*

Boy to experience literature on an introductory, nonthreatening level.

Source: Neil Heims, Critical Essay on *Novio Boy* in *Drama for Students*, Gale, Cengage Learning, 2009.

Lisa Feder-Feitel

In the following interview, Soto answers questions about influences on his writing.

Award-winning author Gary Soto lives with his wife, Carolyn, in the hills above Berkeley, California, but his heart belongs to Fresno. *Scope* talked to Soto about his hometown, his Hispanic heritage, and how both influenced him as a writer.

SCOPE: *Fresno, California, appears in a lot of your work. What was it like when you were a teen?*

Gary Soto: Fresno these days is a much larger city, but when I was a boy, I recall Fresno as an agricultural town. Fruit hung everywhere, and the best way to get it was to pick what you wanted from trees that hung over fences. Plums were there—apricots, peaches, nectarines, grapes, and oranges. I liked walking around, especially in alleys, because I would always find some junky treasure worth my time. Fresno was an ideal place to shape a young writer's mind.

SCOPE: *You've written in many genres—plays, novels, short stories, and poetry. Do you have a favorite kind of writing?*

GS: I'm a poet at heart, and I think in all my other work—novels, short stories, and plays—there is evidence that I think like a poet. I'm a concise writer, I believe, and when I write, say, a novel like *The Afterlife,* I can't seem to write more than 190 pages.

SCOPE: *How valuable is it to write from your own experience?*

GS: Poetry is often about the self, meaning you—a person with an ordinary body, ordinary looks, and ordinary life. I realized this early on, and later carried it over into personal-essay writing. I had a set of experiences as a child, and I wanted to repeat them. It was a time that I could only call back by writing about it.

SCOPE: *What aspects of your Mexican-American heritage make you most proud?*

GS: Without doubt, I'm proud of individuals like Cesar Chavez, founder of the United Farm Workers of America. He was a man who witnessed unfair treatment of field workers and set about to improve their lot. ¡Qué viva Cesar Chavez!

SCOPE: *How important is reading in the process of becoming a better writer?*

GS: Poetry beckoned me while I was a student at Fresno City College. It said, "Hey, you, come on over here." "Here" was a campus library, and I went there in search of poetry, all because I was heartbroken—a girl I liked didn't return any affection.

SCOPE: *Is there a book that changed your life?*

GS: I recall reading John Steinbeck's *The Grapes of Wrath* in tenth grade and thinking that I had encountered a truth about farm workers. I rooted for those poor Okies of *The Grapes of Wrath.* I realized the power of writing and that the poor can have their say, too. It was one of the best reading experiences I have ever had.

Source: Lisa Feder-Feitel, "¡Viva Soto!," in *Scholastic Scope*, Vol. 53, No. 3, October 4, 2004, p. 11.

Annie Ayres

In the following review, Ayres argues that, although the amount of Spanish in Novio Boy *could pose a challenge for some student performers, it is nevertheless a "sweetheart of a play."*

It's not Novio Boy, the cool cat from Soto's *Chato's Kitchen,* but Rudy and Alex from *The Pool Party,* who are featured in this seven-scene play. Rudy, now a ninth-grader, asks an "older woman," an eleventh-grader, out for his first date. In preparation, Rudy seeks advice from his best friend Alex, startles his mother with news of this recent development in his social activities, and asks his "Chicano loafer" and guitar-playing Uncle Juan for financing, but is somehow surprised when they all end up at the restaurant on the night of his big date. Soto's contemporary play is lighthearted and fun to read, but the liberal use of Spanish, which flavors and authenticates the dialogue, requires frequent trips to the extensive glossary at the end and may make the play difficult to perform for students not comfortable speaking Spanish. However, *Novio Boy* is, true to its title, a sweetheart of a play.

Source: Annie Ayres, Review of *Novio Boy: A Play*, in *Booklist*, Vol. 93, No. 16, April 15, 1997, p. 1425.

Miriam Rinn

In the following interview, Soto talks with Rinn about his career, background, and reasons for writing works like Novio Boy *that feature Mexican Americans.*

Gary Soto, the poet, essayist, and fiction writer who has published short stories and novels about Mexican-American teenagers, believes that non-Hispanics have no business writing about this ethnic group. "I feel very strongly that those writing about Mexican Americans should be Mexican American," Soto told the *Book Report*. He doesn't think it's possible for someone who grew up in Philadelphia or a small-town in Georgia to know what life is like for a Latino youngster in Fresno.

As an American of Mexican origin living in California, Soto sets his stories in places he knows intimately, the neighborhoods of Fresno, the surrounding fields, and San Francisco. In doing that, he doesn't feel that's he's any more limited than other American regional writers. After all, Eudora Welty isn't criticized for sticking to her "turf," and he doesn't see why he should see it as a limitation, either.

He doesn't believe in censorship, Soto quickly added, but he truly questions the motivations of the many non-Hispanic writers who have recently published stories with Hispanic themes or main characters. Recently he addressed a group of children's-book professionals and used several picture books to make his point. Each one of the books portrayed Hispanic characters working in the fields and smiling. "I don't trust their observations. I don't trust their motivations," Soto said about the authors. Soto himself has worked as a laborer and so can say with some authority, "You can't write about field work in a picture book and have kids smiling." Instead, those writers should record the cancer rate in the San Joaquin Valley, where field workers inhale pesticides year after year, Soto suggested.

Even when Anglo writers discuss the hardships of the field workers, Soto dismisses their efforts. "Unauthentic tearjerkers" is the way he describes them. There's a saying, Soto added; no tears in the writer, no tears in the reader.

In contrast, Soto's stories are filled with the flavors of Mexican-American life and culture. He worked as a field laborer during his childhood summers. His first book for children, *Baseball in April,* is a collection of short stories that tell of Alfonso's desperation to borrow his

SOTO THINKS OFTEN ABOUT HIS LATINO READERS, THOSE CHILDREN WHO NEED TO SEE THEMSELVES AND THEIR LIVES IN THE BOOKS THEY READ."

brother's bicycle for his first date, Hector's grandfather's dreams of buying a house, Yollie's mother's decision to use money she was saving for college to buy her daughter new clothes.

The kids in Soto's stories dream of brand-new clothes for school instead of hand-me-downs, a real Barbie instead of a cheaper replica, going on expensive amusement-park rides instead of playing baseball in a dusty field. Their fathers work in factories and drink too much. Their mothers cook tortillas and frijoles and threaten their children with straps when they misbehave. Backbreaking work in the fields to make some extra money is always a real option. These are the Latino working poor, neither sentimentalized nor prettified. Children roam the streets unsupervised, do foolish, destructive things, and emerge unscathed. Soto has borrowed a phrase from Ezra Pound—the unkillable children of the poor—to describe them.

In the many letters from readers in response to his first collection of stories based on his own life, *Living Up the Street,* Soto picked up a sense of recognition and yearning for more. They heard what he was saying, he explained, and now he hears from young readers all the time, as well as meeting them in schools in California and the Southwest. Mexican-American kids invariably see themselves in the work, and sometimes they correct the Spanish words and phrases sprinkled throughout his writing. Chuckling, Soto defended his Spanish, and explained that regionalism accounts for the so-called errors.

After the publication of *Living Up the Street* in the mid 80s and another collection of short stories based on his youthful experiences, *A Summer Life,* Soto realized that Latino youngsters needed to see themselves and their lives validated in print. He wanted to put together a book of short stories specifically for children.

Unfortunately, no major publishing houses were interested, citing the form and the limited audience as drawbacks. Traditionally, short stories have been difficult to sell, and in the mid 80s, the publishing industry was not yet aware of the growing market in the Latino community. When Harcourt Brace published *Baseball in April and Other Stories* in 1990, it received glowing reviews. It was chosen an ALA Best Book for Young Adults, a Horn Book Fanfare Selection, and a Judy Lopez Memorial Honor Book.

Once his "young adult" books began to sell well, Soto found himself pursued by other publishers. With an agent to represent him, he began to publish children's books regularly with several different major houses. Soto now devotes most of his time to children's literature, while continuing to write adult poetry.

The connection Latino teens feel to his work is mainly one of pride, Soto believes. Although Mexican Americans do not have an extensive literary tradition, Soto said, "One thing we do have is an incredible pride in who we are." According to Soto, *Pocho,* by Jose Villareal, published in 1959, was the first truly Mexican American novel. It was a coming of age story about second- and third-generation-out-of-Mexico Americans. Now in the 1990s, a real body of literature exists. The plethora of Latino writers now publishing is due to the maturation of the writers themselves and to the growth of the Hispanic audience. Many of the writers now being published by large houses have been around since the 1970s, Soto said, publishing in small presses. They have been honing their skills and getting to be better writers and business people.

Soto himself went to Fresno City College to avoid the draft in 1970. After completing the two-year curriculum, he transferred to California State University at Fresno. At this time, he was writing poetry while working different jobs and living at home. Although he had no idea what he wanted to do, he wrote down urban planner as a career goal. "It sounded good," he recalls. An experienced and skilled student by then, he went on to California State University at Irvine and earned a master's of fine arts degree in creative writing.

In an interview for the first volume of *Speaking of Poets: Interviews with Poets Who Write for Children and Young Adults* (NCTE, 1993), Soto says he first became interested in writing poetry when he discovered the work of Allen Ginsberg and other poets of the "Beat" generation. By the mid 1970s, he began to receive recognition for his poetry, which appeared in magazines and was also published by the University of Pittsburgh Press.

After he received his master's degree, Soto lived in Mexico City for a while. He began teaching at the University of California, Berkeley in 1977. Soto was there until 1991, when he left to write full-time.

Soto's body of works includes children's picture and chapter books, novels for readers from middle grades to high school, poetry and essays for all ages, and film. He has made three short films for Spanish-speaking children, *The Bike, Novio Boy,* and *Pool Party,* which is based on his book. He has put aside filmmaking for theater, and is now searching for high school drama departments to perform his play *Novio Boy,* a young Mexican-American romance.

As one might expect, his books for children have been translated into Spanish, but his poetry and short stories are available in German, Italian, French, Estonian, and Yugoslavian as well.

Soto, who has just finished a novel about gang life in Fresno, knows a little about gangs from personal experience. Present-day Fresno, where he still has relatives, is a different city from the one where he grew up. "There's a lot of anger that comes up" from the street now. "A lot of race problems in that city." Playgrounds in Fresno are dangerous places today, in contrast to the relatively innocent spots they were in the 60s.

Although Soto's essays and stories are filled with scraps and squabbles, children suffer little more than bloody noses and wounded pride. The emotional fuel that drives Latino gang members today is the desire for revenge, Soto believes. He quoted another Latino writer and former gang member, Luis Rodriguez, who said "it's the power to bring people to their knees" that is so intoxicating. That appetite for power is peculiarly American, according to Soto. "Generosity won't get you anywhere. Ruthlessness will get you somewhere. Greed will get you somewhere," he said. In a society where intelligence and the arts are not valued, gang members represent frontier values. Adolescents are the purest believers in those values. "It's a time when you can prove yourself," Soto said, a time when family is not nearly as important as friends.

Soto remembers when he dreamed of physically overwhelming opponents, and his study of karate plays a central part in his novel set in Japan, *Pacific Crossing,* What first interested him in the martial art was "the mystery, the idea of destruction, of being able to beat up the kid across the street." Although he has friends who got hooked on the spiritual component of karate, Soto lost interest after a while. Even though his wife is of Japanese ancestry, the book was based on research rather than visiting the Asian country.

Soto pointed out that sticking to his own ethnic group in his writing doesn't prevent him from exploring the wider world. *Pacific Crossing* recounts the adventures of two Mexican-American boys who go on an exchange trip to Japan. The hero of that book, Lincoln Mendoza, is also the central character in an earlier book, *Taking Sides.* There, Linc and his divorced mother move to a quiet, predominantly white suburb of San Francisco.

Soto thinks often about his Latino readers, those children who need to see themselves and their lives in the books they read. "My big ambition is to provide high-level literature for Mexican-American kids." But that isn't enough to rescue many poor children from lives of disappointment and drudgery. "What they need more than anything is someone to be with them. They need to be loved more," Soto said. He teaches English at his church to Spanish speaking children, and he acknowledges it's a challenge. He participates in the Coalinga Huron House project, a six-week intensive academic program for young people from the Central Valley of California. That program has sent dozens of youngsters to college who, Soto is positive, would never have gone without intervention. These kinds of children "need a very strong curriculum outside the school," along with direction and supervision. They need books that reflect their lives, and nonfamilial adults who value them. "They need to feel part of something."

Source: Miriam Rinn, "Gary Soto," in *Book Report*, Vol. 14, No. 4, January–February 1996, p. 27.

Don Lee

In the following interview, Soto discusses his decision to become a writer and the critical reception of his work.

In one of his essays, Gary Soto writes that as a child, he had imagined he would "marry Mexican

> INSTINCTIVELY, HE KNEW THAT THE MORE PERSONAL HE WAS IN HIS WORK, CONCENTRATING SOLELY ON HIS INDIVIDUAL EXPERIENCES, THE MORE UNIVERSALITY HE COULD ATTAIN."

poor, work Mexican hours, and in the end die a Mexican death, broke and in despair." The statement might seem surprising, coming as it does from such a well-established writer. Considered one of the best Chicano poets of his time, Soto has published over twenty books, including seven volumes of poetry, the latest of which is *New and Selected Poems* (Chronicle Books). In addition to fellowships from the Guggenheim Foundation, the NEA, and the California Arts Council, he has received the American Book Award from the Before Columbus Foundation, the Andrew Carnegie Medal from the American Library Association, and the Levinson Award from *Poetry,* among numerous other honors.

But it is a desperate fate that anyone who grew up with Soto would have predicted for him as well. Recently, Soto attended his junior high school reunion, and he was disheartened to learn how many of his childhood friends had ended up in prison or been killed. Yet no one seemed particularly shocked by the news. His own outcome as an author and a senior lecturer in Berkeley's English department provoked more disbelief. "No, that's gotta be somebody else, man," his classmates said. "You must be copying this stuff out of a book, Gary."

Soto was born in 1952 in Fresno, California, the center of the San Joaquin Valley's agricultural industry, and everyone in his family was a field or factory worker. His father packed boxes at the Sunmaid Raisin Company, and his mother peeled potatoes at Redi-Spuds. Soto himself picked grapes and oranges, collected aluminum, hoed cotton and beets—anything he could do to help out. Red-lining was still legal then, and they were confined to Mexican-American neighborhoods. When Soto was five, his father was killed in an industrial accident. His mother eventually remarried and moved the family to a mostly Anglo area of Fresno, but nonetheless, Soto could never envision a future absent of border-line poverty and violence. "The likelihood of going beyond that was minuscule," he says.

In turn, not much was expected of Soto—a wild, mischievous kid who got into his share of trouble at school. "One of the aspirations was that if we stayed out of prison, we would be fine. As long as we did that, there was a reason to be proud." What might have saved him, just as he was flirting with real danger, was a school program called the Cadets, a military club. Through it, he learned some discipline, although it could hardly be said that the drills improved his academics. Indeed, he finished high school with a D average.

It was somewhat of a miracle, then, that he didn't flunk out of Fresno City College, where he enrolled in 1970 to avoid the draft. Initially, he chose to study geography. "I figured I'd just look at maps, study some rivers, take multiple-choice tests, and that'd be that. Being semi-illiterate, I didn't want to be forced to write anything." He was, after all, a pocho, a Mexican American who was neither here nor there, who didn't belong to either culture, whose Spanish and English were both poor, whose family did not and does not, to this day, read books—not even Soto's work, although they are the first to boast about his accomplishments.

Thus, it took enormous faith—and perhaps a little arrogance—for Soto to believe he could write poetry after being introduced to it by happenstance. At a library, he picked up an anthology, *The New American Poetry,* edited by Donald Allen. The poems—by Edward Field, Gregory Corso, Kenneth Koch, Allen Ginsberg, and Lawrence Ferlinghetti—were lively, irreverent, and audacious, and Soto was hooked. "I thought, Wow, wow, wow. I wanted to do this thing." He transferred to California State University, took workshops with Philip Levine, and fell in with a group that would eventually be known as the Fresno School of poets, which included Leonard Adame, Omar Salinas, Ernesto Trejo, and Jon Veinberg.

In 1974, Soto graduated magna cum laude from Cal State with a degree in English, then received his M.F.A. from the University of California, Irvine, in 1976. The next year, Soto's first book of poems, *The Elements of San Joaquin,* was published by the University of Pittsburgh Press. Critics praised the book—as well as the volumes that followed, *The Tale of Sunlight* and *Where*

Sparrows Work Hard—for Soto's frank, desolate portrait of migrant life, his short, enjambed lines and idiomatic diction, and his ability to shift from naturalism to magic realism, from the apocalyptic to the transcendent.

However, the reception to his work was not completely free of reproach. One of the respected veteranos of Chicano literature now, Soto was occasionally admonished in the seventies for not overtly addressing the socio-economic aspects of Mexican-American life. The movimiento—the movement begun by Cesar Chavez when he organized California food harvesters into the United Farm Workers—was still raging in the San Joaquin Valley, and the Vietnam War, though winding down, was still extant, and Chicano artists were being pressured to adopt the zeitgeist of cultural nationalism and anti-establishment rhetoric. "There were a lot of people who couldn't quite understand what I was doing," Soto recalls. "They'd say, 'Hey, man, how come you're not talking about things that are political?' I was really groping at the time, and if I had gotten lost in that, I don't think I would have recovered." Instinctively, he knew that the more personal he was in his work, concentrating solely on his individual experiences, the more universality he could attain.

If anything, Soto turned more and more inward as the years went by. He published three books of essays—narrative recollections," he called them—in the eighties: *Living Up the Street, Small Faces,* and *Lesser Evils.* Writing prose, he discovered a new freedom. "I felt I could be louder, more direct, also sloppier, whereas with poetry, I believed you had to control your statement, not be so obvious." The prose collections, which were almost strictly autobiographical, also presented something else that was different: a more mature, ironic, and humorous view of his childhood, finding celebrations of joy amid the hardships of growing up in the barrio.

Unexpectedly, he began receiving fan letters, one or two a week, from teenaged Mexican Americans, which convinced him to try writing for children and young adults. In 1990, he came out with *Baseball in April,* which won the Beatty Award and was recognized as the American Library Association's "Best Book for Young Adults." To date, 80,000 copies of *Baseball in April* have been sold. "I began to feel like I was doing something valuable," Soto says. "I thought I might be able to make readers and writers out of this group of kids." He has continued writing—in addition to his literary work—short stories, poems, and novels for young adults and picture books for children, and he has amassed an extraordinary audience for them, selling over half a million copies of his books. He has also produced three short films for Mexican-American kids.

Yet paradoxically, Soto can't quite shake the insecurity of being a pocho from Fresno. He follows a comfortable daily routine at his house in Berkeley, writing in the morning, tackling correspondence in the afternoon, then working out (he has a black belt in tae kwon do and is now studying aikido); in the evening, he spends time with his wife of twenty years, Carolyn, whom he met in college, and their daughter, Mariko. By all measures, Soto should feel assured about his place in the world, but he still doubts his ability to write, still fears that his latest poem will be his last good one—anxieties exemplified by a game he used to play with his wife:

"I would be working on a book of poems, and I'd say to her, 'Do you like this?' and she would nod her head. I would decide, more or less, which poems to save by how many nods she gave me. But I'd be so nervous, waiting for her reaction. I'd think, Oh my God, maybe I'm a fraud, maybe this woman's going to call the Bureau of Consumer Fraud on me. I have to keep reminding myself that after all these books over all these years, I must be doing something right."

Source: Don Lee, "About Gary Soto," in *Ploughshares*, Vol. 21, No. 1, Spring 1995, p. 188.

SOURCES

Agosto, Denise E., "Novio Boy: A Play," *School Library Journal*, Vol. 43, No. 6, June 1997, p. 146.

La Fuentes, Patricia de, "Ambiguity in the Poetry of Gary Soto," *Revista Chicano-Riqueña*, Vol. XI, No. 2, Summer 1983, pp. 34–39.

Olivares, Julian, "The Streets of Gary Soto," *Latin American Literary Review*, Vol. XVIII, No. 35, January–June 1990, pp. 32–49.

Soto, Gary, *Novio Boy*, Harcourt, 1997.

Suarez, Virgil, "Hispanic American Literature: Divergence and Commonality," U.S. Department of State Web site, http://usinfo.state.gov/journals/itsv/0200/ijse/latino1.htm (accessed September 29, 2008).

Torres, Héctor Avalos, "Gary Soto," in *Dictionary of Literary Biography*, Vol. 82, *Chicano Writers, First Series*, edited by Francisco A. Lomelí and Carl R. Shirley, Gale Research, 1989, pp. 246–52.

FURTHER READING

Chavez, Ernesto, ¡*Mi raza primero! (My People First): Nationalism, Identity, and Insurgency in the Chicano Movement in Los Angeles, 1966–1978*, University of California Press, 2002.

In a study of the development of Chicano nationalism in Los Angeles, Chavez focuses on the collaborations and conflicts between several major Chicano political organizations in Los Angeles.

Duarte, Stella Pope, *Let Their Spirits Dance: A Novel*, HarperCollins, 2002.

In *Let Their Spirits Dance*, a Mexican American mother travels from Arizona to Washington, D.C., the site of the Vietnam War memorial, in search of the spirit of her son, who died in the war.

Gutiérrez, David G., *Walls and Mirrors: Mexican Americans, Mexican Immigrants, and the Politics of Ethnicity*, University of California Press, 1995.

Gutiérrez explores the effects of Mexican immigration on the cultural and political development of the American Southwest, particularly that of California.

Ramos, Manuel, *Moony's Road to Hell*, University of New Mexico Press, 2002.

Ramos is a lawyer and a teacher of Chicano studies in Denver, Colorado. He is also known as the founder of the Chicano mystery genre. *Moony's Road to Hell* is a detective novel about illegal immigration, murder, and the U.S. Immigration and Naturalization Service. The book is a noir thriller that incorporates social commentary.

The Post Office

RABINDRANATH TAGORE

1913

Rabindranath Tagore, an Indian writer of all forms of literature (as well as a painter and composer), predominantly wrote in Bengali, though several of his poems and plays have been translated into English. Originally written in Bengali in 1912, *Dak Ghar* was translated into English as *The Post Office* and performed in 1913 by the Abbey Theatre Company in Dublin, Ireland, and London, England. The play was then published in English in 1914. To this day, *The Post Office* is the most renowned and beloved of Tagore's dramatic works, and it is still regularly produced in the United States and abroad. The play is about a small boy who is chronically ill. On account of his sickness, the boy is confined to his bed, and he sits by his window, watching life go by without him. Only by dying is the boy finally set free. In this manner, the play is primarily a metaphor for spiritual freedom, for death as a beginning rather than an ending. The play also presents a social commentary on class structure through the servants who surround the boy during his illness. Having remained in print for almost one hundred years, *The Post Office* is available in a 1998 paperback edition of *Rabindranath Tagore: An Anthology*.

AUTHOR BIOGRAPHY

Rabindranath Tagore was born on May 7, 1861, in Calcutta, India, which was then under British rule. His mother was named Sarada Devi, and his

Rabindranath Tagore *(Public Domain)*

father, Debendranath Tagore, was a scholar, religious reformer, philosopher, and writer. Tagore began writing at an early age, publishing poetry in various magazines and journals by the age of thirteen. By the age of sixteen he had already gained recognition for his poetry. He is the author of the first short story ever to be written in Bengali, "Bhikharini" (1877, "The Beggar Woman"). He continued to write poetry and verse plays at this time, and he also began composing Hindu devotionals. In 1879, Tagore left India to pursue his studies at the University College of London, but he did not enjoy attending school and returned home without a degree in 1880.

Tagore married Mrinalini Devi Raichaudhuri on December 9, 1883. The couple had three daughters, Madhurilata (nicknamed Bela), Renuka, and Mira; and two sons, Rathindranath and Samindranath. Two of the children did not live until adulthood; his wife died around 1902. While his family was still young, Tagore began managing some of the family estates, traveling to villages that are now part of Bangladesh. His experiences and travels over this period are reflected in *Sonar Tari* (1894), his first significant collection of poems (the collection was translated into English and published as *The Golden Boat* in

1932). The short stories he wrote at this time also portrayed village life. This period, running from the 1880s to 1910, was the most prolific of Tagore's life. He wrote not only poems and short stories but also novels, plays, and children's books. Over this time, his style evolved from romanticism to realism, and he experimented with different literary forms never before attempted in Bengali literature, assuring his place as a prominent Bengali writer.

By 1911, only a small portion of Tagore's prolific output had been translated into English. Planning his own trip to England, but being too ill to travel, Tagore instead worked on translating his Bengali works into English. He particularly worked on translating the prose poems from his 1910 collection *Gitanjali*. By early 1912, Tagore was well enough to travel to England with his completed translations. There, his work was championed by famed poets W. B. Yeats and Ezra Pound, and Yeats wrote the introduction to the 1912 English-language edition of *Gitanjali*. During the early twentieth century, the Nobel Prize was awarded for a single work of literature, and in 1913, Tagore received the prize for *Gitanjali*. He was the first Asian Nobel laureate.

Leaving England in late 1912 for a lecture tour in America, Tagore returned to London in April of 1913. There, he saw the Abbey Theatre Company's performance of *The Post Office*. Originally written in Bengali in 1912 as *Dak Ghar*, the play was translated and performed in English shortly thereafter. It was then published in English in 1914. By this time, given his receipt of the Nobel Prize and his prominent literary advocates in England and America, Tagore became an internationally renowned literary figure, traveling the world and giving lectures. In 1915, Tagore was knighted by the British government.

Aside from his writing, Tagore had progressive views on education, politics, and religion; he founded an *ashram* (a spiritual community) and associated school in 1901. In 1919, he resigned his knighthood as an act of political protest, following the Amritsar massacre, in which British troops fired on Indian protestors, killing 400 people. In 1921, he co-founded the Institute for Rural Reconstruction (later renamed Shrineketan). The school largely promoted philosophies that diverged from those of political leader Mahatma Gandhi, as Tagore did not always agree with Gandhi's ideals. During the 1930s, Tagore began protesting Hindu caste structure. Notably, his work as a composer is still very much a part of Indian culture; he is the author of the national anthem of India *and* of the national anthem of Bangladesh. His paintings, which Tagore began to work on in his later years, were exhibited throughout Europe.

Tagore's popularity abroad began to wane later in his career, especially after he renounced his knighthood and publicly criticized Britain's colonialist culture and constant warfare. Indeed, by 1920, when Tagore again traveled to England and America, he was not warmly received. Notably, his cool reception was based on political and not artistic values. For this reason, his work in English translation is still read and studied in the twenty-first century. Regardless, Tagore never again achieved the international success that he had accomplished with *Gitanjali*. His work, however, was still gaining recognition outside of Europe, and Tagore spent much of the 1920s traveling to such countries as China and Peru. By the late 1930s, World War II put an end to his travels, as did his advancing age. Tagore died at the age of eighty on August 7, 1941, in Calcutta. His remains were cremated.

PLOT SUMMARY

Act 1

The Post Office, a three-act play, begins with Madhav Dutta speaking with the Doctor about a young boy with a fever. The Doctor says the boy cannot go outside or he will get worse. The Doctor quotes scripture and proverbs that support his recommended treatment. After he leaves, Thakurda, a wanderer with whom Madhav is acquainted, comes in. Madhav tells Thakurda that his wife has wanted to adopt a son and now they have finally done so. The boy is an orphan who is distantly related to them, something of a nephew on his wife's side of the family. Madhav confides to Thakurda that he did not want to adopt a son lest the boy foolishly spend all the money Madhav has worked so hard to earn all of his life. Now, however, he loves the boy so much that he does not care. Madhav also makes Thakurda promise not to allow the boy to play outside, and not to excite him too much. Thakurda agrees and promises to come back and only play quietly with the boy indoors.

After Thakurda leaves, the sick boy, who is named Amal, speaks with his uncle and adopted father Madhav. Amal questions the Doctor's orders, but Madhav says that the Doctor knows best because he is well-read and is an educated man. Amal concedes that he has not read anything and therefore must not know anything. Madhav then tells Amal that he can sit and read his whole life and become a pundit (a learned man who shapes public opinion because of his expertise). Amal scoffs at the suggestion because he does not want to sit still, as he is being forced to do now. Instead, he wants to travel the world and see all there is to see. Madhav laughs at this, tells Amal he has to go to work, and makes the boy promise not to go outside while he is gone.

Act 2

Amal sits at the window when the Curdseller passes by, singing out his wares. Amal beckons to him, but then says he has no money. Amal does not want to buy *dai* (curds); he wants to hear about the Curdseller's village and to be taught the song that the man uses to sell his curds. He wants to learn how to sell curds when he grows up, walking around and singing. The Curdseller tells the boy that he should become a pundit instead. Amal says "I will never become a pundit." Amal talks about how he feels exhilarated when he hears the Curdseller's song. The Curdseller is touched and gives Amal some dai. He then continues on his way and Amal sings the merchant's song after he leaves.

The Watchman passes by and Amal calls him over. The Watchman tells Amal that the boy should not yell to him; he should be scared of him because he can arrest the boy and take him away. Rather than being scared by this, the thought excites Amal. The boy asks the Watchman about his gong, which is used to announce the time. From this conversation, the Watchman makes a pun about mortality, though Amal does not appear to understand it. If he does understand the joke, then his answer indicates that he wants to die in order to be "free." Amal asks the Watchman about the building across the street, which the Watchman says is the new post office. The boy is entranced by the idea of becoming a mail carrier for the *Raja* (the local monarch, or ruler), traveling the world and delivering messages. The Watchman sees the Headman (the local boss) coming their way and he leaves before getting into trouble for stopping to chat. He promises to return the next day.

As the Headman approaches, Amal talks to himself, imagining what it would be like to receive letters from the Raja. Amal cannot read, so he hopes his "Auntie" will read the letters to him. Better yet, he'll save them and read them once he's older and has learned to read himself. Amal then calls out to the Headman. The boy asks the Headman to tell the mail carriers his name and address in case the Raja sends him a letter. The Headman, who is not very nice, teases Amal about being the Raja's friend. He says to himself that Madhav and his family have gone too far, pretending to be acquainted with royalty just because Madhav has been successful in business. He wants to be sure that they get their "comeuppance" for such audacity. The Headman promises, insincerely, to speak with the Raja and have his letter delivered to Amal. In reality, he plans to speak to the Raja about Madhav's pretensions.

After the Headman goes, a girl walks by and Amal calls her over. She says her name is Shudha. She is on her way to pick flowers for her father, who sells the garlands she makes from them. Amal wishes he could go with her and says he would pick the best and hardest to reach flowers for her. Shudha says she would love to sit all day like Amal, but she must go before all the best flowers have been picked. Amal makes Shudha promise to return, and he asks her to bring him a flower, promising to pay her once he is grown up and has money of his own. Shudha agrees, swearing not to forget, and saying, "You will be remembered."

Next, a group of Village Boys wanders by. Amal asks where they are going and what they are going to play. The boys invite him to come along, but Amal tells them he is not allowed outside because he is ill. Instead, he says he will give the boys all of his toys as long as they promise to come and play outside of his window every morning. He also asks them to send one of the mail carriers to see him. The boys agree and continue on their way. Although it is early in the day, Amal already feels tired, and the effects of his fever begin to show.

Act 3

Madhav says that Amal looks weak from spending all day by the window befriending most of the townspeople. Madhav says that the Doctor will no longer allow Amal to sit by the window. Amal protests because the Fakir (a mystical holy man) is coming to see him. As it turns out, the Fakir is really Thakurda in costume. Madhav lets the man in and Thakurda sits on Amal's bed. Thakurda tells the boy stories of the fantastical Parrot Island. He promises to take Amal there when he is well.

Amal asks Madhav about the Curdseller, who has stopped by and left some dai for him. Madhav says the man's niece is getting married so he will be too busy to stop by for a while. Amal replies that the Curdseller promised him that he could marry his niece. Thakurda jokes that the man probably has many nieces. Exasperated with their nonsense, Madhav leaves the room. Amal then asks Thakurda if the Raja has sent him a letter yet, and Thakurda says he heard that it has been sent. They talk about meeting with the Raja and of the art of begging. Amal declares that he will beg the Raja to be made into a mail carrier. Thakurda then asks Amal why it makes him so unhappy to stay at home. Amal replies that the thought of waiting for the Raja's letter makes it more bearable.

Madhav comes back into the room and worries that they will get into trouble because the Headman has written to the Raja. Madhav states that, according to the Headman, Amal is "saying that the Raja has established his post office only to correspond with you." Amal is worried by this, but Thakurda says the Raja cannot possibly be mad with a little boy. Amal starts to feel faint; his eyesight is beginning to fail him and it is hard for him to see. As the three sit there, the Doctor comes in to check on Amal, who says, "All my pain seems to be going away." The Doctor says that this is not a good sign. He thinks the boy has gotten too much air and sun through the window, and that he's had too many visitors.

Amal appears to fall asleep, and Madhav asks the Doctor, "This child who is not my own but whom I have loved as my own, will he be taken from me?" Before the Doctor is able to answer, he sees the Headman coming and hurries to leave before the Headman sees him. The Doctor promises to send some medicine. When the Headman enters, he calls for Amal, but Thakurda tells the man to be quiet because the child is sleeping. Amal then appears to awake and says that he was not actually asleep, that he could hear everything going on around him, and he could even hear his dead parents speaking to him.

The Headman accuses Madhav and his family of being pretentious. He ridicules them and hands Amal a blank page, saying that it is a letter from the Raja. Amal says he doesn't see any writing, but he thinks that this is because his eyes are failing him. Thakurda pretends to read the fake letter, telling Amal that it says the Raja will come to see him, along with the Royal Physician. Amal replies that he can already hear the Raja's Herald announcing the Raja's arrival. The Headman laughs, believing Amal to be delirious.

Soon, however, someone is banging on the door, and the Raja's Herald enters, announcing that the Raja will be arriving at midnight. In the meantime, he has sent his Physician ahead of him. The Physician enters and says that the room must be opened up, that the boy needs fresh air. Amal tells the Physician that he feels fine. "My illness is gone, my pain is gone. Now everything is open—I can see all the stars, shining on the far side of darkness."

Madhav whispers to Amal that when the Raja comes, he should be sure to ask him for something for the family, indicating that he would like money or favors from the Raja. Amal says that he will ask to be made a mail carrier. Madhav groans. The Herald tells the family to prepare a meal for the Raja when he arrives, but then the Physician says there is "no need," and he tells everyone to be "calm." He says that Amal's "sleep is coming. I will sit beside his pillow as he drifts off. Blow out the lamp; let the starlight come in; his sleep has arrived." Oblivious, Madhav asks Thakurda why he is "so hushed, with your palms pressed together like a statue?" Madhav says, "I feel a kind of dread....Why has the room been darkened? What use is starlight?" Thakurda responds, "Be quiet, unbeliever! Do not speak."

Shudha arrives and asks for Amal, but the Physician says "he has fallen asleep," though he really means that Amal is dead. Shudha puts the flowers she brought for Amal into his hand. She asks the Physician to whisper something in his ear; she says to the Physician, "Tell him, 'Shudha has not forgotten you.'"

CHARACTERS

Amal

Amal is the protagonist of the *The Post Office*. A young village orphan adopted by his distant aunt and uncle, Amal is new to town and is excited by all that it has to offer. He is innocent and naive and has a rich imagination. His chief desire is to see the world, which makes being confined to the house even more painful for him. Since Amal is sweet-natured, he does not complain. Instead, he makes the best of his situation by befriending several of the townspeople who pass by his window. Amal is also somewhat prophetic, or at the very least accurate, in his imaginings. For instance, when Amal asks the Curdseller about his village, the boy imagines what it must be like and the Curdseller admits that his vision of the village is exact. He even goes so far as to ask the boy whether he has been there before. Amal also accurately predicts where the Village Boys are going and what they are going to do.

Amal is well-liked by all who meet him. Madhav, a miserly and greedy man who does not want to adopt a child who will spend his money, loves Amal despite his baser inclinations. Thakurda cares for him so much that he dresses in costume and pretends to be a Fakir. All of the townspeople Amal befriends are touched by him. The Curdseller is touched by the boy's interest in his work. Shudha laughs at his stories and brings him flowers. The Watchman, who at first threatens the boy, grows to like him and promises to return the following day with the town gossip. Even the Headman, who relentlessly makes fun of Amal, says that Amal "has a good heart." It is for all of these reasons that Amal's passing is so poignant. His death is not mourned; it is not even referred to in exact terms. Through his death, Amal is finally set free from his confinement. Even as he succumbs, Amal is able to see and hear everything.

Auntie

Auntie is the unnamed wife of Madhav Dutta and is also Amal's adoptive mother. She is mentioned just a few times in the play, and only by Madhav and Amal. All that is known of her is that she wanted to adopt a son and that she likes to read. She does not actually appear or speak. It is odd that the adoptive mother of a boy who is clearly dying has no interaction with her son in the days leading up to his death.

Curdseller

The Curdseller is one of the townspeople who befriends Amal. He tells Amal of his village and teaches the boy how to sing the song he uses to sell his dai. He also gives Amal free dai on more than one occasion. He tells the boy that his questions and excitement "have shown me the joy in selling dai."

Doctor

The Doctor cares for Amal by ordering his confinement and quoting scripture. Although it is clear to modern readers that the Doctor is ignorant, the characters treat the Doctor as wise and learned, following his every order. The Doctor's nonsense is most evident when he makes the claim that "the greater the suffering, the happier the outcome." The Doctor, like many of the other townspeople, is afraid of the Headman. His fear is greater than his desire to care for his patient, and he leaves Madhav's house as soon as he sees the Headman approaching. He does not finish his examination and promises to send medicine instead. Furthermore, the Doctor does not take any responsibility for Amal's health. When it is clear the boy's illness is getting worse, the Doctor says that his orders have not been followed, though, in fact, they have been.

Madhav Dutta

Madhav Dutta is Amal's adoptive father and also Amal's foil. Where Amal is a dreamer, Madhav is the opposite, a businessman. Although Madhav did not want to adopt a child for fear that he would spend all of his hard-earned money, he has done so for the sake of his wife. Madhav has grown to love Amal so much that he no longer cares if the boy spends his money. He says, "Before, I was addicted to making money. . . . But now my reward is the knowledge that whatever I earn will be his." At the same time, Madhav is a practical businessman. He often leaves Amal alone in order to go to work, despite the fact the boy is sick and bored by his enforced confinement. Madhav's practicality is shown in several ways; he wants Amal to become a pundit and laughs at the boy's ambitions to become a traveler. He sees the tall hills that Amal wants to climb as "forbidding," and he feels they appear that way because they are not meant to be traversed. Amal, however, sees them as "the earth . . . raising up her hands . . . and calling us." Madhav wants Amal to ask the Raja for something when he arrives. While Madhav indicates that he wants money or favors from the Raja, Amal is oblivious to this, and the boy only wants to ask the Raja to make him a mail carrier.

Madhav takes everything at face value. He fears for Amal's life and asks for reassurances from the Doctor. Yet, he does not really see or acknowledge the fact that Amal is declining before his very eyes. Even as Amal dies, Madhav refuses to accept the truth of what is happening. Instead, he asks Thakurda why he is "so hushed."

Fakir

See Thakurda

Headman

The Headman is the town bully, akin to the modern version of a mob boss. Most of the townspeople are afraid of him. Both the Watchman and the Doctor head in the opposite direction as soon as they see him coming. Even Madhav begs the Headman to be kind to them. The Watchman says that the Headman's "entire job seems to be trouble-making, for everyone." This assessment proves true when the Headman takes it upon himself to report Amal's perceived insolence to the Raja. However, the Headman's plan backfires, and instead of being upset, the Raja decides to visit the boy and to send the Royal Physician to care for him. The only people who are not afraid of the Headman are Thakurda and the Royal Physician; in the last act, both indicate that the Headman should leave the house. Thakurda also defies the Headman by pretending to read the fake letter he has brought to Amal.

Raja

The Raja, like Amal's Auntie, does not appear or speak during the play; however, references to him drive much of the plot. Amal wants to work as a mail carrier for the Raja, and he also hopes to receive a letter from him someday. His hopes cause the Headman to complain to the Raja, but this only results in the monarch's plans to visit Amal. Though Amal dies and the story ends before the Raja appears, his emissaries stand beside Amal's deathbed.

Raja's Herald

The Raja's Herald enters to announce the Raja's impending visit, as well as the Royal Physician's presence.

Royal Physician

The Royal Physician is likely more talented than the town Doctor, and he immediately contradicts the Doctor's orders, demanding that the room be opened up to allow the fresh air in. He also talks to Amal about meeting the Raja. The Physician wants the Headman to leave before the Raja arrives, but he relents when the innocent boy says that the Headman is his friend. The Physician knows that Amal is dying, and he is kind to the boy, telling everyone to be "calm." He says that Amal's "sleep is coming. I will sit beside his pillow as he drifts off. Blow out the lamp; let the starlight come in." The Physician is also kind to Shudha; he tells her that Amal "has fallen asleep," and he agrees to whisper into Amal's ear at her request.

Shudha

Shudha is one of the townspeople whom Amal befriends. She picks flowers and makes them into garlands that her father then sells. Although Shudha would like to stay and talk to Amal, she must go to do her work. She likes Amal and the two children tease each other and flirt with one another. She promises to return and to bring Amal flowers even though he cannot pay her for them. Although Shudha arrives after Amal has died, she still wants to give him the flowers as she has promised. She also wants the doctor to whisper into Amal's ear that "Shudha has not forgotten you."

Thakurda

Thakurda is a wanderer who is acquainted with Madhav. At Madhav's request he promises not to excite Amal or allow him to play outside. For this reason, he dresses as a Fakir and tells the boy stories of his mystical travels while Amal lies in bed. Although he seems somewhat silly, Thakurda has more sense than Madhav. Unlike Madhav, he knows that the Raja cannot be mad at a small child's imaginings, and he knows that Amal is dying. For this reason, he sits "hushed," his "palms pressed together" as he holds a vigil for the boy. Finally, Thakurda grows impatient with Madhav's obliviousness to the situation, snapping, "Be quiet, unbeliever! Do not speak."

Village Boys

The Village Boys are a group of children who pass by Amal's window. The boys invite him to join them and, when he says that he cannot, they encourage him to disobey. Despite this, the boys are wary when Amal offers them his toys. They want to know if he will regret giving them away, if they can really keep the toys, and that no one

will punish Amal for giving them away. When Amal dispels their doubts, they agree to come and play with the toys outside of Amal's window each morning.

Watchman

The Watchman is one of the passersby whom Amal speaks with. Although the Watchman tries to frighten Amal by threatening to arrest him, Amal thinks that this would be a great adventure. The boy asks the Watchman about his gong, which is used to announce the time. From this conversation, the Watchman makes a pun about mortality, though Amal does not appear to understand it. If Amal does understand the joke, then his answer indicates that he wants to die in order to be "free." The Watchman responds by observing that he "shouldn't say such things." The Watchman also tells Amal about the post office nearby, and this sets the plot in motion.

THEMES

Death as Release

The main theme of *The Post Office* is that of death as a release, both physical and spiritual, even though the word *death* (and all of its variants) never appears in the play. However, death is constantly referenced. Madhav, particularly, talks around the subject. In the opening act, the Doctor tells Madhav that if the boy "is fated for long life, then he shall have it." When the Doctor begins to speak about the alternative, Madhav cuts him off. Even when Amal is clearly dying before everyone's eyes, the word is not uttered. Madhav refuses to understand what is happening. The Royal Physician says the boy is going to sleep. Thakurda sits in reverent silence and demands the same of Madhav. No one cries or mourns. The playwright seems to be asking: what is there to mourn if suffering has ended and freedom has been granted?

Perhaps death is never directly mentioned to underscore the theme. Death is conventionally viewed as an end to life, rather than a beginning in some unknown realm. Therefore, relying upon the term would undermine the play's message of death as freedom. For this reason, the word *sleep* becomes more appropriate, and it is indeed used throughout as a euphemism for that he feels better, that he feels no pain. At the very least, then, death can be seen as freedom from the body and its constraints. Some of Amal's final words also indicate that death is a beginning and not an ending; he says, "Now everything is open—I can see all the stars, shining on the far side of darkness."

TOPICS FOR FURTHER STUDY

- Imagine that Amal lives long enough to speak with the Raja. What would their conversation be like? Try to mimic the style of the play and write a brief dialogue depicting Amal and the Raja when they first meet.

- Study Indian society in 1913 and the early twenty-first century. Conduct a class presentation comparing and contrasting the two eras, and be sure to use visual aids.

- Critics have cited *The Post Office* as being representative of Tagore's overarching themes and subject matter. Read several of Tagore's other plays and poetry. In an essay, discuss the respective themes and subject matter of each work, and provide an analysis of whether or not you agree that *The Post Office* is representative of Tagore's other works.

- In two separate instances during the play, Amal references the tale of the "seven *champak*-flower brothers." Using the Internet and your local library, research everything you can about the tale and share your findings in a class presentation. Does the tale relate to the play in any way? Discuss why or why not.

death. To sleep is to be in a state that is not living but is certainly not death. It opens up the possibility for dreams or an alternative state of being.

Besides the wordplay that underscores this theme, there are several concrete instances in the play that address death as a form of freedom. First and foremost, when the Watchman and Amal obliquely discuss mortality, the Watchman describes time as going "onwards," and though no one no knows where it is going, everyone "will go there one day." The Watchman also says that perhaps one day "the doctor will hold your hand and take you there." When Amal says that the doctor doesn't let him go anywhere, the Watchman replies that he is referring to a "greater doctor," one "who can set you free." In other instances, as Amal is dying, he says

Class Structure

The secondary theme in *The Post Office* is that of class structure. Madhav is a member of a tenuous middle class. He has done well for himself in business, but he is not rich enough to live a life of leisure. He has enough to provide for an adopted son and for his medical care, albeit not the best care available. This is shown by the Doctor's treatments, which are derived from religious proverbs. Madhav is afraid of the Headman's power to make the Raja displeased with him and his family. He wants to ingratiate himself with the Headman; he is polite to him and asks for his mercy. Yet, when it is clear that the Raja is not displeased, Madhav wishes to take full advantage of the monarch's visit, asking Amal to beg the Raja for a gift.

Other class structures are explored via Amal's interactions with the passersby. The Curdseller, the Watchman, and Shudha are all in the midst of taking care of their daily business, and they view Amal's enforced leisure as a privilege and not a punishment. Because Amal is privileged to become a learned man, both Madhav and the Curdseller encourage him to do so. Yet, Amal sees this fate as a form of imprisonment. Thus, in an interesting inversion of class power, Amal sees freedom in the daily tasks of people passing outside his window where the townspeople only see themselves as attending to their daily drudgery.

The figure of the Headman also illustrates class structure. He is a town bully with connections to the Raja, and almost everyone—from the Watchman to the Doctor—is afraid of him. The Headman wields his power like a bully, and those who are beneath him in social status must suffer this. Yet, those who are above him in status remain unaffected, and thus the Royal Physician is free to insult him by asking him to leave Madhav's house. Thakurda, who, as a wanderer, exists outside of social rules, is also unafraid of the Headman.

STYLE

Foreshadowing

Foreshadowing, or indicating that an event is about to take place, is used throughout the play, especially in reference to Amal's impending death. As the play opens, Madhav voices his fears that Amal will not survive. When Amal interacts with the townspeople, several notice that he does not look well. Shudha says that "to look at you reminds me of the fading morning star." One particularly striking instance of foreshadowing occurs when Amal declares, "I will never become a pundit." Indeed, he will never become anything. In yet another instance, Amal unwittingly foreshadows his death by poignantly asking Shudha, "You won't forget me?" Though Amal is ostensibly asking Shudha to visit him again, on a deeper level, he is asking for her to memorialize him, which, at the play's end, she does. Amal's exchange with the Watchman about time and death and being "free" are all meant to foreshadow his coming death. In a more straightforward form of foreshadowing, as the play progresses, both the Doctor and Madhav comment that Amal's illness appears to be worsening.

Allusion

In literary terms, an allusion is an indirect reference to something outside the work in hand, adding a layer of meaning and complexity. Often, allusions refer to other literary works, works of art, or historical events. They imbue the fictional work in which they appear with a more concrete sense of reality, and they enhance the work's theme or tone by association. Allusions can be overt, simply mentioning a work or event, or they can be subtle, mentioning a character in the work or hinting at an obscure fact related to the item being alluded to. Allusions often require that the reader is already knowledgeable with the works or events that are referred to in order for them to be effective.

There are three straightforward allusions in *The Post Office*. The first is to *Ayurveda*, an ancient Hindu medicinal practice that the doctor quotes as his source for his treatments in the beginning of the play. The second allusion is to the *Ramayana*, which Amal says his Auntie is always reading. The *Ramayana* is an ancient Hindu epic that is believed to have been written by Valmiki. It is comparable culturally to Homer's epic *The Odyssey*. The third is to the "seven *champak*-flower brothers," a fairy tale that is mentioned twice in the play. Furthermore, there is also a secondary allusion to the champak-flower brothers; Amal asks Shudha to "be Parul," one of the characters in the tale.

HISTORICAL CONTEXT

Colonial India and the Movement for Independence

Though the *The Post Office* does not directly address colonial India, it was written while India was under British rule, and its form is very much influenced by this fact. Tagore was educated in England and was the first Bengali author to write in Western forms such as the short story. This sort of cross-cultural interaction is why Indian literature is inextricably linked to its colonial context.

Initially a collection of warring nation-states, India was not unified until it was under British rule, which began in the mid-1700s. The country was first governed by the British East India Company. By the mid-1800s, after being subjugated racially and economically for an entire century, Indian citizens began movements toward independence. The Sepoy Rebellion of 1857 was the first such significant demonstration. Though the rebellion was not successful, some improvements were made, including the passage of the Government of India Act of 1858, which transferred power of rule from the British East India Company to the British Crown. Indians were also given minor governmental control on a local level.

Great Britain planted cotton in India to the point where land for cultivating rice was usurped and India's food stores were endangered. Indians were also employed as cheap labor. Thus, in 1885 the Indian National Congress was formed to communicate Indian interests to Britain and to promote India's independence. During World War I, Britain increased its control of India via the Defense of India Act in 1915. Indian citizens hoped that by participating in the war, they would gain increased governmental control. This did not turn out to be the case, and the British secured even greater powers through the Rowlatt Acts in 1919. Protests led to the Amritsar massacre, in which British troops fired on Indian protestors, killing four hundred people.

COMPARE & CONTRAST

- **1913:** In India, mortality rates from disease are extremely high, and Amal very well could have succumbed to a number of infectious diseases common in India, including typhoid fever, dengue fever, or malaria.

  Today: In India, the average life span is sixty-nine years, and while the aforementioned diseases are still present, they are no longer as deadly. For instance, a vaccine for malaria has been developed.

- **1913:** India has been under British rule since the mid-1700s, but growing dissatisfaction fuels the movement for independence.

  Today: Having gained independence in 1947, India is now a federal republic.

- **1913:** Medical practice in India largely follows Ayurvedic principles. The philosophy is several thousand years old.

  Today: Ayurvedic medicine is still utilized in India, though this is often in tandem with modern or Western medicinal practices. However, roughly two-thirds of people living in rural India still rely on Ayurveda as their primary mode of treatment.

Tagore resigned his knighthood as an act of political protest following this event.

The national outrage following the massacre further fueled India's drive for independence. The country was predominantly led by Mahatma Gandhi and Jawaharlal Nehru (who fought not only for India's independence but for India as a Hindu nation). A smaller faction of Muslim Indians was led by Mohammed Ali Jinnah, and they ultimately wished to create a separate Muslim nation. The British government succeeded in delaying the move for independence by playing the two factions off of one another. Yet, under the increased costs of governing the region, the British Parliament drafted a new Indian constitution in 1935 that granted the colony greater political freedom.

While the Muslim faction supported Britain during World War II, the larger Hindu faction did not. This led the Hindu faction to demand their independence in 1942, and Britain responded by disbanding the Indian National Congress and imprisoning Gandhi and Nehru. India was on the cusp of widespread rioting, and Gandhi was released in 1944 as a means to stave off such an event. Political unrest continued until 1945, when the ruling British party was replaced by the Labour party, which was more amenable to India's demands. The party announced its intentions to grant India's independence, and on August 15, 1947, this became a reality. The country was divided into India and Pakistan, the latter conceived as a Muslim nation.

The Hindu Religion

Hinduism is integral to India's national identity, socially and culturally. Tagore was a Hindu and Hindu teachings heavily influenced his work, especially *The Post Office*. Indeed, one of the core tenets of the Hindu religion is reincarnation, the idea that one's soul lives in many physical bodies during its journey. This tenet coincides with Tagore's exploration of death in the play. The caste system (which posits that enlightened souls are born into higher castes while unenlightened souls are born in lower castes) is a rigid class system that is also a part of Hindu teachings. Tagore opposed this belief system, and this can be seen in the class structures that are explored in the play.

The third largest religion in the world, Hinduism has no clear founder or easily defined practice. Instead, it is an amalgamation of spiritual beliefs formed from 4,000 to 2,000 BCE. Hinduism is predominantly henotheistic, which

Child's arm lying in leaves (© Neil Guegan / zefa / Corbis)

means that it worships a single god who is also manifested in the form of several smaller deities. The main god, Brahma, is the creator of the universe. He is constantly creating, and one great aspect of his personality is Vishnu (or Krishna), who protects these creations. His other aspect is Shiva, a destructive being with sexual undertones. *Dharma*, which is the balance of all things, is maintained by the tenuous balance between the three deities, particularly by Vishnu. There are an infinite number of interpretations of these fundamentals.

Other fundamental beliefs include *Karma*, which influences reincarnation. All of the good or bad that a person does in one life is reflected by their status in the next life. There are also two Hindu factions: the *pravritti*, who embrace the world, and the *nivritti*, who renounce it. The former's religious goals are *Dharma*, virtue or righteousness; *artha*, material wealth; and *kama*, pleasure. The latter's goals are *moksa*, freedom from *samsara* (continued reincarnation), which can only be achieved by reaching enlightenment.

CRITICAL OVERVIEW

In the Western world, *The Post Office* is Tagore's most successful play and his second most successful work overall (after *Gitanjali*). Written in 1912 and first performed in 1913, the play was an immediate success; it was translated into English, performed internationally, and published in English, all within a few years of its original release in Bengali. In an introduction to the play in *Rabindranath Tagore: An Anthology*, Krishna Dutta and Andrew Robinson write that W. B. Yeats called the *The Post Office* a "masterpiece," and that Mahatma Gandhi wrote that he was "enraptured" by a 1917 performance of the play. Dutta and Robinson also note that "Tagore's insight into death is perhaps at its deepest" in the *The Post Office*. The play is generally considered a shining example of Tagore's work, and Dutta and Robinson state in their general introduction to *Rabindranath Tagore* that the play is the first selection in their collection because it "seems to distil the thoughts and feelings that mattered most of all to its author into a vessel of timeless and universal appeal."

Sitansu Sekhar Chakravarti, writing in *Hindu Sprituality: Postclassical and Modern*, sees the play as a religious and spiritual allegory. Through this lens, he finds that the play demonstrates that "however much social customs ... try to segregate us from our real nature, the attempts are doomed to failure." S. K. Desai, writing in *Perspectives on Indian Drama in English*, wishes to avoid allegorical interpretations in his essay. Instead, Desai observes that "structurally, *The Post Office* is amazingly simple." Nirmal Mukerji, also writing in *Perspectives on Indian Drama in English*, finds that "with *The Post Office* Tagore reaches the peak of dramatic excellence. It is rightly considered by nearly all of Tagore's critics to be his best."

CRITICISM

Leah Tieger

Tieger is a freelance writer and editor. In this essay, she explores the symbolism in The Post Office.

Although *The Post Office* is a simple play, it is deceptively so. The play is roughly twenty-five pages long, consists of three brief acts (each containing only one scene), and tells the straightforward story of a boy who is sick and then dies. Beneath this framework lies a carefully wrought meditation on death. The play's simplicity, in some ways, stems from its vagueness. Amal's exact age and illness remain a mystery, as do his aunt's name, his uncle's profession, the town in which he lives, the village from whence he came, the illness that killed his parents, and the time period in which the play takes place. This deliberate lack of detail gives the play a universal feeling and appeal, but it also heightens its symbolic import. The play's diction, or language, is also exceedingly simple. For instance, in a play about death, the word *death* (and all of its variants) never once appears. This conspicuous absence only underscore's the play's theme. Furthermore, the simple storyline heightens the symbolic effect; it lacks suspense or an intricate plot, it lacks significant historical or political context, and it presents static characters who do not experience any discernible emotional or spiritual growth. Indeed, the characters do not contain much depth beyond their allegorical purpose. What, then, can be gleaned from the play besides symbolism?

WHAT DO I READ NEXT?

- *Gitanjali* (1910) was translated into English in 1912 and earned Tagore the Nobel Prize for Literature in 1913. The book is a collection of prose poems and it is one of Tagore's most definitive works.
- The second revised edition of *Ayurvedic Healing: A Comprehensive Guide* (2000), by David Frawley, provides a good starting place for students interested in learning more about *Ayurveda*.
- While *The Post Office* is a literary meditation on death, *On Death and Dying* (1969), by Elisabeth Kubler-Ross, is a groundbreaking psychological study of how people perceive and cope with death.
- Although *Indian Fairy Tales* (2007), by Joseph Jacobs, does not contain the tale of the champak-flower bothers, it still provides insight into the fairy tales of the region, and of the type of stories that were likely to have shaped Amal's character.

The first interaction weighted with symbol occurs when Madhav and Amal discuss the nearby mountains. Amal tells Madhav that he "would so love to cross over them." The term "cross over" is often used to describe death and/or the ensuing passage of the soul to a different realm. Madhav, however, finds the mountains "forbidding." Here, Amal's spiritual nature is contrasted with Madhav's practical, and decidedly unspiritual, point of view. From a slightly different angle one could interpret this exchange in the following manner: On a subconscious level, Amal, on the cusp of death, is being called to the great beyond. Madhav, on the other hand, is healthy, and he is being instinctually warned away.

The second exchange, which is of a very similar nature, takes place between Amal and the Watchman when the two obliquely discuss mortality. The boy asks the Watchman about his gong, which is used to announce the time. From

> **IF THE RAJA IS DEATH, THEN AMAL'S DESIRE TO BE MADE INTO A MAIL CARRIER MAY BE EQUATED WITH A DESIRE TO BE REINCARNATED."**

this conversation, the Watchman makes a pun about mortality, though Amal does not appear to understand the joke. If he does, then his answer clearly indicates that he wants to die in order to be "free." Indeed, the Watchman describes time as going "onwards," and though no one no knows where it is going, everyone "will go there one day." He also says that perhaps one day "the doctor will hold your hand and take you there." When Amal replies that the doctor doesn't let him go anywhere, the Watchman says that he is referring to a "greater doctor," one "who can set you free." Here, Amal responds with enthusiasm, "When will this Great Doctor come for me? I'm so tired of staying here." The Watchman responds by observing that the boy "shouldn't say such things." In this manner, the Watchman takes on Madhav's role of being fearful of death and the afterlife, or at least filled with trepidation at the thought of it. Amal, however, continues to demonstrate his desire for the great beyond. Given this, the boy's constant yearning to be outside, to travel and to see and do everything can be viewed as his soul's yearning for the afterlife.

Another interesting aspect of this interpretation is mentioned by Nirmal Mukerji in *Perspectives on Indian Drama in English*. He states that the Raja "obviously symbolizes death," and adds that the "moment of death for the child is the moment of his union with the King." Indeed, when he dies, Amal believes he has received the letter he has been waiting for and he knows the Raja's approach is imminent. Mukerji also equates the Raja with God, therefore linking death and God. Thus, according to Mukerji, *The Post Office* "is about the yearning of the soul for the oversoul or the king symbolizing God. Death brings the fulfillment of such a yearning." Following this line of reasoning, Mukerji observes that "death is visualized as the liberator which frees man from all earthly

pain." Certainly, this statement aligns itself with most assessments of the play's meaning.

Returning again to the notion of the Raja as the symbolic representation of death, what other textual elements support or enhance this? If the Raja is death, then Amal's desire to be made into a mail carrier may be equated with a desire to be reincarnated. If the Raja is God, then perhaps Amal quite literally wishes to become one of his messengers. Indeed, Amal consistently uses the term *messenger* when referring to the Raja's mailmen. These closely related interpretations are further reinforced by Amal's conversation with the Village Boys. Amal asks the boys if they know any of the Raja's mail carriers, and when the boys reply that they do, Amal asks, "Who are they? What are their names?" The Village Boys answer, "One's called Badal, another's called Sharat, and there are others." Literally translated, *badal* is a Bengali word meaning "rain," "cloud," or "thunder." *Sharat*, or more commonly *sarat*, is the Bengali word for "autumn." Certainly, if the messengers are meant to represent seasons or natural phenomena, then this reinforces the interpretation positing that the Raja is God.

The exchange between Amal and the Village Boys—and its resulting revelation—has been commented upon by S. K. Desai in *Perspectives on Indian Drama in English*. Though Desai dismisses predominantly symbolic interpretations of *The Post Office* (such as the one offered by this essay), he nevertheless concedes that the symbolism found in the messengers' names is too explicit to ignore. Acknowledging that "the King might be God," Desai states that "nature, with her seasons, like Badal and Sarat, might be the agents through whom God sends his messages." Desai even goes so far as to posit that if the Raja can be God, then "the post office might be the whole universe." Though this latter statement is something of a stretch, it could explain the Headman's anger at Amal's perceived arrogance. If Amal really does think that the post office exists only so he can receive letters from it, then he thinks that the universe exists only so that he can receive messages from it. To the Headman, this is the ultimate effrontery; it places Amal, rather than the Headman, at the center of the universe!

Regardless of whether or not the post office can be seen as the universe, it is fair to view the Raja as death or God, and it is more than fair to view death in the play as being synonymous with freedom. This latter interpretation is reinforced at the end of *The Post Office* when Madhav says to Thakurda, "Why so hushed, with your palms pressed together like a statue? I feel a kind of dread. These do not seem like good omens." Yet, they are exactly that, which is why Thakurda responds vehemently, "Be quiet, unbeliever! Do not speak." Even Tagore acknowledged that the play was meant to communicate that death frees the soul. Mukerji quotes a letter from Tagore in which the author comments that death in the material world, in the "world of hoarded wealth and certified creeds," is that which "brings him [Amal] awakening in the world of spiritual freedom."

Source: Leah Tieger, Critical Essay on *The Post Office*, in *Drama for Students*, Gale, Cengage Learning, 2009.

Samir Dayal

In the following essay, Dayal explores Tagore's philosophical, political, and ethical vision, emphasizing the case his works made for India, his anti-nationalism notwithstanding.

If this is an era of globalization, it is also an age in which resistance to the culturally and economically disadvantageous aspects of a unipolar, Western-oriented globalization seems increasingly urgent. From an Asianist perspective, it is not histrionic or frivolous to ask the question: what is, or will be, left of Asia if globalization processes complete their homogenizing drive and in that limited sense arrive at the "end of history"? Further, the acceleration of globalization lends urgency to contemporary projects of interrogating or resisting Eurocentric constructions of Asia, particularly the works of Asians themselves who have conceptualized Asia in other ways. Looking backward, it is instructive to revisit the example of Rabindranath Tagore (1861–1941) as an early, if problematic, example of resistance to the presumed fait accompli of globalization: for Tagore proposed a different route to social justice and democratic processes to those on offer within presumptively modular forms of Western modernity.

India's first Nobel Laureate in Literature (1913), Tagore was political enough to envision an alternative modernity for India, yet his vision has been marginalized—partly because of its constitutive fragility as the embodiment of a utopic literary sensibility and partly because of the anemic (especially when compared to the muscular nationalism then ascendant) and seemingly

> **COULD HE BE AN ANTINATIONALIST AND UNIVERSAL HUMANIST, WHILE SIMULTANEOUSLY PROMOTING REGIONALISM AND INDIA'S EXCEPTIONAL DESTINY?"**

sentimental discourse of love in which it was couched. His vision and discourse were premised on a variety of exceptionalism proceeding from the idea that modernity is not everywhere homogeneous or symmetrical, but takes its form from the specific cultural or civilizational matrix in which it is engendered: there is a plurality of ways to imagine humanity's progress into the future. In Tagore's mind, an ethicopolitical principle that might be counterposed to the megalomania at the core of the Western drive for progress was love, precisely because love implied an other-directed principle for thought and action in the world. He proposed a universal humanism in a future in which "those who are gifted with the moral power of love and vision of spiritual unity ... and the sympathetic insight to place themselves in the position of others, will be the fittest to take their permanent place in the age ... lying before us, and those who are constantly developing their instinct of fight and intolerance of aliens will be eliminated."

The contemporary geopolitical situation makes Tagore's vision rather more attractive, and prescient: today's ethnonationalisms in Bosnia-Herzegovina, Rwanda, Chechnya, Darfur, India, and Iraq are, if anything, more dangerous than those to which the poet was responding. Tagore believed that India could occupy a nodal point between the West and the East in a diachronic trajectory, as well as on a synchronic scale. It could inhabit a spatiotemporal mediating node of cultural development—or, at least, that was India's destiny.

Exploring this vision, this essay highlights three crucial aspects of Tagore's philosophical, political, and ethical project. The first is his antinationalism: Tagore believed in a proper and judicious cultural pride as an alternative to chauvinistic nationalism. The second is his program of repositioning India and Asia in a global frame, to promote the idea of India having a special, mediating mission—and the related idea of pan-Asian solidarity. Tagore proposed that India could be a spiritually potent fulcrum, mediating between Western Enlightenment models of modernity and Eastern ideas of what it meant to be enlightened, and in so doing develop a modern identity into the future, relativizing modernity itself in the Indian context. The third is Tagore's desire to refashion an erotic economy of love, conceptualized not only as a culturally specific idiom but also as a universal humanist allegory of community. This erotic economy was not limited to the register of emotion but open to the ambiguities of gender—and the gendered categories of home and world, private and public. These are, of course, interconnected themes: critiquing nationalism, repositioning India, and reaffirming love as ethical allegory together constitute a program of universal humanism. It is precisely their imbrication that I develop by demonstrating how these interpenetrating elements emerge as the skein or text-ile of Tagore's major work of fiction in translation: as a vision of an alternative Asian modernity.

The first component of Tagore's project—his trenchant critique of nationalism—was consistently evident in his writings and talks presented not only in India, but also in Japan circa 1916 and China circa 1924. In Japan, for instance, Tagore's antinationalism contrasted with the fairly extreme nationalism of Japanese social thinker Yukichi Fukuzawa (1835–1901), who moved toward "a more nationalistic and chauvinistic attitude between about 1875 and 1895" and even toward an advocacy of violent resistance against Western imperialism where necessary. Tagore's cautions against nationalism in Japan would have been understood by the Japanese against the exemplum of their influential compatriot. The famous Tagore–Yone Noguchi correspondence of 1938, in which the correspondents exchanged strong opinions on Noguchi's defense of Japanese intervention in China, captures the tetchiness of Japanese responses to Tagore's critique of Japanese militaristic nationalism. Tagore repudiated Noguchi's doctrine of "Asia for Asia"; he felt that as "an instrument of political blackmail, [it] has all the virtues of the lesser Europe which I repudiate and nothing of the larger humanity that makes us one across the barriers of political labels and divisions." In response to Noguchi's pleas to soften his criticism, Tagore wrote back, "I suffer intensely

not only because the reports of Chinese suffering batter against my heart, but because I can no longer point out with pride the example of a great Japan."

Tagore unleashed an equally blistering critique of a presumptively normative or modular Western nationalism. He re-presented "the nation" of Western invention as a tyrannical creature: "This abstract being, the Nation, is ruling India," he wrote, "[an] octopus of abstractions . . . fixing its innumerable suckers even into the far-away future." In opposition to the presumption of the Western nation as the originary sign of "the modern," Tagore asserted the need for "discriminations between Westernization and modernization" and counterposed to Western modernity his "pioneering affirmation of non-Western modernities." While Tagore, writing today, would have been vulnerable to the charge of underestimating the postcolony's "national longing for form," his attempt to reorient discourses of modernity in the East anticipates contemporary (and especially postcolonial) critique in instructive ways.

The second salient element of Tagore's project was his attempt to reposition Asia and India vis-à-vis both West and East. Tagore proposed that India could legitimately and usefully offer itself as a cultural mediator between the (Asian) pre- or non-modern forms of society and (Western or Enlightenment) modernity: this would not be an entirely new dispensation but a retrieval and renewal of what remained of a long cultural pattern in Asia. It is in this utopian, reformist spirit, I suggest, that Tagore wished to transvalue what was "left of Asia" and particularly—or synecdochically—India as occupying a pivotal geopolitical and cultural position between the West and the East.

Tagore argued that India's experience of colonial domination was a clear instance of the need for rethinking the meaning of the contact between the West and the East—a contact emblematic of globality. After all, India had been trying for "about fifty centuries at least" to "live peacefully and think deeply, the India of no nations, whose one ambition has been to know this world as of soul"; it was this country into which the "Nation of the West burst in . . . driving its tentacles of machinery deep down into the soil." Tagore was an idealist, but he favored neither "the colourless vagueness of cosmopolitanism," nor "the fierce self-idolatry of nation-worship." He endorsed the Indian approach of "social regulation of differences, on the one hand, and the spiritual recognition of unity on the other."

While Tagore himself might be accused of chauvinism for thinking that India could provide an answer to the travails of encroaching modernity, he was not alone. Intellectuals and others in China and Japan were equally proud of their respective countries and about Asia as a counterweight to the West, especially the former colonial powers in the region. In this connection, one of the significant parallels is that between Tagore and Kazuo Okakura, one of Japan's most important nationalist intellectuals. They were about the same age and knew each other well, Okakura having spent a year (1901) in India in the Tagore family's house in Calcutta. As Christopher Bentley has noted, both thinkers founded experimental schools that tried to instill national traditions while cautiously discussing Western ideas. Like Tagore, the Japanese thinker "insisted on the original 'ideals' of Asian culture in order to counter the widespread view . . . that the Japanese were a nation of copyists, clever imitators who mimicked the material surface of things." They shared the notion, expressed in Okakura's 1903 *Ideals of the East,* that "Asia is one" (the opening line of Okakura's book). Okakura also concluded his exposition with this pan-Asianist line of argument—arguing that Asia was the counterpoint to the increasing fragmentation and alienation that he saw as characteristic of European civilization of the time.

At this point we might pause to reconsider Tagore's apparently contradictory argument in support of pan-Asian solidarity: For is regionalism not cut from the same cloth as nationalism? Is it not an equally divisive category? And what about the contradiction implied by Tagore's apparently exceptionalist argument that India had a special mission in a geopolitical and moral sense? Could he be an antinationalist and universal humanist, while simultaneously promoting regionalism and India's exceptional destiny?

Tagore was neither parochial nor doctrinaire in his reformist idealism. If his pan-Asianism was a strategic counter to narrow nationalism, it was also paradoxically closer to cosmopolitanism, as when he wrote to the Reverend C. F. Andrews, the clergyman-activist who was a mutual friend of Gandhi and Tagore, that "whatever we understand and enjoy in human products instantly becomes ours, wherever they might have their origin." He reaffirmed that Japan also had "the

mission of the East to fulfill. She must infuse the sap of a fuller humanity into the heart of modern civilization." Similarly, providence had conferred upon India a particular mission to present a counternarrative to the noisily promulgated myth of the West's "civilizing mission." Was it not "providential," he remarked, "that the West has come to India"? But this also conferred a burden of responsibility: "And yet someone must show the East to the West, and convince the West that the East has her contribution to make to the history of civilization." Since Asia was a diverse region, there were as many different visions of pan-Asianism as there were proponents of it— the Bushido or militaristic form in Japan, for instance, was distinct from the religiously inflected Hindu variety. In any event, pan-Asian unity did not mean that India might not claim a special role in world historical terms. For, as Tagore put it, "what India has been, the whole world is now." Tagore frequently turns to this theme in *Nationalism*.

This exemplary mission was not to be collapsed into the exoticizing clichés and Western fantasies imposed on "the Orient," in which "the East" becomes a mystical Shangri-La or the nonmaterialistic (and immaterial) other, reassuring and consolidating the Western self. Tagore would clearly have resisted this sort of sentimentalized Orientalism, even as he suggested that India could be a model for the world's cultures in an increasingly globalized future: "The whole world," he said, "is becoming one country through scientific facility. And the moment is arriving when you also must find a basis of unity which is not political. If India can offer to the world her solution, it will be a contribution to humanity."

The third salient feature of Tagore's project was his reaffirmation of *love* as an ethicopolitical category. This represented a commitment to a universal humanism that remains worthy of our attention despite the problems associated with the familiar opposition between universalism/cosmopolitanism and particularism/localism. Avoiding this dilemma altogether, Tagore reconceptualized love most powerfully in his fiction as an allegory: for if love was at the heart of the strongest and most intimate personal bonds, it had an analogous role to play in forming the ties that hold the whole of humanity together against such divisive forces as greed, selfishness, war, and nationalism. In short, love had an ethicopolitical role in the public sphere—just as it did in the private. This allegory projected a deconstruction of divisions between private and public, home and world, even West and East. The recuperation of the discourse of love carried the potential for a culturally specific role for India and simultaneously for a deconstructed-and-reconstructed Asia in a global cultural economy, beyond being merely the West's civilizational other.

Modalities of Love

Tagore's discursive recuperation of love had two modalities: the affective and the ethicopolitical. In affective terms, Tagore understood love to refer to the spontaneous feelings that bind or draw people together in an authentic human bond, higher than any other afforded in human society, and beyond the reach of ideological interpellation. The solution India was seeking, he wrote, "depends not merely upon tactfulness but upon *sympathy* and true realization of the unity of man." The category of sympathy (etymologically, "suffering with") figured prominently in the moral-lexical universe with which Tagore would have been familiar, and was expressed as *shahanubhuti* or *sahridayata*—a culturally specific version of universalized sympathy. The latter principle (*sahridayata*) required one to approach all fundamental matters from a perspective of sympathy rather than on the basis of a materialist calculus—and was subscribed to by the late-nineteenth-century Hindu social reformers Rammohun Roy and Ishwarchandra Vidyasagar. Their shared theory of sentiments, as Dipesh Chakrabarty has argued, was different from, but supplementary to, the version of sympathy developed by Adam Smith or David Hume. It was also different from "the view of Romanticism in late-eighteenth-century Europe" that "'love at first sight' is typical of true love." This other notion of sympathy was an alternative that Schlegel, Novalis, and other German Romantics, for example, had actively sought from India.

Tagore's recuperation of the discourse of love also invites comparisons with the moral-philosophical tradition in Western philosophy that emphasizes love as a sine qua non in the pursuit of social or political truth. There is a contemporary relevance in Tagore's problematizations of nationalism and repositioning of Asia on the basis of a worldview in which sympathy was a core value, rather than profit or power. Without assimilating his rejection of nationalism

to a postmodernist antinationalism *avant la lettre,* one could posit that his reemphasis on love is a resonant counternarrative against the contemporary crisis of Indian ethnonationalism. Giorgio Agamben reminds us that Pascal, Augustine, and even Heidegger insisted that we enter into truth only through charity, which is false if not done out of selfless love. Since society is a complex relationship among people, it is the quality of the relationship that should be a primary focus. Love should neither be dismissed as a romantic fancy nor subsumed under legal, political, or governmental considerations. As Agamben notes, furthermore, Heidegger argued that love (or its opposite, hatred) cannot be categorized as mere affect (*Affekte*). For Heidegger, passions (*Leidenschaften*) such as love and hatred are not transient or spontaneous: unlike the affects, they are "always already present and traverse our Being from the beginning."

Tagore sought to underscore the significance of passions in all social life. His focus on love as the most complete and desirable relationship among people is an instructive complement to the usual emphases (for example on "masculine" self-assertion, Asian scientific achievement and rationality, or technological modernity) in the social and political discourse of his time and, by extension, a bracing corrective in ours.

It was not insignificant, then, that Tagore presented the erotic relationship as an allegory for the political. He was not oblivious to the fact that his take on love was an unfashionable alternative to the upsurge of nationalist feeling against the British rule in India. In invoking this allegory he was, as Sugata Bose has noted, echoing the defiant assertion against Lord Curzon made by Surendranath Banerjee, a dissident member of "the Bengali political generation of 1905 [which] strenuously sought to 'unsettle' the 'settled fact' of Curzon's partition of Bengal" through the recuperation of the discourse of the nation as a mother, the love of whom should inspire the nationalists to resist such a dismemberment as Curzon mandated. If Tagore's conceptualizations seem old-fashioned and sentimental today, it is to some degree because they do not correspond to contemporary ideas of love as belonging to a realm of life separate from the public sphere, let alone to the psychoanalytic conceptualization of it as a response to an originary and irredeemable loss. Yet his notion of love subtends a cohesive system of thought and action that might counterbalance our own relatively privatized and depoliticized conceptualization of the sentiment. This is especially important in an age when varieties of predatory transnationalism imperil state protections for disadvantaged communities and when vitiated nationalisms are in the ascendant, threatening the fabric of community in many regions of the globe. Tagore's exhortations against the "abstract force" of the nation were not expressed only on behalf of his own country, "but as it affects the future of all humanity." In brief, his idealist recuperation of love offers a rare, culturally grounded yet universalist, humanist accent in Asian discourse on the nation.

I say "recuperation" precisely because Tagore did not invent out of whole cloth the discourse of love on which he draws. His father and grandfather were members of the Brahmo Samaj, for instance, and in the tradition of this progressive Hinduism, there was already a universalist humanist strand. There was also a preexisting language of love of the motherland that Tagore found far more attractive than the strident ideological discourse of nationalism that was emerging around him. Bankimchandra's hymn to the mother, *Bande Mataram,* was first sung publicly by Tagore himself in 1896, so from the beginning Tagore's preferred version of patriotism was couched in the rhetoric of love, rather than the received modality of aggressive nationalist self-affirmation. In the struggle against the Bengal partition, love had been effectively mobilized as a political force. When the specter of partition loomed again as India lurched toward independence (which would be achieved in 1947 under Mountbatten, six years after Tagore's death), Tagore wanted to recuperate this preexisting discourse, exhorting the nationalists not to forget that true patriotism was also founded on love. This was perhaps the clearest example of how love could be a political principle. Yet it also had other dimensions, as I will suggest below.

Not only does Tagore's work make the case for India assuming an in-between geopolitical position within the region of the East, and between East and West, so that it could function as a source for imagining an alternative modernity—or relativizing it in the Asian context. His work is also characterized by ambivalent recodings of social and political codes, not because he was a moral relativist, but because he had a strong sense of the importance of adhering to ethical principles.

Tagore delights in liminal social spaces and psychological zones, in borderline states of cultural mores where the received notions of home (internal, personal, and therefore authentic) and world (external, public, and therefore difficult to regulate) are complicated by more ambivalent ethicopolitical judgments of value. Against the passionate and often anarchic intensities of the nationalist discourse of his time, Tagore added a note of caution about the complexities and ambiguities of Right— as I show in a discussion below of one of his best-known works of fiction—because he recognized that above received moral codes reigned the imperative of universal humanism. Today, when universalisms of all kinds are often thought to be in bad odor, Tagore's work stands as a complex instance of an alternative cosmopolitanism that unabashedly promotes an ethical universal, a universal that takes love as its political principle....

Source: Samir Dayal, "Repositioning India: Tagore's Passionate Politics of Love," in *Positions: East Asia Cultures Critique*, Vol. 15, No. 1, 2007, pp. 165-208.

Edgardo Canton

In the following letter to scholar Gilbert Murray, Tagore discusses the numerous problems facing India and mankind in 1934, issues which informed such plays as The Post Office.

The letter published below, in abridged form, appeared in *Correspondence,* a journal published (in French) by the International Institute of Intellectual Co-operation. It was sent in 1934 by Rabindranath Tagore to the British classical scholar Gilbert Murray. In response to Murray's "friendly appeal" for a "closer comprehension of the problems faced by our common humanity", the great Bengali writer, who had won the Nobel Prize for Literature in 1913, set out to "deal with some details of our present problems of India and put them in relation to the larger aspect of international relationship as I view it". For Tagore, then aged seventy-three, it was an opportunity to express yet again his unshakable confidence in humanity.

"Uttarayan",

Santiniketan, Bengal.

September 16th, 1934.

My Dear Professor Murray,

... I must confess at once that I do not see any solution of the intricate evils of disharmonious relationship between nations, nor can I point

> " I MUST CONFESS AT ONCE THAT I DO NOT SEE ANY SOLUTION OF THE INTRICATE EVILS OF DISHARMONIOUS RELATIONSHIP BETWEEN NATIONS, NOR CAN I POINT OUT ANY PATH WHICH MAY LEAD US IMMEDIATELY TO THE LEVELS OF SANITY."

out any path which may lead us immediately to the levels of sanity. Like yourself, I find much that is deeply distressing in modern conditions, and I am in complete agreement with you again in believing that at no other period of history has mankind as a whole been more alive to the need of human co-operation, more conscious of the inevitable and inescapable moral links which hold together the fabric of human civilization. I cannot afford to lose my faith in this inner spirit of man, nor in the sureness of human progress which following the upward path of struggle and travail is constantly achieving, through cyclic darkness and doubt, its ever-widening ranges of fulfilment. . . .

Now that mutual intercourse has become easy, and the different peoples and nations of the world have come to know one another in various relations, one might have thought that the time had arrived to merge their differences in a common unity. But the significant thing is that the more the doors are opening and the walls are breaking down outwardly, the greater is the force which the consciousness of individual distinction is gaining within. . . .

Individuality is precious, because only through it can we realize the universal. Unfortunately there are people who take enormous pride in magnifying their speciality and proclaiming to the world that they are fixed forever on their pedestal of uniqueness. They forget that only discords are unique and therefore can claim their own separate place outside the universal world of music.

It should be the function of religion to provide us with this universal ideal of truth and maintain it in its purity. But men have often made perverse use of their religion, building with it permanent walls to ensure their own

separateness. Christianity, when it minimizes its spiritual truth, which is universal, and emphasizes its dogmatic side, which is a mere accretion of time, has the same effect of creating a mental obstruction which leads to the misunderstanding of people who are outside its pale. . . .

We have seen Europe cruelly unscrupulous in its politics and commerce, widely spreading slavery over the face of the Earth in various names and forms. And yet, in this very same Europe, protest is always alive against its own iniquities. Martyrs are never absent whose lives of sacrifice are the penance for the wrongs done by their own kindred. The individuality which is Western is not to be designated by any sect-name of a particular religion, but is distinguished by its eager attitude towards truth, in two of its aspects, scientific and humanistic. This openness of mind to truth has also its moral value and so in the West it has often been noticed that, while those who are professedly pious have sided with tyrannical power, encouraging repression of freedom, the men of intellect, the sceptics, have bravely stood for justice and the rights of man. . . .

In India we have ourselves become material-minded. We are wanting in faith and courage. Since in our country the gods are sleeping, therefore, when the Titans come, they devour all our sacrificial offerings-there is never a hint of strife. The germs of disease are everywhere; but man can resist disease only when his vital force is active and powerful.

So, too, even when the worship of the blood-thirsty and false gods of self-seeking are rampant on all sides, man can lift up his head to the skies if his spirit is awake. Both matter and spirit are active. They alone become entirely materialistic who are only half men, who cripple the native majesty of the spirit before the blind repetition of unintelligent activities; who are niggardly in knowledge and palsied in action; who are ever insulting themselves by setting up a meaningless ritual in the place of true worship . . .

BEGGARS AT THE GATE

In India, what is needed more than anything else is the broad mind which, only because it is conscious of its own vigorous individuality, is not afraid of accepting truth from all sources . . . I have come to feel that the mind which has been matured in the atmosphere of a profound knowledge of its own country, and of the perfect thoughts that have been produced in that land, is ready to accept and assimilate the cultures that come from foreign countries. He who has no wealth of his own can only beg, and those who are compelled to follow the profession of beggary at the gate of the intellectually rich may gain occasional scraps of mental food, but they are sure to lose the strength of their intellectual character and their minds are doomed to become timid in thought and in creative endeavour.

A certain number of us do not admit that our culture has any special features of value. These good people I leave out of account. But the number of those others is not few, who while admitting this value in theory, ignore it more or less in practice. Very often, the flourishing of the banner of this culture is not for the sake of the love of truth but for that of national vaingloriousness-like brandishing a musical instrument in athletic display before one's own admiring family, instead of using it to make music...

The evolving Hindu social ideal has never been present to us as a whole, so that we have only a vague conception of what the Hindu has achieved in the past, or can attempt in the future. The partial view before us at any moment appears at the time to be the most important, so we can hardly bring ourselves to the true ideal, but tend to destroy it. And there we stand fasting and telling beads, emaciated with doing penance, shrinking into a corner away from the rest of the world.

We forget that Hindu civilization was once very much alive, crossing the seas, planting colonies, giving to and taking from all the world. It had its arts, its commerce, its vast and strenuous field of work. In its history, new ideas had their opportunity. Its women also had their learning, their bravery, their place in the civic life. In every page of the Mahabharata we shall find proofs that it was no rigid, cast-iron type of civilization. The men of those days did not, like marionettes, play the same set piece over and over again. They progressed through mistakes, made discoveries through experiment, and gained truth through striving...

Man shows his mental feebleness when he loses his faith in life because it is difficult to govern, and is only willing to take the responsibility of the dead because they are content to lie still under an elaborately decorated tombstone of his own make. We must know that life carries its own weight, while the burden of the dead is heavy to bear—an intolerable burden which has been pressing upon our country for ages.

The fact stands out clearly today that the Divinity dwelling within the heart of man cannot be kept immured any longer in the darkness of particular temples. The day of the Ratha-yatra the Car Festival, has arrived when He shall come out on the highway of the world, into the thick of the joys and sorrows, the mutual commerce, of the throng of men. Each of us must set to work to build such a car as we can, to take its place in the grand procession. The material of some may be of value, of others cheap. Some may break down on the way, others last till the end. But the day has come at last when all the cars must set out.

THE GREAT AWAKENING

Your letter has been a confirmation to me of the deep faith in the ultimate truths of humanity which we both try to serve and which sustains our being. I have tried to express how religion today as it exists in its prevalent institutionalized forms both in the West and the East has failed in its function to control and guide the forces of humanity; how the growth of nationalism and wide commerce of ideas through speeded-up communication have often augmented external differences instead of bringing humanity together. Development of organizing power, mastery over Nature's resources have subserved secret passions or the openly flaunted greed of unashamed national glorification. And yet I do not feel despondent about the future, for the great fact remains that man has never stopped in his urge for self-expression, in his brave quest for knowledge; not only so, there is today all over the world in spite of selfishness and unreason a greater awareness of truth....

In India, too, there is a great awakening everywhere, mainly under the inspiration of Mahatma Gandhi's singular purity of will and conduct, which is creating a new generation of clear-minded servers of our peoples....

I feel proud that I have been born in this great Age. I know that it must take time before we can adjust our minds to a condition which is not only new, but almost exactly the opposite of the old. Let us announce to the world that the light of the morning has come, not for entrenching ourselves behind barriers, but for meeting in mutual understanding and trust on the common field of co-operation; never for nourishing a spirit of rejection, but for that glad acceptance which constantly carries in itself the giving out of the best that we have.

Yours sincerely, Rabindranath Tagore

Source: Edgardo Canton, "A Greater Awareness of Truth," in *UNESCO Courier*, Vol. 47, No. 1, January 1994, p. 44.

Satyajit Ray
In the following essay, Ray provides a brief historical context for Tagore's career.

With a wordly wisdom unusual in a poet but characteristic of the Tagores, Rabindranath set out in a practical way to improve the lot of the poor peasants of his estates. But his own gain from this intimate contact with the fundamental aspects of life and nature, and the influence of this contact on his own life and work, are beyond measure.

Living mostly in his boat and watching life through the window, a whole new world of sights and sounds and feelings opened up before him. It was a world in which the moods of people and the moods of nature were inextricably interwoven. The people found room in a succession of great short stories, and nature, in an outpouring of exquisite songs and poems. Dominant was the mood of the rains, exultant and terrible.

Rabindranath Tagore received the Nobel Prize in 1913, and a knighthood in 1915, while war was raging in Europe. Touring the United States and Japan in 1916, the poet made eloquent appeals for peace. He felt that world peace could be achieved only through intellectual co-operation between nations. He said, "The call has come to every individual in the present age to prepare himself for the dawn of a new era, when man shall discover his soul in the spiritual unity of all human beings."

While peace had been restored in Europe, in India there was unrest. The occasion was the Rowlatt Bill, designed to suppress all political movements. It dashed India's hopes of gaining the self-government that the British rulers had kept promising through the war years.

Dominating the Indian political scene at this time was Gandhi. As a protest against the Rowlatt Bill, Gandhi launched a movement of passive resistance. But the masses misinterpreted the movement and, following a rumour of Gandhi's arrest, violence broke out in many parts of the country.

In the Punjab, martial law was declared. In charge of the troops at Amritsar was Brigadier General Dyer. On the first day of the month of Vaisakh, a crowd gathered in Jallianwallabagh, as it had done every other year. It was a peaceful crowd. But Dyer was taking no chances. Machine guns rattled.

Rabindranath wrote to the Viceroy, Lord Chelmsford, and the letter was published in the newspapers. Condemning the Government for the killing at Jallianwallabagh, he concluded: "And I for my part wish to stand, shorn of all special distinctions, by the side of my countrymen who for their so-called insignificance are liable to suffer degradation not fit for human beings. And these are the reasons which have painfully compelled me to ask your Excellency to relieve me of my title of knighthood."

The next ten years of Rabindranath's life were filled with ceaseless activity. The necessity to collect funds for his university took him to all parts of the world, and the West as much as the East welcomed him with open arms.

Wherever he went, he spread the message of peace and stressed the importance of intellectual co-operation between nations. He said: "We ought to know that isolation of life and culture is not a thing of which any nation can be proud. In the human world, giving is exchanging, it is not one-sided.'

On 7 May 1941, Rabindranath was eighty years old. For the occasion, he had composed a message—his last message to the world—which concerned itself with the state of so-called modern civilization, a civilization that was being shaken to its very roots by barbaric wars of aggression:

"I had at one time believed that the springs of civilization could issue out of the heart of Europe. But today, when I am about to leave the world, that faith has deserted me. I look around and see the crumbling ruins of a proud civilization strewn like a vast heap of futility. And yet, I shall not commit the previous sin of losing faith in man. I shall await for the day when the holocaust will end and the air will be rendered clean with the spirit of service and sacrifice. Perhaps that dawn will come from this horizon, from the East, where the sun rises. On that day will unvanquished man retrench his path of conquest, surmounting all barriers, to win back his lost human heritage.'

Source: Satyajit Ray, "Potrait of a Man," in *UNESCO Courier*, May–June 1986, p. 63.

SOURCES

Central Intelligence Agency, *World Factbook*, s.v. "India," https://www.cia.gov/library/publications/the-world-factbook/geos/in.html (accessed July 16, 2008).

Chakravarti, Sitansu Sekhar, "The Spirituality of Rabindranath Tagore: 'The Religion of an Artist,'" in *Hindu Sprituality: Postclassical and Modern*, edited by K. R. Sundararajan and Bithika Mukerji, Motilal Banarsidass, 2004, pp. 268–82.

"Colonial India, Gandhi, and Eventual Independence," in *Colonial & Postcolonial Literary Dialogues*, http://www.wmich.edu/dialogues/themes/indiagandhi.html (accessed July 16, 2008).

Desai, S. K., "*The Post Office*," in *Perspectives on Indian Drama in English*, edited by M. K. Naik and S. Mokashi-Punekar, Oxford University Press, 1977, pp. 76–85.

Dutta, Krishna, and Andrew Robinson, Introduction to *Rabindranath Tagore: An Anthology*, St. Martin's Press, 1997, pp. 1–16.

Dutta, Krishna, and Andrew Robinson, Introduction to *The Post Office*, in *Rabindranath Tagore: An Anthology*, St. Martin's Press, 1997, pp. 21–23.

Fakrul, Alam, "Rabindranath Tagore," in *Dictionary of Literary Biography*, Vol. 332, *Nobel Prize Laureates in Literature, Part 4: Quasimodo-Yeats*, Thomson Gale, 2007, pp. 436–53.

Keay, John, *India: A History*, Grove Press, 2001.

Mukerji, Nirmal, "The Plays of Rabindranath Tagore," in *Perspectives on Indian Drama in English*, edited by M. K. Naik and S. Mokashi-Punekar, Oxford University Press, 1977, pp. 50–75.

Robinson, B. A., "Hinduism: A General Introduction," in *Religious Tolerance.org*, August 26, 2005, http://www.religioustolerance.org/hinduism2.htm (accessed July 15, 2008).

———, "Hinduism: The World's Third Largest Religion," in *Religious Tolerance.org*, November 11, 2005, http://www.religioustolerance.org/hinduism.htm (accessed July 15, 2008).

Tagore, Rabindranath, *The Post Office*, in *Rabindranath Tagore: An Anthology*, translated by Krishna Dutta and Andrew Robinson, St. Martin's Press, 1997, pp. 24–50.

"What is Ayurvedic Medicine?," in *National Center for Complementary and Alternative Medicine*, http://nccam.nih.gov/health/ayurveda (accessed July 16, 2008).

FURTHER READING

Bhaskarananda, Swami, *The Essentials of Hinduism: A Comprehensive Overview of the World's Oldest Religion*, 2nd ed., Viveka Press, 2002.

> Hinduism is one of the most prominent religions in India, and worldwide. This thorough introduction will give students further insight into *The Post Office*.

Chaudhuri, Amit, ed., *The Vintage Book of Modern Indian Literature*, Vintage Books, 2004.

> This collection contains Indian literature written from 1850 up to the twenty-first century. Aside from including works by Tagore, the anthology also includes selections from famed Indian writers such as Salman Rushdie and R. K. Narayan.

Luce, Edward, *In Spite of the Gods: The Strange Rise of Modern India*, Little, Brown, 2006.

> *The Post Office* was written less than thirty years before the end of colonial rule in India, and Tagore lived to see the beginning of the end of this era. Luce's book picks up where the British Empire left off, tracing the history of India's emerging independence up to the present day.

Menon, Ramesh, *The Ramayana: A Modern Retelling of the Great Indian Epic*, North Point Press, 2003.

> This modernized version of Valmiki's *Ramayana* is accessible to students. The *Ramayana* has shaped Indian literature as much as the Bible and Homer's *The Odyssey* have shaped Western literature.

Sorry, Wrong Number

LUCILLE FLETCHER

1943

Lucille Fletcher's drama *Sorry, Wrong Number* was first performed as a radio play in 1943. In the preface to the published version, Fletcher writes, "This play was originally designed as an experiment in sound and not just as a murder story." The voices on the telephone were to be the play's main focus. However, when her play was performed, the playwright realized that the drama had even more potential. The drama, in the hands of her actress, took on the quality of a character study—a look into the mind of a desperate and helpless woman. As it was performed, the drama became a thriller, which, the dramatist writes, was much more than she "had originally intended."

According to Lawrence Van Gelder, writing Fletcher's obituary for the *New York Times*, the playwright "transfixed a national audience with her radio drama." The drama was so popular, according to Van Gelder, that it was "broadcast nationally seven times from 1943 to 1948 and was ultimately translated into 15 languages." Later Fletcher adapted the radio play to a film script. Barbara Stanwyck, who portrayed the protagonist, earned an Academy Award nomination for her performance. The play also won the 1960 Edgar Allan Poe Award from the Mystery Writers of America for best radio play, was remade for cable television in 1989, and inspired an opera by Jack Beeson in 1996. *Sorry, Wrong Number* is considered by many critics to be, if not her best, at least the most popular of Fletcher's works.

AUTHOR BIOGRAPHY

Fletcher was born in Brooklyn, New York, on March 28, 1912. She later attended Vassar College and graduated with a bachelor's degree in 1933. Shortly afterward, she worked at the Columbia Broadcasting System (CBS), typing up radio plays, managing the music library, and writing publicity. She became convinced during this time that she could write radio dramas at least as good as the plays she was typing.

Fletcher is best known for the thrillers she would go on to write for radio. Her most notable play is *Sorry, Wrong Number*, which first aired in 1943. She later adapted the radio play into a screenplay, which was produced in 1948. Her 1946 drama *Hitch-Hiker* is often considered her second most popular play. *Hitch-Hiker* was adapted as a television drama. Her radio-, screen-, and teleplays attracted some of the most outstanding actors of her generation, including Orson Wells, Vincent Price, Agnes Moorehead, Ida Lupino, and Elizabeth Taylor.

Fletcher also wrote novels, beginning with *The Daughter of Jasper Clay*, published in 1958. Other novels include *Blindfold* (1960), adapted to film in 1965, starring Rock Hudson; *Presumed Dead* (1963); *The Girl in Cabin B54* (1968); *Eighty Dollars to Stamford* (1975), which was adapted to film in 1982 as *Hit and Run*; and her last novel *Mirror Image* (1988), about a young woman who follows false leads in her search for her kidnapped sister.

In 1939, Fletcher married Bernard Hermann, who composed music scores for movies, most notably *Psycho*, *Citizen Kane*, *Cape Fear*, and *Taxi Driver*. Fletcher wrote the libretto for Hermann's 1951 opera, which was based on the novel *Wuthering Heights*. The couple had two daughters before they were divorced in 1948.

Fletcher was married a second time, in 1949, to John Douglass Wallop, an author. Wallop was made famous by his 1954 novel *The Year the Yankees Lost the Pennant*, upon which the 1955 Broadway musical *Damn Yankees* was based. Fletcher was still married to Wallop when he died in 1985.

Fletcher lived much of her younger years in New York. After marrying Wollop, she moved with her husband to the Washington, D.C. area. Later, they settled in Oxford, Maryland, where she lived for thirty years. She was living in Pennsylvania when she died of a stroke on August 31, 2000.

PLOT SUMMARY

Fletcher's *Sorry, Wrong Number* begins with directions for the one and only act and scene of the play. The stage is to be divided into three sections. In the center is a large bed. This is where the main character, Mrs. Stevenson, will remain throughout the play. The other characters, who appear only briefly and play minor roles, will be seen on either side of the bed in the separated sections. Mrs. Stevenson interacts with these characters (except for the murderer) indirectly, while she is talking on the phone.

Mrs. Stevenson (whom the playwright refers to as "a querulous, self-centered neurotic,") is attempting to make a phone call. She slams the receiver down in frustration. She is trying to call her husband, who is supposed to be working late. But every time she dials the number, she receives a busy signal. After calling her husband for almost an hour, Mrs. Stevenson dials the operator. She requests that the operator try the number, hoping the operator will be able to get through. When the operator is successful, Mrs. Stevenson does not recognize the man who answers. She repeatedly asks who the man is then asks for her husband, but the man does not hear her. Instead, the man begins a conversation with a second male, who is also not Mrs. Stevenson's husband. In the course of the conversation, Mrs. Stevenson learns that the second man's name is George.

As the dialogue between the two men continues, Mrs. Stevenson learns much more. The first man tells George that their client has told him that "the coast is clear for tonight." The first man then gives George instructions about what he needs to do. The pertinent details are the time that the guard who patrols the neighborhood leaves his post to get a drink, which is at eleven in the evening. Exactly fifteen minutes later, a subway train crosses a bridge nearby, which the first man states will cover any noises the woman might make should she scream. The murder, the man says, should be done quickly and with as little blood as possible. Their client does not want the woman to "suffer long." The man then tells George to steal the woman's jewelry. He tells George exactly where the jewelry is located, then explains that this will make the act look like a robbery.

Mrs. Stevenson, who listens to the entire phone conversation, is completely distraught.

MEDIA ADAPTATIONS

- A television version of *Sorry, Wrong Number*, starring Mildred Natwick and G. Swayne Gordon and directed by Frances Buss and John Houseman, aired on a local station in New York City in 1946.

- A film version of *Sorry, Wrong Number*, with a screenplay by Fletcher, was released in 1948 by Hal Wallis Productions. Barbara Stanwyck played Mrs. Stevenson and was nominated for an Academy Award (Oscar) for her performance. Burt Lancaster played in an extended role as Mr. Stevenson. Hal Wallis produced the film. It is available on DVD from Paramount.

- In 1954, Fletcher's television adaptation of the radio play was broadcast live on the Columbia Broadcasting Service (CBS) as part of the *Climax!* series. It starred Lillian Bronson.

- In 1989, Ann Louise Bardach adapted Fletcher's play for television. Loni Anderson played the role of Mrs. Stevenson. This adaptation was directed by Tony Wharmby.

- In 1996, Jack Beeson adapted *Sorry, Wrong Number* to a forty-minute conversational chamber opera performed in one act. It is available on CD from Albany Records.

She is convinced that she must save this anonymous woman who is about to be killed. She calls the operator again and becomes frustrated when the operator tells her that it is impossible to trace the phone call Mrs. Stevenson had been mistakenly connected to. Mrs. Stevenson replies by calling the operator "stupid." The operator redials the same number that Mrs. Stevenson had previously requested, but the line is once again busy. Mrs. Stevenson tells the operator that of course the line is busy. It has been busy for over an hour. The operator must have mistakenly dialed a different number when Mrs. Stevenson overheard the conversation about the murder. She wants the operator to try to call the wrong number again. The operator does not know how to do this and Mrs. Stevenson is turned over to the chief operator.

When the chief operator comes to the phone, Mrs. Stevenson repeats her story of how she has overheard a murder plot, but she can provide no names nor can she tell the operator the number where these men can be called. Despite this, Mrs. Stevenson demands that the chief operator trace the phone call. When the chief operator discovers that Mrs. Stevenson has no official police or government title, that she is just an ordinary private citizen, she tells Mrs. Stevenson that she should call the police first. Mrs. Stevenson finally hangs up and then calls the local police station.

Sgt. Duffy is on duty when Mrs. Stevenson calls. Just before Duffy answers the phone, he has ordered a snack. He is disappointed when a delivery boy gives him the wrong type of pastry. He is about to eat the snack when Mrs. Stevenson calls. At the mention of a murder, Duffy forgets about the food and gives Mrs. Stevenson his full attention. Mrs. Stevenson provides all the details she has overheard. She knows that two men are involved and what time the murder is planned. But she only has vague hints about the location. The more Duffy questions Mrs. Stevenson, the less interested he is in her story. He starts eating his pastry while Mrs. Stevenson continues. She does not know the telephone number that the men called from. All she knows about the address of the proposed murder is that it is close to Second Avenue. Duffy reminds her how long Second Avenue is and, since she does not know what city these men were talking about, it could be taking place anywhere. Duffy also tells her that there are many murders committed in the city every day. If the police could do something to prevent them, they would. But with the scant information that Mrs. Stevenson has provided, there is nothing else that Duffy can do. He then adds: "Unless, of course, you have some reason for thinking this call is phony—and that someone may be planning to murder *you*?" Mrs. Stevenson finds this statement preposterous. Who would want to kill her? She tells Duffy that her husband is "crazy" about her. She continues by telling Duffy that her husband has hardly ever left her alone since she "took sick twelve years ago." Duffy says that since her husband is so devoted, Mrs. Stevenson has nothing to worry about, and she should just relax and let the police handle the situation. He promises to take care of things. After hanging up, Duffy returns his full attention to the food in front of him.

Mrs. Stevenson becomes even more frustrated. Her husband's business line continues to be busy, so she cannot get through to him. Then her phone starts ringing. But no one answers at the other end of the line. She calls the operator to complain again. After hanging up, the phone rings again. This time it is a Western Union operator with a telegram for her. It is from her husband. Mr. Stevenson explains in the telegram that he is sorry, but he is not coming home that night. He writes that he has been trying to call her, but her line was constantly busy. He is on his way to Boston on urgent business and will not be back until tomorrow afternoon. Mrs. Stevenson cannot believe her husband would leave her alone. He has been so attentive to her all these years. She is unable to take care of herself. She laments that this particular night she really needs him. She feels he has abandoned her.

Mrs. Stevenson is more unsettled than ever. She wants someone to be with her. She is concerned that she will go crazy if she is left alone any longer. Then she remembers an experience she had two years ago. She was in the hospital for an operation. She stayed at the Henchley Hospital. She dials the hospital's number and asks for a nurse, no one in particular. She just wants a professional to come to her house. However, the receptionist who answers the phone tells Mrs. Stevenson that their nursing staff is short of people and she has been told to send out nurses only in cases of emergency. In order to have a nurse come to Mrs. Stevenson's house, she would have to have a doctor's permission.

Mrs. Stevenson is in a deep panic. She yells at the woman on the phone and tells her about the murder plan she has overheard. She also tells the woman that she is an invalid. She is afraid she will go out of her mind if someone does not come. The woman on the phone says that it is possible that a nurse by the name of Miss Phillips might be able to come, but Miss Phillips went out for dinner at eleven o'clock. Mrs. Stevenson is caught off guard. She had no idea it was so late. She also remembers that the patrolman that the murderers had discussed goes to a local bar at eleven. When Mrs. Stevenson asks what time it is, the person at the hospital tells her it is fourteen minutes after eleven. At that moment,

Mrs. Stevenson hears a click on her telephone line, as if someone downstairs has picked up the receiver. Mrs. Stevenson tells the receptionist that she fears that someone is in her kitchen. Mrs. Stevenson hangs up the phone. She is torn between calling for help and keeping quiet, hoping that whoever it is will not come upstairs. She cannot stand it another minute, though, and calls the operator. She whispers into the receiver. When she hears another click on her line, she screams, "He's coming."

The operator calls the police, but it is too late. A shadowy figure has entered Mrs. Stevenson's bedroom. There is a struggle and a scream as the subway train goes by outside the bedroom window. Then there is a shot of Mrs. Stevenson's lifeless hand hanging over the side of the bed. The man, dressed in black, picks up the receiver and tells Duffy, whom the operator has called and is now on the other end of the line, "Sorry. Wrong number." The murderer replaces the receiver, and Duffy hangs up with a shrug.

CHARACTERS

Chief Operator

The chief operator is the manager at the phone service. She is described as being cool and professional. This operator is also efficient. She asks for details from Mrs. Stevenson. When she discovers that Mrs. Stevenson has not yet contacted the police about the telephone conversation Mrs. Stevenson overheard, she informs her that without the official sanction of the police, the telephone company cannot trace a phone call.

Delivery Boy

The delivery boy appears when Mrs. Stevenson telephones Sgt. Duffy. The delivery boy is in the background, bringing Duffy a pastry. As Mrs. Stevenson is talking to Duffy, the boy and the police officer discuss the pastry, which isn't the kind that Duffy had ordered. Later, as the phone conversation between Duffy and Mrs. Stevenson is ending, the boy reappears with the correct pastry, which makes Duffy forget all about the phone call with Mrs. Stevenson.

Sgt. Duffy

Sgt. Duffy is the police officer on duty when Mrs. Stevenson calls the local precinct to get help in preventing the murder plan she has overheard on the telephone. He is uninterested for most of the call, eating his pastry and talking to the delivery boy, and does not appear to take Mrs. Stevenson seriously. However, it is Duffy who first plants the idea in Mrs. Stevenson's head that the murder plot she overheard might be focused on her. Even as Duffy makes this statement, Mrs. Stevenson can hardly ponder such a conclusion, but with time, Duffy's insinuation takes root. Duffy is also present at the end of the story, when the operator calls the police department and puts the call through to Mrs. Stevenson's line, but it is too late. Mrs. Stevenson is dead.

George

George is the second man in the telephone conversation that Mrs. Stevenson has overheard. George is the murderer. He takes his orders from the first man, who remains anonymous. The first man gives George directions on how the murder will be acted out, giving him the best time to act and telling George how to kill his victim. George makes an appearance at the end of the play as a shadowy figure who enters Mrs. Stevenson's bedroom and wrestles with her before killing her. He delivers the last line in the play when he picks up Mrs. Stevenson's phone after he has killed her and tells Sgt. Duffy, "Sorry. Wrong number."

Fifth Operator

The fifth and last operator is described as being lethargic. Mrs. Stevenson calls this operator near the end of the play. Mrs. Stevenson is desperate. She whispers on the phone because she suspects someone is downstairs and she does not want that person to hear her. Mrs. Stevenson cries out for the operator to call the police, which she does.

First Man on the Phone

The first man on the phone remains anonymous in the conversation that Mrs. Stevenson overhears. This man states that he has been in contact with the client and that the murder should go ahead as planned. This man also tells the second man (George) the details of how the murder is to take place, including the fact that the murderer should steal the woman's jewels to make the motive of the crime look like a robbery.

First Operator

The first operator that Mrs. Stevenson talks to attempts to help Mrs. Stevenson get through to Mr. Stevenson's office. Instead, this operator incorrectly dials the wrong number or else somehow the telephone lines are crossed, and Mrs. Stevenson overhears a conversation between two men who are plotting a murder.

Fourth Operator

The fourth operator takes Mrs. Stevenson's call and responds by honoring her request to call Mr. Stevenson's business number. This time the call goes through. There is no busy signal, but no one answers. Mrs. Stevenson now knows that her husband is gone.

Hospital Receptionist

The receptionist at the hospital that Mrs. Stevenson telephones explains to Mrs. Stevenson that she is under orders not to send out any nurses to private homes unless that request has been made by a doctor. When Mrs. Stevenson more fully explains her situation, the receptionist attempts to help her, telling Mrs. Stevenson that there is one possibility. She could ask Miss Phillips, who is a nurse but has stepped out for dinner. When Miss Phillips comes back, the receptionist plans to ask her to go to Mrs. Stevenson's house; however, the receptionist's plan does not go forward. When she tells Mrs. Stevenson it is almost a quarter after eleven, Mrs. Stevenson hears someone downstairs. Mrs. Stevenson slams down the receiver on the receptionist shortly afterward to call the telephone operator to get help.

Miss Phillips

Miss Phillips is the nurse who the hospital receptionist suggests to Mrs. Stevenson as a possible candidate for coming to her house. Miss Phillips never makes an appearance in the play. She is supposedly out eating dinner. The fact that Miss Phillips left the hospital at eleven makes Mrs. Stevenson realize that the appointed hour of the planned murder is upon her.

Second Operator

After Mrs. Stevenson overhears the conversation about the murder plot, she calls the phone service and talks to a second operator. This second operator attempts to call Mr. Stevenson's office, but the line is busy. Mrs. Stevenson then requests that this operator call the misdialed previous phone number, which, of course, this operator has no knowledge of. When Mrs. Stevenson continues to insist that this operator call the wrong number that the previous operator had dialed, the operator decides to turn Mrs. Stevenson over to her manager, referred to as the Chief Operator.

Mrs. Stevenson

Mrs. Stevenson is the main character in Fletcher's play. She is a sickly woman who tends to blame those around her for her frustrations. When she speaks to other people on the phone, she uses an arrogant tone. Though the requests that she makes do not always make much sense, when others cannot, or do not, comply with her wishes, she calls them stupid. In truth, Mrs. Stevenson does not live in a practical world. It is implied that she is deficient in worldly experience. This could be caused by her dependence on her husband as well as the sheltered life she has lived, confined for several years to her bed. These aspects of her personality are displayed when she wants the police to find the men for whom she has no names and no addresses. She also wants the telephone operators to first re-dial a number she does not know and then to trace a phone call that has already ended. She also demands that a nurse come to her home, not because she is sick but because she is nervous.

Because of the selfish and arrogant tones of Mrs. Stevenson's conversations, she is not a very likeable character. She makes unreasonable demands and is very ungrateful for any attempts that are made to appease her. Though sympathy for her may arise at the end of the play when she is murdered, up until that point, audiences may have trouble empathizing with her. The one redeeming aspect of this character is that in the beginning Mrs. Stevenson believes that she is taking all these efforts to save some other anonymous woman who is about to be killed. It is not until the end of the play that she realizes that she is the victim of the murder plot she has overheard.

Mr. Elbert Stevenson

Mr. Elbert Stevenson is Mrs. Stevenson's husband. Though he never makes an appearance in this play, he is a pivotal character. It is Mr. Stevenson that Mrs. Stevenson desperately attempts to call on the phone. Mrs. Stevenson believes that her husband is devoted to her. He has taken care of her and never left her alone until this one night. Mr. Stevenson is talked about in the phone conversation that Mrs. Stevenson overhears. He is the client that the two men discuss, the person who has asked that his wife be mercifully killed. Later,

Mr. Stevenson is heard in a telegram that he sends to his wife. In it, he tells her that he will not be coming home that night. His so-called urgent business in Boston will ultimately provide him with an alibi when his wife is murdered.

Third Operator

The third operator is described as young and sweet. Mrs. Stevenson calls this operator to complain about her phone ringing. When Mrs. Stevenson answers it, there is no one on the other end of the line. The operator tells Mrs. Stevenson to hang up so she can test the line. This is not what Mrs. Stevenson wants. She asks this operator to put through the call that keeps ringing her phone. The operator explains that is impossible.

Western Union Operator

The Western Union operator calls Mrs. Stevenson and reads the telegram that her husband has sent. Through the telegram, Mrs. Stevenson learns that her husband will not be coming home that night.

THEMES

Helplessness and Arrogance

The main ingredient in Mrs. Stevenson's terror in Fletcher's play is that of helplessness. Whether the protagonist's dependence is caused by real or imagined illness, Mrs. Stevenson believes she is at the mercy of those around her. She cannot get out of bed. She cannot get through to her husband. She cannot make the telephone operators, the police officer, or the hospital receptionist understand just how helpless she is. She cannot do anything. She wants someone to come over to soothe her nerves and, later, to protect her from the man who is coming to her bedroom. Instead, everyone brushes her off in one way or the other, including Mrs. Stevenson's husband. Because of her helplessness, Mrs. Stevenson makes the perfect victim. Her only defense is her voice. Her screams are easily muffled and her only connection to the outside world is through the telephone, which can easily be disconnected.

It is interesting to note that Mrs. Stevenson's helplessness does not humble her in any way, however. To the contrary, it is coupled with an unbecoming arrogance and sense of self-righteousness. The combination of these

TOPICS FOR FURTHER STUDY

- Reread *Sorry, Wrong Number*, paying special attention to the lack of modern devices, such as cell phones. Research how telephone, telegraph, and emergency services worked in the early 1940s, and present your findings to the class in an oral report. Conclude your report by discussing how using a modern setting would affect the drama.

- When reviewers discuss Fletcher's play, they often refer to the fear of the unknown. Rent the 1948 movie adaptation of this play along with a contemporary thriller. Watch the two films and compare the effects that the written play, the movie adaptation, and the contemporary film have on you. Which is scarier? Why? Write an analytical essay about your findings.

- Take a survey of students at your school. Ask them to write their age and their greatest fear on a piece of paper and submit it to you anonymously. Then ask members of your family, people in your neighborhood, and your friends to do the same. Tally your findings and place them in a graph tracking both type of fear and age of the respondent. Before presenting this information to your class, ask them to guess the most frequently occurring fear that people stated in your research. Then share the information you have gathered. Is there a pattern based on age? Can you distinguish between fears of things known versus fears of the unknown? Ask your classmates to help you make these distinctions from the data.

- Imagine a trial in which Mr. Stevenson is accused of orchestrating the murder of his wife. Pretend you are the prosecuting attorney making your final appeal to the jury. Write and deliver your closing remarks to your class. What clues might you have discovered to prove Mr. Stevenson's guilt? How might you persuade the jury? You do not have to confine yourself to the details of the play, but make your arguments believable.

---

character flaws might have been what drove Mr. Stevenson to have his wife killed. When a person is dependent on others as Mrs. Stevenson appears to be, gratitude and humility often follow. Instead Mrs. Stevenson is rude and impatient. She is quick to find fault with the answers people give her. She carelessly insults and degrades others, often implying that she knows more about other people's jobs than they do. This arrogance leads her to initially misinterpret the clues. She does not consider her own mortality; someone else must be the intended victim.

Abandonment

An undercurrent of abandonment flows through Fletcher's drama. The first hint of this occurs in the beginning of the scene when Mrs. Stevenson cannot get through to her husband's office.

From her remarks and the resultant frustration, the audience can tell that this situation is new for Mrs. Stevenson. She cannot believe that her husband's phone line could be busy for almost an hour. Surely there must be something wrong with the phone. That is why she dials the operator and asks for help.

As the play continues, on more subtle levels, everyone Mrs. Stevenson talks to eventually abandons her in some way. No one takes her seriously. Her story about overhearing a murder plot sounds too fantastic to be true. As seen through Sgt. Duffy's eyes, Mrs. Stevenson's story lacks concrete details, therefore, there is nothing he can do to help. He cannot send out policemen to investigate based merely on Mrs. Stevenson's hunch that a murder might take place. Besides, Duffy is too hungry to dig any deeper into her story and he, too, abandons her.

Barbara Stanwyck as Leona in the 1948 film adaptation of Sorry, Wrong Number *(Paramount / The Kobal Collection)*

Also, the phone operators cannot trace the phone call without the policeman's authority. The hospital receptionist cannot send out a nurse without a doctor's orders. Mrs. Stevenson is left alone. Either no one believes her or no one cares enough to investigate further. Thus she rightfully feels abandoned.

The most significant example of abandonment, though, lies squarely on Mr. Stevenson's shoulders. Toward the end of the play, it becomes evident that not only is he leaving her, but he is planning to permanently get rid of her. His phone line is probably purposefully kept busy so he will not have to talk to her. Then he plans his alibi by sending a telegram, which would leave a paper trail, unlike a simple call home. He is leaving her for the night, he tells her through the telegram. The audience knows by then that Mr. Stevenson has no plans of seeing her again.

Technology and Isolation

For the duration of *Sorry, Wrong Number*, Mrs. Stevenson is confined to her room. Her only method of communicating with the outside world is through technology, specifically the telephone. Mrs. Stevenson's reliance on this technology, which is meant to enable communication, ironically becomes an obstacle to her ability to communicate meaningfully. She is unable to reach her husband and spends most of her time talking to various operators. The telephone also makes Mrs. Stevenson privy to a conversation she was not meant to hear—that of the very men planning her murder. When she depends on the same technology to help her address the situation, it fails. Instead, it reinforces her isolation, as she is unable to make meaningful connections to the outside world. Ultimately, her isolation is broken by the intruder who brings her life to an end. He reinforces technology's failure with his final statement: "Sorry. Wrong number."

STYLE

Radio Play

Many of the published scripts for Fletcher's play provide stage directions, but the original production of *Sorry, Wrong Number* was written for the radio. The directions for a radio play focus on sound. Footsteps, the closing of a door, the ringing of a telephone, the roar of a subway train, and, naturally, the sound of different voices are the ingredients necessary to make the radio play come alive. In a radio play, one person might play different roles by altering the pitch of their voice or creating a new accent. Sound effects professionals are employed to provide a more realistic setting and to deepen the tension in the drama. Some radio plays use background music to support the psychological states of mind of the characters. Radio plays, as opposed to stage plays performed in front of an audience, have no need for sets. Many of the visual effects of a radio play are left to the imaginations of the listeners.

Suspense Drama

Most literature, whether novel, short story, or play, includes some element of suspense. Suspense keeps the reader, or the audience, involved in the work; however, in some pieces of literature, such as Fletcher's play, suspense is the defining characteristic of the work. As a genre, suspense has been particularly popular in drama that is designed to be broadcast—in the early twenty-first century via television and film and, before their advent, via radio—most likely because it strongly involves the audience and therefore has a wide appeal.

In *Sorry, Wrong Number*, suspense is created through a variety of techniques. First, the audience, as well as the main character, becomes aware of a murder that is about to take place. The thought of murder is frightening and therefore adds tension to the play. The author also employs a time frame for when this murder is to take place. As the hour of the proposed murder draws near, the suspense increases. In the final moments, when the intruder is heard inside Mrs. Stevenson's home and she finally realizes that she is the victim, the suspense reaches a climax. Whereas throughout most of the play, the audience and Mrs. Stevenson experience suspense by trying to figure out who is about to be murdered, even as the victim is named, the suspense does not ease. As the end approaches, the audience knows that it is Mrs. Stevenson who is being threatened. They also know who has arranged the murder, but the suspense continues until Mrs. Stevenson is actually dead. Up until that very last moment, the audience might still be wondering if she will be saved. The suspense builds from beginning to end, keeping the audience guessing.

HISTORICAL CONTEXT

The United States in the 1940s

The decade of the 1940s was a turbulent time for citizens of the United States. The people and the country were still struggling to get out of the Great Depression as the decade began and then fell right into World War II. This made the first half of the decade very trying. There was the rationing of food and fuel and the constant despair for those killed in the war. There was also a fear that the United States would be attacked. Japanese Americans were forced from their homes and interred in war relocation camps because they were considered a threat. But with the second half of the decade came the end of a victorious but bloody war and a time of prosperity.

It was during the 1940s, because of World War II, that the major powers of the world rushed to create more potent weapons. Many Jewish scientists, escaping from Nazi Germany, immigrated to the United States and helped to boost U.S. efforts to develop the most powerful of weapons, the atomic bomb. This massive weapon, eventually dropped on Hiroshima and Nagasaki, Japan, forced the end of the war. Though other countries, such as the Soviet Union, would duplicate these efforts, once the power of the atomic bomb was demonstrated, people feared an atomic war would destroy the world. The weapon, therefore, became more of a threat than something of practical use in warfare.

Both the United Nations and the North American Treaty Organization (NATO) were established in the 1940s, with the hope that through these organizations the world would be able to maintain peace. The discovery of penicillin, which revolutionized medicine in fighting common disease and infections, came about in this decade. With the return of soldiers at the end of this decade, families were reunited and babies born, giving rise to what later became known as the baby boom.

COMPARE
&
CONTRAST

- **1940s:** Telephone operators play a major role in communication technology. They handle everything from connecting long distance phone calls to reporting the need for phone repairs. In the case of an emergency, they connect callers to the police.

  Today: Telephone operators no longer play a critical role in communication technology. Direct dialing, sophisticated touch-tone voice menus, and the Internet have made telephone operators almost obsolete. In the case of an emergency, individuals can reach the police department quickly and directly by dialing 911 in most parts of the United States.

- **1940s:** Suspense dramas often rely on psychological tensions such as the fear of murder.

  Today: Thriller movies frequently include not only psychological tensions typical of suspense drama but also very realistic and brutal depictions of violence.

- **1940s:** Radios are a major source of entertainment in the home. The 1940s are considered the golden age for radio.

  Today: Radio stations focus on music and news to attract audiences. Dramas are rarely presented on radio. The major source of home entertainment comes from video and computer games, television, and movies on DVD.

Women and the Workplace in the 1940s

Not unlike Mrs. Stevenson in Fletcher's play, most middle- and upper-class women in the United States before the 1940s stayed home and took care of the house and children while their husbands went to work. Although Mrs. Stevenson was confined to bed, thus disallowing her the freedom to leave the house, had she not been infirm, chances are that in the very early 1940s she would not have held a job. Women were not encouraged to take on roles outside of the house.

This all changed as the United States became involved in World War II. With thousands of men sent overseas to fight in the war, jobs in the United States were left unfilled. In an attempt to keep factories fully functioning, the U.S. government created a publicity campaign that enticed women to join the workforce. One of the ads featured Rosie the Riveter, a strong, attractive woman who conveyed the idea that women working outside the home were symbols of patriotism. The campaign was successful as over six million women signed up for and maintained jobs such as in the manufacturing of weapons and military equipment. They held other manufacturing jobs as well. When the soldiers returned and reclaimed most of the job market, women had learned new skills. They also had discovered the pleasure of working outside of the home and making their own money. This was a relatively new idea for women in the United States, one that sparked big changes for women in the business world in the coming decades.

The Golden Age of Radio

The history of radio plays begins in the 1920s. As time passed, this source of entertainment grew, spreading across the globe. This growth continued and reached its peak in the 1940s, which is often called the Golden Age of Radio. One of the greater attractions on radio was the production of plays. Some of these plays were broadcast from New York radio stations and transmitted to other radio stations all over the country. In some cases, the entire cast of a play that was being produced on Broadway took part in the radio production. In other versions, a single actor might deliver a popular monologue from a play in which he or she was staring at the time. One of the most popular dramas on radio was Orson Welles's *The War of the Worlds*, which

Barbara Stanwyck as Leona with Burt Lancaster as Henry in Sorry, Wrong Number*, 1948*
(© Photos 12 / Alamy)

was produced in 1938 and unknowingly frightened some of the audience so greatly they thought the world had actually been invaded by aliens. Other well-known dramatic playwrights were Rod Serling and Tom Stoppard.

The war changed the listening habits of radio audiences as they tuned in to hear the news, wanting to know how the war was progressing. But war-weary listeners also turned to the radio to be distracted from the war. They needed a worthwhile and entertaining escape. This is when comedies grew in popularity, as with comedians like Bud Abbott and Lou Costello, who made people laugh throughout the entire decade with their routines. Thrillers, such as Fletcher's plays, also enjoyed enthusiastic responses. Programs such as *Bell Telephone Hour, Author's Playhouse, Inner Sanctum Mysteries, Mystery Theater,* and *Murder at Midnight*

provided many of the dramas and thrillers during this decade. By the 1950s, television virtually replaced the radio as the main instrument of communication in the homes of many Americans, and the radio was slowly relegated to the sidelines.

CRITICAL OVERVIEW

In a 1947 *New York Times* article, Howard Taubman refers to Fletcher's play *Sorry, Wrong Number* as a "a melodramatic tour de force in radio terms." Taubman was writing about the play because Decca, a record producing company, had just announced that they were selling a recorded version of *Sorry, Wrong Number,* due to its immense popularity. The radio play was later adapted into a novel and a film. Taubman states that Fletcher's play "has everything a good thriller should have, all of it managed with compression and tension."

Several obituaries written when the playwright died in 2000 mention the popularity of *Sorry, Wrong Number*. An anonymous writer for London's *Economist* states that *Sorry, Wrong Number* was first produced on radio in 1943 "and, in one form or another, in some part of the world, has been running almost continuously ever since."

In an obituary for the *Washington Post*, Adam Bernstein refers to Fletcher's play as the "venerable 1940s radio suspense drama." In an anonymous obituary for the *Los Angeles Times*, the writer describes Fletcher as a "versatile writer" and stated that "her forte" was the radio thrillers that made her famous. In mentioning Fletcher's most popular work, this reporter writes that *Sorry, Wrong Number* has become "a perennial [production] of high school and community stages."

CRITICISM

Joyce Hart

Hart is an author and freelance writer. In this essay, she explores the emotional progression that Fletcher's protagonist and the audience undergo throughout Sorry, Wrong Number.

In Fletcher's radio thriller, *Sorry, Wrong Number*, the protagonist, Mrs. Stevenson, experiences an increasingly agitated state of mind. The play begins with Mrs. Stevenson mildly annoyed at a constant busy signal as she attempts to place a phone call, and ends with her in a state of complete panic. Fletcher has Mrs. Stevenson's emotions evolve subtly at first, but as the play builds toward the climax, Mrs. Stevenson's mental state quickly and dramatically deteriorates. Examining the progression of Fletcher's dramatic tension reveals the critical role of the audience in giving the events meaning.

With Mrs. Stevenson's slamming down the telephone receiver in the opening moments of this play, the audience immediately detects the protagonist's unrest. "Oh—*dear*!" Mrs. Stevenson says as an exclamation of her inability to connect with her husband's office. Then immediately afterward, she dials the operator and communicates her slight concern and frustration at not being able to reach her husband. Her

WHAT DO I READ NEXT?

- Fletcher's radio play *The Hitch-Hiker* (1946) was inspired by the author's true-life experience on a road trip with her husband. In this radio play, a man encounters a hitch-hiker who constantly reappears during the man's long trip across the country. Fletcher wrote this play for the famed actor Orson Welles. The play was later adapted to screen for an episode on the television series, *The Twilight Zone*.

- Alfred Hitchcock, the master of terror in films, also collected short stories. *Portraits of Murder: 47 Short Stories Chosen by the Master of Suspense* (2006) is an anthology of mysteries with all the plot twists and turns that Hitchcock was famous for. These short stories were collected from Hitchcock's *Mystery Magazine*.

- Stephen King is considered one of the modern masters of the thriller. His novel *Cell* (2006) has been called one of his best, or at least one of his goriest. The novel is about terrorists attacking millions of people through their cell phones, depriving them of all sense of humanity as they innocently talk to their friends.

- One of the great contemporary American playwrights is Tom Stoppard. In the book *The Plays of Tom Stoppard for Stage, Radio, TV and Film* (2002), editor Terry Hodgson provides a reader's guide to Stoppard's life works. Hodgson focuses on Stoppard's themes, a background into how Stoppard's works have been received by critics, as well as interviews with the playwright.

concern is not for her husband or for herself at this point. Rather she just thinks that something is wrong with the phone. She is put off by this inconvenience, which is just that—a slight setback in her desire to talk to her husband. She is slightly annoyed but not much else. At this point, the audience likewise has little feeling of tension. The woman's attempts to communicate

WHILE THE AUDIENCE ONCE THOUGHT MRS.
STEVENSON WAS ATTEMPTING TO SAVE ANOTHER
WOMAN'S LIFE, AND SO WERE INVESTED IN HER
CAUSE, SHE NOW SEEMS TO BE A FOOL."

with someone have been blocked, but that happens to everyone. There is very little to worry about. After all, it is just a busy signal.

The tension picks up in the next conversation. First, Mrs. Stevenson tells the operator she has been nervous all day. Since the author has described her protagonist as a neurotic woman, the audience's emotions still are not very aroused. They could dismiss Mrs. Stevenson's nervousness as a product of the woman's neurotic imagination. The tension increases shortly afterward when Mrs. Stevenson overhears the conversation about the murder plot. The emotional mood in both Mrs. Stevenson and the audience is heightened. Murder is, of course, a serious threat. Although the tension is heightened, it is still at a relatively low level. The details of this overheard conversation are vague. Neither Mrs. Stevenson nor the audience knows the men who are plotting this crime and they do not have much concrete knowledge of who the victim is. Without a name, a face, or a shared history, the woman who is the focus of this murder remains an abstraction. The audience experiences compassion, but no real or immediate fear. Mrs. Stevenson would like to help this woman by preventing the murder, but at this point there is no danger for her. Mrs. Stevenson's response to this news of a murder plot is: "Oh . . . ! How awful!" She is taken aback. The author suggests that Mrs. Stevenson is "overcome for a few seconds."

When Mrs. Stevenson calls the operator to report what she has overheard, the first thing she says is, "I—I've just been cut off." This is a strange reaction. Mrs. Stevenson's first reaction is about herself and what has happened to her. If she were concerned about the unknown woman, the logical first response would be that someone's life is threatened, not that she was inconvenienced by being cut off from a phone

conversation. It is only in her next comment that Mrs. Stevenson tells the operator about the planned murder. Mrs. Stevenson's emotions then take a new turn. She becomes haughty. She commands "imperiously" that the operator trace the previous call. Someone, she insists, must do something about this.

This new attitude of Mrs. Stevenson's grows. It is as if her fears have been quelled by an inner anger. She begins to look down on everyone she talks to. She concludes that the operator is stupid and does not know how to do her job. During this sequence of conversations, the tension that was building in the audience has been dissipated. While the audience once thought Mrs. Stevenson was attempting to save another woman's life, and so were invested in her cause, she now seems to be a fool. Mrs. Stevenson's responses to the operator's questions do not improve the situation. She does not know the number that was dialed, though she insists that the operator redial it. She does not know the names of the men she has overheard. She does not know who the woman is nor where she lives. Her story has many holes in it, but she demands that the operators solve the problem. When someone acts arrogantly, it is easy to dismiss that person's concern. The audience at this point of the play is more annoyed than fearful.

The conversation between Mrs. Stevenson and Sgt. Duffy changes the course of emotions again. The audience sees how uninvolved the police officer is in dealing with Mrs. Stevenson. Only for a few moments does he take her call seriously. Once Mrs. Stevenson tells him the few vague details, Duffy turns his full attention back to his stomach. He writes Mrs. Stevenson off completely. He has no intention of following through on her story of murder because, in his mind, it would lead nowhere. How do you find a murderer without practical clues?

When Sgt. Duffy suggests that he might send a patrol car around if Mrs. Stevenson has "some reason for thinking this call is phony—and that someone may be planning to murder *you*," Mrs. Stevenson's confidence is shaken and the dramatic tension is heightened. Her first response is one of disbelief. "*Me*? Oh—no—I hardly think so. I—I mean—why should anybody?" This question hangs in the air. It affects both Mrs. Stevenson and the audience. A shadow has been cast. Fear has been stirred again. Is this a possibility? Could the client that the men spoke about be Mr. Stevenson? The details fit. Mrs. Stevenson is all alone and extremely vulnerable. Even though Mrs. Stevenson appears to refuse the possibility, the audience might not. Or maybe Mrs. Stevenson does put the clues together, at least on a subconscious level, because she becomes much more nervous.

The telegram from Mr. Stevenson stating that he is unexpectedly going out of town and will not be home that evening, forces the audience closer to the edge of their seats. Mrs. Stevenson cannot believe that her husband would leave her alone. However, there is a rising suspicion in the audience that he would. Mrs. Stevenson seems to realize this possibility when she exclaims, "No—no—it isn't true! He couldn't do it!" With the train roaring by outside her bedroom window, the tension is closer to a full pitch. The audience, as well as Mrs. Stevenson, has been set up by the author. The subway train signals the time has come for the meeting of the murderer and his victim. There is still a slight doubt that the victim is Mrs. Stevenson, but this doubt is removed when Mrs. Stevenson hears someone downstairs. Everyone knows it is not her husband. Who else could it be?

In complete terror by the end of the play, Mrs. Stevenson makes one last call to an operator. The author suggests that Mrs. Stevenson is desperate. The protagonist is weak. All her arrogance is gone. The audience is pulled deeply into her plight. They know her and all her faults. She is completely at the mercy of the man coming up the stairs. The audience knows what is coming next, but they cannot save her. Her plight reveals their own vulnerability. The play ends and the anticipation of both the fear and the hope of saving her is extinguished as Mrs. Stevenson's still body lies across the bed.

When the fear has been fully realized and, like Mrs. Stevenson, the audience can hardly breathe, the playwright ends the story. The audience is left without satisfaction. Why did Mrs. Stevenson have to die? How could Mr. Stevenson be so cruel? American audiences, in particular, are accustomed to a resolution or explanation of events. This play catches them off-guard. What is the lesson to be learned? Where is justice? Worst of all, audiences may ask the ultimate question: could this ever happen to me?

Source: Joyce Hart, Critical Essay on *Sorry, Wrong Number*, in *Drama for Students*, Gale, Cengage Learning, 2009.

SOURCES

Balk, Alfred, *The Rise of Radio, from Marconi through the Golden Age*, McFarland, 2005.

Bernstein, Adam, "Lucille Fletcher Dies; Radio Suspense Writer," in the *Washington Post*, September 4, 2000, p. B06.

Fletcher, Lucille, Preface to *Sorry, Wrong Number*, in *Sorry, Wrong Number and The Hitch-Hiker*, Dramatists Play Service, 1980, p. 3.

———, *Sorry, Wrong Number and The Hitch-Hiker*, Dramatists Play Service, 1980.

"Lucille Fletcher," in *St. James Guide to Crime and Mystery Writers*, 4th ed., St. James Press, 1996.

"Obituaries; Lucille Fletcher; Wrote 'Sorry, Wrong Number,'" in the *Los Angeles Times*, September 5, 2000, p. 4.

"Obituary: Lucille Fletcher," in the *Economist* (London), September 16, 2000, Vol. 356, No. 8188, p. 96.

Taubman, Howard, "Records: Thriller," in the *New York Times*, December 14, 1947, p. X7.

Van Gelder, Lawrence, "Lucille Fletcher, 88, Author of 'Sorry, Wrong Number,'" in the *New York Times*, September 6, 2000, p. C24.

Watson, Wilbur, "Death by Wire," in the *New York Times*, March 21, 1948, p. BR25.

Wills, Charles A., *America in the 1940s*, Facts on File, 2005.

FURTHER READING

Craig, Carolyn Casey, *Women Pulitzer Playwrights: Biographical Profiles and Analyses of the Plays*, McFarland, 2004.

> Women playwrights not only were scarce until the late twentieth century, they were seldom awarded for their efforts. Since the beginning of the Pulitzer Prize, only eleven women have won this prize for drama. In this collection, Craig brings the reader into the world of such female dramatists as Susan Glaspell, Zoe Akins, Beth Henley, and the other women who were honored by this prize.

Crook, Tim, *Radio Drama*, Routledge, 1999.

> Crook offers practical skills needed for producing radio plays. He includes tips on how to write, to direct, and to provide sound. Included in this book is a history of radio from the early broadcasts of 1914 through the influence of Orson Welles, specifically Welles's famous radio drama *War of the Worlds* of 1938.

Hicks, Neill D., *Writing the Thriller Film: The Terror Within*, Michael Wiese Productions, 2002.

Hicks gives fellow writers tips on how to keep the audience on the edge of their seats when writing a script for movies. This book can also be used to understand the psychology behind thriller movies and why they make movie-goers feel tense.

Kaledin, Eugenia, *Daily Life in the United States, 1940–1959: Shifting Worlds*, Greenwood Press, 2000.

What was life for ordinary U.S. citizens in the 1940s and 1950s? Kaledin presents interesting facts about this historical time during World War II and after. People were going through critical changes, pulling away from the Great Depression, going into the war, and then landing in one of the greatest economic booms in the country. Some of the questions answered are: How did the role of women change? What were the popular pastimes? What was the impact of politics? How did teenagers help the war effort? From the war age to the atomic age, great changes were taking place. Kaledin provides a deep exploration into two very important decades.

Shafer, Yvonne, *American Women Playwrights, 1900–1950*, Peter Lang Publishing, 1995.

Thirty-five female playwrights and their works are explored in Shafer's book. Some who are included in this work are Edna Ferber, Lillian Hellman, Gertrude Stein, and Dorothy Parker. The author connects the playwrights' works to their lives and the time in which they lived.

The Trials of Brother Jero

WOLE SOYINKA

1960

The Trials of Brother Jero is a play by Nigerian writer Wole Soyinka. It was first produced in the dining hall at Mellanby Hall, University College, Ibadan, Nigeria, in April 1960. Notable productions were staged at the Hampstead Theatre Club in London during June 1966, and at the Mews Theatre, New York City, beginning at the end of October 1967. The play was first published in Nigeria in 1963 and by Oxford University Press in 1964. It is available from the same publisher as one of five plays in Soyinka's *Collected Plays 2.*

The Trials of Brother Jero is a light satiric comedy that takes aim at religious hypocrisy in the form of a charlatan, or fraud, named Brother Jero, who preaches to his followers on Bar Beach in Lagos, Nigeria. Jero is a master of manipulation and keeps his followers in a subservient position because he understands what they long for—money, social status, and power—and convinces them that they will soon be able to fulfill these materialistic desires. For their part, they are gullible enough to believe him. The vitality of the rogue Jero makes him a popular figure with audiences, and this rambunctious, humorous play is one of the best-known and most frequently performed of Soyinka's early works.

AUTHOR BIOGRAPHY

Nigerian playwright, poet, novelist, and essayist Wole Soyinka, whose given name was Akinwande

Wole Soyinka (AP Images)

Oluwole, was born on July 13, 1934, in Isara, Nigeria. Born into the Yoruba tribe, he was the son of Ayo and Eniola Soyinka; his father was a headmaster of a school established by the British. At the time, Nigeria was under British rule.

Soyinka attended the University of Ibadan and continued his education at the University of Leeds, England. He graduated with honors, with a bachelor of arts degree in English in 1957 and then spent over a year as a play reader at the Royal Court Theatre in London. His early plays *The Swamp Dwellers*, *The Lion and the Jewel*, and *The Invention* all received productions in London in 1958 and 1959.

Returning to Nigeria in 1960, just after Nigeria became independent, Soyinka's career as a dramatist flourished. He established a reputation for blending Yoruba influences with Western dramatic styles. He founded theater groups and produced and acted in his own plays. *The Trials of Brother Jero* was first produced at Ibadan's University College in April 1960, the same year *A Dance of the Forests* was produced. Soyinka's first novel was *The Interpreters* (1965).

During the 1960s, in addition to holding various teaching positions at universities in Nigeria, Soyinka was also a political activist, working to combat government corruption and censorship. When a civil war broke out in 1967, Soyinka was arrested and imprisoned for more than two years, spending fifteen months in solitary confinement. Several of his writings were influenced by this period of imprisonment, including the play *Madmen and Specialists* (1971); a poetry collection, *A Shuttle in the Crypt* (1972); and a novel, *Season of Anomy* (1973).

After his release in 1969, Soyinka went into exile for six years, living in Ghana, England, and the United States. His plays *Jero's Metamorphoses* (1974), *The Bacchae of Euripides* (1973)—an adaptation of Euripides' work and one of Soyinka's best-known plays—and *Death and the King's Horseman* (1975) date from this period.

Soyinka returned to Nigeria in 1975 and remained politically active. He spoke out against repression under the military government that ruled Nigeria from 1979 to 1983. During this period, Soyinka was professor of comparative literature and dramatic arts at the University of Ife; he was also a visiting professor at Yale University and the University of Ghana.

In 1984, another of his most popular plays, *A Play of Giants*, was produced, and in 1986, Soyinka was awarded the Nobel Prize for Literature, the first African writer to receive this award. In 1994, Soyinka was accused of treason by the Nigerian military government, and he once again went into exile, traveling and lecturing in Europe and the United States. He returned to Nigeria in 1998, where a new government was promising to release political prisoners and hold elections. Since his return home, Soyinka has published a collection of essays, *The Burden of Memory, The Muse of Forgiveness* (1998), and a memoir, *You Must Set Forth at Dawn* (2006).

PLOT SUMMARY

Scene 1

The Trials of Brother Jero begins with a single spotlight illuminating an otherwise dark stage. In the spotlight is the main character, Brother Jeroboam, who speaks directly to the audience. He identifies himself as a prophet, by which he means preacher. He has been a prophet for a long time, he says. His parents thought he was ideally suited to such a role because of his long, thick hair. He enjoys his work, which comes naturally to him. Then he reveals that in recent years, many preachers have taken to the local beach (Bar Beach, Lagos) to preach and attract converts, and there is aggressive competition among them for available space. The Town Council had to go to the beach to settle the disputes and allocate a territory to each preacher. Jeroboam helped a preacher he refers to as his Master gain a large portion of the beach, although he admits he was only doing so because he thought it would work to his own advantage. Jero then goes on to say that there are few worshippers coming to the beach these days. Many people prefer to stay at home and watch television.

He tells the audience that his purpose is to tell them about the events of one particular day in his life, which disturbed him. He also mentions how he was cursed by his Master. He is interrupted by the sudden appearance of his Master, Old Prophet, who reprises his original curse, accusing Jero of having driven him off his piece of land on the beach. Jeroboam, known to his followers as Brother Jero, pays no attention. He tells the audience that the old man was a fool not to realize that he, Jero, was really only out for himself. Old Prophet continues his curse, saying that Jero will be ruined by his appetite for women, and then exits. Jero admits the old man knows that his one weakness is for women, so he has decided to avoid women.

Scene 2

It is early morning in a fishing village. Chume enters on a bicycle, with his wife Amope sitting on the crossbar. The bicycle stops abruptly in front of Jero's house, and Amope is aggrieved at what she considers Chume's inconsiderateness. They squabble, with Amope complaining that the bumpy landing hurt her foot. It is clear that they are not happily married. The squabble continues as Chume unloads the bag containing their lunch. She tells him to make sure he does not spill it. Chume says he has to go because otherwise he will be late for work. Amope responds by chiding him for his lack of ambition.

Jero looks out from his window and sees Amope. He tries to escape from his house without Amope seeing him, but he is not successful. Amope confronts him, saying that he owes her money and that he promised to pay her three months ago. Jero makes an excuse and goes back into the house.

A woman trader passes by on her way to the market. She is selling smoked fish. Amope speaks to her in a surly manner and the two women exchange insults. No sale is made. Amope then catches sight of Jero escaping from his house through the window. She hurls abuse at him and also at the trader, who has now disappeared. A boy walks past her, beating on a drum, and she insults him, too. The scene ends with Amope complaining about Jero, the fish-seller, and the boy, whom she calls a beggar.

Scene 3

A short while later, Jero, at his church on the beach, speaks directly to the audience. He says that he bought a velvet cape from Amope, and he hopes people will start calling him by some impressive name because of it, such as "Velvet-hearted Jeroboam." He wants a name that will appeal to the imaginations of his congregation. He also complains about Amope, cursing her and saying that the cape was not worth what she was asking for it. He confesses that he likes to keep his followers dissatisfied with their lives, so that they will keep coming to him. For example, he refuses to give his assistant, Chume, permission to beat his wife, because he wants Chume to remain feeling helpless.

Jero watches as an attractive girl passes, and then prays that he will be able to resist temptation. Chume enters and prays with him. Jero is surprised that Chume is not at work, and Chume says he is sick. Out of Chume's hearing, Jero reveals his contempt for Chume, and is satisfied that this simple man will never try to become his equal. He is also glad that Chume has found him on the beach this early in the morning, because he likes to pretend that he sleeps on the beach, whereas in fact he sleeps in a bed in his house.

Chume asks permission to beat his wife, just once. Jero refuses and establishes his authority over Chume by reminding him that he predicted he would become Chief Messenger. Now he predicts he will become Chief Clerk. Chume continues to complain vigorously about his wife, while Jero asks God to forgive him. The congregation starts to arrive, and Jero comments about how he has cynically prophesied to two of them that they will advance their political careers. Then he tells Chume once more not to beat his wife. The congregation begins to sing a hymn, dancing and clapping with the rhythm. The Boy Drummer enters, chased by a scantily dressed woman.

They pass by several times, and Jero goes to intercept the woman, whom he recognizes as his neighbor. This leaves Chume to continue the service, which he is incompetent to do. He repeatedly asks God to forgive one penitent woman, who is having a kind of fit, as the congregation says, "Amen." The woman eventually becomes still, and Chume, encouraged by the support he is getting from the congregation, continues his prayer, asking God to provide them with more money and more status in their work.

The angry woman reappears, this time in possession of the boy's drums, while he follows her. He denies that he was abusing her father by drumming, which is why she is angry with him.

Jero returns. He clothes are torn and his face is bleeding; he has been attacked by the woman. He complains about being tormented by women, and Chume, with his own wife in mind, readily agrees. From something Chume says, Jero realizes that Chume's wife is the woman he owes money to. Hoping to free himself from her request for payment, he authorizes Chume to take her home and beat her. He also informs Chume that the Son of God has given him, Jero, a new title: the Immaculate Jero, Articulate Hero of Christ's Crusade.

Scene 4

It is later that day in front of Jero's house. Amope and Chume are quarreling again, and Chume tells his wife it is time to go home. She replies that she is not moving until she gets her money. Jero enters, hides, and observes them, as Amope taunts Chume about his humble station in life. Chume tells her to shut up, which astonishes Amope, who thinks her husband must have gone mad. Chume tries to force her to come with him, but she resists and bangs on the door of Jero's house, calling for help. Jero ignores her cries. Chume tries to force Amope on to the bicycle while she protests loudly. Neighbors gather to watch the scene. Amope dares her husband to kill her and calls on Jero again, saying that if Jero will curse Chume, she will absolve Jero of his debt. Chume questions his wife, discovering that they are outside Jero's house and that it is the preacher who owes his wife money. He had not suspected this before, but now he realizes why Jero finally agreed to allow Chume to beat Amope. It was for the preacher's own convenience. Angry, he gets on his bicycle and rides off, telling Amope to remain where she is.

Scene 5

It is nightfall at the beach. A man is practicing giving a speech, and Jero observes him. He says the man is an ambitious politician who comes to the beach to rehearse his speeches for Parliament, but he never has the courage to make them. Jero then thinks of Chume, assuming that by now he will have beaten his wife. This means that he will be confident and no longer need Jero, but at least it will have rid Jero of the woman's demands for payment.

Jero then turns his attention back to the politician and decides to recruit him as a follower. At first the man is not interested, but Jero gets his attention by saying that he had a vision in which he saw this man elevated to the position of Minister for War. He suggests that God might withdraw His favor if the man does not become a believer, and he suggests that they pray together.

While Jero is working his wiles on the politician, Chume enters, talking to himself. He is furious with Jero, now that he can see through all the preacher's lies. He wonders whether the preacher and Amope have some kind of relationship that he knows nothing of, and he soon convinces himself that they are in fact lovers. He exits.

The politician is kneeling, eyes closed, at the feet of Jero as the preacher asks God to protect him. Chume rushes in, brandishing a cutlass and accusing Jero of adultery. Jero runs away, with Chume chasing him. The politician, unaware of what has taken place, opens his eyes. Finding that Jero has vanished, he thinks that God has mysteriously spirited him away, and he bows his head in reverence.

Jero returns and speaks to the audience, saying that soon the whole town will hear from the politician about the preacher's miraculous disappearance. The politician sits down, hoping that if he has faith, Jero will reappear to him.

Jero tells the audience that he has contacted the police and arranged for Chume to be sent to a lunatic asylum for a year. He notices that the politician has fallen asleep and says that when he wakes, he, Jero, will tell him that Chume is an agent of Satan and must be put in a straitjacket. He picks up a pebble and throws it at the politician, who wakes up, sees Jero, and hails him as Master.

CHARACTERS

Amope

Amope is the shrewish wife of Chume, well practiced at adopting the role of a martyr and indulging in constant bickering. She complains about her ill-treatment at Chume's hands and taunts him for his laziness and lack of ambition, reminding him that his old school friends are now government ministers. They ride in cars, but he still gets around on a bicycle. Later she compares his job unfavorably to that of a sanitary inspector, who at least has a motorcycle. Amope supplements the meager salary Chume brings home by trading various items, and she says she works hard for whatever money she can make. She sold a velvet cape to Jero, for example, although he has yet to pay for it.

Amope does not appear to live in abject poverty, although certainly she and her husband have limited financial resources and she longs for something better. Her husband's passive acceptance of his humble role in life is a constant goad to her. She has no respect for him and loses no opportunity to ridicule him and sneer at him. Amope is an assertive, combative woman, chronically dissatisfied and frustrated. For no apparent reason, she picks a quarrel with a passing female trader, and they trade insults for a while. She also confronts Jero about the non-payment of his debt. Unlike others, she is not awed by his claim to be a man of God; she sees through him immediately. She is also determined to get her money.

When Chume, who has finally received permission from Jero to beat his wife, stands up to her, talks back, and tries to force her to go home with him, she is convinced that he has gone mad. She probably never guesses that her weak husband has been harboring such anger against her. She creates a noisy scene, daring him again and again to kill her, which she must know he will not, but it does give her the chance once more to act the martyr, and in front of others, too.

Boy Drummer

The Boy Drummer appears in scene 2, carrying a drum on each shoulder. He walks toward Amope, banging his drums, but Amope shoos him away. He appears again in scene 3, running across the stage as he is being chased by a woman. When the two characters reappear, the woman is in possession of the drums, and the Boy Drummer pleads for their return.

Chume

Chume is Amope's husband and an assistant to Brother Jero. He used to be a laborer, but now he works as chief messenger in the local government office. Chume is a simple, ineffective man who feels he does not have any power or control in his life. He is nagged and taunted by his wife for his lack of ambition, and he would dearly love to assert himself by beating her, but Jero will not give him permission to do so. Chume clings to Jero because he is weak, and the cynical Jero, who has only contempt for his assistant, gives him hope that his life may improve. Although it is highly unlikely that Chume will ever be more than a chief messenger, he is so bitterly conscious of his weakness and his lowly status that he believes Jero's prophecy that he will eventually become chief clerk, with power over others. Chume is, in fact, a fairly decent man. He does not drink, smoke, or take bribes—Amope says the only reason he does not drink is because he cannot afford it—and his emotions run deep. When he gets excited, he lapses into pidgin English. But Chume simply does not know how to deal with his wife. Nothing he does satisfies her. He eventually manages to get Jero's permission to beat Amope, and he also becomes convinced that Amope and Jero are having an affair. This makes him furious, and he goes after Jero, brandishing a cutlass. But he is no match for Jero's powers of manipulation, since the preacher arranges for Chume to be locked up in a lunatic asylum for a year. Chume therefore pays the price for being the gullible victim of the wily preacher.

Brother Jero

Brother Jero is described as a "beach divine." He is a preacher who has no bricks-and-mortar church but preaches to his followers on the beach, as many other low-status preachers do. Jero is a cynical, manipulative charlatan who appears to have no genuine religious beliefs at all. But he has long had a talent for preaching, which showed up even when he was a child. His family encouraged him to become a preacher, and he attached himself to an established divine, Old Prophet, who acted as his spiritual mentor. Jero worked hard for Old Prophet, securing him a territory on the beach where he could preach, but then he forced Old Prophet off his patch and took over the ministry himself, a move he had been planning from the beginning.

Jero has no ethical values at all, and he preys upon the weak. He is very effective at this because he has a good understanding of human psychology, especially of those who come within his orbit. He knows that people are generally unhappy with their lot in life and want more. He reels them in by prophesying that they will prosper in their careers and become important. He tells the insignificant politician, for example, that he will become a minister, and he also reports that one of his favorite prophecies is to tell people that they will live to be eighty. If they do not, they are hardly in a position to complain to him that he was wrong. Jero does not really want to empower any of his congregation. In truth, he cares nothing for them. He likes to keep them dependent on him, so it is in his interests to keep them weak and unable to help themselves. He refuses to allow Chume to beat his wife, for example, because he thinks that would give Chume a sense of fulfillment and he would no longer look to Jero for guidance. Jero likes others to think he is important, which is why he makes up all kinds of names for himself that he hopes the congregation will adopt, such as Immaculate Jero and Articulate Hero of Christ's Crusade. He likes to be distinctive, to stand out from the crowd. He has a very high opinion of himself, although he does acknowledge that he has a weakness for women.

Jero may be unscrupulous, but he is good at what he does. When Amope relentlessly comes after him for his money, he cunningly uses Chume to get the better of her. When Chume chases after Jero, believing that the preacher is having an affair with his wife, Jero soon turns the situation to his advantage, arranging for Chume to be sent to a lunatic asylum. By the end of the play, Jero has attracted into his orbit the Member of Parliament, a far more influential figure than Chume. This suggests that Jero is about to move up in the world, at least in terms of the stature of the people he is able to manipulate and control.

Despite his many faults, Jero is an amusing character. His redeeming quality is that he is fully aware of what he is doing, does not fool himself, and openly confesses his cynicism and selfish motives to the audience.

Brother Jeroboam

See Brother Jero

Member of Parliament

The Member of Parliament is an ambitious but timid politician of little political importance. He goes to the beach to rehearse the fiery speeches he plans to give in Parliament, but he is too frightened actually to deliver them. He is, at first, hostile to Jero, but Jero soon outwits him by playing on the man's ambition. He is so flattered when Jero tells him that he will become minister for war that he is then easily manipulated. Jero convinces him that fervent prayer would advance his cause with God, and the man complies without hesitation. He thinks Jero is a real prophet and man of God. Jero, of course, plans only to use him for his own ends, but all the politician can think about is his future elevation to the rank of minister for war.

Old Prophet

Old Prophet is the preacher who acted as Jero's spiritual mentor. With Jero's help, Old Prophet staked out a territory for himself on the beach. But then Jero betrayed him by driving him away from his patch. Furious, Old Prophet cursed him, declaring that women would be Jero's downfall. Jero pretends to take no notice of the curse, although in fact it worries him. He has no respect for his former tutor, referring to him as a foolish "old dodderer."

Penitent

The Penitent is a woman in Jero's congregation who has a paroxysm, a kind of emotional fit, during a religious service. She lies on the ground moaning as Chume and the congregation pray for her.

Tough Mamma

The Tough Mamma is an angry woman who chases after the Boy Drummer, accusing him of using the drum to abuse her father. She is Jero's neighbor. Offstage, she gets the drums from the boy, leaving him to follow her onstage pleading for his drums back. The woman is aggressive. When Jero tries to intervene in the dispute, she scratches his face and he ends up with his clothes torn as well. (This incident takes place offstage, and the woman's role throughout is a non-speaking one.)

Trader

The Trader is a woman who passes by Amope while Amope waits outside Jero's house. She is on her way to the market to sell fish. She and Amope exchange angry words. Amope appears to believe that the woman is trading in stolen property.

Young Girl

The Young Girl frequents the beach near the spot where Jero preaches, and he observes her. When she goes to swim, he thinks she looks dirty, but when she returns she looks much more attractive. Jero observes the same transformation in the girl every day and tries to resist his lustful thoughts about her.

THEMES

Hypocrisy and Religious Charlatanism

The play is a satirical attack on religious charlatans or frauds, like Brother Jero, who make a mockery of genuine religion. Jero appears to have no genuine faith at all. Even though he prays for and with his congregation, he does not believe a word of what he tells others. Everything he says is to secure his own position and keep his followers in a subordinate place. He intuits that what people want is not spiritual knowledge but material advancement, and this is what he promises God will deliver for them. A hypocrite is a person who preaches one thing but does another, and this is a perfect description of Jero. No doubt he speaks to his congregation about the need for honest and upright living, but he buys a cloak from Amope and it appears he has no intention of paying for it. He is little more than a crook, always alert for new ways of impressing his gullible followers and keeping them within the fold, as can be seen by his musings about acquiring some grand title for himself that would make his congregation even more malleable in his hands. Jero knows that he is a dreadful example of a preacher (or prophet, which is the term he uses). Near the beginning of the play he quotes a proverb: "There are eggs and there are eggs. Same thing with prophets." He means that not all prophets are the same; some may be good, some bad; some may be genuine, while others are fakes. Jero well knows that he is a fake, but he feels no twinge of conscience about it. Although his followers are not actually shown giving him money, they probably do, since Jero refers to them as "customers": "I always get that feeling every morning that I am a shopkeeper waiting for customers." He also refers to his religious calling as a "trade." In other words, Jero is running a business; he merely pretends to be communicating knowledge about the spiritual realm. He is a fraud, but a clever one, and the audience is amused by his antics and his plots.

Misogyny

The play presents some misogyny, or negative attitudes toward women, on the part of the male characters, and the women themselves are portrayed as either aggressive or as chronic complainers. Jero sets the tone. He worries about his

TOPICS FOR FURTHER STUDY

- Soyinka draws on stock character types in his play, such as the lovable rogue and the shrew. Research the origin of stock types in the drama of ancient Greece and Rome and the sixteenth century Italian *Commedia dell'Arte*. What were the principle stock characters? How does Soyinka make these stock types into believable human beings? Make a class presentation in which you explain your findings.

- Pick one of Jero's speeches, possibly his opening speech in scene 3; rehearse it; and deliver it in front of the class. (There is no need to learn it by heart.) Remember that Jero may be a rascal but he is an amusing one and audiences tend to like him. Try to bring out the humor in his words and attitudes.

- Imagine that Old Prophet returns to the beach and observes Jero's interaction with the Member of Parliament. Write a speech for Old Prophet in which he addresses the audience (the other characters do not hear him). In writing Old Prophet's speech, review his speeches from scene 1 and study his character. What do you think he would say after observing the chicanery of his former pupil?

- One theme of the play is that society is too materialistic. Is this a criticism that could be made of American society? In what sense? Can a person have material ambitions and still lead a life of faith? What are spiritual values? How might they contribute to a person's sense of well being? Write an essay in which you discuss these questions in terms of contemporary American society.

weakness for women and sees them as temptresses who will lead him into trouble. He refers to them, following Old Prophet, as Daughters of Discord; he disparages Amope as a "daughter of Eve" (Eve fell prey to the temptations of the serpent and then tempted Adam in the Garden of Eden); and he mentions the Biblical characters Delilah and Jezebel: "How little women have changed since Eve,

Villagers on a beach in Nigeria (© *Robert Harding Picture Library Ltd.* / *Alamy*)

since Delilah, since Jezebel." Jezebel, the wife of King Ahab in ancient Israel, led the Israelites away from God. Her name has since come to symbolize a wicked woman. Delilah was the woman who betrayed Samson, as recorded in the Book of Judges in the Old Testament.

As for Chume's attitude toward women, he wants nothing more than to beat his wife. Amope is presented as a shrew, a woman who always thinks of herself as a martyr whether she has something to complain about or not, and she certainly makes Chume feel miserable with her taunts. The angry woman who pursues the Boy Drummer and attacks Jero is another example of a negative portrayal of women. It is as if all the women are presented through the eyes of the men who fear them.

Materialism

It is not only Jero who lacks spiritual values. No one else in the play has such values either. The people in the congregation want more material goods and greater success in the world rather than any spiritual salvation. The play therefore satirizes the materialism of the culture. This is amusingly presented in the incident in which

Chume briefly takes over the service in Jero's absence. In his prayer he asks for God to give them all "money to have a happy home." He then sets out a list for the Almighty to act upon, consisting entirely of material desires:

> Those who are petty trader today, make them big contractor tomorrow. Those who dey sweep street today, give them their own big office tomorrow. If we dey walka today, give us our own bicycle tomorrow....Those who have bicycle today, they will ride their own car tomorrow.

STYLE

Satire and Farce

The play combines elements of satiric comedy and farce. Satire pokes clever fun at the failings of humanity; a satiric comedy, according to M. H. Abrams in *A Glossary of Literary Terms*, "ridicules political policies or philosophical doctrines, or else attacks the disorders of society by making ridiculous the violators of its standards of morals or manners." Through the character of Brother Jero,

COMPARE & CONTRAST

- **1960s:** The main religions in Nigeria are Islam and Christianity, while a substantial minority practice some form of indigenous religion. During the decade, tensions develop between Muslim and Christian groups.

  Today: In a trend that is shared in Africa as a whole, the two major religions, Islam and Christianity, continue to grow in Nigeria. Muslims account for 50 percent of the population, Christians constitute 40 percent, and adherents of indigenous religions account for 10 percent. Christians are concentrated in southeastern Nigeria; Muslims dominate in the north.

- **1960s:** Nigeria achieves independence from Britain in 1960. However, the new nation does not achieve political stability and, in 1966, there is a military coup, followed in 1967 by a civil war.

  Today: Nigeria has a civilian government and is enjoying the longest period of civilian rule since independence. Ethnic and religious tensions remain.

- **1960s:** Led by Soyinka and Chinua Achebe, Nigeria develops an impressive body of literature written in English.

  Today: Nigeria continues to produce writers working in English who are making an impact on world literature. Several of these writers, such as novelists Chimamanda Ngozi Adichie and Uzodinma Iweala, are now based in the United States.

Soyinka ridicules the churches of his day, although Jero himself, because of his shameless admission of his own low motives, becomes not so much a ridiculous figure as one whom the audience is likely to enjoy. This does not lessen the satirical point the dramatist wishes to convey. Farce is a form of comedy in which stock characters are put in exaggerated situations with the intention of eliciting laughter. The humor is often coarse and physical. In this play, there are farcical elements in scene 3, when the angry woman chases the Boy Drummer across the stage, and the two of them keep reappearing while the bewildered Chume takes over the religious service and the Penitent starts writhing around on the ground. Other farcical moments happen when Chume grabs Amope and tries to put her on the bicycle (scene 4), and when Chume chases Jero across the stage, brandishing a cutlass (scene 5).

Pidgin English

When Chume gets emotionally excited or involved, his speech lapses into what is called pidgin English. Pidgin English is a combination of English with a local language. In Nigeria, the languages combined with English are mainly Hausa, Yoruba, and Igbo, and several million people speak different forms of pidgin English. A good example comes in scene 5, when Chume finally realizes that Jero is a hypocrite and even thinks that the preacher is having an affair with Amope:

> O God, my life done spoil. My life done spoil finish. O God a no' get eyes for my head. Na lie. Na big lie. Na pretence 'e de pretend that wicked woman! She no' go collect nutin! She no' mean to sleep for outside house. The Prophet na 'in lover.

Jero has a contemptuous attitude to Chume's pidgin English, which he calls "animal jabber" and sees as a sign of Chume's inferiority.

HISTORICAL CONTEXT

The Emergence of West African Literature in English

West African literature in English has a comparatively short history. It can be said to have begun with the publication of Amos Tutuola's *The Palm-Wine Drinkard* in 1952, which was a telling of Yoruba folktales in an unorthodox English style.

Yorubas (© *Owen Franken / Corbis*)

Like Soyinka, Tutuola came from the Yoruba area in western Nigeria. His second book, *My Life in the Bush of Ghosts*, was published in 1954. Chinua Achebe's novel, *Things Fall Apart* (1958), achieved international recognition.

In drama, the work of the physician and playwright James Ene Henshaw marked a significant beginning. Henshaw's plays dealt with important issues in Nigerian social and political life in the 1950s and 1960s. His first play, *This Is Our Chance* (1957), was highly popular, and he wrote many more successful plays, including *Jewels of the Shrine* (1957), *Children of the Goddess* (1964), *Magic in the Blood* (1964), *Medicine for Love* (1964), and *Dinner for Promotion* (1967). In the 1960s, Soyinka emerged as the dominant figure in Nigerian drama, but other playwrights also made significant contributions to the emerging literary culture. These include John Pepper Grant, whose plays produced in the 1960s were *Song of a Goat* (1961), *The Masquerade* (1964), *The Raft* (1964), and *Ozidi* (1966); and Ola Rotimi, whose first play, *The Gods Are Not to Blame* (1968), is based on Sophocles' play *Oedipus Rex* but set in fifteenth-century Nigeria.

Christianity in Nigeria

Christianity in Nigeria dates from the 1840s when Anglicans, Methodists, the United Presbyterian Church of Scotland, and the Southern U.S. Baptists established missions there. These early Christian churches ignored African traditions and used European forms of worship and practice; therefore, Africans did not fully embrace these churches as their own. In the second decade of the twentieth century, as a result of African dissatisfaction with the European-centered mission churches, a Pentecostal movement spread through western portions of Nigeria, incorporating more indigenous African beliefs and practices. These spiritualist, Pentecostal churches flourished in western Nigeria during the 1960s, and they are the main targets of Soyinka's satire in *The Trials of Brother Jero*. These churches are known in Nigeria as *Aladura*, a Yoruba word that means "praying people." Emphasizing prayer and faith healing, and incorporating a more lively form of service in which there was hand-clapping and dancing (as in Soyinka's play), the Aladura churches quickly attracted thousands of converts. Aladura churches are sometimes known as "white garment" churches because of the way their preachers dress. The "white flowing gown" that Jero wears clearly identifies him as an Aladura preacher. The four best-known Aladura churches during this period were the Christ Apostolic Church, the Eternal Sacred Order of Cherubim and Seraphim, the Church of the Lord (Aladura), and the Celestial Church of Christ. The second of these, the Eternal Sacred Order of Cherubim and Seraphim, is actually named in the first scene of the play as one of the many churches jostling for space on the beach. Founded in Lagos, Nigeria, in 1925 as a prayer group within the Anglican church, the sect became an independent church in 1928 and soon made a name for itself by crusading against witches. It also underwent many schisms, and by the 1960s there were ten different divisions of the church.

CRITICAL OVERVIEW

The Trials of Brother Jero was produced at the Hampstead Theatre Club in London in June 1966, performed by an African company from the Transcription Centre Theatre Workshop. In his review of this production, the drama critic for the London *Times* comments that Soyinka "appears as an extremely sophisticated crafts-man working within a rich folk tradition." He describes the play as a "harsh, unforgiving comedy, but it makes its point entirely through structure and language." In terms of language, the reviewer notes the "contrast between the half-educated rhetoric and natural speech [which] perfectly conveys the power of the confidence man over the gullible victims." As for structure, "the story-telling technique...allows Jero to gossip about his methods to the audience, [which] takes the place of explicit moral comment." This production also included some insertions, perhaps by Soyinka but possibly by the director, Athol Fugard, to the speech given by the Member of Parliament, alluding to some political issues of the day in southern Africa.

The play was first produced in the United States in Cleveland, Ohio, in 1964, and then in San Francisco in 1965. It reached New York City in a production at the Mews Theatre during October and November 1967. In a review of this production for *Time* magazine, a critic describes the play as "a broad spoof of a religious humbug, a con man of prophecy who lives by mulcting his worshipers, or 'customers,' as he calls them in

moments of absent-minded lucidity." The reviewer has high praise for Harold Scott, the actor who played Brother Jero: "The title role is played with unerring finesse by Harold Scott, who is sly, playful, sanctimonious or lecherous, as the occasion demands."

Since the 1960s, the play has had many productions in Africa, the United States, and the United Kingdom, and it continues to receive attention from scholars of Soyinka's work, although it is generally considered one of his slighter plays.

CRITICISM

Bryan Aubrey

Aubrey holds a Ph.D. in English. In this essay, he examines the archetypal characters in The Trials of Brother Jero *and also discusses Soyinka's development of the title character in his later play,* Jero's Metamorphosis.

In order to accomplish his satirical goals in *The Trials of Brother Jero*, Soyinka drew on a long tradition in literature (and later in film) of the lovable rogue, the character who repeatedly cheats and schemes to his own advantage but does so with wit, verve, and often such great charm that the reader or audience cannot help but find him amusing and may even admire him, even if they cannot admire what he actually does. The lovable rogue *par excellence* is Shakespeare's Sir John Falstaff, who appears in *Henry IV, Part One*, *Henry IV, Part Two*, and *The Merry Wives of Windsor*. Shakespeare's character Autolycus, the peddler in *The Winter's Tale*, comes from the same tradition. The Artful Dodger, the boy pickpocket in Charles Dickens's *Oliver Twist* (1838), is a lovable rogue, as is Tom Sawyer in Mark Twain's *The Adventures of Tom Sawyer* (1876). Later examples include Augie March in Saul Bellow's *The Adventures of Augie March* (1953), and Alfie, in Bill Naughton's play *Alfie* (1963), which was made into the well-known movie of the same name, starring Michael Caine, in 1966. The film *Dirty Rotten Scoundrels* (1988) stars Michael Caine and Steve Martin as two lovable rogues.

Soyinka was therefore not working in a vacuum when he created one of his most popular characters to make his satirical points: the hypocrisy of the preachers who plied their trade on the Bar Beach in Lagos and the superficiality of the culture that produced their followers, who identified their life goals solely in terms of the

WHAT DO I READ NEXT?

- Soyinka's *Aké: The Years of Childhood* (1989) is a memoir of Soyinka's childhood in the village of Aké, up to the age of eleven. It has been praised by reviewers as one of the finest memoirs of childhood ever written.
- Molière's *Tartuffe*, translated into English verse by Richard Wilbur (1963) is a classic comedy, first performed in France in 1669. The play is a satire on religious hypocrisy, centering around the confidence trickster, Tartuffe.
- *West African Trickster Tales* (1995), adapted by Martin Bennett, is a collection of thirteen trickster tales, retold in a modern, Western setting. The collection will be of interest to readers of *The Trials of Brother Jero* since a number of commentators have noted similarities between Jero and the tricksters of these tales, such as Ananse the Spider and the Tortoise.
- *Elmer Gantry* (1927), a novel by Sinclair Lewis, is an entertaining satire on Protestant fundamentalist religion in the American Midwest. Elmer Gantry is a successful but corrupt and hypocritical preacher who denounces vice in others but shows little inclination to reform his own immoral behavior. The novel caused a sensation when first published and was banned in several cities. It still makes for lively reading in the early twenty-first century.

accumulation of material rewards and social position. Such naïve people, the play seems to say, in some sense warrant deception. They get the preacher their shallow minds deserve.

Brother Jero stands high in the pantheon of lovable rogues. He manipulates his followers shamelessly and appears not to have an ounce of integrity. He would no doubt regard integrity as an impediment to good business. He is a very suave operator who has his act down completely: his imposing appearance with his heavy beard,

> THE AUDIENCE GETS THE FEELING THAT CHUME, WHATEVER HE DOES, WILL NEVER GET THE SATISFACTION OF BREAKING HIS WIFE'S SPIRIT BY PHYSICAL FORCE. THIS IS ONE SHREW WHO, UNLIKE SHAKESPEARE'S KATHARINA, WILL NOT BE TAMED."

the sleek white gown with the white velvet cape that he still has not paid for, the divine rod that further marks out his authority as a man of God, and his lofty way of speaking, complete with all the usual flourishes of the silver-tongued preacher. His words beguile his congregation. Brother Jero is a master manipulator and he clearly knows it; he is much smarter, and, when he has to be, more ruthless, than not only the other preachers he outwitted in order to secure his beach territory, but also his simple followers, such as Chume, who have no idea that they are being played for fools. Poor Chume is the archetypal dupe who cannot get the better of the charlatan even when he finally realizes the truth about him. Chume is an easy victim of the man who took the measure of him a long time ago and who well knows his own superior cunning. The hold the preacher has over his assistant, and the meaninglessness of the charade he calls a religious service is shown clearly in scene 3, when Jero gets Chume to pray with him against his one weakness, which is for women. Jero calls on the names of various figures in Christian tradition, including Abraham, David, Samuel, Elijah, and even Adam. Then as Chume joins in and becomes more and more excited, Jero repeats, "Abraka, Abraka, Abraka." As Chume joins the chant, Jero continues, "Abraka, Abraka, Hebra, Hebra, Hebra, Hebra, Hebra, Hebra, Hebra, Hebra." In this context, *Abraka* and *Hebra* are nonsense words; they have no meaning. Indeed, Abraka is close in sound to the cry of the stage magician, "Abracadabra" (sometimes spelled Abrakadabra) as he is about to perform some piece of entertaining trickery in front of an audience, which is close to what Jero is doing here—putting on a show of piety for the benefit of his witless disciple, who is so caught up in the emotionalism of the situation that he has no rational power to question the appropriateness of the incantation.

If Jero is the lovable rogue and Chume his perpetual dupe, the other main character, Amope, is the archetypal shrew. Like the lovable rogue, the stock character of the shrew has a long history in literature. Shakespeare's Katharina in *The Taming of the Shrew* is perhaps the most famous. Paulina in *The Winter's Tale* is another, as is Zeena in Edith Wharton's novel, *Ethan Frome*. The shrew is easy to spot; she is the character who is perpetually nagging her husband, showering him with verbal abuse. Sometimes the husband meekly knuckles under; sometimes he rebels and finally shows the troublesome lady who is the boss. Chume would dearly love to take the latter course, but the truth of the matter is that, in what is no doubt a long and unhappy relationship, Amope is the stronger personality and dominates her hapless husband whatever he might do to challenge her. Long skilled at playing the martyr, she accuses him of abusing her if he offers her even the mildest of rebukes. Nothing he does makes any difference to this situation, which is why he entertains fantasies of giving her a beating. When Jero gives him the go-ahead to teach her a lesson, he starts to assert himself like he never has before: "Shut your big mouth!" he yells, and he lifts her bodily in an attempt to put her on his bicycle so he can take her home and beat her. After she protests and he puts her down, he raises a clenched fist, telling her once more to keep silent. Amope appears to be at his mercy, but in fact the quick-witted woman soon finds a way of regaining the upper hand, repeatedly telling him to kill her, even as a crowd gathers to watch. She is still playing the martyr, and her gamble that he will in fact do nothing seems a fairly safe one. The audience gets the feeling that Chume, whatever he does, will never get the satisfaction of breaking his wife's spirit by physical force. This is one shrew who, unlike Shakespeare's Katharina, will not be tamed.

The Trials of Brother Jero proves to be one of Soyinka's most popular and frequently performed plays. As a light satire, it produces more fun and laughter than serious thought, and Soyinka liked his charlatan of a hero enough to bring him back in a later play, *Jero's Metamorphosis* (first produced in Lagos in 1972). However, the tone of the later play presents a stark contrast to that of the earlier one. Much had happened in

Nigeria in the intervening twelve years. The hopes of the newly independent nation had not been fulfilled and, in 1966, there were several military coups. The following year, civil war broke out when Biafra, the eastern region of the country, declared its independence from Nigeria. The civil war ended in 1970, but during the 1970s the country remained under repressive military rule. Bar Beach, Lagos, the scene of Jero's petty chicanery, was used for public executions.

Soyinka was imprisoned for over two years during the civil war, and when he turned his creative attention back to Brother Jero, his vision had darkened. The earlier play ended with Jero pulling into his fold the ambitious but timid Member of Parliament, who wants to become minister for war, thus suggesting that the preacher is about to widen his sphere of influence into the political realm. *Jero's Metamorphosis* takes up this hint of an alliance between religious quackery and the political rulers to present a bitter satire with Jero at its center. In his office, Jero displays a portrait of the country's military ruler, so the changed conditions under wich the country is operating are clear at the outset. The plot centers around the plan of the authorities to evict the rag-tag group of preachers from the beach and develop it for tourism. They also have plans to build a large stadium on the beach where they would hold public executions. Part of the plan involves issuing a license to just one religious group to operate on the beach. The role of the favored church would be to say prayers before and after the executions and give sermons to the crowds pointing out that perpetrators of crime will meet with a bad end. Jero fears that the Salvation Army is about to be appointed as the state-approved sect, so he gathers all the preachers together and announces he is forming a new church in the image of the country's military rulers. Everyone is given a military title, including Chume, who, it turns out, spent only three months in the lunatic asylum and was soon won back into Jero's fold by the preacher's promise of rapid promotion. Chume is immediately appointed a brigadier in the new church, and Jero persuades the head of the Tourist Board to grant them their desired spiritual monopoly on the beach. Jero thus sets himself up as the spiritual wing of the ruling military junta, creating an ugly alliance between religion and the repressive rulers of the state that has the people at its mercy. Jero has grown from petty con man to a state-sanctioned leader of a militarized church that does the bidding of a regime that executes its enemies in public as a form of mass entertainment. For Jero, this represents progress, but for Nigeria, Soyinka suggests, it represents the opposite.

Source: Bryan Aubrey, Critical Essay on *The Trials of Brother Jero*, in *Drama for Students*, Gale, Cengage Learning, 2009.

Alan Jacobs

In the following excerpt, Jacobs provides an overview of Soyinka's life and oeuvre, including The Trials of Brother Jero, *and emphasizes the playwright's significance to contemporary literature.*

1

Like many teachers of literature, I am sometimes asked to name the Greatest Living Writer. (I can hear the capital letters in the voices of those who ask.) Invariably I name two candidates: the Polish-Lithuanian poet Czeslaw Milosz and the Nigerian playwright Wole Soyinka. These names are usually greeted by puzzlement, for, though both have won the Nobel Prize for Literature—Milosz in 1980 and Soyinka in 1986—and both have been on *The McNeil-Lehrer Newshour,* neither has entered the American public consciousness in a potent way. Milosz is more likely to be familiar, though, and apparently my interlocutors think him a more plausible choice; my claim for Soyinka almost always earns skeptical looks.

I imagine that this skepticism derives from the still-common picture of Africa as the dark continent, full of illiterate savages (a picture that the Western media do little to dispel); and also from the suspicion that any African Nobel laureate must be the beneficiary of multicultural affirmative action. But if anything, Soyinka is a more comprehensive genius even than Milosz. Here is a writer of spectacular literary gifts; he is an acclaimed lyric and satirical poet, a brilliant novelist of ideas, a memoirist both nostalgic and harrowing, and almost certainly the greatest religious dramatist of our time. The assumption that he has come to our attention only because of academic politics is profoundly unjust—though perhaps understandable, considering the number of mediocre talents who have assumed recent prominence for just such reasons.

That assumption also carries a heavy load of irony, given the distance between the triviality of American academic politics—what Henry Louis Gates, Jr. has aptly called our "marionette

> HERE IS A WRITER OF SPECTACULAR LITERARY GIFTS; HE IS AN ACCLAIMED LYRIC AND SATIRICAL POET, A BRILLIANT NOVELIST OF IDEAS, A MEMOIRIST BOTH NOSTALGIC AND HARROWING, AND ALMOST CERTAINLY THE GREATEST RELIGIOUS DRAMATIST OF OUR TIME."

theater of the political"—and the *real* political crises which have continually afflicted Soyinka and his work. Soyinka's 1996 book on the political collapse of his native Nigeria, *The Open Sore of a Continent,* teaches us how absurdly misbegotten our whole literary-political conversation tends to be. Through this book, and through the shape his career has assumed, Soyinka brings compelling messages to our warring parties. To the traditionalists who deplore "the politicization of literary discourse," Soyinka serves as a living reminder that writers in some parts of the world don't get to *choose* whether their work will be political; that is a privilege enjoyed by those who happen to be born into stable and relatively peaceable societies. Others have politics thrust upon them. But Soyinka also tells our Young Turks that their cardinal principle—Everything is Political—is true only in an utterly trivial sense. To adapt a famous phrase from George Orwell, if everything is political, some things are a hell of a lot more political than others.

Whichever side of this dispute one tends to be on, or even if one isn't on either side, Soyinka's story is worth paying attention to, because his career has been virtually derailed by the collapse of his native country into political tyranny and social chaos. Soyinka has not eagerly thrown his energies into protest and polemic in the way that, for instance, Aleksandr Solzhenitsyn did in the days of the Soviet empire; unlike Solzhenitsyn, he is no *natural* polemicist. However, Soyinka has also been unable to follow the route of Solzhenitsyn's older contemporary Boris Pasternak, which was to combat political tyranny by ignoring it, by cultivating a realm of personal feeling impervious to the corrosive solvent of Politics. (As Czeslaw Milosz writes of

Pasternak, "confronted by argument, he replied with his sacred dance.") Soyinka has felt called upon to respond to the collapse of Nigeria, and as a result his career has taken a very different direction than it once promised to do. It is hard to question his choice; it is equally hard to celebrate it, for it has led a fecund and celebratory poetic mind into an abyss of outrage.

Soyinka's homeland has suffered from the same consequences of colonialism that have afflicted almost every modern African state. The area now called Nigeria is occupied by many peoples, the most prominent among them being the Hausa, the Yoruba, and the Ibo. The boundaries of the country do not reflect the distribution of these ethnic populations; there are Ibo people in Cameroon, Yoruba in Benin, Hausa in Niger. The physical shape of Nigeria is an administrative fiction deriving from the way the colonial powers parceled out the "dark continent" in the nineteenth century. (Somalia alone among African countries is ethnically homogeneous.) So when the British granted independence to Nigeria in 1960, this most populous of African nations had some considerable work to do to make itself *into* a real nation, as opposed to a collection of adversarial ethnicities. These problems have been exacerbated by almost continually increasing tensions between Christians and Muslims in the country.

No wonder, then, that civic rule has been the exception rather than the norm in Nigeria's history, and that civilian governments have served only at the behest of the military, who have been quick to take over and impose martial law whenever they have sensed the coming of chaos, or genuine democracy—for them the two amount to more or less the same thing. And with martial law has always come strict censorship of all the media, which makes it difficult for even the most apolitical writer to avoid politics. Besides, respect for intellectuals is so great in most African cultures that writers can scarcely resist the pleas of their people for help.

2

Wole Soyinka's people, in the ethnic sense, are the Yoruba, and there is no culture in the world more fascinating. The Yoruba are traditionally among the greatest sculptors in Africa, and their labyrinthine mythology is so coherent and compelling that even the selling of many Yoruba people into slavery could not eradicate

it: especially in places where great numbers of Yoruba were transported (most notably Brazil and Haiti) it survived by adapting itself, syncretistically, to certain Catholic traditions. The chief Yoruba gods (the *orisa*) became conflated with the popular saints; the results can be seen even today in religions, or cults, like Santeria. The notorious Haitian practice of voodoo is largely an evil corruption of Yoruba medicine, which typically seeks to confuse the evil spirits who cause illness and draw them from the ill person into a doll or effigy, which is then beaten or destroyed. This form of medical treatment is crucial to one of Soyinka's earliest and most accessibly powerful plays, *The Strong Breed* (1959).

Perhaps not surprisingly, the Yoruba have long practiced the arts of drama, and Soyinka is an heir of that tradition. It is really inaccurate to say that Yoruba drama is religious, because even to make such a statement one must employ a vocabulary which distinguishes between religion and other forms of culture in a way alien to Africa. For the Yoruba, as for almost all Africans, every aspect of culture is religious through and through—it simply *is* worship or celebration or healing or teaching—and religion is thoroughly cultural. In Africa, the notion of "the aesthetic" as a distinct category of experience is unthinkable. No Yoruba arts can be identified as part of the human realm as distinct from that of the gods and spirits. In part this is because of the animism of Yoruba culture, but such a complete integration of religion and culture does not require animism. It seems to have characterized ancient Israel, for instance: the poetry of the Israelites is inseparable from their covenantal relationship with Yahweh. Similarly, Westerners seem to have difficulty understanding why Muslims insist upon the universal application of *sharia,* or Islamic law, and tend to think that Muslims don't know how to respect the appropriate cultural boundaries. Yoruba drama arises from what one might call such a "total culture."

Soyinka, though, was raised in a Christian home. His mother's brand and intensity of piety may be guessed at from this: in his memoirs he refers to her almost exclusively as "Wild Christian." But it seems that his chief interest in the doctrines and practices of Christianity derives from their similarities to Yoruba traditions. Biblical themes always echo in his work, especially early in his career: the story of the Prodigal Son in *The Swamp Dwellers* (about 1958), the Passion (with staggering force) in *The Strong Breed*. But, as in his fascinating adaptation of Euripides's *The Bacchae* [*The Bacchae of Euripides: A Communion Rite*] (1973), so do the themes of classical tragedy. It is clear that Soyinka has been interested in the primordial mythic truths that lie behind the doctrines and practices of particular religions: he shares the Jungian view that all religions are concretized and particularized versions of universal experiences. Moreover, he seems to espouse the Feuerbachian projection theory of religion as he says in his critical book *Myth, Literature, and the African World* (1976), "myths arise from man's attempt to externalise and communicate his inner intuitions," and more recently he has written, in oracular tones. "THE WILL of man is placed beyond surrender. . . . ORISA reveals Destiny as—SELF-DESTINATION."

These universalistic and syncretistic tendencies are more easily reconcilable with Yoruba than with Christian or Muslim beliefs, as Soyinka observes in the essay "Reparations, Truth, and Reconciliation," one of a series of lectures given at Harvard University in 1997 and published as *The Burden of Memory, the Muse of Forgiveness* (1999):

> Just what is *African*, for a start, about any section of that continent that arrogantly considers any change of faith an apostasy, punishable even by death? What is *African* about religious intolerance and deadly fanaticism? The spirituality of the black continent, as attested, for instance, in the religion of the *orisa*, abhors such principles of coercion or exclusion, and recognizes all manifestations of spiritual urgings as attributes of the complex disposition of the godhead. *Tolerance* is synonymous with the spirituality of the black continent, *intolerance* is anathema!

Soyinka's imagination is thus secondarily and derivatively Christian at best, despite his upbringing and his long-term fascination with Christian doctrine. And as we shall see, he has sought to exorcise that fascination in rather frightening ways.

When, as a young man, he came to study in England at the University of Leeds, it is not at all surprising that Soyinka fell under the influence of the controversial Shakespearean scholar G. Wilson Knight. For Knight's career was devoted chiefly to the contention that Shakespeare's plays, however "secular" they might appear, were really Christian (in a mythic or archetypal sort of way) through and through. It must have seemed perfectly natural to Soyinka, coming

from his Yoruba world, that such would be the case, indeed it must have been hard for him to think of drama in any other terms. No wonder he ultimately decided to adapt *The Bacchae:* the Euripedean original, so obviously shaped by and angrily responsive to the Athenian worship of Dionysos, was a clear picture of what he had always understood drama to be. Soyinka's version, a turbulent tragic fantasy half-Greek and half-African, is one of the most striking and provocative plays of our time, and in its exploration of irreconcilable worldviews often seems a veiled commentary on the troubles of modern Africa.

3

Soyinka's plays are often said to be about the modern "clash of cultures" in Africa between Western and African traditional ways, but this is a phrase for which Soyinka has a singular contempt. In an "Author's Note" to what may well be his greatest play, the tragedy *Death and the King's Horseman* (1975), which is based on a historical event, he complains that "the bane of themes of this genre is that they are no sooner employed creatively than they acquire the facile tag of 'clash of cultures,' a prejudicial label which, quite apart from its frequent misapplication, presupposes a potential equality in every given situation of the alien culture and the indigenous, on the actual soil of the latter."

One might think that Soyinka is here reminding us that the British came to Africa with technologies and forces that traditional African cultures could not hope to resist; in other words, that he is reminding us of his people's status as victims. That would be a misreading. The British did indeed bring superior physical force to Nigeria; but Soyinka is more concerned to point out that the spiritual and cultural forces upon which the Yoruba relied were far more impressive. Now, Soyinka is never shy about offering potent critiques of his culture, and not just in its modern manifestations; from those early plays, *The Swamp Dwellers* and *The Strong Breed*, we can see a fierce indictment of how power corrupts even at the level of the village, where leaders pervert their people's traditions and manipulate them for their own gain. But those traditions themselves, Soyinka is always eager to say, have enormous power, and when rightly used and respectfully employed can overcome the humiliations inflicted upon the Yoruba by British imperialism. This is indeed the central theme of *Death* and the King's Horseman, where tradition finds a way to rescue the dignity of a people even when the colonial power seems to have things well under control.

In Nigeria during World War II, a king has died. Oba Elesin, the king's horseman and a lesser king himself ("Oba" means "king" or "chief"), is expected, at the end of the month of ceremonies marking the king's passing, to follow his master into the spirit world of the ancestors. In other words, he is to commit ritual suicide. It is his greatest wish to do so, and in the village marketplace, surrounded by people who love and respect him, he awaits the appointed time.

> All is prepared. Listen! [*A steady drum-beat from the distance.*] Yes. It is nearly time. The King's dog has been killed. The King's favourite horse is about to follow his master. My brother chiefs know their task and perform it well.... My faithful drummers, do me your last service. This is where I have chosen to do my leave-taking, in this heart of life, this hive which contains the swarm of the world in its small compass.... Just then I felt my spirit's eagerness.... But wait a while my spirit. Wait. Wait for the coming of the courier of the King.

But Simon Pilkings, the district officer in this British colonial outpost, intervenes to prevent the suicide, which violates British law and which he considers to be a barbaric custom. And his intervention succeeds in part because at the crucial moment Elesin hesitates, and thereby cooperates with Pilkings in bringing shame upon himself, his people, and his king (who is by Elesin's cowardice "condemned to wander in the void of evil with beings who are the enemies of life"). Elesin's son Olunde—who had been in England studying medicine and returned when he heard of the death of the king—explains this to Simon Pilkings's wife Jane before he knows that the interference has succeeded. When she suggests that Elesin "is entitled to whatever protection is available to him"—that is, available from her husband as instrument of the colonial Law—Olunde quickly replies,

> How can I make you understand? He *has* protection. No one can undertake what he does tonight without the deepest protection the mind can conceive. What can you offer him in place of his peace of mind? In place of the honour and veneration of his own people?

And it is Olunde—the one who Elesin feared would in England forget or repudiate the old tribal ways—who finds a way to rescue his people and his king from the shame brought by Elesin.

In his preface Soyinka is determined to insist that the colonial situation of the play be seen as a catalyst for an exploration of what is permanent in Yoruba society; the play is about "transition," the transition from this world to the world of the spirits and the ancestors, and as such cannot be reduced to a single historical moment. The colonial era simply troubles the waters, it cannot dam the river of Yoruba tradition. "The confrontation in the play," Soyinka writes, "is largely metaphysical, contained in the human vehicle which is Elesin and the universe of the Yoruba mind—the world of the living, the dead, and the unborn." Simon Pilkings thinks he holds the power in this situation, that he participates in a story which his people are writing and of which they are the protagonists; but Soyinka reveals him as merely a plot device, a means by which "the universe of the Yoruba mind" is explored.

This potent tragedy marked a return to Soyinka's early themes and concerns, arresting a drift toward political satire that had begun some years before. One sees this tendency in his two wickedly funny plays about the shyster preacher and self-proclaimed prophet Brother Jeroboam (*The Trials of Brother Jero* [1960] and *Jero's Metamorphosis* [1968]), who ultimately becomes the "general" of a Nigerian version of the Salvation Army, sending his "troops" out into a dangerous world while he remains secure in his office. Lingering just below the surface of these plays is a commentary on the ambitions and absurdities of Nigeria's hyperactive military. The Jero plays were followed by Soyinka's darkest, bitterest play, *Madmen and Specialists* (1970), which reveals his disgust at the crisis of Biafra in 1969.

Biafra was the new country proclaimed by leaders of the Ibo people of eastern Nigeria; but their attempt to secede from Nigeria ended when they were beaten and starved into submission. Soyinka's sympathy for the Biafran rebels led to his arrest and lengthy detainment, an experience chronicled in his searing memoir, *The Man Died* (1972).

Madmen and Specialists emphasizes the ways that the lust for power, and not just power itself, corrupts gifted men and turns them into tyrants who cannot abide dissent or even questioning. One can easily see why after writing this play and *The Man Died*, Soyinka would produce *Death and the King's Horseman*, with its passionate commitment to the maintenance of a great spiritual tradition that cannot be extinguished or even derailed by the traumas of political history. But as passionately as Soyinka expresses that commitment, what speaks still louder than the brilliance of the play is that in the quarter-century since it appeared Soyinka has severely curtailed his theatrical writing. (And most of the plays he has written are topical political satires, like *The Beatification of Area Boy*.) It is hard to imagine a greater loss for modern drama....

Source: Alan Jacobs, "Wole Soyinka's Outrage: The Divided Soul of Nigeria's Nobel Laureate," in *Books & Culture*, Vol. 7, No. 6, November–December 2001, pp. 28–31.

Dale Byam

In the following interview, Soyinka details how his Nigerian and Yoruba heritage and his mood influence his work, including The Trials of Brother Jero.

Even the briefest of encounters with Wole Soyinka—celebrated playwright, essayist, activist and winner of the 1986 Nobel Prize for Literature—is enough to make evident the qualities that are at the crux of his accomplishments. A formidable and centered man, he speaks with a quiet and utter confidence—a confidence that belies his personal fury for the events of June 12, 1993, which rendered him into exile from his native Nigeria.

It was on that day that a military coup prevented a newly elected civilian government from assuming power. Large numbers of Nigerians had voted across ethnic and regional lines in what was widely seen as the country's most democratic election ever—an event that, in Soyinka's eyes, was his homeland's last best hope of becoming a free and viable nation. But the military strongman Gen. Ibrahim Babangida, who had ruled Nigeria for eight years (in the process building one of Africa's largest private fortunes), forbade publication of the voting results and, in place of the election's ostensible winner, installed his own deputy, the brutal Gen. Sani Abacha, as head of state. Soyinka celebrated his 60th birthday with a protest march against Abacha's takeover, an action that led to threats of house arrest and the writer's movement into exile.

From this vantage, stateless but hardly alienated, Soyinka has continued to bring the issues of Africa to the table, so to speak. His most recent play, *The Beatification of Area Boy,* arrived in America in October at the Brooklyn Academy of Music, following its debut in Leeds, England last year; his impassioned philosophical essay *The*

> OH, SOME PEOPLE FIND, FOR INSTANCE, MY SPOOF *BROTHER JERO* OFFENSIVE—IT'S OFFENSIVE TO THE CHRISTIAN RELIGION, ALTHOUGH OTHERS OF MY PLAYS HAVE SPOOFED RELIGIOUS EXTREMISM ALL OVER THE PLACE. BUT THERE HAS BEEN NO PRICE ON MY HEAD YET."

Open Sore of a Continent: A Personal Narrative of the Nigerian Crisis, was published last August by Oxford. The two works illuminate distinctly different but complementary sides of Soyinka: the anecdotal, celebratory playwright with a penchant for portraiture and whimsy, and the fiercely angry polemicist, producing what he once called "monster prodigies of spleen."

A full measure of the writer's righteous anger cannot be taken without considering a second incident of outrage: On Nov. 10, 1995, Ken Saro-Wiwa, Soyinka's friend and fellow dissident writer, was executed by the military government, along with eight other members of the Ogoni ethnic minority. Soyinka, himself a member of the Yoruba majority, had arduously campaigned throughout the world community for their release, and for the cause of the Ogoni, who have waged a desperate battle for survival against overdevelopment and international oil interests.

Soyinka's plays—the best-known of which is the Yoruban epic *Death and the King's Horseman,* which was directed by the author in an acclaimed 1987 production starring Earle Hyman at Lincoln Center Theater—keep such practical political matters at arm's length, or at a poetic remove. *The Beatification of Area Boy* takes the form of a lively slice of life as it explores the condition of Nigeria's urban poor, young boys who survive in the environs of a shopping complex in Lagos through a savvy that almost always involves hoodwinking the unwitting, innocent shopper or tourist. Sanda, a failed revolutionary, surreptitiously manages the "boys" while serving as the complex's chief security guard. Street vendors and madmen are the play's other principal characters. The plot thickens when Sanda encounters Miseyi, a former lover and college student, on the eve of her wedding to a key military officer. But flowing like a stream beneath the play's buoyant surface is an underlying awareness of the offstage exodus of a million people, forcibly resettled at the whim of the military government.

Soyinka the dramatist clearly shies away from prescribing solutions to the wretched conditions in the play, reserving his ideas about correctives for *Open Sore of a Continent*. There Soyinka summons the international community to discuss the urgent problems of African nationhood, fashioning a philosophic imperative to do the right thing in Africa. The Nigerian people, he points out, did not repudiate nationhood—they voted their hunger for it, only to see their will criminally denied. "A nation is a collective enterprise," he writes; "outside of that, it is mostly a gambling space for the opportunism and adventurism of power."

As one talks with Soyinka about his art—an art indelibly linked to his ideas of nationhood in this age of Nigerian uncertainty, and to the rich and complex mythology of Yoruba culture—his countenance betrays neither lament nor brooding. Rather his indomitable spirit is a nourishing symbol of African perseverance.

DALE BYAM: Do you write in response to something, or can it simply be a mood?

WOLE SOYINKA: A mood, or just an idea in my head. I know there are writers who get up every morning and sit by their typewriter or word processor or pad of paper and wait to write. I don't function that way. I go through a long period of gestation before I'm even ready to write. Take *Death and the King's Horseman*. The story of that play [based on a true incident in 1946, in which the horseman of the title was prevented by resident colonial authorities from following his deceased king to the grave by committing ritual suicide] is something I had known for about 10 years before I got down to writing it. One day it was just ready to be written. The muse had mounted my head, shall we say, and I sat down and wrote the play, and that was that.

When you write a play, is there a particular audience that you have in mind?

It would be more accurate to say I have a company in mind to perform the play. I used to work very closely with two different companies in Nigeria, and while I'm not writing the plays as vehicles for them, in certain cases I do have certain actors in mind for certain roles. One of the companies I used to run did what I call

guerrilla theatre—we made instant improvisations on themes of the day and gave performances in market places, outside civil service offices, outside the houses of assembly members. Obviously the plays were targeted not merely at the specific audience, which is Nigerian, but also created for a specific time when certain events are fresh in the mind.

There are other plays like *Opera Wonyusi*, my adaptation of Brecht's *Threepenny Opera*, which are particularly targeted at Nigerian audiences. Even though this play was written before the hanging of Ken Saro-Wiwa and the eight Ogoni people, there's no way anybody would see this play—which involved the military, and takes place in Nigeria without immediately thinking of this universally traumatizing event. I know that for me, who went to speak to heads of state after the sentences were confirmed, it was so disquieting that I couldn't function for about three days.

It is pleasant to find that even though *Opera Wonyusi* was produced outside Nigeria, it is receiving a tremendous response. I saw it in Zurich with mixed audiences, and it's amazing how people responded to it.

Do political events direct your work, or are they a distraction from work that you ideally want to do?

My creative temperament is rather eclectic. I find I'm in the mood some days to write a densely mythological play like *Death and the King's Horseman*; at other times, I write lighthearted "scoops" like the Jero plays [such as *The Trials of Brother Jero,* about the power trips of a prophet who feeds on his followers' dissatisfaction]; then there are ritualistic plays like *Strong Breed*. Anything which agitates me sufficiently to start conceiving of an event to strike a feeling of revenge, a projection in creative terms—that's what gets onto the paper.

Are there any plays that have worked better on paper than on stage?

For me a play can never work better on paper than in performance. You can say, perhaps, that the performance has not quite fulfilled the expectations of the play; the performance may understate the playwright's intentions, or distort them completely. But the play on paper isn't working yet. You can enjoy reading it like a piece of literature, yes, that's true. Some read better than others, but they don't come to life until they're on stage.

I understand the director of Area Boy, Jude Kelly, actually visited Nigeria to find actors. Is it necessary to have Nigerians in the play?

Well, yes, even when I direct my plays outside Nigeria I always do everything possible to bring a core of my company—four, five or six actors—to participate in the production. It makes a difference with certain plays. You try to create a certain atmosphere in the kind of plays which involve community. To create the atmosphere, the color, the tone, to infect the others who are alienated from that environment, you cannot guess the difference it makes to have a community of actors. Also, in this kind of play I use a lot of local music.

Because you are of the Yoruba culture but very representative of the whole of Nigeria, have you managed to straddle the ethnic contradictions?

First of all, I don't believe in ethnic contradictions. (There are, however, collisions of ethnic interests which the government orchestrates.) Take *Strong Breed,* for instance—the ritual of the carrier I used in that play is not a Yoruba ritual at all. It is a ritual from the Ibo, in the eastern part of Nigeria. Others of my plays incorporate many things which most Nigerian ethnic groups will recognize. But essentially, my culture dominates my plays, and naturally it is the Yoruba culture.

No one considers it a transgression when you incorporate ethnic rituals in your work?

They have no right. Culture is not their property. Culture is universal.

Even when it is attached to a religious framework?

Oh, some people find, for instance, my spoof *Brother Jero* offensive—it's offensive to the Christian religion, although others of my plays have spoofed religious extremism all over the place. But there has been no price on my head yet.

Sitting in a New York cab driven by a Nigerian, I mentioned your *Beatification of Area Boy.* This taxi driver became so excited by the mere mention of your name. He had read your work during his school years in Nigeria. How do you reconcile your celebration in that society with the present reality that you are in virtual alienation . . . exile?

My condition is not one of permanent exile. There's no question at all, though, that my condition is one of partial alienation. That alienation, of course, triggers off the need to respond in some fashion—in some creative way. If you're a painter, you respond as a painter; if you're a musician, you respond as a musician. It's no surprise that some musicians have been jailed by this dictatorship for their music. [The Nigerian pop idol] Fela has been persecuted by a number of regimes—that's become his way of life. It's not just writers who are in exile.

But there is no conflict: If you live in a state of social disjunction, on certain levels that becomes your reality. You operate within it, you critique it. From time to time, you act as a citizen and join others in resisting it. You become part of an oppositional movement which cuts across your profession. During the protestations to remove [former Nigerian President] Babangida, you would see all sorts of people there—civil servants, union members, policemen, market women. There were the "touts," the area boys, as well, some of whom were totally committed, others who took the opportunity to pick a few pockets. The whole society is involved, and the question is which is the real society at that moment? Is it the predators who are sitting on top, immune in their fortifications? Or is it those masses on the street? Which is the reality?

Which is the reality?

Oh, the people on the streets . . . with whom I find myself.

Even though a culture of silence prevails amongst these oppressed people?

No, it is not a culture of silence. Sometimes, yes, there is stasis, a seeming acquiescence. But, believe me, there is simmering ferment going on all the time. People may be hobbled by the superior power, the ruthlessness, of a regime like Abacha's. But talk to those taxi drivers—even those who are here in the U.S.; talk to people who come out from time to time; look at the vibrant underground press in Nigeria, the risks that they take. They are jailed, they are brutalized by the police, their families are sometimes taken hostage. For me, this is the reality, this underground reality. The culture of resistance begins gathering force, sometimes slowly, sometimes suddenly. You never can tell which way it will go.

As a Yoruba, how do you see yourself in relation to Nigeria?

I am undeniably a Yoruba because I was born into Yoruba; I am a Nigerian because I was born into a certain definable entity called Nigeria. What I am saying is that when you compare that entity called Yoruba—or Ogun, or Hausa, or Ibo—when you compare it to the entity called Nigeria, you see that one is not the result of any artificial creation or agreement. It happens to be. It's like your blood. The other, however, something called Nigeria, was not there 50 years ago. It was invented. What was the purpose of that invention? Was it simply to supply raw material to Great Britain and to the international and commercial world? Or was Nigeria invented in order to cohere all the disparate elements into a single entity, where all have the right to life, liberty, means of education, health, etc., etc.? You must decide, what should be my definition of a nation?

Are both Open Sore of a Continent and Area Boy responding to the military rule in Nigeria?

Open Sore of a Continent is a large discourse. *The Beatification of Area Boy* is a vignette, a microcosm of society. The characters in the play are not concerned with issues of nationhood—they're concerned with issues of community and how best to survive; they are responding to the cruelty of a singularly insensitive regime. I wouldn't say the two works cover the same ground.

The military expulsion, the removal of a million people, which actually happened there, horrified me—it made me feel ashamed to be a Nigerian in a time when such things could happen. One wonders how there can be a nation where people could wake up and be rendered homeless in peacetime, for no reason other than greed. But I'm not asking that question in the play.

Having now traveled so extensively, do you see parallels between the Nigerian condition and elsewhere?

Oh, yes, no question at all there are many such spots on the African continent, and look at what's happening in some of the Latin American countries—look at "class sanitation," which takes place in Brazil when the police go and round up all these area boys, little ones, not even the grown-up ones, and shoot them because they think they will grow up into thugs and thieves. Repression is not peculiar to Nigeria.

So what can the performing artist do?

The performing artist is at a disadvantage, as his resources are limited. All an actor can do is join forces. He or she may also decide, "I will not do this kind of play, it's reactionary or corrupt." Remember, a writer, a musician, a painter, a sculptor, an architect—these are first of all citizens. Their responsibility is no different from any other citizen. There should be no unfair burden

being placed on the artists in society—each artist must choose the degree and capability of his or her commitment to certain issues. You cannot say an artist 24 hours, 7 days a week, must be politically engaged. That's madness. You cannot make that imposition on a bricklayer or a craftsman; you cannot make it on the artist.

But you find yourself in that position?

It doesn't mean that I believe that this is the best life. I do what I do because I'm temperamentally inclined to do it. All writers are not the same, just like all preachers are not the same. Some preachers believe that religion should be an instrument of social change, and thank God for that; but there are others who believe that their function is simply to minister to the spirit. Similarly, you have artists who believe that their function is to be revelatory, to open up certain horizons for human striving. I'm an artist and a producer, a creative person, but I'm also a consumer—I like to go into galleries, to listen to music, to read books—and I don't recall screaming in outrage if a work is not politically engaged, because what I'm consuming at that moment fulfills a certain part of me. The kind of spiritual elevation that is also a part of the function of the artist should never, never be underestimated.

Does your condition overwhelm you?

Oh, yes, sometimes.

How do you temper that?

I go for a drink. At home I'll pick up my gun and go hunting. The thing I miss here is getting lost in the bush. I just go. I call it sometimes "just taking my gun for a walk." I can get lost in the bush for hours. Come back very much refreshed, feeling more benevolent towards life in general, because I've seen animals who act better than human beings.

Source: Dale Byam, "Art, Exile and Resistance: An Interview with Wole Soyinka," in *American Theatre*, Vol. 14, No. 1, January 1997, p. 26.

SOURCES

Abrams, M. H., *A Glossary of Literary Terms*, 4th ed., Holt, Rinehart, and Winston, 1981, p. 25.

Central Intelligence Agency, *World Factbook*, s.v. "Nigeria," https://www.cia.gov/library/publications/the-world-factbook/print/ni.html (accessed August 12, 2008).

"Festival of Death," in *Time*, March 22, 1976, http://www.time.com/time/magazine/article/0,9171,911769,00.html (accessed August 12, 2008).

Gibbs, James, "Wole Soyinka," in *Dictionary of Literary Biography*, Vol. 332, *Nobel Prize Laureates in Literature, Part 4: Quasimodo-Yeats*, Thomson Gale, 2007, pp. 341–78.

"Harsh Comedy on a Lagos Beach," in *Times* (London), No. 56670, June 29, 1966, p. 7.

"Infectious Humanity," in *Time*, Vol. 90, November 17, 1967, p. 50.

Ositelu, Rufus Okikiolaolu Olubiyi, *African Instituted Churches: Diversities, Growth, Gifts, Spirituality and Ecumenical Understanding of African Initiated Churches*, Lit Verlag, 2002.

St. Jorre, John de, *The Brothers' War: Biafra and Nigeria*, Houghton Mifflin, 1972.

Soyinka, Wole, *The Trials of Brother Jero*, in *Collected Plays 2*, Oxford University Press, 1974, pp. 143–71.

———, *Jero's Metamorphosis*, in *Collected Plays 2*, Oxford University Press, 1974, pp. 173–213.

FURTHER READING

Falola, Toyin, and Matthew M. Heaton, *A History of Nigeria*, Cambridge University Press, 2008.

> This is a history of Nigeria from pre-colonial times to the present. The authors' discussion of Nigerian politics, nationalism, and the economy and their presentation of Nigerian culture, including art, music, literature, and drama, shed light on the cultural environment in which Soyinka was raised and in which he produced much of his life's work.

Msiska, Mpalive-Hangson, *Wole Soyinka*, Northcote House, 1998, pp. 18–21.

> Msiska discusses both Jero plays in terms of the corruption in society that they reveal. He argues that *The Trials of Brother Jero* also targets the false promises of the nationalist ideology of the early 1960s.

Obilade, Tony, "The Stylistic Function of Pidgin English in African Literature: Achebe and Soyinka," in *Research on Wole Soyinka*, edited by James Gibbs and Bernth Lindfors, Africa World Press, 1993, pp. 13–24.

> Obilade examines the use Soyinka makes of pidgin English, concluding that it is an indispensable part of *The Trials of Brother Jero*.

Ogunba, Oyin, *The Movement of Transition: A Study of the Plays of Wole Soyinka*, Ibadan University Press, 1975, pp. 55–68.

> This is the most detailed critical essay on the play. Oguna argues that the play is a satire on a materialistic society and that the characters are stock types, but Soyinka injects them with a vitality that is fresh and interesting.

Wright, Derek, *Wole Soyinka Revisited*, Twayne Publishers, 1993.

> Wright presents a comprehensive examination of Soyinka's work. His treatment of *The Trials of Brother Jero* discusses the elements of satiric comedy that Soyinka uses and also argues that the play should be regarded as a light comedy and not seen as a prelude to the darker *Jero's Metamorphosis*. However, Wright also argues that Soyinka created an ending to the play that revealed his serious misgivings about the future political leaders of Nigeria.

A Walk in the Woods

LEE BLESSING

1987

A Walk in the Woods is set in what turned out to be the last years of the cold war, although Lee Blessing could not have known that when he first presented the play as a staged reading in 1986. At this time, the nuclear arsenals of both the United States and the Soviet Union were bursting with weaponry of massive and incalculable destructive capacity, a circumstance that caused widespread and international anxiety.

A Walk in the Woods was originally produced by the Yale Repertory Theatre in New Haven, Connecticut, in 1987, and was later produced on Broadway in New York, New York, in 1988. It is a two-character play composed in the form of a dialogue between United States and Soviet negotiators in a serene wooded area in Switzerland. A country known historically for its order, social peace, and neutrality in international conflicts, Switzerland, consequently, is an ideal venue for negotiations between hostile powers. Despite its political themes and geopolitical context, however, *A Walk in the Woods* is less concerned with particular political issues than with the climate of alienation generated by the cold war. The encounter between the negotiators becomes a study of how two personalities deal with the frustration and hopelessness that the arms race generated in people of conscience. The two must go through the motions of attempting to negotiate an agreement that, ultimately, neither of their governments will authorize. Although *A Walk in the Woods* is entirely fictional, Blessing

derived the idea for the situation of his play from an actual event. Formal arms control negotiations took place in Geneva, Switzerland, in 1982, and U.S. negotiator Paul Nitze and Soviet negotiator Yuli Kvitsinsky met in a wooded area to approach the issue privately. In this peaceful environment, they drafted a proposal for arms reduction that was later rejected by both the U.S. and the Soviet governments.

A Walk in the Woods was published in 1988 by Dramatic Play Service and reprinted in 1998.

AUTHOR BIOGRAPHY

Lee Blessing was born in Minneapolis, Minnesota, on October 4, 1949. He received a B.A. from Reed College in 1971, and after graduation, he traveled to the Soviet Union. Upon his return, Blessing enrolled in the University of Iowa and earned a master of fine arts degree in English in 1976, and another in speech and theater in 1979. From 1977 to 1979, Blessing taught playwriting at the University of Iowa. From 1986 to 1988, he taught playwriting at the Playwright's Center in Minneapolis. Since then, he has been the head of the Mason Gross School of the Arts graduate playwriting program at Rutgers University in New Brunswick, New Jersey, and in 1986, he married Jeanne Blake. Although Blessing has sometimes seen Broadway productions, his plays have enjoyed the kind of popularity that makes them regularly produced in regional and amateur theaters.

Besides *A Walk in the Woods*, first produced in 1987 and published in 1988, Blessing has written many other plays, including *The Authentic Life of Billy the Kid, Eleemosynary, Cobb, Fortinbras, Going to St. Ives, Black Sheep,* and *Flag Day.* Like *A Walk in the Woods*, most of Blessing's works draw upon social and political issues but focus on human struggles, especially efforts to forge meaningful interpersonal relations under socially and politically hostile circumstances. Blessing has won a number of awards; *A Walk in the Woods* earned an American Theater Critics Association Award and nominations for a Pulitzer Prize and an Antoinette Perry (Tony) Award in 1987. Blessing has also received the American College Theater Festival Award, 1979; a Jerome Foundation grant, 1981, 1982; a McKnight Foundation grant, 1983, 1989; the Great American Play Award, 1984; a National Endowment for the Arts (NEA) grant, 1985, 1988; a Bush Foundation fellowship, 1987; the Marton Award, 1988; the Dramalogue Award, 1988; and a Guggenheim fellowship, 1989.

PLOT SUMMARY

Little action occurs in *A Walk in the Woods*; most of the play consists of conversation. Although the ostensible purpose of the meeting between the diplomats is to negotiate a treaty, the men discuss a wide variety of topics. Their conversation reveals their personalities and reflects the growth of their relationship.

Act 1
SCENE 1
In *A Walk in the Woods*, Andrey Botvinnik, a diplomat for the Soviet Union, and John Honeyman, a negotiator for the United States, are walking through a forest outside Geneva, Switzerland. They have been sent by their respective governments to try to negotiate a nuclear weapons nonproliferation treaty, which would limit the production of weapons of mass destruction. Botvinnik tells Honeyman how he jokingly told an American television reporter that the Soviet leader Leonid Brezhnev, when he was in power, would begin meetings of the Politburo (political bureau) by saying that Soviet survival depended upon the "total annihilation of America." The reporter believed that Botvinnik was serious and filed the report. When the reporter's chief discovered where the information originated from, he canceled the story, knowing that Botvinnik was inclined to joke.

Botvinnik's story, in addition to demonstrating his personality, sets the tone and rhythm for the rest of the play. Honeyman is relatively new to his position, replacing the previous U.S. negotiator, Mr. McIntyre. Botvinnik is an experienced diplomat who has worked with many U.S. negotiators. The walk in the woods is his idea, and Honeyman understands their walk to be an extension of their concurrent formal negotiation sessions in an atmosphere more favorable to reaching an agreement than the traditional meeting setting. It is not clear, however, that this is Botvinnik's intention. He seems prone to make small talk and avoid serious negotiation. When Honeyman asks Botvinnik if they are taking a walk to discuss the American proposal,

MEDIA ADAPTATIONS

- In 1988, Kirk Browning directed a made-for-television film of *A Walk in the Woods*, featuring the original Broadway cast, Robert Prosky and Sam Waterston.

Botvinnik, while assuring him that the American proposal is a good one, explains that they have come to the woods not to negotiate but to relax, to "talk about trees, lakes, whatever." Honeyman responds that the reporters waiting at the edge of the woods will be disappointed, because they are expecting the two to get some "real work done." In response, Botvinnik turns the conversation to what constitutes real work and suggests that it is important for them to become friends. Honeyman counters, "But is that, strictly speaking, our job?" Characteristically, Botvinnik responds to Honeyman not by addressing his objections but by discussing seemingly trivial matters unrelated to their current situation. Botvinnik leads Honeyman through this *pas des deux*, or well-staged dance for two, and several others, frustrating him with feints, generalities, digressions, and irrelevancies. Honeyman makes a heartfelt and impassioned plea for a "mutual commitment to the hard work of negotiating a treaty," yet Botvinnik continues to change the subject. He points out that Honeyman has a string on his suit. Immediately Honeyman corrects him: he means a thread, not a string. Botvinnik agrees, and Honeyman picks the thread off his suit, mentioning that he has heard Botvinnik is fond of changing the subject. Botvinnik apologizes and then talks about changing the subject before asking if Honeyman's suit is Italian. Finally, Honeyman steers him back to the subject, which is not about nuclear disarmament proposals but whether or not the two should be friends. In response, Botvinnik talks in circles and continually contradicts himself. He says he agrees that the two of them should *not* be friends and then says he wants to agree because they are friends. Honeyman attempts to clarify Botvinnik's statements and points out the contradictions inherent in his speech. Botvinnik admits to Honeyman's claim and offers as an excuse that he "will go to any length to keep a friend." Before the discussion can proceed, Botvinnik uses eye drops, which leads the men into a conversation about Botvinnik's dry eyes.

Once the exchange is finished, Honeyman suggests it is time for them to leave the woods. Botvinnik, though, wonders why they should do so, asking if Honeyman does not like where they are. Honeyman responds that he "need[s] some seriousness," that they owe it to their governments. Botvinnik responds by asking Honeyman if he likes him. Entirely frazzled, Honeyman states that he is leaving. Botvinnik, in response, points out that the reporters waiting for them will question his behavior and asks him if he is embarrassed to be an American. When Honeyman states that he is not ashamed, Botvinnik says he is embarrassed to be Russian, because year after year both governments engage in negotiations to end the nuclear threat and never really accomplish anything. The blame, Botvinnik explains, lies not with either party but with Switzerland. Switzerland is so lovely and peaceful that the negotiators do not feel a sense of urgency to come to an agreement. He adds that negotiations should be held at the bottom of a missile silo instead of Switzerland. Honeyman can only respond by asking Botvinnik why he has not been replaced as the Soviet diplomat. He then answers his own question by acknowledging that Botvinnik is charming and cultured and, most importantly, he is an expert at saying "no" graciously. Honeyman also notes that his predecessor, Mr. McIntyre, was not sure whether Botvinnik's digressions were a deliberate ploy or a character flaw he could not control. Honeyman asserts that Botvinnik is fully in control of what he does, and Botvinnik gently taunts Honeyman for his lack of long-term experience as a negotiator. Honeyman counters by describing his effectiveness and expressing his belief that they will ultimately come to an agreement. Botvinnik responds with a tangent comparing the air in Leningrad, Russia, with the air in Geneva. Both parties say they are about to leave the woods but begin to argue again. Honeyman tries to convince Botvinnik that they are beginning to understand each other. Botvinnik says they agree because they are friends, once more frustrating Honeyman, who is looking for a counterpart to work with, not a friend. On another tangent, Botvinnik turns his attention to Honeyman's shoes. When Honeyman asks if Botvinnik will work with him, Botvinnik responds by asking him where he purchases his ties. When he asks Honeyman when they should take their next walk, Honeyman declares, "Never." Botvinnik, responding with the same tortuous charm he has employed throughout the first act of the play, states, "Very well.... After all, we are here to agree."

SCENE 2

Two months have passed. Botvinnik is sitting on a bench in the woods, and Honeyman is pacing and expressing his impatience with Botvinnik, who has been stalling by arguing about details of a proposal from Washington, D.C. Botvinnik remains calm and disarming, taking nothing Honeyman says seriously and offering no satisfactory explanation for his objections. He also cites the Russian people's suffering forty years earlier during World War II as a reason for Moscow's reluctance. Heatedly, Honeyman rejects this argument, and Botvinnik expresses pleasure at the degree of Honeyman's passion. Just as Honeyman attempts to make a point about Moscow's position, Botvinnik holds up a leaf and asks him what kind it is. Honeyman identifies it as a linden leaf, and Botvinnik asks him if there are such leaves in Wisconsin, where Honeyman comes from. With growing frustration, Honeyman answers, and Botvinnik continues to sidetrack the conversation, repeatedly mispronouncing the name of Honeyman's hometown. Honeyman asks Botvinnik if he is trying to frustrate him in order to gain "the upper hand" and reminds him that if they fail to come to an agreement, they will both be perceived negatively by their countries' media and governments. Botvinnik is unfazed and says he has failed before. Honeyman retorts, however, that *he* has not.

Honeyman asks when Botvinnik believes his government will be able to make a decision about the American proposal. With Botvinnik's answer of "five weeks," Honeyman threatens him, asking, "What if we [the United States] force the matter?" Botvinnik answers quite seriously that by doing so, Honeyman will "lose the proposal." When Honeyman asks him to be quiet, Botvinnik offers to leave. Honeyman, though, notes that if they go back too soon, the reporters will think they are having trouble coming to an agreement. Botvinnik taunts him, saying they are in trouble, and asks if he does not believe in freedom of the press. As the two continue to argue, Botvinnik asks

what they should talk about. Honeyman says they do not have to talk about anything; they just need to stay in the woods for a reasonable interval of time. After a period of silence, Honeyman asks Botvinnik what the U.S. government can do to get him to advocate for the U.S. proposal, an action which Botvinnik says will put his job at risk. Botvinnik replies that there is nothing it can do, but that Honeyman can do something which might make him act—stop being serious and be "frivolous." He explains that the jargon of his profession, including phrases like "test ban" and "Star Wars," profoundly alienate him from a sense of contact with the earth, and he feels like an astronaut floating away from it. He wants to discuss cartoon characters and country music—"anything that is not serious." Honeyman tries but is not good at making frivolous conversation. He can only say that he hates brown suits. He is, Botvinnik remarks, only boring, not frivolous.

Since Honeyman cannot be frivolous, Botvinnik decides to be serious and asks him if he believes there is a difference between Russians and Americans. Honeyman answers that a difference does exist, and Botvinnik proceeds to demonstrate the contrary. He asks Honeyman what would have happened if the Russians had settled in the New World, rather than the English, and answers himself with, "They would have killed all the Indians and taken all the land." He then draws a distinction between Russians and Americans based on the geography of each country. Bounded by oceans that keep enemies at a distance, the Americans were able to engage in "conquest without competition." As Russia is a country of "flat, broad plains," it is open to invasion. Thus, the country engaged in "conquest *because* of competition." Botvinnik continues, stating that Americans developed an ideology of individual freedom, calling conquest "settling the West." Russians developed an ideology of control, channeling "the many wills of the people into one will" in order to vanquish neighboring nations. Botvinnik concludes that Americans believe they are "idealists," because they have "never had to confront themselves as conquerors," whereas Russians, who were forced to do so, define themselves as "realists." When Honeyman calls him "profoundly cynical," Botvinnik responds that he is only "clear-eyed." He has come to understand that no one, "not even the man on the street" wants them to succeed. The ordinary citizens of each country, he asserts, do not want to "give up [their] country's power, prestige and predominance in the world," even though they will deny it. In this situation, Botvinnik argues, nuclear weapons are essential—without nuclear weapons, the countries could not be empires. Botvinnik completes his argument by saying, "The most exciting thing in the world is to know we can destroy the world. Like that. In a day." When Honeyman tries to distinguish between governments and people, recognizing that governments pursue war but people prefer peace, Botvinnik retorts that if this idea is true, the people would make themselves heard. Despite Botvinnik's insistence, Honeyman begs for his help in forging an agreement, asking him to talk to his superiors in the Russian government. Honeyman delivers an impassioned speech about the totality of nuclear annihilation and pleads with Botvinnik to realize the fundamental identity of all humanity: "We look across the table, and we see ourselves." Botvinnik remains unmoved by Honeyman's eloquence, but he gives in when Honeyman makes his help the condition of their friendship. He promises to suggest that his superiors consider Honeyman's proposal without delay.

Act 2

SCENE 1

It is a gloomy winter afternoon. The scene opens as Botvinnik tries unsuccessfully to catch a rabbit running past him. He recalls his prowess in catching rabbits as a boy and how later, during the war, he caught rats for food. Having recently returned to Switzerland from Moscow, Botvinnik tells Honeyman that the Russian government rejected not the proposal itself, but "what [the U.S.] President has turned the proposal into." The president has announced the proposal even though an agreement was not forged, which Botvinnik calls "a cynical public relations scheme." Honeyman defends the president, saying he was forced to announce his plan because the Soviets would not agree to it before the U.S. presidential elections; the president needed to look like he had accomplished something. In addition, Honeyman says he tried to stop the president from making the announcement but does not believe it was wrong to publicize the proposal. Botvinnik explains that the announcement makes the Russians look weak by supposedly agreeing to an American plan and that the negotiations are not a "quest for peace" but a "quest for the appearance of the quest for peace." When Honeyman asks what the Kremlin did not like about the proposal, Botvinnik explains that it "was . . . too good." He adds that the treaty proposed might have actually led to

arms reduction, and while his government wants that, they are also afraid of it. Honeyman does not understand this reasoning and notes that the Soviets have made previous treaties with the United States. Botvinnik objects—they were not really treaties. Rather, they were agreements about which weapons each superpower was going to scrap and which ones they were going to permit each other to build: "We trade obsolete technology for state-of-the-art, we take weapons out of Europe so we can put up new ones in space." By making such agreements, the United States and the Soviet Union appear to exercise restraint while really continuing the arms race. New weapons become "bargaining chips" for the next round of negotiations, and the superpowers look like they are trying to achieve something. However, Botvinnik explains, if the superpowers were to sign a real treaty, they would appear to dishonor the treaty when they created new, more devastating weapons. Without a treaty in place, they could still maintain an appearance of striving for peace. Introducing new weapons after signing a treaty would make the superpowers look like "warmongers who can't keep a treaty."

Still, Honeyman insists, how can they let this small step toward disarmament slip away? Botvinnik responds by assessing the problem of trust. Not only can they not trust each other's governments, they do not even really know what their own governments might secretly be doing. In addition, Botvinnik argues that governments are irrational and are incapable of becoming rational. As he speaks, he reveals his anger about the impasse. When Honeyman points out Botvinnik's anger, he denies it. Botvinnik suggests that it is time for them to speak about things other than their work. Honeyman, however, states that since they are both frustrated, they should discuss their frustration. Botvinnik responds that when two people are dying of cancer, they do not meet to talk about cancer. Honeyman insists that they have a job to do, and Botvinnik passionately responds, "Yes, and now you know what it is," suggesting that their task is precisely not to accomplish anything but only to make a show of attempting to do so. Honeyman cannot accept this answer; he tells Botvinnik of how he visited the nuclear silos in the United States before leaving for Geneva. They are located in the exact center of the North American continent beneath a barren landscape. Honeyman relates that he experienced the emptiness of the place as his own emptiness. He liked the weapons, because they filled the emptiness.

Despite the fact that he wanted to see more weapons built, Honeyman realized this very desire had to be stifled, like an addict's desire for drugs. He refuses to surrender to the hopelessness he sees in Botvinnik.

Although his proposal has been defeated, Honeyman takes the actual papers from his pocket and, giving them to Botvinnik to look at, suggests they simply rename it as if it were another proposal and submit it to their governments again. Botvinnik takes the proposal and makes some changes to it, changes Honeyman finds acceptable. They agree to bring the revised proposal to their governments, Botvinnik convinced it will fail, Honeyman determined to fight for its success.

SCENE 2

It is early spring, six weeks later. Honeyman sits dejectedly on a bench as Botvinnik picks flowers. The American president has rejected the proposal, telling Honeyman not to "try so hard." Botvinnik explains that the president meant that he should not do anything. He recalls how, many years earlier with one of Honeyman's predecessors, he forged an agreement they were both enthusiastic about; it was rejected. This is a climactic moment in the play, revealing the root cause of Botvinnik's cool cynicism. He is a resigned man, whose ardor has been defeated, continuing in a job he knows to be a mockery.

In distress, Honeyman takes the flowers that Botvinnik picked and tosses them on the ground. Botvinnik picks them up and says, "Control yourself. Switzerland has strict laws about littering." This remark surprisingly leads Honeyman to relate an out-of-character incident that occurred that morning. He threw a gum wrapper on the sidewalk, and when an old Swiss police officer told him to pick it up, he made a scene and even pushed the officer. He avoided arrest only after showing the officer his diplomat's identification papers. He is overwrought by the futility of his position as a negotiator; he realizes that he is attempting to settle an overwhelmingly important arms control agreement that his government does not want him to settle. In exasperation, he asks, "What are we doing here?" Botvinnik tells him he is asking "too large" a question and wishes to ask a "smaller one." Botvinnik asks him what his favorite color is, and they riff on this theme at considerable length, as they have throughout the play on various apparently frivolous subjects. Botvinnik reveals the reason for his questioning—he wants to give Honeyman a tie as a parting gift. He is leaving

his position and returning to Leningrad, aware that his work is futile and that intense arms build-ups follow every agreement. Honeyman tries to dissuade him from leaving, but Botvinnik suggests that Honeyman quit too, emphasizing the pointless nature of the negotiator position. Honeyman, though, insists on continuing his role and having hope. The play ends as they decide not to talk anymore. Sitting together silently in the woods, they are aware that their failure to come to an agreement has been successful. They are also conscious that they are two men frustrated by their work; they both have a conscience in a job that has no use for a conscience.

CHARACTERS

Andrey Botvinnik

Botvinnik, the Soviet diplomat, is a tired, somewhat rumpled man who has been able to endure his years as a negotiator with his self-deprecating sense of humor and apparent nonchalance. Botvinnik must face his negotiation counterparts and also navigate the perils of being a Soviet diplomat and satisfying his superiors in the Kremlin. Beneath his carefree exterior, he is frustrated with his work, particularly because it demands that he remain in a futile position. He has metaphorically "dried up," as emphasized by his use of eye drops. It is evident that he was once a lively, curious, and adventurous person; he tells Honeyman how he used to chase rabbits, and he has a love of nature. Working for many years as a diplomat who is instructed not to resolve problems, he is disillusioned with the process of negotiation; this notion makes him an effective negotiator for negotiations that are actually intended to remain unresolved. Botvinnik has abandoned any hope that a real arms control treaty between the Soviet Union and the United States can be possible because of the unstated policy of each government to maintain the upper hand militarily and guard against any possible subterfuge from the opposition. Botvinnik's major skill is changing the subject in a discussion. Essentially, he believes that neither the people nor the governments really want to control the destructive powers that guarantee their geopolitical positions as superpowers. Despite his cynicism, or, as he calls it, "clarity," Botvinnik is a pleasant man, as is shown in both his gift of friendly conversation and his appreciation for nature. He desires friendship with his

American counterpart and a respite from the impasse created by world-threatening, international, political conflicts. With a wry sense of humor and a seeming delight in teasing people, Botvinnik's first anecdote describes how he misled a television reporter to believe that the stereotypical idea of a fierce Soviet desire to destroy the West is absolutely true. The reader may wonder if, beneath his cynicism and despair, Botvinnik believes the fruitless negotiations in which he is involved are actually useful. One may interpret the scene in which Botvinnik imagines that all the trees in the forest are cut down to make negotiation tables as a suggestion that as long as negotiations continue—even though they are unproductive—both sides will remain nonviolent by talking about weapons, rather than launching them at each other.

John Honeyman

Honeyman, the American negotiator, is relatively new in his position as a negotiator. He is a somewhat proud, self-controlled man who apparently needs to prove himself as a competent and strong negotiator. He has a no-nonsense air in his attitude and even in his attire. With a personality far less colorful than that of Botvinnik, Honeyman is loathe to steer off course and lose his focus on the negotiation at hand. Serious and focused, Honeyman is determined to come to an agreement with Botvinnik, despite the two governments' previous difficulties. He seems to be motivated by a sense of pride as well as duty—he does not like to lose. Frustrated by Botvinnik's apparent indifference and resignation, Honeyman believes progress can be made incrementally. Despite the frustration of the discussion, he mainly keeps himself under control—until he ultimately explodes. The underlying cause of his explosion does not lie in his relationship with Botvinnik but with his own government. He experiences unexpected obstacles from U.S. authorities who indirectly convey to him that his mission is not to succeed in obtaining an agreement with the Soviet diplomat. Honeyman cannot concede to the idea of futility as Botvinnik does. Believing that his work is to create peace, particularly because he has experienced and partially overcome his own attraction to the weapons systems, he hopes to dismantle the system and is resolved to overcome his inclination toward violence and domination. He is, however, willful and stubborn when frustrated, as he tells Botvinnik about his encounter with a Swiss police officer over littering. Honeyman states that he tossed a gum wrapper on the sidewalk, which is a civil crime in Geneva. Apprehended by an older police officer for the offense, Honeyman made a scene and drew a crowd of onlookers. Unable to defy the greater authority of his government, Honeyman rebelled against a lesser form of power. Only during the last moments of the play is he able to rest in his sense of futility, and only by sitting silently on a bench with Botvinnik, at peace with him, does Honeyman become at peace with himself.

THEMES

Citizen versus Bureaucrat

To an observer or a reader of newspapers, Botvinnik and Honeyman would seem to be rather powerful men with high-ranking positions in their respective governments. Yet they are actually powerless functionaries performing a public relations charade to maintain each country's peace-seeking image. They do not have the power to bring about change, and their suggestions do not make an impact on the nuclear arms situation. In fact, the leaders of their respective governments dismiss their suggestions, as Blessing suggests, because their governments do not really want peace. The two are frustrated men who must surrender their roles as citizens when they become bureaucrats, or government public servants. Such a situation was to be expected regarding Botvinnik, given the authoritarian nature of the Soviet regime. But in *A Walk in the Woods*, Blessing asserts the situation in the United States is the same.

Cynicism

Cynicism about the motives of governments and their actions is an implicit and pervasive theme in *A Walk in the Woods*. Botvinnik knows that his government does not want him to make progress in his negotiations with Honeyman. Consequently, his diversionary strategies as a negotiator can be seen as the cynical acts of a man who does not believe in what he is doing. His sense of humor, as is evident in his story about how he teased a news reporter about Soviet belligerence, also appears to be driven by cynicism. Honeyman, unlike Botvinnik, is inexperienced and acquires a certain cynicism during the play. He is forced to surrender a naïve idealism when he learns of his government's hypocrisy in negotiations with the Soviet Union. Honeyman must face the reality of his situation; the U.S. government does not appreciate his dedicated efforts to establish a workable plan. Like the Soviet government, the U.S. government wishes to

TOPICS FOR FURTHER STUDY

- In the course of their discussions, Honeyman and Botvinnik refer to a number of acronyms, such as SALT, START, BMD, ASAT, SDI, CEP, MX, SLBM, and SLCM. Research what the acronyms stand for and choose four of them as the subject of a report. Describe each acronym in detail, including any political or military significance. Prepare both a written report and an oral presentation.

- With a classmate, identify an unresolved issue at your school that has two possible resolutions. Choose opposing sides and negotiate with each other to find a solution that you mutually agree on. Write a proposal and present it to one of your school's governing bodies, such as your student council or a group of school officials. Is your proposal accepted, rejected, or returned for modification? What are the reasons for the governing body's decision? Videotape the entire process for screening in your class.

- Write a two-character scene involving a conversation between a representative of the U.S. government and a representative of a country such as Iran, Iraq, or North Korea. In the play, the two representatives should discuss measures to end current international military, political, and cultural conflicts. Perform the scene in front of your class.

- When the United States and the Soviet Union were engaged in negotiating nuclear arms control treaties in the 1980s, a large, citizen-led movement in the United States and other countries advocating a freeze on nuclear weapons acquisition and development was taking place. Research this movement, how it was organized, what its specific objectives were, and what influence it had on nuclear arms controversy. Write a report detailing your findings.

- A. J. Muste, Barbara Demming, Dorothy Day, David Dellinger, Bayard Rustin, Grace Paley, Mohandas K. Gandhi, Judith Malina, David McReynolds, and Julian Beck were some of the leading pacifists (individuals who advocate nonviolence and oppose violent conflict) of the twentieth century. Choose one of the above people as a subject for research and write a biography focusing on the intersection of his or her life and work as a pacifist.

---

maintain the appearance of ongoing negotiations without any actual accomplishment.

Destruction

The encounter between Botvinnik and Honeyman is dramatic and powerful, because of the context in which they meet and the world circumstances that shape that context. They are both aware, as is the audience, that the stakes of their negotiations involve the complete and utter destruction of the world in the event of nuclear war. The magnitude of destruction possible is historically of an order never before realized.

Resignation

Although the term *resignation* is not uttered in *A Walk in the Woods*, the play is very much about the attitude of resigning, or giving in to others. It takes nearly the entire play to realize that Botvinnik's behavior, his deviations and tangents, are actually expressions of resignation to the fact that his task is essentially to make sure that he does not accomplish the task—he must pretend to agree to an arms control agreement. From the start of the play he knows this, unlike Honeyman, since he is an experienced diplomat. Honeyman is new to his job and has high hopes for their discussion. At first, he considers Botvinnik to be cynical. After his best efforts to reach an agreement are thwarted, though, he cracks under the strain of frustration at his inability to move toward his goal. Finally, he surrenders to the facts of his professional life: the play ends as the two negotiators have come to an agreement, not for their governments and not about weaponry, but to sit with each other in a still, silent

Paul Nitze shakes the hand of Juli Kvitsinski at the nuclear arms limitations talks in Switzerland, Geneva, 1981 (AP Images)

center of resignation within the chaos of a discord that has defeated them.

Trust

The theme of trust is implicit throughout *A Walk in the Woods*, which presents negotiators from the United States and the Soviet Union in a delicate battle of wits. Each is attempting to influence the other and secure an agreement to reduce an accumulation of nuclear weapons. The problem of trust is openly discussed. Each man is suspicious of the other, considering him an untrustworthy man who is merely using an agreement on nuclear arms control to gain an advantage in the arms race. In the play, trust is not only intergovernmental; it is also interpersonal, involving the negotiators' ability to trust the integrity of each other. The Soviet negotiator, although an apparently warm, friendly man, can seem cagey and devious. His standard method is to change the subject and prevent them from coming to an agreement. The American negotiator, while appearing more business-like and inflexible, is

idealistic in his dedication to his task and is also set on proving his prowess as a negotiator. The negotiators have trouble trusting each other and the opposing government. Also, they are not positive they can trust their own governments to support decisions made in the negotiation.

STYLE

Digression

Although sections of *A Walk in the Woods* are devoted to the subject of war, weaponry, polemics (passionate argument), and realpolitik (hard-headed practical politics), much of the dialogue in the play does not concern these subjects and can be considered entirely ordinary. These exchanges address favorite colors, French versus Italian shoes, childhood recollections, and bouts of bickering more appropriate to an off-kilter, domestic comedy like Neil Simon's *The Odd Couple* than to

COMPARE & CONTRAST

- **1980s:** The United States is engaged in an ongoing nuclear arms race with the competing imperial superpower, the Soviet Union.

  Today: After the dissolution of the Soviet Union, the United States is no longer in overt competition with Russia and continues to be a nuclear superpower. In 2003 the United States invades Iraq because the country's leader, Saddam Hussein, is allegedly developing weapons of mass destruction.

- **1980s:** The United States holds high-level diplomatic meetings with the Soviet Union; U.S. President Ronald Reagan meets with the Soviet leader, Mikhail Gorbachev, in Reykjavik, Iceland.

  Today: Whether or not leaders of the U.S. government should meet with leaders of countries they designate as adversaries, such as Cuba or Iran, is a hotly debated political issue.

- **1980s:** American citizens mobilize in great numbers and join with citizens of other coun-

  tries to protest the manufacture and stockpiling of nuclear weapons.

  Today: American citizens mobilize in great numbers to oppose the U.S. invasion and occupation of Iraq and are joined in their protests by citizens of other countries around the world.

- **1980s:** The possibility of the use of nuclear weapons in a massive attack causes widespread anxiety in the United States. Due to the threat of mutual annihilation between the United States and Russia, though, nuclear weapons are not deployed.

  Today: The U.S. military uses weapons powered by depleted uranium ammunition, made with low-level radioactive waste, in Fallujah, Iraq. Unlike the nuclear weapons of the 1980s, these are strategically limited weapons. However, their damage goes beyond human injury and raises the level of radiation in the environment.

---

a drama about the fate of the world. Most of these conversations are introduced through the technique of digression, or an apparent change of the subject, which seems to be a unique skill that Botvinnik has cultivated. The drama of much of the dialogue results from the frustration that Honeyman and the audience suffer as apparently trivial conversation replaces what should be life and death discussions. It slowly becomes obvious that Botvinnik's digressions are not really substitutions for other, more serious subjects but the only topics they can really talk about, given the real desire of their governments, as postulated in the play, not to reach an agreement.

Polemics

A Walk in the Woods involves two men at an impasse and how they cope with each other and with their mandates, which they discover to be futile. However, there are several sections in which each of them makes serious speeches of a polemical

nature about the political situation they are in and about the dangers of nuclear annihilation that the world faces because of the arms race between the United States and the Soviet Union. Botvinnik delivers an important lecture on the allure of having the power to cause unlimited destruction. Honeyman delivers a passionate speech about his own attraction to nuclear hardware and on the overwhelming importance of forging agreements that can prevent world-ending catastrophe.

HISTORICAL CONTEXT

The Cold War, the Nuclear Arms Race, and Nuclear Deterrence

During World War II, despite their political and ideological differences, the United States and the Soviet Union formed a military alliance against Nazi Germany. After the war, however, the two

Robert Prosky and Sam Waterston in a 1988 production of A Walk in the Woods *(Peter Cunningham / Time & Life Pictures / Getty Images)*

nations became adversaries, competing with each other to secure spheres of influence and extend their political, economic, and social systems around the world. While numerous proxy military confrontations occurred between the two super-powers in smaller countries, including Greece, Korea, Vietnam, and Afghanistan, a direct military confrontation between them did not take place. Thus, their ongoing opposition was called the cold war. Nevertheless, both the United States and the Soviet Union devoted enormous resources to the development of continually more sophisticated and dangerous nuclear weaponry. They reasoned that the only way to prevent all-out war was to be so heavily armed that neither side would dare attack the other for fear of a mutually assured destruction, a theory called deterrence. While "ban the bomb" movements were strong throughout Europe and the United States since the 1950s, in the 1980s the nuclear freeze movement, calling for a halt in the production of nuclear weapons by both superpowers, became widespread throughout the world.

Glasnost

From 1929 to 1953 the Soviet Union under Joseph Stalin was an absolute dictatorship with all the machinery of totalitarianism, including secret police; show trials; torture; random, politically motivated incarceration and execution; and government secrecy. At the Twentieth Party Congress in February 1956, Nikita Khrushchev denounced Stalin's rule. While there was some denial of the most heinous Stalinist tactics, a real change in regard to the loosening of state control of everyday rights to free expression and of government secrecy began in 1985 with Mikhail Gorbachev's accession to power. Gorbachev introduced the policy of *glasnost*, or openness, and *perestroika*, a policy of economic restructuring, again reducing the control of the state over citizens' activities. The effects of Gorbachev's policies were startling. What had once been a closed society became open. Western popular culture was permitted to flourish openly, rather than remain underground. Newspapers, radio, and television became far less restricted. The Soviet Union was also opened to foreign capitalist investors, businesspeople, and speculators. Ultimately glasnost led to the end of the cold war and the dissolution of the Soviet Union in 1991.

The Meeting between Paul Nitze and Yuli Kvitsinsky

In 1981, U.S. President Ronald Reagan appointed Paul Nitze, a businessman, career diplomat, and arms control negotiator, to head the U.S. delegation to an arms control conference in Geneva, Switzerland. The negotiations, which took place over the course of a year, did not produce an agreement. In desperation, Nitze asked his Soviet counterpart, Yuli Kvitsinsky, to accompany him on a walk through the Jura Mountains. On July 16, 1982, walking in the woods, the two men agreed on a plan to limit the number of intermediate range missiles held by both superpowers. Their governments, though, rejected the plan. In the intervening years, the Soviet Union's leadership went through several changes as one leader after another died, until Mikhail Gorbachev came to power in March 1985. In 1986, Nitze accompanied Reagan to Reykjavik, Iceland, to a summit conference with Gorbachev. Nitze almost succeeded in establishing a nuclear treaty with Sergei Akhromeyev, the Soviet negotiator, but that, too, failed to be approved. On December 8, 1987, the two powers finally reached a nuclear arms limitation treaty.

CRITICAL OVERVIEW

Nominated for a Pulitzer Prize, *A Walk in the Woods* received mostly positive reviews. Writing about a 1987 production of the play staged at the Yale Repertory Theater, *New York Times* contributor Mel Gussow praises the play for being "neither a polemic nor a cartoon, but an engrossing attempt to humanize a situation of awesome portentousness." One of the play's virtues, he argues, is that "there is no artificial enlargement of the two characters into emblematic figures. Mr. Blessing makes us sympathize with them." However, Frank Rich, reviewing the Broadway production in February 1988 for the *New York Times*, views the play as a failed polemic against the arms race. Rich argues that *A Walk in the Woods* "fudges the distinctions of actual international politics and arms negotiations, choosing instead to telescope the messy, life-or-death conflict into a sentimental relationship between two

likable envoys." He adds, "Blessing has made a subject as volatile as the bomb seem as pleasantly cool—and as safely remote—as his neutral forest setting." Rich finds the characters "nearly as generic as their vague negotiating positions." In a March 1988 review for *Time* magazine, William A. Henry, III, calls *A Walk in the Woods* "a work of passion and power with the ring of political truth." *A Walk in the Woods* remains a popular play and has been staged repeatedly by small professional and amateur groups.

CRITICISM

Neil Heims

Heims is a freelance writer living in Paris and the author or editor of over two dozen books on literary subjects. In the following essay, he argues that A Walk in the Woods *is a drama about the absurdity that results when a rational need, nuclear disarmament, and an irrational policy, maintaining the status of a superpower, come into conflict.*

Despite its manifest subject, *A Walk in the Woods* is not really about the nuclear arms race or an unorthodox attempt at arms control negotiations. It is a play about how the continuous pursuit of more powerful weapons systems and the resulting transformation of nations into empires renders rationality irrational, life not only precarious but absurd, and men impotent, or powerless. To be absurd means to be involved in a purposeless, irrational, or meaningless pursuit. This is exactly the condition of Botvinnik and Honeyman, and their respective governments, the Soviet Union and the United States. Even though they want to come to an agreement, Botvinnik and Honeyman cannot advance to the rational goal of limiting the production of nuclear weapons, because although their governments' public positions support arms limitation, their actual policies are to continue to develop deadlier weapons. The leaders of both countries are dedicated to the irrational goal of building more and more sophisticated nuclear weapons of massive destructive capability, of such devastating power that, unlike in the past, Honeyman explains,

> no matter what stupid, gaping terror [men] created, it was always *survivable*. But no more. If we fail now [to come to an agreement] history itself will disappear. Time will stop.... There will be no *here*.

WHAT DO I READ NEXT?

- *The Last Flower* by James Thurber, written in 1939, is an illustrated fable about the destructiveness of war and the folly of mankind.

- *Making Do*, published in 1963, is a novel by Paul Goodman depicting the effect of the cold war and the nuclear arms race on American culture.

- *Insect Dreams: The Half Life of Gregor Samsa*, written by Marc Estrin and published in 2002, is a wry epic novel. Gregor Samsa, the hero-victim of Franz Kafka's story "The Metamorphosis," is resurrected and becomes a participant in the creation of the atomic bomb in Los Alamos, New Mexico.

- *Waiting for Godot*, written by Samuel Beckett and published in 1949, depicts the conversation of two apparently aimless characters in an absurd world who seem to be waiting fruitlessly for a meaningful conclusion to a meaningless situation.

Botvinnik suggests two reasons for this unreasonable quest for limitless power. The first explanation, from the realm of realpolitick, is that neither side is able to trust the other. But Botvinnik, in the course of their dialogue, offers what appears to be a more fundamental reason. "The most exciting thing in the world," he says, "is to know we can destroy the world." With this sentence, Botvinnik removes the problem from the realm of politics or sociology and locates it squarely in the realms of biology and psychology.

The consequence of the awesome weaponry and power of each nation involved in the arms race is that nature is no longer within reach. At best, nature is a lost memory of a past possibility. Botvinnik recalls what it was like, when he was a boy, to be a swift and integral part of nature and, consequently, to be able to catch rabbits with his bare hands. Honeyman, ever an idealist, recalls,

> THEY ARE ABSURD AND FUTILE MEN, HIGHLY
> PLACED BUT POWERLESS, INVOLVED IN A PROCESS
> THAT IS COUNTER TO THEIR CONSCIENCES."

> When I was young, I used to think if you ate a lot of wild things—you know if you went to the woods and gathered things: blueberries, mushrooms, asparagus—I thought eating those things would somehow make you ... wild. Not wild-behaving, just more a part of that world.

Now they are two men in the woods but not a part of the woods. Rather, they are souls lost in the woods. They are absurd and futile men, highly placed but powerless, involved in a process that is counter to their consciences. Botvinnik knows this from the moment the play opens. Honeyman comes to realize it as the play comes to an end. Absurdity and futility are the results of such an international society as the one presented in *A Walk in the Woods*.

Both the conversation and the international climate are defined by Botvinnik's opening lines. The audience catches him in the middle of a story he is telling Honeyman. It is a story characteristic of him, showing not only his negotiation technique of ensnaring his participant's interest and keeping him off balance, but also what has become his technique for survival. As a man who has been rendered absurd, who must work for something he knows he must not achieve, Botvinnik has become a master at constructing digressions promising a result that never materializes. He has turned futility into an art and a pastime. In this sense, the world is absurd because its rulers refuse to take what is serious—total destruction—seriously. Since this absurd world has rendered Botvinnik absurd, he has become a master of absurdity. Not just with this opening anecdote but with everything Botvinnik says, it is difficult to know if he is being serious or facetious. If he is being facetious, it is hard to discern whether his lightheartedness points to something deeper.

Botvinnik tells Honeyman that he once told a network news reporter that "when [Leonid] Brezhnev was in power, he always began Politburo meetings by saying, 'The survival of the

Soviet Union depends on the total annihilation of America.'" The reporter believed him and ran with the story until his senior editor, discovering Botvinnik was the source of the story, canceled it, aware of Botvinnik's tendency to joke. In his statement to the reporter, Botvinnik had been playing on the worst fears of the paranoid cold war mentality. His joke succeeded, because it quite possibly, in the common mind, might not have been a joke. Although Botvinnik now, a sophisticate playing the innocent, says, "How was I to know he'd believe it?" He does not actually deny the truth of what he said. Given the intense propaganda of the cold war and the way each side demonized the other in the media, the reporter was not to blame for believing him. Undoubtedly, many Americans, at the time the play was first produced, and some even now, would have no difficulty believing it either. As noted in a 1956 *Time* magazine article, Soviet Union Prime Minister Nikita Khrushchev famously stated at the Polish embassy on November 18, 1956, "We will bury you," addressing the capitalist West. Khrushchev spoke with a coyness similar to Botvinnik. In a speech in Yugoslavia given on August 24, 1963, he seems to have backtracked. Khrushchev, as quoted in *Simpson's Contemporary Quotations: The Most Notable Quotes since 1960*, explained, "I once said, 'We will bury you,' and I got into trouble with it. Of course we will not bury you with a shovel. Your own working class will bury you." It is in this climate of taunts and maneuvers, and rumors and threats of overwhelming and impenetrable catastrophe, that the conversation between Honeyman and Botvinnik takes place.

The dimensions of the looming disaster are rendered within the conversation. Botvinnik appears to be dedicated to mitigating the scope of the looming threat by refusing to treat it seriously or, sometimes, to acknowledge it at all. Honeyman's passionate intensity, while making him appear to be truly naïve given Botvinnik's sophisticated nonchalance, is really a form of hardheaded outrage. When he is frustrated, that outrage becomes pure rage, which is released in his absurd altercation with an old Swiss police officer who stops him for littering. Refusing to pick up the gum wrapper he dropped in the street, he pushes the police officer and barely avoids being arrested. In this event, something comes full circle. Botvinnik has asked Honeyman to speak of frivolous and trivial things. The anecdote of the chewing gum wrapper meets this

requirement. Yet within it, the profound frustration of being an absurd man is revealed. That is why Botvinnik identifies this event as "crucial" when Honeyman tells him about it. Honeyman's rage is the consequence of being in a position in which, as far as his government is concerned, failure to accomplish what he is apparently supposed to accomplish—and what he is actually dedicated to accomplishing—is the measure of success. Baffled, he tells Botvinnik about his conversation with the U.S. president after he showed him the proposed agreement. "He looked me straight in the eye," Honeyman states, "and said, 'Don't try so hard.'" That, Botvinnik explains, "was only a euphemism" for "don't try at all."

A Walk in the Woods focuses on dialogue and debate, sometimes presenting comments that sound like successful political opinion pieces. Its drama and suspense, if it has either, must come from how its two actors connect with each other and bring their own characters to life. Conversation is the only action of the play, if conversation, especially conversation that leads nowhere, can be called action. The brief interlude in which Botvinnik scampers about the stage trying unsuccessfully to catch a rabbit, can hardly be considered action. Honeyman's aggressive encounter with the Swiss police officer happens offstage and, like an act of violence in a Greek tragedy, is narrated rather than shown to the audience. His confrontation with the U.S. president also happens offstage and is later recounted. Paradoxically, the only action of the play that happens on stage is the action that does not happen. No arms control agreement is achieved, which Botvinnik states, makes their "time together... a very great failure. *But*—a successful one." They have achieved what their governments wanted them to achieve: nothing. How does a play that involves all talk and no action end? In the case of *A Walk in the Woods*, it ends in silence. Silence is what the two achieve, and silence is the play's message, because all of its words are meaningless. They are futile, because they do not lead to action. The only action that their words can possibly lead to, given the intransigent world of the nuclear threat in which they are spoken, is silence.

"Shall we go back?" Botvinnik suggests in the last lines of *A Walk in the Woods*, as they both realize they have nothing else to discuss. They have neither the serious talk of negotiations to pursue, nor the frivolous or "small talk" that has regularly sidetracked or interrupted their conversation, as there is no serious talk to avoid. "Let's stay awhile," however, Honeyman says. "What do you want to talk about?" Botvinnik asks, surprised. "Nothing," Honeyman answers. On this note, they sit in the woods staring out "into the distance" together. Botvinnik puts some drops into his eyes, as he has done throughout the play. Even the act of crying is impossible and can only be rendered by this absurd mechanism. The stage lights fade as they sit in silence, in the heart of nature, two denatured men in a denatured world. They have arrived at an impasse and resolutely acknowledge and yield to it. At this moment, like the Chinese sages in W. B. Yeats's poem "Lapis Lazuli," who sit in a landscape of the mind composed of mountain and sky staring at tragedy, they are no longer absurd. It is a grim comedy.

Source: Neil Heims, Critical Essay on *A Walk in the Woods*, in *Drama for Students*, Gale, Cengage Learning, 2009.

Thomas M. Disch

In the following review, Disch compares A Walk in the Woods *to Larry Shue's* Wenceslas Square, *Len Jenkins's* American Notes, *and Loren-Paul Caplin's* A Subject of Childhood, *remarking that the scenes in Blessing's play are "laboriously contrived and unconvincing."*

Of the two new plays about East meeting West and the resulting strains, I must confess my preference for the ostensibly less serious, Larry Shue's *Wenceslas Square* at the Public Theater. That's not to say that Lee Blessing's *A Walk in the Woods* (at the Booth Theater) fails to engage the attention or command respect, but ultimately these simulated meetings between a U.S. and a Russian arms negotiator seemed as laboriously contrived and unconvincing as Bill Clarke's set, with its lean, limbless tree trunks and recyclable autumn leaves posing in front of the three white walls of an enormous room decorated with a photo of real woods. This unnaturalness was never put to any theatrical use except to remind us, at every moment, that what we were watching was symbolic. Unfortunately, that didn't need underlining.

The problem with *A Walk in the Woods* inheres in its central merit. It is a calm, lucid, nonpartisan scale model of the frustration generated by decades of disarmament negotiations

> BLESSING'S CHARACTERS DO CHANGE AND EVOLVE IN THE COURSE OF *A WALK IN THE WOODS*, AS THE DRAMA RULEBOOK REQUIRES, BUT SHUE'S CHARACTERS BECOME MORE COMPLICATED AS WE GET TO KNOW THEM."

that both the United States and the Soviet Union use as window dressing for the reality of an unstoppable arms race. Robert Prosky (who was *Hill Street Blues*'s Sgt. Jablonski) plays the Soviet negotiator, a lovably gruff teddy bear whose pleasure in rubbing more disingenuous noses in the dirt of geopolitical reality provides the driving force of the plot, such as it is. As the U.S. negotiator whose nose Prosky abuses, Sam Waterston proves once again that not even James Stewart is more like James Stewart than he. Stiff, laconic, lanky and soon to play the title role in an NBC miniseries of Gore Vidal's *Lincoln*, Waterston is the quintessential Yankee. He rebuffs Prosky's overtures of friendship, refuses to play trivia games with him and delivers the show's one overt sermon on the horror of the nuclear arms race, a serviceable paraphrase of Jonathan Schell's *The Fate of the Earth*. However, the play's last word on the subject savors more of Samuel Beckett than of any crusader for disarmament. The negotiators' best efforts prove futile, and they part ways (much as the audience leaves the theater), knowing the nuclear nightmare will go on. Such a muted curse on both superpowers' houses is probably the most commonly used aspirin for frazzled nuclear-age nerves, and *A Walk in the Woods* has enjoyed a fair success with critics and audiences for saying what is universally thought but almost always repressed: We all live in a nuclear submarine.

Wenceslas Square, though more diffident in trundling out the big guns of the *Zeitgeist,* has the merits that sort with modesty: It is lifelike and full of warmth. It takes the form of a travelogue through Prague some five years after the brief political thaw of 1968. The protagonist is a drama teacher (played by Jonathan Hadary) from "Cementville College," who is revisiting Prague to research a "Where Are They Now?"

epilogue to his book about the Czech theater during the thaw; with him is an undergraduate who acts as his photographer and straight man (Bruce Norris, as pleasantly ingenuous in blue jeans in this role as he was as Demetrius in the Public Theater's recent *Midsummer Night's Dream*). As the citizens and officials of Prague, Dana Ivey and Victor Garber tend to steal most scenes, and how could they do otherwise with so many plumm character roles to flit about in? As in his much broader farce, *The Foreigner,* Larry Shue has a lot of fun with the strangeness of language, foreigners' and ours, but unlike that play or his even more frenetic hit (still on Broadway) *The Nerd,* Shue's aim has not been to create some juggernaut laugh machine but simply to recount his experiences as an innocent abroad. (I assume, from its varied textures, that Shue's Prague is based on personal acquaintance. Blessing's "pleasant woods on the outskirts of Geneva" are as generic as the Forest of Arden.) The effect is not unlike Spalding Gray's *Swimming to Cambodia,* with the addition of actors, props and a modicum of scenery.

But let me get back to "lifelike and full of warmth," those bromidic evasions (as they must seem) of the critical responsibility to account precisely for one's applause. Actors as good as Waterston and Prosky can do much to invest wooden characters with seeming vitality, and when the wood used in their construction is of the best quality, illusion can go far. Blessing has given his dialogue a smooth veneer of Shavian high gloss ("Formality," harrumphs his Russian, "is simply anger with its hair combed") and he's taken great pains in the engineering of the two characters' interactions so that there is always a varying tension between them. But: These are not men with lives that continue when they leave the stage, and their major interpersonal dilemma (Can we be friends even though our countries are enemies?) is the kind of happy problem that only exists in the theater and in movies, where it is solved in just two hours after an emotional outburst has prepared the ground for Sympathy and Understanding. Blessing's play shows what arms negotiations would be like if they were conducted by you or me or Everyman; arms negotiators in the real world would have solved Blessing's happy problem years before they got to Geneva. For this reason, Blessing's play ends up delivering a feel-good message despite its ostensibly downbeat ending: If Sam Waterston and Robert Prosky

can become friends, then maybe someday so can America and the Soviet Union. Who would want to contest this Aquarian wisdom, or fail to be comforted by it?

Wenceslas Square is lifelike much in the manner of those evermore exfoliating designs generated by the Mandelbrot set of complex numbers, crystalline lattices of potentially infinite intricacy. Blessing's characters do change and evolve in the course of *A Walk in the Woods,* as the drama rulebook requires, but Shue's characters become more complicated as we get to know them. Part of this is the actors' doing; Hadary, for instance, modulates his laughter through a range from sneaky aggression to self-abnegation that is as finely gradated as Sam Waterston's spectrum of smiles. The difference is that Hadary's characterization is generated by a text that is literally lifelike in its potential for provoking any amount of valid embellishment. Waterston's smiles, like a model's, are a professional accouterment.

Of warmth as a dramatic criterion, though our aesthetic antennae respond to it in art as our skin does in nature, I am reduced to mere finger pointing, head nodding and phatic noises. Shue's play has considerable warmth; Blessing's is lukewarm—but Len Jenkin's *American Notes* (also at the Public Theater) is positively chilly. Its microcosm of ten representative Americans includes: two hookers, a pimp, a U.F.O. fanatic, a carnival pitchman, a zombielike derelict and a mysterious stranger in a trench coat who pays sinister court to the coed night clerk of a seedy motel. These and other lowlifes all speak the argot peculiar to serious theater, a poesy as stereotyped as the lyrics of country and western ballads, and not that different. In Jenkin's America, women are either victims or whores, men are sinister creeps or pathetic wimps, no one works (except the zombie), people survive on fast food and booze, and the TV is always on, rotting minds. No one goes anywhere, no one listens to anyone else, and the program comes with an epigraph from Blake's *America:* "Tho' obscur'd, this is the form of the Angelic land." This is the mindset of a 16-year-old refugee from Winnetka still wet behind the ears with the blood from his or her first piercing. Jenkin is scarcely the first to confuse the safety pin in his cheek with political savvy, nor even the callowest.

The most distressing thing about *American Notes* was the wealth of theatrical talent that has been squandered on its production: an elaborate, two-tiered honeycomb of a set designed by John Arnone and the services of ten actors with enough prior credits among them to constitute a brief history of Off Broadway. But had they been the Royal Shakespeare Company they couldn't have kept *American Notes* afloat, so there's not much point blaming (or naming) them. The nature and degree of producer Joseph Papp's responsibility is a matter of conjecture. My own, based upon a sampling of such recent Papp productions as David Hare's fatal *The Knife* and Reinaldo Povod's *La Puta Vida,* is that Papp, being of a bilious disposition, will settle for the near-beer of petulance when genuine wrath or malice isn't on tap. It may also be the case that near-beer is a more marketable commodity, but I doubt it.

A Subject of Childhood at the WPA Theater is a horse so redolently dead that one hesitates to whip its gruesome carcass. Playwright Loren-Paul Caplin writes dialogue that would make even the hastiest soap-opera hack cringe. Like the immortal Florence Foster Jenkins, he possesses a voice that grates throughout its range. Whether he's being gooey about love, or purveying psychobabble, or having people quarrel like toddlers ("No, you're not!" "Yes, I am!" "Not, not, not!" is a fair paraphrase of one big scene), Caplin gets it wrong. As his tired plot plods to its Act I curtain (rarely does a play this bad offer an intermission in which to escape one's seat), the luckless onlooker's wandering mind inevitably begins to speculate on *how* such a turkey ever came to be served up by a theatrical company with the track record of the WPA Theater, the originator of last season's entirely stageworthy *Steel Magnolias.* Admittedly, it's got a high-concept story line: parents debating whether their little boy is a genuine Bad Seed, or did his little friend fall to his death by accident? But this viable idea doesn't survive five minutes of Caplin's heavy-handed treatment. Surely a professional, in reading the script, would have known what anyone but Caplin's mother would have to say about *A Subject of Childhood*—i.e., that it was certain to bomb. But where there's a part, no matter how bad, somewhere there'll be an actor hungry enough to take it. (One of the actresses in *Subject* is making her Off Broadway debut, and my advice to her is to change her name and start from scratch.) But why would a *director* ask for this kind of trouble? The answer appears in the program notes, where we're informed that

director Bill Castellino co-wrote the book for *City Muzik* with its composer-lyricist, none other than Loren-Paul Caplin. From that point, what one is seeing on stage begins to make sense.

The reason *Subject* is worth discussing at all is the set by Edward T. Gianfrancesco, one of Off Broadway's most capable scene designers. It represents the living room, staircase and upstairs hallway of a house said to be in Brooklyn. Gianfrancesco's idea was to universalize his domestic interior by surrounding gray stuffed furniture on a gray carpet with bookshelves, a TV, a child's plastic tricycle and other impedimenta, all spackled gray. Ditto the walls and the pictures on the walls. It was hard not to suppose that this was Gianfrancesco's veiled comment on the character of the text he'd been set to illustrate rather than a sincere aesthetic faux pas. After all, if a dead horse needn't be beaten, neither does it require much in the way of equipage, so why not just paint it gray?

However, this particular style of design has become, with some trivial modifications, a commonplace among Off Broadway theaters, and it cannot represent in all such cases the set designer's cryptic commentary on the text. The Second Stage's recent *Loose Ends* and several productions at Circle Rep have adopted this generic solution to the problem of low-budget set decoration. It is almost always a false solution, for gray paint, gray carpets and gray sofas do not create a Platonic living room inhabitable by any cast of characters; they represent the negation of the forms over which they cast their pall. A designer would do better to scavenge authentic furniture off the streets than to fob off another such dentist's waiting room as a set design. It's simply an excuse for not thinking.

Loren Sherman, who designed the set for *Wenceslas Square,* was under (I would guess) budgetary constraints comparable to those at WPA, but Sherman's every prop and stick of furniture was expressive and characterful. Even the piece of steel scaffolding that signified a construction site was individualized by a red-trimmed metal trough for mixing concrete, which had the expressive individuality of a piece of sculpture. A set designer doesn't need a big budget to create great sets, only a live imagination, a good eye and an understanding of the secret language of cloth, wood and papier-mâché.

Source: Thomas M. Disch, Review of *A Walk in the Woods,* in *Nation,* April 9, 1988, pp. 510–12.

Leo Sauvage

In the following review, Sauvage provides a generally positive critique of A Walk in the Woods *and comments in particular on the play's characterization.*

A Walk in the Woods can unambiguously be welcomed to New York's Booth Theater. Whether it lasts for years or, because of its unconventional subject, has a more limited run, it will surely rank among the most interesting plays of many a Broadway season.

Disarmament negotiations tend to be a crabbed and difficult business—hardly an obvious source for show material. There is a certain tediousness, moreover, to the strategics involved: Diplomatic teams are perfectly capable of rejecting a provision they agree with and would have liked to have proposed themselves simply because it has been broached by the other side.

Happily, the American playwright Lee Blessing has kept the technicalities and convolutions inherent in such exchanges to a minimum. He also has supplied enough sharp and shiny lines to give *Woods* plenty of dramatic drive. The play manages to teach us something without being the least bit didactic. Thanks to Blessing's sure touch, we avidly follow the twisting path through the Geneva landscape, smiling all the while.

That is not to say this production—which came to New York from the La Jolla Playhouse in California via Yale—is perfect in every respect. Indeed, some might be disturbed that Blessing and director Des McAnuff have endowed the Russian official with qualities of subtlety, depth and humor that far surpass those discernible in the American. Andrey Botvinnik (Robert Prosky) is older and more experienced than his interlocutor. He has been hardened by disappointment, and his wryly cynical tone suggests an underlying hopelessness. Paired with the youngish, eager John Honeyman (Sam Waterston), whose impulsive sincerity frequently erupts in fits of righteous shouting, Botvinnik is the one who inevitably fascinates us. It is as though in responding to the challenge of humanizing the unorthodox Soviet diplomat, Blessing and McAnuff got carried away and made his counterpart into a bit of a foil.

Lest this asymmetry in the two characters be taken as a reflection of political bias, it should be added that Botvinik—whose disciplined sarcasm does not adequately mask an absence of illusions about his own country—is finally removed from the negotiations by his suspicious bosses. The ever hopeful Honeyman stays on in Geneva to deal with his successor.

The play was inspired by a well-known incident: In the summer of 1982, Yuli A. Kvitsinsky and Paul H. Nitze stepped away from a deadlocked arms reduction session in Geneva for a stroll in a nearby park, and returned with a break-through compromise (which ultimately proved unacceptable to hardliners on both sides). Yet it was evidently not Blessing's intention merely to give a dramatized account of this: His four half-acts see Botvinnik and Honeyman having four different conversations in the glade— one in each season of the year—and the American character is in many ways the antithesis of Nitze.

A Walk in the Woods marks a promising Broadway debut for Blessing, who has an undeniable flair for stage writing. Rather than getting lost in a jungle of issues and meanings, he uses the Geneva talks as an occasion for scrutinizing the minds and hearts of the opposed parties, drawing out their shared need to convince and be convinced as well as to prevail. McAnuff's direction is admirable, and Robert Prosky turns in one of the most skillful performances of his long career. Bill Clarke's stylish set cleverly extends the almost Chekhovian presence of the trees, paths and bench in the foreground by means of a framed painting of woods upstage.

To avoid giving the impression that I was utterly overcome with pleasure by a Broadway play simply because it was well enough turned out not to require roller skates, let me end by registering a tiny cavil: Why is the winter scene signaled by an unbelievably dense fog that has as little to do with Geneva weather as it does with the clarity of *Woods'* insight into the minds of the negotiators?

Source: Leo Sauvage, Review of *A Walk in the Woods*, in *New Leader*, Vol. 71, No. 5, March 21, 1988, p. 23.

SOURCES

Blessing, Lee, *A Walk in the Woods*, Dramatists Play Service, 1998.

Gussow, Mel, "Theater: Bilateral Talks in *A Walk in the Woods*," in the *New York Times*, March 8, 1987, p. 66.

Henry, William A., III, "To Survive, Just Keep Talking: *A Walk in the Woods*," in *Time*, March 14, 1988, p. 91.

"Lee Blessing, Playwright," in the Indiana University Web site, http://www.indiana.edu/~thtr/guests/bio/blessing.html (accessed October 8, 2008).

"Lee (Knowlton) Blessing," in *Contemporary Dramatists*, 6th ed., St. James Press, 1999.

McCauley, Martin, "Union of Soviet Socialist Republics," in *Encyclopaedia Britannica Online*.

"Paul Nitze: Master Strategist of the Cold War," in *Academy of Achievement*, February 25, 2005, http://www.achievement. org/autodoc/page/nit0bio-1 (accessed August 1, 2008).

"Quote 192," in *Simpson's Contemporary Quotations: The Most Notable Quotes since 1950*, compiled by James Beasley Simpson, Houghton Mifflin, 1988.

Rich, Frank, "Stage: *A Walk in the Woods*," in *New York Times*, February 29, 1988, p. 18.

"We Will Bury You!," in *Time*, November 26, 1956.

FURTHER READING

Alinsky, Saul, *Rules for Radicals: A Pragmatic Primer for Realistic Radicals*, Random House, 1971.

> Alinsky, 1909–1972, was a community organizer who pioneered many techniques for disenfranchised people to attain social and economic power in their communities through negotiation.

Kahn, Herman, *On Thermonuclear War*, Princeton University Press, 1960, Transaction Publishers, 2007.

> One of the principle works justifying the building and stockpiling of nuclear weapons, this book also calculates the degree of destruction in a nuclear war that can be considered acceptable.

Knebel, Fletcher, and Charles W. Bailey, II, *Seven Days in May*, Harper & Row, 1962.

> This cold war thriller is about the reaction of a unit of military hawks to a nuclear arms control treaty implemented by the United States and the Soviet Union.

McReynolds, David, *We Have Been Invaded by the 21st Century*, Praeger, 1970.

> McReynolds is a pacifist and a socialist who worked as field secretary for the War Resisters League and has written extensively about the cold war and the nuclear threat.

Glossary of Literary Terms

A

Abstract: Used as a noun, the term refers to a short summary or outline of a longer work. As an adjective applied to writing or literary works, abstract refers to words or phrases that name things not knowable through the five senses. Examples of abstracts include the *Cliffs Notes* summaries of major literary works. Examples of abstract terms or concepts include "idea," "guilt" "honesty," and "loyalty."

Absurd, Theater of the: See *Theater of the Absurd*

Absurdism: See *Theater of the Absurd*

Act: A major section of a play. Acts are divided into varying numbers of shorter scenes. From ancient times to the nineteenth century plays were generally constructed of five acts, but modern works typically consist of one, two, or three acts. Examples of five-act plays include the works of Sophocles and Shakespeare, while the plays of Arthur Miller commonly have a three-act structure.

Acto: A one-act Chicano theater piece developed out of collective improvisation. *Actos* were performed by members of Luis Valdez's Teatro Campesino in California during the mid-1960s.

Aestheticism: A literary and artistic movement of the nineteenth century. Followers of the movement believed that art should not be mixed with social, political, or moral teaching.

The statement "art for art's sake" is a good summary of aestheticism. The movement had its roots in France, but it gained widespread importance in England in the last half of the nineteenth century, where it helped change the Victorian practice of including moral lessons in literature. Oscar Wilde is one of the best-known "aesthetes" of the late nineteenth century.

Age of Johnson: The period in English literature between 1750 and 1798, named after the most prominent literary figure of the age, Samuel Johnson. Works written during this time are noted for their emphasis on "sensibility," or emotional quality. These works formed a transition between the rational works of the Age of Reason, or Neoclassical period, and the emphasis on individual feelings and responses of the Romantic period. Significant writers during the Age of Johnson included the novelists Ann Radcliffe and Henry Mackenzie, dramatists Richard Sheridan and Oliver Goldsmith, and poets William Collins and Thomas Gray. Also known as Age of Sensibility

Age of Reason: See *Neoclassicism*

Age of Sensibility: See *Age of Johnson*

Alexandrine Meter: See *Meter*

Allegory: A narrative technique in which characters representing things or abstract ideas are used to convey a message or teach a lesson.

Allegory is typically used to teach moral, ethical, or religious lessons but is sometimes used for satiric or political purposes. Examples of allegorical works include Edmund Spenser's *The Faerie Queene* and John Bunyan's *The Pilgrim's Progress.*

Allusion: A reference to a familiar literary or historical person or event, used to make an idea more easily understood. For example, describing someone as a "Romeo" makes an allusion to William Shakespeare's famous young lover in *Romeo and Juliet.*

Amerind Literature: The writing and oral traditions of Native Americans. Native American literature was originally passed on by word of mouth, so it consisted largely of stories and events that were easily memorized. Amerind prose is often rhythmic like poetry because it was recited to the beat of a ceremonial drum. Examples of Amerind literature include the autobiographical *Black Elk Speaks,* the works of N. Scott Momaday, James Welch, and Craig Lee Strete, and the poetry of Luci Tapahonso.

Analogy: A comparison of two things made to explain something unfamiliar through its similarities to something familiar, or to prove one point based on the acceptedness of another. Similes and metaphors are types of analogies. Analogies often take the form of an extended simile, as in William Blake's aphorism: "As the caterpillar chooses the fairest leaves to lay her eggs on, so the priest lays his curse on the fairest joys."

Angry Young Men: A group of British writers of the 1950s whose work expressed bitterness and disillusionment with society. Common to their work is an anti-hero who rebels against a corrupt social order and strives for personal integrity. The term has been used to describe Kingsley Amis, John Osborne, Colin Wilson, John Wain, and others.

Antagonist: The major character in a narrative or drama who works against the hero or protagonist. An example of an evil antagonist is Richard Lovelace in Samuel Richardson's *Clarissa,* while a virtuous antagonist is Macduff in William Shakespeare's *Macbeth.*

Anthropomorphism: The presentation of animals or objects in human shape or with human characteristics. The term is derived from the Greek word for "human form." The fables of Aesop, the animated films of Walt Disney, and Richard Adams's *Watership Down* feature anthropomorphic characters.

Anti-hero: A central character in a work of literature who lacks traditional heroic qualities such as courage, physical prowess, and fortitude. Anti-heros typically distrust conventional values and are unable to commit themselves to any ideals. They generally feel helpless in a world over which they have no control. Anti-heroes usually accept, and often celebrate, their positions as social outcasts. A well-known anti-hero is Yossarian in Joseph Heller's novel *Catch-22.*

Antimasque: See *Masque*

Antithesis: The antithesis of something is its direct opposite. In literature, the use of antithesis as a figure of speech results in two statements that show a contrast through the balancing of two opposite ideas. Technically, it is the second portion of the statement that is defined as the "antithesis"; the first portion is the "thesis." An example of antithesis is found in the following portion of Abraham Lincoln's "Gettysburg Address"; notice the opposition between the verbs "remember" and "forget" and the phrases "what we say" and "what they did": "The world will little note nor long remember what we say here, but it can never forget what they did here."

Apocrypha: Writings tentatively attributed to an author but not proven or universally accepted to be their works. The term was originally applied to certain books of the Bible that were not considered inspired and so were not included in the "sacred canon." Geoffrey Chaucer, William Shakespeare, Thomas Kyd, Thomas Middleton, and John Marston all have apocrypha. Apocryphal books of the Bible include the Old Testament's Book of Enoch and New Testament's Gospel of Peter.

Apollonian and Dionysian: The two impulses believed to guide authors of dramatic tragedy. The Apollonian impulse is named after Apollo, the Greek god of light and beauty and the symbol of intellectual order. The Dionysian impulse is named after Dionysus, the Greek god of wine and the symbol of the unrestrained forces of nature. The Apollonian impulse is to create a rational, harmonious world, while the Dionysian is to express the irrational forces of personality. Friedrich Nietzche uses these terms in *The*

Birth of Tragedy to designate contrasting elements in Greek tragedy.

Apostrophe: A statement, question, or request addressed to an inanimate object or concept or to a nonexistent or absent person. Requests for inspiration from the muses in poetry are examples of apostrophe, as is Marc Antony's address to Caesar's corpse in William Shakespeare's *Julius Caesar*: "O, pardon me, thou bleeding piece of earth, That I am meek and gentle with these butchers!... Woe to the hand that shed this costly blood!..."

Archetype: The word archetype is commonly used to describe an original pattern or model from which all other things of the same kind are made. This term was introduced to literary criticism from the psychology of Carl Jung. It expresses Jung's theory that behind every person's "unconscious," or repressed memories of the past, lies the "collective unconscious" of the human race: memories of the countless typical experiences of our ancestors. These memories are said to prompt illogical associations that trigger powerful emotions in the reader. Often, the emotional process is primitive, even primordial. Archetypes are the literary images that grow out of the "collective unconscious." They appear in literature as incidents and plots that repeat basic patterns of life. They may also appear as stereotyped characters. Examples of literary archetypes include themes such as birth and death and characters such as the Earth Mother.

Argument: The argument of a work is the author's subject matter or principal idea. Examples of defined "argument" portions of works include John Milton's *Arguments* to each of the books of *Paradise Lost* and the "Argument" to Robert Herrick's *Hesperides*.

Aristotelian Criticism: Specifically, the method of evaluating and analyzing tragedy formulated by the Greek philosopher Aristotle in his *Poetics*. More generally, the term indicates any form of criticism that follows Aristotle's views. Aristotelian criticism focuses on the form and logical structure of a work, apart from its historical or social context, in contrast to "Platonic Criticism," which stresses the usefulness of art. Adherents of New Criticism including John Crowe Ransom and Cleanth Brooks utilize and value the basic ideas of Aristotelian criticism for textual analysis.

Art for Art's Sake: See *Aestheticism*

Aside: A comment made by a stage performer that is intended to be heard by the audience but supposedly not by other characters. Eugene O'Neill's *Strange Interlude* is an extended use of the aside in modern theater.

Audience: The people for whom a piece of literature is written. Authors usually write with a certain audience in mind, for example, children, members of a religious or ethnic group, or colleagues in a professional field. The term "audience" also applies to the people who gather to see or hear any performance, including plays, poetry readings, speeches, and concerts. Jane Austen's parody of the gothic novel, *Northanger Abbey,* was originally intended for (and also pokes fun at) an audience of young and avid female gothic novel readers.

Avant-garde: A French term meaning "vanguard." It is used in literary criticism to describe new writing that rejects traditional approaches to literature in favor of innovations in style or content. Twentieth-century examples of the literary *avant-garde* include the Black Mountain School of poets, the Bloomsbury Group, and the Beat Movement.

B

Ballad: A short poem that tells a simple story and has a repeated refrain. Ballads were originally intended to be sung. Early ballads, known as folk ballads, were passed down through generations, so their authors are often unknown. Later ballads composed by known authors are called literary ballads. An example of an anonymous folk ballad is "Edward," which dates from the Middle Ages. Samuel Taylor Coleridge's "The Rime of the Ancient Mariner" and John Keats's "La Belle Dame sans Merci" are examples of literary ballads.

Baroque: A term used in literary criticism to describe literature that is complex or ornate in style or diction. Baroque works typically express tension, anxiety, and violent emotion. The term "Baroque Age" designates a period in Western European literature beginning in the late sixteenth century and ending about one hundred years later. Works of this period often mirror the qualities of works more generally associated with the label "baroque" and sometimes feature elaborate conceits. Examples of Baroque works include John

Lyly's *Euphues: The Anatomy of Wit,* Luis de Gongora's *Soledads,* and William Shakespeare's *As You Like It.*

Baroque Age: See *Baroque*

Baroque Period: See *Baroque*

Beat Generation: See *Beat Movement*

Beat Movement: A period featuring a group of American poets and novelists of the 1950s and 1960s—including Jack Kerouac, Allen Ginsberg, Gregory Corso, William S. Burroughs, and Lawrence Ferlinghetti—who rejected established social and literary values. Using such techniques as stream of consciousness writing and jazz-influenced free verse and focusing on unusual or abnormal states of mind—generated by religious ecstasy or the use of drugs—the Beat writers aimed to create works that were unconventional in both form and subject matter. Kerouac's *On the Road* is perhaps the best-known example of a Beat Generation novel, and Ginsberg's *Howl* is a famous collection of Beat poetry.

Black Aesthetic Movement: A period of artistic and literary development among African Americans in the 1960s and early 1970s. This was the first major African-American artistic movement since the Harlem Renaissance and was closely paralleled by the civil rights and black power movements. The black aesthetic writers attempted to produce works of art that would be meaningful to the black masses. Key figures in black aesthetics included one of its founders, poet and playwright Amiri Baraka, formerly known as LeRoi Jones; poet and essayist Haki R. Madhubuti, formerly Don L. Lee; poet and playwright Sonia Sanchez; and dramatist Ed Bullins. Works representative of the Black Aesthetic Movement include Amiri Baraka's play *Dutchman,* a 1964 Obie award-winner; *Black Fire: An Anthology of Afro-American Writing,* edited by Baraka and playwright Larry Neal and published in 1968; and Sonia Sanchez's poetry collection *We a BaddDDD People,* published in 1970. Also known as Black Arts Movement.

Black Arts Movement: See *Black Aesthetic Movement*

Black Comedy: See *Black Humor*

Black Humor: Writing that places grotesque elements side by side with humorous ones in an attempt to shock the reader, forcing him or her to laugh at the horrifying reality of a disordered world. Joseph Heller's novel *Catch-22* is considered a superb example of the use of black humor. Other well-known authors who use black humor include Kurt Vonnegut, Edward Albee, Eugene Ionesco, and Harold Pinter. Also known as Black Comedy.

Blank Verse: Loosely, any unrhymed poetry, but more generally, unrhymed iambic pentameter verse (composed of lines of five two-syllable feet with the first syllable accented, the second unaccented). Blank verse has been used by poets since the Renaissance for its flexibility and its graceful, dignified tone. John Milton's *Paradise Lost* is in blank verse, as are most of William Shakespeare's plays.

Bloomsbury Group: A group of English writers, artists, and intellectuals who held informal artistic and philosophical discussions in Bloomsbury, a district of London, from around 1907 to the early 1930s. The Bloomsbury Group held no uniform philosophical beliefs but did commonly express an aversion to moral prudery and a desire for greater social tolerance. At various times the circle included Virginia Woolf, E. M. Forster, Clive Bell, Lytton Strachey, and John Maynard Keynes.

Bon Mot: A French term meaning "good word." A *bon mot* is a witty remark or clever observation. Charles Lamb and Oscar Wilde are celebrated for their witty *bon mots.* Two examples by Oscar Wilde stand out: (1) "All women become their mothers. That is their tragedy. No man does. That's his." (2) "A man cannot be too careful in the choice of his enemies."

Breath Verse: See *Projective Verse*

Burlesque: Any literary work that uses exaggeration to make its subject appear ridiculous, either by treating a trivial subject with profound seriousness or by treating a dignified subject frivolously. The word "burlesque" may also be used as an adjective, as in "burlesque show," to mean "striptease act." Examples of literary burlesque include the comedies of Aristophanes, Miguel de Cervantes's *Don Quixote,,* Samuel Butler's poem "Hudibras," and John Gay's play *The Beggar's Opera.*

C

Cadence: The natural rhythm of language caused by the alternation of accented and unaccented syllables. Much modern poetry—notably free verse—deliberately manipulates cadence to create complex rhythmic effects. James Macpherson's "Ossian poems" are richly cadenced, as is the poetry of the Symbolists, Walt Whitman, and Amy Lowell.

Caesura: A pause in a line of poetry, usually occurring near the middle. It typically corresponds to a break in the natural rhythm or sense of the line but is sometimes shifted to create special meanings or rhythmic effects. The opening line of Edgar Allan Poe's "The Raven" contains a caesura following "dreary": "Once upon a midnight dreary, while I pondered weak and weary...."

Canzone: A short Italian or Provencal lyric poem, commonly about love and often set to music. The *canzone* has no set form but typically contains five or six stanzas made up of seven to twenty lines of eleven syllables each. A shorter, five- to ten-line "envoy," or concluding stanza, completes the poem. Masters of the *canzone* form include Petrarch, Dante Alighieri, Torquato Tasso, and Guido Cavalcanti.

Carpe Diem: A Latin term meaning "seize the day." This is a traditional theme of poetry, especially lyrics. A *carpe diem* poem advises the reader or the person it addresses to live for today and enjoy the pleasures of the moment. Two celebrated *carpe diem* poems are Andrew Marvell's "To His Coy Mistress" and Robert Herrick's poem beginning "Gather ye rosebuds while ye may...."

Catharsis: The release or purging of unwanted emotions—specifically fear and pity—brought about by exposure to art. The term was first used by the Greek philosopher Aristotle in his *Poetics* to refer to the desired effect of tragedy on spectators. A famous example of catharsis is realized in Sophocles' *Oedipus Rex,* when Oedipus discovers that his wife, Jacosta, is his own mother and that the stranger he killed on the road was his own father.

Celtic Renaissance: A period of Irish literary and cultural history at the end of the nineteenth century. Followers of the movement aimed to create a romantic vision of Celtic myth and legend. The most significant works of the Celtic Renaissance typically present a dreamy, unreal world, usually in reaction against the reality of contemporary problems. William Butler Yeats's *The Wanderings of Oisin* is among the most significant works of the Celtic Renaissance. Also known as Celtic Twilight.

Celtic Twilight: See *Celtic Renaissance*

Character: Broadly speaking, a person in a literary work. The actions of characters are what constitute the plot of a story, novel, or poem. There are numerous types of characters, ranging from simple, stereotypical figures to intricate, multifaceted ones. In the techniques of anthropomorphism and personification, animals—and even places or things—can assume aspects of character. "Characterization" is the process by which an author creates vivid, believable characters in a work of art. This may be done in a variety of ways, including (1) direct description of the character by the narrator; (2) the direct presentation of the speech, thoughts, or actions of the character; and (3) the responses of other characters to the character. The term "character" also refers to a form originated by the ancient Greek writer Theophrastus that later became popular in the seventeenth and eighteenth centuries. It is a short essay or sketch of a person who prominently displays a specific attribute or quality, such as miserliness or ambition. Notable characters in literature include Oedipus Rex, Don Quixote de la Mancha, Macbeth, Candide, Hester Prynne, Ebenezer Scrooge, Huckleberry Finn, Jay Gatsby, Scarlett O'Hara, James Bond, and Kunta Kinte.

Characterization: See *Character*

Chorus: In ancient Greek drama, a group of actors who commented on and interpreted the unfolding action on the stage. Initially the chorus was a major component of the presentation, but over time it became less significant, with its numbers reduced and its role eventually limited to commentary between acts. By the sixteenth century the chorus—if employed at all—was typically a single person who provided a prologue and an epilogue and occasionally appeared between acts to introduce or underscore an important event. The chorus in William Shakespeare's *Henry V* functions in this way. Modern dramas rarely feature a chorus, but T. S. Eliot's *Murder in the Cathedral* and Arthur Miller's *A View from the Bridge* are notable exceptions. The Stage Manager in Thornton Wilder's *Our Town* performs a role similar to that of the chorus.

Chronicle: A record of events presented in chronological order. Although the scope and level of detail provided varies greatly among the chronicles surviving from ancient times, some, such as the *Anglo-Saxon Chronicle,* feature vivid descriptions and a lively recounting of events. During the Elizabethan Age, many dramas— appropriately called "chronicle plays"—were based on material from chronicles. Many of William Shakespeare's dramas of English history as well as Christopher Marlowe's *Edward II* are based in part on Raphael Holinshead's *Chronicles of England, Scotland, and Ireland.*

Classical: In its strictest definition in literary criticism, classicism refers to works of ancient Greek or Roman literature. The term may also be used to describe a literary work of recognized importance (a "classic") from any time period or literature that exhibits the traits of classicism. Classical authors from ancient Greek and Roman times include Juvenal and Homer. Examples of later works and authors now described as classical include French literature of the seventeenth century, Western novels of the nineteenth century, and American fiction of the mid-nineteenth century such as that written by James Fenimore Cooper and Mark Twain.

Classicism: A term used in literary criticism to describe critical doctrines that have their roots in ancient Greek and Roman literature, philosophy, and art. Works associated with classicism typically exhibit restraint on the part of the author, unity of design and purpose, clarity, simplicity, logical organization, and respect for tradition. Examples of literary classicism include Cicero's prose, the dramas of Pierre Corneille and Jean Racine, the poetry of John Dryden and Alexander Pope, and the writings of J. W. von Goethe, G. E. Lessing, and T. S. Eliot.

Climax: The turning point in a narrative, the moment when the conflict is at its most intense. Typically, the structure of stories, novels, and plays is one of rising action, in which tension builds to the climax, followed by falling action, in which tension lessens as the story moves to its conclusion. The climax in James Fenimore Cooper's *The Last of the Mohicans* occurs when Magua and his captive Cora are pursued to the edge of a cliff by Uncas. Magua kills Uncas but is subsequently killed by Hawkeye.

Colloquialism: A word, phrase, or form of pronunciation that is acceptable in casual conversation but not in formal, written communication. It is considered more acceptable than slang. An example of colloquialism can be found in Rudyard Kipling's *Barrack-room Ballads:* When 'Omer smote 'is bloomin' lyre He'd 'eard men sing by land and sea; An' what he thought 'e might require 'E went an' took— the same as me!

Comedy: One of two major types of drama, the other being tragedy. Its aim is to amuse, and it typically ends happily. Comedy assumes many forms, such as farce and burlesque, and uses a variety of techniques, from parody to satire. In a restricted sense the term comedy refers only to dramatic presentations, but in general usage it is commonly applied to nondramatic works as well. Examples of comedies range from the plays of Aristophanes, Terrence, and Plautus, Dante Alighieri's *The Divine Comedy,* Francois Rabelais's *Pantagruel* and *Gargantua,* and some of Geoffrey Chaucer's tales and William Shakespeare's plays to Noel Coward's play *Private Lives* and James Thurber's short story "The Secret Life of Walter Mitty."

Comedy of Manners: A play about the manners and conventions of an aristocratic, highly sophisticated society. The characters are usually types rather than individualized personalities, and plot is less important than atmosphere. Such plays were an important aspect of late seventeenth-century English comedy. The comedy of manners was revived in the eighteenth century by Oliver Goldsmith and Richard Brinsley Sheridan, enjoyed a second revival in the late nineteenth century, and has endured into the twentieth century. Examples of comedies of manners include William Congreve's *The Way of the World* in the late seventeenth century, Oliver Goldsmith's *She Stoops to Conquer* and Richard Brinsley Sheridan's *The School for Scandal* in the eighteenth century, Oscar Wilde's *The Importance of Being Earnest* in the nineteenth century, and W. Somerset Maugham's *The Circle* in the twentieth century.

Comic Relief: The use of humor to lighten the mood of a serious or tragic story, especially in plays. The technique is very common in

Elizabethan works, and can be an integral part of the plot or simply a brief event designed to break the tension of the scene. The Gravediggers' scene in William Shakespeare's *Hamlet* is a frequently cited example of comic relief.

Commedia dell'arte: An Italian term meaning "the comedy of guilds" or "the comedy of professional actors." This form of dramatic comedy was popular in Italy during the sixteenth century. Actors were assigned stock roles (such as Pulcinella, the stupid servant, or Pantalone, the old merchant) and given a basic plot to follow, but all dialogue was improvised. The roles were rigidly typed and the plots were formulaic, usually revolving around young lovers who thwarted their elders and attained wealth and happiness. A rigid convention of the *commedia dell'arte* is the periodic intrusion of Harlequin, who interrupts the play with low buffoonery. Peppino de Filippo's *Metamorphoses of a Wandering Minstrel* gave modern audiences an idea of what *commedia dell'arte* may have been like. Various scenarios for *commedia dell'arte* were compiled in Petraccone's *La commedia dell'arte, storia, technica, scenari,* published in 1927.

Complaint: A lyric poem, popular in the Renaissance, in which the speaker expresses sorrow about his or her condition. Typically, the speaker's sadness is caused by an unresponsive lover, but some complaints cite other sources of unhappiness, such as poverty or fate. A commonly cited example is "A Complaint by Night of the Lover Not Beloved" by Henry Howard, Earl of Surrey. Thomas Sackville's "Complaint of Henry, Duke of Buckingham" traces the duke's unhappiness to his ruthless ambition.

Conceit: A clever and fanciful metaphor, usually expressed through elaborate and extended comparison, that presents a striking parallel between two seemingly dissimilar things—for example, elaborately comparing a beautiful woman to an object like a garden or the sun. The conceit was a popular device throughout the Elizabethan Age and Baroque Age and was the principal technique of the seventeenth-century English metaphysical poets. This usage of the word conceit is unrelated to the best-known definition of conceit as an arrogant attitude or behavior. The conceit figures prominently in the works of John Donne, Emily Dickinson, and T. S. Eliot.

Concrete: Concrete is the opposite of abstract, and refers to a thing that actually exists or a description that allows the reader to experience an object or concept with the senses. Henry David Thoreau's *Walden* contains much concrete description of nature and wildlife.

Concrete Poetry: Poetry in which visual elements play a large part in the poetic effect. Punctuation marks, letters, or words are arranged on a page to form a visual design: a cross, for example, or a bumblebee. Max Bill and Eugene Gomringer were among the early practitioners of concrete poetry; Haroldo de Campos and Augusto de Campos are among contemporary authors of concrete poetry.

Confessional Poetry: A form of poetry in which the poet reveals very personal, intimate, sometimes shocking information about himself or herself. Anne Sexton, Sylvia Plath, Robert Lowell, and John Berryman wrote poetry in the confessional vein.

Conflict: The conflict in a work of fiction is the issue to be resolved in the story. It usually occurs between two characters, the protagonist and the antagonist, or between the protagonist and society or the protagonist and himself or herself. Conflict in Theodore Dreiser's novel *Sister Carrie* comes as a result of urban society, while Jack London's short story "To Build a Fire" concerns the protagonist's battle against the cold and himself.

Connotation: The impression that a word gives beyond its defined meaning. Connotations may be universally understood or may be significant only to a certain group. Both "horse" and "steed" denote the same animal, but "steed" has a different connotation, deriving from the chivalrous or romantic narratives in which the word was once often used.

Consonance: Consonance occurs in poetry when words appearing at the ends of two or more verses have similar final consonant sounds but have final vowel sounds that differ, as with "stuff" and "off." Consonance is found in "The curfew tolls the knells of parting day" from Thomas Grey's "An Elegy Written in a Country Church Yard." Also known as Half Rhyme or Slant Rhyme.

Convention: Any widely accepted literary device, style, or form. A soliloquy, in which a character reveals to the audience his or her private thoughts, is an example of a dramatic convention.

Corrido: A Mexican ballad. Examples of *corridos* include "Muerte del afamado Bilito," "La voz de mi conciencia," "Lucio Perez," "La juida," and "Los presos."

Couplet: Two lines of poetry with the same rhyme and meter, often expressing a complete and self-contained thought. The following couplet is from Alexander Pope's "Elegy to the Memory of an Unfortunate Lady": 'Tis Use alone that sanctifies Expense, And Splendour borrows all her rays from Sense.

Criticism: The systematic study and evaluation of literary works, usually based on a specific method or set of principles. An important part of literary studies since ancient times, the practice of criticism has given rise to numerous theories, methods, and "schools," sometimes producing conflicting, even contradictory, interpretations of literature in general as well as of individual works. Even such basic issues as what constitutes a poem or a novel have been the subject of much criticism over the centuries. Seminal texts of literary criticism include Plato's *Republic,* Aristotle's *Poetics,* Sir Philip Sidney's *The Defence of Poesie,* John Dryden's *Of Dramatic Poesie,* and William Wordsworth's "Preface" to the second edition of his *Lyrical Ballads.* Contemporary schools of criticism include deconstruction, feminist, psychoanalytic, poststructuralist, new historicist, postcolonialist, and reader-response.

D

Dactyl: See *Foot*

Dadaism: A protest movement in art and literature founded by Tristan Tzara in 1916. Followers of the movement expressed their outrage at the destruction brought about by World War I by revolting against numerous forms of social convention. The Dadaists presented works marked by calculated madness and flamboyant nonsense. They stressed total freedom of expression, commonly through primitive displays of emotion and illogical, often senseless, poetry. The movement ended shortly after the war, when it was replaced by surrealism. Proponents of Dadaism include Andre Breton, Louis Aragon, Philippe Soupault, and Paul Eluard.

Decadent: See *Decadents*

Decadents: The followers of a nineteenth-century literary movement that had its beginnings in French aestheticism. Decadent literature displays a fascination with perverse and morbid states; a search for novelty and sensation—the "new thrill"; a preoccupation with mysticism; and a belief in the senselessness of human existence. The movement is closely associated with the doctrine Art for Art's Sake. The term "decadence" is sometimes used to denote a decline in the quality of art or literature following a period of greatness. Major French decadents are Charles Baudelaire and Arthur Rimbaud. English decadents include Oscar Wilde, Ernest Dowson, and Frank Harris.

Deconstruction: A method of literary criticism developed by Jacques Derrida and characterized by multiple conflicting interpretations of a given work. Deconstructionists consider the impact of the language of a work and suggest that the true meaning of the work is not necessarily the meaning that the author intended. Jacques Derrida's *De la grammatologie* is the seminal text on deconstructive strategies; among American practitioners of this method of criticism are Paul de Man and J. Hillis Miller.

Deduction: The process of reaching a conclusion through reasoning from general premises to a specific premise. An example of deduction is present in the following syllogism: Premise: All mammals are animals. Premise: All whales are mammals. Conclusion: Therefore, all whales are animals.

Denotation: The definition of a word, apart from the impressions or feelings it creates in the reader. The word "apartheid" denotes a political and economic policy of segregation by race, but its connotations— oppression, slavery, inequality—are numerous.

Denouement: A French word meaning "the unknotting." In literary criticism, it denotes the resolution of conflict in fiction or drama. The *denouement* follows the climax and provides an outcome to the primary plot situation as well as an explanation of secondary plot complications. The *denouement* often involves a character's recognition of his or her state of mind or moral condition. A well-known example of *denouement* is the last scene of the play *As You Like It* by William Shakespeare, in which couples are married, an evildoer repents, the identities of two disguised characters are revealed, and a ruler is restored to power. Also known as Falling Action.

Description: Descriptive writing is intended to allow a reader to picture the scene or setting in which the action of a story takes place. The form this description takes often evokes an intended emotional response—a dark, spooky graveyard will evoke fear, and a peaceful, sunny meadow will evoke calmness. An example of a descriptive story is Edgar Allan Poe's *Landor's Cottage,* which offers a detailed depiction of a New York country estate.

Detective Story: A narrative about the solution of a mystery or the identification of a criminal. The conventions of the detective story include the detective's scrupulous use of logic in solving the mystery; incompetent or ineffectual police; a suspect who appears guilty at first but is later proved innocent; and the detective's friend or confidant—often the narrator—whose slowness in interpreting clues emphasizes by contrast the detective's brilliance. Edgar Allan Poe's "Murders in the Rue Morgue" is commonly regarded as the earliest example of this type of story. With this work, Poe established many of the conventions of the detective story genre, which are still in practice. Other practitioners of this vast and extremely popular genre include Arthur Conan Doyle, Dashiell Hammett, and Agatha Christie.

Deus ex machina: A Latin term meaning "god out of a machine." In Greek drama, a god was often lowered onto the stage by a mechanism of some kind to rescue the hero or untangle the plot. By extension, the term refers to any artificial device or coincidence used to bring about a convenient and simple solution to a plot. This is a common device in melodramas and includes such fortunate circumstances as the sudden receipt of a legacy to save the family farm or a last-minute stay of execution. The *deus ex machina* invariably rewards the virtuous and punishes evildoers. Examples of *deus ex machina* include King Louis XIV in Jean-Baptiste Moliere's *Tartuffe* and Queen Victoria in *The Pirates of Penzance* by William Gilbert and Arthur Sullivan. Bertolt Brecht parodies the abuse of such devices in the conclusion of his *Threepenny Opera.*

Dialogue: In its widest sense, dialogue is simply conversation between people in a literary work; in its most restricted sense, it refers specifically to the speech of characters in a drama. As a specific literary genre, a "dialogue" is a composition in which characters debate an issue or idea. The Greek philosopher Plato frequently expounded his theories in the form of dialogues.

Diction: The selection and arrangement of words in a literary work. Either or both may vary depending on the desired effect. There are four general types of diction: "formal," used in scholarly or lofty writing; "informal," used in relaxed but educated conversation; "colloquial," used in everyday speech; and "slang," containing newly coined words and other terms not accepted in formal usage.

Didactic: A term used to describe works of literature that aim to teach some moral, religious, political, or practical lesson. Although didactic elements are often found in artistically pleasing works, the term "didactic" usually refers to literature in which the message is more important than the form. The term may also be used to criticize a work that the critic finds "overly didactic," that is, heavy-handed in its delivery of a lesson. Examples of didactic literature include John Bunyan's *Pilgrim's Progress,* Alexander Pope's *Essay on Criticism,* Jean-Jacques Rousseau's *Emile,* and Elizabeth Inchbald's *Simple Story.*

Dimeter: See *Meter*

Dionysian: See *Apollonian and Dionysian*

Discordia concours: A Latin phrase meaning "discord in harmony." The term was coined by the eighteenth-century English writer Samuel Johnson to describe "a combination of dissimilar images or discovery of occult resemblances in things apparently unlike." Johnson created the expression by reversing a phrase by the Latin poet Horace. The metaphysical poetry of John Donne, Richard Crashaw, Abraham Cowley, George Herbert, and Edward Taylor among others, contains many examples of *discordia concours.* In Donne's "A Valediction: Forbidding Mourning," the poet compares the union of himself with his lover to a draftsman's compass: If they be two, they are two so, As stiff twin compasses are

two: Thy soul, the fixed foot, makes no show
To move, but doth, if the other do; And
though it in the center sit, Yet when the
other far doth roam, It leans, and hearkens
after it, And grows erect, as that comes home.

Dissonance: A combination of harsh or jarring
sounds, especially in poetry. Although such
combinations may be accidental, poets sometimes intentionally make them to achieve
particular effects. Dissonance is also sometimes used to refer to close but not identical
rhymes. When this is the case, the word functions as a synonym for consonance. Robert
Browning, Gerard Manley Hopkins, and
many other poets have made deliberate use
of dissonance.

Doppelganger: A literary technique by which a
character is duplicated (usually in the form of
an alter ego, though sometimes as a ghostly
counterpart) or divided into two distinct, usually opposite personalities. The use of this
character device is widespread in nineteenth-
and twentieth- century literature, and indicates
a growing awareness among authors that the
"self" is really a composite of many "selves." A
well-known story containing a *doppelganger*
character is Robert Louis Stevenson's *Dr.
Jekyll and Mr. Hyde,* which dramatizes an
internal struggle between good and evil. Also
known as The Double.

Double Entendre: A corruption of a French phrase
meaning "double meaning." The term is used
to indicate a word or phrase that is deliberately
ambiguous, especially when one of the meanings is risque or improper. An example of a
double entendre is the Elizabethan usage of the
verb "die," which refers both to death and to
orgasm.

Double, The: See *Doppelganger*

Draft: Any preliminary version of a written
work. An author may write dozens of drafts
which are revised to form the final work, or
he or she may write only one, with few or no
revisions. Dorothy Parker's observation that
"I can't write five words but that I change
seven" humorously indicates the purpose of
the draft.

Drama: In its widest sense, a drama is any work
designed to be presented by actors on a stage.
Similarly, "drama" denotes a broad literary
genre that includes a variety of forms, from
pageant and spectacle to tragedy and comedy,
as well as countless types and subtypes. More
commonly in modern usage, however, a
drama is a work that treats serious subjects
and themes but does not aim at the grandeur
of tragedy. This use of the term originated
with the eighteenth-century French writer
Denis Diderot, who used the word *drame* to
designate his plays about middle- class life; thus
"drama" typically features characters of a less
exalted stature than those of tragedy. Examples
of classical dramas include Menander's comedy *Dyscolus* and Sophocles' tragedy *Oedipus
Rex*. Contemporary dramas include Eugene
O'Neill's *The Iceman Cometh,* Lillian Hellman's *Little Foxes,* and August Wilson's
Ma Rainey's Black Bottom.

Dramatic Irony: Occurs when the audience of a
play or the reader of a work of literature
knows something that a character in the
work itself does not know. The irony is in
the contrast between the intended meaning of
the statements or actions of a character and
the additional information understood by the
audience. A celebrated example of dramatic
irony is in Act V of William Shakespeare's
Romeo and Juliet, where two young lovers
meet their end as a result of a tragic misunderstanding. Here, the audience has full
knowledge that Juliet's apparent "death" is
merely temporary; she will regain her senses
when the mysterious "sleeping potion" she
has taken wears off. But Romeo, mistaking
Juliet's drug-induced trance for true death,
kills himself in grief. Upon awakening, Juliet
discovers Romeo's corpse and, in despair,
slays herself.

Dramatic Monologue: See *Monologue*

Dramatic Poetry: Any lyric work that employs
elements of drama such as dialogue, conflict,
or characterization, but excluding works that
are intended for stage presentation. A monologue is a form of dramatic poetry.

Dramatis Personae: The characters in a work of
literature, particularly a drama. The list of
characters printed before the main text of a
play or in the program is the *dramatis personae*.

Dream Allegory: See *Dream Vision*

Dream Vision: A literary convention, chiefly of
the Middle Ages. In a dream vision a story is
presented as a literal dream of the narrator.
This device was commonly used to teach
moral and religious lessons. Important works

of this type are *The Divine Comedy* by Dante Alighieri, *Piers Plowman* by William Langland, and *The Pilgrim's Progress* by John Bunyan. Also known as Dream Allegory.

Dystopia: An imaginary place in a work of fiction where the characters lead dehumanized, fearful lives. Jack London's *The Iron Heel,* Yevgeny Zamyatin's *My,* Aldous Huxley's *Brave New World,* George Orwell's *Nineteen Eighty-four,* and Margaret Atwood's *Handmaid's Tale* portray versions of dystopia.

E

Eclogue: In classical literature, a poem featuring rural themes and structured as a dialogue among shepherds. Eclogues often took specific poetic forms, such as elegies or love poems. Some were written as the soliloquy of a shepherd. In later centuries, "eclogue" came to refer to any poem that was in the pastoral tradition or that had a dialogue or monologue structure. A classical example of an eclogue is Virgil's *Eclogues,* also known as *Bucolics.* Giovanni Boccaccio, Edmund Spenser, Andrew Marvell, Jonathan Swift, and Louis MacNeice also wrote eclogues.

Edwardian: Describes cultural conventions identified with the period of the reign of Edward VII of England (1901-1910). Writers of the Edwardian Age typically displayed a strong reaction against the propriety and conservatism of the Victorian Age. Their work often exhibits distrust of authority in religion, politics, and art and expresses strong doubts about the soundness of conventional values. Writers of this era include George Bernard Shaw, H. G. Wells, and Joseph Conrad.

Edwardian Age: See *Edwardian*

Electra Complex: A daughter's amorous obsession with her father. The term Electra complex comes from the plays of Euripides and Sophocles entitled *Electra,* in which the character Electra drives her brother Orestes to kill their mother and her lover in revenge for the murder of their father.

Elegy: A lyric poem that laments the death of a person or the eventual death of all people. In a conventional elegy, set in a classical world, the poet and subject are spoken of as shepherds. In modern criticism, the word elegy is often used to refer to a poem that is melancholy or mournfully contemplative. John Milton's

"Lycidas" and Percy Bysshe Shelley's "Adonais" are two examples of this form.

Elizabethan Age: A period of great economic growth, religious controversy, and nationalism closely associated with the reign of Elizabeth I of England (1558-1603). The Elizabethan Age is considered a part of the general renaissance—that is, the flowering of arts and literature—that took place in Europe during the fourteenth through sixteenth centuries. The era is considered the golden age of English literature. The most important dramas in English and a great deal of lyric poetry were produced during this period, and modern English criticism began around this time. The notable authors of the period—Philip Sidney, Edmund Spenser, Christopher Marlowe, William Shakespeare, Ben Jonson, Francis Bacon, and John Donne—are among the best in all of English literature.

Elizabethan Drama: English comic and tragic plays produced during the Renaissance, or more narrowly, those plays written during the last years of and few years after Queen Elizabeth's reign. William Shakespeare is considered an Elizabethan dramatist in the broader sense, although most of his work was produced during the reign of James I. Examples of Elizabethan comedies include John Lyly's *The Woman in the Moone,* Thomas Dekker's *The Roaring Girl, or, Moll Cut Purse,* and William Shakespeare's *Twelfth Night.* Examples of Elizabethan tragedies include William Shakespeare's *Antony and Cleopatra,* Thomas Kyd's *The Spanish Tragedy,* and John Webster's *The Tragedy of the Duchess of Malfi.*

Empathy: A sense of shared experience, including emotional and physical feelings, with someone or something other than oneself. Empathy is often used to describe the response of a reader to a literary character. An example of an empathic passage is William Shakespeare's description in his narrative poem *Venus and Adonis* of: the snail, whose tender horns being hit, Shrinks backward in his shelly cave with pain. Readers of Gerard Manley Hopkins's *The Windhover* may experience some of the physical sensations evoked in the description of the movement of the falcon.

English Sonnet: See *Sonnet*

Enjambment: The running over of the sense and structure of a line of verse or a couplet into the following verse or couplet. Andrew Marvell's "To His Coy Mistress" is structured as a series of enjambments, as in lines 11-12: "My vegetable love should grow/Vaster than empires and more slow."

Enlightenment, The: An eighteenth-century philosophical movement. It began in France but had a wide impact throughout Europe and America. Thinkers of the Enlightenment valued reason and believed that both the individual and society could achieve a state of perfection. Corresponding to this essentially humanist vision was a resistance to religious authority. Important figures of the Enlightenment were Denis Diderot and Voltaire in France, Edward Gibbon and David Hume in England, and Thomas Paine and Thomas Jefferson in the United States.

Epic: A long narrative poem about the adventures of a hero of great historic or legendary importance. The setting is vast and the action is often given cosmic significance through the intervention of supernatural forces such as gods, angels, or demons. Epics are typically written in a classical style of grand simplicity with elaborate metaphors and allusions that enhance the symbolic importance of a hero's adventures. Some well-known epics are Homer's *Iliad* and *Odyssey,* Virgil's *Aeneid,* and John Milton's *Paradise Lost.*

Epic Simile: See *Homeric Simile*

Epic Theater: A theory of theatrical presentation developed by twentieth-century German playwright Bertolt Brecht. Brecht created a type of drama that the audience could view with complete detachment. He used what he termed "alienation effects" to create an emotional distance between the audience and the action on stage. Among these effects are: short, self-contained scenes that keep the play from building to a cathartic climax; songs that comment on the action; and techniques of acting that prevent the actor from developing an emotional identity with his role. Besides the plays of Bertolt Brecht, other plays that utilize epic theater conventions include those of Georg Buchner, Frank Wedekind, Erwin Piscator, and Leopold Jessner.

Epigram: A saying that makes the speaker's point quickly and concisely. Samuel Taylor Coleridge wrote an epigram that neatly sums up the form: What is an Epigram? A Dwarfish whole, Its body brevity, and wit its soul.

Epilogue: A concluding statement or section of a literary work. In dramas, particularly those of the seventeenth and eighteenth centuries, the epilogue is a closing speech, often in verse, delivered by an actor at the end of a play and spoken directly to the audience. A famous epilogue is Puck's speech at the end of William Shakespeare's *A Midsummer Night's Dream.*

Epiphany: A sudden revelation of truth inspired by a seemingly trivial incident. The term was widely used by James Joyce in his critical writings, and the stories in Joyce's *Dubliners* are commonly called "epiphanies."

Episode: An incident that forms part of a story and is significantly related to it. Episodes may be either self- contained narratives or events that depend on a larger context for their sense and importance. Examples of episodes include the founding of Wilmington, Delaware in Charles Reade's *The Disinherited Heir* and the individual events comprising the picaresque novels and medieval romances.

Episodic Plot: See *Plot*

Epitaph: An inscription on a tomb or tombstone, or a verse written on the occasion of a person's death. Epitaphs may be serious or humorous. Dorothy Parker's epitaph reads, "I told you I was sick."

Epithalamion: A song or poem written to honor and commemorate a marriage ceremony. Famous examples include Edmund Spenser's "Epithalamion" and e. e. cummings's "Epithalamion." Also spelled Epithalamium.

Epithalamium: See *Epithalamion*

Epithet: A word or phrase, often disparaging or abusive, that expresses a character trait of someone or something. "The Napoleon of crime" is an epithet applied to Professor Moriarty, arch-rival of Sherlock Holmes in Arthur Conan Doyle's series of detective stories.

Exempla: See *Exemplum*

Exemplum: A tale with a moral message. This form of literary sermonizing flourished during the Middle Ages, when *exempla* appeared in collections known as "example-books." The works of Geoffrey Chaucer are full of *exempla.*

Existentialism: A predominantly twentieth-century philosophy concerned with the nature and perception of human existence. There are two major strains of existentialist thought: atheistic and Christian. Followers of atheistic existentialism believe that the individual is alone in a godless universe and that the basic human condition is one of suffering and loneliness. Nevertheless, because there are no fixed values, individuals can create their own characters—indeed, they can shape themselves—through the exercise of free will. The atheistic strain culminates in and is popularly associated with the works of Jean-Paul Sartre. The Christian existentialists, on the other hand, believe that only in God may people find freedom from life's anguish. The two strains hold certain beliefs in common: that existence cannot be fully understood or described through empirical effort; that anguish is a universal element of life; that individuals must bear responsibility for their actions; and that there is no common standard of behavior or perception for religious and ethical matters. Existentialist thought figures prominently in the works of such authors as Eugene Ionesco, Franz Kafka, Fyodor Dostoyevsky, Simone de Beauvoir, Samuel Beckett, and Albert Camus.

Expatriates: See *Expatriatism*

Expatriatism: The practice of leaving one's country to live for an extended period in another country. Literary expatriates include English poets Percy Bysshe Shelley and John Keats in Italy, Polish novelist Joseph Conrad in England, American writers Richard Wright, James Baldwin, Gertrude Stein, and Ernest Hemingway in France, and Trinidadian author Neil Bissondath in Canada.

Exposition: Writing intended to explain the nature of an idea, thing, or theme. Expository writing is often combined with description, narration, or argument. In dramatic writing, the exposition is the introductory material which presents the characters, setting, and tone of the play. An example of dramatic exposition occurs in many nineteenth-century drawing-room comedies in which the butler and the maid open the play with relevant talk about their master and mistress; in composition, exposition relays factual information, as in encyclopedia entries.

Expressionism: An indistinct literary term, originally used to describe an early twentieth-century school of German painting. The term applies to almost any mode of unconventional, highly subjective writing that distorts reality in some way. Advocates of Expressionism include dramatists George Kaiser, Ernst Toller, Luigi Pirandello, Federico Garcia Lorca, Eugene O'Neill, and Elmer Rice; poets George Heym, Ernst Stadler, August Stramm, Gottfried Benn, and Georg Trakl; and novelists Franz Kafka and James Joyce.

Extended Monologue: See *Monologue*

F

Fable: A prose or verse narrative intended to convey a moral. Animals or inanimate objects with human characteristics often serve as characters in fables. A famous fable is Aesop's "The Tortoise and the Hare."

Fairy Tales: Short narratives featuring mythical beings such as fairies, elves, and sprites. These tales originally belonged to the folklore of a particular nation or region, such as those collected in Germany by Jacob and Wilhelm Grimm. Two other celebrated writers of fairy tales are Hans Christian Andersen and Rudyard Kipling.

Falling Action: See *Denouement*

Fantasy: A literary form related to mythology and folklore. Fantasy literature is typically set in non-existent realms and features supernatural beings. Notable examples of fantasy literature are *The Lord of the Rings* by J. R. R. Tolkien and the Gormenghast trilogy by Mervyn Peake.

Farce: A type of comedy characterized by broad humor, outlandish incidents, and often vulgar subject matter. Much of the "comedy" in film and television could more accurately be described as farce.

Feet: See *Foot*

Feminine Rhyme: See *Rhyme*

Femme fatale: A French phrase with the literal translation "fatal woman." A *femme fatale* is a sensuous, alluring woman who often leads men into danger or trouble. A classic example of the *femme fatale* is the nameless character in Billy Wilder's *The Seven Year Itch*, portrayed by Marilyn Monroe in the film adaptation.

Fiction: Any story that is the product of imagination rather than a documentation of fact. characters and events in such narratives may be based in real life but their ultimate form and configuration is a creation of the author. Geoffrey Chaucer's *The Canterbury Tales,* Laurence Sterne's *Tristram Shandy,* and Margaret Mitchell's *Gone with the Wind* are examples of fiction.

Figurative Language: A technique in writing in which the author temporarily interrupts the order, construction, or meaning of the writing for a particular effect. This interruption takes the form of one or more figures of speech such as hyperbole, irony, or simile. Figurative language is the opposite of literal language, in which every word is truthful, accurate, and free of exaggeration or embellishment. Examples of figurative language are tropes such as metaphor and rhetorical figures such as apostrophe.

Figures of Speech: Writing that differs from customary conventions for construction, meaning, order, or significance for the purpose of a special meaning or effect. There are two major types of figures of speech: rhetorical figures, which do not make changes in the meaning of the words, and tropes, which do. Types of figures of speech include simile, hyperbole, alliteration, and pun, among many others.

Fin de siecle: A French term meaning "end of the century." The term is used to denote the last decade of the nineteenth century, a transition period when writers and other artists abandoned old conventions and looked for new techniques and objectives. Two writers commonly associated with the *fin de siecle* mindset are Oscar Wilde and George Bernard Shaw.

First Person: See *Point of View*

Flashback: A device used in literature to present action that occurred before the beginning of the story. Flashbacks are often introduced as the dreams or recollections of one or more characters. Flashback techniques are often used in films, where they are typically set off by a gradual changing of one picture to another.

Foil: A character in a work of literature whose physical or psychological qualities contrast strongly with, and therefore highlight, the corresponding qualities of another character. In his Sherlock Holmes stories, Arthur Conan Doyle portrayed Dr. Watson as a man of normal habits and intelligence, making him a foil for the eccentric and wonderfully perceptive Sherlock Holmes.

Folk Ballad: See *Ballad*

Folklore: Traditions and myths preserved in a culture or group of people. Typically, these are passed on by word of mouth in various forms—such as legends, songs, and proverbs—or preserved in customs and ceremonies. This term was first used by W. J. Thoms in 1846. Sir James Frazer's *The Golden Bough* is the record of English folklore; myths about the frontier and the Old South exemplify American folklore.

Folktale: A story originating in oral tradition. Folktales fall into a variety of categories, including legends, ghost stories, fairy tales, fables, and anecdotes based on historical figures and events. Examples of folktales include Giambattista Basile's *The Pentamerone,* which contains the tales of Puss in Boots, Rapunzel, Cinderella, and Beauty and the Beast, and Joel Chandler Harris's Uncle Remus stories, which represent transplanted African folktales and American tales about the characters Mike Fink, Johnny Appleseed, Paul Bunyan, and Pecos Bill.

Foot: The smallest unit of rhythm in a line of poetry. In English-language poetry, a foot is typically one accented syllable combined with one or two unaccented syllables. There are many different types of feet. When the accent is on the second syllable of a two syllable word (con- *tort*), the foot is an "iamb"; the reverse accentual pattern (*tor* -ture) is a "trochee." Other feet that commonly occur in poetry in English are "anapest", two unaccented syllables followed by an accented syllable as in in-ter-*cept*, and "dactyl", an accented syllable followed by two unaccented syllables as in *su*-i- cide.

Foreshadowing: A device used in literature to create expectation or to set up an explanation of later developments. In Charles Dickens's *Great Expectations,* the graveyard encounter at the beginning of the novel between Pip and the escaped convict Magwitch foreshadows the baleful atmosphere and events that comprise much of the narrative.

Form: The pattern or construction of a work which identifies its genre and distinguishes it from other genres. Examples of forms include the different genres, such as the lyric form or the short story form, and various patterns for poetry, such as the verse form or the stanza form.

Formalism: In literary criticism, the belief that literature should follow prescribed rules of construction, such as those that govern the sonnet form. Examples of formalism are found in the work of the New Critics and structuralists.

Fourteener Meter: See *Meter*

Free Verse: Poetry that lacks regular metrical and rhyme patterns but that tries to capture the cadences of everyday speech. The form allows a poet to exploit a variety of rhythmical effects within a single poem. Free-verse techniques have been widely used in the twentieth century by such writers as Ezra Pound, T. S. Eliot, Carl Sandburg, and William Carlos Williams. Also known as *Vers libre*.

Futurism: A flamboyant literary and artistic movement that developed in France, Italy, and Russia from 1908 through the 1920s. Futurist theater and poetry abandoned traditional literary forms. In their place, followers of the movement attempted to achieve total freedom of expression through bizarre imagery and deformed or newly invented words. The Futurists were self-consciously modern artists who attempted to incorporate the appearances and sounds of modern life into their work. Futurist writers include Filippo Tommaso Marinetti, Wyndham Lewis, Guillaume Apollinaire, Velimir Khlebnikov, and Vladimir Mayakovsky.

G

Genre: A category of literary work. In critical theory, genre may refer to both the content of a given work—tragedy, comedy, pastoral—and to its form, such as poetry, novel, or drama. This term also refers to types of popular literature, as in the genres of science fiction or the detective story.

Genteel Tradition: A term coined by critic George Santayana to describe the literary practice of certain late nineteenth- century American writers, especially New Englanders. Followers of the Genteel Tradition emphasized conventionality in social, religious, moral, and literary standards. Some of the best-known writers of the Genteel Tradition are R. H. Stoddard and Bayard Taylor.

Gilded Age: A period in American history during the 1870s characterized by political corruption and materialism. A number of important novels of social and political criticism were written during this time. Examples of Gilded Age literature include Henry Adams's *Democracy* and F. Marion Crawford's *An American Politician.*

Gothic: See *Gothicism*

Gothicism: In literary criticism, works characterized by a taste for the medieval or morbidly attractive. A gothic novel prominently features elements of horror, the supernatural, gloom, and violence: clanking chains, terror, charnel houses, ghosts, medieval castles, and mysteriously slamming doors. The term "gothic novel" is also applied to novels that lack elements of the traditional Gothic setting but that create a similar atmosphere of terror or dread. Mary Shelley's *Frankenstein* is perhaps the best-known English work of this kind.

Gothic Novel: See *Gothicism*

Great Chain of Being: The belief that all things and creatures in nature are organized in a hierarchy from inanimate objects at the bottom to God at the top. This system of belief was popular in the seventeenth and eighteenth centuries. A summary of the concept of the great chain of being can be found in the first epistle of Alexander Pope's *An Essay on Man,* and more recently in Arthur O. Lovejoy's *The Great Chain of Being: A Study of the History of an Idea.*

Grotesque: In literary criticism, the subject matter of a work or a style of expression characterized by exaggeration, deformity, freakishness, and disorder. The grotesque often includes an element of comic absurdity. Early examples of literary grotesque include Francois Rabelais's *Pantagruel* and *Gargantua* and Thomas Nashe's *The Unfortunate Traveller,* while more recent examples can be found in the works of Edgar Allan Poe, Evelyn Waugh, Eudora Welty, Flannery O'Connor, Eugene Ionesco, Gunter

Grass, Thomas Mann, Mervyn Peake, and Joseph Heller, among many others.

H

Haiku: The shortest form of Japanese poetry, constructed in three lines of five, seven, and five syllables respectively. The message of a *haiku* poem usually centers on some aspect of spirituality and provokes an emotional response in the reader. Early masters of *haiku* include Basho, Buson, Kobayashi Issa, and Masaoka Shiki. English writers of *haiku* include the Imagists, notably Ezra Pound, H. D., Amy Lowell, Carl Sandburg, and William Carlos Williams. Also known as *Hokku*.

Half Rhyme: See *Consonance*

Hamartia: In tragedy, the event or act that leads to the hero's or heroine's downfall. This term is often incorrectly used as a synonym for tragic flaw. In Richard Wright's *Native Son,* the act that seals Bigger Thomas's fate is his first impulsive murder.

Harlem Renaissance: The Harlem Renaissance of the 1920s is generally considered the first significant movement of black writers and artists in the United States. During this period, new and established black writers published more fiction and poetry than ever before, the first influential black literary journals were established, and black authors and artists received their first widespread recognition and serious critical appraisal. Among the major writers associated with this period are Claude McKay, Jean Toomer, Countee Cullen, Langston Hughes, Arna Bontemps, Nella Larsen, and Zora Neale Hurston. Works representative of the Harlem Renaissance include Arna Bontemps's poems "The Return" and "Golgotha Is a Mountain," Claude McKay's novel *Home to Harlem*, Nella Larsen's novel *Passing*, Langston Hughes's poem "The Negro Speaks of Rivers," and the journals *Crisis* and *Opportunity*, both founded during this period. Also known as Negro Renaissance and New Negro Movement.

Harlequin: A stock character of the *commedia dell'arte* who occasionally interrupted the action with silly antics. Harlequin first appeared on the English stage in John Day's *The Travailes of the Three English Brothers*. The San Francisco Mime Troupe is one of the few modern groups to adapt Harlequin to the needs of contemporary satire.

Hellenism: Imitation of ancient Greek thought or styles. Also, an approach to life that focuses on the growth and development of the intellect. "Hellenism" is sometimes used to refer to the belief that reason can be applied to examine all human experience. A cogent discussion of Hellenism can be found in Matthew Arnold's *Culture and Anarchy*.

Heptameter: See *Meter*

Hero/Heroine: The principal sympathetic character (male or female) in a literary work. Heroes and heroines typically exhibit admirable traits: idealism, courage, and integrity, for example. Famous heroes and heroines include Pip in Charles Dickens's *Great Expectations*, the anonymous narrator in Ralph Ellison's *Invisible Man*, and Sethe in Toni Morrison's *Beloved*.

Heroic Couplet: A rhyming couplet written in iambic pentameter (a verse with five iambic feet). The following lines by Alexander Pope are an example: "Truth guards the Poet, sanctifies the line,/ And makes Immortal, Verse as mean as mine."

Heroic Line: The meter and length of a line of verse in epic or heroic poetry. This varies by language and time period. For example, in English poetry, the heroic line is iambic pentameter (a verse with five iambic feet); in French, the alexandrine (a verse with six iambic feet); in classical literature, dactylic hexameter (a verse with six dactylic feet).

Heroine: See *Hero/Heroine*

Hexameter: See *Meter*

Historical Criticism: The study of a work based on its impact on the world of the time period in which it was written. Examples of postmodern historical criticism can be found in the work of Michel Foucault, Hayden White, Stephen Greenblatt, and Jonathan Goldberg.

Hokku: See *Haiku*

Holocaust: See *Holocaust Literature*

Holocaust Literature: Literature influenced by or written about the Holocaust of World War II. Such literature includes true stories of survival in concentration camps, escape, and life after the war, as well as fictional works and poetry. Representative works of Holocaust literature include Saul Bellow's

Mr. Sammler's Planet, Anne Frank's *The Diary of a Young Girl,* Jerzy Kosinski's *The Painted Bird,* Arthur Miller's *Incident at Vichy,* Czeslaw Milosz's *Collected Poems,* William Styron's *Sophie's Choice,* and Art Spiegelman's *Maus.*

Homeric Simile: An elaborate, detailed comparison written as a simile many lines in length. An example of an epic simile from John Milton's *Paradise Lost* follows: Angel Forms, who lay entranced Thick as autumnal leaves that strow the brooks In Vallombrosa, where the Etrurian shades High over-arched embower; or scattered sedge Afloat, when with fierce winds Orion armed Hath vexed the Red-Sea coast, whose waves o'erthrew Busiris and his Memphian chivalry, While with perfidious hatred they pursued The sojourners of Goshen, who beheld From the safe shore their floating carcasses And broken chariot-wheels. Also known as Epic Simile.

Horatian Satire: See *Satire*

Humanism: A philosophy that places faith in the dignity of humankind and rejects the medieval perception of the individual as a weak, fallen creature. "Humanists" typically believe in the perfectibility of human nature and view reason and education as the means to that end. Humanist thought is represented in the works of Marsilio Ficino, Ludovico Castelvetro, Edmund Spenser, John Milton, Dean John Colet, Desiderius Erasmus, John Dryden, Alexander Pope, Matthew Arnold, and Irving Babbitt.

Humors: Mentions of the humors refer to the ancient Greek theory that a person's health and personality were determined by the balance of four basic fluids in the body: blood, phlegm, yellow bile, and black bile. A dominance of any fluid would cause extremes in behavior. An excess of blood created a sanguine person who was joyful, aggressive, and passionate; a phlegmatic person was shy, fearful, and sluggish; too much yellow bile led to a choleric temperament characterized by impatience, anger, bitterness, and stubbornness; and excessive black bile created melancholy, a state of laziness, gluttony, and lack of motivation. Literary treatment of the humors is exemplified by several characters in Ben Jonson's plays *Every*

Man in His Humour and *Every Man out of His Humour.* Also spelled Humours.

Humours: See *Humors*

Hyperbole: In literary criticism, deliberate exaggeration used to achieve an effect. In William Shakespeare's *Macbeth,* Lady Macbeth hyperbolizes when she says, "All the perfumes of Arabia could not sweeten this little hand."

I

Iamb: See *Foot*

Idiom: A word construction or verbal expression closely associated with a given language. For example, in colloquial English the construction "how come" can be used instead of "why" to introduce a question. Similarly, "a piece of cake" is sometimes used to describe a task that is easily done.

Image: A concrete representation of an object or sensory experience. Typically, such a representation helps evoke the feelings associated with the object or experience itself. Images are either "literal" or "figurative." Literal images are especially concrete and involve little or no extension of the obvious meaning of the words used to express them. Figurative images do not follow the literal meaning of the words exactly. Images in literature are usually visual, but the term "image" can also refer to the representation of any sensory experience. In his poem "The Shepherd's Hour," Paul Verlaine presents the following image: "The Moon is red through horizon's fog;/ In a dancing mist the hazy meadow sleeps." The first line is broadly literal, while the second line involves turns of meaning associated with dancing and sleeping.

Imagery: The array of images in a literary work. Also, figurative language. William Butler Yeats's "The Second Coming" offers a powerful image of encroaching anarchy: Turning and turning in the widening gyre The falcon cannot hear the falconer; Things fall apart....

Imagism: An English and American poetry movement that flourished between 1908 and 1917. The Imagists used precise, clearly presented images in their works. They also used common, everyday speech and aimed for conciseness, concrete imagery, and the creation of new rhythms. Participants in the Imagist movement included Ezra Pound, H. D. (Hilda Doolittle), and Amy Lowell, among others.

In medias res: A Latin term meaning "in the middle of things." It refers to the technique of beginning a story at its midpoint and then using various flashback devices to reveal previous action. This technique originated in such epics as Virgil's *Aeneid*.

Induction: The process of reaching a conclusion by reasoning from specific premises to form a general premise. Also, an introductory portion of a work of literature, especially a play. Geoffrey Chaucer's "Prologue" to the *Canterbury Tales,* Thomas Sackville's "Induction" to *The Mirror of Magistrates,* and the opening scene in William Shakespeare's *The Taming of the Shrew* are examples of inductions to literary works.

Intentional Fallacy: The belief that judgments of a literary work based solely on an author's stated or implied intentions are false and misleading. Critics who believe in the concept of the intentional fallacy typically argue that the work itself is sufficient matter for interpretation, even though they may concede that an author's statement of purpose can be useful. Analysis of William Wordsworth's *Lyrical Ballads* based on the observations about poetry he makes in his "Preface" to the second edition of that work is an example of the intentional fallacy.

Interior Monologue: A narrative technique in which characters' thoughts are revealed in a way that appears to be uncontrolled by the author. The interior monologue typically aims to reveal the inner self of a character. It portrays emotional experiences as they occur at both a conscious and unconscious level. images are often used to represent sensations or emotions. One of the best-known interior monologues in English is the Molly Bloom section at the close of James Joyce's *Ulysses.* The interior monologue is also common in the works of Virginia Woolf.

Internal Rhyme: Rhyme that occurs within a single line of verse. An example is in the opening line of Edgar Allan Poe's "The Raven": "Once upon a midnight dreary, while I pondered weak and weary." Here, "dreary" and "weary" make an internal rhyme.

Irish Literary Renaissance: A late nineteenth- and early twentieth-century movement in Irish literature. Members of the movement aimed to reduce the influence of British culture in Ireland and create an Irish national literature. William Butler Yeats, George Moore, and Sean O'Casey are three of the best-known figures of the movement.

Irony: In literary criticism, the effect of language in which the intended meaning is the opposite of what is stated. The title of Jonathan Swift's "A Modest Proposal" is ironic because what Swift proposes in this essay is cannibalism—hardly "modest."

Italian Sonnet: See *Sonnet*

J

Jacobean Age: The period of the reign of James I of England (1603-1625). The early literature of this period reflected the worldview of the Elizabethan Age, but a darker, more cynical attitude steadily grew in the art and literature of the Jacobean Age. This was an important time for English drama and poetry. Milestones include William Shakespeare's tragedies, tragicomedies, and sonnets; Ben Jonson's various dramas; and John Donne's metaphysical poetry.

Jargon: Language that is used or understood only by a select group of people. Jargon may refer to terminology used in a certain profession, such as computer jargon, or it may refer to any nonsensical language that is not understood by most people. Literary examples of jargon are Francois Villon's *Ballades en jargon,* which is composed in the secret language of the *coquillards,* and Anthony Burgess's *A Clockwork Orange,* narrated in the fictional characters' language of "Nadsat."

Juvenalian Satire: See *Satire*

K

Knickerbocker Group: A somewhat indistinct group of New York writers of the first half of the nineteenth century. Members of the group were linked only by location and a common theme: New York life. Two famous members of the Knickerbocker Group were Washington Irving and William Cullen Bryant. The group's name derives from Irving's *Knickerbocker's History of New York.*

L

Lais: See *Lay*

Lay: A song or simple narrative poem. The form originated in medieval France. Early French *lais* were often based on the Celtic legends and other tales sung by Breton minstrels—thus the name of the "Breton lay." In fourteenth-century England, the term "lay" was used to describe short narratives written in imitation of the Breton lays. The most notable of these is Geoffrey Chaucer's "The Minstrel's Tale."

Leitmotiv: See *Motif*

Literal Language: An author uses literal language when he or she writes without exaggerating or embellishing the subject matter and without any tools of figurative language. To say "He ran very quickly down the street" is to use literal language, whereas to say "He ran like a hare down the street" would be using figurative language.

Literary Ballad: See *Ballad*

Literature: Literature is broadly defined as any written or spoken material, but the term most often refers to creative works. Literature includes poetry, drama, fiction, and many kinds of nonfiction writing, as well as oral, dramatic, and broadcast compositions not necessarily preserved in a written format, such as films and television programs.

Lost Generation: A term first used by Gertrude Stein to describe the post-World War I generation of American writers: men and women haunted by a sense of betrayal and emptiness brought about by the destructiveness of the war. The term is commonly applied to Hart Crane, Ernest Hemingway, F. Scott Fitzgerald, and others.

Lyric Poetry: A poem expressing the subjective feelings and personal emotions of the poet. Such poetry is melodic, since it was originally accompanied by a lyre in recitals. Most Western poetry in the twentieth century may be classified as lyrical. Examples of lyric poetry include A. E. Housman's elegy "To an Athlete Dying Young," the odes of Pindar and Horace, Thomas Gray and William Collins, the sonnets of Sir Thomas Wyatt and Sir Philip Sidney, Elizabeth Barrett Browning and Rainer Maria Rilke, and a host of other forms in the poetry of William Blake and Christina Rossetti, among many others.

M

Mannerism: Exaggerated, artificial adherence to a literary manner or style. Also, a popular style of the visual arts of late sixteenth-century Europe that was marked by elongation of the human form and by intentional spatial distortion. Literary works that are self-consciously high-toned and artistic are often said to be "mannered." Authors of such works include Henry James and Gertrude Stein.

Masculine Rhyme: See *Rhyme*

Masque: A lavish and elaborate form of entertainment, often performed in royal courts, that emphasizes song, dance, and costumery. The Renaissance form of the masque grew out of the spectacles of masked figures common in medieval England and Europe. The masque reached its peak of popularity and development in seventeenth-century England, during the reigns of James I and, especially, of Charles I. Ben Jonson, the most significant masque writer, also created the "antimasque," which incorporates elements of humor and the grotesque into the traditional masque and achieved greater dramatic quality. Masque-like interludes appear in Edmund Spenser's *The Faerie Queene* and in William Shakespeare's *The Tempest*. One of the best-known English masques is John Milton's *Comus*.

Measure: The foot, verse, or time sequence used in a literary work, especially a poem. Measure is often used somewhat incorrectly as a synonym for meter.

Melodrama: A play in which the typical plot is a conflict between characters who personify extreme good and evil. Melodramas usually end happily and emphasize sensationalism. Other literary forms that use the same techniques are often labeled "melodramatic." The term was formerly used to describe a combination of drama and music; as such, it was synonymous with "opera." Augustin Daly's *Under the Gaslight* and Dion Boucicault's *The Octoroon, The Colleen Bawn,* and *The Poor of New York* are examples of melodramas. The most popular media for twentieth-century melodramas are motion pictures and television.

Metaphor: A figure of speech that expresses an idea through the image of another object. Metaphors suggest the essence of the first object by identifying it with certain qualities of the second object. An example is "But soft, what light through yonder window breaks?/ It is the east, and Juliet is the sun" in William Shakespeare's *Romeo and Juliet*.

Here, Juliet, the first object, is identified with qualities of the second object, the sun.

Metaphysical Conceit: See *Conceit*

Metaphysical Poetry: The body of poetry produced by a group of seventeenth-century English writers called the "Metaphysical Poets." The group includes John Donne and Andrew Marvell. The Metaphysical Poets made use of everyday speech, intellectual analysis, and unique imagery. They aimed to portray the ordinary conflicts and contradictions of life. Their poems often took the form of an argument, and many of them emphasize physical and religious love as well as the fleeting nature of life. Elaborate conceits are typical in metaphysical poetry. Marvell's "To His Coy Mistress" is a well-known example of a metaphysical poem.

Metaphysical Poets: See *Metaphysical Poetry*

Meter: In literary criticism, the repetition of sound patterns that creates a rhythm in poetry. The patterns are based on the number of syllables and the presence and absence of accents. The unit of rhythm in a line is called a foot. Types of meter are classified according to the number of feet in a line. These are the standard English lines: Monometer, one foot; Dimeter, two feet; Trimeter, three feet; Tetrameter, four feet; Pentameter, five feet; Hexameter, six feet (also called the Alexandrine); Heptameter, seven feet (also called the "Fourteener" when the feet are iambic). The most common English meter is the iambic pentameter, in which each line contains ten syllables, or five iambic feet, which individually are composed of an unstressed syllable followed by an accented syllable. Both of the following lines from Alfred, Lord Tennyson's "Ulysses" are written in iambic pentameter: Made weak by time and fate, but strong in will To strive, to seek, to find, and not to yield.

Mise en scene: The costumes, scenery, and other properties of a drama. Herbert Beerbohm Tree was renowned for the elaborate *mises en scene* of his lavish Shakespearean productions at His Majesty's Theatre between 1897 and 1915.

Modernism: Modern literary practices. Also, the principles of a literary school that lasted from roughly the beginning of the twentieth century until the end of World War II. Modernism is defined by its rejection of the literary conventions of the nineteenth century and by its opposition to conventional morality, taste, traditions, and economic values. Many writers are associated with the concepts of Modernism, including Albert Camus, Marcel Proust, D. H. Lawrence, W. H. Auden, Ernest Hemingway, William Faulkner, William Butler Yeats, Thomas Mann, Tennessee Williams, Eugene O'Neill, and James Joyce.

Monologue: A composition, written or oral, by a single individual. More specifically, a speech given by a single individual in a drama or other public entertainment. It has no set length, although it is usually several or more lines long. An example of an "extended monologue"—that is, a monologue of great length and seriousness—occurs in the one- act, one-character play *The Stronger* by August Strindberg.

Monometer: See *Meter*

Mood: The prevailing emotions of a work or of the author in his or her creation of the work. The mood of a work is not always what might be expected based on its subject matter. The poem "Dover Beach" by Matthew Arnold offers examples of two different moods originating from the same experience: watching the ocean at night. The mood of the first three lines—The sea is calm tonight The tide is full, the moon lies fair Upon the straights.... is in sharp contrast to the mood of the last three lines—And we are here as on a darkling plain Swept with confused alarms of struggle and flight, Where ignorant armies clash by night.

Motif: A theme, character type, image, metaphor, or other verbal element that recurs throughout a single work of literature or occurs in a number of different works over a period of time. For example, the various manifestations of the color white in Herman Melville's *Moby Dick* is a "specific" *motif*, while the trials of star-crossed lovers is a "conventional" *motif* from the literature of all periods. Also known as *Motiv* or *Leitmotiv*.

Motiv: See *Motif*

Muckrakers: An early twentieth-century group of American writers. Typically, their works exposed the wrongdoings of big business and government in the United States. Upton

Sinclair's *The Jungle* exemplifies the muckraking novel.

Muses: Nine Greek mythological goddesses, the daughters of Zeus and Mnemosyne (Memory). Each muse patronized a specific area of the liberal arts and sciences. Calliope presided over epic poetry, Clio over history, Erato over love poetry, Euterpe over music or lyric poetry, Melpomene over tragedy, Polyhymnia over hymns to the gods, Terpsichore over dance, Thalia over comedy, and Urania over astronomy. Poets and writers traditionally made appeals to the Muses for inspiration in their work. John Milton invokes the aid of a muse at the beginning of the first book of his *Paradise Lost:* Of Man's First disobedience, and the Fruit of the Forbidden Tree, whose mortal taste Brought Death into the World, and all our woe, With loss of Eden, till one greater Man Restore us, and regain the blissful Seat, Sing Heav'nly Muse, that on the secret top of Oreb, or of Sinai, didst inspire That Shepherd, who first taught the chosen Seed, In the Beginning how the Heav'ns and Earth Rose out of Chaos....

Mystery: See *Suspense*

Myth: An anonymous tale emerging from the traditional beliefs of a culture or social unit. Myths use supernatural explanations for natural phenomena. They may also explain cosmic issues like creation and death. Collections of myths, known as mythologies, are common to all cultures and nations, but the best-known myths belong to the Norse, Roman, and Greek mythologies. A famous myth is the story of Arachne, an arrogant young girl who challenged a goddess, Athena, to a weaving contest; when the girl won, Athena was enraged and turned Arachne into a spider, thus explaining the existence of spiders.

N

Narration: The telling of a series of events, real or invented. A narration may be either a simple narrative, in which the events are recounted chronologically, or a narrative with a plot, in which the account is given in a style reflecting the author's artistic concept of the story. Narration is sometimes used as a synonym for "storyline." The recounting of scary stories around a campfire is a form of narration.

Narrative: A verse or prose accounting of an event or sequence of events, real or invented. The term is also used as an adjective in the sense "method of narration." For example, in literary criticism, the expression "narrative technique" usually refers to the way the author structures and presents his or her story. Narratives range from the shortest accounts of events, as in Julius Caesar's remark, "I came, I saw, I conquered," to the longest historical or biographical works, as in Edward Gibbon's *The Decline and Fall of the Roman Empire,* as well as diaries, travelogues, novels, ballads, epics, short stories, and other fictional forms.

Narrative Poetry: A nondramatic poem in which the author tells a story. Such poems may be of any length or level of complexity. Epics such as *Beowulf* and ballads are forms of narrative poetry.

Narrator: The teller of a story. The narrator may be the author or a character in the story through whom the author speaks. Huckleberry Finn is the narrator of Mark Twain's *The Adventures of Huckleberry Finn.*

Naturalism: A literary movement of the late nineteenth and early twentieth centuries. The movement's major theorist, French novelist Emile Zola, envisioned a type of fiction that would examine human life with the objectivity of scientific inquiry. The Naturalists typically viewed human beings as either the products of "biological determinism," ruled by hereditary instincts and engaged in an endless struggle for survival, or as the products of "socioeconomic determinism," ruled by social and economic forces beyond their control. In their works, the Naturalists generally ignored the highest levels of society and focused on degradation: poverty, alcoholism, prostitution, insanity, and disease. Naturalism influenced authors throughout the world, including Henrik Ibsen and Thomas Hardy. In the United States, in particular, Naturalism had a profound impact. Among the authors who embraced its principles are Theodore Dreiser, Eugene O'Neill, Stephen Crane, Jack London, and Frank Norris.

Negritude: A literary movement based on the concept of a shared cultural bond on the part of black Africans, wherever they may be in the world. It traces its origins to the former French colonies of Africa and the Caribbean. Negritude poets, novelists, and essayists generally stress four points in their writings: One, black alienation from traditional African culture can lead to feelings of inferiority. Two, European colonialism and Western education should be resisted. Three, black Africans should seek to affirm and define their own identity. Four, African culture can and should be reclaimed. Many Negritude writers also claim that blacks can make unique contributions to the world, based on a heightened appreciation of nature, rhythm, and human emotions—aspects of life they say are not so highly valued in the materialistic and rationalistic West. Examples of Negritude literature include the poetry of both Senegalese Leopold Senghor in *Hosties noires* and Martiniquais Aime-Fernand Cesaire in *Return to My Native Land.*

Negro Renaissance: See *Harlem Renaissance*

Neoclassical Period: See *Neoclassicism*

Neoclassicism: In literary criticism, this term refers to the revival of the attitudes and styles of expression of classical literature. It is generally used to describe a period in European history beginning in the late seventeenth century and lasting until about 1800. In its purest form, Neoclassicism marked a return to order, proportion, restraint, logic, accuracy, and decorum. In England, where Neoclassicism perhaps was most popular, it reflected the influence of seventeenth- century French writers, especially dramatists. Neoclassical writers typically reacted against the intensity and enthusiasm of the Renaissance period. They wrote works that appealed to the intellect, using elevated language and classical literary forms such as satire and the ode. Neoclassical works were often governed by the classical goal of instruction. English neoclassicists included Alexander Pope, Jonathan Swift, Joseph Addison, Sir Richard Steele, John Gay, and Matthew Prior; French neoclassicists included Pierre Corneille and Jean-Baptiste Moliere. Also known as Age of Reason.

Neoclassicists: See *Neoclassicism*

New Criticism: A movement in literary criticism, dating from the late 1920s, that stressed close textual analysis in the interpretation of works of literature. The New Critics saw little merit in historical and biographical analysis. Rather, they aimed to examine the text alone, free from the question of how external events—biographical or otherwise—may have helped shape it. This predominantly American school was named "New Criticism" by one of its practitioners, John Crowe Ransom. Other important New Critics included Allen Tate, R. P. Blackmur, Robert Penn Warren, and Cleanth Brooks.

New Negro Movement: See *Harlem Renaissance*

Noble Savage: The idea that primitive man is noble and good but becomes evil and corrupted as he becomes civilized. The concept of the noble savage originated in the Renaissance period but is more closely identified with such later writers as Jean-Jacques Rousseau and Aphra Behn. First described in John Dryden's play *The Conquest of Granada,* the noble savage is portrayed by the various Native Americans in James Fenimore Cooper's "Leatherstocking Tales," by Queequeg, Daggoo, and Tashtego in Herman Melville's *Moby Dick,* and by John the Savage in Aldous Huxley's *Brave New World.*

O

Objective Correlative: An outward set of objects, a situation, or a chain of events corresponding to an inward experience and evoking this experience in the reader. The term frequently appears in modern criticism in discussions of authors' intended effects on the emotional responses of readers. This term was originally used by T. S. Eliot in his 1919 essay "Hamlet."

Objectivity: A quality in writing characterized by the absence of the author's opinion or feeling about the subject matter. Objectivity is an important factor in criticism. The novels of Henry James and, to a certain extent, the poems of John Larkin demonstrate objectivity, and it is central to John Keats's concept of "negative capability." Critical and journalistic writing usually are or attempt to be objective.

Occasional Verse: poetry written on the occasion of a significant historical or personal event. *Vers de societe* is sometimes called occasional verse although it is of a less serious nature. Famous examples of occasional verse include Andrew Marvell's "Horatian Ode upon Cromwell's Return from England," Walt Whitman's "When Lilacs Last in the Dooryard Bloom'd"—written upon the death of Abraham Lincoln—and Edmund Spenser's commemoration of his wedding, "Epithalamion."

Octave: A poem or stanza composed of eight lines. The term octave most often represents the first eight lines of a Petrarchan sonnet. An example of an octave is taken from a translation of a Petrarchan sonnet by Sir Thomas Wyatt: The pillar perisht is whereto I leant, The strongest stay of mine unquiet mind; The like of it no man again can find, From East to West Still seeking though he went. To mind unhap! for hap away hath rent Of all my joy the very bark and rind; And I, alas, by chance am thus assigned Daily to mourn till death do it relent.

Ode: Name given to an extended lyric poem characterized by exalted emotion and dignified style. An ode usually concerns a single, serious theme. Most odes, but not all, are addressed to an object or individual. Odes are distinguished from other lyric poetic forms by their complex rhythmic and stanzaic patterns. An example of this form is John Keats's "Ode to a Nightingale."

Oedipus Complex: A son's amorous obsession with his mother. The phrase is derived from the story of the ancient Theban hero Oedipus, who unknowingly killed his father and married his mother. Literary occurrences of the Oedipus complex include Andre Gide's *Oedipe* and Jean Cocteau's *La Machine infernale,* as well as the most famous, Sophocles' *Oedipus Rex.*

Omniscience: See *Point of View*

Onomatopoeia: The use of words whose sounds express or suggest their meaning. In its simplest sense, onomatopoeia may be represented by words that mimic the sounds they denote such as "hiss" or "meow." At a more subtle level, the pattern and rhythm of sounds and rhymes of a line or poem may be onomatopoeic. A celebrated example of onomatopoeia is the repetition of the word "bells" in Edgar Allan Poe's poem "The Bells."

Opera: A type of stage performance, usually a drama, in which the dialogue is sung. Classic examples of opera include Giuseppi Verdi's *La traviata,* Giacomo Puccini's *La Boheme,* and Richard Wagner's *Tristan und Isolde.* Major twentieth- century contributors to the form include Richard Strauss and Alban Berg.

Operetta: A usually romantic comic opera. John Gay's *The Beggar's Opera,* Richard Sheridan's *The Duenna,* and numerous works by William Gilbert and Arthur Sullivan are examples of operettas.

Oral Tradition: See *Oral Transmission*

Oral Transmission: A process by which songs, ballads, folklore, and other material are transmitted by word of mouth. The tradition of oral transmission predates the written record systems of literate society. Oral transmission preserves material sometimes over generations, although often with variations. Memory plays a large part in the recitation and preservation of orally transmitted material. Breton lays, French *fabliaux,* national epics (including the Anglo- Saxon *Beowulf,* the Spanish *El Cid,* and the Finnish *Kalevala*), Native American myths and legends, and African folktales told by plantation slaves are examples of orally transmitted literature.

Oration: Formal speaking intended to motivate the listeners to some action or feeling. Such public speaking was much more common before the development of timely printed communication such as newspapers. Famous examples of oration include Abraham Lincoln's "Gettysburg Address" and Dr. Martin Luther King Jr.'s "I Have a Dream" speech.

Ottava Rima: An eight-line stanza of poetry composed in iambic pentameter (a five-foot line in which each foot consists of an unaccented syllable followed by an accented syllable), following the abababcc rhyme scheme. This form has been prominently used by such important English writers as Lord Byron, Henry Wadsworth Longfellow, and W. B. Yeats.

Oxymoron: A phrase combining two contradictory terms. Oxymorons may be intentional or unintentional. The following speech from William Shakespeare's *Romeo and Juliet* uses several oxymorons: Why, then, O brawling love! O loving hate! O anything, of nothing first create! O heavy lightness! serious vanity! Mis-shapen chaos of well-seeming forms! Feather of lead, bright smoke, cold fire, sick health! This love feel I, that feel no love in this.

P

Pantheism: The idea that all things are both a manifestation or revelation of God and a part of God at the same time. Pantheism was a common attitude in the early societies of Egypt, India, and Greece—the term derives from the Greek *pan* meaning "all" and *theos* meaning "deity." It later became a significant part of the Christian faith. William Wordsworth and Ralph Waldo Emerson are among the many writers who have expressed the pantheistic attitude in their works.

Parable: A story intended to teach a moral lesson or answer an ethical question. In the West, the best examples of parables are those of Jesus Christ in the New Testament, notably "The Prodigal Son," but parables also are used in Sufism, rabbinic literature, Hasidism, and Zen Buddhism.

Paradox: A statement that appears illogical or contradictory at first, but may actually point to an underlying truth. "Less is more" is an example of a paradox. Literary examples include Francis Bacon's statement, "The most corrected copies are commonly the least correct," and "All animals are equal, but some animals are more equal than others" from George Orwell's *Animal Farm.*

Parallelism: A method of comparison of two ideas in which each is developed in the same grammatical structure. Ralph Waldo Emerson's "Civilization" contains this example of parallelism: Raphael paints wisdom; Handel sings it, Phidias carves it, Shakespeare writes it, Wren builds it, Columbus sails it, Luther preaches it, Washington arms it, Watt mechanizes it.

Parnassianism: A mid nineteenth-century movement in French literature. Followers of the movement stressed adherence to well-defined artistic forms as a reaction against the often chaotic expression of the artist's ego that dominated the work of the Romantics. The Parnassians also rejected the moral, ethical, and social themes exhibited in the works of French Romantics such as Victor Hugo. The aesthetic doctrines of the Parnassians strongly influenced the later symbolist and decadent movements. Members of the Parnassian school include Leconte de Lisle, Sully Prudhomme, Albert Glatigny, Francois Coppee, and Theodore de Banville.

Parody: In literary criticism, this term refers to an imitation of a serious literary work or the signature style of a particular author in a ridiculous manner. A typical parody adopts the style of the original and applies it to an inappropriate subject for humorous effect. Parody is a form of satire and could be considered the literary equivalent of a caricature or cartoon. Henry Fielding's *Shamela* is a parody of Samuel Richardson's *Pamela.*

Pastoral: A term derived from the Latin word "pastor," meaning shepherd. A pastoral is a literary composition on a rural theme. The conventions of the pastoral were originated by the third-century Greek poet Theocritus, who wrote about the experiences, love affairs, and pastimes of Sicilian shepherds. In a pastoral, characters and language of a courtly nature are often placed in a simple setting. The term pastoral is also used to classify dramas, elegies, and lyrics that exhibit the use of country settings and shepherd characters. Percy Bysshe Shelley's "Adonais" and John Milton's "Lycidas" are two famous examples of pastorals.

Pastorela: The Spanish name for the shepherds play, a folk drama reenacted during the Christmas season. Examples of *pastorelas* include Gomez Manrique's *Representacion del nacimiento* and the dramas of Lucas Fernandez and Juan del Encina.

Pathetic Fallacy: A term coined by English critic John Ruskin to identify writing that falsely endows nonhuman things with human intentions and feelings, such as "angry clouds" and "sad trees." The pathetic fallacy is a required convention in the classical poetic form of the pastoral elegy, and it is used in the modern poetry of T. S. Eliot, Ezra Pound, and the Imagists. Also known as Poetic Fallacy.

Pelado: Literally the "skinned one" or shirtless one, he was the stock underdog, sharp-witted picaresque character of Mexican vaudeville and tent shows. The *pelado* is found in such works as Don Catarino's *Los effectos de la crisis* and *Regreso a mi tierra.*

Pen Name: See *Pseudonym*

Pentameter: See *Meter*

Persona: A Latin term meaning "mask." *Personae* are the characters in a fictional work of literature. The *persona* generally functions as a mask through which the author tells a story in a voice other than his or her own. A *persona* is usually either a character in a story who acts as a narrator or an "implied author," a voice created by the author to act as the narrator for himself or herself. *Personae* include the narrator of Geoffrey Chaucer's *Canterbury*

Tales and Marlow in Joseph Conrad's *Heart of Darkness.*

Personae: See *Persona*

Personal Point of View: See *Point of View*

Personification: A figure of speech that gives human qualities to abstract ideas, animals, and inanimate objects. William Shakespeare used personification in *Romeo and Juliet* in the lines "Arise, fair sun, and kill the envious moon,/ Who is already sick and pale with grief." Here, the moon is portrayed as being envious, sick, and pale with grief—all markedly human qualities. Also known as *Prosopopoeia.*

Petrarchan Sonnet: See *Sonnet*

Phenomenology: A method of literary criticism based on the belief that things have no existence outside of human consciousness or awareness. Proponents of this theory believe that art is a process that takes place in the mind of the observer as he or she contemplates an object rather than a quality of the object itself. Among phenomenological critics are Edmund Husserl, George Poulet, Marcel Raymond, and Roman Ingarden.

Picaresque Novel: Episodic fiction depicting the adventures of a roguish central character ("picaro" is Spanish for "rogue"). The picaresque hero is commonly a low-born but clever individual who wanders into and out of various affairs of love, danger, and farcical intrigue. These involvements may take place at all social levels and typically present a humorous and wide-ranging satire of a given society. Prominent examples of the picaresque novel are *Don Quixote* by Miguel de Cervantes, *Tom Jones* by Henry Fielding, and *Moll Flanders* by Daniel Defoe.

Plagiarism: Claiming another person's written material as one's own. Plagiarism can take the form of direct, word-for- word copying or the theft of the substance or idea of the work. A student who copies an encyclopedia entry and turns it in as a report for school is guilty of plagiarism.

Platonic Criticism: A form of criticism that stresses an artistic work's usefulness as an agent of social engineering rather than any quality or value of the work itself. Platonic criticism takes as its starting point the ancient Greek philosopher Plato's comments on art in his *Republic.*

Platonism: The embracing of the doctrines of the philosopher Plato, popular among the poets of the Renaissance and the Romantic period. Platonism is more flexible than Aristotelian Criticism and places more emphasis on the supernatural and unknown aspects of life. Platonism is expressed in the love poetry of the Renaissance, the fourth book of Baldassare Castiglione's *The Book of the Courtier,* and the poetry of William Blake, William Wordsworth, Percy Bysshe Shelley, Friedrich Holderlin, William Butler Yeats, and Wallace Stevens.

Play: See *Drama*

Plot: In literary criticism, this term refers to the pattern of events in a narrative or drama. In its simplest sense, the plot guides the author in composing the work and helps the reader follow the work. Typically, plots exhibit causality and unity and have a beginning, a middle, and an end. Sometimes, however, a plot may consist of a series of disconnected events, in which case it is known as an "episodic plot." In his *Aspects of the Novel,* E. M. Forster distinguishes between a story, defined as a "narrative of events arranged in their time-sequence," and plot, which organizes the events to a "sense of causality." This definition closely mirrors Aristotle's discussion of plot in his *Poetics.*

Poem: In its broadest sense, a composition utilizing rhyme, meter, concrete detail, and expressive language to create a literary experience with emotional and aesthetic appeal. Typical poems include sonnets, odes, elegies, *haiku,* ballads, and free verse.

Poet: An author who writes poetry or verse. The term is also used to refer to an artist or writer who has an exceptional gift for expression, imagination, and energy in the making of art in any form. Well-known poets include Horace, Basho, Sir Philip Sidney, Sir Edmund Spenser, John Donne, Andrew Marvell, Alexander Pope, Jonathan Swift, George Gordon, Lord Byron, John Keats, Christina Rossetti, W. H. Auden, Stevie Smith, and Sylvia Plath.

Poetic Fallacy: See *Pathetic Fallacy*

Poetic Justice: An outcome in a literary work, not necessarily a poem, in which the good are rewarded and the evil are punished, especially in ways that particularly fit their virtues or crimes. For example, a murderer may himself be murdered, or a thief will find himself penniless.

Poetic License: Distortions of fact and literary convention made by a writer—not always a poet—for the sake of the effect gained. Poetic license is closely related to the concept of "artistic freedom." An author exercises poetic license by saying that a pile of money "reaches as high as a mountain" when the pile is actually only a foot or two high.

Poetics: This term has two closely related meanings. It denotes (1) an aesthetic theory in literary criticism about the essence of poetry or (2) rules prescribing the proper methods, content, style, or diction of poetry. The term poetics may also refer to theories about literature in general, not just poetry.

Poetry: In its broadest sense, writing that aims to present ideas and evoke an emotional experience in the reader through the use of meter, imagery, connotative and concrete words, and a carefully constructed structure based on rhythmic patterns. Poetry typically relies on words and expressions that have several layers of meaning. It also makes use of the effects of regular rhythm on the ear and may make a strong appeal to the senses through the use of imagery. Edgar Allan Poe's "Annabel Lee" and Walt Whitman's *Leaves of Grass* are famous examples of poetry.

Point of View: The narrative perspective from which a literary work is presented to the reader. There are four traditional points of view. The "third person omniscient" gives the reader a "godlike" perspective, unrestricted by time or place, from which to see actions and look into the minds of characters. This allows the author to comment openly on characters and events in the work. The "third person" point of view presents the events of the story from outside of any single character's perception, much like the omniscient point of view, but the reader must understand the action as it takes place and without any special insight into characters' minds or motivations. The "first person" or "personal" point of view relates events as they are perceived by a single character. The main character "tells" the story and may offer opinions about the action and characters which differ from those of the author. Much less common than omniscient, third person, and first person is the "second person" point of view, wherein the author tells the story as if it is happening to the reader. James Thurber employs the omniscient point of view in his short story "The Secret Life of Walter Mitty." Ernest Hemingway's "A Clean, Well-Lighted Place" is a short story told from the third person point of view. Mark Twain's novel *Huck Finn* is presented from the first person viewpoint. Jay McInerney's *Bright Lights, Big City* is an example of a novel which uses the second person point of view.

Polemic: A work in which the author takes a stand on a controversial subject, such as abortion or religion. Such works are often extremely argumentative or provocative. Classic examples of polemics include John Milton's *Aeropagitica* and Thomas Paine's *The American Crisis*.

Pornography: Writing intended to provoke feelings of lust in the reader. Such works are often condemned by critics and teachers, but those which can be shown to have literary value are viewed less harshly. Literary works that have been described as pornographic include Ovid's *The Art of Love*, Margaret of Angouleme's *Heptameron*, John Cleland's *Memoirs of a Woman of Pleasure; or, the Life of Fanny Hill*, the anonymous *My Secret Life*, D. H. Lawrence's *Lady Chatterley's Lover*, and Vladimir Nabokov's *Lolita*.

Post-Aesthetic Movement: An artistic response made by African Americans to the black aesthetic movement of the 1960s and early '70s. Writers since that time have adopted a somewhat different tone in their work, with less emphasis placed on the disparity between black and white in the United States. In the words of post-aesthetic authors such as Toni Morrison, John Edgar Wideman, and Kristin Hunter, African Americans are portrayed as looking inward for answers to their own questions, rather than always looking to the outside world. Two well-known examples of works produced as part of the post-aesthetic movement are the Pulitzer Prize-winning novels *The Color Purple* by Alice Walker and *Beloved* by Toni Morrison.

Postmodernism: Writing from the 1960s forward characterized by experimentation and continuing to apply some of the fundamentals of modernism, which included existentialism and alienation. Postmodernists have gone a step further in the rejection of tradition begun with the modernists by also rejecting traditional forms, preferring the anti-novel over the novel and the anti-hero over the hero. Postmodern writers include Alain Robbe-Grillet, Thomas Pynchon, Margaret Drabble, John Fowles, Adolfo Bioy-Casares, and Gabriel Garcia Marquez.

Pre-Raphaelites: A circle of writers and artists in mid nineteenth-century England. Valuing the pre-Renaissance artistic qualities of religious symbolism, lavish pictorialism, and natural sensuousness, the Pre-Raphaelites cultivated a sense of mystery and melancholy that influenced later writers associated with the Symbolist and Decadent movements. The major members of the group include Dante Gabriel Rossetti, Christina Rossetti, Algernon Swinburne, and Walter Pater.

Primitivism: The belief that primitive peoples were nobler and less flawed than civilized peoples because they had not been subjected to the tainting influence of society. Examples of literature espousing primitivism include Aphra Behn's *Oroonoko: Or, The History of the Royal Slave,* Jean-Jacques Rousseau's *Julie ou la Nouvelle Heloise,* Oliver Goldsmith's *The Deserted Village,* the poems of Robert Burns, Herman Melville's stories *Typee, Omoo,* and *Mardi,* many poems of William Butler Yeats and Robert Frost, and William Golding's novel *Lord of the Flies.*

Projective Verse: A form of free verse in which the poet's breathing pattern determines the lines of the poem. Poets who advocate projective verse are against all formal structures in writing, including meter and form. Besides its creators, Robert Creeley, Robert Duncan, and Charles Olson, two other well-known projective verse poets are Denise Levertov and LeRoi Jones (Amiri Baraka). Also known as Breath Verse.

Prologue: An introductory section of a literary work. It often contains information establishing the situation of the characters or presents information about the setting, time period, or action. In drama, the prologue is spoken by a chorus or by one of the principal characters. In the "General Prologue" of *The Canterbury Tales,* Geoffrey Chaucer describes the main characters and establishes the setting and purpose of the work.

Prose: A literary medium that attempts to mirror the language of everyday speech. It is distinguished from poetry by its use of unmetered, unrhymed language consisting of logically related sentences. Prose is usually grouped into paragraphs that form a cohesive whole such as an essay or a novel. Recognized masters of English prose writing include Sir Thomas Malory, William Caxton, Raphael Holinshed, Joseph Addison, Mark Twain, and Ernest Hemingway.

Prosopopoeia: See *Personification*

Protagonist: The central character of a story who serves as a focus for its themes and incidents and as the principal rationale for its development. The protagonist is sometimes referred to in discussions of modern literature as the hero or anti-hero. Well-known protagonists are Hamlet in William Shakespeare's *Hamlet* and Jay Gatsby in F. Scott Fitzgerald's *The Great Gatsby.*

Protest Fiction: Protest fiction has as its primary purpose the protesting of some social injustice, such as racism or discrimination. One example of protest fiction is a series of five novels by Chester Himes, beginning in 1945 with *If He Hollers Let Him Go* and ending in 1955 with *The Primitive.* These works depict the destructive effects of race and gender stereotyping in the context of interracial relationships. Another African American author whose works often revolve around themes of social protest is John Oliver Killens. James Baldwin's essay "Everybody's Protest Novel" generated controversy by attacking the authors of protest fiction.

Proverb: A brief, sage saying that expresses a truth about life in a striking manner. "They are not all cooks who carry long knives" is an example of a proverb.

Pseudonym: A name assumed by a writer, most often intended to prevent his or her identification as the author of a work. Two or more authors may work together under one pseudonym, or an author may use a different name for each genre he or she publishes in. Some publishing companies maintain "house pseudonyms," under which any number of authors may write installations in a series. Some authors also choose a pseudonym over their real names the way an actor may use a stage name. Examples of pseudonyms (with the author's real name in parentheses) include Voltaire (Francois-Marie Arouet), Novalis (Friedrich von Hardenberg), Currer Bell (Charlotte Bronte), Ellis Bell (Emily Bronte), George Eliot (Maryann

Evans), Honorio Bustos Donmecq (Adolfo Bioy-Casares and Jorge Luis Borges), and Richard Bachman (Stephen King).

Pun: A play on words that have similar sounds but different meanings. A serious example of the pun is from John Donne's "A Hymne to God the Father": Sweare by thyself, that at my death thy sonne Shall shine as he shines now, and hereto fore; And, having done that, Thou haste done; I fear no more.

Pure Poetry: poetry written without instructional intent or moral purpose that aims only to please a reader by its imagery or musical flow. The term pure poetry is used as the antonym of the term "didacticism." The poetry of Edgar Allan Poe, Stephane Mallarme, Paul Verlaine, Paul Valery, Juan Ramoz Jimenez, and Jorge Guillen offer examples of pure poetry.

Q

Quatrain: A four-line stanza of a poem or an entire poem consisting of four lines. The following quatrain is from Robert Herrick's "To Live Merrily, and to Trust to Good Verses": Round, round, the root do's run; And being ravisht thus, Come, I will drink a Tun To my *Propertius.*

R

Raisonneur: A character in a drama who functions as a spokesperson for the dramatist's views. The *raisonneur* typically observes the play without becoming central to its action. *Raisonneurs* were very common in plays of the nineteenth century.

Realism: A nineteenth-century European literary movement that sought to portray familiar characters, situations, and settings in a realistic manner. This was done primarily by using an objective narrative point of view and through the buildup of accurate detail. The standard for success of any realistic work depends on how faithfully it transfers common experience into fictional forms. The realistic method may be altered or extended, as in stream of consciousness writing, to record highly subjective experience. Seminal authors in the tradition of Realism include Honore de Balzac, Gustave Flaubert, and Henry James.

Refrain: A phrase repeated at intervals throughout a poem. A refrain may appear at the end of each stanza or at less regular intervals. It may be altered slightly at each appearance. Some refrains are nonsense expressions—as with "Nevermore" in Edgar Allan Poe's "The Raven"—that seem to take on a different significance with each use.

Renaissance: The period in European history that marked the end of the Middle Ages. It began in Italy in the late fourteenth century. In broad terms, it is usually seen as spanning the fourteenth, fifteenth, and sixteenth centuries, although it did not reach Great Britain, for example, until the 1480s or so. The Renaissance saw an awakening in almost every sphere of human activity, especially science, philosophy, and the arts. The period is best defined by the emergence of a general philosophy that emphasized the importance of the intellect, the individual, and world affairs. It contrasts strongly with the medieval worldview, characterized by the dominant concerns of faith, the social collective, and spiritual salvation. Prominent writers during the Renaissance include Niccolo Machiavelli and Baldassare Castiglione in Italy, Miguel de Cervantes and Lope de Vega in Spain, Jean Froissart and Francois Rabelais in France, Sir Thomas More and Sir Philip Sidney in England, and Desiderius Erasmus in Holland.

Repartee: Conversation featuring snappy retorts and witticisms. Masters of *repartee* include Sydney Smith, Charles Lamb, and Oscar Wilde. An example is recorded in the meeting of "Beau" Nash and John Wesley: Nash said, "I never make way for a fool," to which Wesley responded, "Don't you? I always do," and stepped aside.

Resolution: The portion of a story following the climax, in which the conflict is resolved. The resolution of Jane Austen's *Northanger Abbey* is neatly summed up in the following sentence: "Henry and Catherine were married, the bells rang and every body smiled."

Restoration: See *Restoration Age*

Restoration Age: A period in English literature beginning with the crowning of Charles II in 1660 and running to about 1700. The era, which was characterized by a reaction against Puritanism, was the first great age of the comedy of manners. The finest literature of the era is typically witty and urbane, and often lewd. Prominent Restoration Age writers include

William Congreve, Samuel Pepys, John Dryden, and John Milton.

Revenge Tragedy: A dramatic form popular during the Elizabethan Age, in which the protagonist, directed by the ghost of his murdered father or son, inflicts retaliation upon a powerful villain. Notable features of the revenge tragedy include violence, bizarre criminal acts, intrigue, insanity, a hesitant protagonist, and the use of soliloquy. Thomas Kyd's *Spanish Tragedy* is the first example of revenge tragedy in English, and William Shakespeare's *Hamlet* is perhaps the best. Extreme examples of revenge tragedy, such as John Webster's *The Duchess of Malfi,* are labeled "tragedies of blood." Also known as Tragedy of Blood.

Revista: The Spanish term for a vaudeville musical revue. Examples of *revistas* include Antonio Guzman Aguilera's *Mexico para los mexicanos,* Daniel Vanegas's *Maldito jazz,* and Don Catarino's *Whiskey, morfina y marihuana* and *El desterrado.*

Rhetoric: In literary criticism, this term denotes the art of ethical persuasion. In its strictest sense, rhetoric adheres to various principles developed since classical times for arranging facts and ideas in a clear, persuasive, appealing manner. The term is also used to refer to effective prose in general and theories of or methods for composing effective prose. Classical examples of rhetorics include *The Rhetoric of Aristotle,* Quintillian's *Institutio Oratoria,* and Cicero's *Ad Herennium.*

Rhetorical Question: A question intended to provoke thought, but not an expressed answer, in the reader. It is most commonly used in oratory and other persuasive genres. The following lines from Thomas Gray's "Elegy Written in a Country Churchyard" ask rhetorical questions: Can storied urn or animated bust Back to its mansion call the fleeting breath? Can Honour's voice provoke the silent dust, Or Flattery soothe the dull cold ear of Death?

Rhyme: When used as a noun in literary criticism, this term generally refers to a poem in which words sound identical or very similar and appear in parallel positions in two or more lines. Rhymes are classified into different types according to where they fall in a line or stanza or according to the degree of similarity they exhibit in their spellings and sounds. Some major types of rhyme are "masculine" rhyme, "feminine" rhyme, and "triple"

rhyme. In a masculine rhyme, the rhyming sound falls in a single accented syllable, as with "heat" and "eat." Feminine rhyme is a rhyme of two syllables, one stressed and one unstressed, as with "merry" and "tarry." Triple rhyme matches the sound of the accented syllable and the two unaccented syllables that follow: "narrative" and "declarative." Robert Browning alternates feminine and masculine rhymes in his "Soliloquy of the Spanish Cloister": Gr-r-r—there go, my heart's abhorrence! Water your damned flower-pots, do! If hate killed men, Brother Lawrence, God's blood, would not mine kill you! What? Your myrtle-bush wants trimming? Oh, that rose has prior claims— Needs its leaden vase filled brimming? Hell dry you up with flames! Triple rhymes can be found in Thomas Hood's "Bridge of Sighs," George Gordon Byron's satirical verse, and Ogden Nash's comic poems.

Rhyme Royal: A stanza of seven lines composed in iambic pentameter and rhymed *ababbcc.* The name is said to be a tribute to King James I of Scotland, who made much use of the form in his poetry. Examples of rhyme royal include Geoffrey Chaucer's *The Parlement of Foules,* William Shakespeare's *The Rape of Lucrece,* William Morris's *The Early Paradise,* and John Masefield's *The Widow in the Bye Street.*

Rhyme Scheme: See *Rhyme*

Rhythm: A regular pattern of sound, time intervals, or events occurring in writing, most often and most discernably in poetry. Regular, reliable rhythm is known to be soothing to humans, while interrupted, unpredictable, or rapidly changing rhythm is disturbing. These effects are known to authors, who use them to produce a desired reaction in the reader. An example of a form of irregular rhythm is sprung rhythm poetry; quantitative verse, on the other hand, is very regular in its rhythm.

Rising Action: The part of a drama where the plot becomes increasingly complicated. Rising action leads up to the climax, or turning point, of a drama. The final "chase scene" of an action film is generally the rising action which culminates in the film's climax.

Rococo: A style of European architecture that flourished in the eighteenth century, especially in France. The most notable features of *rococo* are its extensive use of ornamentation and its themes of lightness, gaiety, and intimacy. In literary criticism, the term is often used disparagingly to refer to a decadent or over-ornamental style. Alexander Pope's "The Rape of the Lock" is an example of literary *rococo*.

Roman à clef: A French phrase meaning "novel with a key." It refers to a narrative in which real persons are portrayed under fictitious names. Jack Kerouac, for example, portrayed various real-life beat generation figures under fictitious names in his *On the Road*.

Romance: A broad term, usually denoting a narrative with exotic, exaggerated, often idealized characters, scenes, and themes. Nathaniel Hawthorne called his *The House of the Seven Gables* and *The Marble Faun* romances in order to distinguish them from clearly realistic works.

Romantic Age: See *Romanticism*

Romanticism: This term has two widely accepted meanings. In historical criticism, it refers to a European intellectual and artistic movement of the late eighteenth and early nineteenth centuries that sought greater freedom of personal expression than that allowed by the strict rules of literary form and logic of the eighteenth-century neoclassicists. The Romantics preferred emotional and imaginative expression to rational analysis. They considered the individual to be at the center of all experience and so placed him or her at the center of their art. The Romantics believed that the creative imagination reveals nobler truths—unique feelings and attitudes—than those that could be discovered by logic or by scientific examination. Both the natural world and the state of childhood were important sources for revelations of "eternal truths." "Romanticism" is also used as a general term to refer to a type of sensibility found in all periods of literary history and usually considered to be in opposition to the principles of classicism. In this sense, Romanticism signifies any work or philosophy in which the exotic or dreamlike figure strongly, or that is devoted to individualistic expression, self-analysis, or a pursuit of a higher realm of knowledge than can be discovered by human reason. Prominent Romantics include Jean-Jacques Rousseau, William Wordsworth, John Keats, Lord Byron, and Johann Wolfgang von Goethe.

Romantics: See *Romanticism*

Russian Symbolism: A Russian poetic movement, derived from French symbolism, that flourished between 1894 and 1910. While some Russian Symbolists continued in the French tradition, stressing aestheticism and the importance of suggestion above didactic intent, others saw their craft as a form of mystical worship, and themselves as mediators between the supernatural and the mundane. Russian symbolists include Aleksandr Blok, Vyacheslav Ivanovich Ivanov, Fyodor Sologub, Andrey Bely, Nikolay Gumilyov, and Vladimir Sergeyevich Solovyov.

S

Satire: A work that uses ridicule, humor, and wit to criticize and provoke change in human nature and institutions. There are two major types of satire: "formal" or "direct" satire speaks directly to the reader or to a character in the work; "indirect" satire relies upon the ridiculous behavior of its characters to make its point. Formal satire is further divided into two manners: the "Horatian," which ridicules gently, and the "Juvenalian," which derides its subjects harshly and bitterly. Voltaire's novella *Candide* is an indirect satire. Jonathan Swift's essay "A Modest Proposal" is a Juvenalian satire.

Scansion: The analysis or "scanning" of a poem to determine its meter and often its rhyme scheme. The most common system of scansion uses accents (slanted lines drawn above syllables) to show stressed syllables, breves (curved lines drawn above syllables) to show unstressed syllables, and vertical lines to separate each foot. In the first line of John Keats's *Endymion,* "A thing of beauty is a joy forever:" the word "thing," the first syllable of "beauty," the word "joy," and the second syllable of "forever" are stressed, while the words "A" and "of," the second syllable of "beauty," the word "a," and the first and third syllables of "forever" are unstressed. In the second line: "Its loveliness increases; it will never" a pair of vertical lines separate the foot ending with "increases" and the one beginning with "it."

Scene: A subdivision of an act of a drama, consisting of continuous action taking place at a single time and in a single location. The beginnings and endings of scenes may be indicated by clearing the stage of actors and props or by the entrances and exits of important characters. The first act of William Shakespeare's *Winter's Tale* is comprised of two scenes.

Science Fiction: A type of narrative about or based upon real or imagined scientific theories and technology. Science fiction is often peopled with alien creatures and set on other planets or in different dimensions. Karel Capek's *R.U.R.* is a major work of science fiction.

Second Person: See *Point of View*

Semiotics: The study of how literary forms and conventions affect the meaning of language. Semioticians include Ferdinand de Saussure, Charles Sanders Pierce, Claude Levi-Strauss, Jacques Lacan, Michel Foucault, Jacques Derrida, Roland Barthes, and Julia Kristeva.

Sestet: Any six-line poem or stanza. Examples of the sestet include the last six lines of the Petrarchan sonnet form, the stanza form of Robert Burns's "A Poet's Welcome to his love-begotten Daughter," and the sestina form in W. H. Auden's "Paysage Moralise."

Setting: The time, place, and culture in which the action of a narrative takes place. The elements of setting may include geographic location, characters' physical and mental environments, prevailing cultural attitudes, or the historical time in which the action takes place. Examples of settings include the romanticized Scotland in Sir Walter Scott's "Waverley" novels, the French provincial setting in Gustave Flaubert's *Madame Bovary*, the fictional Wessex country of Thomas Hardy's novels, and the small towns of southern Ontario in Alice Munro's short stories.

Shakespearean Sonnet: See *Sonnet*

Signifying Monkey: A popular trickster figure in black folklore, with hundreds of tales about this character documented since the 19th century. Henry Louis Gates Jr. examines the history of the signifying monkey in *The Signifying Monkey: Towards a Theory of Afro-American Literary Criticism,* published in 1988.

Simile: A comparison, usually using "like" or "as", of two essentially dissimilar things, as in "coffee as cold as ice" or "He sounded like

a broken record." The title of Ernest Hemingway's "Hills Like White Elephants" contains a simile.

Slang: A type of informal verbal communication that is generally unacceptable for formal writing. Slang words and phrases are often colorful exaggerations used to emphasize the speaker's point; they may also be shortened versions of an often-used word or phrase. Examples of American slang from the 1990s include "yuppie" (an acronym for Young Urban Professional), "awesome" (for "excellent"), wired (for "nervous" or "excited"), and "chill out" (for relax).

Slant Rhyme: See *Consonance*

Slave Narrative: Autobiographical accounts of American slave life as told by escaped slaves. These works first appeared during the abolition movement of the 1830s through the 1850s. Olaudah Equiano's *The Interesting Narrative of Olaudah Equiano, or Gustavus Vassa, The African* and Harriet Ann Jacobs's *Incidents in the Life of a Slave Girl* are examples of the slave narrative.

Social Realism: See *Socialist Realism*

Socialist Realism: The Socialist Realism school of literary theory was proposed by Maxim Gorky and established as a dogma by the first Soviet Congress of Writers. It demanded adherence to a communist worldview in works of literature. Its doctrines required an objective viewpoint comprehensible to the working classes and themes of social struggle featuring strong proletarian heroes. A successful work of socialist realism is Nikolay Ostrovsky's *Kak zakalyalas stal (How the Steel Was Tempered)*. Also known as Social Realism.

Soliloquy: A monologue in a drama used to give the audience information and to develop the speaker's character. It is typically a projection of the speaker's innermost thoughts. Usually delivered while the speaker is alone on stage, a soliloquy is intended to present an illusion of unspoken reflection. A celebrated soliloquy is Hamlet's "To be or not to be" speech in William Shakespeare's *Hamlet*.

Sonnet: A fourteen-line poem, usually composed in iambic pentameter, employing one of several rhyme schemes. There are three major types of sonnets, upon which all other variations of the form are based: the "Petrarchan" or "Italian" sonnet, the "Shakespearean" or

"English" sonnet, and the "Spenserian" sonnet. A Petrarchan sonnet consists of an octave rhymed *abbaabba* and a "sestet" rhymed either *cdecde, cdccdc,* or *cdedce.* The octave poses a question or problem, relates a narrative, or puts forth a proposition; the sestet presents a solution to the problem, comments upon the narrative, or applies the proposition put forth in the octave. The Shakespearean sonnet is divided into three quatrains and a couplet rhymed *abab cdcd efef gg.* The couplet provides an epigrammatic comment on the narrative or problem put forth in the quatrains. The Spenserian sonnet uses three quatrains and a couplet like the Shakespearean, but links their three rhyme schemes in this way: *abab bcbc cdcd ee.* The Spenserian sonnet develops its theme in two parts like the Petrarchan, its final six lines resolving a problem, analyzing a narrative, or applying a proposition put forth in its first eight lines. Examples of sonnets can be found in Petrarch's *Canzoniere,* Edmund Spenser's *Amoretti,* Elizabeth Barrett Browning's *Sonnets from the Portuguese,* Rainer Maria Rilke's *Sonnets to Orpheus,* and Adrienne Rich's poem "The Insusceptibles."

Spenserian Sonnet: See *Sonnet*

Spenserian Stanza: A nine-line stanza having eight verses in iambic pentameter, its ninth verse in iambic hexameter, and the rhyme scheme ababbcbcc. This stanza form was first used by Edmund Spenser in his allegorical poem *The Faerie Queene.*

Spondee: In poetry meter, a foot consisting of two long or stressed syllables occurring together. This form is quite rare in English verse, and is usually composed of two monosyllabic words. The first foot in the following line from Robert Burns's "Green Grow the Rashes" is an example of a spondee: Green grow the rashes, O.

Sprung Rhythm: Versification using a specific number of accented syllables per line but disregarding the number of unaccented syllables that fall in each line, producing an irregular rhythm in the poem. Gerard Manley Hopkins, who coined the term "sprung rhythm," is the most notable practitioner of this technique.

Stanza: A subdivision of a poem consisting of lines grouped together, often in recurring patterns of rhyme, line length, and meter. Stanzas may also serve as units of thought in a poem much like paragraphs in prose.

Examples of stanza forms include the quatrain, *terza rima, ottava rima,* Spenserian, and the so-called *In Memoriam* stanza from Alfred, Lord Tennyson's poem by that title. The following is an example of the latter form: Love is and was my lord and king, And in his presence I attend To hear the tidings of my friend, Which every hour his couriers bring.

Stereotype: A stereotype was originally the name for a duplication made during the printing process; this led to its modern definition as a person or thing that is (or is assumed to be) the same as all others of its type. Common stereotypical characters include the absent-minded professor, the nagging wife, the troublemaking teenager, and the kindhearted grandmother.

Stream of Consciousness: A narrative technique for rendering the inward experience of a character. This technique is designed to give the impression of an ever-changing series of thoughts, emotions, images, and memories in the spontaneous and seemingly illogical order that they occur in life. The textbook example of stream of consciousness is the last section of James Joyce's *Ulysses.*

Structuralism: A twentieth-century movement in literary criticism that examines how literary texts arrive at their meanings, rather than the meanings themselves. There are two major types of structuralist analysis: one examines the way patterns of linguistic structures unify a specific text and emphasize certain elements of that text, and the other interprets the way literary forms and conventions affect the meaning of language itself. Prominent structuralists include Michel Foucault, Roman Jakobson, and Roland Barthes.

Structure: The form taken by a piece of literature. The structure may be made obvious for ease of understanding, as in nonfiction works, or may obscured for artistic purposes, as in some poetry or seemingly "unstructured" prose. Examples of common literary structures include the plot of a narrative, the acts and scenes of a drama, and such poetic forms as the Shakespearean sonnet and the Pindaric ode.

Sturm und Drang: A German term meaning "storm and stress." It refers to a German literary movement of the 1770s and 1780s that reacted against the order and rationalism of the enlightenment, focusing instead on the intense experience of extraordinary individuals. Highly romantic, works of this movement, such as Johann Wolfgang von Goethe's *Gotz von Berlichingen,* are typified by realism, rebelliousness, and intense emotionalism.

Style: A writer's distinctive manner of arranging words to suit his or her ideas and purpose in writing. The unique imprint of the author's personality upon his or her writing, style is the product of an author's way of arranging ideas and his or her use of diction, different sentence structures, rhythm, figures of speech, rhetorical principles, and other elements of composition. Styles may be classified according to period (Metaphysical, Augustan, Georgian), individual authors (Chaucerian, Miltonic, Jamesian), level (grand, middle, low, plain), or language (scientific, expository, poetic, journalistic).

Subject: The person, event, or theme at the center of a work of literature. A work may have one or more subjects of each type, with shorter works tending to have fewer and longer works tending to have more. The subjects of James Baldwin's novel *Go Tell It on the Mountain* include the themes of father-son relationships, religious conversion, black life, and sexuality. The subjects of Anne Frank's *Diary of a Young Girl* include Anne and her family members as well as World War II, the Holocaust, and the themes of war, isolation, injustice, and racism.

Subjectivity: Writing that expresses the author's personal feelings about his subject, and which may or may not include factual information about the subject. Subjectivity is demonstrated in James Joyce's *Portrait of the Artist as a Young Man,* Samuel Butler's *The Way of All Flesh,* and Thomas Wolfe's *Look Homeward, Angel.*

Subplot: A secondary story in a narrative. A subplot may serve as a motivating or complicating force for the main plot of the work, or it may provide emphasis for, or relief from, the main plot. The conflict between the Capulets and the Montagues in William Shakespeare's *Romeo and Juliet* is an example of a subplot.

Surrealism: A term introduced to criticism by Guillaume Apollinaire and later adopted by Andre Breton. It refers to a French literary and artistic movement founded in the 1920s. The Surrealists sought to express unconscious thoughts and feelings in their works. The best-known technique used for achieving this aim was automatic writing—transcriptions of spontaneous outpourings from the unconscious. The Surrealists proposed to unify the contrary levels of conscious and unconscious, dream and reality, objectivity and subjectivity into a new level of "super-realism." Surrealism can be found in the poetry of Paul Eluard, Pierre Reverdy, and Louis Aragon, among others.

Suspense: A literary device in which the author maintains the audience's attention through the buildup of events, the outcome of which will soon be revealed. Suspense in William Shakespeare's *Hamlet* is sustained throughout by the question of whether or not the Prince will achieve what he has been instructed to do and of what he intends to do.

Syllogism: A method of presenting a logical argument. In its most basic form, the syllogism consists of a major premise, a minor premise, and a conclusion. An example of a syllogism is: Major premise: When it snows, the streets get wet. Minor premise: It is snowing. Conclusion: The streets are wet.

Symbol: Something that suggests or stands for something else without losing its original identity. In literature, symbols combine their literal meaning with the suggestion of an abstract concept. Literary symbols are of two types: those that carry complex associations of meaning no matter what their contexts, and those that derive their suggestive meaning from their functions in specific literary works. Examples of symbols are sunshine suggesting happiness, rain suggesting sorrow, and storm clouds suggesting despair.

Symbolism: This term has two widely accepted meanings. In historical criticism, it denotes an early modernist literary movement initiated in France during the nineteenth century that reacted against the prevailing standards of realism. Writers in this movement aimed to evoke, indirectly and symbolically, an order of being beyond the material world of the five senses. Poetic expression of personal emotion figured strongly in the movement, typically by means of a private set of symbols uniquely identifiable with the individual poet. The principal aim of the Symbolists was to express in words the highly complex feelings that grew out of everyday contact with the world. In a broader sense, the term "symbolism" refers to the use of one object to represent another. Early members of the Symbolist movement included the French authors Charles Baudelaire and Arthur Rimbaud; William Butler Yeats, James Joyce, and T. S. Eliot were influenced as the movement moved to Ireland, England, and the United States. Examples of the concept of symbolism include a flag that stands for a nation or movement, or an empty cupboard used to suggest hopelessness, poverty, and despair.

Symbolist: See *Symbolism*

Symbolist Movement: See *Symbolism*

Sympathetic Fallacy: See *Affective Fallacy*

T

Tale: A story told by a narrator with a simple plot and little character development. Tales are usually relatively short and often carry a simple message. Examples of tales can be found in the work of Rudyard Kipling, Somerset Maugham, Saki, Anton Chekhov, Guy de Maupassant, and Armistead Maupin.

Tall Tale: A humorous tale told in a straightforward, credible tone but relating absolutely impossible events or feats of the characters. Such tales were commonly told of frontier adventures during the settlement of the west in the United States. Tall tales have been spun around such legendary heroes as Mike Fink, Paul Bunyan, Davy Crockett, Johnny Appleseed, and Captain Stormalong as well as the real-life William F. Cody and Annie Oakley. Literary use of tall tales can be found in Washington Irving's *History of New York,* Mark Twain's *Life on the Mississippi,* and in the German R. F. Raspe's *Baron Munchausen's Narratives of His Marvellous Travels and Campaigns in Russia.*

Tanka: A form of Japanese poetry similar to *haiku.* A *tanka* is five lines long, with the lines containing five, seven, five, seven, and seven syllables respectively. Skilled *tanka* authors include Ishikawa Takuboku, Masaoka Shiki, Amy Lowell, and Adelaide Crapsey.

Teatro Grottesco: See *Theater of the Grotesque*

Terza Rima: A three-line stanza form in poetry in which the rhymes are made on the last word of each line in the following manner: the first and third lines of the first stanza, then the second line of the first stanza and the first and third lines of the second stanza, and so on with the middle line of any stanza rhyming with the first and third lines of the following stanza. An example of *terza rima* is Percy Bysshe Shelley's "The Triumph of Love": As in that trance of wondrous thought I lay This was the tenour of my waking dream. Methought I sate beside a public way Thick strewn with summer dust, and a great stream Of people there was hurrying to and fro Numerous as gnats upon the evening gleam,...

Tetrameter: See *Meter*

Textual Criticism: A branch of literary criticism that seeks to establish the authoritative text of a literary work. Textual critics typically compare all known manuscripts or printings of a single work in order to assess the meanings of differences and revisions. This procedure allows them to arrive at a definitive version that (supposedly) corresponds to the author's original intention. Textual criticism was applied during the Renaissance to salvage the classical texts of Greece and Rome, and modern works have been studied, for instance, to undo deliberate correction or censorship, as in the case of novels by Stephen Crane and Theodore Dreiser.

Theater of Cruelty: Term used to denote a group of theatrical techniques designed to eliminate the psychological and emotional distance between actors and audience. This concept, introduced in the 1930s in France, was intended to inspire a more intense theatrical experience than conventional theater allowed. The "cruelty" of this dramatic theory signified not sadism but heightened actor/audience involvement in the dramatic event. The theater of cruelty was theorized by Antonin Artaud in his *Le Theatre et son double (The Theatre and Its Double)*, and also appears in the work of Jerzy Grotowski, Jean Genet, Jean Vilar, and Arthur Adamov, among others.

Theater of the Absurd: A post-World War II dramatic trend characterized by radical theatrical innovations. In works influenced by the Theater of the absurd, nontraditional, sometimes grotesque characterizations, plots, and stage sets reveal a meaningless universe in which human values are irrelevant. Existentialist themes of estrangement, absurdity, and futility link many of the works of this movement. The principal writers of the Theater of

the Absurd are Samuel Beckett, Eugene Ionesco, Jean Genet, and Harold Pinter.

Theater of the Grotesque: An Italian theatrical
movement characterized by plays written
around the ironic and macabre aspects of
daily life in the World War I era. Theater
of the Grotesque was named after the play
The Mask and the Face by Luigi Chiarelli,
which was described as "a grotesque in three
acts." The movement influenced the work of
Italian dramatist Luigi Pirandello, author of
Right You Are, If You Think You Are. Also
known as *Teatro Grottesco.*

Theme: The main point of a work of literature.
The term is used interchangeably with the-
sis. The theme of William Shakespeare's
Othello—jealousy—is a common one.

Thesis: A thesis is both an essay and the point
argued in the essay. Thesis novels and thesis
plays share the quality of containing a thesis
which is supported through the action of the
story. A master's thesis and a doctoral dissertation are two theses required of graduate
students.

Thesis Play: See *Thesis*

Three Unities: See *Unities*

Tone: The author's attitude toward his or her
audience may be deduced from the tone of
the work. A formal tone may create distance
or convey politeness, while an informal tone
may encourage a friendly, intimate, or intru-
sive feeling in the reader. The author's attitude toward his or her subject matter may
also be deduced from the tone of the words
he or she uses in discussing it. The tone of
John F. Kennedy's speech which included
the appeal to "ask not what your country
can do for you" was intended to instill feelings of camaraderie and national pride in
listeners.

Tragedy: A drama in prose or poetry about a
noble, courageous hero of excellent character
who, because of some tragic character flaw or
hamartia, brings ruin upon him- or herself.
Tragedy treats its subjects in a dignified and
serious manner, using poetic language to help
evoke pity and fear and bring about catharsis, a purging of these emotions. The tragic
form was practiced extensively by the ancient
Greeks. In the Middle Ages, when classical
works were virtually unknown, tragedy came
to denote any works about the fall of persons

from exalted to low conditions due to any
reason: fate, vice, weakness, etc. According
to the classical definition of tragedy, such
works present the "pathetic"—that which
evokes pity—rather than the tragic. The classical form of tragedy was revived in the sixteenth century; it flourished especially on the
Elizabethan stage. In modern times, dramatists have attempted to adapt the form to the
needs of modern society by drawing their
heroes from the ranks of ordinary men and
women and defining the nobility of these
heroes in terms of spirit rather than exalted
social standing. The greatest classical example of tragedy is Sophocles' *Oedipus Rex.* The
"pathetic" derivation is exemplified in "The
Monk's Tale" in Geoffrey Chaucer's *Canterbury Tales.* Notable works produced during
the sixteenth century revival include William
Shakespeare's *Hamlet, Othello,* and *King Lear.*
Modern dramatists working in the tragic tradition include Henrik Ibsen, Arthur Miller,
and Eugene O'Neill.

Tragedy of Blood: See *Revenge Tragedy*

Tragic Flaw: In a tragedy, the quality within the
hero or heroine which leads to his or her
downfall. Examples of the tragic flaw include
Othello's jealousy and Hamlet's indecisive-
ness, although most great tragedies defy
such simple interpretation.

Transcendentalism: An American philosophical
and religious movement, based in New England from around 1835 until the Civil War.
Transcendentalism was a form of American
romanticism that had its roots abroad in the
works of Thomas Carlyle, Samuel Coleridge,
and Johann Wolfgang von Goethe. The
Transcendentalists stressed the importance
of intuition and subjective experience in
communication with God. They rejected
religious dogma and texts in favor of mysticism and scientific naturalism. They pursued truths that lie beyond the "colorless"
realms perceived by reason and the senses
and were active social reformers in public
education, women's rights, and the abolition of slavery. Prominent members of the
group include Ralph Waldo Emerson and
Henry David Thoreau.

Trickster: A character or figure common in Native
American and African literature who uses his
ingenuity to defeat enemies and escape difficult
situations. Tricksters are most often animals,

such as the spider, hare, or coyote, although they may take the form of humans as well. Examples of trickster tales include Thomas King's *A Coyote Columbus Story,* Ashley F. Bryan's *The Dancing Granny* and Ishmael Reed's *The Last Days of Louisiana Red.*

Trimeter: See *Meter*

Triple Rhyme: See *Rhyme*

Trochee: See *Foot*

U

Understatement: See *Irony*

Unities: Strict rules of dramatic structure, formulated by Italian and French critics of the Renaissance and based loosely on the principles of drama discussed by Aristotle in his *Poetics.* Foremost among these rules were the three unities of action, time, and place that compelled a dramatist to: (1) construct a single plot with a beginning, middle, and end that details the causal relationships of action and character; (2) restrict the action to the events of a single day; and (3) limit the scene to a single place or city. The unities were observed faithfully by continental European writers until the Romantic Age, but they were never regularly observed in English drama. Modern dramatists are typically more concerned with a unity of impression or emotional effect than with any of the classical unities. The unities are observed in Pierre Corneille's tragedy *Polyeuctes* and Jean-Baptiste Racine's *Phedre.* Also known as Three Unities.

Urban Realism: A branch of realist writing that attempts to accurately reflect the often harsh facts of modern urban existence. Some works by Stephen Crane, Theodore Dreiser, Charles Dickens, Fyodor Dostoyevsky, Emile Zola, Abraham Cahan, and Henry Fuller feature urban realism. Modern examples include Claude Brown's *Manchild in the Promised Land* and Ron Milner's *What the Wine Sellers Buy.*

Utopia: A fictional perfect place, such as "paradise" or "heaven." Early literary utopias were included in Plato's *Republic* and Sir Thomas More's *Utopia,* while more modern utopias can be found in Samuel Butler's *Erewhon,* Theodor Herzka's *A Visit to Freeland,* and H. G. Wells' *A Modern Utopia.*

Utopian: See *Utopia*

Utopianism: See *Utopia*

V

Verisimilitude: Literally, the appearance of truth. In literary criticism, the term refers to aspects of a work of literature that seem true to the reader. Verisimilitude is achieved in the work of Honore de Balzac, Gustave Flaubert, and Henry James, among other late nineteenth-century realist writers.

Vers de societe: See *Occasional Verse*

Vers libre: See *Free Verse*

Verse: A line of metered language, a line of a poem, or any work written in verse. The following line of verse is from the epic poem *Don Juan* by Lord Byron: "My way is to begin with the beginning."

Versification: The writing of verse. Versification may also refer to the meter, rhyme, and other mechanical components of a poem. Composition of a "Roses are red, violets are blue" poem to suit an occasion is a common form of versification practiced by students.

Victorian: Refers broadly to the reign of Queen Victoria of England (1837-1901) and to anything with qualities typical of that era. For example, the qualities of smug narrowmindedness, bourgeois materialism, faith in social progress, and priggish morality are often considered Victorian. This stereotype is contradicted by such dramatic intellectual developments as the theories of Charles Darwin, Karl Marx, and Sigmund Freud (which stirred strong debates in England) and the critical attitudes of serious Victorian writers like Charles Dickens and George Eliot. In literature, the Victorian Period was the great age of the English novel, and the latter part of the era saw the rise of movements such as decadence and symbolism. Works of Victorian literature include the poetry of Robert Browning and Alfred, Lord Tennyson, the criticism of Matthew Arnold and John Ruskin, and the novels of Emily Bronte, William Makepeace Thackeray, and Thomas Hardy. Also known as Victorian Age and Victorian Period.

Victorian Age: See *Victorian*

Victorian Period: See *Victorian*

W

Weltanschauung: A German term referring to a person's worldview or philosophy. Examples of *weltanschauung* include Thomas Hardy's view of the human being as the victim of fate, destiny, or impersonal forces and circumstances, and the disillusioned and laconic cynicism expressed by such poets of the 1930s as W. H. Auden, Sir Stephen Spender, and Sir William Empson.

Weltschmerz: A German term meaning "world pain." It describes a sense of anguish about the nature of existence, usually associated with a melancholy, pessimistic attitude. *Weltschmerz* was expressed in England by George Gordon, Lord Byron in his *Manfred* and *Childe Harold's Pilgrimage,* in France by Viscount de Chateaubriand, Alfred de Vigny, and Alfred de Musset, in Russia by Aleksandr Pushkin and Mikhail Lermontov, in Poland by Juliusz Slowacki, and in America by Nathaniel Hawthorne.

Z

Zarzuela: A type of Spanish operetta. Writers of *zarzuelas* include Lope de Vega and Pedro Calderon.

Zeitgeist: A German term meaning "spirit of the time." It refers to the moral and intellectual trends of a given era. Examples of *zeitgeist* include the preoccupation with the more morbid aspects of dying and death in some Jacobean literature, especially in the works of dramatists Cyril Tourneur and John Webster, and the decadence of the French Symbolists.

Cumulative Author/Title Index

Numerical

36 Views (Iizuka): V21
84, Charing Cross Road (Hanff): V17

A

Abe Lincoln in Illinois (Sherwood,
    Robert E.): V11
Abe, Kobo
    The Man Who Turned into a
      Stick: V14
Accidental Death of an Anarchist
    (Fo): V23
Ackermann, Joan
    Off the Map: V22
The Advertisement (Ginzburg): V14
Aeschylus
    Agamemnon: V26
    Prometheus Bound: V5
    Seven Against Thebes: V10
Agamemnon (Aeschylus): V26
Ajax (Sophocles): V8
Albee, Edward
    The American Dream: V25
    A Delicate Balance: V14
    Seascape: V13
    Three Tall Women: V8
    Tiny Alice: V10
    Who's Afraid of Virginia Woolf?: V3
    The Zoo Story: V2
The Alchemist (Jonson): V4
Alison's House (Glaspell): V24
All My Sons (Miller): V8
Amadeus (Shaffer): V13
The Amen Corner (Baldwin): V11
American Buffalo (Mamet): V3
The American Dream (Albee): V25

Anderson, Maxwell
    Both Your Houses: V16
    Winterset: V20
Angels Fall (Wilson): V20
Angels in America (Kushner): V5
Anna Christie (O'Neill): V12
Anna in the Tropics (Cruz): V21
Anonymous
    Arden of Faversham: V24
    Everyman: V7
    The Second Shepherds' Play: V25
Anouilh, Jean
    Antigone: V9
    Becket, or the Honor of God: V19
    Ring Around the Moon: V10
Antigone (Anouilh): V9
Antigone (Sophocles): V1
Arcadia (Stoppard): V5
Arden, John
    Serjeant Musgrave's Dance: V9
Arden of Faversham (Anonymous):
    V24
Aristophanes
    Lysistrata: V10
Arms and the Man (Shaw): V22
Arsenic and Old Lace (Kesselring): V20
Art (Reza): V19
Artaud, Antonin
    The Cenci: V22
As Bees in Honey Drown (Beane): V21
The Au Pair Man (Leonard): V24
Auburn, David
    Proof: V21
Ayckbourn, Alan
    A Chorus of Disapproval: V7

B

The Bacchae (Euripides): V6
The Balcony (Genet): V10
The Bald Soprano (Ionesco, Eugène):
    V4
Baldwin, James
    The Amen Corner: V11
    One Day, When I Was Lost: A
      Scenario: V15
The Baptism (Baraka): V16
Baraka, Amiri
    The Baptism: V16
    Dutchman: V3
    Slave Ship: V11
The Barber of Seville (de
    Beaumarchais): V16
Barnes, Peter
    The Ruling Class: V6
Barrie, J(ames) M.
    Peter Pan: V7
Barry, Philip
    The Philadelphia Story: V9
The Basic Training of Pavlo Hummel
    (Rabe): V3
Beane, Douglas Carter
    As Bees in Honey Drown: V21
The Bear (Chekhov): V26
Beautiful Señoritas (Prida): V23
Becket, or the Honor of God
    (Anouilh): V19
Beckett, Samuel
    Endgame: V18
    Krapp's Last Tape: V7
    Waiting for Godot: V2
Behan, Brendan
    The Hostage: V7

Behn, Aphra
  The Forc'd Marriage: V24
  The Rover: V16
Beim, Norman
  The Deserter: V18
The Belle's Stratagem (Cowley): V22
Bent (Sherman): V20
Beyond the Horizon (O'Neill): V16
Biloxi Blues (Simon): V12
The Birthday Party (Pinter): V5
Blank, Jessica
  The Exonerated: V24
Blessing, Lee
  Eleemosynary: V23
  A Walk in the Woods: V26
Blood Relations (Pollock): V3
Blood Wedding (García Lorca): V10
Blue Room (Hare): V7
Blue Surge (Gilman): V23
Blues for an Alabama Sky
  (Cleage): V14
Boesman & Lena (Fugard): V6
Bolt, Robert
  A Man for All Seasons: V2
Bond, Edward
  Lear: V3
  Saved: V8
Bonner, Marita
  The Purple Flower: V13
Both Your Houses (Anderson): V16
The Boys in the Band (Crowley): V14
Brand (Ibsen): V16
Brecht, Bertolt
  The Good Person of Szechwan: V9
  *Mother Courage and Her
    Children:* V5
  The Threepenny Opera: V4
Brighton Beach Memoirs (Simon): V6
Brooks, Mel
  The Producers: V21
The Browning Version (Rattigan): V8
Buero Vallejo, Antonio
  The Sleep of Reason: V11
Buried Child (Shepard): V6
Burn This (Wilson): V4
Bus Stop (Inge): V8
Bye-Bye, Brevoort (Welty): V26

C

Calderón de la Barca, Pedro
  Life Is a Dream: V23
Calm Down Mother (Terry): V18
Capek, Josef
  The Insect Play: V11
Capek, Karel
  The Insect Play: V11
  R.U.R.: V7
Carballido, Emilio
  I, Too, Speak of the Rose: V4
The Caretaker (Pinter): V7
Cat on a Hot Tin Roof (Williams): V3

The Cenci (Artaud): V22
The Chairs (Ionesco, Eugène): V9
The Changeling (Middleton): V22
Chase, Mary
  Harvey: V11
A Chaste Maid in Cheapside
  (Middleton): V18
Chayefsky, Paddy
  Marty: V26
Chekhov, Anton
  The Bear: V26
  The Cherry Orchard: V1
  The Seagull: V12
  The Three Sisters: V10
  Uncle Vanya: V5
The Cherry Orchard (Chekhov): V1
Children of a Lesser God (Medoff): V4
The Children's Hour (Hellman): V3
Childress, Alice
  Florence: V26
  Trouble in Mind: V8
  The Wedding Band: V2
  Wine in the Wilderness: V14
A Chorus of Disapproval
  (Ayckbourn): V7
Christie, Agatha
  The Mousetrap: V2
Churchill, Caryl
  Cloud Nine: V16
  Serious Money: V25
  Top Girls: V12
Clark, John Pepper
  The Raft: V13
Cleage, Pearl
  Blues for an Alabama Sky: V14
  Flyin' West: V16
Cloud Nine (Churchill): V16
Coburn, D. L.
  The Gin Game: V23
The Cocktail Party (Eliot): V13
Cocteau, Jean
  Indiscretions: V24
Come Back, Little Sheba (Inge): V3
Congreve, William
  Love for Love: V14
  The Way of the World: V15
Connelly, Marc
  The Green Pastures: V12
Copenhagen (Frayn): V22
Corneille, Pierre
  Le Cid: V21
Coward, Noel
  Hay Fever: V6
  Private Lives: V3
Cowley, Hannah
  The Belle's Stratagem: V22
Crimes of the Heart (Henley): V2
Cristofer, Michael
  The Shadow Box: V15
The Critic (Sheridan): V14
Crossroads (Solórzano): V26
Crouse, Russel
  State of the Union: V19

Crowley, Mart
  The Boys in the Band: V14
The Crucible (Miller): V3
Cruz, Migdalia
  Telling Tales: V19
Cruz, Nilo
  Anna in the Tropics: V21
Curse of the Starving Class
  (Shepard): V14
Cyrano de Bergerac (Rostand): V1

D

Da (Leonard): V13
Dancing at Lughnasa (Friel): V11
de Beaumarchais, Pierre-Augustin
  The Barber of Seville: V16
  The Marriage of Figaro: V14
de Hartog, Jan
  The Fourposter: V12
Death and the King's Horseman
  (Soyinka): V10
Death and the Maiden (Dorfman): V4
Death of a Salesman (Miller): V1
Delaney, Shelagh
  A Taste of Honey: V7
A Delicate Balance (Albee): V14
The Deserter (Beim): V18
The Desperate Hours (Hayes): V20
Detective Story (Kingsley): V19
The Diary of Anne Frank
  (Goodrichand Hackett): V15
Dinner with Friends (Margulies): V13
Dirty Blonde (Shear): V24
Doctor Faustus (Marlowe): V1
Dogg's Hamlet, Cahoot's Macbeth
  (Stoppard): V16
A Doll's House (Ibsen): V1
Dorfman, Ariel
  Death and the Maiden: V4
Doubt (Shanley): V23
Driving Miss Daisy (Uhry): V11
The Duchess of Malfi (Webster): V17
Duffy, Maureen
  Rites: V15
The Dumb Waiter (Pinter): V25
Duras, Marguerite
  India Song: V21
Dutchman (Baraka): V3

E

Edgar, David
  *The Life and Adventures of
    Nicholas Nickleby:* V15
Edson, Margaret
  Wit: V13
*Edward II: The Troublesome Reign
  and Lamentable Death of
  Edward the Second, King of
  England, with the Tragical Fall of
  Proud Mortimer* (Marlowe): V5

The Effect of Gamma Rays on Man-in-the-Moon Marigolds (Zindel): V12
Electra (Sophocles): V4
Electra (von Hofmannsthal): V17
Eleemosynary (Blessing): V23
The Elephant Man (Pomerance): V9
Eliot, T. S.
   The Cocktail Party: V13
   Murder in the Cathedral: V4
The Emperor Jones (O'Neill): V6
Endgame (Beckett): V18
An Enemy of the People (Ibsen): V25
Ensler, Eve
   Necessary Targets: V23
Entertaining Mr. Sloane (Orton): V3
Ephron, Nora
   Imaginary Friends: V22
Equus (Shaffer): V5
Euripides
   The Bacchae: V6
   Hippolytus: V25
   Iphigenia in Taurus: V4
   Medea: V1
Everyman (Anonymous): V7
The Exonerated (Blank and Jensen): V24

F

Fabulation; or, The Re-Education of Undine (Nottage): V25
Feeding the Moonfish (Wiechmann): V21
Fefu and Her Friends (Fornes): V25
Fences (Wilson): V3
Fiddler on the Roof (Stein): V7
Fierstein, Harvey
   Torch Song Trilogy: V6
The Firebugs (Frisch): V25
Fires in the Mirror (Smith): V22
Fletcher, Lucille
   Sorry, Wrong Number: V26
The Flies (Sartre): V26
Florence (Childress): V26
Flyin' West (Cleage): V16
Fo, Dario
   Accidental Death of an Anarchist: V23
Fool for Love (Shepard): V7
Foote, Horton
   The Young Man from Atlanta: V20
for colored girls who have considered suicide/when the rainbow is enuf (Shange): V2
For Services Rendered (Maugham): V22
The Forc'd Marriage (Behn): V24
Ford, John
   'Tis Pity She's a Whore: V7
The Foreigner (Shue): V7
Fornes, Marie Irene
   Fefu and Her Friends: V25

The Fourposter (de Hartog): V12
Frayn, Michael
   Copenhagen: V22
Friel, Brian
   Dancing at Lughnasa: V11
Frisch, Max
   The Firebugs: V25
The Front Page (Hecht and MacArthur): V9
Frozen (Lavery): V25
Fugard, Athol
   Boesman & Lena: V6
   A Lesson from Aloes: V24
   "Master Harold". . . and the Boys: V3
   Sizwe Bansi is Dead: V10
Fuller, Charles H.
   A Soldier's Play: V8
Funnyhouse of a Negro (Kennedy): V9

G

Gale, Zona
   Miss Lulu Bett: V17
García Lorca, Federico
   Blood Wedding: V10
   The House of Bernarda Alba: V4
Gardner, Herb
   I'm Not Rappaport: V18
   A Thousand Clowns: V20
Gems, Pam
   Stanley: V25
Genet, Jean
   The Balcony: V10
Gerstenberg, Alice
   Overtones: V17
The Ghost Sonata (Strindberg): V9
Ghosts (Ibsen): V11
Gibson, William
   The Miracle Worker: V2
Gilman, Rebecca
   Blue Surge: V23
Gilroy, Frank D.
   The Subject Was Roses: V17
The Gin Game (Coburn): V23
Ginzburg, Natalia
   The Advertisement: V14
Glaspell, Susan
   Alison's House: V24
   Trifles: V8
   The Verge: V18
The Glass Menagerie (Williams): V1
Glengarry Glen Ross (Mamet): V2
Gogol, Nikolai
   The Government Inspector: V12
Golden Boy (Odets): V17
Goldman, James
   The Lion in Winter: V20
Goldsmith, Oliver
   She Stoops to Conquer: V1
The Good Person of Szechwan (Brecht): V9

Goodnight Desdemona (Good Morning Juliet) (MacDonald): V23
Goodrich, Frances
   The Diary of Anne Frank: V15
Gorki, Maxim
   The Lower Depths: V9
The Government Inspector (Gogol): V12
The Great God Brown (O'Neill): V11
The Great White Hope (Sackler): V15
The Green Pastures (Connelly): V12
Greenberg, Richard
   Take Me Out: V24
Guare, John
   The House of Blue Leaves: V8
   Six Degrees of Separation: V13

H

Habitat (Thompson): V22
Hackett, Albert
   The Diary of Anne Frank: V15
The Hairy Ape (O'Neill): V4
Hammerstein, Oscar II
   The King and I: V1
Hanff, Helene
   84, Charing Cross Road: V17
Hansberry, Lorraine
   A Raisin in the Sun: V2
Hare, David
   Blue Room: V7
   Plenty: V4
   The Secret Rapture: V16
Hart, Moss
   Once in a Lifetime: V10
   You Can't Take It with You: V1
Harvey (Chase): V11
Havel, Vaclav
   The Memorandum: V10
Hay Fever (Coward): V6
Hayes, Joseph
   The Desperate Hours: V20
Hecht, Ben
   The Front Page: V9
Hedda Gabler (Ibsen): V6
Heggen, Thomas
   Mister Roberts: V20
The Heidi Chronicles (Wasserstein): V5
Hellman, Lillian
   The Children's Hour: V3
   The Little Foxes: V1
   Watch on the Rhine: V14
Henley, Beth
   Crimes of the Heart: V2
   Impossible Marriage: V26
   The Miss Firecracker Contest: V21
Highway, Tomson
   The Rez Sisters: V2
Hippolytus (Euripides): V25
The Homecoming (Pinter): V3
The Hostage (Behan): V7

Hot L Baltimore (Wilson): V9
The House of Bernarda Alba
    (GarcíaLorca, Federico): V4
The House of Blue Leaves (Guare): V8
How I Learned to Drive (Vogel): V14
Hughes, Langston
    Mulatto: V18
    Mule Bone: V6
Hurston, Zora Neale
    Mule Bone: V6
Hwang, David Henry
    M. Butterfly: V11
    The Sound of a Voice: V18

I

I Am My Own Wife (Wright): V23
I, Too, Speak of the Rose (Carballido):
    V4
Ibsen, Henrik
    Brand: V16
    A Doll's House: V1
    An Enemy of the People: V25
    Ghosts: V11
    Hedda Gabler: V6
    The Master Builder: V15
    Peer Gynt: V8
    The Wild Duck: V10
The Iceman Cometh (O'Neill): V5
An Ideal Husband (Wilde): V21
Idiot's Delight (Sherwood): V15
I Hate Hamlet (Rudnick): V22
Iizuka, Naomi
    36 Views: V21
Ile (O'Neill): V26
I'm Not Rappaport (Gardner): V18
Imaginary Friends (Ephron): V22
The Imaginary Invalid (Molière): V20
The Importance of Being Earnest
    (Wilde): V4
Impossible Marriage (Henley): V26
Inadmissible Evidence (Osborne):
    V24
India Song (Duras): V21
Indian Ink (Stoppard): V11
Indians (Kopit): V24
Indiscretions (Cocteau): V24
Inge, William
    Bus Stop: V8
    Come Back, Little Sheba: V3
    Picnic: V5
Inherit the Wind (Lawrence and
    Lee): V2
The Insect Play (Capek): V11
Into the Woods (Sondheim and
    Lapine): V25
Ionesco, Eugène
    The Bald Soprano: V4
    The Chairs: V9
    Rhinoceros: V25
Iphigenia in Taurus (Euripides): V4

J

J. B. (MacLeish): V15
Jarry, Alfred
    Ubu Roi: V8
Jensen, Erik
    The Exonerated: V24
Jesus Christ Superstar (Webber and
    Rice): V7
The Jew of Malta (Marlowe): V13
Joe Turner's Come and Gone
    (Wilson): V17
Jones, LeRoi
    see Baraka, Amiri
Jonson, Ben(jamin)
    The Alchemist: V4
    Volpone: V10

K

Kaufman, George S.
    Once in a Lifetime: V10
    You Can't Take It with You: V1
Kaufman, Moisés
    The Laramie Project: V22
Kennedy, Adrienne
    Funnyhouse of a Negro: V9
The Kentucky Cycle (Schenkkan): V10
Kesselring, Joseph
    Arsenic and Old Lace: V20
The King and I (Hammerstein and
    Rodgers): V1
Kingsley, Sidney
    Detective Story: V19
    Men in White: V14
Kopit, Arthur
    Indians: V24
    *Oh Dad, Poor Dad, Mamma's
       Hung You in the Closet and I'm
       Feelin' So Sad:* V7
    Y2K: V14
Kramm, Joseph
    The Shrike: V15
Krapp's Last Tape (Beckett): V7
Kushner, Tony
    Angels in America: V5
Kyd, Thomas
    The Spanish Tragedy: V21

L

Lady Windermere's Fan (Wilde): V9
Lapine, James
    Into the Woods: V25
The Laramie Project (Kaufman): V22
Larson, Jonathan
    Rent: V23
The Last Night of Ballyhoo (Uhry): V15
Lavery, Bryony
    Frozen: V25
Lawrence, Jerome
    Inherit the Wind: V2
    The Night Thoreau Spent in Jail: V16

Le Cid (Corneille): V21
Lear (Bond): V3
Lee, Robert E.
    Inherit the Wind: V2
    The Night Thoreau Spent in Jail: V16
Leight, Warren
    Side Man: V19
Leonard, Hugh
    The Au Pair Man: V24
    Da: V13
Lessing, Doris
    Play with a Tiger: V20
A Lesson from Aloes (Fugard): V24
*The Life and Adventures of Nicholas
    Nickleby* (Edgar): V15
A Life in the Theatre (Mamet): V12
Life Is a Dream (Calderón de la
    Barca): V23
Lindsay, Howard
    State of the Union: V19
The Lion in Winter (Goldman): V20
The Little Foxes (Hellman): V1
Lonergan, Kenneth
    This Is Our Youth: V23
Long Day's Journey into Night
    (O'Neill): V2
Look Back in Anger (Osborne): V4
Lost in Yonkers (Simon): V18
Love for Love (Congreve): V14
Love! Valour! Compassion!
    (McNally): V19
The Lower Depths (Gorki): V9
Luce, Clare Boothe
    The Women: V19
Luther (Osborne): V19
Lysistrata (Aristophanes): V10

M

M. Butterfly (Hwang): V11
Ma Rainey's Black Bottom (Wilson):
    V15
MacArthur, Charles
    The Front Page: V9
MacDonald, Ann-Marie
    *Goodnight Desdemona (Good
       Morning Juliet):* V23
Machinal (Treadwell): V22
MacLeish, Archibald
    J. B.: V15
Major Barbara (Shaw): V3
Mamet, David
    American Buffalo: V3
    Glengarry Glen Ross: V2
    A Life in the Theatre: V12
    Reunion: V15
    Speed-the-Plow: V6
Man and Superman (Shaw): V6
A Man for All Seasons (Bolt): V2
The Man Who Turned into a Stick
    (Abe): V14
Marat/Sade (Weiss): V3

Margulies, Donald
  Dinner with Friends: V13
Marlowe, Christopher
  Doctor Faustus: V1
  Edward II: The Troublesome Reign and Lamentable Death of Edward the Second, King of England, with the Tragical Fall of Proud Mortimer: V5
  The Jew of Malta: V13
  Tamburlaine the Great: V21
The Marriage of Figaro (de Beaumarchais): V14
Martin, Steve
  WASP: V19
Marty (Chayefsky): V26
The Master Builder (Ibsen): V15
Master Class (McNally): V16
"Master Harold": . . . and the Boys (Fugard): V3
The Matchmaker (Wilder): V16
Maugham, Somerset
  For Services Rendered: V22
McCullers, Carson
  The Member of the Wedding: V5
  The Square Root of Wonderful: V18
McNally, Terrence
  Love! Valour! Compassion!: V19
  Master Class: V16
Medea (Euripides): V1
Medoff, Mark
  Children of a Lesser God: V4
The Member of the Wedding (McCullers): V5
The Memorandum (Havel): V10
Men in White (Kingsley): V14
Middleton, Thomas
  The Changeling: V22
  A Chaste Maid in Cheapside: V18
Miller, Arthur
  All My Sons: V8
  The Crucible: V3
  Death of a Salesman: V1
Miller, Jason
  That Championship Season: V12
The Miracle Worker (Gibson): V2
The Misanthrope (Molière): V13
The Miss Firecracker Contest (Henley): V21
Miss Julie (Strindberg): V4
Miss Lulu Bett (Gale): V17
Mister Roberts (Heggen): V20
Molière
  The Imaginary Invalid: V20
  The Misanthrope: V13
  Tartuffe: V18
A Month in the Country (Turgenev): V6
Mother Courage and Her Children (Brecht): V5
The Mound Builders (Wilson): V16
Mountain Language (Pinter): V14

Mourning Becomes Electra (O'Neill): V9
The Mousetrap (Christie): V2
Mrs. Warren's Profession (Shaw): V19
Mulatto (Hughes): V18
Mule Bone (Hurston and Hughes): V6
Murder in the Cathedral (Eliot): V4

N

Necessary Targets (Ensler): V23
Nicholson, William
  Shadowlands: V11
'night, Mother (Norman): V2
The Night of the Iguana (Williams): V7
The Night Thoreau Spent in Jail (Lawrence and Lee): V16
No Exit (Sartre, Jean-Paul): V5
Norman, Marsha
  'night, Mother: V2
Nottage, Lynn
  Fabulation; or, The Re-Education of Undine: V25
Novio Boy (Soto): V26

O

O'Casey, Sean
  Red Roses for Me: V19
The Odd Couple (Simon): V2
Odets, Clifford
  Golden Boy: V17
  Rocket to the Moon: V20
  Waiting for Lefty: V3
Oedipus Rex (Sophocles): V1
Off the Map (Ackermann): V22
Oh Dad, Poor Dad, Mamma's Hung You in the Closet and I'm Feelin' So Sad (Kopit): V7
On Golden Pond (Thompson): V23
Once in a Lifetime (Hart): V10
Once in a Lifetime (Kaufman): V10
One Day, When I Was Lost: A Scenario (Baldwin): V15
O'Neill, Eugene
  Anna Christie: V12
  Beyond the Horizon: V16
  The Emperor Jones: V6
  The Great God Brown: V11
  The Hairy Ape: V4
  The Iceman Cometh: V5
  Ile: V26
  Long Day's Journey into Night: V2
  Mourning Becomes Electra: V9
  Strange Interlude: V20
Orpheus Descending (Williams): V17
Orton, Joe
  Entertaining Mr. Sloane: V3
  What the Butler Saw: V6

Osborne, John
  Inadmissible Evidence: V24
  Look Back in Anger: V4
  Luther: V19
Othello (Shakespeare): V20
The Other Shore (Xingjian): V21
Our Town (Wilder): V1
Overtones (Gerstenberg): V17

P

Parks, Suzan-Lori
  Topdog/Underdog: V22
Patrick, John
  The Teahouse of the August Moon: V13
Peer Gynt (Ibsen): V8
Peter Pan (Barrie): V7
The Petrified Forest (Sherwood): V17
The Philadelphia Story (Barry): V9
The Piano Lesson (Wilson): V7
Picnic (Inge): V5
Pinter, Harold
  The Birthday Party: V5
  The Caretaker: V7
  The Dumb Waiter: V25
  The Homecoming: V3
  Mountain Language: V14
Pirandello, Luigi
  Right You Are, If You Think You Are: V9
  Six Characters in Search of an Author: V4
Play with a Tiger (Lessing): V20
The Playboy of the Western World (Synge): V18
Plenty (Hare): V4
Pollock, Sharon
  Blood Relations: V3
Pomerance, Bernard
  The Elephant Man: V9
The Post Office (Tagore): V26
Prida, Dolores
  Beautiful Señoritas: V23
The Prisoner of Second Avenue (Simon): V24
Private Lives (Coward): V3
The Producers (Brooks): V21
Prometheus Bound (Aeschylus): V5
Proof (Auburn): V21
The Purple Flower (Bonner): V13
Pygmalion (Shaw): V1

R

R.U.R. (Capek): V7
Rabe, David
  The Basic Training of Pavlo Hummel: V3
  Sticks and Bones: V13
  Streamers: V8
The Raft (Clark): V13
A Raisin in the Sun (Hansberry): V2

Rattigan, Terence
  The Browning Version: V8
The Real Thing (Stoppard): V8
Rebeck, Theresa
  Spike Heels: V11
Red Roses for Me (O'Casey): V19
Rent (Larson): V23
Reunion (Mamet): V15
The Rez Sisters (Highway): V2
Reza, Yasmina
  Art: V19
Rhinoceros (Ionesco): V25
Rice, Elmer
  Street Scene: V12
Rice, Tim
  Jesus Christ Superstar: V7
Right You Are, If You Think You Are
  (Pirandello): V9
Ring Around the Moon (Anouilh): V10
Rites (Duffy): V15
The Rivals (Sheridan): V15
The River Niger (Walker): V12
Rocket to the Moon (Odets): V20
Rodgers, Richard
  The King and I: V1
Romeo and Juliet (Shakespeare): V21
Rose, Reginald
  Twelve Angry Men: V23
The Rose Tattoo (Williams): V18
Rosencrantz and Guildenstern Are
  Dead (Stoppard): V2
Rostand, Edmond
  Cyrano de Bergerac: V1
The Rover (Behn): V16
Rudnick, Paul
  I Hate Hamlet: V22
The Ruling Class (Barnes): V6

S

Sackler, Howard
  The Great White Hope: V15
Saint Joan (Shaw): V11
Salome (Wilde): V8
Saroyan, William
  The Time of Your Life: V17
Sartre, Jean-Paul
  The Flies: V26
  No Exit: V5
Saved (Bond): V8
Schary, Dore
  Sunrise at Campobello: V17
Schenkkan, Robert
  The Kentucky Cycle: V10
School for Scandal (Sheridan): V4
The Seagull (Chekhov): V12
Seascape (Albee): V13
The Second Shepherds' Play
  (Anonymous): V25
The Secret Rapture (Hare): V16
Serious Money (Churchill): V25

Serjeant Musgrave's Dance (Arden):
  V9
Seven Against Thebes (Aeschylus): V10
The Shadow Box (Cristofer): V15
Shadowlands (Nicholson): V11
Shaffer, Anthony
  Sleuth: V13
Shaffer, Peter
  Amadeus: V13
  Equus: V5
Shakespeare, William
  Othello: V20
  Romeo and Juliet: V21
Shange, Ntozake
  for colored girls who have
    considered suicide/when the
    rainbow is enuf: V2
Shanley, John Patrick
  Doubt: V23
Shaw, George Bernard
  Arms and the Man: V22
  Major Barbara: V3
  Man and Superman: V6
  Mrs. Warren's Profession: V19
  Pygmalion: V1
  Saint Joan: V11
She Stoops to Conquer (Goldsmith):
  V1
Shear, Claudia
  Dirty Blonde: V24
Shepard, Sam
  Buried Child: V6
  Curse of the Starving Class: V14
  Fool for Love: V7
  True West: V3
Sheridan, Richard Brinsley
  The Critic: V14
  The Rivals: V15
  School for Scandal: V4
Sherman, Martin
  Bent: V20
Sherwood, Robert E.
  Abe Lincoln in Illinois: V11
  Idiot's Delight: V15
  The Petrified Forest: V17
The Shrike (Kramm): V15
Shue, Larry
  The Foreigner: V7
Side Man (Leight): V19
Simon, Neil
  Biloxi Blues: V12
  Brighton Beach Memoirs: V6
  Lost in Yonkers: V18
  The Odd Couple: V2
  The Prisoner of Second Avenue: V24
The Sisters Rosensweig
  (Wasserstein): V17
Six Characters in Search of an Author
  (Pirandello): V4
Six Degrees of Separation (Guare): V13
Sizwe Bansi is Dead (Fugard): V10
The Skin of Our Teeth (Wilder): V4

Slave Ship (Baraka): V11
The Sleep of Reason (Buero Vallejo):
  V11
Sleuth (Shaffer): V13
Smith, Anna Deavere
  Fires in the Mirror: V22
  Twilight: Los Angeles, 1992: V2
A Soldier's Play (Fuller, Charles H.):
  V8
Solórzano, Carlos
  Crossroads: V26
Sondheim, Stephen
  Into the Woods: V25
Sophocles
  Ajax: V8
  Antigone: V1
  Electra: V4
  Oedipus Rex: V1
  Women of Trachis: Trachiniae: V24
Sorry, Wrong Number (Fletcher): V26
Soto, Gary
  Novio Boy: V26
The Sound of a Voice (Hwang): V18
Soyinka, Wole
  Death and the King's Horseman: V10
  The Trials of Brother Jero: V26
The Spanish Tragedy (Kyd): V21
Speed-the-Plow (Mamet): V6
Spike Heels (Rebeck): V11
The Square Root of Wonderful
  (McCullers): V18
Stanley (Gems): V25
State of the Union (Crouse and
  Lindsay): V19
Stein, Joseph
  Fiddler on the Roof: V7
Sticks and Bones (Rabe): V13
Stoppard, Tom
  Arcadia: V5
  Dogg's Hamlet, Cahoot's
    Macbeth: V16
  Indian Ink: V11
  The Real Thing: V8
  Rosencrantz and Guildenstern Are
    Dead: V2
  Travesties: V13
Strange Interlude (O'Neill): V20
Streamers (Rabe): V8
Street Scene (Rice): V12
A Streetcar Named Desire
  (Williams): V1
Strindberg, August
  The Ghost Sonata: V9
  Miss Julie: V4
The Subject Was Roses (Gilroy): V17
Sunrise at Campobello (Schary): V17
Sweeney Todd: The Demon Barber of
  Fleet Street (Wheeler): V19
Sweet Bird of Youth (Williams): V12
Synge, J. M.
  The Playboy of the Western
    World: V18

T

Tagore, Rabindranath
  The Post Office: V26
Take Me Out (Greenberg): V24
Talley's Folly (Wilson): V12
Tamburlaine the Great (Marlowe): V21
Tartuffe (Molière): V18
A Taste of Honey (Delaney): V7
The Teahouse of the August Moon
    (Patrick): V13
Telling Tales (Cruz): V19
Terry, Megan
  Calm Down Mother: V18
That Championship Season (Miller):
    V12
This Is Our Youth (Lonergan): V23
Thompson, Ernest
  On Golden Pond: V23
Thompson, Judith
  Habitat: V22
A Thousand Clowns (Gardner): V20
The Three Sisters (Chekhov): V10
Three Tall Women (Albee): V8
The Threepenny Opera (Brecht): V4
The Time of Your Life (Saroyan): V17
Tiny Alice (Albee): V10
'Tis Pity She's a Whore (Ford): V7
Topdog/Underdog (Parks): V22
Top Girls (Churchill): V12
Torch Song Trilogy (Fierstein): V6
The Tower (von Hofmannsthal): V12
Travesties (Stoppard): V13
Treadwell, Sophie
  Machinal: V22
The Trials of Brother Jero (Soyinka):
    V26
Trifles (Glaspell): V8
Trouble in Mind (Childress): V8
True West (Shepard): V3
Turgenev, Ivan
  A Month in the Country: V6
Twelve Angry Men (Rose): V23
Twilight: Los Angeles, 1992 (Smith):
    V2
Two Trains Running (Wilson): V24

U

Ubu Roi (Jarry): V8
Uhry, Alfred
  Driving Miss Daisy: V11
  The Last Night of Ballyhoo: V15
Uncle Vanya (Chekhov): V5

V

Valdez, Luis*Zoot Suit:* V5
The Verge (Glaspell): V18
Vidal, Gore
  Visit to a Small Planet: V2
Visit to a Small Planet (Vidal): V2
Vogel, Paula
  How I Learned to Drive: V14
Volpone (Jonson, Ben(jamin)): V10
von Hofmannsthal, Hugo
  Electra: V17
  The Tower: V12

W

Waiting for Godot (Beckett): V2
Waiting for Lefty (Odets): V3
A Walk in the Woods (Blessing):
    V26
Walker, Joseph A.
  The River Niger: V12
WASP (Martin): V19
Wasserstein, Wendy
  The Heidi Chronicles: V5
  The Sisters Rosensweig: V17
Watch on the Rhine (Hellman): V14
The Way of the World (Congreve):
    V15
Webber, Andrew Lloyd
  Jesus Christ Superstar: V7
Webster, John
  The Duchess of Malfi: V17
  The White Devil: V19
The Wedding Band (Childress): V2
Weiss, Peter
  Marat/Sade: V3
Welty, Eudora
  Bye-Bye, Brevoort: V26
What the Butler Saw (Orton): V6
Wheeler, Hugh
  Sweeney Todd: The Demon Barber
    of Fleet Street: V19
The White Devil (Webster): V19
Who's Afraid of Virginia Woolf?
    (Albee): V3
Wiechmann, Barbara
  Feeding the Moonfish: V21
The Wild Duck (Ibsen): V10
Wilde, Oscar
  An Ideal Husband: V21
  The Importance of Being Earnest:
    V4
  Lady Windermere's Fan: V9
  Salome: V8

Wilder, Thornton
  The Matchmaker: V16
  Our Town: V1
  The Skin of Our Teeth: V4
Williams, Tennessee
  Cat on a Hot Tin Roof: V3
  The Glass Menagerie: V1
  The Night of the Iguana: V7
  Orpheus Descending: V17
  The Rose Tattoo: V18
  A Streetcar Named Desire: V1
  Sweet Bird of Youth: V12
Wilson, August
  Fences: V3
  Joe Turner's Come and Gone: V17
  Ma Rainey's Black Bottom: V15
  The Piano Lesson: V7
  Two Trains Running: V24
Wilson, Lanford
  Angels Fall: V20
  Burn This: V4
  Hot L Baltimore: V9
  The Mound Builders: V16
  Talley's Folly: V12
Wine in the Wilderness (Childress):
    V14
Winterset (Anderson): V20
Wit (Edson): V13
The Women (Luce): V19
Women of Trachis: Trachiniae
    (Sophocles): V24
Wright, Doug
  I Am My Own Wife: V23

X

Xingjian, Gao
  The Other Shore: V21

Y

Y2K (Kopit): V14
You Can't Take It with You (Hart): V1
You Can't Take It with You
    (Kaufman): V1
The Young Man from Atlanta
    (Foote): V20

Z

Zindel, Paul
  The Effect of Gamma Rays on
    Man-in-the-Moon Marigolds:
    V12
The Zoo Story (Albee): V2
Zoot Suit (Valdez): V5

Cumulative
Nationality/Ethnicity Index

Anonymous
Everyman: V7

African American
Baldwin, James
The Amen Corner: V11
One Day, When I Was Lost:
A Scenario: V15
Baraka, Amiri
The Baptism: V16
Dutchman: V3
Slave Ship: V11
Bonner, Marita
The Purple Flower: V13
Childress, Alice
Florence: V26
Trouble in Mind: V8
The Wedding Band: V2
Wine in the Wilderness: V14
Cleage, Pearl
Blues for an Alabama Sky: V14
Flyin' West: V16
Fuller, Charles H.
A Soldier's Play: V8
Hansberry, Lorraine
A Raisin in the Sun: V2
Hughes, Langston
Mulatto: V18
Mule Bone: V6
Hurston, Zora Neale
Mule Bone: V6
Kennedy, Adrienne
Funnyhouse of a Negro: V9
Nottage, Lynn
Fabulation; or, The Re-Education
of Undine: V25

Shange, Ntozake
for colored girls who have
considered suicide/when the
rainbow is enuf: V2
Smith, Anna Deavere
Twilight: Los Angeles, 1992: V2
Wilson, August
Fences: V3
Joe Turner's Come and Gone: V17
Ma Rainey's Black Bottom: V15
The Piano Lesson: V7
Two Trains Running: V24

American
Albee, Edward
The American Dream: V25
A Delicate Balance: V14
Seascape: V13
Three Tall Women: V8
Tiny Alice: V10
Who's Afraid of Virginia
Woolf?: V3
The Zoo Story: V2
Anderson, Maxwell
Both Your Houses: V16
Winterset: V20
Auburn, David
Proof: V21
Baldwin, James
The Amen Corner: V11
One Day, When I Was Lost: A
Scenario: V15
Baraka, Amiri
The Baptism: V16
Dutchman: V3
Slave Ship: V11

Barry, Philip
The Philadelphia Story: V9
Beane, Douglas Carter
As Bees in Honey Drown: V21
Beim, Norman
The Deserter: V18
Blank, Jessica
The Exonerated: V24
Blessing, Lee
Eleemosynary: V23
A Walk in the Woods: V26
Bonner, Marita
The Purple Flower: V13
Brooks, Mel
The Producers: V21
Chase, Mary
Harvey: V11
Chayefsky, Paddy
Marty: V26
Childress, Alice
Florence: V26
Trouble in Mind: V8
The Wedding Band: V2
Wine in the Wilderness: V14
Cleage, Pearl
Blues for an Alabama Sky: V14
Flyin' West: V16
Coburn, D. L.
The Gin Game: V23
Connelly, Marc
The Green Pastures: V12
Cristofer, Michael
The Shadow Box: V15
Crouse, Russel
State of the Union: V19
Crowley, Mart
The Boys in the Band: V14

Cruz, Migdalia
  Telling Tales: V19
Cruz, Nilo
  Anna in the Tropics: V21
Edson, Margaret
  Wit: V13
Eliot, T. S.
  The Cocktail Party: V13
  Murder in the Cathedral: V4
Ensler, Eve
  Necessary Targets: V23
Ephron, Nora
  Imaginary Friends: V22
Fierstein, Harvey
  Torch Song Trilogy: V6
Fletcher, Lucille
  Sorry, Wrong Number: V26
Foote, Horton
  The Young Man from Atlanta: V20
Fornes, Maria Irene
  Fefu and Her Friends: V25
Fuller, Charles H.
  A Soldier's Play: V8
Gale, Zona
  Miss Lulu Bett: V17
Gardner, Herb
  I'm Not Rappaport: V18
  A Thousand Clowns: V20
Gerstenberg, Alice
  Overtones: V17
Gibson, William
  The Miracle Worker: V2
Gilman, Rebecca
  Blue Surge: V23
Gilroy, Frank D.
  The Subject Was Roses: V17
Glaspell, Susan
  Alison's House: V24
  Trifles: V8
  The Verge: V18
Goldman, James
  The Lion in Winter: V20
Goodrich, Frances
  The Diary of Anne Frank: V15
Greenberg, Richard
  Take Me Out: V24
Guare, John
  The House of Blue Leaves: V8
  Six Degrees of Separation: V13
Hackett, Albert
  The Diary of Anne Frank: V15
Hammerstein, Oscar II
  The King and I: V1
Hanff, Helene
  84, Charing Cross Road: V17
Hansberry, Lorraine
  A Raisin in the Sun: V2
Hart, Moss
  Once in a Lifetime: V10
  You Can't Take It with You: V1
Hayes, Joseph
  The Desperate Hours: V20

Hecht, Ben
  The Front Page: V9
Heggen, Thomas
  Mister Roberts: V20
Hellman, Lillian
  The Children's Hour: V3
  The Little Foxes: V1
  Watch on the Rhine: V14
Henley, Beth
  Crimes of the Heart: V2
  Impossible Marriage: V26
  The Miss Firecracker Contest:
    V21
Hughes, Langston
  Mulatto: V18
Hurston, Zora Neale
  Mule Bone: V6
Hwang, David Henry
  M. Butterfly: V11
  The Sound of a Voice: V18
Iizuka, Naomi
  36 Views: V21
Inge, William
  Bus Stop: V8
  Come Back, Little Sheba: V3
  Picnic: V5
Jensen, Erik
  The Exonerated: V24
Kaufman, George S.
  Once in a Lifetime: V10
  You Can't Take It with You: V1
Kesselring, Joseph
  Arsenic and Old Lace: V20
Kingsley, Sidney
  Detective Story: V19
  Men in White: V14
Kopit, Arthur
  Indians: V24
  Oh Dad, Poor Dad, Mamma's
    Hung You in the Closet and I'm
    Feelin' So Sad: V7
  Y2K: V14
Kramm, Joseph
  The Shrike: V15
Kushner, Tony
  Angels in America: V5
Lapine, James
  Into the Woods: V25
Larson, Jonathan
  Rent: V23
Lawrence, Jerome
  Inherit the Wind: V2
  The Night Thoreau Spent in Jail:
    V16
Lee, Robert E.
  Inherit the Wind: V2
  The Night Thoreau Spent in Jail:
    V16
Leight, Warren
  Side Man: V19
Lindsay, Howard
  State of the Union: V19

Lonergan, Kenneth
  This Is Our Youth: V23
Luce, Clare Boothe
  The Women: V19
MacArthur, Charles
  The Front Page: V9
MacLeish, Archibald
  J. B.: V15
Mamet, David
  American Buffalo: V3
  Glengarry Glen Ross: V2
  A Life in the Theatre: V12
  Reunion: V15
  Speed-the-Plow: V6
Margulies, Donald
  Dinner with Friends: V13
Martin, Steve
  WASP: V19
McCullers, Carson
  The Member of the Wedding: V5
  The Square Root of Wonderful: V18
McNally, Terrence
  Love! Valour! Compassion!: V19
  Master Class: V16
Medoff, Mark
  Children of a Lesser God: V4
Miller, Arthur
  All My Sons: V8
  The Crucible: V3
  Death of a Salesman: V1
Miller, Jason
  That Championship Season: V12
Norman, Marsha
  'night, Mother: V2
Nottage, Lynn
  Fabulation; or, The Re-Education
    of Undine: V25
O'Neill, Eugene
  Anna Christie: V12
  Beyond the Horizon: V16
  The Emperor Jones: V6
  The Great God Brown: V11
  The Hairy Ape: V4
  The Iceman Cometh: V5
  Ile: V26
  Long Day's Journey into Night: V2
  Mourning Becomes Electra: V9
  Strange Interlude: V20
Odets, Clifford
  Golden Boy: V17
  Rocket to the Moon: V20
  Waiting for Lefty: V3
Parks, Suzan-Lori
  Topdog/Underdog: V22
Patrick, John
  The Teahouse of the August Moon:
    V13
Pomerance, Bernard
  The Elephant Man: V9
Rabe, David
  The Basic Training of Pavlo
    Hummel: V3

Sticks and Bones: V13
Streamers: V8
Rebeck, Theresa
Spike Heels: V11
Rice, Elmer
Street Scene: V12
Rodgers, Richard
The King and I: V1
Rose, Reginald
Twelve Angry Men: V23
Rudnick, Paul
I Hate Hamlet: V22
Sackler, Howard
The Great White Hope: V15
Saroyan, William
The Time of Your Life: V17
Schary, Dore
Sunrise at Campobello: V17
Schenkkan, Robert
The Kentucky Cycle: V10
Shange, Ntozake
for colored girls who have
considered suicide/when the
rainbow is enuf: V2
Shanley, John Patrick
Doubt: V23
Shear, Claudia
Dirty Blonde: V24
Shepard, Sam
Buried Child: V6
Curse of the Starving Class: V14
Fool for Love: V7
True West: V3
Sherman, Martin
Bent: V20
Sherwood, Robert E.
Abe Lincoln in Illinois: V11
Idiot's Delight: V15
The Petrified Forest: V17
Shue, Larry
The Foreigner: V7
Simon, Neil
Biloxi Blues: V12
Brighton Beach Memoirs: V6
Lost in Yonkers: V18
The Odd Couple: V2
The Prisoner of Second Avenue: V24
Smith, Anna Deavere
Fires in the Mirror: V22
Twilight: Los Angeles, 1992: V2
Soto, Gary
Novio Boy: V26
Sondheim, Stephen
Into the Woods: V25
Stein, Joseph
Fiddler on the Roof: V7
Terry, Megan
Calm Down Mother: V18
Thompson, Ernest
On Golden Pond: V23
Treadwell, Sophie
Machinal: V22

Uhry, Alfred
Driving Miss Daisy: V11
The Last Night of Ballyhoo: V15
Valdez, Luis
Zoot Suit: V5
Vidal, Gore
Visit to a Small Planet: V2
Vogel, Paula
How I Learned to Drive: V14
Walker, Joseph A.
The River Niger: V12
Wasserstein, Wendy
The Heidi Chronicles: V5
The Sisters Rosensweig: V17
Welty, Eudora
Bye-Bye, Brevoort: V26
Wiechmann, Barbara
Feeding the Moonfish: V21
Wilder, Thornton
The Matchmaker: V16
Our Town: V1
The Skin of Our Teeth: V4
Williams, Tennessee
Cat on a Hot Tin Roof: V3
The Glass Menagerie: V1
The Night of the Iguana: V7
Orpheus Descending: V17
The Rose Tattoo: V18
A Streetcar Named Desire: V1
Sweet Bird of Youth: V12
Wilson, August
Fences: V3
Joe Turner's Come and Gone: V17
Ma Rainey's Black Bottom: V15
The Piano Lesson: V7
Two Trains Running: V24
Wilson, Lanford
Angels Fall: V20
Burn This: V4
Hot L Baltimore: V9
The Mound Builders: V16
Talley's Folly: V12
Wright, Doug
I Am My Own Wife: V23
Zindel, Paul
*The Effect of Gamma Rays on Man-
in-the-Moon Marigolds:* V12

Argentinian
Dorfman, Ariel
Death and the Maiden: V4

Asian American
Hwang, David Henry
M. Butterfly: V11
The Sound of a Voice: V18

Austrian
von Hofmannsthal, Hugo
Electra: V17
The Tower: V12

Bohemian (Czechoslovakian)
Capek, Karel
The Insect Play: V11

Canadian
Highway, Tomson
The Rez Sisters: V2
MacDonald, Ann-Marie
*Goodnight Desdemona (Good
Morning Juliet):* V23
Pollock, Sharon
Blood Relations: V3
Thompson, Judith
Habitat: V22

Chilean
Dorfman, Ariel
Death and the Maiden: V4

Chinese
Xingjian, Gao
The Other Shore: V21

Cuban
Cruz, Nilo
Anna in the Tropics: V21
Fornes, Maria Irene
Fefu and Her Friends: V25
Prida, Dolores
Beautiful Señoritas: V23

Cuban American
Cruz, Nilo
Anna in the Tropics: V21

Czechoslovakian
Capek, Joseph
The Insect Play: V11
Capek, Karel
The Insect Play: V11
R.U.R.: V7
Havel, Vaclav
The Memorandum: V10
Stoppard, Tom
Arcadia: V5
*Dogg's Hamlet, Cahoot's
Macbeth:* V16
Indian Ink: V11
The Real Thing: V8
*Rosencrantz and Guildenstern Are
Dead:* V2
Travesties: V13

Dutch
de Hartog, Jan
The Fourposter: V12

English

Anonymous
  Arden of Faversham: V24
  The Second Shepherds' Play: V25
Arden, John
  Serjeant Musgrave's Dance: V9
Ayckbourn, Alan
  A Chorus of Disapproval: V7
Barnes, Peter
  The Ruling Class: V6
Behn, Aphra
  The Forc'd Marriage: V24
  The Rover: V16
Bolt, Robert
  A Man for All Seasons: V2
Bond, Edward
  Lear: V3
  Saved: V8
Christie, Agatha
  The Mousetrap: V2
Churchill, Caryl
  Cloud Nine: V16
  Serious Money: V25
  Top Girls: V12
Congreve, William
  Love for Love: V14
  The Way of the World: V15
Coward, Noel
  Hay Fever: V6
  Private Lives: V3
Cowley, Hannah
  The Belle's Stratagem: V22
Delaney, Shelagh
  A Taste of Honey: V7
Duffy, Maureen
  Rites: V15
Edgar, David
  *The Life and Adventures of
    Nicholas Nickleby:* V15
Ford, John
  'Tis Pity She's a Whore: V7
Frayn, Michael
  Copenhagen: V22
Gems, Pam
  Stanley: V25
Goldsmith, Oliver
  She Stoops to Conquer: V1
Hare, David
  Blue Room: V7
  Plenty: V4
  The Secret Rapture: V16
Jonson, Ben(jamin)
  The Alchemist: V4
  Volpone: V10
Kyd, Thomas
  The Spanish Tragedy: V21
Lavery, Bryony
  Frozen: V25
Lessing, Doris
  Play with a Tiger: V20
Marlowe, Christopher
  Doctor Faustus: V1

*Edward II: The Troublesome Reign
  and Lamentable Death of
  Edward the Second, King of
  England, with the Tragical Fall
  of Proud Mortimer:* V5
The Jew of Malta: V13
Tamburlaine the Great: V21
Maugham, Somerset
  For Services Rendered: V22
Middleton, Thomas
  The Changeling: V22
  A Chaste Maid in Cheapside: V18
Nicholson, William
  Shadowlands: V11
Orton, Joe
  Entertaining Mr. Sloane: V3
  What the Butler Saw: V6
Osborne, John
  Inadmissible Evidence: V24
  Look Back in Anger: V4
  Luther: V19
Pinter, Harold
  The Birthday Party: V5
  The Caretaker: V7
  The Dumb Waiter: V25
  The Homecoming: V3
  Mountain Language: V14
Rattigan, Terence
  The Browning Version: V8
Rice, Tim
  Jesus Christ Superstar: V7
Shaffer, Anthony
  Sleuth: V13
Shaffer, Peter
  Amadeus: V13
  Equus: V5
Shakespeare, William
  Othello: V20
  Romeo and Juliet: V21
Stoppard, Tom
  Arcadia: V5
  *Dogg's Hamlet, Cahoot's Mac
    beth:* V16
  Indian Ink: V11
  The Real Thing: V8
  *Rosencrantz and Guildenstern Are
    Dead:* V2
  Travesties: V13
Webber, Andrew Lloyd
  Jesus Christ Superstar: V7
Webster, John
  The Duchess of Malfi: V17
  The White Devil: V19
Wheeler, Hugh
  *Sweeney Todd: The Demon Barber
    of Fleet Street:* V19

French

Anouilh, Jean
  Antigone: V9
  Becket, or the Honor of God: V19
  Ring Around the Moon: V10

Artaud, Antonin
  The Cenci: V22
Beckett, Samuel
  Endgame: V18
  Krapp's Last Tape: V7
  Waiting for Godot: V2
Cocteau, Jean
  Indiscretions: V24
Corneille, Pierre
  Le Cid: V21
de Beaumarchais, Pierre-Augustin
  The Barber of Seville: V16
  The Marriage of Figaro: V14
Duras, Marguerite
  India Song: V21
Genet, Jean
  The Balcony: V10
Ionesco, Eugène
  The Bald Soprano: V4
  The Chairs: V9
  Rhinoceros: V25
Jarry, Alfred
  Ubu Roi: V8
Molière
  The Imaginary Invalid: V20
  The Misanthrope: V13
  Tartuffe: V18
Reza, Yasmina
  Art: V19
Rostand, Edmond
  Cyrano de Bergerac: V1
Sartre, Jean-Paul
  The Flies: V26
  No Exit: V5

German

Brecht, Bertolt
  The Good Person of Szechwan: V9
  *Mother Courage and Her
    Children:* V5
  The Threepenny Opera: V4
Weiss, Peter
  Marat/Sade: V3

Greek

Aeschylus
  Agamemnon: V26
  Prometheus Bound: V5
  Seven Against Thebes: V10
Aristophanes
  Lysistrata: V10
Euripides
  The Bacchae: V6
  Hippolytus: V25
  Iphigenia in Taurus: V4
  Medea: V1
Sophocles
  Ajax: V8
  Antigone: V1
  Electra: V4
  Oedipus Rex: V1
  Women of Trachis: Trachiniae: V24

Guatemalan

Solórzano, Carlos
Crossroads: V26

Hispanic

Cruz, Nilo
Anna in the Tropics: V21
Fornes, Maria Irene
Fefu and Her Friends: V25
Valdez, Luis
Zoot Suit: V5

Indian

Tagore, Rabindranath
The Post Office: V26

Indochinese

Duras, Marguerite
India Song: V21

Irish

Beckett, Samuel
Endgame: V18
Krapp's Last Tape: V7
Waiting for Godot: V2
Behan, Brendan
The Hostage: V7
Friel, Brian
Dancing at Lughnasa: V11
Leonard, Hugh
The Au Pair Man: V24
Da: V13
O'Casey, Sean
Red Roses for Me: V19
Shaw, George Bernard
Arms and the Man: V22
Major Barbara: V3
Man and Superman: V6
Mrs. Warren's Profession: V19
Pygmalion: V1
Saint Joan: V11
Sheridan, Richard Brinsley
The Critic: V14
The Rivals: V15
School for Scandal: V4
Synge, J. M.
Playboy of the Western World: V18
Wilde, Oscar
An Ideal Husband: V21
*The Importance of Being
Earnest:* V4
Lady Windermere's Fan: V9
Salome: V8

Italian

Fo, Dario
Accidental Death of an Anarchist:
V23
Ginzburg, Natalia
The Advertisement: V14

Pirandello, Luigi
*Right You Are, If You Think You
Are:* V9
*Six Characters in Search of an
Author:* V4

Japanese

Abe, Kobo
The Man Who Turned into a Stick:
V14
Iizuka, Naomi
36 Views: V21

Jewish

Chayefsky, Paddy
Marty: V26
Gardner, Herb
A Thousand Clowns: V20
Mamet, David
Reunion: V15
Odets, Clifford
Rocket to the Moon: V20
Sherman, Martin
Bent: V20
Simon, Neil
Biloxi Blues: V12
Brighton Beach Memoirs: V6
Lost in Yonkers: V18
The Odd Couple: V2
The Prisoner of Second Avenue: V24
Uhry, Alfred
Driving Miss Daisy: V11
The Last Night of Ballyhoo: V15

Mexican

Carballido, Emilio
I, Too, Speak of the Rose: V4
Solórzano, Carlos
Crossroads: V26
Soto, Gary
Novio Boy: V26

Native Canadian

Highway, Tomson
The Rez Sisters: V2

Nigerian

Clark, John Pepper
The Raft: V13
Soyinka, Wole
Death and the King's Horseman: V10
The Trials of Brother Jero: V26

Norwegian

Ibsen, Henrik
Brand: V16
A Doll's House: V1
An Enemy of the People: V25
Ghosts: V11
Hedda Gabler: V6
The Master Builder: V15

Peer Gynt: V8
The Wild Duck: V10

Romanian

Ionesco, Eugène
The Bald Soprano: V4
The Chairs: V9
Rhinoceros: V25

Russian

Chekhov, Anton
The Bear: V26
The Cherry Orchard: V1
The Seagull: V12
The Three Sisters: V10
Uncle Vanya: V5
Gogol, Nikolai
The Government Inspector: V12
Gorki, Maxim
The Lower Depths: V9
Turgenev, Ivan
A Month in the Country: V6

Scottish

Barrie, J(ames) M.
Peter Pan: V7

South African

Fugard, Athol
Boesman & Lena: V6
A Lesson from Aloes: V24
"Master Harold" . . . and the Boys:
V3
Sizwe Bansi is Dead: V10

Spanish

Buero Vallejo, Antonio
The Sleep of Reason: V11
Calderón de la Barca, Pedro
Life Is a Dream: V23
García Lorca, Federico
Blood Wedding: V10
The House of Bernarda Alba: V4

Swedish

Strindberg, August
The Ghost Sonata: V9
Miss Julie: V4

Swiss

Frisch, Max
The Firebugs: V25

Ukrainian

Chayefsky, Paddy
Marty: V26

Venezuelan

Kaufman, Moisés
The Laramie Project: V22

Subject/Theme Index

*Boldfaced
Denotes discussion in **Themes**
section

Numerical

1940s
Sorry, Wrong Number: 254–255

A

Abandonment
Sorry, Wrong Number: 252–253
Abstract
Crossroads: 63
Absurdism
Crossroads: 70–71, 72, 75, 79–82
A Walk in the Woods: 295
Achievement
Ile: 147
Adultery
The Bear: 26, 31
African Americans
Florence: 110, 125–127, 128–133
African Literature
The Trials of Brother Jero: 269–270
Afterlife
The Post Office: 236
Age versus Maturity
Novio Boy: 212–213
Aging
Crossroads: 68–69, 73
Impossible Marriage: 164
Aging
Bye-Bye, Brevoort: 47
Alienation
Crossroads: 99

Ile: 135, 148
A Walk in the Woods: 283
Allegory
Crossroads: 71
Allusion
Bye-Bye, Brevoort: 47–48
The Post Office: 232
American Negro Theatre
Florence: 118–119, 124
American Northeast
Marty: 192
American South
Bye-Bye, Brevoort: 41, 50, 56–59
Impossible Marriage: 162, 165, 167, 168–169, 175, 181
Anagnorisis
Crossroads: 97, 98–99
Antagonist
Impossible Marriage: 164
Anti-Romantic Sentiment
Impossible Marriage: 165–166
Archetypes
Impossible Marriage: 168
Archteypes
The Trials of Brother Jero: 273
Arrogance
Sorry, Wrong Number: 251–252
Assimilation
Novio Boy: 217
Author Interviews
Bye-Bye, Brevoort: 56–61
The Flies: 106–109
Impossible Marriage: 173–181
Novio Boy: 218–223
The Trials of Brother Jero: 278–281
Avant-Garde
Crossroads: 63, 69–70, 71, 80

B

Beauty and Ugliness
Marty: 186–187
Beauty and Ugliness
Marty: 191–192
Betrayal
The Bear: 31, 32
Bitterness
The Bear: 31
Black Comedy
Impossible Marriage: 158
Black Self-Determinism Theater
Florence: 125–127
Breakdown in Communication
Ile: 148
Brutality
Ile: 148
Brute Strength
Ile: 153–154

C

Catharsis
Crossroads: 97
The Flies: 99
Change
Bye-Bye, Brevoort: 55
Change
Bye-Bye, Brevoort: 45–46
Characterization
The Bear: 30
Crossroads: 72–73
Impossible Marriage: 181
Marty: 202–203
A Walk in the Woods: 300

Charlatanism
  The Trials of Brother Jero:
    265–266, 267
Chicano Culture
  Novio Boy: 207, 213, 214–215,
    217–221, 222–223
Christianity
  The Trials of Brother Jero:
    270–271, 275–276
Citizen versus Bureaucrat
  A Walk in the Woods: 289
Civilization versus Passion
  Impossible Marriage: 158, 167,
    170, 171, 172
Civilization versus Passion
  Impossible Marriage: 165
Class Structure
  The Post Office: 224
Class Structure
  The Post Office: 231
Cold War
  A Walk in the Woods: 283, 292–293
Collective Rights
  Agamemnon: 12
Colonialism
  Bye-Bye, Brevoort: 50–53
  The Post Office: 232–234
Comedy
  The Bear: 27, 29–30
Comedy of Manners
  Impossible Marriage: 158, 163,
    167, 175
Coming of Age
  Novio Boy: 212–213
Community
  Marty: 191
  Novio Boy: 213
Compassion
  Ile: 150
Competition
  A Walk in the Woods: 286
Conformity
  Impossible Marriage: 168, 170
Connection
  Crossroads: 67
Conquest
  A Walk in the Woods: 286
Contradiction
  The Bear: 24
  Crossroads: 74
Conversation
  A Walk in the Woods: 296
Courage
  Florence: 114
  Impossible Marriage: 164
Creativity
  Ile: 147
Cruelty
  Marty: 197
Cultural Assimilation
  Novio Boy: 217
Culture Clash
  The Trials of Brother Jero: 276–277

Cynicism
  Impossible Marriage: 164
  A Walk in the Woods: 288–289, 300
Cynicism
  A Walk in the Woods: 289–290

D
Day-to-Day Existence
  Marty: 200, 204
Death
  The Bear: 20
  Bye-Bye, Brevoort: 52
  Impossible Marriage: 164
Death and Mourning
  The Bear: 25
Death as a Beginning
  The Post Office: 224
Death as a Release
  The Post Office: 228, 235–237
Death as a Release
  The Post Office: 230–231
Decency
  Marty: 190, 205
Deception
  Agamemnon: 1
  The Bear: 24, 26
  Crossroads: 75
Decorum
  Impossible Marriage: 162
Dedication to Family
  Marty: 191
Delusion
  Crossroads: 66, 68
Democracy
  Agamemnon: 16
Denial
  Bye-Bye, Brevoort: 50, 55
Desire
  Crossroads: 73
Despair
  A Walk in the Woods: 288–289
Destruction
  A Walk in the Woods: 295, 296
Destruction
  A Walk in the Woods: 290
Destruction of the Old
  Bye-Bye, Brevoort: 41, 46, 55
Dialect
  Novio Boy: 214
Dialogue
  Agamemnon: 9
  Impossible Marriage: 169–170
  Marty: 202–203, 203
Digression
  A Walk in the Woods: 291–292
Disappointment
  Crossroads: 68
Discipline
  Ile: 147
Disillusionment
  Crossroads: 73, 74

Domestic Tragedy
  Agamemnon: 16
Dramatic Tension
  Marty: 195–197
  Sorry, Wrong Number: 254,
    257–259
Dramatic Unity
  Ile: 143
Duty
  A Walk in the Woods: 289

E
Elusiveness of Identity
  Crossroads: 74
Emotional Development
  Impossible Marriage: 164
Emotions
  Agamemnon: 12
Epigrammatic Dialogue
  Impossible Marriage: 167–168
Everyday Life
  Marty: 200, 204
Existentialism
  Crossroads: 75–79, 98, 99
  The Flies: 84, 91, 94, 100, 101, 102,
    104–106, 105
Expectation
  Ile: 139
  Impossible Marriage: 165

F
Faithfulness
  The Bear: 31, 32
Family
  Marty: 191
Family
  Marty: 191
Farce
  The Bear: 20, 27, 29, 31
  Bye-Bye, Brevoort: 45, 47, 50, 55
  The Trials of Brother Jero:
    268–269
Fascism
  The Flies: 104–105
Fear
  Crossroads: 63
Femininity
  Impossible Marriage: 168
Fickleness
  The Bear: 24, 27
Fidelity
  The Bear: 25–26, 32
Folk Tradition
  The Trials of Brother Jero:
    271
Folklore
  Ile: 152–156
The Fool
  Bye-Bye, Brevoort: 44–45
Foreshadowing
  The Post Office: 232

France
  The Flies: 94–96
Fraud
  The Trials of Brother Jero: 261, 265
Free Will
  The Flies: 84
Freedom
  Crossroads: 98
  The Flies: 84, 90, 91, 99, 101, 102, 104–105
  The Post Office: 228, 236–237
Freedom
  The Flies: 92–93
French Vaudeville
  The Bear: 20, 27
Frustration
  A Walk in the Woods: 283
Futility
  A Walk in the Woods: 289

G

Gender Roles
  Agamemnon: 8
  Ile: 26–27, 147–148
  Impossible Marriage: 165–167
  Novio Boy: 217
  Sorry, Wrong Number: 255
Gender Roles
  Novio Boy: 213–214
Generational Relationships
  Marty: 196
  Glasnost
  A Walk in the Woods: 293–294
Globalization
  The Post Office: 237
God
  The Post Office: 236–237
Good and Evil
  Agamemnon: 17–18
Goodness
  Marty: 205
Greek Chorus
  Agamemnon: 9
Greek Tragedy
  Crossroads: 97–99
  The Flies: 94
Grief
  The Bear: 20, 30–31
Grotesque
  Impossible Marriage: 175

H

Helplessness and Arrogance
  Sorry, Wrong Number: 251–252
Hinduism
  The Post Office: 234, 243–244
Honesty
  Bye-Bye, Brevoort: 45
Hope
  Impossible Marriage: 172

Hopelessness
  Crossroads: 63
  A Walk in the Woods: 283, 300
Hubris
  Agamemnon: 14, 15, 16
Humanism
  The Post Office: 237–238
Humans versus Nature
  Ile: 135, 144–145, 149–150
Humans versus Nature
  Ile: 141–142
Humor
  The Bear: 24, 30, 35–36
  Bye-Bye, Brevoort: 41, 44–45, 47
  Marty: 204–205
  The Trials of Brother Jero: 261
Hybrid Culture
  Novio Boy: 213
Hypocrisy and Religious
    Charlatanism
  The Trials of Brother Jero: 261, 271–272
**Hypocrisy and Religious
    Charlatanism**
  The Trials of Brother Jero: 267

I

Idealism versus Realism
  A Walk in the Woods: 286
Imagery
  Agamemnon: 16
Imagination
  The Post Office: 228
Individual Rights
  Agamemnon: 12
Infidelity
  The Bear: 31
Intellectual Cooperation
  The Post Office: 244–245
Irony
  Bye-Bye, Brevoort: 44
  Impossible Marriage: 171
  Marty: 192
Isolation
  Impossible Marriage: 163
  Sorry, Wrong Number: 253

J

Jealousy
  Agamemnon: 7–8
Jim Crow Laws
  Florence: 117
Justice
  Agamemnon: 14, 16
Justice
  Agamemnon: 6–7

K

Kinship
  Agamemnon: 1

L

Language
  Bye-Bye, Brevoort: 52, 55
  Crossroads: 73
  Ile: 143, 155–156
  Novio Boy: 214
  The Post Office: 235
  The Trials of Brother Jero: 269
Law
  Agamemnon: 16
Light and Dark
  Agamemnon: 16
Limitations and Opportunities
  Florence: 114, 121–122
Loneliness
  Crossroads: 67–68, 69, 73
  Marty: 186, 200, 202, 203
Longing
  Crossroads: 63
**Longing, Loneliness, and Idealized
    Love**
  Crossroads: 67–68
Loss
  The Bear: 32
Lovable Rogue
  The Trials of Brother Jero: 271–273
Love
  The Bear: 20, 31, 32
  Ile: 147–148
  Impossible Marriage: 164
  Marty: 200
  The Post Office: 237, 240–241
Love and Faithfulness
  The Bear: 25–26
Love and Hate
  Agamemnon: 17
Lower Class
  Marty: 198, 200

M

Madness
  Ile: 146, 147, 148
Manipulation
  The Bear: 31
Marriage
  Ile: 147–148
Marriage and Courtship
  Marty: 183, 197, 200
Marriage and Courtship
  Marty: 190–191
Martyrdom
  The Trials of Brother Jero: 265, 273
Masculine and Feminine
  Ile: 147–148
Mastery
  Ile: 147
Materialism
  Impossible Marriage: 164
  The Trials of Brother Jero: 272

Materialism
The Trials of Brother Jero: 268
Meaning
Crossroads: 73–75
Melodrama
The Bear: 31
Impossible Marriage: 167
Metaphor
Agamemnon: 16
Mexican Americans
Novio Boy: 213, 217–221, 222–223
Mexico
Crossroads: 70
Military Occupation
Crossroads: 97
The Flies: 94–96, 100, 102–105
Misogyny
The Trials of Brother Jero:
267–268
Modernism
Bye-Bye, Brevoort: 46, 50
Moral Relativity
The Flies: 102
Mother/Daughter-in-Law
Relationship
Marty: 196–197
Mourning
The Bear: 20, 24, 30–31

N

Names
Impossible Marriage: 168
National Guilt
The Flies: 100
Nihilism
Crossroads: 73–75
Nuclear Arms Race
A Walk in the Woods: 292–293

O

Obstinacy
Agamemnon: 14
Old and New
Bye-Bye, Brevoort: 50
Old and Young
Bye-Bye, Brevoort: 47
One-Act Dramatic Structure
Florence: 116–117
Ordinary Life
Marty: 200
Ordinary Speech
Marty: 202
Ostracism
Marty: 204
Outcast
Marty: 204
Outspokenness
Impossible Marriage: 166

P

Pan-Asianism
The Post Office: 239
Paradox
Crossroads: 74
Parody
Bye-Bye, Brevoort: 47, 48, 52
Passage of Time
Bye-Bye, Brevoort: 50, 55
Passion
Impossible Marriage: 158, 164,
165, 170, 171
Passivity
Ile: 147
Peace
Ile: 147
Pidgin English
The Trials of Brother Jero: 269
Polemics
A Walk in the Woods: 292
Power
Agamemnon: 1
A Walk in the Woods: 294–295
Practicality
The Post Office: 229
Pretense
Impossible Marriage: 165, 170,
171, 172
Pride
Agamemnon: 16
Ile: 147
Ile: 140, 150
A Walk in the Woods: 289
Propriety
Impossible Marriage: 172
Psychological Inevitability
The Bear: 29–30

R

Racism
Florence: 110, 112–113, 120, 127
Racism
Florence: 114–115
Radio Plays
Sorry, Wrong Number: 254,
255–256
Realism
The Bear: 20, 29
Florence: 110, 116
Ile: 143, 145
Impossible Marriage: 165
Marty: 200
Reality
Ile: 139
Impossible Marriage: 170
Rebelliousness
Impossible Marriage: 165–166
Redemption
Impossible Marriage: 163,
170–173
Rejection
Marty: 186

Religion
Ile: 147
The Post Office: 234, 243–244
The Trials of Brother Jero: 261,
265, 267, 270–271, 271–272,
275–276, 280
Remorse
The Flies: 91, 99, 100, 101,
102, 104
Remorse
The Flies: 93
Repose
Ile: 147
Representation
Crossroads: 70, 73
Repression
Impossible Marriage: 168
Repression and Liberation of Women
Impossible Marriage: 165–167
Resignation
A Walk in the Woods: 297
Resignation
A Walk in the Woods:
290–291
Resistance
The Flies: 102–105
Respectability
Impossible Marriage: 162
Responsibility
Agamemnon: 1
Restoration Comedy
Impossible Marriage: 167
Revenge
Agamemnon: 1, 12, 16, 18
Crossroads: 98
The Flies: 88, 100–101
Revenge
Agamemnon: 7
Reversal of Fortune
Crossroads: 98
Revolution
Bye-Bye, Brevoort: 52–53
Rhetoric
The Flies: 93–94
Ritual
Bye-Bye, Brevoort: 41
Rules
Agamemnon: 12

S

Saccharine Quality
Marty: 205
Sailor Life
Ile: 152–156
Satire
Bye-Bye, Brevoort: 47, 49, 55
Impossible Marriage: 167
The Trials of Brother Jero: 261,
268–269, 271, 273
Scientific Determinism
Ile: 149

Segregation
  Florence: 112–113, 114–115,
    117–118, 120–122
Self-Awareness
  Crossroads: 75
Self-Delusion
  Crossroads: 66, 68
Self-Denial
  Impossible Marriage: 172
Self-Righteousness
  Sorry, Wrong Number:
    251–252
  Séquestré
  The Flies: 107–108
Seriousness
  Impossible Marriage: 175
Servitude
  Bye-Bye, Brevoort: 46
Sexism
  Agamemnon: 14
Sexism
  Agamemnon: 8
Silence
  Ile: 148
Slang
  Marty: 192
  Novio Boy: 214
Social Class
  Bye-Bye, Brevoort: 44–45, 49,
    50–53
  Impossible Marriage: 167, 168
  Marty: 198, 200
  The Post Office: 224, 231
Social Class
  Bye-Bye, Brevoort: 46–47
Social Conventions
  Impossible Marriage: 165
Social Issues
  Agamemnon: 12
  Florence: 127
Solitude
  The Flies: 101
Southern Belle Archetype
  Impossible Marriage: 168
Spanish American Literature
  Crossroads: 75–79
Spiritual Freedom
  The Post Office: 224

Spontaneity
  Impossible Marriage: 165, 170
Stereotypes
  Bye-Bye, Brevoort: 47
  Florence: 110, 114, 122
Stereotypes
  Florence: 115–116
Storytelling
  Bye-Bye, Brevoort: 53
Stychomathia
  Novio Boy: 214
Subplot
  Marty: 203
Success
  Ile: 147
Superiority
  Bye-Bye, Brevoort: 46
Suspense Drama
  Sorry, Wrong Number: 254, 257
Symbolic Setting
  Impossible Marriage: 167
Symbolism
  Bye-Bye, Brevoort: 45, 46, 52
  Crossroads: 63, 70, 71, 72, 74–75
  The Flies: 91
  Florence: 121
  Ile: 149
  Impossible Marriage: 165, 168,
    171
  The Post Office: 235–237
Sympathy
  A Walk in the Woods: 298

T

Technology and Isolation
  Sorry, Wrong Number: 253
Television
  Marty: 192–194
Theater of the Absurd
  Crossroads: 70–71, 73, 79–82
Time and Aging
  Crossroads: 68–69
Tradition
  Bye-Bye, Brevoort: 50
  Impossible Marriage: 165
Traditional Gender Roles
  Ile: 26–27

Tragic Flaw
  Crossroads: 98
Transference
  The Bear: 24
Transformation
  The Bear: 24
  Impossible Marriage: 172
Trust
  A Walk in the Woods: 287
Trust
  A Walk in the Woods: 291

U

Understanding
  A Walk in the Woods: 298
Upper Class
  Bye-Bye, Brevoort: 44–45, 49, 52
  Impossible Marriage: 167, 168
Urban Life
  Marty: 198

V

Vaudeville
  Crossroads: 70
Vulnerability
  Marty: 189

W

War
  Agamemnon: 9–10, 16
Weakness
  Ile: 147
  The Trials of Brother Jero: 265
Wisdom
  Bye-Bye, Brevoort: 45
Wordplay
  Bye-Bye, Brevoort: 47–48, 55
Writer's Role
  Florence: 126
Writing Process
  Bye-Bye, Brevoort: 57–59, 60–61
  The Trials of Brother Jero: 279–280

Y

Youth
  Impossible Marriage: 164